All Children Read

Teaching for Literacy in Today's Diverse Classrooms

Fifth Edition

Charles Temple
Hobart and William Smith Colleges

Donna Ogle
National-Louis University

Alan Crawford
California State University, Los Angeles

Codruta Temple
State University of New York College at Cortland

330 Hudson Street, NY NY 10013

Vice President and Editor in Chief: Kevin M. Davis
Portfolio Manager: Drew Bennett
Content Producer: Miryam Chandler
Portfolio Management Assistant: Maria Feliberty
Development Editor: Carolyn Schweitzer
Executive Product Marketing Manager: Christopher Barry
Executive Field Marketing Manager: Krista Clark
Procurement Specialist: Deidra Smith
Cover Designer: Cenveo, Carie Keller
Cover Art: Lorena Fernandez/Shutterstock
Media Producer: Allison Longley
Editorial Production and Composition Services: Cenveo Publisher Services
Full-Service Project Manager: Revathi Viswanathan and Yasmita Hota, Cenveo Publisher Services
Text Font: Palatino LT Pro

Cataloging-in-Publication data is on file with the Library of Congress.

1 18

Bound Book
ISBN-10:   0-13-489465-0
ISBN-13: 978-0-13-489465-2

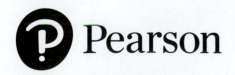

About the Authors

• CHARLES TEMPLE is a professor of education at Hobart and William Smith Colleges in Geneva, New York, where he teaches courses on literacy, children's literature, storytelling, and international education. He has written books on emergent literacy, invented spelling, writing instruction, language arts, diagnosis and remediation of reading disabilities, and children's literature, as well as books for children. He codirects Critical Thinking International, Inc., a nonprofit organization that does children's book development and literacy work around the world.

• DONNA OGLE is Emerita Professor of Reading and Language at National-Louis University (NLU) in Chicago, Illinois, and is active in research and professional development projects. She served as senior consultant to the Chicago Striving Readers Project, was CoDirector of the Literacy Partners Project, and codirects the Reading Leadership Institute. Donna also serves as a literacy consultant internationally and is part of Critical Thinking International and an editorial reviewer for Grupo SM in Latin America, *The Reading Teacher*, and the *Journal of Adolescent and Adult Literacy*. Donna is a past president of the International Reading Association (IRA) and an elected member of the Reading Hall of Fame. She is the author of many books, book chapters, professional articles, and curriculum materials.

• ALAN CRAWFORD is Emeritus Professor of Education at California State University, Los Angeles. He has served as President of the California Reading Association, a Fulbright Senior scholar in Ecuador and Morocco, and a Researcher in Residence at the American Embassy in Baku, Azerbaijan. He has done extensive teaching, consulting, and writing on teaching reading in the elementary school, especially for second language learners. Alan has written curriculum for teaching reading in Spanish and served on the Editorial Review Board of *Lectura y Vida*. He served as IRA's representative to UNESCO for many years and was a Senior Literacy Specialist at UNESCO in Paris during International Literacy Year (1989–90). He is currently a director of Critical Thinking International. He frequently presents seminars and workshops on a volunteer basis for international development projects in Latin America, Europe, Asia, and Africa.

• CODRUTA TEMPLE is associate professor of second language education at the State University of New York College at Cortland. She has coauthored two college textbooks, *The Beginnings of Writing* and *Understanding Reading Problems: Assessment and Instruction*, as well as several articles and book chapters on literacy development in mathematics classrooms.

Brief Contents

Contents

5   Phonics and Word Knowledge   95

6   Helping Readers Build Fluency   116

7   The Importance of Vocabulary Development   132

8 Reading Comprehension, Part I: Making Sense of Literature 157

9 Reading Comprehension, Part II: Understanding and Learning with Informational Texts 185

12 Assessing Literacy 286

13 Integrating Language and Literacy Instruction Across the Grades 321

Preface

New to This Edition

Since you are most likely reading these words on a screen, you are experiencing one feature that distinguishes this fifth edition of *All Children Read: Teaching for Literacy in Today's Diverse Classrooms*. And of course there are updates to the contents that respond to significant developments in the literacy field and build upon the strengths our readers have found in previous editions of our book.

The fifth edition includes:

- **Learning outcomes open each chapter and are linked to the sections where they are discussed.** The end-of-chapter reviews link you back to where the information was presented within the chapter, too.

- **Illustrative video clips** bring content to life, allowing you to view real classrooms taught by master teachers and receive in-depth information from subject matter experts. Video clips are accompanied by Video Exploration short-answer questions with answer feedback that encourage you to think critically about chapter concepts.

- **New, interactive glossary** helps you keep track of important terms that are used throughout the book.

- **Check Your Understanding multiple-choice quizzes** are located at the end of every major section of all chapters and provide immediate feedback about correct and incorrect answers, helping you to self-assess your learning before moving on to new concepts.

- **Separate chapters on teaching reading fluency and vocabulary** have been prepared for greater coverage of both topics.

- **Updated explanations of concepts about language** prepare teachers to teach foundational concepts for reading as called for in the Common Core State Standards, and equip teachers-in-training with what they are expected to know on professional qualifying examinations.

Carried over from the previous edition are:

- *An emphasis on the Common Core State Standards (CCSS) throughout the book*, highlighted by icons in the margins alongside content that aligns with these Standards, as well as boxed features.

- *Updated content is provided throughout the book on teaching English language learners, along with an updated chapter on teaching these students in Chapter 14.* There is an opening discussion in Chapter 2 on sociocultural and legal factors in teaching reading to English language learners, background content in Chapter 3 on the English language, and then subsequent chapters address the topic as appropriate, including those on assessing and teaching reading and writing.

- *Expanded emphasis on teaching close reading for comprehension in the primary grades*, in response to the Common Core State Standards' insistence that children from the earliest grades be guided to read repeatedly to get the message, the details, and the devices used in both fiction and nonfiction.

- *An appendix correlating chapters with Common Core State Standards* that pinpoints which chapters correspond to which Standards, and identifies what students should know and be able to do.

- *An expanded focus on Response to Intervention (RTI)* further explores this important initiative in practical ways in Chapter 2.

- *Elaborate coverage of new literacies throughout the book* that provides information about the impact of technology on the teaching of reading and writing. This content is highlighted by a margin note icon.

- *A Developmental Milestones feature* that appears in Chapters 3 and 4. The Developmental Milestones feature provides at-a-glance summaries of typical behaviors in children's development of emergent literacy and phonological awareness.

- Students from California who use *All Children Read* will find that key terms from the **Reading Instruction Competence Assessment (RICA)** are fully developed in the text and also appear in the index. In addition, major concepts related to the assessment of students are also developed to support our readers in other aspects of the RICA.

- *The Teach It! lesson plan booklet* appears as an Appendix containing a wide variety of ready-to-use, classroom-tested activities for teaching critical concepts in literacy education. Teach It! feature boxes appear throughout the text, linking content to correlated activities in Appendix B.

- *Chapter 1: Approaches to Teaching Reading* chronicles recent major changes in the field, including a trend toward integrating instruction across the curriculum, that are affecting classroom practice. Response to Intervention (RTI), the federal initiative to support readers with a range of needs, is introduced in Chapter 1.

- *Chapter 2: The Social and Cultural Contexts for Teaching All Children to Read* includes regulations and implementation guidelines about the federal Response to Intervention (RTI) initiative and insights about teaching reading and writing to children whose home language is African American Vernacular English. A classroom vignette about Getting Parents and the Community Involved is included.

- *Chapter 3: What Reading Teachers Need to Know about Language* includes careful treatments of the sounds of the English language, vocabulary, morphology or word structure, syntax (grammar), and text structure.

- *Chapter 4: Emergent Literacy* includes practices based on current research on assessing and teaching for emergent literacy, including teaching concepts about print and the language units that print represents, including phonemes.

- *Chapter 5: Phonics and Word Knowledge* treats phonics more generally as knowledge of words—knowledge that begins with teaching letter-to-sound correspondences and advances to include morphemes and derivational relationships among words.

- *Chapter 6: Helping Readers Build Fluency* is a new chapter devoted entirely to teaching students to read fluently with approaches that range from direct instruction to creative performances—voice choirs and readers' theater.

- *Chapter 7: The Importance of Vocabulary Development* is now a chapter all its own, with updated strategies for teaching many dimensions of word meanings. It connects general vocabulary and content specific vocabulary learning to the CCSS.

- *Chapter 8: Reading Comprehension, Part I: Making Sense of Literature* includes more teaching strategies to boost the comprehension of younger students, and an update of major concepts. It also includes strategies for close reading.

- *Chapter 9: Reading Comprehension, Part II: Understanding and Learning with Informational Texts* provides reliable suggestions for teaching students to comprehend and learn from informational text. It is rich with suggested Web- and computer-based resources. One section introduces teachers to the importance of helping students learn to use the basic structure of Web sites and identifying the sources of the sites.

- *Chapter 10: Critical Thinking and Critical Literacy* provides explanations of critical thinking and critical literacy and discusses their importance at all levels. The chapter explores ways of teaching students to conduct critical discussion of fictional and informational texts, and also addresses the special and urgent challenges of applying critical thinking to electronic texts.

- *Chapter 11: Teaching Children to Spell and Write* provides updates of research-supported practices for assessing and teaching spelling, including the work of Donald Bear, Robert Schlagal, Richard Gentry, and Kathy Ganske. The chapter also includes writing supports for English language learners.

- *Chapter 12: Assessing Literacy* explains the many kinds of assessments of reading and their purposes. It includes a section on administering the Informal Reading Inventory and subsections on scoring and interpreting the outcomes.

- *Chapter 13: Integrating Language and Literacy Instruction Across the Grades* provides updated information about research-based approaches to teaching students at grade levels K–8. Chapter 13 also includes information about the important relationship between oral language development and written language. References to the Common Core State Standards are made throughout the chapter.

- *Chapter 14: Models and Strategies for Teaching ESL and for Teaching Reading in the Mother Tongue* is our anchor chapter on teaching students with limited English proficiency. The chapter introduces research and information about legal policies for English language learners, as well as a section on building vocabulary with read-alouds.

Our Rationale for This Book

Teaching all children to read is a central responsibility of our elementary and middle schools. This book shares the knowledge and skills needed to do that work well. What kind of skills? Many of them could be called "traditional." There are things good teachers of reading have done successfully for a long time: student-centered teaching, immersing children in good literature—both fiction and nonfiction, and combining reading and writing, to name a few. We will pass on the best of those practices here. Traditional teaching won't take us far enough, though, because the circumstances of teaching have changed and are still changing.

We are facing enormous pressure to educate better. Changes in society beyond the classroom are insisting that every student learn to read and think critically—every student. There are fewer and fewer places in our society and in the workplace for the undereducated. By law, children with special needs are guaranteed the right to be educated in the least restrictive environment, and all teachers are invited to team together to plan and carry out instruction that helps every child learn. All of us are educating all or nearly all of the children.

Four hundred sixty. That is the number of different languages children in our classrooms speak at home. Fourteen million is the number of English language learners in our schools. North Carolina, South Carolina, and Indiana are some of the states that have recently seen 200% to 300% increases in English language learners. But 55% is the share of Spanish-speaking children who entered Los Angeles County schools last year. Most teachers at one time or another will teach a child who doesn't have strong English ability, and a large number will teach many English language learners every year.

A few years ago, teachers could complain of working in a lonely profession: When they closed the door in the morning they were alone all day with the kids. The Response to Intervention Initiative (RTI) is asking teachers who teach reading to work in teams with fellow teachers and other educational professionals in the school, sharing data and ideas and finding solutions to learning problems together.

When teachers plan together, they often speak of ways to combine or integrate the teaching of many subjects. As long as students are reading for comprehension and writing to learn, it makes sense to focus reading and writing some of the time on social studies, science, and mathematics. Integrating curriculum makes good use of teaching time. Also, with the greater attention being paid to reading instruction, integrating curriculum buys more teaching time for social studies and science.

Not long ago, teaching students to understand what they read was the pinnacle of reading instruction. Now we must go further and teach students not only to understand what they read but also to make sure it is credible and to examine it for biases and manipulation. Critical literacy and critical thinking are taking their place alongside reading comprehension.

The technology affecting what students read, how they read it, and how we should teach has been changing so rapidly that literacy educators now refer to the "new literacies." The recognition of new literacies acknowledges that as students continue to encode and decode messages, and store and search for information, the technologies that they use to do these things will have a profound effect on the skills they need.

Finally, the Common Core State Standards for the English Language Arts have now been with us for a while, after having been adopted with dramatic suddenness a decade ago by 45 states and the District of Columbia. The CCSS call on teachers to understand and be able to teach the details of the English language, to teach children to read closely for literary details, and to read and learn from informational texts. All of these topics had been addressed for years in previous editions of *All Children Read*, and the coverage has been strengthened in this fifth edition.

Special Features

Throughout the book, special features focus on issues of recurring importance to reading teachers and extend understanding of key concepts in reading instruction.

- **Common Core State Standards (CCSS) features** illustrate chapter content that aligns with Common Core State Standards.

CCSS

Common Core State Standards and Vocabulary for Literary Discussions

As part of the comprehension of literature, the Common Core State Standards include having vocabulary to discuss characters and their feelings and motives, settings, and actions (CCSS, Comprehending Literature: Key Ideas and Details, Standards 2 and 3). Students should also have control of literary terms, so that they can talk about an author's craft (CCSS, Comprehending Literature: Craft and Structure, Standard 5). Teachers should be careful to model and also explicitly teach the words students will need in order to discuss stories from the inside out (as if the characters were real people and the events actually happened) and from the outside in (as if they were writers and were interested in the way the author created the work).

Anticipation Guide

The following statements will help you begin thinking about the topics covered in this chapter. Answer *true* or *false* in response to each statement. As you read and learn more about the topics mentioned in these statements, double-check your answers. See what interests you and prompts your curiosity toward more understanding.

_____ **1.** Literacy makes you smarter because the vocabulary, the information, and the habit of learning from text make you better able to learn new things.

_____ **2.** Among adults, there is little correlation between people's reading ability and their income level.

_____ **3.** American children read fairly well. Fourth graders scored in the top eighth in the world on one recent international comparison of basic reading skill.

_____ **4.** Most reading disabilities are caused by malfunctions of the brain, and children with reading problems need a wholly different kind of teaching from that provided to normally developing readers.

_____ **5.** Research shows that 86% of the children who get a poor start in learning to read do not catch up with their peers.

_____ **6.** Differences in the amount of reading children do are not significant. What matters in teaching reading are the skills students learn.

_____ **7.** Giving parents ideas for helping their children at home with literacy experiences makes a considerable difference in the children's success in school.

_____ **8.** Reading ability develops through stages in this order: beginning reading, emergent literacy, reading to learn and for pleasure, building fluency, and mature reading.

_____ **9.** The debate between advocates of phonics instruction and advocates of whole-word instruction began in the 1980s in the United States, during the Reagan Administration.

_____ **10.** Because the U.S. Constitution leaves the governance of education up to the states, standards for education, including reading, vary widely from state to state.

- **An Anticipation Guide** at the start of each chapter provides readers with the opportunity to assess their level of understanding prior to reading the chapter.

A Classroom Story

Literacy Activities in a First-Grade Classroom

Maria Gupta plans to show her first-grade students how words are constructed by building them from consonants and vowels. On a digital overhead projector, she places cut-out consonants in one row and vowels in another. She has chosen the letters the children can recognize and name. The children are ready to study ways those letters can combine and spell words.

Poised to begin, she calls the children's attention to the screen. "Class," she says, "here is a way I think you'll find interesting to learn how words are made. Watch me make a word and take that word apart, and make another word!" Ms. Gupta moves the consonant s from the row of consonants. She thinks out loud as she does this, and she continues to think aloud as she moves through the modeled lesson.

"Okay, I'm moving the s. What sound does this letter make?" The children respond with the sssss sound, and she asks for the name of this letter as well. "Correct. I'm putting it down here where I'm going to build a word. But, I think I need more letters to make a word. Now I'm getting a vowel; I'm going to try a, hmm . . . okay, we have sa. I'm going to think of a word that begins with sa; you try, too, and I'll get another letter. I'm going to try t because I may have thought of a word spelled s a t." She moves the letter t beside s and a, and asks the class if they know this word. Many of the children respond correctly, but not all of them. Ms. Gupta says, "Yes! It's the word sat. Let's say all three sounds. We can hear them and then put them together to make sat. Sat is a word!" Ms. Gupta says, "Its nice to learn to make words."

For the next step, Ms. Gupta takes the letters away one by one beginning with the s. She then asks if they can pronounce the at that is left and guides them in deciding together if a word can be made with just two letters. In talk that ensues, Ms. Gupta makes teaching points at each opportunity. For example, she says, "Yes, we can make a word with just these two letters this time because at is a word. But we nearly always need more letters to make a real word in English because we don't have many two-letter words!" Ms. Gupta repeats word building in the same way with other consonants and vowels.

- Every chapter begins with a narrative **Classroom Story** that shares a reading teacher's experience in an active classroom. Each vignette models key concepts from the chapter and demonstrates the challenges of today's classrooms and considerations for addressing children's needs.

The World of Reading

Using Taxonomies in Questioning

As we take time to consider the role of questioning in learning, we need ways to categorize and analyze the nature of our questions. There are some commonly used frameworks that can be used to help us in this activity. The most widely used is probably one developed by Benjamin Bloom and his colleagues in the 1950s and revised in 2010. Bloom's **taxonomy** was not initially created for use by teachers, but was developed as a taxonomy of educational objectives to measure school goals and assessment. However, teachers saw its value and have used it as a tool to help them reflect on their classroom questioning patterns. The taxonomy has seven levels of questions: memory, translation, interpretation, application, analysis, evaluation, and synthesis.

In research studies of classroom talk, it is not uncommon to see analyses of the levels of teacher questions. In some descriptions of reading comprehension and reading assessment, Bloom's seven levels have been chunked into three or four levels. For example, one common way of describing reading is by thinking of literal, interpretive, applied, and critical levels of comprehension to define kinds of questions in relation to text.

Raphael (1986) has helped students to think about sources of information for questions they are to answer by creating four categories:

- *Right there:* Questions that can be answered directly from the text
- *Think and search:* Questions that require more than one piece of information from the text
- *Author and you:* Questions that go beyond the text
- *On your own:* Questions that rely on the reader

The whole strategy is called Question-Answer-Relationships (**QAR**) and provides very practical definitions that make it easy for students to become more involved in both planning their strategies for responding and becoming aware metacognitively of the range of responses they need to be able to make to the text.

Taxonomies provide a helpful language to think about questioning and the kinds of thinking we want to help stimulate in students. Some teachers keep the levels of questions in their teacher manuals or put them on the bulletin boards so that both they and students are more aware of the need to go beyond the literal or memory level. Other teachers do not like to use taxonomies to evaluate comprehension. Rather than conceiving of them as a hierarchy, these teachers see taxonomies as an array of options that are available to use as appropriate.

- **World of Reading** boxes investigate a wide array of subjects as they pertain to the field of reading.

Teach It! 39

Discussion Web

Promoting thoughtful discussion and interpretation of shared literature with peers, this activity asks students to consider both sides of an argument.

- **Teach It!** boxes link to correlating activities from the Teach It! appendix that can be used to teach the concepts discussed.

- **Differentiated Instruction** features highlight ways to differentiate instruction so that all students are engaged positively and productively, acknowledging the increasing diversity of today's students.

> ### Differentiating Instruction
> #### English Language Learners
>
> Measures of reading fluency count the number of words read in a period of time and subtract from that number a reader's errors in word reading. Fluency scores may be reported as words read correctly per minute (WCPM) or the reading may be characterized qualitatively on a rubric such as Rasinski and Zutell's *Multidimension Index* (Rasinski, 2003). When fluency assessment is conducted with native speakers, we assume we are testing children's speed and accuracy at reading words, whether the children read words as wholes or decode them. We are also indirectly assessing their understanding of the materials, since being able to follow the syntax of the sentences, the structure of the text, and the meaning of the ideas contribute to the rate and accuracy of reading.
>
> Be aware, though, that English language learners may score poorly on reading fluency measures, but not for the same reasons that native speakers do. English language learners' poorer performance on both rate and accuracy can be caused by difficulties in rapidly pronouncing words in an unfamiliar language (Ockey, 2010). The good news is that such readers may comprehend words that they mispronounce.
>
> The methods in this chapter that provide practice in fluent reading may be challenging for English language learners. The practice of repeated oral reading can be helpful for English language learners, but teachers should take extra care to avoid making it embarrassing. English language learners may read faster silently than they do orally, so practices like Scaffolded Silent Reading are recommended for them.

- **For Review** sections conclude each chapter and offer a convenient study tool in the form of a brief recap of the learning outcomes covered.
- **For Your Journal** sections offer ideas for using material learned in each chapter to inform development of a personal teaching journal.
- **Taking It to the World** exercises challenge readers to apply chapter material to authentic classroom situations.

This is the first edition of *All Children Read: Teaching for Literacy in Today's Diverse Classrooms* offered in REVEL™.

REVEL™ is Pearson's newest way of delivering our respected content. Fully digital and highly engaging, REVEL offers an immersive learning experience designed for the way today's students read, think, and learn. Enlivening course content with media interactives and assessments, REVEL empowers educators to increase engagement with the course, and better connect with students.

REVEL Offers:

Dynamic content matched to the way today's students read, think, and learn:

- **Videos**
  Integrated within the narrative, videos empower students to engage with concepts and take an active role in learning. REVEL's unique presentation of media as an intrinsic part of course content brings the hallmark features of Pearson's bestselling titles to life.

- **Quizzing**
  Located throughout REVEL, quizzing affords students opportunities to check their understanding at regular intervals before moving on.

Support Materials for Instructors

The following resources are available for instructors to download on www.pearsonhighered.com/educators. Instructors enter the author or title of this book, select this particular edition of the book, and then click on the "Resources" tab to log in and download textbook supplements.

- Instructor's Resource Manual and Test Bank (0-13-451598-6)

The Instructor's Resource Manual and Test Bank includes suggestions for learning activities, additional Experiencing Firsthand exercises, supplementary lectures, case study analyses, discussion topics, group activities, and a robust collection of test items. Some items (lower-level questions) simply ask students to identify or explain concepts and principles they have learned. But many others (higher-level questions) ask students to apply those same concepts and principles to specific classroom situations—that is, to actual student behaviors and teaching strategies.

- PowerPoint Slides (0-13-451600-1)

The PowerPoint slides include key concept summarizations, diagrams, and other graphic aids to enhance learning. They are designed to help students understand, organize, and remember core concepts and theories.

- TestGen (0-13-451599-4)

TestGen is a powerful test generator that instructors install on a computer and use in conjunction with the TestGen testbank file for the text. Assessments, including equations, graphs, and scientific notation, may be created for both print or testing online.

TestGen is available exclusively from Pearson Education publishers. Instructors install TestGen on a personal computer (Windows or Macintosh) and create tests for classroom testing and for other specialized delivery options, such as over a local area network or on the Web. A test bank, which is also called a Test Item File (TIF), typically contains a large set of test items, organized by chapter and ready for use in creating a test, based on the associated textbook material.

The tests can be downloaded in the following formats:

TestGen file - PC

TestGen file - MAC

TestGen - Blackboard 9

TestGen - Blackboard CE/Vista (WebCT)

D2L

Moodle

Sakai Test Bank

Acknowledgments

We would like to thank the reviewers who took time out from busy schedules to share with us their support and expertise and provided us with the valuable feedback that helped to shape this project: Thangi Appanah, Ed.D., Gallaudet University; Dr. Clarissa Gamble Booker, Prairie View A&M University; Michele Repass, Ph.D., George Mason University Valerie Wright, Saint Leo University; Laurence Zoeckler, Utica College.

For hanging in through five editions Charles Temple thanks his coauthors on this book, which was conceived in a kitchen in Brasov, Romania, seventeen years ago. Thanks, also, to colleagues and students at HWS and to the good teachers in the Finger Lakes and elsewhere for inspiration and insights, to the International Literacy Association for offering a clearinghouse for teachers' ideas, to the Open Society Institute and to CODE-Canada for many great adventures over the years, and of course to Codruța and our family. He joins his co-authors in thanking our dear copy editor Kathy Smith for keeping us grammatical through so many editions; our production team at Cenveo in India, Revathi Viswanathan and Yasmita Hota; our current editors at Pearson, Drew Bennett, Carolyn Schweitzer, Miryam Chandler, and Hope Madden; and the previous editors who believed in this book and helped it on its way: especially Aurora Martinez, Kathryn Boice, Janet Domingo, Karen Mason, Kathy Smith, Bryce Bell, and Meredith Fossel.

Donna Ogle wants to thank her husband, niece, and colleagues for their contributions to this book. Bud has provided incredible support for this project and is a model "critical reader." Kjersten Kuhlman, teaching in Massachusetts, helps Donna stay current. The teachers with whom Donna works in the Chicago area and in international contexts energize her to share their exemplary practices.

Alan Crawford thanks his colleagues and students in the public schools of East Los Angeles and Cal State Los Angeles for inspiration over the years; the teachers with whom he's worked—in California, Latin America, Central Asia, Central Europe, and Africa; good friends at UNESCO, the International Literacy Association, and the Open Society Institute; and, of course, Linda.

Codruta Temple thanks her husband, Charles Temple, and the other coauthors, Donna Ogle and Alan Crawford, for trusting her to be able to contribute to this new edition of a textbook that she has used in her classes for many years, and for inviting her to do so. She also thanks all her former linguistics and literacy professors for teaching her much of what she knows today. Finally, she thanks her students at SUNY Cortland for learning so much from this text.

All of the authors send a grateful farewell to our long-time coauthor, Professor Penny Freppon, and wish her a happy retirement of teaching in Guatemala and hiking the mountains of Montana.

Chapter 1
Approaches to Teaching Reading

 ## Learning Outcomes

After reading this chapter you should be able to:

1. Define literacy and its importance in students' lives
2. Summarize the current state of literacy in the United States
3. List and describe the components of reading ability
4. Name the phases of reading development
5. Outline the recent history of reading instruction

Anticipation Guide

The following statements will help you begin thinking about the topics covered in this chapter. Answer *true* or *false* in response to each statement. As you read and learn more about the topics mentioned in these statements, double-check your answers. See what interests you and prompts your curiosity toward more understanding.

_____ 1. Literacy makes you smarter because the vocabulary, the information, and the habit of learning from text make you better able to learn new things.

_____ 2. Among adults, there is little correlation between people's reading ability and their income level.

_____ 3. American children read fairly well. Fourth graders scored in the top eighth in the world on one recent international comparison of basic reading skill.

_____ 4. Most reading disabilities are caused by malfunctions of the brain, and children with reading problems need a wholly different kind of teaching from that provided to normally developing readers.

_____ 5. Research shows that 86% of the children who get a poor start in learning to read do not catch up with their peers.

_____ 6. Differences in the amount of reading children do are not significant. What matters in teaching reading are the skills students learn.

_____ 7. Giving parents ideas for helping their children at home with literacy experiences makes a considerable difference in the children's success in school.

_____ 8. Reading ability develops through stages in this order: beginning reading, emergent literacy, reading to learn and for pleasure, building fluency, and mature reading.

_____ 9. The debate between advocates of phonics instruction and advocates of whole-word instruction began in the 1980s in the United States, during the Reagan Administration.

_____ 10. Because the U.S. Constitution leaves the governance of education up to the states, standards for education, including reading, vary widely from state to state.

A Classroom Story

What Makes a Good Teacher of Reading and Writing?

Good teachers of reading and writing are multitalented people. They know a great many teaching methods, but they also have a solid background in the science of language and literacy, and they proudly keep up with new developments in their field. They are keen observers of children's learning, and inventive designers of lessons and techniques. They can connect with children, and children of all backgrounds like them, trust them, and are inspired by them. They make unusual efforts to connect with their students' families, too, and help the families feel comfortable with the school environment and practices. Good teachers of reading and writing love to read and write, and they gladly demonstrate their enthusiasm and share their knowledge with their students.

Good teachers of reading and writing work everywhere—in classrooms from Los Angeles to New York City, from the Rio Grande Valley to the fields of Saskatchewan, and all around the world. Some work in carpeted classrooms equipped with smartboards and tablets, while others make cheerful places out of storage rooms, hallways, or even tropical shelters with rattling tin roofs and open walls—always thoughtfully orchestrating the learning of an individual child or of many different children. You will find them teaching in English, Spanish, French, Tagalog, Arabic, or many languages at once. In North America, some good teachers of reading have the title of reading specialists, some are reading coaches, and some are teachers of children with special needs; many are classroom teachers at all levels, including teachers of English to speakers of other languages as well as teachers of social studies, science, and other subjects who recognize the need to help students learn to read and learn from materials in their disciplines. Many are active in their professional associations, and share their experiences and learn from others at the state, regional, and national conventions of the International Literacy Association and the National Council of Teachers of English.

The authors of this book hope that you will share with those good teachers a passion for bringing the gift of literacy to young people, that you will have a fascination for the intricacies of the task and an appreciation of the scholarship necessary to understand how reading works and how it is taught, and that you will continue to grow in your knowledge of reading and reading instruction.

Teaching every child to read and write is the most important mission of the elementary and middle school teacher. Science, mathematics, and social studies; art, physical education, and vocational preparedness; anti-drug abuse and conflict resolution education; civic education and education for self-awareness—all contribute to the making of the well-rounded child (and all of them require literacy in their own ways, too). But teaching children to read and write and to use the thinking processes that accompany literacy prepare them to learn their other school subjects and to educate themselves for the rest of their lives. The skills of literacy are centrally important for other reasons, too: Being able to read and write makes children smarter and ultimately makes their lives better.

Why Does Literacy Matter?

Literacy. Think about that word for a minute. If you describe a friend or relative as "literate," chances are you mean that person has read many important books and been affected by them. But if you say someone is "not literate," or, worse yet, "illiterate," you mean that person cannot read this sentence. There is a lot of territory in between! When we attach the word *literate* to "technological" or "financial," then literacy means to have the concepts and vocabulary that enable us to make sense of technology or financial information, and to have the skills to use that knowledge to operate successfully in the fields of technology or finance. Those uses of literacy come close to what we mean by the term *literacy* in this book. We define **literacy** *as a set of concepts and skills that enable a person to read and write: that is, to make sense of and communicate messages through the medium of written language.*

Teaching children to read and write not only gives them access to knowledge from print but also makes them better able to use that knowledge. Children who read store up background knowledge about the things they read about, whether it be nature, science, history, current events, or geography (Schwanenflugel, P. J., & Knapp, N. F., 2016; Stanovich, 1992). This knowledge helps them make better sense of the new things they read (Anderson & Pearson, 1984) and encounter in their everyday lives; in other words, it makes them smarter (Acheson, Wells, & MacDonald, 2008). Children who read gain bigger vocabularies, too (Smith, 1997), and having bigger vocabularies enables them to notice things (Brown, 1955) and to make finer distinctions in their perceptions of the world (Beck, McKeown, & Kucan, 2013).

Literacy helps children to think in more sophisticated ways. Studies have shown that reading proficiency makes profound differences in people's reasoning, their awareness of language, their understanding of themselves, and even their ability to formulate questions and learn about things they didn't know (Luria, 1976). Children who read and talk about books with others show greater self-awareness and critical thinking (Almasi, 1995), demonstrate increased empathy and social understanding (Lysaker, Tonge, Gauson, & Miller, 2011), tend to engage ideas more deeply (Eeds & Wells, 1989; Goatley, Brock, & Raphael, 1995), and are more likely to perceive themes in stories; that is, they are more likely to get the message (Lehr, 1991).

Among adults, literacy is associated with better health, greater job opportunities, and higher incomes (National Center for Education Statistics, 2015). Surveys show that people who can read and write well tend to have a wider range of options in life. But surveys also show that people need fairly sophisticated levels of literacy to benefit in terms of better jobs and other quality of life indicators (OECD and Statistics Canada, 2005).

This discussion may seem remote to anyone teaching kindergarten or third grade, but please pay attention: Students' early experiences as readers have a huge effect on their eventual success or failure to learn to read and write. Those of you who are fortunate enough to be teachers are in a privileged position to make sure your children have better choices available to them both sooner and later. You can teach them to read and write. But be aware that people with limited literacy do not usually see themselves as having a literacy problem (National Center for Education Statistics, 2015). The task of a teacher of reading, then, will not only be to teach but also to motivate. Even though reading ability is a ticket to a better future for all students, they might not know that, and their families might not know it either. Teachers have to make special efforts to encourage every child to *want* to be a reader, and for their parents to support them in their efforts to learn.

Check Your Understanding 1.1: Gauge your understanding of the skills and concepts in this section.

How Well Do Children in the United States Read?

For years, the media have clamored about the poor state of reading in American schools. But the critics have mostly gotten it wrong. They have missed both the considerable achievements as well as the most serious challenges in our nation's efforts to teach all children to read (Klenk & Kibby, 2000). In a nutshell, two things are true about the way children read in the United States:

1. American students in elementary schools do fairly well at basic reading compared to those in other countries. But—

2. Success in reading among American students is spread unevenly among our children.

Global Reading Scores

According to the latest international comparison of reading achievement, the **PIRLS** (Progress in International Reading Literacy), in 2011 American fourth graders scored sixth compared to children in the 45 countries around the world who participated in the test, and that rank was up from eleventh in 2006 (see Figure 1.1).

The **PISA** (Programme for International Student Assessment) test samples students' ability to solve real-world problems using a variety of realistic texts. In 2012 American 15-year-olds scored above the world's average in reading on the PISA test, but students in more than 21 countries scored better than students in the United States.

Discrepancies in Reading Achievement Among American Students

Our most successful students do well in basic literacy tasks, but there are many students who do not. For example, the National Assessment of Educational Progress (**NAEP**) defines a fourth-grade "proficient reading level" this way:

> *Fourth-grade students performing at the* Proficient *level should be able to integrate and interpret texts and apply their understanding of the text to draw conclusions and make evaluations.* (National Center for Education Statistics, 2015)

In 2015, 40% of all U.S. fourth graders could read at or above the proficient level, though that number dropped to one in five black students and Hispanic students. What about the rest? A "basic level" of reading ability on the NAEP was described this way:

> *Fourth-grade students performing at the* Basic *level should be able to locate relevant information, make simple inferences, and use their understanding of the text to identify details that support a given interpretation or conclusion. Students should be able to interpret the meaning of a word as it is used in the text.* (National Center for Education Statistics, 2015)

In 2015, 42% of all fourth graders could read at a basic level; 31% read below that level. Again, performance was different for different ethnic groups. Nearly half of all black and Hispanic students read below the basic level in 2015.

In 2015, a third of all U.S. eighth graders were at or above the proficient level, compared to 15% and 20% of black students and Hispanic students, respectively.

At the eighth grade level, NAEP defines basic reading this way:

> *Eighth-grade students performing at the* Basic *level should be able to locate information; identify statements of main idea, theme, or author's purpose; and make simple inferences from texts. They should be able to interpret the meaning of a word as it is used*

Figure 1.1 PIRLS Scores for Fourth Grades, 2011

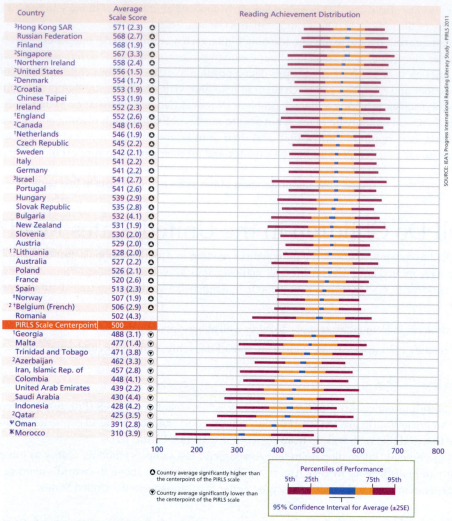

in the text. Students performing at this level should also be able to state judgments and give some support about content and presentation of content. (National Center for Education Statistics, 2015).

In 2015, 42% of all eighth graders read at a basic level. But it's troubling again that a fourth of all eighth graders could not do so, and that proportion rose to 42% and 35% of black and Hispanic students, respectively.

DIFFERENCES IN READING ACHIEVEMENT BY SOCIOECONOMIC STATUS Differences in reading achievement are often related to socioeconomic status. That is not good news for American children, since a third of them live in poverty, according to *The Washington Post* (Ingraham, 2015). The *Post's* definition of a person living in poverty is anyone who makes below 60% of the national average income. When that criterion is tightened to below 50% of the national average, still over 23% of children in the United States are considered to be poor. By either criterion, that is a terrible statistic. It looks even worse when compared to other developed countries. As you can see from Figure 1.2, according to UNICEF, our child poverty rate in the United States at over 23% was second highest of the world's 35 richest countries. Lowest was Iceland, with 4.7%.

Poor children now make up a slight majority of the children who attend public schools in the United States (Layton, 2014). American students' standing on at least one international comparison is pulled down by high rates of poverty, one critic claims (Martin Carnoy, in Rabinovitz, 2013). The gap between U.S. 15-year olds' scores on the PISA test, on which we

Figure 1.2 Child Poverty Rates in Developed Countries

Child poverty rate
(% of children living in households with equivalent income lower than 50% of national median)

Note: Data refer to children aged 0 to 17.
Sources: Calculations based on EU-SILC 2009, HILDA 2009, SLID 2009, SHP 2009, PSID 2007. Results for New Zealand are from Perry (2011). Results for Japan are from Cabinet Office, Gender Equality Bureau (2011).

now rank behind more than 20 countries, would be cut in half if the students in U.S. schools were compared with samples of students with similar demographics in other countries.

Poverty complicates children's learning in a host of ways that we will consider in Chapter 2. It is not surprising that poor children—those from families who are eligible for free or reduced cost lunches—tend to score well below other children in reading (see Figure 1.3).

Low family income does not necessarily mean students should perform poorly in reading. **Resilient students** are those who overcome difficult circumstances and learn to read in school. Poor children living in Asia are likely to be resilient—50% to 70% of them (PISA, 2009). But they are less so in the United States, where only about 5% of children from poor family backgrounds tend to be resilient (Center on International Education Benchmarking, 2013).

DIFFERENCES IN READING ACHIEVEMENT BY STATE AND LANGUAGE BACKGROUND   There are also sizable differences in reading achievement levels among the states. In 2015, the state with the highest scores had 50% of fourth graders reading at or above the proficient level, while in the lowest scoring state only half that many read proficiently. In the lowest scoring state nearly half of the fourth graders read below the basic level, compared to 18% reading below basic in the state with the highest scores. In the highest scoring state, 14% of the children read at the advanced level, but only 4% did so in the lowest performing state (National Center for Education Statistics, 2015).

Figure 1.3 Relation Between Poverty and Reading Achievement

SOURCE: NAEP *Nation's Report Card*, 2011: http://nces.ed.gov/nationsreportcard/pdf/main2011/2012457.pdf

English language learners (ELLs) are defined by the NAEP as "[S]tudents who are in the process of acquiring English language skills and knowledge" (National Center for Education Statistics, 2015). English Language Learners score well below native English speakers (see Figure 1.4).

Who Are the Struggling Readers?

If success in reading in the United States is spread unevenly, how many of our children have "reading disabilities"? A reading disability is said to be present when a child who can see and hear well, has normal intelligence, and who has had adequate instruction fails to learn to read. Or to be more specific, the federal Individuals With Disabilities Education Act (IDEA) defines a Specific Learning Disability, of which a reading disability is a subcategory, as "a disorder in one or more of the basic psychological processes involved in understanding or in using language, spoken or written, which disorder may manifest itself in the imperfect ability to listen, think, speak, read, write, spell, or do mathematical calculations. Such term includes such conditions as perceptual disabilities, brain injury, minimal brain dysfunction, dyslexia, and developmental aphasia. Such term does not include a learning problem that is primarily the result of visual, hearing, or motor disabilities, of mental retardation, of emotional disturbance, or of environmental, cultural, or economic disadvantage" (National Center for Learning Disabilities, 2014, p. 2).

By this definition, perhaps 5% of all school children—2.4 million of them—have Specific Learning Disabilities (National Center for Learning Disabilities, 2014). The majority of those disabilities affect reading. The percentage of children with learning disabilities has shrunk in recent years, but whether the decline is due to earlier and more effective reading interventions or because of refinements in identifying children with learning disabilities is a subject of debate.

Early Reading Experiences Matter

Why are early reading experiences important? The value of a good beginning in reading—and the damage that can be done by a poor beginning—was underscored by Connie Juel (1988). Juel surveyed a group of first graders in a Texas public school, found the 20% who read least well, and carefully tracked the reading progress of 54 of these students for three years. At the end of the study, 86% of those children were still in the bottom half of the class. Although reading problems had not been severe in first grade, they were serious by fourth grade. Juel worried that these children would not close the gap in later years.

Why?

"MATTHEW EFFECTS" IN READING   In a famous essay, Keith Stanovich (1986) showed that in learning to read, "The rich get richer and the poor get poorer." He called this phenomenon the "**Matthew Effect**," after the Bible verse, "For unto every one that hath shall be given, and he shall have abundance: but from him that hath not shall be taken away even that which he hath" (Matthew 25:29). Stanovich meant that students who get off to a good start in reading are likely to practice reading and get better and better. But for others, relatively small reading problems in the early years can discourage students from practicing their reading; and if they don't practice, their reading ability won't grow, so those small problems are compounded and grow into severe reading disabilities after three or four years. Watch this video in which Dr. Stanovich explains the Matthew Effect and answer the question that follows.

FIGURE 1.4 Reading Scores of English Language Learners Compared to Others

SOURCE: National Assessment of Education Progress, *Nation's Report Card Reading and Mathematics Assessment 2015*. http://www.nationsreportcard.gov/reading_math_2015/#reading/acl?grade=4

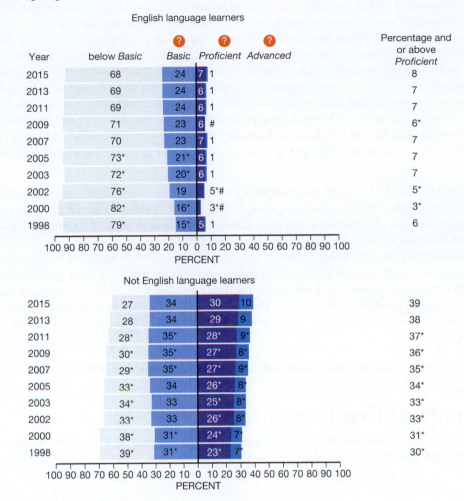

Year	below *Basic*	*Basic*	*Proficient*	*Advanced*	Percentage and or above *Proficient*
English language learners					
2015	68	24	7	1	8
2013	69	24	6	1	7
2011	69	24	6	1	7
2009	71	23	6	#	6*
2007	70	23	7	1	7
2005	73*	21*	6	1	7
2003	72*	20*	6	1	7
2002	76*	19	5*#		5*
2000	82*	16*	3*#		3*
1998	79*	15*	5	1	6

100 90 80 70 60 50 40 30 20 10 0 0 10 20 30 40 50 60 70 80 90 100
PERCENT

Year	below *Basic*	*Basic*	*Proficient*	*Advanced*	Percentage and or above *Proficient*
Not English language learners					
2015	27	34	30	10	39
2013	28	34	29	9	38
2011	28*	35*	28*	9*	37*
2009	30*	35*	27*	8*	36*
2007	29*	35*	27*	9*	35*
2005	33*	34	26*	8*	34*
2003	34*	33	25*	8*	33*
2002	33*	33	26*	8*	33*
2000	38*	31*	24*	7*	31*
1998	39*	31*	23*	7*	30*

100 90 80 70 60 50 40 30 20 10 0 0 10 20 30 40 50 60 70 80 90 100
PERCENT

 Video Exploration 1.1: Watch the video (www.youtube.com/watch?v=IF6VKmMVWEc) and answer questions that reflect the content you have read.

Children learn to read by reading. The amount of reading children do closely correlates with reading achievement at all levels (Garan & DeVoogd, 2008), since children who read more tend to read better (Allington, 2014). That is why teachers need to consider the Matthew Effect as they plan instruction. Watch this video and think about the ways that the Matthew Effect might influence a teacher's daily classroom routine. Then, answer the question that follows.

Video Exploration 1.2: Watch the video and answer questions that reflect the content you have read.

Family and Community Involvement

Families make a difference in children's preparation to learn to read and write. On the average, children from poor families have more difficulty learning to be literate than children from middle-class homes do (Vernon-Feagans, Hammer, Miccio, & Manlove, 2001). But the exact reasons for this can be difficult to tease out. If a family is poor, then poverty itself presents a complex set of stress factors (Ehrenreich, 2001). If you are poor, it is hard to raise a healthy and competent child.

It is hard to buy and prepare nutritious food. It is hard to afford good-quality childcare. It is hard to find the time and energy between jobs to spend time with your child.

Nonetheless, researchers have identified family literacy practices related to children's success in learning to read and write. Many of these may be influenced by the school or by the school working in concert with community partners. The National Research Council (Snow, Burns, & Griffin, 1998) found that families help children become readers in four ways: by showing children that they (the family members) place value on literacy, by expecting children to work hard to achieve goals and motivating and encouraging them to do so, by making sure there are accessible reading materials in the home, and by reading with the children. Family literacy projects that encourage families to read to children and talk with them can have success (Vernon-Feagans et al., 2001). But helping families nurture their children's literacy is not a simple matter. Communication patterns within families are hard to change—even if we agreed that educators had any business trying to change them! A famous study showed that poor families offer children less verbal interaction than middle-class families do, and the shortage of interaction has a strong effect on the children's vocabulary size (Hart & Risley, 1995), which in turn shortchanges the store of meanings available to them as they try to learn to read and write.

GIVING ALL FAMILIES ACCESS TO READING MATERIALS   It is known that children's preschool experiences with books and print also contribute to their success in learning to read once they arrive in school (Snow et al., 1998; Teale & Sulzby, 1987). But families who live in low-income areas have far less access to books than middle-class families do—fewer libraries, open fewer hours (Bornstein, 2011, unpaged; Neuman & Celano, 2012).

Nearly all families in the United States have some contact with literacy materials, but many low-literacy families really do not seriously engage with print enough to provide experiences for children that teach them (Purcell-Gates, 1996). Even when low-income families visit libraries, the visits don't necessarily result in their finding materials to read (Neuman & Celano, 2010). Family literacy work is not always easy, but the title of Purcell-Gates' book about the illiterate mother and the semi-literate son—*The Cycle of Low Literacy*—underscores how important it is for educators to include families in their plans for promoting literacy.

Check Your Understanding 1.2: **Gauge your understanding of the skills and concepts in this section.**

Components of Reading Ability

What exactly are you teaching when you teach a child to read? Reading ability can be broken down into several different sets of concepts and skills. The most widely recognized ones are outlined below.

Concepts About Print

Imagine a child who had never watched someone read. If that child were in your kindergarten or first-grade class, you would need to show her what a book is, how to hold it, what is print and what is a picture, the direction of the print across from left to right and down the page, that print contains letters and the identities of those letters, that letters combine into words and that words are groups of letters with a space on either end, that the same words are spoken each time someone reads the same page, and—above all!—that those words add up to interesting information or a good story. Taken together, all of these facts are called **concepts about print**. Most children enter kindergarten with at least some concepts about print intact. But children vary widely in their exposure to print, so assessing and teaching concepts about print should be part of the repertoire of every teacher of preschool, kindergarten, and first grade—and just about every teacher of special education in the primary grades.

Word Recognition and Phonics

Recognizing the words on the page is the next important reading skill. This skill has two parts. One is recognizing words instantly, as you would recognize the face of a friend. This is called **sight word** *recognition*, or recognizing words *at sight*. A word that has been seen many times, particularly if it refers to something interesting and its meaning is familiar, becomes a word a reader can recognize instantly. A good reader has many thousands of sight words in memory.

The other aspect of word recognition is puzzling out the identity of words readers can't yet recognize, and this is called **decoding**. When you read nonsense words like *glatz, charl, splane,* and *clorption,* you are decoding. A young reader uses decoding to figure out how to read the unfamiliar word *stripe* when he already knows how to read *stop* and *ripe;* or *dot* when he can read hardly any words at all, but knows the sounds represented by the consonants *D* and *T*, and the vowel *O* when it comes right before a consonant. The sort of knowledge a reader applies when he decodes is called **phonics.** Phonics is knowledge of the relations between letters or groups of letters and speech sounds.

Phonics knowledge, in turn, has two parts. One is knowing the relationship between letters and clusters of letters called **graphemes** (a grapheme is a small unit of written language) and the speech sounds they represent. The other is awareness of those speech sounds, called **phonemes** (a phoneme is the smallest unit of speech that differentiates meanings). This latter sort of awareness is known as **phonological awareness** (which is the awareness of speech sounds in general, including syllables) and **phonemic awareness** (awareness of phonemes specifically).

Reading Fluency

Reading fluency has four aspects:

- recognizing words *automatically and accurately,*
- reading text *with appropriate speed,*
- reading *with meaningful inflection* (the voice goes higher and lower, louder and softer, depending on the meaning or the emotions evoked by what is read), and
- *grouping words meaningfully* (for example, "Austin, [pause] the capital of Texas, [pause] is the home of the University of Texas.").

Reading fluency is closely related to comprehension. First, reading fluently *contributes to* comprehension because having the ability to read strings of words smoothly and accurately leaves the mind plenty of capacity to think about the meaning of the text (Perfetti, 1992; Pressley, 2000). Second, reading fluency *benefits from* comprehension because a reader can only read with good voice inflection and meaningful pauses if she understands what she is reading. Bear in mind that fluent reading can be silent as well as oral—we just can't hear the inflection and the word grouping when students are reading silently.

Like any other skill that we want to be able to perform automatically—be it tying a shoe, driving an automobile, sailing a boat, or hitting a tennis ball—reading fluency improves with practice. That is why thoughtful teachers provide children plenty of opportunities to read texts that are fairly easy for them, even as they sometimes assign more challenging texts, too. It's not surprising that our best readers are the ones who read often for pleasure (see Figure 1.5).

Vocabulary

Vocabulary is the store of words and their meanings in memory. Having an adequate vocabulary helps reading in several ways. First, when you encounter words such as *epithalamion, ecclesiastical, primogeniture, dodecahedron,* or *unicameral,* you may struggle to decide what the letters are adding up to, only to discover you don't know the word they spell anyway. On the other hand, when you come across words like *muthuh, sista,* and *solja,* you can easily work through the unfamiliar street spellings because you do know the words they spell. Vocabulary helps us read by facilitating word recognition in just that way: You may more successfully puzzle through the spelling of a word you don't immediately recognize in written form if you already have the word in your vocabulary.

FIGURE 1.5 Children Who Read for Pleasure Score Higher on Reading Tests.

SOURCE: NAEP *Nation's Report Card,* 2011: http://nces.ed.gov/nationsreportcard/pdf/main2011/2012457.pdf

Average Fourth Grade Reading Scores on the National Assessment of Reading Progress Sorted by Self-Reported Reading for Pleasure.

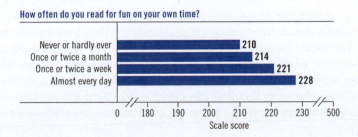

Vocabulary aids comprehension, too. Words are tokens of meaning. They are both labels for the facts and concepts we have learned and mental identifiers that we retain and will use to make sense of future experiences—whether reading or in real life. It's not surprising that students' vocabulary size correlates positively with their reading comprehension scores. Monolingual English-speaking students vary widely in their vocabulary size, and for English language learners, limited vocabulary can be a debilitating problem.

Reading Comprehension

Reading comprehension is the act of understanding the meaning, of making sense of what is read. Comprehending what we read is the main point of reading, of course, but for decades, research has reported that comprehension has received less attention in the classroom than other aspects of reading, especially word recognition and phonics.

When a student does it well, comprehension may look like a single competence, but there are many factors that contribute to it and many skills that comprise it.

- *Background knowledge.* It may seem odd to say that your capacity to understand something depends on how much you already know about it, but scholars find that is largely true. A time-honored model of comprehension known as *schema theory* (Pearson & Anderson, 1985) argues that to understand something, you need to interpret the new information using the knowledge you already had, and then sort the new information into your existing mental frameworks, or what is called your *schemes* or *schemata* of prior knowledge. Moreover, the better organized your prior knowledge is, the more likely you are to pay attention to aspects of the new information that will be helpful to know in the long run—and will help you comprehend still more new information (Alexander & Jetton, 2000). **Background knowledge** implies having labels or *vocabulary* for those things that are already known. We have mentioned vocabulary as a separate aspect of reading skill because it is often treated as such, but it is an important part of comprehension, too.

- *Visualizing, or imaging.* Being able to picture what is suggested by the words in a text is another aspect of comprehension. Not all text invites imaging to the same degree, but readers should be ready to come up with images in their mind when the words suggest them.

- *Main ideas.* A competent reader can find *main ideas* or recognize what is most essential in a passage—the main claim or assertions, and also what details are used to support it—almost as if she were able to construct an outline of the text in her head.

- *Summarizing.* A competent reader can repeat back to you the essential points in a passage, with the less important information left out of the summary.

- *Making inferences.* "Reading between the lines" or making inferences is a key aspect of comprehension, since a good reader can put together cues from the text with what he knows from experience to construct meaning, even when that meaning is not expressed explicitly.

- *Following the pattern of a text.* Whether the pattern is the plot of a story, the pattern of a poem, the structure of an argument, or the organization of an explanation, following the pattern of a text is also important in comprehension. As students move up through the grades, they must be able to read intelligently in different genres that have different patterns. Stories usually introduce a setting in which characters encounter a problem, try different solutions, and experience an outcome with a consequence from which readers might derive some moral lesson. Most stories are not literally true, and they may range from highly fanciful (think *Harry Potter*) to highly realistic (think Walter Dean Myers's *Monster*, or R.J. Polacio's *Wonder*). Their language can be full of imagery, dialogue, struggles between right and wrong, appeals to emotion, and evocations of suspense and relief. Nonfiction texts from science are quite different, with specialized and exact vocabulary, structures of claim and support or explanation, and no protagonists and antagonists.

- *Reading comparatively across texts.* Adults read different, and often competing, texts that compare automobiles, insurance policies, vacation destinations, and political candidates. They look for insights on the same topic even when different texts don't share the same structure or address topics in the same way. They consider the author's point of view or perspective, possible biases, and credibility when they try to decide how to interpret statements and whether to accept them. Even students in the primary grades can get a multidimensional view of the Civil Rights era by reading a novel such as Rita Williams-Garcia's *One Crazy Summer,* then articles on the Civil Rights movement in *Cobblestone Magazine,* and also poems on black themes in collections such as Arnold Adoff's *The Poetry of Black America.*

Critical Reading

The Common Core State Standards are calling the attention of teachers at all levels to techniques of literary criticism, ways of exploring the meanings of texts, and ways texts have meaning. The approach that has been most popular since the 1970s and 1980s has been *reader response criticism* (Bleich, 1975; Rosenblatt, 1978), which holds that the meaning of a text is actively created by the reader with suggestions supplied by the print on the page. Teachers who follow this approach encourage students to talk about what a text means to them, and the teachers are not disturbed if different children respond somewhat differently to the same text. The Common Core State Standards have called for renewed attention to an older kind of criticism variously known as *formalism* or *New Criticism*. Formalism focuses on the text and not the reader, and calls for close reading that carefully scrutinizes the structure and parts of the literary work: reading, rereading, and studying the text much as a biologist would examine a living organism—the parts, relationships among the parts, and their overall function in a meaningful work.

There are good reasons to support both approaches. Reader response teaching tends to be more engaging; in addition, listening to different responses to the same text mirrors what happens in society, where conservatives and liberals, black citizens and white citizens, or women and men respond differently to the same event. Even though we respond differently, we need to understand and get along with each other, and classroom discussions that are run along the lines of reader response criticism can help develop interpersonal understanding and promote engaged and tolerant citizenship. Formalism and its method of close reading, on the other hand, require readers to look carefully at genres, text structures, word meanings, connotations, allusions, and many other literary devices in order to understand how they work together to form a meaningful whole. Formalism and close reading require disciplined thought and hard work, and they develop students' investigative skills.

Check Your Understanding 1.3: Gauge your understanding of the skills and concepts in this section.

Phases of Reading Development

Using the word *development* to describe growth in reading ability implies that the learner doesn't simply wait passively to take in reading instruction from a teacher, but rather undergoes an interaction among growth, experience, and discovery that can be called *developmental learning*. Developmental learning proceeds according to these factors:

- Cognitive growth of learners, which opens up capacities for learning
- Exposure to relevant models of skilled performance and challenges in learners' own performances from their surroundings
- Active discoveries initiated by the learners themselves
- Opportunities for learners to practice what they learn, and to work it into their ways of knowing and acting

Calling learning to read *developmental* suggests that all children go through roughly the same set of stages as they learn to read. It suggests that their maturation—simply getting older—plays a part, but that the stimulation, encouragement, modeling, and opportunities to practice reading and writing are important, too. Developmental learning follows fairly predictable pathways, although a learner's development along those pathways is usually more predictable in the early stages than in later ones.

Emergent Literacy

The earliest period or stage of learning to read and write has come to be called *emergent literacy*. In early childhood, before children enter formal instruction, they discover useful insights about literacy; these insights become the basis on which their later learning can be built, even the learning that is orchestrated by their teachers in school. In the emergent stage, learning about literacy involves:

- Learning about the nature of reading
- Learning what books are, what kinds of experiences come from them, and how they are put together
- Learning about language itself, that it comes in patterns like stories and poems, and that even though you cannot see it, it is real enough to be captured in books and revisited again and again
- Learning that language comes in units of words and even smaller units, and that the language one speaks while reading bears some kind of relationships to marks on a page.

In the field of literacy, as our awareness of emergent literacy has grown, teachers have promoted practices among families that help children's literacy to emerge. Head Start, the federally funded early childhood education program for disadvantaged children, now includes as part of its programming reading to children and other literacy activities that are embedded in children's daily play and learning activities. In some communities, parents are given a children's book when they leave the hospital with a newborn, to underscore the importance of reading to children and to make the point that it is never too early to begin reading to a child.

With their growing awareness of emergent literacy, teachers have developed ways to observe and assess children's early concepts of literacy. These include approaches such as Marie Clay's *Concepts about Print Test*, Elizabeth Sulzby's *Emergent Storybook Reading Inventory*, Darrell Morris's *Early Reading Screening Inventory*, and studies of invented spelling, as described by Richard Gentry or Temple, Nathan, and Temple (2013). Using these investigative approaches often yields amazing profiles of what children have discovered about literacy. However, they also give cause for concern when it turns out that important concepts about literacy have not yet emerged in one child or another, because we know that these children will need to have the concepts in place as they learn to read.

Learning to read in school without a fully developed foundation of emergent literacy concepts has been likened to trying to climb stairs when the first several steps are missing. Because teachers are aware of the importance of emergent literacy, they are now able to teach all children in a way that gives them another chance to develop emergent concepts about literacy. They can also provide finely tuned tutoring to children who need it so that more children can get off to the best possible start in learning to read and write.

Beginning Reading

In late kindergarten and first grade, most children enter the phase of beginning reading. Most prominent in this stage is their learning to read words, but children are also learning to understand what they read. The task of learning to read words from different combinations of letters on the page is so challenging that teachers often must remind children to "go back and read that line so it sounds like talk" or ask them, "Does that make sense?"

The stage of beginning reading comes after much prior learning. As we already noted, emergent readers must come to understand that print, and not pictures, talks (Clay, 1985) and that a reader is not free to say just any words when paging through a text but must come up with pronunciations of the words whose representations are printed there (Sulzby, 1985). They have a sense of the patterns of stories and poems, and they know how to follow them to make meaning.

With these understandings in place, children are able to concentrate on words and develop strategies for sounding them out, as well as develop sight vocabularies. They are ready, though they often need reminding, to find humor, suspense, and surprise in what they read—in other words, to make meaning from print. But their reading is still hesitant, and they still need much support from adults. They also need carefully crafted materials, with few words per page, predictable language patterns, and illustrations that help carry the meaning.

Building Fluency and Comprehension

Through late first and early second grade, most children have enough experience in reading words and following messages that their reading is becoming more and more fluent: more rapid and more accurate. For children who were read to often in early childhood, this period can be a joyful "catch up" moment: After a period of struggling to read texts that were far simpler and less meaningful than the stories they had long heard read to them, children are at last able to do for themselves what adults had to do for them. For children who are not so lucky as to have been read to, however, this period can be a hard trek through unfamiliar territory, as the fascinations of reading materialize only gradually. For the first type of child, teachers will find that their main task is to keep providing more books on the right levels to a hungry reader. For the second type of child, the teacher will have to celebrate gains but also gently and insistently push the child to read—and to read gradually more challenging texts.

If the teacher is successful, then all children will steadily amass sight words and increase both the quantity and the speed of their reading. They will be preparing themselves for the next stage of reading, which is called *reading for learning and pleasure*. Even so, wide differences will begin to open up here in the amount of reading children do and the size of their sight vocabularies.

Readers in this "fledgling" stage, as it is often called, are usually so preoccupied with getting the words right that they may forget about what the words are saying. However, they can, and should, be reminded to talk about the meaning of what they read. Teachers must make special efforts to make print meaningful through this stage.

Reading for Learning and Pleasure

By the beginning of third grade, and increasingly in fourth grade, something of a threshold is crossed, and the emphasis shifts from learning to read to reading to learn—and also reading for pleasure. By this time, children are expected to read and follow directions and to gain information from texts. In addition, they read chapter books and novels and have

Teach It! 60
The Writing Workshop
Learn how the workshop format supports young learners as they become familiar with the writing process: rehearsing, drafting, revising, editing, and publishing.

something to say about them in their response journals and in their book clubs, or wherever they discuss what they are reading.

A period for reading and writing instruction is still provided every day, but more and more time is given to free reading and discussion, as well as to writing workshops.

These activities are essential, because children must practice literacy to develop it. Nonetheless, there is still a place for teaching students how to comprehend, interpret, and compose. There is also still a need to make students aware of the structure of written words and the way our English vocabulary works. This is necessary because word knowledge is not gained only in the early years. The collection of words children encounter in text changes significantly at around fourth grade (primarily from words derived from Anglo-Saxon to words derived from Latin and Greek). At this point there are new features to be learned about words through the remainder of the elementary grades.

It is in fourth grade that problems in reading have traditionally become obvious because reading ability affects students' learning in other subjects. It is also because the unsuccessful struggles to learn to read well have led children to frustration and low motivation. Indeed, children's self-esteem might have begun to suffer because they haven't succeeded in a skill that is highly valued in school (Stanovich, 1986). Although troubled readers can and certainly should be helped to overcome their difficulties, doing so is time consuming at this stage, especially since by this time there is much content to be learned throughout the school day. Because they understand how earlier experiences contribute to children's reading abilities, many teachers, and whole programs such as Reading Recovery, are placing their greatest emphasis on getting children off to a good start in reading, so that the problem of the "fourth-grade slump" can be avoided wherever possible.

Mature Reading

After fifth grade and certainly by sixth grade, children who have made normal progress as readers have gradually developed additional abilities that are characterized as mature reading. They read with an appreciation of the author's style, and they enjoy reading passages aloud to friends or try to imitate an author's style in their own writing. They read beyond the details of a work, and can summarize its main point, argument, or theme. They read with an awareness of the author's take on the subject and may see a work as a metaphorical commentary on life. They can venture an intelligent interpretation of the meaning of a work and support it with careful reference to the text. They can read several works on a theme and talk perceptively on the ways different authors' views affect the different presentations. They might practice critical literacy, argue back against the theme of a book, or take issues with its sexist or racist overtones. In any case, they are more analytical and more philosophical in what they look for in texts and in the ways they respond to them.

Mature readers are also more strategic. They can read for information, and they have strategies for previewing, questioning, marking, note taking, reviewing, and studying books they read for information.

As we noted at the outset of this section, one characteristic of developmental learning is that the earlier periods of development are more predictable and more commonly experienced than the later ones. That is clearly true with respect to mature reading. Some readers show evidence of mature reading by the time they enter fourth grade. Many more show it by seventh or eighth grade. But many others rarely do this kind of reading.

Check Your Understanding 1.4: **Gauge your understanding of the skills and concepts in this section.**

The Recent History of Reading Instruction: How We Got Where We Are

The past 20 years have seen many changes to reading and writing instruction in the United States, and in most schools you will find teachers who have fascinating stories to tell of past movements and instructional practices. Your college library surely has methods books on the shelves written in earlier eras, with different assumptions and different practices than what you will be learning now (although it is true that many good teaching practices have been in use for a long time). We offer the following as a way to keep track of what has gone before in the reading field.

Early Modern Descriptions of Reading

In 1908, Edmund Burke Huey (1908) chronicled the major approaches to teaching reading that were practiced in American schools in his time. He found an unreconciled difference between teachers who preferred to emphasize words as wholes and teachers who taught students the relationships between letters and sounds. As Huey noted, this distinction was already very old—perhaps 350 years old, according to one of his sources. Huey offered research—his own and that of others—that showed that the eye and brain take just as long to recognize a single letter as they do a whole word. This finding, building on a reaction to the heavy drill orientations of reading approaches in the late nineteenth century, encouraged a movement toward whole-word teaching approaches that lasted through the mid-1960s. Even then, the issue was not settled, and between Huey's time and ours, there has been an intense outpouring of research on the issue. Hundreds of conferences have been attended by thousands of educators, yet the tension between different approaches to teaching beginning reading remains.

Phonics Versus Whole-Word Reading

In the 1960s, Jeanne Chall (1967) reviewed the available research on the question of the best approaches to beginning reading. She found that in the decades leading up to the time when she was writing, most children in the United States were taught to read in basal reading programs, that is, in textbooks composed of short reading passages with graduated difficulty levels. For the most part, the basal reading programs, such as the popular Dick and Jane series, used whole-word approaches (what Chall called a "meaning emphasis") and did not teach phonics (what Chall called a "code emphasis"). According to the studies she reviewed, however, reading approaches that did use phonics showed better results than programs that did not. Following the appearance of Chall's influential book, publishers began to include phonics instruction in their basal reading programs.

But that did not settle the matter. Many teachers, such as New Zealander Sylvia Ashton-Warner (1963), continued to favor whole-word approaches and argued that their use emphasized meaning, whereas the phonics approaches could lead children to focus on the small parts of reading—the letters and sounds—without an adequate appreciation of what the letters were supposed to add up to. Indeed, some of the reading materials that came into use during the 1960s focused so much on letter-to-sound regularities that they left very little meaning to be pursued. "Linguistic readers" contained text like this: "A man had a tin pin. It's a pin for a cap. It's a cap for Dan." Advocates of meaning-centered reading instruction worried that if children mostly read text as pointless as this, they could easily become confused about the true purpose of reading: to construct meaning from print.

The Cognitive Revolution

The 1970s saw a revolution in the way scholars thought of language learning. The field of psycholinguistics was developing, largely under the influence of the ingenious linguist Noam Chomsky. The researchers whom Chomsky inspired began to find evidence that children learn language by exercising a built-in capacity for discovery. As long as they are in the company of people who talk to them and who model language, and as long as those around them honor children's own needs to communicate, children will learn to talk. Gradually, by stages, through an amazing exercise of finely tuned linguistic discovery processes, children learn language.

Almost immediately, theorists began to see ways to apply psycholinguistic theory to the acquisition of reading. Frank Smith wrote an influential book called *Psycholinguistics and Reading* (1973), in which he and others argued that children could learn to read in large part by discovery and encouragement. One of the contributors to that book, Kenneth Goodman (1967), had offered a conception of reading as "a psycholinguistic guessing game." Goodman's work, along with that of some imaginative Australians such as Don Holdaway (1979) and Andrea Butler and Jan Turbill (1985), gave rise to what came to be known as the *whole language movement*.

Whole Language

Whole language advocates embraced many child-centered approaches to teaching. The *writing process approach* popularized by Donald Graves (1982) and Lucy Calkins (1996) was taken up by whole language advocates and became part of the movement. So did the literature-based approaches of Dorothy Strickland (1991) and Nancie Atwell (1985). Whole language classrooms were (and are) bursting with children's creativity, as children have rich experiences that stimulate talk, as they read and listen to much good literature, and as they write and act out their own ideas.

On the psychological front, the new field of cognitive psychology yielded studies of comprehension that greatly expanded our understanding of reading. A U.S. government grant to the University of Illinois created the Center for the Study of Reading, where Richard Anderson, David Pearson (1984), and others elaborated on a theory of comprehension called *schema theory*, which stresses the reader's active role in making meaning. Schema theory was highly compatible with the work of both the psycholinguists inspired by Noam Chomsky and the constructivist theories of intellectual development inspired by Swiss psychologist Jean Piaget and others. The theory found ready acceptance in the 1970s and 1980s, and most reading experts still accept it today in some form or another as our guiding theory of how comprehension works. Like psycholinguistic research before it, schema theory lent support to the child-centered, discovery-oriented beliefs of the whole language movement.

Research-Based Emphasis

Still, the disagreements between the meaning-centered advocates and the code-centered advocates continued. In the late 1980s, the U.S. Department of Education commissioned another examination of beginning reading instruction. The resulting work was *Beginning to Read* (1990), by a psychologist, Marilyn Jaeger Adams. In it, Adams concluded that exposure to print and enthusiastic encouragement might work in some cases but that they were not sufficient to teach all children to read. Like the evidence Jeanne Chall had reviewed 20 years before, the evidence Adams collected led her to conclude that reading approaches that explicitly and systematically taught children the code that links speech sounds to patterns of letters in words were more successful than those that did not. Adams urged teachers to give primacy to teaching children to decode and recognize words, even as they immersed the children in print and encouraged them to write.

Adams also highlighted another finding from research on reading: the importance of children's awareness of phonemes, the smallest sound units in spoken words. In a host of studies, phonemic awareness in first grade was found to make an important difference in whether children learned to read successfully. Adams urged teachers to emphasize phonemic awareness and letter-to-sound correspondences in their early reading instruction.

In the late 1990s, a study of early reading difficulties was undertaken by the Committee on the Prevention of Reading Difficulties in Young Children, a group of reading experts assembled under the auspices of the National Science Foundation. The resulting report, *Preventing Reading Difficulties in Young Children* (Snow et al., 1998), recommended that teachers encourage students' growth in language and general knowledge, their exposure to and appreciation of literature, and their opportunities to write, while also providing instruction to boost phonemic awareness, knowledge of letter-to-sound relationships, fluency, vocabulary, and comprehension.

In 1997, Congress commissioned yet another group of experts to "assess the effectiveness of different approaches used to teach children to read" (National Reading Panel Web site, 2003). This was the National Reading Panel, organized by the National Institute of Child Health and Human Development (NICHD) at the National Institutes of Health. After reviewing what they considered to be evidence-based studies of reading over a two-year period, the National Reading Panel published their findings in *The Report of the National Reading Panel: Teaching Children to Read* (2000). In it, the panel made a number of recommendations, including a strong push for skills instruction, especially in the recognition of words and the skills that support word recognition: awareness of speech sounds and knowledge of phonics.

No Child Left Behind

With the reauthorization of the Elementary and Secondary Education Act (U.S. Department of Education, 2001) called No Child Left Behind (signed into law on January 8, 2001), the administration of President George W. Bush insisted that every state develop learning standards in reading and test every child annually from third grade up. (Testing was phased in over a four-year period.) The act required that schools receiving federal funding use "evidence-based" instructional practices, and for its source of evidence, the Administration embraced the recommendations of the National Reading Panel, with special focus on five particular areas of focus: *phonological awareness, phonics, fluency, vocabulary*, and *comprehension*.

Armed with the No Child Left Behind legislation, the U.S. Department of Education was aggressive in its insistence that schools receiving federal funds use methods and materials that are backed by "SBRR," or "scientifically-based reading research." Democrats, Republicans, and a majority of the American people supported the emphasis on helping struggling readers, along with the use of state learning standards measured by end-of-year tests—although there was growing unease over the number of schools that were deemed "failures" under the NCLB initiative. The unease over the testing finally won out, and in December of 2015, thirteen years after No Child Left Behind was enacted, President Obama signed into law the Every Student Succeeds Act, or ESSA, which still required testing every year in grades three through eight and once again in high school but sent back to the states responsibility for the testing and for responses to failing schools.

CHANGES IN SPECIAL EDUCATION Until a couple of decades ago, the field of special education and the literacy field had little to do with each other. Special education and reading teachers were trained in different departments, where they learned different theories and practices. In schools, special education teachers and reading teachers—even "remedial" reading teachers—worked separately. The separation has largely collapsed, for two reasons: First, in the latter part of the twentieth century, the framework for understanding reading and reading problems that guided both special educators and reading educators received serious scrutiny, and now both fields have come to work from the same theories of reading and learning. Second, special education law evolved and now requires that children who are identified for special education services be "mainstreamed" into regular classrooms, where they may be taught by a classroom teacher and a special education teacher working together.

Current special education laws have created an approach known as *Response to Intervention,* or RTI, which calls for coordinated instruction for students with varying levels of need for attention, rather than a sharp distinction between children who are identified for special education services and everyone else. The concept of inclusion has evolved considerably in recent years. RTI has been subsumed in the broader construct of *multi-tiered systems of support,* or MTSS, that includes strategies for students with behavioral challenges in addition to academic ones. And after the Individuals with Disabilities Education Act of 2004 (IDEA) schools have broadened the idea of inclusion even further under the term *specially designed instruction* (SDI). (Special educators do love their abbreviations!) Specially designed instruction refers to teaching that is modified for students who require a wide range of accommodations, from those who have cognitive or behavioral challenges, to English language learners, to students who are gifted and talented. Along with the integrating students with special learning and behavioral needs into the mainstream has come the responsibility that they learn what other students learn. The recent Every Student Succeeds Act requires that all students, even those identified with special needs, take the federally mandated state achievement tests in grades 3 through 8—except for up to 1% who have significant cognitive challenges.

ENGLISH LANGUAGE LEARNERS The rights of students with limited English proficiency to be given appropriate education have been guaranteed by federal laws going back to the Civil Rights Act of 1964 and several decisions of the Supreme Court since then. These guarantees were extended to children of undocumented immigrants in 1982 by the Supreme Court ruling on *Plyler v. Doe*. The numbers of school-age children who speak a language other than English at home has doubled since the 1980s, and about 9% of all U.S. students have limited English proficiency (National Center for Education Statistics, 2015). These students are now found in many states, not concentrated in just a few states as in the past.

Many students in the United States do not speak English in their homes. This video discusses ways in which schools can provide services for non-English speaking families. After watching, answer the question that follows.

  Video Exploration 1.3: Watch the video and answer questions that reflect the content you have read.

LEARNING STANDARDS Since the nation's founding, the governance of education in the United States has been the responsibility of the states. In the 1990s, a decade after the founding of the United States Department of Education, the federal government was looking for a mechanism to exert enough influence over the states to lead a reform movement in education. An initiative called America 2000, launched in 1994 during the presidency of George H. W. Bush, introduced the idea of standards-based education. America 2000 called for states to set standards that defined "what all students should know and be able to do." The act set up a bipartisan federal panel to "certify State content standards and State student performance standards … if such standards are comparable or higher in rigor and quality to the voluntary national content standards and voluntary national student performance standards."

Within a decade, all states had set performance standards for children and had developed tests for those standards. But there was considerable variety from state to state in what children were expected to learn and what teachers were expected to teach.

Common Core State Standards

The National Governors Association Center for Best Practices (NGA Center) and Council of Chief State School Officers (CCSSO) set out to address the variety of learning standards found from state to state and came up with a common set of standards that students all over the United States should meet. They convened a panel of experts and in 2010 published the Common Core Standards for English Language Arts and Mathematics. Many corporations and foundations with an interest in education endorsed them, and initially 45 states plus the District of Columbia adopted them—so they apply or did apply to more than 80% of the students in the United States. Testing geared to the standards began in 2014–2015, and there was almost immediately significant pushback from parents' groups, who objected to the tests, the more rigorous expectations for reading, and the unfamiliar approach to mathematics that came in with the standards. While the standards were voted in with bipartisan support, the bipartisan spirit quickly dissolved, and as of this writing, while a majority of states still support them, a number of states are backing away from enforcing the Common Core State Standards.

The Common Core State Standards define the knowledge and skills students should have within their K–12 education careers so that they will graduate high school able to succeed in entry-level, credit-bearing academic college courses and in workforce training programs.

In fact, the Common Core State Standards are a serious departure from past practices in reading instruction. We can summarize the changes this way:

1. Children are pushed hard to read on or close to grade level, based on newly defined measures of "text complexity."

2. Children are required to read a balance of narrative and informational text: 50% informational text at grade 4 and 65% at grade 8.

3. Students are expected to read about the same topic across several texts, often from different genres.

4. Students do close reading of texts and study the ways meanings are conveyed, and they make interpretations of texts and support their interpretations with reasons and evidence.

5. The standards are closely aligned to the skills that are tested on the National Assessment of Educational Progress, the PIRLS, and the PISA, the devices on which American students' reading performance is compared from year to year and from country to country.

6. Writing is used as a means of presenting claims and reasoned arguments.

7. Although technology is not heavily emphasized, students are expected to use technology as a tool for inquiry and research.

8. Since the Common Core State Standards apply to English Language Arts (ELA) and mathematics, but not social studies and science, those latter subjects are being taught in integrated units with ELA and mathematics.

9. The standards make few concessions to children with special needs or students who are English Language Learners.

Students' satisfactory achievement of the Common Core State Standards is measured mainly with two tests that were each developed by representatives of many states.

Smarter Balanced is given to students in 18 states, plus schools administered by the Bureau of Indian Affairs and schools in the U.S. Virgin Islands. The states are California, Connecticut, Delaware, Hawaii, Idaho, Iowa, Michigan, Montana, Nevada, New Hampshire, North Carolina, North Dakota, Oregon, South Dakota, Vermont, Washington, West Virginia, and Wyoming.

The PARCC test (Partnership for Assessment of Readiness for College and Careers) is administered annually to students in grades 3–11. As of this writing, 11 states and the District of Columbia are participating in PARCC. The states are Arkansas, Colorado, Illinois, Louisiana, Maryland, Massachusetts, Mississippi, New Jersey, New Mexico, Ohio, and Rhode Island.

Check Your Understanding 1.5: Gauge your understanding of the skills and concepts in this section.

For Review

At the outset of this chapter we stated that when you reached this point in your reading and studying you should be able to:

• **Define literacy and its importance in students' lives.**

Literacy was defined as *having and using a set of concepts and skills that enable a person to read and write: that is, to make sense of and communicate messages through the medium of written language.* Literacy makes enormous differences in people's lives. We noted that reading a lot quite literally makes children smarter, with bigger vocabularies and greater world knowledge. Literacy gives people concepts and vocabulary that broaden their capacity to notice and think about things. Among adults, literacy is associated with better health, greater job opportunities, and higher incomes; people who can read and write well tend to have a wider range of options in life.

- **Summarize the current state of literacy in the United States**

International comparisons show that U.S. students read fairly well, but the benefits of literacy are not shared equitably among students from different income groups or ethnic groups. When the National Assessment of Educational Progress has assessed reading ability, the findings have revealed unacceptably high numbers of elementary-age students who do not read with adequate comprehension.

- **List and describe the components of reading ability**

The components of reading are interrelated, but reading can be viewed in terms of word recognition, fluency, vocabulary, comprehension, and critical literacy.

- **Name the phases of reading development**

Reading develops normally through stages: emergent literacy, beginning reading, building fluency, reading for learning and pleasure, and mature reading.

- **Outline the recent history of reading instruction**

The history of research on reading instruction is nearly as old as the scientific study of psychology. But debates over instructional methods in literacy—such as the whole word versus phonics debate—have lasted for many generations. Arguments between advocates of holistic approaches and skills-based approaches have been heated in recent decades but appear to be easing with the emphasis on a balance of both. Research supports instruction in the alphabetic writing system—in phonics and the awareness of the sound system that underlies it—at least to those students who don't intuit the system. It also supports holistic instruction so that children see that literacy is meaningful and can understand literacy skills in context. For the past two decades the federal government has pushed for research-based literacy instruction, with accountability monitored by means of standards and regular testing. The first wave of standards was passed by individual states, but a set of Common Core State Standards has set uniform expectations for reading and writing and mathematics in nearly all states, although some states that initially adopted them are reconsidering their commitment.

For Your Journal

Go back to the Anticipation Guide that opened this chapter, and consider your answers to the questions posed. Divide a page of your journal with a vertical line. On the left side, write down one of your answers that you want to think about more. On the right side, write what you think about that topic now. Repeat the exercise with at least two more questions. Take your journal to class with you, and share your comments with your classmates.

Taking It to the World

1. Interview three primary-grade teachers, and ask them how they have seen the emphases in reading instruction change in the past 10 years. What aspects have stayed the same? What changes have they witnessed?

2. Many adults who have poorly developed reading skills don't perceive their limited literacy as a problem. Call the local chapter of Literacy Volunteers of America, and ask whether this has been their experience. Do many of the adults in the community who need help with literacy seek it? (A class might choose to appoint a committee to do this investigation, so as not to inundate the chapter with phone calls.)

3. The National Adult Literacy Survey cited in this chapter noted that prisoners are more likely than the rest of the population to have reading problems. Have a member of your class interview the person in charge of education at a local or regional prison. To what extent are literacy issues related to the problems the inmates have faced?

Chapter 2
The Social and Cultural Contexts for Teaching All Children to Read

 Learning Outcomes

After reading this chapter, you should be able to:

1. Explain some differences in how literacy functions in varied social, cultural, and economic communities.

2. Communicate (or demonstrate) literacy values by organizing a pro-literacy classroom, planning activities for children, and involving parents.

3. Meet the literacy needs of linguistically and culturally diverse students in the classroom.

4. Explain how Response to Intervention (RTI) has changed the role of teachers of reading—both classroom teachers and reading specialists—in working with students with special needs.

5. Incorporate authentic literature and informational text for students from diverse communities in the classroom and discuss their importance to reading instruction beyond traditional reading textbooks and anthologies.

Anticipation Guide

The following statements will help you begin thinking about the topics covered in this chapter. Answer *true* or *false* in response to each statement. As you read and learn more about the topics mentioned in these statements, double-check your answers. See what interests you and prompts your curiosity toward more understanding.

_____ 1. Reading and writing are both social and individual forms of communicating.

_____ 2. Differences among students in classrooms have little effect on how teachers work with children.

_____ 3. Cultural groups have distinct values regarding the importance of reading and writing.

_____ 4. Almost all English language learners are found in large urban centers in the Southwest.

_____ 5. African American Vernacular English is a dialect of English.

_____ 6. Children's culture is reflected in their body language, the way they manage time, and the distance they maintain between themselves and others.

_____ 7. A gifted child who is reading at grade level probably has a reading problem.

_____ 8. Boys tend to have more reading problems than girls do.

_____ 9. Children should be considered for special education only if they are two years behind their age level in expected achievement.

_____ 10. Children with special needs benefit from being in general education classrooms for part of the school day.

A Classroom Story

Getting Parents and the Community Involved in the Classroom

Marguerite has been teaching seventh grade for several years. Recently, many of her students have come from newly arrived immigrant families, especially from Asia and Eastern Europe. She wants to help these students understand American society and local community life, so she uses a resource unit on community biography from the state department of education. This unit integrates language arts and history as students study their own community members. She likes this project because it helps both her new students and the rest of the class understand how local communities, schools, religious groups, businesses, and government work together. As they do their projects and learn from each other, students develop pride in being part of their community.

Marguerite also uses this project to give her students a real purpose for developing their oral and written language skills. They use language by interviewing, collecting data, and writing biographies. Each student selects a special person in the community about whom he or she will write a biography. To complete the project, students need to develop questions to use in their interviews, conduct the interviews, and write up their findings. In addition, they conduct research on the national and international events that occurred during this person's life, create a timeline of important events that correlate with the person's life, and collect pictures and other artifacts that pertain to the report. The results of their research will be presented on a three-part bulletin board that will be exhibited at the Special Persons Fair, *which is open to the public. As she organizes the time frame for this unit, she works closely with the school librarian to locate resources that will help students gain more information about the local community, its history, and community leadership. The librarian introduced her to the collection of local newspapers on file and suggested that the public library also had a wealth of materials that students could use.*

Confident because of her careful planning and well-organized resources, Marguerite quickly engages her students in the unit. The students benefit from her preparation and become very excited about what they learn about their own community during their research and interviews. In fact, throughout the unit students share what they are learning with each other. The enthusiasm and insights shared by students often spark new ideas and questions from others. They make connections between their own families' experiences and those of other individuals in their community. One student who chose the school custodian as his subject developed a great history of the school through the custodian's eyes and saw how much this man had given to many generations of students. This significant contributor to the community finally received the special recognition he deserved.

The class shares their project results during Special Persons Night *at school, to which they invite the subjects of their projects and other local community members. The large turnout of adults interested in the recognition of local community members lets students know the value of the project. The students learn a great deal about their own community: Both students and community members are proud of the students' accomplishments.*

The activity creates a positive connection between the various parts of the community—old and new, those in leadership roles and many other (less noticed, but very important) contributors, and the students and teachers in the school.

We learn from those around us. We learn to act like them, to talk like them, to dress like them, to become part of a culture. Think of how you, as an infant and young child, learned to speak by following the models of those who nurtured you or how, as a teenager, you watched and then tried to talk and look just like your friends. The power of the social context is also very strong as people develop their literacy interests and behaviors. Children who come from families in which reading is a part of the fabric of their lives—in which family members keep books by their beds to read in quiet moments, where even bathrooms have piles of magazines, and where children are read to nightly—know that reading is important. They come to school with the expectation that they will become readers like the rest of their family members. Some students enter kindergarten facile with using computers and able to read and write. Other children, however, come to school without such extensive experiences and foundations for becoming literate. Yet, they want to learn and have also probably experienced the value of family members using smartphones to send text messages, observed relatives reading religious materials, noted environmental print, watched adults write and read, and played with video games. Their experiences with literacy may be different, but all can provide strong motivation for learning to read and write.

In getting acquainted with our students, it is part of our job as teachers to find out about their literacy history as readers and writers. Students want to learn to read and write and to communicate well with others. We can make better connections to their expectations and experiences when we know about their lives and understand their personal purposes for literacy. The more we know about their literacy experiences, the more we can ensure that all students become part of a social network of children and adults who value literacy and who use it in many ways and for many purposes.

As teachers we also know the importance of the social nature of literacy beyond the home. Children compare themselves to those around them. Just ask students who are the best readers in their class—they know. Ask who should write the letter of thanks to the author who visited the school, and they will direct you to the best writer. Children in classrooms can easily fall into categories of participators and non-participators, achievers and non-achievers. Teachers need to know how to make the social dynamics of the classroom work positively for all students, so all can be engaged and succeed.

Twenty-first-century schools have fewer and fewer classrooms composed of children from one ethnic or cultural group who all speak English as their mother tongue and who are otherwise similar to each other. In fact, about 20% of the children in the United States have immigrant parents, and this percentage is increasing regularly (Suárez-Orozco, Suárez-Orozco, & Todorova, 2008). One in six students in American classrooms is African American, and soon one in five will be Hispanic, but still nine out of ten teachers are white. In most American schools, teachers are working with students whose ethnic backgrounds and possibly home languages are different from their own. As cultural and linguistic diversity are increasing, educators are finding ways to make schools and classrooms inviting learning communities where families and children learn from and with each other. This chapter highlights the research and best practices that emphasize the importance of reading and writing as social activities, not just as individual skills to be acquired.

The Social Contexts of Literacy

Communities and families vary in their approaches and orientations to literacy, and many of these variations are grounded in historical and cultural circumstance. Not all Americans value the same forms of literacy in their lives. Research in mainstream American communities, as well as in varied cultural settings, has highlighted both the commonalities and the differences across families and among communities.

Cultural Experiences and Their Relationships to Literacy in Communities

A classic study of variations in literacy was done by Heath (1983) and reported in her book *Ways with Words*. In this comparison of literacy in three different cultural groups in a mill town near Charlotte, North Carolina, Heath illustrates how the two working-class communities, Tracton and Roadville, provided their children with different cultural experiences related to reading and writing from those of the townspeople, whose use of literacy was more compatible with that of the schools. Roadville families' literacy was anchored in their fundamentalist church. They saw written works as creations that they themselves were unfit to question, and they discouraged their children from asking questions or telling stories. Tracton families were more playful and collaborative when it came to reading—it was not unusual to hear a mother standing on her front stoop reading aloud a line of a letter, and have neighbors up and down the block chime in with their ideas of what it meant. At school, children from Roadville seldom ventured ideas about texts. Their teacher saw them as dull and unimaginative. The children from Tracton eagerly helped each other read aloud, even though only one child had been called upon. Their teachers saw them as unruly and even prone to cheating. Heath was able to work with the teachers to help them better connect the children's home lives and their reading tasks in school, and everyone felt more successful as a result.

Since that early work of Heath, others have explored underlying values and styles associated with literacy. Delpit (1995) has provided insights about African American cultural variations in literacy. She argues that African American children are accustomed to a more direct form of teaching and discipline and that they need that kind of clarity for success. According to Delpit, the more indirect forms of teaching and discipline preferred by many middle-class teachers leave some students out. These students often don't understand the cues that teachers provide about what is important and what their roles should be.

Research by Kelly (2000) with a group of Mexican American mothers revealed the high level of respect they accord teachers and schools. Even when they have had few opportunities for formal schooling themselves, they want their children to succeed. Their high regard for teachers, however, has a potential negative effect. They do not want to interfere with the teachers' role by helping their children learn to read before going to school. Because of this respect for teachers and their lack of a tradition of home literacy, their children often do not enter school with the same story reading and writing experiences that other children have. These families also thought that their children could learn English in school but that Spanish would remain the language used at home. This has both advantages and disadvantages. It poses a problem in giving English language learners enough opportunities to speak and use English to become proficient. It also means that the language of intimacy and familiarity is not English, so the school associations with English need to be very positive if students are going to learn it easily. Students who speak languages other than English can be encouraged to work and talk together so that they can practice English more regularly.

Because students are coming from increasingly diverse cultural traditions with varying literacy experiences, it is valuable to try to understand something of their family and cultural values, particularly those related to literacy and schooling.

Social Context of
Community

It is also important to find good ways to communicate with the parents and adjust to their needs (Gandara, 2010; Rueda, August, & Goldenberg, 2006). For example, some Hispanic parents feel intimidated when asked to come to school for parent conferences. They are unfamiliar with the traditions of U.S. schools and the customary relationships between teachers and families. In an attempt to honor the different experiences of the parents, one school district in California changed its format for parent nights. Instead of having each family come alone for conferencing, the schools have small-group conferencing. After the teachers lead a discussion of students' work and curriculum expectations, they answer questions from the parents. The teachers then make themselves available to individual families who wish to talk privately. This format has worked very well. The parents feel much more secure discussing issues of school learning in a group setting rather than alone with a teacher. Instead of creating high levels of anxiety among the parents, teachers' sensitivity led to a more comfortable and relaxed way to connect with parents in small groups.

The more teachers learn about the social contexts of their community, the better able they will be to respond appropriately to their students and to build new expectations and competence so that all students can attain the levels of literacy needed today. Despite the traditional values that many communities place on literacy, teachers who reach all their students successfully take time to learn about their students and expand their horizons to become versatile in their use of literacy in a wide variety of settings.

The Need for a Learning Community: Linking Home, School, and Community

Becoming aware of the relationship between community values and students' motivation and interests is a good starting place for understanding the setting in which one teaches. The cultural importance of literacy activities and the ways adults and children communicate affect how teachers can help their students most effectively.

New teachers should think of themselves as working in a community, not just in a school. Before entering the school and closing out the rest of the world, take time to become acquainted with the resources around you. For example, are there libraries you can link with to help provide the variety of reading materials you will want your students to have available to them? What resources are particularly relevant to the families you will be working with, such as community clubs, religious and ethnic centers, and local organizations and their leaders?

Your most powerful opportunities, however, come from within the school. As a teacher, you have a very important role for the parents and families of the children in your classroom. How you meet and relate to them is critical. Understanding the families' attitudes and values will help you work with the families as partners in developing their children's literacy. You want to know them as well as possible to communicate effectively with them. Think of their needs and ways to build bridges between the school and their homes. What do they want to know? How can you support them in their efforts to help their children? Think of how you can involve them in the life of the school and the classroom. What is appropriate and beneficial for both you and them?

As a teacher, you will be part of a school community, too. The more you can participate as part of the professional team, sharing your own literacy and learning and growing with others in the building, the more successful you will be as a teacher. Do not wait until you have your classroom under control before you think about building your roles within this larger support team. Begin to envision yourself as a committed professional sharing with others.

Check Your Understanding 2.1: Gauge your understanding of the skills and concepts in this section.

Planning for a Literate Classroom

Along with the variation among communities in the way they express the values and functions of literacy, there is also great variation within schools in the way the value of literacy is expressed. A part of creating a community is designing an inviting and purposeful space in the classroom, one that maximizes the possibilities for establishing a real literacy community among students. Whether adjusting the physical environment or adapting the structure of reading and writing activities, each teacher can do a great deal to contribute to a school culture that stimulates literacy and honors students' contributions.

Create a Literate Culture

One of the first statements you make to students about what is important in school is found in the classroom environment. Are desks grouped together? Are books and print materials displayed and easily accessible? Think about the classroom environment you want to create during your first year of teaching. What will the classroom look like? Remember, you will have a great deal to do in determining the kind of context you create for your students. Think of your classroom space as a visual and physical opportunity to invite your students to enjoy reading and writing. Think about some of the classrooms you have visited in recent years. How did the teachers make a clear statement that they valued reading and writing? The visual survey below indicates how this was done.

The classroom contains:

1. Special places for reading and writing—a reading corner, a computer center, a writers' corner, etc.

2. A classroom library of books students can use regularly

3. A collection of books students have written either individually or in groups (these could be big books, bound books added to the classroom library, etc.)

4. A rack with magazines and newspapers appropriate for the students

5. An author's chair and/or a reader's and writer's chair from which the students read to the rest of the class

6. Books and magazines the teacher is reading, both professional and personal

7. Examples on the walls or ledges of students' responses to materials they are reading—reviews of books, story maps of key points, sketches of interesting parts of stories, shared responses, etc.

8. Charts and other visuals that serve as strategy guides for students learning to read and write—reading strategies, fix-up strategies, steps in writing, word walls with key vocabulary students are learning, a guide to spelling using key patterns, etc.

9. Visual "in process" charts of students' work—K-W-L and I-charts, matrices of learning, responses to questions for reflection, etc.

10. Illustrations of what students are studying and learning in content areas—science process journals and social studies artifacts

11. Books, magazines, and other materials that reflect cultures represented in your class or school

12. Examples of writing in different orthographies so that students can explore the varieties of written languages

One of the easiest and most important ways in which you can invite your students into literacy is by providing them with places where they can participate with others in literate activities. Every classroom with a library of appropriate books, magazines, and newspapers encourages the habit of reading. As you begin to create a library, determine the range of reading levels likely among the students, identify key themes and authors that children of this age enjoy, and begin building the collection. Many schools provide sets of books for each classroom. However, you will still want to evaluate the collection and make it as appealing as possible. It should contain material on a wide range of topics of interest to your students, and some of the collection should connect to the science, social studies, and special topics that the children will be studying. Ensure that there are books representing the various cultures from which students in the school come. All students deserve to find and see themselves in the books and magazines in their classrooms. Watch this video to learn how multicultural children's literature is having an impact in American classrooms and answer the question that follows.

activities ✓

 Video Exploration 2.1: Watch the video and answer questions that reflect the content you have read.

Another important step is to create an attractive place for literacy activities. If space is available, create reading, computer, and writing corners or centers. In the reading corner, house the classroom library and additional inviting reading materials in a space where students can browse through the books and curl up on the floor or in comfortable chairs to read. Some teachers find soft chairs, pillows, or even bathtubs in which children can relax and read. You can add small bins for paper so students can make notes about special ideas they find while reading and for stick-on notes so they can mark places for sharing with each other. Some teachers involve students in creating bookmarks so they can easily access their point of reading and have extra bookmarks available in the reading center.

The writing space needs a table and comfortable chairs. The space becomes more attractive when students can enjoy a range of writing tools and a supply of writing materials. Depending on the students' age, these will vary, but a selection of colored pencils and pens, some wooden ink blocks with special designs, and a variety of kinds of paper, some with designs, make writing more fun. Computers can be housed in this area or in a separate space. If computers are located in the writing corner, they can be used for writing and editing support by families and volunteers in early primary classes and by students as they become adept at using them. In addition, dictionaries, thesauruses, and other writing aids should be displayed prominently for students' use. This area can house students' writing folders or flash drives so that when they are ready to write, they can enter the process easily and, when finished, can refile or save their works in process.

Ensure the Sharing of Literacy

A key to helping students become lifelong readers and writers is to develop the social nature of literacy by providing regular opportunities for children to engage with each other around literacy events. Too often, as students move up in the grades, opportunities to talk with others about what they are reading and writing disappear. Yet it is through sharing with others that students realize how central literacy can become in their own lives as part of their own enjoyment and learning. As you begin to plan for your literacy program, think carefully about including regular opportunities for students to engage with each other without the teacher dominating the discussion or exchange. Students need opportunities to work in paired reading and writing activities. They need to learn how to function as part of small cooperative literacy groups, knowing that they should be prepared with their own ideas to share and willing to listen and connect with what others say. They also need to have experiences in larger groups and whole-class discussions that build from their partner or small-group experiences.

For many students who are new to this country, talking in a whole-class setting is extremely difficult because they lack confidence in their command of English and of the culture of the school. Teachers can ease these students into the classroom academic life by using paired reading and talking as a first step before involving the students in larger group activities. As you think about all the literacy learning activities you will structure for your students, make sure students have frequent and regular opportunities to talk and share with their peers in nonthreatening settings.

Don't assume that students know what it is like to discuss a book or piece of text. You might need to spend a significant amount of time helping students become familiar with "talk about text." One way to develop more book discussion is to begin a Great Books shared inquiry program. There is full training for teachers and group leaders in this program and materials that guide students' thinking about the rich stories and texts that are included at each grade level (Plecha, 1992). Many teachers now use some form of book club (Raphael & McMahon, 1994) or literature circle (Daniels, 2002) as a way of involving students in focused talk about what they are reading.

Another support for book talk is to help parents learn how to elicit reflection from their children. Some school districts have developed videotapes of the kinds of questions and follow-up comments that parents can use to help children talk about their reading. Others have prepared guides for parents to follow. One example is shown in Figure 2.1.

It is useful to help students share literacy with each other at all ages and grade levels. In this way, the shared, cultural aspects of reading and writing can become more alive for all the students in the school. A very simple way to do this is for two different grades to become partners. Students are also joined into buddy pairs for reading and writing and meet regularly (e.g., weekly, every two weeks, monthly). The children begin to share their literate activities with students older and/or younger than they are. The older readers help the younger ones as they read from books they want to share; the older students might also help write responses to the reading—what the two like about the story, characters, or information. When the younger students write their own descriptions of a trip to the nature center, the older student buddies take dictation and help to create personal accounts of the experiences.

In some schools, the students who struggle with reading also get help from older students who are trained in some basic reading strategies. In this way, both groups of students gain, and the shared understanding of literacy develops naturally. One particular program, Tall Friends, pairs middle-grade, below-level readers with second graders who are also

Teach It! 45

Think–Pair–Share

Appropriate for both English speakers and English language learners, this comprehension-building activity supports student talk as they reflect on questions and share responses with peers.

Figure 2.1 Tips for Reading with Your Child

TIPS FOR READING WITH YOUR CHILD

1. Find a relaxed time and setting.

2. Talk about the book as you read.
   * Look over the cover, title, author, and picture and predict
     what you think may happen and why you like the book.
   * As you read, share connections to your life.
     "Doesn't this seem like Aunt Dorothy?"
     "This picture reminds me of our trip!"
     "Oh, I remember feeling like this!"
   * Ask questions of your child. For example:
     "Do you know anyone like this?"
     "How would you feel?"
   * After reading, share your favorite parts. For example:
     "I really liked . . ."
     ". . . was so funny!"

3. Reread favorite books.

4. Read many kinds of books—real world, poetry, folktales, humor,
   & fiction.

having trouble. The reading teacher works with the older students to develop some activities that will help the second graders focus on the phonetic regularities of English by doing controlled word sorts and by learning to listen to and support students as they read orally from their instructional-level materials.

If a school does not have a vibrant shared literacy culture, think about how to bring in some new focus to stimulate students' attention to reading and writing. There are many ways in which this can be done. One is to celebrate special days, from International Literacy Day, September 8, to Dr. Seuss's birthday, March 2. Some states have their own awards for good children's books. Illinois holds a contest each year to select students' favorite books as part of the Rebecca Caudill Awards Program. California's Young Reader Medal is similar. School participation in the selection of these books creates a new focus for the celebration of books. Other programs that recognize student writing can also help to add emphasis to

Teach It! 37

Literature Circles

Learn how this structured format supports student engagement in thoughtful small-group discussions around a shared text.

Teach It! 27

Paired Reading

In this fluency-building activity, less fluent readers are paired with more fluent readers to read (and reread) a text together.

---

school literacy. Inviting authors to visit the school and speak with different groups of students can make literacy and the process of writing and reading very real. Most states have some beloved and respected authors who are willing to visit schools, and bookstores will often help to bring authors to area schools.

Each of these examples highlights the importance of thinking of literacy as a community activity in the school. The more there is a climate of support for and interest in how students read and write, the more all students benefit. In addition, the more students talk with each other about their reading, the more they identify with books and reading.

Start the Year Out Right

Just as teachers can do much to create a warm, supportive literacy climate in the classroom, they can also help to model the importance and joy of literacy even before students start the year. Consider writing a letter to each of your new students before the year begins, introducing yourself and telling a little about your expectations for the fall. You can suggest that students bring with them an example of their own writing (if they are beyond the second grade) or a favorite book or poem. Some teachers ask students to bring pictures of themselves doing something they enjoy to put on a board for the first day. Each of these activities is an example of using literacy as a bridge to building relationships. Students love to receive mail, and some of the apprehension of starting a new year can be melted away with such simple, yet profound, gestures.

Teachers can also involve parents in events at the start of the year. By sending a letter home during the first week, introducing themselves, and describing what they will be doing in the classroom, teachers can build a bridge from school to home. Parents respond positively to a note from the teacher explaining what to expect for the fall. After an initial letter, the teacher might publish a weekly or monthly newsletter of class events, with explanations of aspects of the reading and writing programs. Parents need to know how they can contribute. When they feel that they are important and are helping their children, most parents will become more involved in their children's developing literacy.

During the first week of school, literacy activities can also help the class to become better acquainted. Ask each student to bring a favorite book or magazine to share, give the students time to explain why they have selected the particular material, and listen carefully to them. This can be a good way to find out even more about the students' personal and home uses of literacy. For students for whom such selection and sharing might not be comfortable, conduct a book talk about several books and magazines in the classroom library and ask students to select the one they think they will like most. Having time to scan the materials gives each student an opportunity to share responses.

Getting to know the students quickly is important. Asking them to draw or write something about themselves is another way to elicit shared literacy activity. The bulletin board that can be created from this activity then becomes an invitation to read and learn about classmates. In one school, parents created the covers for the writing journals that the kindergarten and first-grade children were given the first week of school. Imagine the children's surprise when they realized that they would be holding a creation of their parents each time they wrote! Parents knew their children would be using their developmental spelling abilities as well as drawing to write messages each day when they spent time at the writing table.

Involve Parents in the Reading Program of the School

It is impossible to discuss social contexts of literacy without focusing on parents, for they are the children's first and most important teachers. Teachers need to know as much as possible about the parents' cultural values and styles of communicating with their children so that the necessary adjustments to the school culture and style of each teacher can be made. Even the ability to talk about different ways of thinking, talking, reading, and writing can be useful to students, parents, and teachers. For example, you might suggest to a parent, "At school, we are trying to get the children to be independent in their reading by giving them time to figure out unfamiliar words for themselves. We ask them to look for three sources of information: visual, grammatical, and meaningful. Of course, you want them to read perfectly and fluently. Giving them the correct pronunciation of words helps this. However, right now we are trying to get the children to be more independent. If you could help reinforce our teaching strategy for the next few months, your child will feel more comfortable and, I think, reach the goal we both share." Accept that what the parents value and think is important, and then help them understand how they can assist the instructional program.

As already mentioned, relationships between parents and schools vary tremendously. In some communities, parents feel too intimidated to join the school culture. They want teachers to do their jobs and will support this as best they can. In other communities, parents are very involved in the schools, serving on curriculum committees, working on standards development, and visiting classrooms regularly. They might want to know a great deal about how reading is taught and might have a wealth of experience themselves guiding their own children's literacy development. When this is the case, home–school letters can be more specific with explanations of research and instructional priorities. Creating videotapes and having Parents' Nights and programs that explain how literacy develops can help to build good communication in these situations. Dealing with the variations in parent knowledge and expectations is a concern of the whole school and should be a shared decision of the faculty and administration. A key in all situations is being open to, and interested in, the parents' perspectives and concerns.

Check Your Understanding 2.2: **Gauge your understanding of the skills and concepts in this section.**

Meeting the Literacy Needs of All Children

Classrooms in the twenty-first century are in a period of dynamic change. The classroom of middle-class white children is no longer the norm around which reading programs and textbooks are designed. Multilingual, multiethnic, and multicultural classrooms are the new reality. These children from various backgrounds bring diverse strengths that add to the richness of the classroom. They also bring new challenges as a result of the representation of languages in addition to English and standard American English. Children from a variety of ethnic groups bring cultural lives and customs that are expressed not only in language but also in nonverbal communication, how they express feelings and emotions through body language. Teachers will encounter many struggling readers, requiring them to examine the ways that language and culture are addressed in the classroom.

The needs of at-risk and struggling readers are also a topic of great interest. Major categories of interest are the following:

- Those who arrive in their classrooms without English proficiency—English language learners
- Those whose dialect of English is not Standard American English, mainly African American students who arrive at school speaking African American Vernacular English (AAVE)
- Students with special needs, those whose needs were formerly met entirely in programs of special education

An Urban Classroom

Farah Al Jabar's fourth-grade class is located in a low-income area of a major urban center. Her 36 students represent, in about equal numbers, four major ethnic/language groups: African American, Asian, Hispanic, and Anglo. Almost half of the children entered kindergarten speaking another language or a dialect of English. Although all are at least minimally proficient in English now, many have gaps in their oral language vocabularies and in the background knowledge that corresponds to that of the middle-class children for whom the school curriculum and textbooks are typically designed. According to the results of informal reading inventories that Farah administered in the fall, many are reading below grade level, and a few are reading markedly below grade level.

Today, one group of 10 children, all reading at grade level, is beginning to read a novel by Spinelli (1990a) entitled *Maniac Magee*, which was awarded the prestigious Newbery Medal. It is not a particularly difficult story, but many vocabulary words are new to the children. In addition, some children lack background knowledge about substantive issues that underlie the story.

Farah ensured that she was incorporating the elements of the four-block **guided reading model** she applies in her classroom: guided reading, writing, working with words, and **self-selected reading**. Before the children begin, she leads them through several brief anticipatory reading activities that prepare them to read the story with good understanding. First, she says, "Let's read the title of the book and look at the illustration on the cover," demonstrating and modeling how she makes predictions about text she will read. She asks, "What predictions can you make about this book?" One child tries to sound out the word "maniac," saying "m-m-maniac—what does it mean?" Another child quickly responds, "It's a word for a crazy person, somebody out of control." Another notices the shoes on the cover and asks, "Do those shoes belong to a boy or a girl?" Farah says, "Let's find out." She reads the two-page foreword of the book aloud to the children. She then explains, "The main character is Jeffrey Magee, but they call him 'Maniac Magee.' He's a boy about your age. Now what do you think the story might be about?"

Farah has already prepared the beginning of a semantic map to introduce the term *dump*, which the children will encounter early in the story. She asks, "What do you know about this word?" The children share the information they already have, and Farah records it in appropriate categories on the graphic organizer.

She then has the children close their books with their finger in place at the first page of the first chapter, and she asks them a question that will guide their silent reading of that page, beginning the guided reading part of her lesson where they will build knowledge through reading. She asks, "How does Jeffrey's life suddenly change?" They listen to the question, and then they open their books and begin reading silently. (Jeffrey is orphaned when his parents are killed in an automobile accident. He lives with an aunt and uncle for a short time and then runs away to live in a dump.)

As they read, Farah circulates around the group, motivating them by touching shoulders, smiling, and offering encouraging comments. Some children ask for assistance with words that are unfamiliar, even after the anticipatory reading activities. She quickly provides help so they can maintain their comprehension. This activity also provides an opportunity for her to briefly circulate around the classroom and supervise the work of other children who are working independently as they wait for their own small-group lessons.

As the children finish reading the page and begin to raise their hands to respond to the question, Farah returns to her seat. She repeats the question and calls on a child who says, "He went to live with his aunt and uncle—they weren't too cool." Another adds, "His mom and dad were killed in a car accident." Yet another says, "He ran away." Other children add new information and share other points of view. Finally, Farah asks one student to read aloud the sentence that provides evidence for the answer that all the students finally agreed on. She then asks another **comprehension-level question** about the same page, following this procedure through the three pages of this first chapter of the story.

In a consolidation activity at the end of the lesson, Farah asks, "How did the story begin?" A child responds, "Jeffrey's parents were killed, and he went to live with his uncle and his aunt." She asks, "What happened next?" The children continue to retell the story up to that point in their own words. Farah then says, "Write a short paragraph, and predict what you think will happen in the next chapter of the story. While I teach the other group and when you finish your short paragraph, please read your library books." She moves on to work with another small group of children that is reading from an **anthology**.

Farah has exhibited many behaviors that tell us she is an outstanding teacher, some of which relate to her strong instructional program. She uses teaching strategies that support or scaffold comprehension and that help children build confidence. In reading aloud, she provided a model both of fluent reading and of thinking about what she read, as revealed in her follow-up question. Farah gave attention to working with words in analyzing a crucial word in the story, *dump*, whose meaning was a key to understanding the circumstances in which Maniac Magee was living. She provided explicit guidance that scaffolded comprehension by asking higher-order questions before the children read. She provided an application and extension activity: writing a short paragraph to predict what might happen in the next chapter. And, finally, she provided time for self-selected reading.

Equally important are aspects of her approach that motivate the children, that indicate her high expectations and affection for them, and that demonstrate her deep understanding of the cultures from which they come. Choosing appropriate literature for the children is an important part of her planning. The main character of *Maniac Magee* is a boy who has very positive interactions with African American children in the story. She has also provided a large-print version of the book from LRS Large Print Publications (Spinelli, 1990b) for a student with a vision impairment. Farah's next literature choice for this group is *By the Lake of Sleeping Children: The Secret Life of the Mexican Border* (Urrea, 1996), about life in a dump in Tijuana, Mexico, which parallels and connects with the setting of *Maniac Magee*. She takes much care to ensure that all children in her class see themselves in many different roles in the literature she provides for them. She directs the major part of her small discretionary budget each year to the purchase of sets of trade books to supplement her basal reading program.

Valuing Diversity or Coping With Differences?

We can view the diversity in Farah's classroom, and in most American classrooms, from at least two perspectives. On the one hand, teachers can consider that associating with people who are different enriches everyone. On the other hand,

Teach It! 42

Story Maps

These graphic organizers enhance children's text comprehension by familiarizing them with story grammar as they identify and sequence key story elements and events.

because diversity means that differences between children are greater than just the ordinary individual differences found among homogeneous groups of children, some teachers perceive it as a problem. Different languages can make it difficult to meet needs, group students efficiently for instruction, and provide materials that are appropriate for all children. Cultural differences arise, making teaching a complex and demanding act. These are legitimate concerns, but they should be viewed as challenges instead of as problems. Teachers who view it as a challenge consider diversity an asset to be valued for the benefit of the children—one that enriches the learning of all—the students and the teacher.

CULTURAL DIVERSITY, BACKGROUND KNOWLEDGE, AND LITERACY   According to Gollnick and Chinn (2012), the pervasive culture in U.S. schools is primarily based on the perspective of Northern and Western Europe. Many believe that this culture is apparent in textbooks and curricula and in the cadre of teachers who staff most schools. It characterizes what teachers expect students to know when they come to school, and it serves as the basis for teachers' assessments of student outcomes. It often characterizes how teachers reinforce children's behavior, both positively and negatively; how they ask children questions and accept their responses; how they correct children; how they do, or do not, make the classroom safe for children; and how they use gestures and time. Clearly, schools cannot adopt the culture of each and every child, but they can accept the culture of every child, accommodate that culture, and use its presence and teachers' knowledge of it to help teach all children. According to Fitzgerald (1995), teachers must make reading instruction congruent with the background culture that children bring to their lessons.

THE ZONE OF PROXIMAL DEVELOPMENT   The work of Vygotsky (1978) provides another view of social constructivism that underlies children's cognitive development, with particular applications to the teaching of reading and language. The learning community includes culture, language, and important adults who guide children in their learning.

Vygotsky's concept of the **zone of proximal development** is especially important. According to his view, certain tasks can be performed by a student independently; some tasks cannot be performed at all, even with help; and some fall within the "zone," which can be performed with help from others. Those *others* in the classroom are teachers, paraprofessionals, and parent volunteers, or more capable student peers in cooperative learning group settings. Many implications for the effective classroom emerge from these concepts:

- Teachers need to design instruction that is at an appropriate level for each child—not so difficult that they fail, not so simple that there is no gain, but at a level where, with scaffolding (i.e., a support system), they can learn. A one-size-fits-all approach is not appropriate.
- Learning activities need to be carried out in meaningful contexts, not in isolation.
- Children need to construct their own meaning with the help of the teacher and other adults and peers in the role of facilitators.
- Children need to see relationships between what they are learning and the communities in which they live.

CULTURALLY RESPONSIVE CLASSROOM COMMUNICATION   Children's language develops in a sociocultural context. How children use language in their homes and communities also has important effects on their use of language in classrooms, especially when they are learning to read and write. Although language arts and reading curricula often reflect a linear assumption about all literacy development in all of its forms, ethnographers remind teachers that they must view how parents use language in rearing their children, the range of types of language use in the home, and the amount of exposure that children experience with respect to the diversity of languages, speakers of languages, and ways of using language outside of their homes (Heath, 1986). Culturally responsive teachers apply their knowledge of the many cultures in their classroom to the way they respond to children, both verbally and nonverbally.

Verbal Communication   Providing feedback to students is a vital teacher activity. When feedback is given across cultures, there is always potential for misunderstanding. Scarcella (1990) provides several categories of feedback behavior:

- *Interpreting student feedback* (how they indicate that they are paying attention). Most Americans nod their heads to indicate that they are listening. Asian students often nod to indicate that they are listening, but this does not necessarily indicate understanding.
- *Complimenting and criticizing* (how this is interpreted from both perspectives). Asian students might reject too many compliments as being insincere, whereas Hispanic students usually welcome praise.
- *Teacher correction of student errors* (how students view the way the teacher corrects errors). Students from some cultures want to be corrected and are concerned at a lack of correction. In other cultures, correction can be a humiliation. It is important for the teacher to consider how to treat this issue with each student in the classroom.

- *Student requests for clarification* (how, or if, students ask for help and how teachers interpret these requests). Teachers should carefully monitor the comprehension of their students, checking for understanding and watching for nonverbal behavior that might indicate a question that has not been expressed.

- *Spotlighting, or calling attention to a student's behavior in front of others.* Many children do not appreciate having attention called to them, especially from across the room. Teachers might be more effective if they walk over to students and softly give instructions, especially if student misbehavior is involved or even praise for older students. The teacher can avoid turning a small problem of inattention into a major problem of defiance.

- *Questioning and answering* (the purpose of questions). Asking questions is an important teacher instructional behavior. American teachers tend to ask many questions for the purpose of motivating critical thinking on the part of the students. But Heath (1983) has found that African American children are often confused by why teachers ask questions when the teachers already know the answers. She recommends that these children be asked questions of the type they are asked at home, such as "What's that like?" or "What's happening?" To promote higher-order thinking, teachers often ask for opinions about what a character did in a story or how an author expressed an idea. Children from some cultures are uncomfortable in offering opinions; they can gain experience and confidence in acquiring this ability in small-group work before they express themselves in front of the entire class.

- *Pausing* (wait-time). Teachers tend to provide insufficient **wait-time** for students. They need to allow students time to think about their responses before going on to another student or accepting a response from students who always seem to know the correct answer before anyone else. According to Rowe (1974), teachers usually wait slightly more than one second. She found that when children were provided with at least three seconds of undisturbed wait-time, they responded more completely and correctly, the number of nonresponses decreased, and the number of volunteered responses increased.

Nonverbal Communication   Communication is often thought of only as a verbal process, but the important impact of nonverbal communication is considerable, especially when teachers work with children from many different cultures. For example, a frequent type of interaction between teacher and child is the teacher's need to correct the inappropriate behavior of a child. To show respect, an Anglo child usually looks in the teacher's eyes when being corrected. The same child shows defiance by looking at the floor instead of looking the teacher in the face. Conversely, a Hispanic child often shows respect to the teacher by looking at the floor, whereas he shows defiance by looking the teacher in the eyes. What message does the teacher send by saying to the Hispanic child, "Look me in the eye when I talk to you"? In this case, the teacher might be asking the student to demonstrate defiance. This is only one of many examples of the potential for cross-cultural misunderstandings between teacher and child, even when both are behaving appropriately for their own cultures.

Nonverbal communication is a form of paralanguage, which includes many aspects of behavior that teachers should understand. These behaviors are the clues that tell us someone is from another culture, and sometimes even what country they are from, although we might not be able to hear them speaking. You cannot be familiar with all culturally based **nonverbal behaviors** in your diverse classroom, but you can begin to reflect about the reactions of children to your nonverbal behaviors and about your own reactions to puzzling nonverbal behaviors of students. When student reactions to a teacher's behavior are counterintuitive, there is often a cultural explanation.

As children's experiences with life in the United States expand, they also begin to learn the appropriate nonverbal behaviors of the new language and culture they are assimilating. When they are successful, they are able to function comfortably in two cultures, which makes them bicultural. Teachers need to be sensitive to children as they go about the complicated task of becoming bicultural.

Linguistic Diversity: Today's Classroom Demographics

Who are the English language learners? Where are they? Everywhere! The 2010 census revealed a growing diversity in American classrooms in almost all parts of the country. Perhaps the most important aspect of this change is the number of children classified as English language learners, children who arrive in American classrooms with no English or insufficient English for learning to read and write in English. When teachers think of English language learners, they likely think of Hispanic children; indeed, Hispanics make up the largest population of English language learners. According to the 2010 U.S. census, the Hispanic population of the United States has risen from 12.5% to 16.3% of the total population (U.S. Census Bureau, 2011).

Data from the National Clearinghouse for English Language Acquisition and Language Instruction Educational Programs (NCELA, 2011) indicate that the most dramatic difference in the growth of Hispanic populations in the 2010 census was the continuing dissemination to smaller population centers. In 2008–2009, more than 10% of K–12 school populations were English language learners in Alaska, Oregon, California, Nevada, Arizona, Colorado, New Mexico, Texas, Illinois, Florida, and Puerto Rico. In Minnesota, Arkansas, Michigan, North and South Carolina, New York, Rhode Island, Massachusetts, Connecticut, Washington, Idaho, Utah, Kansas, Nebraska, and Oklahoma, the proportion ranged from 5% to 10%. The growth in numbers of English language learners in Colorado, Arkansas, Illinois, Kentucky, Mississippi, Georgia, and North and South Carolina was over 200% from 1997–1998 to 2008–2009. English language learners are not a monolithic population. Some are very proficient in speaking and understanding their mother tongue, and some are literate in that language. Some became literate in their home countries; others do so in programs of bilingual education in the United States. As a result of living in refugee camps for extended periods, some upper elementary and adolescent children arrive in this country with little or no school experience at all. Some English language learners are migrant children from rural areas without educational opportunities, and others were working and contributing to the family income. Some English language learners have limited proficiency even in their mother tongue, just as some native English speakers are limited in their English proficiency. As teachers consider the challenges today's students represent, they also must think in terms of possible solutions.

ENGLISH LANGUAGE LEARNERS   Perhaps the most sweeping policy change to affect the education of English language learners in recent years was the 1974 *Lau v. Nichols* decision of the U.S. Supreme Court, which ruled that equal education did not result from providing exactly the same education to all children (J. Crawford, 1989; *Lau v. Nichols*, 1974). This decision required that school districts take positive steps to overcome the educational barriers experienced by students who did not speak English. Soon afterward, the Elementary and Secondary Education Act was amended with Title VII to make limited English proficient students eligible for federal funds and to permit their enrollment in bilingual education programs.

A 1981 court decision (*Casteñeda v. Pickard*, 1981) established three criteria for determining how programs of bilingual education were to be held accountable for meeting requirements of the Equal Education Opportunity Act of 1974. The criteria included the following:

- The program must be based on sound educational theory.
- The program must be effectively implemented with adequate resources for personnel, instructional materials, and space.
- Following a trial period, the program must be shown to be effective in overcoming language handicaps.

Although the *Lau v. Nichols* decision did not mandate bilingual education as a remedy, school districts found it to be one of the few ways to ensure that English language learners had equal access to education, that is, education in their mother tongue while they were learning English. The No Child Left Behind Act of 2001 replaced the earlier Elementary and Secondary Education Act (ESEA) Title VII, which formerly funded programs of instruction for bilingual children and was rescinded (García, 2005). The new law, Title III, continues to provide resources for what are called *English language learners*. Annual assessments of English-language proficiency are mandated, as well as requirements that these children meet state academic content and student achievement standards in English (Office of English Language Acquisition [OELA], 2004). The term *bilingual* does not appear in the new law, which now stresses skills in English only. There is no federal interest in the development of academic bilingual education programs for these children.

In late 2006, the Department of Education released regulations concerning English language learners (Federal Register, 2006) that allow school districts to delay the testing in reading of English language learners who have been in the United States for less than a year. Unfortunately, no evidence indicates that these children can learn English in one year, so the effect is minimal.

ENGLISH LANGUAGE LEARNERS AND LITERACY   Bilingual education, however, is a subject of much controversy. Initiatives in a number of states, including California (Proposition 227 in 1998), Arizona (Proposition 203 in 2000), and Massachusetts (Question 2 in 2002), have discouraged most bilingual education. They require instead a one-year period of immersion instruction in English as a second language, although the efficacy of this approach is not supported in the literature. In fact, abundant evidence indicates that children need two to five years of instruction in English as a second language before they are ready to learn to read in English (Thomas & Collier, 1997). An analysis of test scores from the 2002 California Stanford 9 test scores reported by the influential League of United Latin American Citizens (LULAC) (O'Leary, 2002) suggested that English language learners were not developing English fluency and that many were falling further behind in academic subjects. O'Leary reported that four years after the passage of California's Unz English Initiative, Proposition 227, more than a million limited-English immigrant students in second through eleventh grades in California still had not been mainstreamed in English-only classes, an indication of the failure of the policy. According to Slavin and

Cheung (2004), bilingual programs don't harm the progress of English language learners in reading, and they usually improve it. Zehr (2008) concluded that there was no difference between bilingual education programs and immersion English programs in the reading achievement of English language learners at the fourth-grade level. In his own research, Jepsen (2009, 2010) found that by grades 3 to 5, there were no differences in the reading achievement of children in bilingual education programs and other programs (immersion). In a five-year study, Slavin, Madden, Calderón, Chamberlain, and Hennessy (2010) found that children in traditional bilingual education learned to read well in Spanish and that they learned to read in English just as well in transitional bilingual education as they did in structured English immersion.

Goodman (1986) reminds us that bilingual children are not disadvantaged in some academic way. They are disadvantaged only if their linguistic strengths are not appreciated and if schools fail to build on their strengths. The International Literacy Association (ILA) has recognized the efficacy of teaching children to read in the mother tongue while they learn to understand and speak English and before they begin learning to read in their second language, English. Their resolution of support includes three major elements: (1) initial literacy instruction should be provided in the child's native language whenever possible; (2) although initial literacy instruction in a second language can be successful, there is a higher risk of reading problems than beginning with a child's first language; and (3) instructional decisions should support the professional judgment of the teachers and administrators who are responsible for teaching students whose first language is not English and who oppose any restrictive federal, state, or local initiatives (International Reading Association, 2001).

Dialects of English and Literacy

English language learners, whose mother tongue is not English and whose English proficiency is limited, are not the only children whose reading instruction is affected by linguistic factors. African American Vernacular English is a dialect of English that is spoken by many urban African American children in the United States. There are other dialects, including Southern Regional Dialect, a mostly rural dialect of both Anglo and African American children.

AFRICAN AMERICAN VERNACULAR ENGLISH (AAVE)   Also known as *black dialect* and *ebonics*, African American Vernacular English is the dialect of the English language that is probably most frequently encountered in American classrooms. According to Labov (1970, 1972), African American Vernacular English is as logical and consistent as Standard American English, it can be reproduced, and it makes sense. It is merely different from Standard American English. A policy statement of the TESOL (Teachers of English to Speakers of Other Languages) (1997) board of directors stipulates that African American Vernacular English has been demonstrated in research to be a rule-governed linguistic system that has its own lexical, phonological, syntactic, and discourse patterns and that it therefore deserves pedagogical recognition. It is not a substandard dialect of English, and it is not poor English. It is a dialect that is widely understood and spoken among many inner city African Americans.

There are many phonological and syntactical differences between African American Vernacular English and Standard American English (Rickford, 1999). Some of those identified by Simons & Johnson (1974) are presented in Table 2.1.

These characteristics of African American Vernacular English appear so consistently that they frequently appear in the oral reading of children who superimpose their dialect over the words written on the page (Johnson & Simons, 1974; Wheeler, Cartwright, & Swords, 2012). Teachers must consider whether there is a negative effect on reading comprehension or only on oral reading accuracy because both are possible, even in a single reading episode by an individual child.

ADDING STANDARD AMERICAN ENGLISH   Teachers demonstrate that they value the language of children when they accept the way the children communicate with each other and with members of their families and communities. In classrooms, however, teachers also need to help students add a second dialect of English: Standard American English, a dialect that supports the children's continuing academic learning and offers access to higher education and desirable employment opportunities (Wheeler, Cartwright, & Swords, 2012). The resulting **bidialectical** children resemble bilingual children in that they can readily switch back and forth between dialects according to the educational or social situation in which they find themselves. Part of the process of being bidialectical is knowing when and where to use each dialect.

In schools where an ESL program is already in place for English language learners, many ESL activities will be of value for children whose home and community language environment is African American Vernacular English. Teachers can use many intermediate and advanced ESL instructional strategies to add Standard American English to the children's repertoire. The children will not require instruction at the basic stages of the natural approach for English language learners (described in Chapter 14), but participation in activities at the third stage of the natural approach will be helpful because they focus on communication, not on grammar. In addition, the activities described for "sheltered English" in Chapter 14 will support, scaffold, and enhance the children's development of background knowledge and vocabulary needed for effective reading comprehension. In schools where such a program is not in place because there are no English

Table 2.1 Some Examples of Differences Between Standard American English and African American Vernacular English

Linguistic Feature	Standard American English	African American Vernacular English
Initial and final sounds of /th/ (modified)	this, those	dis, dose
	both, breathe	bof, breave
Medial /v/ (modified)	seven	seben
Medial or final /r/, /l/ (deleted)	door	doe
	help	hep
Consonant clusters (deleted)	desk	des
	told	tol
Past tense marker	I talked to him.	I talk to him.
Copula deleted (the copula is a form of the verb "to be")	He is tall.	He tall.
Use of verb *be* (habitual)	Tamisha reads every day.	Tamisha be reading.
Subject-verb agreement	We were there.	We was there.
Double negative	Jason doesn't have a football.	Jason don't have no football.
Possessive (deleted)	The girl's skirt	The girl skirt
Question (reversal of subject and verb)	What is that?	What that is?

SOURCES: Based on Johnson and Simons (1974); Wheeler, Cartwright, and Swords (2012)

language learners, an oral language development program should be provided to help children acquire Standard American English in much the same way that English language learners acquire English. This is not an ESL program, but rather a program of oral language development.

Rickford and Rickford (1995) suggest a very direct approach, beginning with an agreement among students that Standard American English is appropriate for classroom interaction and writing. With that understanding, teachers should provide focused activities based on the language needs that children demonstrate. Delpit (1990) suggests that these include dialect contrast activities in which students and teachers agree that learning Standard American English is a goal; this would probably take place in the upper elementary grades and beyond. These dialect contrasts can be incorporated into dialogue journals, class logs, and student portfolios.

LITERACY ISSUES FOR AFRICAN AMERICAN CHILDREN   The issue of mother tongue instruction has important implications for children who speak African American Vernacular English. If learning to read in Spanish while learning to speak English is the most effective program for Spanish-speaking children, then it could follow that speakers of African American Vernacular English should learn to read from materials written in that dialect while they are acquiring Standard American English as a second dialect (Simpkins, Holt, & Simpkins, 1974). Indeed, some educators have advocated for this approach. There are, however, some significant barriers:

- There is not broad acceptance in the African American community for the use of African American Vernacular English as a language of instruction.
- Although some reading instructional materials have been written in African American Vernacular English through the years, they have not been broadly or systematically used.
- Limited research evidence at present supports the use of reading materials written in African American Vernacular English (Simpkins et al., 1974).
- There is a sense among some African Americans and others that the use of African American Vernacular English might be a tool for minimizing opportunities for success among African American children (Williams, 1991).

Given the highly controversial nature of the issue, there are several ways in which teachers can make effective and positive use of the presence of African American Vernacular English—and other dialects of English—in American classrooms:

- Value and acknowledge positively the communication efforts of children who use African American Vernacular English in the classroom.
- Avoid correcting pronunciation and syntactical structures from African American Vernacular English and other dialects of English used by children in their ordinary classroom discourse; such attempts betray a negative valuing of the way the children speak and, by implication, of the children themselves and of their family members and communities.

- Demonstrate valuing of the dialect by accepting it in the dictations of children in key vocabulary and language experience approach activities.

- In addition to using children's literature in which dialogue is in Standard American English for read-aloud activities, incorporate children's literature that includes dialogue in African American Vernacular English and other dialects spoken by children in the classroom (Brooks, 2005, 2006; Sanacore, 2004).

- In activities that are designed to help children acquire Standard American English, avoid references to the standard dialect as the "correct" or "better" way to speak.

- Use storytelling (Sanacore, 2004) and traditional cultural literary structures of the African American community, such as the praise song and the praise poem (Johnson-Coleman, 2001) and trickster tales, which are also a part of the Native American oral tradition. An Internet search will yield dozens of praise song, praise poem, and trickster tale resources.

- Ensure that phonological, morphological, lexical, and syntactical features of African American Vernacular English and other dialects of English are not used to penalize children in assessment activities, especially those that are not related to the purpose of the assessment.

Delpit (1990, 2008) offers suggestions for teachers to consider in educating children of color who are too often failed by our schools. She recommends that teachers do the following:

- Teach these children more, not less.
- Provide critical thinking experiences for them (also Sanacore, 2004).
- Challenge the racist view some individuals hold that these children are incompetent.
- Recognize and build on the children's strengths.
- Use metaphors, analogies, and experiences that are familiar to the children to connect them to school knowledge.
- Ensure that the children feel cared for, as in a family (also Sanacore, 2004).
- Identify the children's needs and meet them with a variety of strategies.
- Honor and respect the culture the children bring to school (also Ladson-Billings, 2009).
- Connect the children to their community, something that is greater than themselves (also Ladson-Billings, 2009).

Several best practices for teaching African American children are recommended by Edwards, McMillon, and Turner (2010):

- Provide texts to read that connect student interests and cultural contexts, especially for male students.
- Use music to tell their stories, including hip-hop.
- Increase the use of informational text.
- Use narratives that touch on sensitive topics.

The reading of elementary-level African American boys is a special concern of educators. Wood and Jocius (2013) offer three dimensions of critical literacy that serve to improve these students' achievement and interest: culturally relevant texts in which students see themselves; collaboration in small supportive groups; and critical conversations about what they are reading, including looking at themselves in the context of these stories. They provide a valuable list of places to look for books that engage young African American boys in literacy activities:

- Coretta Scott King Award book awards
- Brown Sugar & Spice Books & Educational Services
- Scholastic
- Getting Boys to Read

As boys quite consistently perform at lower levels than girls, Wilhelm and Smith (2014) offer suggestions for improving the reading of middle-school boys in this era of Common Core State Standards. In their study of the literate lives of adolescent boys, they recommend what they characterize as flow experiences in five categories:

- Competence and control, for example, by using a computer or self-selected reading
- Appropriate challenge, reading a self-selected book or text that is comprehensible

- Clear goals and feedback in the text that helps them learn who and what they could be
- A focus on the immediate, not on the future
- The importance of the social, working with friends and sharing books of interest

Meier (2015) laments the shortage of literature for engaging African American boys in literacy and recommends the use of books that are relevant in their lives. These books should include references to literacy in the lives of African American men, such as those found in the following books: *Words Set Me Free: The Story of Young Frederick Douglass; Ron's Big Mission; Coming Home: From the Life of Langston Hughes; Jump! From the Life of Michael Jordan; Barack Obama: Son of Promise, Child of Hope; Howard Thurman's Great Hope; My Dream of Martin Luther King;* and *Malcolm Little: The Boy Who Grew Up to Become Malcolm X.*

INCORPORATING STUDENTS' AUTHENTIC LANGUAGE AND CHILDREN'S LITERATURE WITH THE LANGUAGE EXPERIENCE APPROACH   The language experience approach (LEA) to reading is a powerful tool for encouraging reluctant readers by addressing culture and utilizing beginning reading that is based on the oral language of children. The approach centers on language as the vehicle for communicating thoughts and ideas, and incorporates authentic children's literature for culturally diverse children.

The first step is for the teacher to conduct a read-aloud of a piece of children's literature that is culturally appropriate—in this case, for a group of African American first graders—and that is also ideal as a stimulus for a language experience dictation. The book in this example is Patricia McKissack's *Ma Dear's Aprons* (1997), about a little boy living with his mother in a single-parent situation. In the story, David Earl's mother has a different apron for each day of the week, and David knows which day of the week it is by observing the apron his mother is wearing. Although there are seven days and seven aprons, the teacher might decide to read only up through the first three days and aprons. During the read-aloud, share the wonderful illustrations by Floyd Cooper, asking questions about the activities of the three days and the aprons that Ma Dear wears.

Then have the children dictate their brief version of the story. They might come up with something similar to the example seen in the figure. Accept the dictations of the children as stated, regardless of any cultural affectations.

In this collaborative chart story strategy, children negotiate with each other about what they want to dictate on the chart. Some children might suggest changes that result in a dictation reflecting more Standard American English than the original version. The example shows two past tense verbs, *wash* and *iron*, that were written as dictated by the children because no child suggested a change. The word *next* was pronounced as "nex"; the teacher should spell it correctly according to best practice in the language experience approach. The children should have many opportunities to read the text in a shared reading mode as the dictation is recorded and after the children's rendition of the story is completed.

> On Monday, Ma Dear put on the blue apron.
> She wash the clothes.
>
> The next day she wore a yellow apron.
> She iron the clothes on Tuesday.
>
> David likes the green apron on Wednesday.
> It had a treasure pocket.
> There was candy in it.

Differentiating Instruction for At-Risk and Struggling Readers

Another aspect of diversity in American classrooms is a more generic category that incorporates children from all groups that are at risk of not learning to read. Through the years since the Coleman Report (Coleman et al., 1966), many terms have been used to describe students whose school achievement is below expectation, including *at-risk, disadvantaged, low-income,* and others. The constellation of factors often associated with at-risk students includes the following: low income; inner city or rural; ethnic and/or language minority; non-English speaking; nontraditional family structure, including frequent absence of father; and high rate of school dropout.

Many students who exhibit the characteristics just listed have satisfactory or above-average achievement in school, and some students who exhibit none of the characteristics experience failure in school. But it is fair to say that these factors are strongly associated with low school achievement.

As a result of the Coleman Report (Coleman et al., 1966), a variety of federally funded efforts were initiated to alleviate the effects of these factors on low school achievement, especially in reading. These included Head Start, Title I and Title VII of the Elementary and Secondary Education Act (ESEA), and the Reading First and Early Reading First Programs. The most recent of these federally funded programs is the five-year Striving Readers Program, which sponsored eight research projects to determine the most effective ways of lowering the numbers of struggling middle and secondary readers.

The rapidly increasing influx of English language learners and other so-called disadvantaged students in U.S. schools provides a greater challenge than ever before to teachers whose charge is to promote the equitable access of all students to high-quality instruction in reading and writing. These students have generally been placed in compensatory or remedial programs, where they are expected to learn to read and write by acquiring isolated skills through interaction with incomplete fragments of language. Rarely do they emerge successfully from these programs into the mainstream; instead, frequently they leave the programs only when they leave school—all too often as early leavers or dropouts (A. N. Crawford, 1993).

COGNITIVE, AFFECTIVE, AND PSYCHOMOTOR FACTORS Cultural and linguistic diversity are major factors for teachers to consider in planning reading instruction for children. But cognitive, affective, and psychomotor aspects of diversity also have an effect on reading.

The increasing diversity of our classrooms seems to bring with it an increase in the numbers of children who are struggling to read. Duffy-Hester (1999) examined several model reading programs for such children and found common guiding principles that should serve teachers well in working with troubled readers. Among these guiding principles are the following:

- Reading programs should be balanced, drawing on more than a single theoretical perspective. A one-size-fits-all approach to reading instruction inevitably seems to miss meeting the needs of some children. A balanced program touches on all of the learning modalities that diverse groups of children bring to the classroom.

- There should be a well-supported role for every element in a balanced reading program. Several currently popular direct instruction reading programs, for example, make heavy use of decodable text, fragments of unconnected text in which the students are to practice word recognition elements they have been studying. Yet little research supports the use of such text, whereas abundant research supports the use of connected text, especially in the promotion of reading comprehension (Allington, 1997).

- Word recognition, comprehension, and vocabulary development should be taught in the context of authentic reading and writing activities, not in isolation.

- Teacher read-aloud activities serve to build background knowledge and vocabulary, preparing children to understand their own reading of the text later.

- Authentic assessment provides valuable information that teachers can use to inform their instruction. Some assessment does not provide this type of information and takes up valuable time that children could use to read and write. We are reminded of a traditional dictum about assessment: "You don't fatten a pig by weighing it."

- Teachers should use their professional preparation to make instructional decisions about which reading programs they use.

- Staff development activities should provide time for reflection and opportunities to share experiences about best practices.

- The learner-centered goals and strategies that are most effective for troubled readers will serve other children well, too.

Other factors can affect the plight of troubled readers. Allington (2001) offers several research-based accommodations that relate to the organization of the school. Class size is an important factor, with research demonstrating that achievement is higher when classes are smaller, especially with children from low-income families (Achilles, 1999). Allington recommends a class size of 20. Access to appropriate instructional materials is also important. In agreement with Duffy-Hester, he feels that programs should be designed to fit children; we should not force children to fit into programs. He recommends that no more than 20% to 30% of instructional time be devoted to single-source materials, that is, materials that all children in the classroom use in common. A third factor is that of honoring instructional time. No interruptions of the period for teaching reading should occur, not even public address announcements from the principal's office.

Allington then turns his attention to the question of access to intensive, expert instruction. He suggests that one-on-one tutoring is the most intensive type of instruction, but that real small-group instruction (four to seven students) is much more effective than traditional large-group or whole-class instruction. He further observes that pullout remedial reading programs, such as those underwritten by federal funds, frequently offer instruction in periods that are too short, but whose course is extended over too long a time span. He recommends offering a semester of very frequent and intensive support instead of a year of less intensive support. Finally, Allington suggests expanding instruction time for troubled readers. This can be accomplished by adding a second daily lesson, providing extended-day reading instruction through after-school programs, and offering summer school reading support to minimize summer reading loss.

INCLUSION IN GENERAL EDUCATION CLASSROOMS   Federal law calls for inclusion for many children identified for special education services; many are now placed in general education classrooms, although sometimes for only part of the school day. They are educated, to the maximum extent possible, in the same setting as their classmates without disabilities. This means that general education classroom teachers must address the needs of some children who have intellectual disabilities, physical disabilities, hearing impairments, emotional disturbance, or other special needs.

Under provisions of the law, students are identified as requiring assessment if they display any of the following specific conditions: intellectual disabilities; a hearing impairment, including deafness; a speech or language impairment; a visual impairment, including blindness; a serious emotional disturbance; an orthopedic impairment; autism; traumatic brain injury; a specific learning disability; deaf-blindness; or multiple disabilities. These children's needs must be assessed, and an Individual Education Plan (IEP) must be developed for each student (Individuals with Disabilities Education Act, 1997). The plan must include the following elements:

- Current levels of educational performance
- Annual goals and short-term objectives
- Need for special education and related services
- Explanation if the child cannot be mainstreamed in the general education classroom
- Description and schedule of special education services provided
- Description of transition services provided
- Assessment of student progress, including needed accommodations

The Individuals with Disabilities Education Improvement Act of 2004 (IDEA) is carefully aligned with provisions of NCLB (NEA, 2004). Special education teachers are required to be "highly qualified"; students with disabilities are required to be assessed annually in NCLB-required assessments, with some accommodations; and students must meet the same state standards as all other students, including English language learners, with some exceptions for students with severe cognitive disability. Needless to say, these provisions in the law are the subject of much discussion in all school districts as teachers attempt to meet these new requirements.

It is not only the physical needs of these students that should be addressed in inclusion efforts but also the content of the curriculum. If students of color or girls need to see themselves in the literature they read, then so should students with disabilities. According to Landrum (2001), this benefits not only those students, but also students without disabilities, who need to learn about and accept differences. Landrum has developed a set of criteria for the evaluation of novels that feature characters with disabilities. Among her criteria are the following:

- *Plot:* Story events are realistic, not contrived; characters with disabilities are active participants.
- *Character development:* Characters with disabilities are presented as strong and independent, not passive and dependent; the focus is on what they can do, not on what they cannot do.
- *Tone:* The text avoids using such terms as *retarded*, *handicapped*, and *crippled*.

Check Your Understanding 2.3: **Gauge your understanding of the skills and concepts in this section.**

Response to Intervention (RTI)

For many years, it has been common practice to delay intervention in addressing struggling readers' problems until there was a two-year discrepancy between their measured and expected reading achievement. A child who shows signs of being a struggling reader in kindergarten, for example, would not receive any help until second grade. Vaughn and Fuchs (2003) describe this interval as "waiting to fail." Juel (1988) found that students who failed to learn to read before the end of the first grade tended to be unsuccessful in reading throughout the elementary grades, indicating that waiting for two years virtually ensures that the child will fail in reading.

Response to Intervention (RTI) is a set of regulations under the Individuals with Disabilities Education Improvement Act of 2004 (IDEIA) that provides new procedures for identifying and teaching children with learning disabilities. RTI constitutes a welcome change from the previous discrepancy model, permitting intervention based on identification of a struggling reader's needs as soon as a problem is recognized.

No Child Left Behind (NCLB), Reading First, and the Every Student Succeeds Act (ESSA)

The interaction between IDEA and the successive effects of NCLB and Reading First created additional difficulties for the struggling reader. Despite assurances to the contrary, NCLB evolved as a one-size-fits-all approach to instruction. All children were typically provided instruction from the same materials using the same methodology and at the same level. RTI provides increased flexibility so that children receive appropriate reading instruction. The NCLB law has been renamed the Every Student Succeeds Act (ESSA) and there have been major changes in it (Davis, 2015). The most significant is that the authority to improve troubled schools has been returned to the states. High-stakes testing will be de-emphasized and test requirements for English language learners have been eased (Tripplet, 2015). Some provisions of the old law remain, however, including reading and mathematics testing in grades 3–8 and reporting data for schools and subgroups, such as English language learners and special education students. But there is no provision for teacher evaluation based on test results (Klein, 2015). States are authorized to develop their own programs to implement this power.

State education agencies have long wanted to be in charge of planning the use of federal funds. This new authority under ESSA comes at the end of a recession that decimated the staffs of most of them (Burnette II, 2016). They were not well equipped to implement the last revision of ESEA, the No Child Left Behind (NCLB) mandates. They now have a deadline of 2017–2018 to develop accountability plans for submission to the Department of Education that address the following:

- Challenging academic standards
- Accountability for gaps that exist between subgroups of students in academic achievement and English-language proficiency, including interventions in schools that are among the bottom 5%
- Equitable distribution of effective classroom teachers, although test scores are no longer a factor
- Continued testing in grades 3–8
- School improvement grants that are more flexible in the spending of Title I funds, with more available for school turnarounds

Characteristics of RTI: What It Is, What It Isn't

Educators in general and reading educators in particular have long suffered under highly prescriptive government mandates such as NCLB and Reading First. RTI provides considerable discretion to schools and school districts in designing their programs to meet the needs of students with reading difficulties. In this video, listen to associate professor Ellie Young describe how RTI is different from historical models of special education and answer the question that follows.

 Video Exploration 2.2: Watch the video and answer questions that reflect the content you have read.

RTI is not based on the earlier model that required a discrepancy between the student's IQ and his or her level of achievement (Johnston, 2010). Rather, it is designed to identify learning disabilities and ensure that identified students receive appropriate instruction. RTI permits the early identification of reading difficulties, resulting in early intervention instead of waiting for students to fail. It also reduces the overidentification of English language learners and other diverse groups of students. According to Fuchs and Fuchs (2009), the goal of RTI is not to prevent special education, but rather to identify those children who have disabilities and to avoid the negative consequences of children exiting school without academic competence.

RTI programs generally consist of three components:

- Universal screening for the early identification of students at risk of struggling in reading
- Provision of tiers of instruction ranging from the regular classroom program to intensive intervention, sometimes in special education
- Continuous monitoring of student progress

RTI refers to recent changes in the application of special education laws, the Individuals with Disabilities Acts of 1997 and 2004 (IDEA, IDEIA). RTI refines IDEA with an assessment of the effectiveness of a scientific, research-based intervention in improving an identified child's academic performance, assuming that a continuing problem is not related to a visual, hearing, or motor disability, intellectual disability, emotional disturbance, cultural factors, economic disadvantage, or limited English proficiency.

Eight areas of low achievement are used as the basis for identifying specific learning disabilities, of which six are in the language arts: oral expression, listening comprehension, written expression, basic reading skill, reading fluency skills, and reading comprehension (International Reading Association, 2009).

K–3 students are screened in accordance with Reading First. Literacy screening instruments and procedures are used to determine if they are at risk of not meeting prescribed benchmarks. If students do not meet benchmarks after scientifically valid interventions are applied, the RTI models provide for interventions in small groups to provide needed assistance. The children's progress is monitored using measures that are targeted at skills the children need to attain. If progress is not noted, individualized interventions are provided. If these are not effective, then the child's case is reviewed by a team of professionals to determine if he or she is eligible for special education services. According to Mesmer and Mesmer (2008/2009), the RTI process is a useful alternative to a discrepancy model.

An IQ measure is no longer used to assess the discrepancy between expected and actual learning outcomes. In any case, IQ tests are not useful with children whose English is limited (Gillet, Temple, Temple, & Crawford, 2012).

The Multi-Tiered Structure of RTI

RTI programs are organized around a multi-tier system that is designed to prevent reading failure. It usually consists of three tiers, although this structure is not mandated by government regulation. Within this three-tier structure, Tier One is the general education or regular classroom instructional program, including the core curriculum. Tier Two provides additional intervention that is designed to address needs identified through assessment; it usually consists of small-group tutoring. Tier Three consists of intensive intervention that is often individualized or provided in small groups, sometimes by a special education teacher, sometimes by a reading specialist, and sometimes by a team, as seen in Figure 2.2.

TIER ONE: GENERAL EDUCATION PROGRAM   Tier One consists of the general education program that is usually conducted by a well-trained classroom teacher in the regular classroom. According to Taylor (2008), effective reading instruction in grades K–5 includes phonemic awareness and phonics instruction, fluency instruction, vocabulary instruction, and comprehension instruction. Fuchs and Fuchs (2008) describe a benchmark assessment mode within Tier One. A part of the school population that may be at risk for reading failure is identified with a brief screening measure. A cut score for the measure is established, and children scoring below the cut score are identified as at risk. Some districts establish the cut score at about 20% of students, who will have further diagnosis. Tier One includes all students.

TIER TWO: SMALL GROUP INTERVENTION   The purpose of Tier Two is to meet the needs of students who have not made satisfactory progress with supplemental intervention through targeted support in Tier One. A common approach in Tier Two is to provide tutoring in small groups using an evidence-based approach. The focus is on accelerating reading growth, allowing students to catch up. Progress monitoring that shows growth leads to students being returned to the general program in Tier One (Fuchs & Fuchs, 2008). Most students are in Tier Two for a six- to eight-week period of progress monitoring to clarify the identification process.

TIER THREE: INTENSIVE INTERVENTION   Students who make unsatisfactory progress in Tier Two are referred to Tier Three, which involves intensive intervention services, often provided by special education resources. Longer individualized or small-group sessions are provided, including validated treatment protocols (Fuchs & Fuchs, 2008). Progress monitoring and diagnostic assessment continue in Tier Three, with the goal of returning successful students to Tier Two or Tier One. Many fewer students are in Tier Three programs than in Tiers One and Two.

The Role of Assessment in RTI

Assessment is a major part of RTI. It does not include a high-stakes assessment test to inform school districts about how they are doing in their literacy program, but it is instead designed to help teachers meet the needs of individual students at risk of failure in literacy. RTI assessment is conducted in several different modes at different stages and for different purposes, including screening, diagnostics, formative progress monitoring, benchmark progress monitoring, and summative outcome assessment (Wixson & Valencia, 2011). Major categories of assessment include curriculum-based assessment, diagnostic assessment, and progress monitoring.

Figure 2.2 RTI Tiers

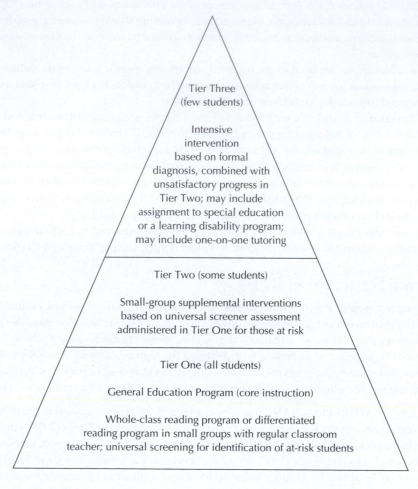

Tier Three
(few students)

Intensive
intervention
based on formal
diagnosis, combined with
unsatisfactory progress in
Tier Two; may include
assignment to special education
or a learning disability program;
may include one-on-one tutoring

Tier Two (some students)

Small-group supplemental interventions
based on universal screener assessment
administered in Tier One for those at risk

Tier One (all students)

General Education Program (core instruction)

Whole-class reading program or differentiated
reading program in small groups with regular classroom
teacher; universal screening for identification of at-risk students

CURRICULUM-BASED MEASUREMENT (CBM) OR BENCHMARK ASSESSMENT CBM and benchmark assessment are often the terms used for the universal screening that takes place in the Tier One general education program. Assessments such as PALS or DIBELS are frequently used. In past approaches to assessment, only data for struggling students were collected and analyzed. In RTI, data are collected for all students in Tier One (Tileston, 2011).

DIAGNOSTIC ASSESSMENT A very thorough diagnostic assessment is used with students who fail to reach the cut score in Tier One assessment. This diagnostic assessment is individualized according to the apparent needs of each student. According to Lipson, Chomsky-Higgins, and Kanfer (2011), it should include the following areas: phonological awareness, letter identification, sight vocabulary, fluency, decoding, vocabulary, comprehension, motivation, stamina, writing about reading, and text level, all of which can lead to effective differentiated instruction.

PROGRESS MONITORING Progress monitoring is an important component of RTI (Moore & Whitfield, 2009). It includes regular and systematic assessment of the progress of students in all tiers.

Evidence-Based Literacy Programs

Many evidence-based literacy curriculum packages or validated treatment protocols are in common use as interventions to meet instructional needs in Tier Two and Tier Three RTI programs. The following are examples of programs frequently used: Peer-Assisted Literacy Strategies (PALS) Series; Read Naturally; and Reading Recovery. Evidence-based strategies also meet criteria for RTI. They are widely used strategies for specific purposes that have a strong research base, but they should not be used as scripted one-size-fits-all programs. As Johnston (2010) reminds us, an intervention effective for most children may not be effective for all.

Allington and Walmsley (1995, 2007) provide important principles that serve to strengthen programs of intervention for identified struggling readers:

- All staff, classroom teachers, special education teachers, and specialists are responsible for the education of all students, with emphasis on the reading expertise of the classroom teacher.

- All children should be provided with the same literacy experiences, materials, and expectations. Poor readers are too often placed in programs that limit access to literacy because their primary focus is on low-level skill development, oral reading, and word recognition—a fragmented program.

- All children should be educated with their peers, an approach characterized by inclusion, not segregation into special classes.

- The literacy curriculum for identified students and struggling readers should contain all of the elements that successful readers are experiencing in their lessons, including silent reading, reading full-length material, and reading for a variety of purposes, including pleasure. Joint planning between general education classroom teachers and those who provide instructional support outside the general education classroom is needed.

- Expert teachers provide high-quality reading instruction. These are usually general education classroom teachers with excellent preparation in the teaching of reading and writing.

- Instructional support programs for struggling readers should function as integrated wholes, rather than as a series of separately funded programs that address different issues: a single, unified instructional support program that involves all of the players in meeting children's literacy needs in an integration of remedial and, when needed, special education services.

Allington (2008) adds other important elements:

- Texts used must be matched to students' reading levels.

- Reading activity must be dramatically expanded—that is, actual reading, rather than studying about reading.

- Interventions must be coordinated with the curriculum in the classroom.

- Meaning and metacognition should be the focus of instruction.

- Needed expert teachers do not include paraprofessionals who use workbooks and low-level worksheets, a common intervention for struggling readers.

Members of the RTI Team and Their Roles

The successful implementation of RTI requires a collaborative team effort. It includes classroom teachers, reading specialists/coaches, special education teachers, school psychologists, building principals, district level administrators, and parents. There must be mutual respect among team members for the different kinds of expertise they bring to the RTI process. RTI provides a newly recognized important role for classroom teachers in that they frequently have more academic preparation and literacy teaching experience than other team members, even though they may not have had a great deal of practice with the processes of assessment and planning for students with reading disabilities.

Bean and Lillenstein (2012) have recommended expanded roles for school personnel in the RTI program. School principals should increase emphasis on empowering others and should be actively involved with implementing and establishing conditions for success. Literacy coaches should manage and coordinate an increased focus on evidence-based instruction in a team approach. Special educators are seen as working with regular students, and not just their customary population, focusing more on literacy, and working collaboratively with other teachers. And classroom teachers should emphasize data-based decision making with students beyond those in their own classrooms. Reading specialists should provide more intervention for selected students with greater needs. In addition, a meta-analysis of research by Galloway and Lesaux (2014) indicates that reading specialists are spending more time on improving classroom instruction in the school through serving as a coaching resource to teachers in diagnosing and teaching students, a teacher of teachers and change agent role. This is most pronounced in elementary schools.

Parents also have a strong role in RTI when they are notified about their children's problems, as they must provide informed consent before any diagnostic assessment or intervention may take place (Fuchs & Mellard, 2007). Parents always have the right to request a comprehensive evaluation of their child.

Special Considerations in Implementing RTI

RTI is implemented in different ways, according to different categories and levels of students and also changes in curriculum.

RTI IN MIDDLE SCHOOLS   Gelzheiser, Scanlon, and Hallgren-Flynn (2010) describe several characteristics of RTI programs that are especially important for middle-school students.

- Instruction that is responsive to their individual needs, as with other students at lower levels, is critical for middle-school students, instead of providing the same packaged program to all.

- It is important to guide middle-grade students toward independence in their own learning, as contrasted with strong teacher-controlled interaction in the earlier grades.

- Reading in the content areas of the curriculum is of great importance in RTI at the middle-school level.

- Students at the middle-school level should focus on coherence in the meanings of all words in order to strengthen their reading comprehension.

- Struggling students benefit from reading at a variety of reading levels for different purposes and from different genres.

- Motivation and attitudes toward reading are especially important at the middle-school level, as many students have already given up.

ENGLISH LANGUAGE LEARNERS AND RTI   There is continuing concern about the overrepresentation of children from linguistic and ethnic minorities in special education classes (Hill, Carjuzaa, Aramburo, & Baca, 1993). According to Damico (1991), referral to special education, and by extension to RTI Tier Three, should not be based on the following:

- Other factors that might explain the child's learning and language difficulties, such as the lack of opportunity to learn, cultural dissonance, and stressful life events, for example, among refugee children

- Language difficulties that affect the student at school, but not at home or in the community

- Ordinary needs of children to acquire English as a second language or the Standard American English dialect

- Cross-cultural interference

- Bias in the assessment process, including data analysis that does not take into account the child's culture, language, and life experiences

The most problematic issue with respect to English language learners is their varying proficiency in English, which can range from speaking no English to being quite competent in their second language, even within the same classroom. Teachers and RTI team members should ask themselves if English language learners would have literacy problems if they were taught to read and write in their mother tongue, instead of English. If they would not, then their intervention should be a strong and formal ESL program. Klingner, Soltero-González, and Lesaux (2010) accordingly recommend that teachers should be knowledgeable about second language acquisition and also about how to teach reading in English to children for whom English is their second language. Fisher, Frey, and Rothenberg (2011) emphasize that all teachers are teachers of language, providing instruction in all four domains: listening, speaking, reading, and writing. Scaffolding must accommodate the language levels of all students.

Many strategies can be used very effectively in teaching children with these needs. According to Gersten and Baker (2000), teachers should do the following:

- Build children's vocabulary and use it as a curricular anchor

- Use visual representations to reinforce major concepts and vocabulary

- Use the children's mother tongue as a support system

- Adapt cognitive and language demands of instruction to the children by using sheltered English strategies

Fisher, Frey, and Rothenberg (2011) additionally recommend that the multidisciplinary RTI team have expertise about children who are English language learners. This will alleviate the problem of overrepresentation of English language learners within special education programs. Conversely, it can also address the problem of underrepresentation of these children when personnel who lack the needed language and cultural skills are not able to accurately assess their needs.

Esparza, Brown, and Sanford (2011) place particular emphasis on the need for the RTI team to have expertise and experience in assessing second language proficiency and also in providing effective second language instruction that recognizes stages of language acquisition (see Chapter 14).

RTI AND THE GIFTED   Teachers often conclude that gifted children do not have reading problems. Many or most learn to read at home if parents read to them, and the rest appear to learn to read quickly in kindergarten or the first grade. But we have found that teachers often make the following erroneous assumptions about gifted children:

- *Gifted children don't have reading problems.* The gifted child reading on grade level has a reading problem that should be diagnosed and addressed. Based on expectations, gifted children should be reading above grade level, usually several grades above their age-expected level. Although gifted children probably won't end up in Tier Three of RTI programs, they might appear in Tier Two.
- *Gifted children have mastered the basic skills of reading.* It isn't unusual to observe the fragmentation of basic skills among gifted children—they may have mastered most basic skills, but gaps may appear. They can be integrated into reading groups that are addressing identified areas of weakness at the time an appropriate lesson or lessons are offered, even though those groups are usually working below the levels of these otherwise more capable students.
- *All gifted children speak English well.* Often, gifted children can read in a language other than English, which means that their greatest need is to learn to understand and speak English.

RTI AND THE COMMON CORE STATE STANDARDS (CCSS)   The CCSS have major implications for RTI. The early emphasis on reading is now expanding beyond basic reading skills of phonemic awareness, phonics, fluency, vocabulary, and comprehension to attention to reading and writing in grades 6 to 12 (Wixson & Lipson, 2012). The trend in assessment is toward comprehending complex texts, analyzing writing sources, conducting and reporting on research, posing questions and gathering and presenting information, and speaking and listening. These higher expectations will result in an increase in the need for differentiated instruction, which reflects RTI.

Check Your Understanding 2.4: **Gauge your understanding of the skills and concepts in this section.**

Finding the Books and Materials They Want to Read

Diversity is important with respect not only to the learning characteristics of all students but also to their need for appropriate texts to read and from which to learn to read.

The Print Environment of Students at Home

As might be expected, the print environment of the home and community is closely related to the factors of diversity described in this chapter. The newspapers, magazines, books, calendars, checkbooks, notes on the refrigerator door, Web site pages on the computer screen, and instructional manuals found in most middle-class homes may be absent from or less frequently encountered in the homes of children from low-income families. There might not be a tradition of reading and writing in the family, or perhaps a Bible or other religious book is the only representation of print in the home.

In a study they conducted, Halle, Kurtz-Costes, and Mahoney (1997) found that access to print was an important factor related to the reading achievement of African American children. In an international study of the relationships among reading achievement, home literacy environment, and school and public library availability of reading material in several countries, Elley (1992, 1996) reported that access to print was the most powerful factor associated with reading achievement, including the size of the school library. He found that frequent silent reading was the next most significant variable affecting reading achievement. McQuillan and Au (2001), consistent with earlier research, found that convenient access to reading material was associated with students reading more frequently. Voluntary and free reading was associated with increased levels of reading proficiency, supporting the need for easy access of students to things of interest to read.

Beyond the presence of text to read, the need for models who read in the home is also of great importance, especially when it is recognized that men and older boys are often less likely to read than are women and girls in the family.

Besides often being a factor in the low-income home, the absence of text also characterizes the low-income communities in which the homes are located. In a study of print resources in two low-income and two middle-income neighborhoods, Neuman and Celano (2001) surveyed the availability of reading materials for purchase, such as newspapers, magazines, and children's books; the quantity of signage; public places where reading took place, such as laundromats and bookstores; the availability of books in child care centers; and the quality of services and materials provided by school and public libraries. They found an overwhelming advantage of print resources in the middle-income neighborhoods, and they concluded that children in the low-income neighborhoods would have difficulty finding books of good quality, whereas those in the middle-income neighborhoods would have difficulty avoiding them.

In addition, the provision of a full-time or even part-time librarian is often related to the income levels of students in the schools. Neuman and Celano (2001) found that there were no trained school librarians in the low-income communities they studied, whereas the schools in the middle-income communities had well-trained and highly experienced school librarians. School libraries in the middle-income communities were also open more days and hours per week than those in the low-income communities. The same disparities were found in public libraries in the communities studied.

They concluded, as did Cunningham and Stanovich (1997), that the children who are most in need of a print-rich environment are the least likely to encounter it, resulting in a spiraling down of environmental opportunities for reading in the community, which in turn results in less motivation to read and still fewer opportunities to read. Allington (1983) adds that this situation is aggravated when these same children are enrolled in public schools in which low-level programs are provided to address their reading problems, resulting in their doing less reading of text than children who read well. These programs involve major time commitments to studying about reading instead of time devoted to reading connected text.

Getting Books, Magazines, and Newspapers Into Children's Hands

Given the diversity of children in our schools, especially children who are at risk of being troubled readers, teachers should take special pains to find books and other print materials that children will enjoy, books with characters and settings with which they can identify, books in which they can see themselves in positive roles, and materials that are of high interest and have visual appeal. A valuable resource of books and other sources of connected text that reflect cultures of diversity is found in Banks's *Teaching Strategies for Ethnic Studies* (2008). Banks categorizes many dozens of books in English for teachers and for children in the following groups: First Americans (American Indians, Native Hawaiians, and African Americans); European Americans (European ethnic groups and Jewish Americans); Hispanic Americans (Mexican Americans, Puerto Rican Americans, and Cuban Americans); and Asian Americans (Chinese Americans, Japanese Americans, Filipino Americans, and Indochinese Americans).

An abundance of books available in Spanish exist for children who want and need to read in that language (Schon, 2000, 2001, 2004; Schon & Corona Berkin, 1996). Isabel Schon has passed on, but California State University, San Marcos, has established the Barahona Center to continue her outstanding work (Barahona Center, 2007). Both children who did not have the opportunity to learn to read in their mother tongue and those who have acquired this ability in another school or country should be provided with opportunities to read more books in that language. It improves self-concept, offers evidence that the school and teacher value that language, and provides practice in reading that builds background knowledge and skills that transfer positively to reading in English later. Teachers should also be very careful about the use of so-called bilingual books that are written in two languages, usually with English and Spanish versions on facing pages. This practice ensures that children will acquire English in terms of Spanish, that is, a very ineffective translation approach. It is better for children to read a story in Spanish from one book and then read the same story in English from another book, as elaborated in later chapters. The children can use their background knowledge from the first experience to support their comprehension and learning of English in the second book.

Gifted children require a rich variety of books and other text materials to maintain their many and changing interests. They will often tackle books at a much higher level than the level at which they are reading because of their motivation and willingness to persist. Given good guidance, they can use the Internet very productively, too. Many sites are now available that are geared to younger children's reading abilities. Teacher sites like Thinkfinity can also help teachers locate stimulating project ideas and resources for these students. This is less of a problem for children in the lower grades of a multi-graded school because they will find reading resources for older children in the school library. But it can be a problem for the gifted sixth grader in a K–6 school, who needs access to a middle or secondary school library or an understanding teacher who is willing to check out books at the public library.

Finding materials that are high interest and low enough vocabulary for troubled readers, especially for boys, is a perennial problem for teachers. The teacher who is always conventional might have difficulty finding books that meet both criteria. A good resource for magazines is Magazines for Kids and Teens at the Madison Public Library Web site under "kids/magazines." It provides descriptions of the content and the reading and interest levels of dozens of magazines on a wide variety of topics, including some that publish students' own writing.

Teach It! 7
Making Individual Small Books

This activity is an inexpensive and accessible way for children to create their own small books to read at school and at home.

School budget problems are often a factor that affects the numbers of books, magazines, and newspapers available to children in the classroom. Some sources of text that teachers can exploit to augment those supplied by the school district are the following:

- School storage rooms, where surplus books are often hidden away
- Secondhand stores, public library book sales, yard sales, and swap meets, where teachers can often negotiate low prices with vendors "for the children"; returning to vendors at the end of the day and offering to buy all remaining books for a bulk price is often an effective way to maximize scarce teacher resources (many teachers spend their own money on books for children)
- Local public libraries that are usually available for walking field trips and that permit children to request library cards so they can check out their own books
- Commercial book clubs, which offer children's books at quantity discounts, usually with soft covers instead of hard covers. Depending on the number of books ordered by the children, many book clubs provide additional books for the teacher's classroom library.
- Newspapers that often sponsor programs to adopt a classroom and also often provide newspapers at no cost
- Support from parent groups, service clubs, and other community sources
- Reading Is Fundamental, which provides sets of books to schools at no cost
- Child-made books that result from collaborative chart stories, language experience approach activities, and other student writing activities

Finally, teachers should ensure that a wide variety of text is readily available for children to take home to read. Too many resources are so protected from loss or abuse that they are never used.

READERS WHO ARE BOYS   Much attention has been given to the roles of girls in literature for children in recent years—and with good effect. Whereas stories in basal readers and current literature anthologies tended to focus on boys in the most active roles in past years, there is now balance in the stories that the children read, not to mention representation of major cultural and linguistic groups as well. You might wonder why boys would be listed as a category of diversity among readers, but boys continue to have problems in reading that are out of proportion to their numbers in the population. Why do boys make up an almost overwhelming proportion of troubled readers? Among the many factors associated with this finding are the greater frequency of left dominance (left-handedness); lack of physical and emotional maturity compared to girls; greater frequency of attention deficit disorder; different cultural expectations for boys, including more physical activity and action; fewer positive reading models for boys; low interest levels of books for boys; and female-dominated environment in schools, with teachers also favoring realistic fiction and character-related stories.

Teachers can take steps to ensure that boys do not continue to be overrepresented among the ranks of troubled readers:

- Provide more time in the initial stages of reading instruction for immature boys, especially those who exhibit signs of left dominance.
- Provide books of interest to boys and nonfiction informational books about nature, history, biography, and sports.
- Provide magazines and newspapers that have more real-world interest and shorter texts.
- Permit more physical movement, for example, letting the children sprawl out on the floor when reading.
- Provide structured opportunities for children to discuss the text they are reading and writing about (Young & Brozo, 2001).
- Recognize the importance of archetypes of masculinity in picture books and story books for boys (Zambo, 2007).

- Provide positive role models for boys: men and older boys who read (Zambo & Brozo, 2009; Brozo, 2010). Watch this video that explains why star basketball player LeBron James and other members of his NBA team bring books to read before and after major games, and answer the question that follows.

 Video Exploration 2.3: Watch the video (https://www.youtube.com/watch?v=kB86T-yS96M) and answer questions that reflect the content you have read.

In a study by Farris, Werderich, Nelson, and Fuhler (2009), the researchers concluded that the following types of books appeal to boys:

- Easy-to-read books with enticing covers (at their independent reading level)
- Realistic fiction and fantasy books that are part of a series and by a favorite author
- Informational books that have short illustrated passages
- Novels and nonfiction books that are graphic

In addition, boys will enjoy recent offerings in the immensely popular Captain Underpants series (Pilkey, 2000): *Captain Underpants and the Invasion of the Incredibly Naughty Cafeteria Ladies from Outer Space, Captain Underpants and the Wrath of the Wicked Wedgie Woman*, and *Captain Underpants and the Attack of the Talking Toilets*. Teachers who understand and appreciate the sense of humor of nine-year-old boys will recognize the appeal of these titles and the opportunities for stimulating those boys' creative writing instincts. A search on "books for boys" on the Internet will yield dozens of additional books that appeal to boys of various ages.

READERS WHO ARE ENGLISH LANGUAGE LEARNERS   Finally, books for English language learners should not be so-called bilingual books, which have, for example, English and Spanish on facing pages. Students will quickly stop looking at the second language and read only in the first language. Adults will do the same. Instead, have the students read the Spanish version of a book first, and then read the English version in the new second language. They won't be tempted to return to Spanish because they don't have it at hand. But they usually have sufficient background knowledge from the Spanish version to understand the English version and to learn from it.

Check Your Understanding 2.5: Gauge your understanding of the skills and concepts in this section.

For Review

This chapter considered the social and cultural contexts of literacy for children in grades K–8. Different social and cultural groups have views of literacy that reflect their own realities and needs, which might vary from the mainstream view. It is important to acknowledge the validity of the various views of literacy as instruction is planned for children from these social and cultural groups. At the outset of this chapter we stated that when you reached this point in your reading and studying you should be able to:

- **Explain some differences in how literacy functions in varied social, cultural, and economic communities**

In some communities written texts are highly respected and not to be questioned; in other communities there is a more playful and interactive engagement with written materials. It is also true that cultural groups vary in what they consider to be the role of teachers. African American parents often prefer directed discipline, while many immigrant parents hold teachers in high esteem and don't want to interfere with their teaching; as a result they don't provide early literacy experiences for their children, nor

do they think of it as their role to engage with their children in doing literacy "homework" during school years.

- **Communicate (or demonstrate) literacy values through organizing a pro-literacy classroom, planning activities for children, and involving parents.**

Some teachers begin the school year writing to their new students and establish a personal connection with literacy even before they meet the children. When children enter the classroom spaces for independent and small-group work, let them know their literacy will be developed in a collaborative way; the variety of books and print materials also provide a strong message about the possibilities of enjoyable and interesting reading geared to individual interests. By including books from a variety of cultures and in different languages, teachers enable children to expand their understanding and appreciation of worldwide literacy.

Most parents want to know what teachers expect of their children and how they can support their learning. By inviting parents to visit and observe actual lessons and by sending information home about the reading and writing students are doing teachers can help parents feel more informed and can also extend those activities. Using videos of classroom interactions, local television programming, and written parent guides all can create close communication.

- **Meet the literacy needs of linguistically and culturally diverse students in the classroom.**

The needs of English language learners in the linguistic area are obvious. In order to learn to read in English, they must be able to understand and speak English. This requires an ESL program that focuses on oral communication. These students may not pronounce English sounds like native speakers, but this does not interfere with their comprehension in reading and in their abilities to write. African American students often speak African American Vernacular English (AAVE) at home. This can interfere with reading comprehension, as they struggle to apply their dialect, grammatical constructions, and pronunciation to reading in Standard American English. Their need is to add the standard dialect to their language repertoire, not to replace AAVE with Standard American English. In the meantime, teachers should consider their dialect as an acceptable form of communication as they learn the new standard dialect and when to use it.

Teachers must also consider that body language varies with different ethnic, cultural, and language groups. Confusion about a message conveyed by the body and facial expressions of students from diverse groups should be viewed as a cultural conflict, not as misbehavior or disrespect. As students become bilingual or bidialectical, they can also become bicultural. Teachers can make the same accommodation, at least in terms of understanding what is being communicated.

- **Explain how Response to Intervention (RTI) has changed the role of teachers of reading, both classroom teachers and reading specialists, in working with students with special needs.**

Students with special needs used to work only with special education teachers and school psychologists. There is now a team approach that includes the regular classrooms teachers, who may work with students in the least restrictive environment, and reading specialists, whose expertise in reading and writing has much more depth than that of special education teachers and school psychologists. Regular classroom teachers and reading specialists now work within a team that also includes school psychologists, special education teachers, administrators, and parents.

- **Incorporate authentic literature and informational text for students from diverse communities in the classroom and discuss their importance to reading instruction beyond traditional reading textbooks.**

Students from diverse communities have the same need for interesting and relevant sources of print as students in advantaged communities, but diverse communities are often characterized by a lack of books and print in their homes, as well as the absence of local libraries. Sometimes, there are no libraries in their schools. Teachers need to scour their environment for appealing and relevant sources of print for these students: their own libraries, classroom libraries stocked with books from garage sales, thrift shops, donations, and also magazines of interest.

Special care is needed to find books of interest for boys—books that they are capable of reading (books at their independent reading level), books about heroes, and success stories about characters who can serve as role models. English language learners will benefit more from reading a mother tongue version of a story first, then English later, instead of a bilingual book that has mother tongue text on one page and English on the facing page.

For Your Journal

1. Now that you have read Chapter 2, return to the Anticipation Guide at the beginning of the chapter. What differences are there in how you would answer the open-ended questions now?

2. The true-false questions in the Anticipation Guide addressed many myths about the demographics of children in our schools and about children's learning. After you read and found answers to the questions, which one(s) surprised you the most? Why?

Taking It to the World

Now that you have considered the implications of classroom diversity, think about your classmates when you were in the third grade. In terms of diversity, how does the student population of the classroom to which you are assigned now compare to that of your own third-grade classroom? Make a list of positive outcomes that the children of today exhibit as a result of the increased classroom diversity they experience.

Chapter 3
What Reading Teachers Need to Know About Language

 Learning Outcomes

After reading this chapter you should be able to:

1. Define vowels, consonants, and syllables, and explain how phonological awareness supports reading and spelling development.

2. Define and classify morphemes, and explain why morpheme awareness is important for reading and spelling development.

3. Identify vocabulary tiers, and explain how knowledge of lexical relationships supports reading comprehension.

4. Distinguish among types of sentences, identify parts of speech, and explain how knowledge of syntax supports reading comprehension.

5. Identify the structure of texts, signal words associated with varied text structures, and explain how awareness of text structure and signal words can support reading comprehension and writing development.

Anticipation Guide

The following statements will help you begin thinking about the topics covered in this chapter. Answer *true* or *false* in response to each statement. As you read and learn more about the topics mentioned in the statements, double-check your answers. See what interests you and prompts your curiosity toward more understanding.

_____ 1. You study French to learn about the French language and Spanish to learn about the Spanish language. The study of languages in general is known as *linguistics*.

_____ 2. Chinese has an ideographic writing system; written characters relate to ideas. English has a syllabic writing system; written characters relate to spoken syllables. And Japanese has an alphabetic writing system; alphabetic letters relate to small sound units called *phonemes*.

_____ 3. Over the centuries, the pronunciation of English sometimes has changed more than the writing system. Many English words are spelled the way they used to be pronounced.

_____ 4. Morphemes can only be purchased with a prescription from licensed pharmacies.

_____ 5. Onsets and rimes are the smallest particles of phonemes.

_____ 6. The words *elect* and *college* are related to each other. Both come from a Latin word meaning "to choose."

_____ 7. Vocabulary words face two ways: they are a record of what you have learned in the past, and they enable you to learn more in the future.

_____ **8.** The emphasis on close reading that comes with the Common Core State Standards will require that teachers think more carefully about grammar—about the ordering and inflection of words.

_____ **9.** A relative pronoun can refer to blood relatives, but not relatives by marriage.

_____ **10.** A proper noun is the correct choice of noun to use in formal situations, dressed in your best clothes.

A Classroom Story

Teachers Use Linguistics

Janet Reardon feels lucky to have been assigned to this second-grade class for her observation period. She will be student teaching next fall, and she has filled a notebook with ideas she can use. Her cooperating teacher is Alan Parsons. It is exciting to watch him interact with children, and he is also generous with his time and advice, especially when Janet asks him about topics she has been studying at the university in her literacy class.

Last Friday she asked him how he assessed phonemic awareness.

"I use the Yopp-Singer phonemic awareness test from time to time. You should try it out yourself. But the truth is, I can tell a lot about how a child is coming along in phonemic awareness by looking at her invented spelling."

"How?"

"For instance, when a child strings a lot of letters in a line without any obvious connection to sounds, I don't expect the child to have a concept of word or much in the way of phonemic awareness. But if a child writes down a few letters for a word—what is called 'early phonemic' spelling—you can be pretty sure that she has started to be aware of phonemes."

"How do you know? What does the spelling tell you?"

"Well, for a kid to invent spellings, she has to be able to break a word down into its phonemes, and then match each one of those phonemes with a letter. But there's more."

"There always is."

"You'll get used to it. When she uses 'letter name spelling' when she writes, we know she's further along in phonemic segmenta-tion. What's more, you can get an idea of what she knows about letter-to-sound correspondences from her early spelling. Look at this spelling: HAK MIK."

"Hack Mick?"

"No. 'Check mark.' That's what Andrea said when she read it back to me. She's pretty far along in phonemic segmentation. See? She spelled the beginning consonant sound, the vowel, and the final consonant on both words. But you can see from the spelling that she doesn't have a clue about digraph consonants yet—see that H for the /ch/ sound? So her invented spelling is a good indication not only of her phonemic segmentation, but also of what she knows about letter-to-sound correspondences."

"Amazing."

"Totally. Go back and tell your classmates to pay attention to linguistics. Especially to phonology."

"What's that?"

"That's for you to find out. Have a great weekend."

"Print is talk written down," teachers say, and in many ways the statement is true. In order to learn to read, children need to realize that print represents spoken language; and you, their reading teacher, will need to help them to understand how speech maps onto print.

One of the first things you will want them to understand is what the characters used in print stand for. In English they stand for speech sounds, but this is not true of all languages. For example, if the language is Chinese, the characters repre-sent ideas. Hence, the Chinese writing system is called **ideographic**, for "ideas written down" (see Figure 3.1).

If the language we spoke were Japanese, the written characters would mostly represent spoken syllables. Each charac-ter that represented a consonant would represent a vowel, too. Each consonant and vowel combination (such as _ka, ki, ke, ko,_ and _ku_) gets a different graphic character. Hence, the Japanese writing system is **syllabic** (see Figure 3.2).

The English writing system, which is _alphabetic_, represents speech at one level smaller than a syllable. Our alphabet letters represent _phonemes_, vowel or consonant sounds. For example, each of the three sounds that make up the word _cat_: /k/, /æ/, and /t/ is a phoneme.

If the English language used ideographs instead of letters of the alphabet, we would need to learn _a million_ characters for all the words, according to the Global Language Monitor. If English used a syllabary instead of an alphabet, we would still need to learn around 2,700 characters to represent all of our syllables (Barker, 2006). Since the English language uses

Figure 3.1 Chinese Ideographs

愛	財	德	吉	美
Love	Wealth	Virtue	Lucky	Beautiful

an alphabet, we can get by with 26 characters—or 52, if you count uppercase and lowercase letters. That's a big advantage in simplicity. But there is a price to pay.

Reading ideographs, matching graphic images with ideas, is easily done. Small children recognize the logos of their favorite soft drinks and fast foods, and soon after learn the Arabic numerals (and those are ideographs, too: *1, 2,* and *3* are called "one," "two," and "three" in English, but "moja," "mbili," and "tatu" in Kiswahili). Matching characters with syllables is harder, but still not very difficult. Middle-school students who struggle to read words spelled alphabetically can be fairly easily taught to read words transcribed by their syllables (Gleitman & Rozin, 1973). But reading alphabetic writing—matching a string of characters with their corresponding speech sounds at the level of phonemes—is the most challenging of all. Many children struggle to break out spoken words into phonemes, and this difficulty causes problems in reading written words (Snow et al., 1998). That's why the economy of having the few graphic symbols in an alphabetic writing system comes at the price of having to focus on smaller bits of sound in language.

Understanding the alphabetic principle—namely, that each speech sound is represented in print by one or more letters—and the intricacies of the English spelling system are by no means the only challenges that children learning to read and write in English face. That is because reading (deriving meaning from print) and writing (conveying meaning through print) require much more than the ability to match sounds to letters.

One of the underlying assumptions of this textbook is that, in order to help your students to become good readers and writers, you, their teachers, need to understand how language works. In this chapter we will pay attention to those aspects of language that matter the most in learning to read and write, and in subsequent chapters we will refer back to them as we highlight their connections to varied reading and writing skills you will want your students to develop. They are:

- *Phonology*, the *sounds of language* that affect the meanings of words
- *Morphology* or *word structure*, the ways words are made
- *Vocabulary*, the ways that words convey meaning
- *Syntax*, the ordering and inflection of words in sentences
- *Text structure*, the way texts are organized.

Figure 3.2 Japanese Hiragana, Syllabic Characters

sa	shi	su	se	so
さ	し	す	せ	そ
ta	chi	tsu	te	to
た	ち	つ	て	と
na	ni	nu	ne	no
な	に	ぬ	ね	の

Phonology: The Sounds of English

Since English has an **alphabetic writing system**, words are written by making matches between speech sounds or *phonemes* and alphabet letters. **Phonemes** are speech sounds that differentiate meanings in a given language, and different languages use different phonemes to differentiate meanings. For example, the words *jam* and *yam* have two different meanings in English because they differ in their first sound, /ʤ/ versus /j/. In Spanish, the word "yo" (= I) will mean the same thing whether the first sound is pronounced /ʤ/, as it is in Latin American countries, or /j/, as it is pronounced in Castilian Spanish. This means that /ʤ/ and /j/ are phonemes in English, but they are interchangeable pronunciations of one and the same phoneme in Spanish—something for you to keep in mind if you are working with students whose home language is Spanish.

English phonemes are classified into vowels and consonants. Let's take a look at how each of the two kinds of phonemes is produced.

How English Vowels Are Made

Vowel sounds are produced when you vibrate your vocal cords and breathe across them without any obstruction. But what makes the difference between one vowel sound and another? That is, what are you doing when you produce the sound of *"EEEE"* as opposed to *"AHHH"*? The answer lies in how and where you hold your tongue in your mouth while you breathe past your vibrating vocal cords. The sound of *"EEEE"* is made with the tongue high in the front of the mouth, while the sound of *"AHHH"* is made with the tongue low in the back of the mouth. But there is more.

VOWELS: LONG AND SHORT, OR TENSE AND LAX?   Teachers use the terms "long" and "short" to refer to the sounds represented by the letter *I* in *kite* (a "long" vowel sound) and the letter *I* in *kit* (a "short" vowel sound). But it doesn't take you any longer to say *kite* than it does to say *kit*. So the expressions "long" and "short" really do not capture the difference between the two kinds of vowel sounds.

What does? Say *feet* and *fit* aloud, and stretch out the vowels as you pronounce them. Notice what happens in your mouth when you say each. Poke your finger firmly into the muscle under your jaw and say them again. This time you should feel your tongue muscle tense up when you say the vowel in *feet* and relax when you say the vowel in *fit*. Because of the tensing and relaxing of the tongue muscle when you make the sound of *ee* and *ih*, linguists call these vowels *tense* for the "long" vowel sound and *lax* for the "short" vowel sound.

Now we have some confusion, because the long and short versions of the same vowel letter, like the letter *I* in *kite* and *kit* and the letter *A* in *mat* and *mate*, sound very different from each other. The short vowel sounds are all lax vowels, as linguists call them. But they are often represented by the same vowel letters that represent long/tense vowel sounds. There are historical reasons for this. Essentially, between the fourteenth and sixteenth centuries the pronunciations of English vowels changed, but their spellings didn't (see Temple, Nathan, and Temple, 2013 for further discussion). And, as we shall see in Chapter 11, the mismatch between vowel sounds and vowel spellings causes problems for beginning readers and writers. For now, just keep in mind that short/lax vowels are usually (though not always!) represented in print by one vowel letter, while long/tense vowels are often represented by "vowel teams" (two or more letters that stand for one vowel sound).

Bear in mind, also, that the distinction between short/lax and long/tense vowels is not phonemic in all languages. For example, the words *fit* and *feet* would sound like one and the same word to a Spanish speaker who does not speak English. That is because the different vowel sounds in the two English words would not change the meaning of a Spanish word. That is also one reason that Spanish has only 5 vowel phonemes, while English has 15.

DIPHTHONGS AND MONOPHTHONGS   Listen to the vowels in *he* and *soil*. *He* contains a single vowel sound and *soil* contains a double vowel sound. The technical term for a single vowel sound is a **monophthong** (a term we almost never hear) and the term for a double vowel sound (two closely pronounced vowel sounds) is a **diphthong**. The vowel sounds in *out* and *soil* are diphthongs. And that is a term you do hear more often. Diphthongs and monophthongs can confuse young writers and English language learners because our spelling acknowledges some diphthongs but not others. The diphthong in *boil* is spelled with two letters. But the vowel in *so* is a diphthong, too (*so-eww*) although it is spelled with only one letter. The same is true with the long sound of *A* (which is spelled with one letter although the actual sound is *ay-ee*), and the long sound of *I* (pronounced *ah-ee*). In many other languages, such as Spanish, diphthongs are consistently represented in print by two vowel letters. That is why your Spanish-speaking students may spell the word *by* as *bai*.

How English Consonants Are Made

We know that vowels are produced when you vibrate your vocal cords while you are breathing out without obstructing the airflow. Consonants are made when you interrupt that flow of breath in some way. There are many ways to interrupt it. If you completely stop it momentarily, you produce what are called *stop consonants,* such as the sounds represented by *p, b, d, t, k,* and *g.* If you buzz the breath slightly, you produce the *fricative* consonants represented by the letters *s, z, th, f,* and *v.* If you stop the air flow and then hiss it, you get *affricate consonants,* such as the sounds represented by the letters *ch* and *j.* And if you direct the airflow out through the nose, you get *nasal consonants,* such as the sounds represented by the letters *m, n,* and *ng.*

Which consonant sounds you produce depends on two more things: where in the mouth you produce the interruption and whether the vocal cords are vibrating when you make the interruption. Let's illustrate. If you stop the airflow through your mouth with the back of the tongue raised against the top of the mouth toward the rear, you get the sound of /g/ or /k/. If your vocal cords are vibrating while you do it, you get the sound of /g/. If they are not vibrating, you get the sound of /k/. Similarly, /b/ and /p/ are made by closing the lips. The sound of /b/ is *voiced* (that is, the vocal cords vibrate the whole time it is made), and the sound of /p/ is unvoiced (the vocal cords don't start vibrating until about 40 thousandths of a second after you start producing the sound). If you want to know whether a consonant sound is voiced or unvoiced, place your hand on your Adam's apple and pronounce it—loudly! If you feel your Adam's apple vibrating, it is because it is a voiced consonant; if you don't, it is because it is an unvoiced consonant sound.

Teachers of primary grades should be aware of the ways speech sounds are made because, as children begin to experiment with spelling, you will see they listen very carefully to speech sounds and their similarities, even when they can't talk about what they are hearing. For example, young children often spell the sound represented by *TH* with the letter *V.* It helps to know that the name of the letter *V* is a "buzzed" (fricative) and voiced sound that's made in the front of the mouth, just as the sound of *TH* in *then* is. (The only difference is that the sound /v/ is made with the upper teeth on the lower lip, and the sound of *TH* in *then* is made with the tongue on the fleshy ridge behind the upper front teeth.) And since children expect a single phoneme to be spelled with a single letter, *V* is a natural choice for the sound of *TH,* which is spelled with two letters. (More on this in Chapter 11.)

English language learners whose home languages are Spanish, Romanian, or Russian may spell the sound of *TH* in *then* as *V,* and the sound of *TH* in *thin* as *S* for the same reasons as native speakers of English do. They may have an additional reason, though: the phonological inventories of their home languages do not include the phonemes represented by *TH* in English; therefore, they perceive those phonemes as approximations of phonemes that their languages do include, /v/ and /s/, and spell them accordingly as *V* or *S.*

Phonemic Awareness and Reading

When children realize that words they speak are made up of small bits of sound called *phonemes,* we say they have **phonemic awareness**. Children usually show phonemic awareness in late kindergarten and early first grade (Goswami, 2000). Some children have trouble with phonemic awareness even into first and second grade, and if they do, it may be hard for them to learn to read. Why is phonemic awareness challenging for children? It is probably because words really cannot be spoken so slowly that each of their phonemes can be heard distinctly.

You may think it's obvious that the phonemes exist in words, but you know that fact from indirect evidence. You know it because you can substitute a /b/ phoneme for the /k/ in c̲at and get b̲at, and you can substitute an /n/ phoneme for the /t/ in ca̲t and get ca̲n. Once you began to read, you saw that letters tended to be matched with phonemes in words such as *CAT,* and that reinforced the idea that phonemes can be heard separately. But young learners without that experience in reading are often challenged by the task of separating or *segmenting* phonemes in words.

Note that we are not saying children cannot hear the phonemes. Of course they can. Most English-speaking three-year-olds can correctly "show you the c̲at" and "show you the b̲at." It's the task of saying slowly the three sounds in *CAT* that young children find difficult.

Most preschool children can't show you that they know words are made up of phonemes, but most second graders can. How does that awareness develop? Hall and Moats (1999) present the pathway taken by normally developing children in kindergarten and first grade (see Figure 3.3).

Teach It! 12

Phonemic Segmentation with Elkonin Boxes

This instructional activity provides a visual to help children segment phonemes.

Figure 3.3 Developmental Milestones in Phonological Awareness

Stages of Literacy Development	Developmental Milestones in Phonological Awareness
At the end of kindergarten:	• At the syllable level: Most children can distinguish single-syllable words from words with two syllables when they hear them. • At the onset and rime level (*p* + *at* = *pat*; *l* + *ight* = *light*—see below): Most children can match a target word with a rhyming word. • At the phoneme level: Most children can pick out words that begin with the same sound as a target word and can tell you the odd word out—the one that does not begin with the same sound as the others.
Two months into first grade:	• Given two letters on cards, most children can combine them and pronounce the word they spell (*in, on, at, it, up*) • Given a three-phoneme word, most children can say the word that is left when the beginning consonant is deleted: *bat/at, sit/it, cup/up.*
By the end of first grade:	• Most children can pronounce two-phoneme words slowly and separate the phonemes: /t/ - /oo/; /b/ - /y/. • Given longer words, most children can leave off the first consonant and pronounce what is left: *b—utterfly.* • Given three isolated phonemes, most children can combine them to make a word: /s/ /æ/ /t/ = *sat.*

SOURCE: After Hall, S. and Moats, C. from *Straight talk about reading: How parents can make a difference in the early years.* (1999). Chicago: Contemporary Books.

Syllables, Onsets, and Rimes

Syllables are rhythmic pulses in words. The word *final* has two of them, *fi* and *nal*, while *awareness* has three: *a* + *ware* + *ness*. In the word *awareness*, you can see that a vowel can stand alone as a syllable, but consonants cannot (at least not in English). Some languages such as Spanish, Japanese, and Kiswahili have relatively few syllables. In Spanish, roughly 50 different syllables can be combined to make most of the words in the language. The words of the English language, though, are made up of a couple of thousand different syllables (Barker, 2006). Few teachers of English would bother to have students learn groups of syllables, as teachers of Spanish, Portuguese, and Kiswahili regularly do.

English syllables can be open or closed. An *open syllable* ends in a vowel, and a *closed syllable* ends in a consonant. All three syllables in *banana* are open syllables, and both syllables in *problem* are closed syllables. When these words are divided at the end of a line of print, the hyphen goes after the vowel in words with open syllables like *final* (*fi-nal*) and *recess* (*re-cess*), and after the consonant in words with closed syllables like *picnic* (*pic-nic*) and *knapsack* (*knap-sack*). The vowel in an open syllable often has its "long" sound, and the vowel in a closed syllable usually has its "short" sound. Compare *capable* and *captain; meter* and *metric;* and *human* and *humble.*

Syllables can be broken into smaller units called *onsets* and *rimes* (Trieman, 1985). The **onset** is the initial consonant sound of a syllable, if there is one, and the **rime** is the vowel plus any consonant sound that comes after it. Any English syllable must have a rime (a vowel, that is, whether or not it is followed by one or more consonants), but not necessarily an onset. For example, in *cat*, the sound represented by *C* is the onset and the sound represented by *AT* is the rime of the syllable. But the word/syllable *at* has only a rime, *AT*. The word/syllable *be*, on the other hand, has an onset, represented by the letter *B*, and a rime that consists of one vowel only (represented by the letter *E*). Children who have experience playing with onsets and rimes—which is what we do when we recite nursery rhymes—have been shown to have an easier time learning to read words (Bradley & Bryant, 1985). Watch this video in which students work with onsets and rimes and then answer the question that follows.

 Video Exploration 3.1: Watch the video and answer questions that reflect the content you have read.

One more thing you should know about syllables is that they are differently stressed in speech, which affects the pronunciation of the vowels in them. If a content word (noun, verb, adjective, or adverb) consists of only one syllable, it will be stressed, and the vowel will be pronounced as a short/lax or as a long/tense vowel (e.g., *can*, or *cane*). In multisyllable words, though, only one syllable is usually stressed, and the vowel in the stressed syllable will be pronounced as a short/lax or long/tense vowel. The vowels in the unstressed syllables will be reduced to what linguists call a "schwa"—a

Teach It! 16

Word Hunts

This word study activity helps children make connections between the spelling and pronunciation of words.

nondescript vowel that only occurs in unstressed syllables in English, and whose symbol in the International Phonetic Alphabet is /ə/. For example, in the word *cannibal*, the first syllable is stressed, while the following two are not. As a consequence, the vowel letter in the first syllable is pronounced as a short/lax /æ/ sound, while the vowels in the next two syllables are reduced to schwas. Why should we care? Well, because the schwa can be represented in writing by any vowel letter. It is represented by the vowel letters "i" and "a" in the word *cannibal*, by "e" and "a" in the second and third syllables of *elephant*, by "u" in *supply*, and by "o" in the second syllable of the word *common*. While vowel reduction poses serious reading and spelling problems for English language learners whose home languages do not exhibit this phenomenon, native speakers of English who are learning to read and write find it challenging as well.

Check Your Understanding 3.1: Gauge your understanding of the skills and concepts in this section.

Morphology: How English Words Are Built

The study of the ways words are built is called *morphology*. Words are built out of **morphemes**, which are the smallest meaningful parts of a language. For example, the word *morpheme* is made up of two morphemes of Greek origin, *morph-* (meaning "form" or "structure") and *-eme* (meaning "element" or "small piece"). Morphemes need not be word parts; they can be whole words as well, such as *cat*, and they can have one or more syllables (e.g., *dog, swallow, crocodile*).

Classification of Morphemes

Morphemes can be classified as free or bound. **Free morphemes** can stand alone as words and cannot be subdivided into other morphemes. **Bound morphemes** cannot stand alone; they need to combine with other morphemes to form words. Thus, *dog, swallow,* and *crocodile* are free morphemes, while *-eme* in *morpheme*, or *-logy* in *morphology* are bound morphemes. When combined with a bound morpheme, free morphemes are often referred to as **base words** or *root words*.

FREE MORPHEMES   When two or more free morphemes combine with one another, as in *houseboat* and *lawnmower,* they make *compound words*. Dictionary writers have three different ways of writing compound words:

Houseboat: Compound words that are frequently spoken together are joined without a space. Those words are made plural by adding *-s* at the end of the last word: *houseboats*.

Mother-in-law: Other compound words are joined with hyphens. When these words are made plural, the *-s* is added to the more important word: *mothers-in-law*.

Boa constrictor: Some compound words are often said together, but are written separately. Nonetheless, to make them plural, you only add *-s* to the second word: *boa constrictors*.

BOUND MORPHEMES   Bound morphemes must combine with other morphemes to form words. Bound morphemes include:

- **Affixes**, which may be **prefixes**, if they precede a free morpheme or a base word (e.g., *pre-* in *preschooler*) or **suffixes**, if they follow one (e.g., *-ful* in *sorrowful*, or *-ed* in *walked*).

- **Roots**, which often come from Latin, and which are the morphemes that carry the major component of the meaning, such as *leg-* (from the Latin *legis* = law) in *legal*.

- *Combining forms*, which usually come from Greek, such as *chrono-* and *-logy* in *chronology*.

All affixes add some information to the base word to which they are attached, but not the same kind of information. Prefixes change the meaning of the base word. For example, *un-, non-,* and *dis-,* all of which mean "not," turn base words into their opposites, as in *unsure, nondescript,* or *disingenuous*.

Table 3.1 Latin Prefixes and Roots

PREFIX	MEANING	EXAMPLES
com- (con-, col-, cor-)	together	collect, commute, connect, correct
ad- (ac-, af-, ag-, al-, ap-, as-, at-)	to, toward	accredit, addiction, affect, aggression, allocate, append, assimilate, attend
in- (il-, im-, ir-)	in, into, not	illegal, immigrant, innate irresponsible

ROOT	MEANING	EXAMPLES
cred	belief	credible, accredit
lect, lege	choose	elect, collect, college
rect	straight, right	direct, correct
tract	pull, draw	contract, traction, attract

Some prefixes of Latin origin change their pronunciation to match the beginning sound of the root to which they are attached. They are called **assimilated prefixes**, and they account for the presence of double consonants in the spelling of many words of Latin origin. For example, the word *attract* is made up of the prefix *ad-* (meaning to or toward) and the root *tract*. The pronunciation of the prefix was changed at some point—the consonant /d/ turned into /t/ so it would be easier to pronounce when followed by a root beginning with the sound /t/, and the spelling of the word reflected the phonetic change. The same thing happened in words such as *attend* and *attach*. Table 3.1 shows some Latin prefixes and their assimilated forms.

Some suffixes, called *derivational suffixes*, change the part of speech of the base word to which they are attached. Thus, *beautiful* is an adjective because the suffix *-ful* has been added to the noun *beauty*; *quickly* is an adverb because *-ly* has been added to the adjective *quick*; and *illness* is a noun because the suffix *-ness* has been added to the adjective *ill*. Table 3.2 shows some common prefixes and derivational suffixes.

Other suffixes, called **inflectional** or **grammatical suffixes**, add grammatical information to the base word without otherwise changing its meaning, and without changing its part of speech. For example, the suffix *-ed* signals the past tense of a verb, and the suffix *-s* may signal the plural of a noun or the third person singular present tense form of a verb.

Morphemes, Reading, and Spelling

Having an awareness of morphemes helps a person read. Even third graders use word parts to recognize words—especially in words like *hilly* and *helpful,* where the original word part is easily visible, or "transparent" (Carlisle & Stone, 2005). To read words that are typically encountered from the fourth grade on, it is more useful to be aware of the morphemes that make up words than to try to match letters with individual sounds (Reichle & Perfetti, 2003). Being aware of morphemes makes it possible to identify as many as 60% of unknown words that are encountered in the middle grades and above (Nagy et al., 1989). So, for example, a reader who knows that *inter* means "between" and *planetary* refers to

Table 3.2 Prefixes and Derivational Suffixes

PREFIX	MEANING	EXAMPLES
sub-	under	submarine, subway, substandard
dis-	not	distrust, disrespect, distasteful
mis-	not	misunderstand, misguided, mislead
inter-	between or among	interstate, international, intercity
pre-	before	preschool, pretest, preview

SUFFIX	MEANING	EXAMPLES
-er	more than	taller, shorter, quicker
-ful	containing	hopeful, wishful, bountiful
-less	without	painless, toothless, penniless
-ly	in the manner of	beautifully, miserly, shortly
-ness	state of being	goodness, highness, badness

"planets" can figure out that *interplanetary* means "between planets." Children beyond the early elementary years who are aware of morphemes in words register better comprehension (Carlisle, 2000). Teachers cannot possibly teach all the words needed to comprehend grade-level text directly, so they must give students tools for learning words on their own. One such tool is morpheme analysis.

Awareness of morphemes also supports children's spelling development. For example, knowing that the inflectional suffix that marks the past tense is always spelled *-ed* irrespective of its pronunciation, will help students to spell words such as *walked, pulled*, and *wanted* correctly. Awareness of assimilated prefixes will help older students remember to double the consonants in academic words such as *immature* or *allocate*. Finally, awareness of roots, and of the fact that the pronunciation of roots often changes when a derivational suffix is added to them, is likely to help students to cope with many challenges of English spelling. Let's look at some examples.

Think of the words *sign* and *signal*. In the word *signal*, each letter of the root is pronounced, unlike in *sign*, where the *g* is silent. Knowing that the two words share a common root may help students to remember how to spell the word *sign* correctly (not phonetically, that is). Knowing that the word *competition* is derived from *compete* is likely to help students to preserve the spelling of the root vowel in *competition* in spite of its being reduced to a schwa.

The strident emphasis on phonics—letter-to-sound correspondences—that the No Child Left Behind legislation ushered in might have distracted teachers from the realization that there are other important things to know about words, especially beyond the primary grades. Some of those things include the parts that make up words and where those words came from.

Etymologies: Word Origins

In many dictionaries, you will find listings for words that look like this:

give. (giv). Vt gave, giv'en, giv'ing. [OE giefan]

What do these notations mean? The part in parentheses is the pronunciation; *vt* means that the word is a transitive verb—that is, a verb that takes an object to complete the meaning. *Gave, given*, and *giving* are the past, past participle (the form used in compound verbs like *have given* or *had given*), and present participle (the form used in compound verbs like *is giving* and *were giving*). The part in brackets means that the word came down to us from an earlier word—in this case from Old English (OE). Words in English are derived from many sources. Nonetheless, it is possible to map out a rough lineage for a great many of the words you use in English. When you trace the origins of a word or look at its history, you are dealing with its **etymology**.

The English language traces its origin to Anglo-Saxon. In the fifth and sixth centuries C.E., Germanic peoples from northern Germany and the Netherlands invaded England and pushed the indigenous Celts north into Scotland and west to Wales and Ireland. They brought their Germanic language with them, and it came to be called *Anglo-Saxon* (*Anglo* comes from Angles, the name of one of the Germanic tribes, and *Saxon* from another of those tribes). In the eighth and ninth centuries, Vikings raided from Scandinavia, and Old English became a mixture of Germanic, Norse, Danish, and Dutch words.

In 1066, the Normans from France conquered England and brought with them not only an early version of the French language but also Latin, which became widely used in the church, the government, and other places of higher culture—to the exclusion of English, which remained the language spoken around the hearth, on the farm, and in the market. Hundreds of words from Latin and Greek (Greek was read in the monasteries), as well as French, were absorbed into English in this period.

In 1476, William Caxton brought the first printing press to England and began printing books in English, giving an enormous boost to the language. The language he wrote, Middle English, had a sort of dual structure, consisting of Anglo-Saxon words and Latinate words. You can see this duality in the English words for food. The animal you call a *pig* (an Anglo-Saxon word) on the farm is called *pork* when it reaches the dining room table. *Pork* is a French word, from Latin. The *cow* (Anglo-Saxon) in the pasture became *beef* (French and Latin) in the dining room. *Sheep* on the farm (Anglo-Saxon word) became *mutton* (French and Latin) in the dining room. This all came about because English was spoken on the farm by workers, but French was spoken in the dining rooms of the ruling class. To this day, our language has a core of words that came through Old English from Anglo-Saxon. These are very often the common, basic items in our vocabulary, the words children learn first, the words you use when you are being most direct. But there is another body of words, from Latin and Greek, that are more specialized, more scientific, and more limited to educated usage. Thus, you find the Anglo-Saxon words *cat* and *dog* and the corresponding Latin words *feline* and *canine*; you also find the Anglo-Saxon word *feel*, the related Latin word *sensitive*, and the related Greek word *sympathy*. Today the English language can be described as having an Anglo-Saxon base and a superimposed Latin vocabulary. About a third of our words are Anglo-Saxon and most of the rest are from Latin (and through Latin, from Greek). There are also many loan words from Spanish, modern French, German, and other languages.

Check Your Understanding 3.2: Gauge your understanding of the skills and concepts in this section.

Vocabulary: Words and Their Meanings

Vocabulary is knowledge of words and their meanings. The more words children have in their spoken vocabularies, the easier it will be for them to learn to read. This is true for three reasons:

- *Having a word in the spoken vocabulary makes it possible to recognize that word in print.* Having the word in their vocabulary allows children to confirm more quickly if they have deciphered a printed word correctly. It is frustrating for beginning readers to struggle to decipher a word from its letters, only to realize that they don't know the word anyway. Having the word in their vocabulary allows children to use meaning-based strategies for word identification strategies, such as, "Think of a word that begins like this one, and which would make sense in this sentence."

- *Having more words in the spoken vocabulary boosts children's language awareness.* The more children are aware of language, the better able they are to read words—to be aware of their parts and their sounds (Wong-Fillmore & Snow, 2000).

- *Having words in the spoken vocabulary boosts reading comprehension.* Words are tokens for concepts. They are units of meaning. The size of children's vocabulary is a measure of their knowledge of the world. It is also a measure of their potential for understanding new information. Let's elaborate on these issues now.

Levels of Vocabulary Knowledge

What do we mean by *knowing* vocabulary? Beck et al. (2002) suggest a continuum of word knowledge that looks like this:

- No knowledge
- General sense, such as knowing *mendacious* has a negative connotation
- Narrow, context-bound knowledge, such as knowing that a *frustrated* person is unhappy because she can't have what she wants, but not knowing that a good defensive player can *frustrate* the other team's efforts to score a touchdown
- Knowledge of a word, but not enough to be able to recall it readily enough to use it in appropriate situations
- Rich, decontextualized knowledge of a word's meaning, its relationship to other words, and its extension to metaphorical uses, such as understanding what someone is doing when she is *devouring* a book (p. 10).

Knowing vocabulary well means not just understanding what words in a book mean, then, but knowing words in a range of contexts, in associations with other words, and in connection with one's experience—to have words as one's own.

Exploring Children's Vocabulary

The job of teaching vocabulary seems truly immense. Nagy and Anderson (1984) estimate that by ninth grade, students have to cope with a total written vocabulary of 88,500 words. Were we to try to teach all those words, the prospect of teaching children nearly 10,000 words a year would be daunting indeed. But Beck et al. (2002) have found a useful way to break down those numbers.

- *Tier One Words.* There are many thousands of words already in children's spoken vocabulary that we won't usually have to teach. Beck et al. call these words *Tier One* words, and they include examples such as *mother, clock,* and *jump.*

- *Tier Three Words.* Then there are many more thousands of words that are so highly specialized that they are almost never used outside of the disciplines in which they are encountered. These *Tier Three* words—like *monozygotic, tetrahedron,* and *bicameral*—are best learned in the science, social studies, and other classes where they are tied to the content under study.

- *Tier Two Words.* That leaves the *Tier Two* words—the words with wide utility that most children don't have in their spoken vocabularies, such as *dismayed, paradoxical, absurd,* and *wary.* Beck et al. (2002) estimate that there may be about 7,000 Tier Two words, and even if we teach children half of them—or about 400 words a year—we will have gone a long way toward growing children's vocabularies and equalizing children's access to learning.

Vocabulary and Reading

The task of teaching vocabulary is further complicated by the fact that a word may have different meanings, and sometimes even different pronunciations, depending on the context in which it is used, or the lexical relationships between a particular word and the words around it. Obviously, awareness of such lexical relationships, which we will say more about in the remainder of this section, can greatly support reading comprehension.

POLYSEMY *Polysemy* means "having multiple meanings." (Speaking of etymologies, *poly-* comes from a Greek word meaning "many" and *sem-* comes from another Greek word meaning "signal" or "meaning.") Many Tier One words are **polysemous**. For example, *can* may mean "to be able to" or "a metal container"; in slang, it can mean "a toilet." The *can can* is a dance. *Tree* can refer to a large plant, or to the act of frightening an animal into climbing one. A *telephone tree* is a network of people who call others, and a *tree diagram* is a graphic organizer that shows taxonomic relationships. Oddly, more Tier One words are polysemous than the words on the upper tiers, and by the time you get to Tier Three, the words have very limited meanings: *monozygotic, polygamous,* and *chiaroscuro* have one meaning each. Words with multiple meanings can be confusing for students to learn and challenging for teachers to teach. Watch this video about teaching multiple meanings and then answer the question that follows.

 Video Exploration 3.2: Watch the video and answer questions that reflect the content you have read.

COLLOCATION **Collocation** refers to words that naturally occur together. (*Col-* means "together" and *loc-* means "place." Both morphemes are from Latin.) In English we say *dine out* and not *dine away*. We say *eat in*, not *dine in*; *best friends*, not *superior friends*; *fast food*, not *quick food*; *commit a crime*, not *perform a crime*. These collocations do not often translate from one language to another: in English we say *think of . . .* but the same expression in Spanish is *think on*. Native speakers have little trouble with collocation, but English language learners often do.

IDIOMS **Idioms** are words or phrases that have a meaning that is not predictable from the literal definition. Many idioms are formed by adding prepositions to verbs. Note the different meanings of these examples: *fall in, fall out, fall to, fall away; run in, run into, run out of, run away, run over, run off* (two meanings), *run about; tell on, tell off; buy in, buy out, buy off, buy up; pay up, pay down, pay out,* and so on. Many idioms have stories connected to them: *To kick the bucket* ("to die") refers to kicking the bucket from under a hanging victim; *three sheets to the wind* is a sailor's term for a drunken person. A sheet is the line (what sailors call ropes) that controls the tension on a sail. If one sheet gets loose in the wind, a boat is a little out of control, and if *three* sheets are loose in the wind, the boat is under no one's control.

DENOTATIONS AND CONNOTATIONS *Denotations* and *connotations* refer to the literal and figurative meanings of words. The **denotation** is the precise definition. The denotation of *dog* is a member of the canine family, often domesticated. The **connotation** is what the word suggests. Oddly, though many of us love our dogs, the denotation of the word *dog* is negative: *Dog* can refer to something that doesn't work very well, or to a person who is treacherous. The denotation of a *bear* is a carnivorous or omnivorous mammal from the *ursidae* family; but the connotation is that what it names is very difficult, as in "That exam was a bear," or "The month of April saw a bear market."

Tier One and sometimes Tier Two words often have connotations, but Tier Three words are all denotations. That exam may have been a *bear*, but not an *ursida*; that treacherous guy you thought was your friend may have been a *dirty dog*, but not a *contaminated canine*.

HOMOPHONES AND HOMOGRAPHS **Homophones** are words that have the same pronunciation but different spellings and different meanings, depending on the context in which they occur. The English language abounds in homophones. Think of *way* and *weigh*; *wait* and *weight*; *ate* and *eight*; *so, sew,* and *sow*; *for, fore,* and *four*; or *by, bye,* and *buy*. Notice, also, that all these examples are Tier One words. This means that, while children may have them in their spoken vocabularies, you will still need to teach your students how to spell them correctly in context.

Homographs are words that have the same spelling but different pronunciations and different meanings. There are many of those in English, too. Some of them are simply coincidences, such as *lead, wound,* or *moped,* and their meanings are not related in any way. Others, such as *insert, contrast,* or *affect,* are related in meaning but differ in pronunciation depending on which of their syllables is stressed. Whether we stress the first or the second syllable in such words depends on whether they are used as nouns or as verbs in context. To teach your students how to figure out whether a word is a noun or a verb, you will need to teach them something about syntax.

Check Your Understanding 3.3: Gauge your understanding of the skills and concepts in this section.

Syntax: Ordering and Inflecting Classes of Words

Syntax, a more precise word for grammar, refers to the set of rules that order words of different types and their inflections meaningfully in sentences. Syntax can be thought of as a kind of code that enables speakers and writers to encode meaning, and hearers and readers to decode meaning. There are many reasons why teachers of literacy need extensive knowledge of syntax. First, and most important, readers rely on their knowledge of syntax to make sense when they listen, speak, read, and write. Second, many young writers struggle to produce sentences in Standard American English. Third, English language learners are in particular need of someone who can answer their questions about English syntax. Fourth, the Common Core State Standards call for students to read and write in Standard American English, and also to be able to do close readings of texts. Close reading often requires an explicit understanding of syntax. The Common Core State Standards also set out grade-level expectations for spoken language that students must meet, and some of those relate to syntax as well.

The renewed attention to syntax that the Common Core State Standards have brought about comes after several decades in which, mostly because of the ineffectiveness of the prescriptive, drill-oriented pedagogy used to teach it, grammar was deemphasized in American schools (Gartland & Smolkin, 2016). It is not surprising therefore that many teachers, who are themselves the products of those decades of education, feel rather uncertain of their own grammar knowledge (Watson, 2013). We hope that this section will boost your confidence in your understanding of English syntax.

Syntax occurs on two levels. At the conscious level, we think of syntax as the common set of rules taught in school, such as "A verb must agree with its subject in person and number." But conscious syntactical knowledge is only a fraction of what you know that enables you to produce and understand sentences. Consider, for example, the following sentences:

- *I would go bike riding if I weren't tired.* (But I won't go bike riding because I am tired.)
- *I will go bike riding if I'm not tired.* (I don't know yet if I will go bike riding.)
- *I go bike riding if I'm not tired.* (When I'm not tired, I usually go bike riding.)
- *I'm going bike riding, and I'm not tired.* (I expected to be tired, but I'm not.)
- *I did go bike riding, and I'm not tired.* (Somebody said I would be tired if I went bike riding, but I went anyway, and, guess what? I'm not tired.)

If you have ever taught English as a second language, you have surely found that although the differences in the meanings of these sentences were obvious to you, it was difficult to tell non-native speakers how to produce sentences that convey those shades of meaning. That phenomenon happens because on a deep level you know the "rules" of syntax (because there really are rules that explain how each of the above sentences is made), but you cannot explain what you know. Linguists call this *tacit knowledge*—we have it, but it's not conscious. The lion's share of our knowledge of syntax is tacit. But if you are going to help children read, write, and speak Standard American English, you will have to make a hefty amount of that knowledge conscious. The following sections will remind you of things you already know about the English language, on some level. But we are betting that some of the explanations, at least, will be new to you.

Kinds of Sentences

To begin at the beginning, sentences have subjects and predicates. The *subject* of a sentence is the noun phrase that is the agent or doer of the action in the sentence. The *predicate* is the verb (the action word) and any noun, adjective, adverb, or prepositional phrase that follows it. Table 3.3 shows some examples of subjects and predicates. All of these examples are *simple sentences*—sentences with one subject and one predicate.

A simple sentence can have a compound subject and also a compound predicate:

The players and the cheerleaders trained in the sun and performed in the rain.

The players and the cheerleaders is the compound subject and *trained in the sun and performed in the rain* is the compound predicate.

Table 3.3 Subjects and Predicates in Simple Sentences

Subject	Predicate
The girl	scored the goal.
The fans	were very happy.
The game	was a triumph.

SENTENCE TYPES   Sentences come in four types and four patterns. The *types* of sentences are declarative, interrogative, imperative, and exclamatory. The first type of sentence, *declarative sentences*, state something straight out.

Juan was a gymnast.
Alicia was impressed by his moves.

are both declarative sentences. (It doesn't make a sentence any less declarative to have the verb in the passive voice.)
Interrogative sentences ask a question.

Was Juan a gymnast?
Was Alicia impressed by his moves?

are both interrogative sentences. Note that interrogative sentences usually place an auxiliary (or "helping") verb, such as *was, were, does,* or *did,* at the beginning of the sentence. Note, too, that interrogative sentences may add an auxiliary verb if they didn't already have one:

Juan was a gymnast. Was Juan a gymnast?
Juan fell. Did Juan fall?

Sentences can also be made interrogative by adding a *tag question* to the declarative form:

Juan was a gymnast, <u>wasn't he</u>?
Juan fell, <u>didn't he</u>?

An *imperative sentence* gives a command.

Watch out!
Don't smoke in here.

are both imperative sentences. Classifying sentences as imperative can get fuzzy when degrees of politeness are involved. For example, a guard in a museum would say, "Don't smoke in here," but a person who is obligated to treat another with respect might say, "Sorry, this is a no-smoking area," or "Would you mind waiting until you are outside before lighting that?" The forms of those two sentences are declarative and interrogative, respectively, even though the intent of both is imperative.

An *exclamatory sentence* shows excitement. It is almost always punctuated with an exclamation point.

We won!
Today is a snow day!

are both exclamatory sentences.

SENTENCE PATTERNS   The *patterns* of sentences are simple, compound, complex, and compound-complex.

A **compound sentence** has two or more independent clauses. An *independent clause*, also called a *main clause* because it expresses a main idea, is a group of words that could stand on their own as a sentence.

The players practiced, but the cheerleaders goofed off.

Take out *but* and both of the clauses would make sense by themselves. These clauses carry equal weights of meaning.

A **complex sentence** is made up of an independent clause and one or more *dependent clauses*. Since an independent clause expresses the main idea in a sentence, a dependent clause comes along to help explain or clarify that main idea.

Women who drive trucks are road warriors, too.

The independent clause here is *Women . . . are road warriors, too.* The dependent clause is *. . . who drive trucks. . . .* The independent clause makes a point about women, and the dependent clause tells which women we are making a point about.

Relative clauses are one kind of dependent clause. Relative clauses can be restrictive or unrestrictive. **Restrictive clauses** add information that is limited to a subset of the subject of the sentence. **Unrestrictive clauses** share information that applies to the whole group. Compare these two sentences:

Women who always say what they want get their way.
Children, who always say what they want, get their way.

In the first sentence the clause *who always say what they want* is restrictive, because it says we are talking only about those women who say what they want—not about all women. In the second sentence the clause is unrestrictive, because it purports to tell us something about all women. Unrestrictive clauses are set off from the rest of the sentence by commas in writing and by very brief pauses in speech. But these commas and minuscule pauses signal a *huge* difference in the meaning of the two sentences.

Compound-complex sentences, as the name implies, are sentences made up of at least two main clauses and at least one dependent clause.

We wanted to watch television because we were exhausted, but they wanted to play football because they'd just woken up.

That is a compound-complex sentence because it has two main clauses—*We wanted to watch television* and *they wanted to play football*, and because it also has dependent clauses—*because we were exhausted* and *because they'd just woken up*.

Parts of Speech

The words that make up sentences can be classified into different categories, or parts of speech, based on the role, or function that they play in a sentence.

NOUNS Let's start with nouns. **Nouns** are names. Historically, that's what the word *noun* means, and it is related to *nominate* ("to put someone's name forward"), *nominal* ("in name only"), and *nomenclature* ("about the naming of things"). *Proper nouns* begin with capital letters, and they name particular people, places, or things. We can say "I like to swim in the *ocean*" (here *ocean* is a common noun), but "Once I swam in the Atlantic *Ocean* (and now *Ocean*, and also *Atlantic*, are proper nouns); or "I want a *drink*" but "I want a *Diet Pepsi*."

Nouns can be *concrete*, things you can touch, throw, or dip your finger into, like *flower*, *football* and *milk*; or *abstract*, general things like *happiness* or *luck*. The difference matters in the way we construct sentences: You can say *I have a football* but not **I have a happiness*. (In linguistics, we conventionally put an asterisk [*] before an ungrammatical sentence.)

We have count nouns and mass nouns, too. *Count nouns* name things that can be counted, like *one duck, two ducks*. *Mass nouns* name things that can't be counted but have to be measured, like *money* and *milk*. You don't say **one money*, **two moneys*. You have to say *some money*, or *much money*. That's why we say *money* and *milk* are not count nouns, but mass nouns. As for count nouns, you say *many ducks* but not **much ducks*, because *ducks*, like *bucks*, *trucks*, and *clucks* (but not *luck* or *muck*), are count nouns. Standard American English would have you say *ten items or fewer* because *items* is a count noun—but tell that to your local supermarket!

Most nouns come in *singular* (for one) and *plural* (for more than one) forms, like *pigeon* and *pigeons*. Abstract nouns only come in the singular form, though: *She has good luck*, but not **They have good lucks*. (The same is true of mass nouns: We say *He has ten dollars*, but not **He has ten moneys*).

Plurals normally add *-s* to a singular noun, as in *dog* and *dogs*. Note, though, that the *-s* or *-es* ending has three pronunciations:

> dog/dogs (the sound is "zzz")
>
> fish/fishes (the sound is "izzz")
>
> duck/ducks (the sound is "sss")

Some plurals are irregular. *Child/children, woman/women, man/men, ox/oxen, mouse/mice, goose/geese, foot/feet, tooth/teeth* all came from Old English, where words commonly changed internally to make plurals. Some plurals change internally but still add *-s*: *wife/wives, dwarf/dwarves, shelf/shelves* (and note that the plural of *roof* [*roofs*] can experience the same internal sound change as *wife/wives* and *knife/knives*, but the *F* spelling doesn't change to *V*). Some nouns don't change at all from singular to plural: *deer/deer, fish/fish, trout/trout, bison/bison*.

Words from Latin often have irregular plurals, too. Latin nouns came in different genders and each made its plural differently (see Table 3.4).

Most *proper names* form plurals just as common nouns do: by adding *-s*. Brad and Angelina can be referred to together as the *Pitts*, and more than one Kennedy are *Kennedys*. (Note that the spelling rule, "Change the *Y* to *I* and add *-es*" does not apply to proper nouns.) When a proper noun ends in *s*, *z*, *ch*, or *sh*, we add *-es* to form the plural. More than one Jones are *Joneses*, the many members of the Bush family are *Bushes*, our friend Chris Hatch and his wife are the *Hatches*, and Miriam Martinez and her husband are the *Martinezes*. None of these plurals needs an apostrophe (which will be news to many mailbox painters in America!).

Note that many other languages don't behave this way. Both French and Spanish pluralize the article (the word corresponding to *the* in English), but not the proper noun (*Los Calderón, Les Sarkozy*). English language learners may be confused by that difference.

Table 3.4 Plurals of Nouns from Latin

Gender	Singular	Plural
Feminine	larva	larvae
	antenna	antennae
	alumna	alumnae
Masculine	nucleus	nuclei
	focus	foci
	syllabus	syllabi
	alumnus	alumni
	fungus	fungi
Neuter	datum (rare)	data
	opus	opera
	medium	media
	millennium	millennia
	memorandum	memoranda
Others	index	indices
	axis	axes
	thesis	theses

There are some rare cases where an apostrophe is used with plurals. The plurals of numbers and letters need apostrophes: *1's, 2's, 3's; A's, B's, C's; M.D.'s* and *Ph.D.'s.* But that's about all. American writing, even in some pretty expensive signs, is rife with inappropriate apostrophes in plurals.

Possessives of nouns are generally straightforward: Add -*'s*. Adding possessives to proper names works the same as with common nouns, with a few exceptions. Proper names ending with an *S* may take an apostrophe only, or take -*'s*: *Charles' book* and *Charles's book* are both acceptable, according Strunk and White's *Elements of Style* (1999)—just be consistent about it.

ARTICLES   Count nouns in English are preceded by *articles*: *a football* or *the football.* Articles don't mean much, except they let us know if we have heard the word before in this conversation. If you say, "I bought *a* football" using the *indefinite article*, your friend might say, "Oh, that's nice." But if you say, "I bought *the* football," using the *definite article*, your friend will say, "Which one?" or "What football?" because by using the definite article you implied that you had already mentioned a football.

The use of articles is not the same in all languages. Some, like Chinese, don't use them at all. Others use them differently from the way English does. For example, in English we say "Love conquers all," but in Spanish they say *El amor lo vence todo*, or "*The love conquers all.*" It is not unusual for a child who is a native speaker of another language to have trouble with definite and indefinite articles in English.

PRONOUNS   *Pronouns* stand for nouns and avoid a lot of tedious repetition. There are many kinds of pronouns, as you can see in Table 3.5. English language learners may need to learn these English pronouns. To native speakers they may be second nature, although in many dialects they may be used in non-standard ways, such as *Me and my brother went fishing, Get your hands off them shoes,* and even *This here is mine; that there is yourn* (although you have to go pretty far out of town to hear that). A problem pronouns cause for comprehension is one of reference, when it is not clear who is meant when a text says *this, that,* or *it.* Consider this passage, for an example of unclear pronoun reference:

> *Alicia was only four feet tall. She had a fierce dog and a wry sense of humor. Her father was a noted politician. This made her feel a little out of place sometimes.*

What made her feel out of place—all of those factors or just one? The use of the pronoun *this* doesn't say, and because it doesn't, the meaning of the passage is unclear.

VERBS   *Verbs* are words that name actions. Verbs come in different *tenses*, too (see Table 3.6). A verb tense refers to the time that the action takes place. In grammatical terminology, *perfect* means that something is completed, so the present perfect means that as of the present, an action has been completed; the past perfect means that in the past an action had already been completed, and so on. *Progressive* means that an action is going on. The present progressive tense means that an action is going on in the present; the past progressive tense (also called the *imperfect* tense) means that an action was going on in the past, and so on.

The forms of verbs vary with their *person* and *number* (see Table 3.7). Their number can be singular or plural, and they may occur in the first, second, or third person.

Table 3.5 Varieties of Pronouns

Personal Pronouns		
Subjective	*I [he, she, it] did it.*	can be subjects of sentences
Possessive	*This is my [your, her, his] book.*	indicate ownership
Objective	*He saw me [you, her, him, us].*	receive actions or follow prepositions
Reflexive	*I cut myself; You cut yourself, etc.*	the action is done to oneself
Intensive	*I like it myself; You like it yourself, etc.*	emphasize the subject
Demonstrative Pronouns		
	I want those [this, them, these]	stand for something that is indicated
As determiners	*These shoes, or That book.*	point to a certain thing
Indefinite Pronouns		
	I want some. I don't have any.	point to a category of unspecified things
Relative Pronouns		
	She wants a dog that hunts. This is the germ which caused the illness.	introduce dependent words or clauses
Interrogative Pronouns		
As pronouns	*Who moved my book? Where is the fire? What caused the smoke?*	stand for an unknown person, place, or thing
As determiners	*What book? Which fire?*	point to an unknown thing
Negative Pronouns		
	Nobody knows the trouble I've seen. This is no one's business. We're going nowhere, but nothing can stop us.	stand for an unknown person, place, or thing

Table 3.6 Verb Tenses

Verb Tense	Example
Simple present	*Juan skates.*
Simple past	*Juan skated.*
Simple future	*Juan will skate.*
Present perfect	*Juan has skated.*
Past perfect	*Juan had skated.*
Future perfect	*Juan will have skated.*
Present progressive	*Juan is skating.*
Past progressive	*Juan was skating.*
Future progressive	*Juan will be skating.*

Table 3.7 Person and Number of Verbs in the Present Tense

	Singular	Plural
First person	*I run.*	*We run.*
Second person	*You run.*	*You (all) run.*
Third person	*She runs.*	*They run.*

People have moods. So do verbs: the conditional mood, the subjunctive mood, and the indicative mood. The *conditional mood* is used in a main or independent clause of a sentence to suggest that an action depends on something else:

I *would run* if I weren't so tired.

I *would have run* if I hadn't been so tired.

The *subjunctive mood* is used with verbs in the dependent clause of a sentence to refer to something that is uncertain, contrary to fact, hypothetical, hoped for, or doubtful:

If I <u>were</u> you, I wouldn't touch that wire.

We insist that our money <u>be</u> refunded.

Often the subjunctive mood sounds archaic, though. When Jack's Giant roared,

Fee, fie, foe, fum! I smell the blood of an Englishman!

<u>Be</u> he alive or <u>be</u> he dead, I'll grind his bones to make my bread!

we knew he was an *old* giant, who lived a long time ago.

The *indicative mood* is the straightforward one we most often use. It is used to make factual statements and to ask questions:

You didn't touch that wire.

Did he refund our money?

There are four classes of verbs: transitive active, transitive passive, intransitive linking, and intransitive complete.

Transitive verbs take objects. *Objects* are receivers of the action named by the verb. Objects can be *direct*—the person or thing that something happens to—or *indirect*—the person or thing who is the beneficiary of the action. Note these sentences:

Sheila collects DVDs. (*DVDs* is a direct object), and

Sheila gave Herbert a DVD. (*Herbert* is an indirect object and *DVD* is a direct object).

In the preceding sentences, the verbs are *transitive active*, because the sentences are framed in the *active voice*. Sentences in the active voice take the form *subject* (the agent or doer of the action) + *verb* + *object* (the receiver of the action). When sentences are framed in the *passive voice*, the verbs are *transitive passive*. Here are some examples:

DVDs are collected by Sheila (which sounds pretty stupid, but is technically correct) and

Herbert was given a DVD by Sheila (which sounds more reasonable).

When a sentence is framed in the passive voice, the grammatical subject of the sentence functions either as a direct or an indirect object. In the sentence, *DVDs are collected by Sheila, DVDs* is the grammatical subject but *DVDs* are still the items given, the receivers of the action. In the second sentence, *Herbert was given a DVD by Sheila, Herbert* is the grammatical subject, but he is the beneficiary of the action, and not the one who did the giving.

Discerning the difference between sentences in the active voice and those in the passive voice can be challenging for young readers and English language learners. These readers often expect the grammatical subject of the sentence to be the agent of the action and not the object or the beneficiary of it.

Passive sentences cause another kind of problem, in that they don't have to mention who is actually behind the action. Politicians famously exclaim, "Mistakes were made!" and the passive construction allows them to slip by without saying who made them. (But try that with your mother!)

Intransitive linking verbs resemble equals signs in arithmetic. In

Juan <u>is</u> a gymnast.

Juan <u>seems</u> happy.

Alicia <u>became</u> ill.

the verbs *is, seems,* and *became* are all linking verbs because they link the subjects of those sentences with either the things they are or their physical or emotional states. The verbs are considered intransitive because in grammatical terms, transitive verbs take objects and intransitive verbs don't.

Intransitive complete verbs don't link anything, and they don't take objects, either. They are complete onto themselves.

Sheila coughed.

Juan sneezed.

The car exploded.

Main verbs, auxiliary verbs, participles, gerunds, and infinitives are all verb forms. In the sentences *DVD's are collected by Sheila*, and *Herbert was given a DVD by Sheila*, the transitive passive verbs took the forms *are collected* and *was given*. *Collected* and *given* were the *main verbs*, and *are* and *was* are *auxiliary verbs*, or *helping verbs*.

The main verb in a passive sentence has the form of a *participle*. Many past participles end in *-ed* and resemble the past tense, but several do not. We say *The food was cooked*, and *He has <u>cooked</u> the food*. But we also say *The medicine was <u>taken</u>* and *She has <u>taken</u> the medicine*—and the underlined forms are all participles. Participles can function as adjectives, too. You can say *The eggs were fried*, and here the sentence is cast in the passive voice using a transitive passive verb consisting of an auxiliary verb and the participial form of the main verb. You can also ask *You want fried eggs, honey?*, and now the participle *fried* functions as an adjective modifying *eggs*. For still more variety, participles come not just in past forms (*fried* in the last sentence is a *past participle*) but also in present forms. In *The sun is baking us*, the verb *baking* is a *present participle* serving as part of a present progressive tense (see above). In the sentence *We stood in the baking sun*, now the present participle *baking* is serving as an adjective.

We can twist verbs into another function called *gerunds*. A gerund is a verb ending in *-ing* that functions grammatically as a noun:

I like <u>baking</u>.

<u>Making</u> mistakes cost Sheila her job.

The **infinitive** form of a verb—*to* + the verb—functions in much the same way a gerund does:

I like <u>to bake</u>.

<u>To err</u> is human; <u>to forgive</u> is divine.

Modal verbs are a special class of auxiliary verbs, and they indicate fine shades of meaning, including the likelihood of something occurring, someone's ability to perform an action, permission to do something, or obligation to do something (Palmer, 2001). Here are some examples:

Ahab <u>might</u> return soon. (likelihood)

Ahab <u>can</u> return as soon as he finds the money for a ticket. (ability)

Ahab <u>may</u> return here any time he likes. (permission)

Ahab <u>must</u> return at once! (obligation)

The differences between these modal verbs is sometimes ambiguous. For instance, not all speakers use *may* and *can* with contrasted meaning, so we hear *Can Rodney come over?* when the question is, does Rodney have permission, not the ability, to come over. Similarly, *Rodney may come over* can be interpreted to mean either that it's possible but not certain that Rodney will come over or that he has permission to do so. Being sensitive to these seemingly minor grammatical features makes a big difference in having the ability to comprehend the meanings of the sentences. (And there's yet another reason for close reading!)

ADJECTIVES AND ADVERBS   *Adjectives* say something about nouns and *adverbs* say something about verbs, adjectives, or other adverbs. The adjective *black* in *She drives a black Porsche* tells us something about the Porsche; and the adverb *recklessly* in *She drives recklessly* tells us something about the way she drives it. Words that mean roughly the same thing have adjectival and adverbial forms, like *a <u>slow</u> car* (adjective) and *a car that goes <u>slowly</u>* (adverb). As in these examples, adverbs are often made by adding *-ly* onto an adjective. People don't always observe the distinction between adjectives and adverbs in speech—we often say *Go slow*. But in writing, and in formal speech, we will prefer *Go slowly*. Children should be aware of the difference, even if they don't always observe it.

Adverbs tell us more about adjectives in sentences like *Shirley is very funny* (where *funny* is an adjective telling us how Shirley is, and *very* is an adverb telling us how funny); or *Shirley drives completely carelessly* (where *carelessly* is an adverb telling us how Shirley drives, and *completely* is another adverb telling us just how carelessly).

CONJUNCTIONS   *Conjunctions* are words that join things—other words, phrases (a group of words), or clauses (a group of words with a subject and a predicate—see above). They come in three varieties: coordinating conjunctions, correlative conjunctions, and subordinating conjunctions. *Coordinating conjunctions* join words, phrases, and clauses that are of equal importance grammatically: *I like tea <u>and</u> coffee; I like tea <u>and</u> I like coffee; I don't like tea <u>but</u> I like coffee; I drink coffee in the morning and after lunch*. *Correlative conjunctions* come in pairs: *I like <u>both</u> tea <u>and</u> coffee; I like <u>neither</u> tea <u>nor</u> coffee; I like <u>not only</u> tea <u>but also</u> coffee*. *Subordinating conjunctions* join dependent clauses to another word or main clause: *I like her <u>because</u> she is nice; She's very wise <u>although</u> she's young; He has been unhappy <u>since</u> he lost his bicycle*.

PREPOSITIONS   Prepositions are words that show relationships between other words. In these sentences, the prepositions are underlined:

> *She was almost hit <u>by</u> a car.*
>
> *That is <u>beside</u> the point.*
>
> *The duchess swept <u>into</u> the room.*
>
> *The Frisbee flew <u>across</u> the lawn.*
>
> *Let me tell you the story <u>about</u> a man named Charlie.*

Prepositions come in phrases, consisting of a preposition followed by a noun (or something like it) plus that noun's modifiers. Prepositional phrases function much like modifiers.

> *We escaped <u>by quickly hiding in the smelly sewer</u>.*

In the above sentence, *by quickly hiding* is a prepositional phrase (*hiding* seems like a verb but in that form it is a gerund, and it functions grammatically like a noun). *In the smelly sewer* is a prepositional phrase, too.

Syntax and Reading

Syntax is important in literacy. First, and most obviously, syntax is needed to make meaning from text. As shown in many examples in the previous section, a reader needs to understand the syntax to derive the right meaning of a sentence. Syntax matters in word recognition, too. Often, teachers will ask a reader who struggles over an unknown word, "What would make sense here?" And if the child is reading the sentence, "The mother hoped the jar would contain money, but it d____," the word *but* will help the reader figure out that the next word should say *didn't*. The conjunction *but* tells the reader to expect those words to convey a meaning counter to the beginning phrase. Syntax matters, too, in writing Standard American English, and, of course, in gaining acceptable scores on tests of knowledge of the English language arts. Finally, students who are English language learners must learn the syntax of English, and they will often be relying on their teachers to clarify problems. The challenge is that most knowledge of syntax is the *tacit knowledge* of native speakers, including teachers. Teachers must work extra hard to understand on a conscious level the syntactic concepts they use, so they can make them explicit to their students.

Check Your Understanding 3.4: Gauge your understanding of the skills and concepts in this section.

Text Structure

The materials children read come in structures that have loose "rules" similar to the rules of syntax we reviewed in the previous section. As students have experiences reading different types of texts, they learn those rules—normally on a tacit or unconscious level. Having the rules in their minds helps readers follow along with the text—just as knowing the order of a religious service or of a football game helps someone follow or take part in the proceedings.

The structures of stories—called story grammars—are the most commonly taught text structures. But informational texts have structures, too: cause-and-effect, question-and-answer, problem-and-solution, taxonomy, chronology, general exposition, and arguments-and-reasons.

Story Grammar

The most thoroughly studied of the structures of discourse (*discourse* roughly means "a body of talk") is story grammar. Consider the story "The Frowning Princess" in Figure 3.4.

Stories such as this one have a set of identifiable elements, or slots, into which the particulars of the story are placed. These slots are almost always organized in a particular order. (The terms *identifiable elements* and *particular order* are signs that one is talking about grammar or syntax.) For example, a story consists of a setting, one or more episodes, and a consequence. An analysis of the story "The Frowning Princess" using this story grammar model is found in Table 3.8.

Children as young as kindergarten age have a sense of story grammar, and they appear to use it to comprehend stories (Stein & Glenn, 1979). Teaching children story grammar improves their comprehension (Olson & Gee, 1988). Such instruction has been found to be especially helpful for children with learning disabilities (Gersten, 1998).

Watch this video of a sample story map lesson for second graders and answer the question that follows.

 Video Exploration 3.3: Watch the video (https://www.youtube.com/watch?v=OAxvDLEkl_w) and answer questions that reflect the content you have read.

Figure 3.4 The Frowning Princess

The Frowning Princess

In a faraway time and a distant place, there lived a king and his daughter. She frowned. From morning to night, she frowned and frowned and frowned. Even if you saw her in her sleep, she would still be frowning.

The royal advisor worried. "This is terrible, your majesty. A frowning princess is like a cloudy day," he said. "The people will think there is something wrong with your kingdom if the princess doesn't stop frowning."

"I pay you well, so I guess you are right," said the king. "We must find a way to make my daughter stop frowning."

The king and the royal advisor told the princess every joke they knew. But kings and royal advisors are not funny people, and after they had told both of their jokes, the princess was still frowning.

They brought a dozen monkeys and three trained hyenas to the palace. Nobody got any sleep for days. The princess frowned even harder.

Then it happened that a chambermaid put her head between her legs to clean under the princess' bed. Seeing the princess from this odd position, the chambermaid discovered something. "The princess is smiling," she thought. She told the princess to stand on her head and look into the mirror. When the princess saw her reflection, she tried to turn her upside-down frown right-side up. So, of course, she smiled.

Now the princess smiles all the day long. The king, his advisor, and the people are happy. It may be that the princess is still trying to frown, but I won't tell if you won't.

Teach It! 42

Story Maps

These graphic organizers enhance children's text comprehension by familiarizing them with story grammar as they identify and sequence key story elements and events.

Table 3.8 Story Grammar Applied

Elements of Story Grammar	Examples
The **setting**, a place and time	"In a faraway time and a distant place . . ."
There are **characters**	". . . a king and his daughter . . ."
An initiating event—something that creates a problem to be solved, and sets further events in motion.	"She frowned. From morning to night, the princess frowned and frowned and frowned."
There is one or more **episodes** that contain . . .	
An attempt to solve the problem	"The king and the royal advisor told the princess every joke they knew."
Which has an **outcome**	". . . the princess was still frowning."
Possibly another **attempt**	"They brought a dozen monkeys and three trained hyenas to the palace."
Which has an **outcome**	"Nobody got any sleep for days. The princess frowned even harder."
Possibly another **attempt**	"A chambermaid put her head between her legs to clean under the princess' bed. Seeing the princess from this odd position, the chambermaid discovered something. 'The princess is smiling,' she thought. She told the princess to stand on her head and look into the mirror."
Which has an **outcome**	"When the princess saw her reflection, she tried to turn her upside-down frown right-side up. So, of course, she smiled."
There is a **resolution**	"Now the princess smiles all the day long."
There is a **consequence**	"The king, his advisor, and the people are happy."

SOURCE: Based on Stein, N. & Glenn, C. An analysis of story comprehension in elementary school children. In R. O. Freedle (Ed.), *New directions in discourse processing* (pp. 53–120). Norwood, NJ: Ablex Publishing Corporation, 2009.

Structures of Informational Texts

The Common Core State Standards have mandated that a large portion of students' reading be done in informational text. Accordingly, the varieties of informational texts used in schools have proliferated greatly. The following are some frequently encountered informational text structures.

QUESTION AND ANSWER   Many popular books for young readers pose questions about outlandish topics, and then provide answers. Melvin Berger's True or False books (e.g., 2009) are good examples. Books for older readers pose larger questions and develop longer answers.

PROBLEM AND SOLUTION; CAUSE AND EFFECT   Some texts pose a problem, engage readers in thinking about how it might be solved, and then explain solutions. Often, the problem is presented in terms of its cause/s and effect/s.

TAXONOMY   A taxonomy is an organizing chart. Some texts explain the varieties of members of a category that are related to each other. Melvin Berger's *Chomp!* (1999) does that for sharks; *Snap!* (2002) does it for crocodiles and alligators.

CHRONOLOGY   A chronology is an unfolding of a series of events through time. Janis Herbert's *American Revolution for Kids* (2002) lays out a series of chapters that are each somewhat self-contained stories about a part of the Revolution, arranged in chronological order. The two dozen books in Franklin Watts Publishers' *Wicked History* series provide the chronology of events in the lives of characters who were deliberately chosen not only for their importance but also for their fascination for young readers, especially boys: Vlad the Impaler, Catherine the Great, Hitler, Genghis Khan, and others.

COMPARISON AND CONTRAST   Many texts are arranged to make comparisons. Steve Jenkins' *What Do You Do with a Tail Like This?* (2008) teaches zoology to young readers by discussing living creatures (monkeys, scorpions, elephants, and more) one at a time and comparing and contrasting them by that feature (tails, eyes, claws).

GENERAL EXPOSITION   A widely used structure for informational texts is similar to the chapter you are reading now. It sets out a main topic, subdivides it into smaller topics, and provides details for those smaller topics.

ARGUMENTS   Arguments are everywhere—in political campaigns, on newspapers' editorial pages, in advertisements, and, increasingly, in texts for children. Argumentative text typically states a claim of something the reader should believe or do or both. Then it lists reasons that support the claim, along with evidence that supports each reason. All of those things are marshaled toward a conclusion by the use of logic. Jen Green's *Why Should I Save Water?* (2005a), and *Why Should I Recycle?* (2005b) are good examples of argumentative works for young readers.

Text Structure, Reading, and Writing

Just as awareness of story grammar can support comprehension of narrative texts, so can awareness of the structure of various types of informational texts help readers take in the information these texts present. Moreover, it can help students to produce similar types of texts. One way to develop such awareness is by drawing students' attention to "discourse markers" or "signal words." These are words and phrases that provide the reader with signposts indicating how the text is developing and how stretches of text are linked to one another (Derewianka, 2013). For example, to signal that a summary is coming up, the writer or speaker may use a phrase such as *to sum up, all in all, briefly,* or *in short*. Here are some more examples of signal words and their associated text structures.

Signal words that occur frequently in texts with a cause-and-effect structure are *because (of), due to, as a result, as a consequence, consequently, for that reason, therefore*. In texts that compare and contrast two items, we often encounter words or phrases such as *similar, both, like, different, unlike, by contrast*. In a text that presents information chronologically, commonly occurring signal words are *then, after, before, next, as soon as, meanwhile, earlier, later, afterwards*. Signal words typically found in argumentative texts are *however, nonetheless, in spite of, moreover, in light of the above*.

General expository texts use a variety of signal words to indicate what the writer/speaker intends to do at different points in the text. For example, to signal that she is about to further clarify an idea by restating it, the author may use *in other words, I mean, to put it another way, to be more precise, that is*. If the clarification is going to be done through examples, the author might use *for example, for instance, to illustrate, a case in point is, in particular*. If the author wants to signal that she is about to begin an exposition, she may choose to do that with *to begin, to start with, for a start, first of all*; if she is adding more information, she may signal it by using *furthermore, in addition, also, moreover, what's more, besides*; if she is about to conclude the exposition, she may warn the audience by using *to conclude, in conclusion, finally, a final point*.

Paying attention to text structure and signal words is likely to result in better comprehension. It is also likely to help students to produce better organized texts by giving them tools for expressing the relationships between and among the ideas they wish to convey orally or in writing.

Check Your Understanding 3.5: **Gauge your understanding of the skills and concepts in this section.**

For Review

If reading is making sense of talk written down, then teachers need more than a passing acquaintance with linguistics, the study of language, in order to teach reading well. In this chapter we explored the main areas of language knowledge, including the sound system of language or *phonology*, the ways words are formed or *morphology*, the collection of words to be learned or *vocabulary*, the ordering and inflecting of classes of words or *syntax*, and the organization of different types of texts, or *text structure*. At the outset of this chapter we stated that when you reached this point in your reading and studying you should be able to:

- **Define vowels, consonants, and syllables and explain how phonological awareness supports reading and spelling development.**

We explained that English uses an alphabetic writing system, so the letters of the alphabet relate to individual speech sounds. Teaching students what vowels, consonants, and syllables are and how they are produced develops their phonological awareness, which, in turn, supports reading and spelling development.

- **Define and classify morphemes, and explain why morpheme awareness is important for students' reading and spelling development.**

The spelling and pronunciation of English words cannot be fully explained or understood in terms of letter-to-sound correspondences. That is because adding morphemes to base words changes the meaning or the part of speech of those words, and often changes their spelling and pronunciation as well. Awareness of morphemes can thus help students to become better comprehenders as well as better spellers.

- **Identify vocabulary tiers, and explain how knowledge of lexical relationships supports reading comprehension.**

"Knowing" a word happens on several levels, and there are also different "tiers" of words to be known. Having the ability to negotiate those tiers can help reduce the burden of teaching and learning the 90,000 different words that are typically used in elementary through high school. Such ability presupposes awareness of multiple lexical relationships.

- **Distinguish among types of sentences, identify parts of speech, and explain how knowledge of syntax supports reading comprehension.**

Most of what we know about syntax is *tacit* knowledge—we can use it but we can't talk about what we know. But nowadays teachers are called on to explain the syntax of

Standard American English to all students on some level, especially to English language learners. That means they need to be familiar with varied types of sentences, able to explain what the different parts of speech are, and understand how syntax supports reading comprehension.

- **Identify the structure of texts, signal words associated with varied text structures, and explain how awareness of text structure and signal words can support reading comprehension and writing development.**

Teachers are also expected to support students' comprehension and ability to produce a variety of oral and written text types. That is why they need to understand text structure and be aware of words and phrases that signal different text structures.

For Your Journal

1. Review the answers to the Anticipation Guide on the first page of this chapter. What answers would you give to those questions now that you have read this chapter?

2. If you still need proof that you have tacit knowledge of English grammar, that is, knowledge that enables you to talk and listen but of which you are largely unaware, try this exercise. Explain what is wrong with this sentence: *Ignacio is playing with a red big ball.* State the rule that you would use in writing the sentence correctly.

3. Families from different social backgrounds think of literacy in strikingly different ways. How did you use literacy in your family when you were growing up? What materials did the people around you read? Did they share or discuss them with each other? If so, how? Was there bedtime reading? If so, what was it like?

Taking It to the World

Interview a guidance counselor at a middle or high school or a counseling psychologist who treats adults. Interview a foreman or manager at a business or manufacturing plant. With regard to their clients or the people they supervise, to what extent do these professionals find that people's problems are related to their difficulties in using language for different purposes—for self-awareness, for getting along with others, for giving and receiving directions clearly? Do these people believe that schools have a role in teaching communication for different purposes?

Chapter 4
Emergent Literacy

 ## Learning Outcomes

After reading this chapter you should be able to:

1. Define emergent literacy.

2. Describe language-based learning as it applies to emergent literacy.

3. Describe print-based aspects of emergent literacy.

4. Explain comprehensive strategies to develop general aspects of emergent literacy.

5. Explain specific strategies for developing targeted emergent literacy concepts and skills.

6. List and explain environmental strategies to support emergent literacy.

7. Describe ways of promoting family literacy and home support for young children's literacy.

Anticipation Guide

The following statements will help you begin thinking about the topics covered in this chapter. Answer *true* or *false* in response to each statement. As you read and learn more about the topics mentioned in these statements, double-check your answers. See what interests you and what prompts your curiosity toward more understanding.

_____ 1. When you get right down to it, learning to read is "natural."

_____ 2. The ability to tap out individual phonemes in words is normally developed by the end of kindergarten.

_____ 3. Some children learn concepts about print, such as the arrangement of print on the page or the fact that people read the print and not the pictures, without having to be taught them, but others need instruction.

_____ 4. Children don't need to be aware of the features of language to learn to talk, but they do need some language awareness in order to learn to read and write.

_____ 5. All children know what words are and that their language is composed of them. We don't need to teach them that.

_____ 6. We can teach children a lot about reading and writing through passive means, such as labeling items in the classroom.

_____ 7. Dialogic reading is a means of teaching children about both printed and spoken language.

_____ 8. Reading aloud to children is a waste of valuable instructional time. If it is to be done at all, it should be left up to parents.

_____ 9. Teaching reading is such a complicated undertaking that parents should be discouraged from taking any part in it.

_____ 10. Parents read to their children much more than they used to. This is true of people from all income groups.

A Classroom Story

Vignette of a Kindergarten Classroom: Emergent Literacy in Context

It is the second Monday in November, and Ignacio Diaz's kindergartners know the morning routine very well. As they enter, they take off their coats, stuff their lunch boxes into their cubbies, and check the job board to see who will give the weather report, who will lead the Pledge of Allegiance, and who will line the children up to go to lunch. Then they go to the task board and see what their rotations are for the language block. Their names are pasted in quadrants with symbols, indicating who will go to the independent study center, who will work with the teacher in the reading circle, who will write, and who will have reading time. Charmaigne enters the room and hands her teacher a book baggie, a plastic bag that holds a book and a group of games and activity sheets.

"Mama said she liked the drawing I did of Toad. Or maybe it was Frog. . . . How do you tell them apart again?" she says. "And she said to tell you we finally figured out how to do the alphabet game."

Ignacio laughs and puts the book baggie into a bin to be repacked for another child to take home.

As children come in from various buses, Charmaigne wanders to the library corner and begins reading a little book about frogs. It is one of her favorites, written by Henry, the boy who taught them all to draw cartoons. Henry's penciled letters make dubious spellings that flow across the page in pencil, but Charmaigne focuses on the neat black letters her teacher has written with a felt-tipped pen. She can read some of the words, and she likes finding the ones she knows. Henry's drawings always make clear what is going on in his books, so when Charmaigne wants to, she can hold the book up and tell the story aloud as if she were reading it, even though she does not yet know many of the words.

The class is all here, and Charmaigne's turn has come to lead the Pledge of Allegiance. She knows what a flag is, but the word flag *is taped underneath it anyway. It begins with F, just like the title of Henry's book,* Frogs. *Now Mr. Diaz calls the children to the rug in front of the chart stand.*

"Who knows what today is?" he asks.

"Monday," says Henry.

"Right," says Ignacio. "And I'm going to write 'Today is Monday' right here on the chart. Let's say that sentence: 'Today is Monday.'"

"Today is Monday," chants the class.

"What's the first word I need to write?"

"Today," Charmaigne offers.

"Good. I'm going to start writing up here," and he points to the upper left hand corner of the sheet. "What's the first sound we hear in 'Today'?" Some children, including Charmaigne, chant the tuh *sound, over and over. After a moment's hesitation, other children join them.*

"Aw, you're champions. Now, what letter will we use to spell the tuh *sound?"*

With the children and Mr. Diaz taking turns offering up sounds and naming letters to spell them with, the morning news is written on the chart. It covers four lines. Ignacio is careful to show the children that he begins writing over on the left side, then writes across to the right, then returns to the left but down one line, and continues writing to the right again.

The children read the sentences through three times as Ignacio points to every word with his "Harry Potter wand," the stick he uses for pointing to words.

What Is Emergent Literacy?

If they grow up in a community where others read and write, children learn a great deal about those things years before they meet their first teacher. They learn by their own efforts, and they employ an amazing capacity to look closely at language, tease out its patterns, and work their way toward competent use through a succession of more and more sophisticated stages, or layers of strategies. Certainly children depend on adults to "put literacy in their way"—surround them with print, read to them, and set up opportunities for them to try out their own versions of reading and writing. These opportunities are a hidden advantage for children who have them, and allow those children to start right into reading instruction with understanding and enthusiasm. But while some children get thousands of hours of early experiences with literacy at home, other children get few. So teachers of children in preschool and in the early school grades have a lot of work to do to prepare all children to make a good start in learning to read and write. We call this whole enterprise *emergent literacy*. It's a mix of what children first discover for themselves and what adults help them learn about literacy.

Emergent literacy means:

- a period in children's experience between the time when they first notice print and wonder what people are doing when they work with it, and the time when they can read words; and also

- the early informal and formal teaching that children receive in preschool and early kindergarten at the hands of careful teachers who make sure that all children understand what reading and writing are and what they are for, so they can benefit fully from reading instruction.

Because print represents spoken language, children must understand the language that comes from print, and know a good deal about that language and about the features of the print that represent that language. Learning language, learning about language, learning about print, and learning how print and language go together in reading and writing are the aspects of emergent literacy that will be explored in this chapter.

Figure 4.1 lists phases of children's development of emergent literacy and matches teaching procedures to each phase.

Check Your Understanding 4.1: Gauge your understanding of the skills and concepts in this section.

Figure 4.1 Developmental Milestones: Emergent Literacy

Stages of Literacy Development	Developmental Milestones	Teaching Strategies
Exploring Print (Beginning Kindergarten)	• May tap out syllables in most words, but not phonemes • Holds a book the right way up and can point to the front. • May know that print "talks" and not pictures. • May recognize some letters and may be able to write a few of them. • Writing shows no relation between letters and sounds. P2X = "little." • After memorizing a short text, cannot voice-point to the words accurately. • When listening to stories, some will respond to parts of them with movements and chants; others will follow the plot with displays of expectation, suspense, and relief. • Can make up a story while paging through a familiar picture book. • May draw pictures and tell you about the scene he or she is describing. • May write captions to pictures or other compositions, using invented symbols and random letters.	• Read-alouds—teachers read daily to children, thinking aloud and emphasizing plot structure (who the characters are, what the problem is, what they do to solve the problem, what happens, how things are at the end). The same story is reread several times and children are later invited to pretend-read it themselves. • Sing-alongs and rhyming games. • Morning message: The teacher asks children to take turns helping introduce and write up the day, date, month, and weather, as well as the day's activities. Rebus symbols are used for weather and names of activities. • Assignment charts: Children's names printed on tagboard are divided among slots in a pocket chart according to their tasks and center assignments for the day. • Shared reading—the teacher carefully points at large print while pronouncing words. The teacher carefully names aspects of reading—"letters," "words," "direction," "top of the page," "bottom of the page," and calls attention to individual letters and words that are repeated. • Teaching the alphabet. • Incorporating print in play activities—post office, grocery store, etc. • Writing Workshop: Children have opportunities to communicate with pencils and colored pencils; encouragement to write captions; opportunities to share what they have drawn and written.
Becoming Familiar with Print (Late Kindergarten) Logographic Reading	• Can begin to tap out phonemes. • Can provide rhyming words. • Still can't confidently voice-point at word units. • Knows way around books. • Can write own name. • Uses invented spelling to write words or phrases as captions to pictures. • Invented spelling begins to represent sounds in words, but only a few: LL = "little." • May recognize most letters and associate upper- and lowercase letters. • Sometimes writes letters and lines of print backwards, unless shown where to start writing. • Less pretend reading—the child often refuses to read, because she knows she doesn't know the words; or reads only the few words she knows.	• Read-alouds—teachers continue to read two or three times daily to children, thinking aloud and inviting the children's comments and predictions. At least one book per day is reread several times and children are invited to pretend-read it themselves. • Children are invited to reenact stories using drama, puppets, or flannel boards. • Sing-alongs and rhyming games. • Morning message: The teacher asks children to take turns helping introduce the day, date, month, and weather, as well as the day's activities. Rebus symbols are used for weather and names of activities. • Assignment charts: Children's names printed on tagboard are divided among slots in a pocket chart according to their tasks and center assignments for the day. • Alphabet teaching activities. • Shared reading, with the children reading lines after the teacher. • Sharing the pen writing. • Writing Workshop: Children have opportunities to communicate with pencils and colored pencils; encouragement to write captions; opportunities to share what they have drawn and written.

Stages of Literacy Development	Developmental Milestones	Teaching Strategies
Beginning Finger-Point Reading (Beginning First Grade) **Early Alphabetic Reading**	• Can tap out phonemes. Many can combine phonemes to make new words: *s + top = stop.* • Many children can voice-point at word units. • Those who can voice-point are learning some words from encounters with print. • Writes with invented spelling, and includes letters for most sounds that are heard. A few high frequency words are spelled conventionally. • LDL = "little." • Still makes active responses to stories, like chanting and moving. Is increasingly following the plot and other patterns, too, as demonstrated by predictions and comments.	• Read-alouds—teacher continues to read two times daily to children, thinking aloud and inviting the children's comments and predictions. The teacher emphasizes parts of the book: the title, the author, the illustrator. • Children are invited to reenact stories using drama, puppets, or flannel boards. • Sing-alongs and rhyming games. • Morning message uses longer sentences and introduces new words. • Charts for tasks and center assignments are still used. • Shared reading, with the children reading lines after the teacher. The teacher calls attention to the title, the author, and the illustrator and introduces other terminology as needed, such as "first word," "bottom of the page," etc. The teacher teaches lessons on letter sounds and word recognition. • Sharing the pen writing teaches letter-to-sound correspondences and conventions of capitalization and punctuation. • Language Experience Approach. • Guided Reading: In small groups, children are led to finger-point read simple texts. • Word study activities (see Chapter 5). • Writing Workshop: Children have opportunities to communicate with pencils and colored pencils; encouragement to write captions; opportunities to share what they have drawn and written
Finger-Point Reading (Mid First Grade) **Alphabetic Reading**	• Can more easily tap out phonemes, and can combine phonemes to make new words: *s + top = stop.* • Can more easily produce rhyming words, in games like "Ding, dong, dell . . ." • Is able to finger-point read simple predictable books with strong picture support. • Continues to acquire sight words from reading activities. • Is able to sound out predictably spelled words, letter by letter. • May write messages of two or three lines. Invented spellings are mixed with more conventionally spelled words. • LEDL or LETL still spell "little." • Is able to take highly predictable books home to read aloud.	• Read-alouds—teacher continues to read two times daily to children, thinking aloud and inviting the children's comments and predictions. The teacher emphasizes parts of the book: the title, the author, the illustrator. • Children are invited to reenact stories using drama, puppets, or flannel boards. • Sing-alongs and rhyming games. • Morning message uses longer sentences and introduces new words. • Charts for tasks and center assignments are still used. • Shared reading, with the children reading lines after the teacher. The teacher calls attention to the title, the author, and the illustrator and introduces other terminology as needed, such as "first word," "bottom of the page," etc. The teacher teaches lessons on letter sounds and word recognition. • Sharing the pen writing teaches letter-to-sound correspondences and conventions of capitalization and punctuation. • Taking dictation; using the Language Experience Approach. • Guided Reading: In small groups, children are led to finger-point read simple texts. • Word study activities (see Chapter 5). • Writing Workshop: Children have opportunities to communicate with pencils and colored pencils; encouragement to write captions; opportunities to share what they have drawn and written. • Focused lessons are offered on both the conventions of writing and strategies for composing (see Chapter 10).

Language-Based Learning and Emergent Literacy

Native speakers have acquired a working knowledge of the English language by the time they enter kindergarten. On average, they have vocabularies of around 2,000 root words (*run* is a root word, but *runs, running,* and *ran* are derived words), although children with limited language exposure may have half that (Biemiller, 2009). They can speak and understand most kinds of simple sentences and follow many stories and explanations. Remember, too, that between one child in every seven and one in every five speaks another language at home, and these children will need help learning the English language.

Understanding and being able to use language is not enough. When children learn to read, they have to be conscious of language, too. Consciousness of language is called *metalinguistic awareness.* Because print represents spoken language, emergent readers need to be aware that their language is real—it is not just noise that accompanies thoughts and actions, but something that can be written down in sentences. They must know that sentences are made up of words, and they must be aware that spoken words consist of syllables and the smaller units called *phonemes.*

They also need to be learning about print—which side of a book is up, that the print is what talks, and that it's arrayed on the page from top to bottom and left to right—at least it is if it's written in English.

Vocabulary

Children in the emergent literacy phase (preschool through early first grade, usually) should know words for common concepts and actions, as well as common adjectives. They should understand nuances of words, the slight differences in synonyms for the same action (*run, jog, dash*), and be able to think of opposites of adjectives and verbs. They also should be able to think of things in terms of categories (*A duck is a kind of bird*).

Syntax

Syntax, or the rules of grammar, has two parts. One is the ordering of words in sentences. The other is the inflectional endings that indicate the number of a noun and whether it is in the possessive form; and the person, number, and tense of verbs.

Children in the emergent literacy stage should be encouraged to speak in complete sentences with Standard American English inflections on verbs and nouns. Some dialects of English, such as African American Vernacular English, do not use inflectional English in the ways Standard American English does. But because written English uses conventional inflections, children need to know them.

Decontextualized Language

Decontextualized language refers to things that are not here in our immediate surroundings. To illustrate, let's suppose you are walking across campus and meet a close friend whose arm is in a cast. You say, "What happened?" and she knows she should explain why she is wearing the cast, especially if the cast is brand new. You just used *contextualized language* because the meeting with your friend, the cast, and your surprise provide a context for understanding your utterance. Now suppose a one-year-old in a high chair stretches out her arm toward a juice bottle and groans "uh-uh-uh!" Her parent knows that the child wants more juice. The thirsty child and a bottle of juice just out of reach provide a context for understanding "uh-uh-uh!" The child is using *contextualized language*—and it allows her to communicate without even using words! But then suppose you read:

> *Daylight crested the dark hill above the village, topped the tarred board wall in front of the little farm compound, filtered through the leaves of the acacia trees, and dappled the faded blue-paint cottage under the shaggy brow of thick thatched roof. Cheery light glowed gold on neat stacks of firewood, low barns with splashed muddy red bases, the clay oven under its woven straw roof, and the long hinged pole hanging a bucket over the tidy round well.*

Now there is no context to help you understand the words, because you may be reading those lines on your laptop sitting in a library, where there is no sun, no fence, no cottage, and no firewood. The words alone, with the help of your imagination, must make the meaning. That is what we mean by understanding *decontextualized language*: making meaning from words alone. Children need to understand decontextualized language in order to listen to or read text with understanding—because unlike most speech, written language is usually unsupported by context.

Social Uses of Language

Social uses of language are not strictly related to literacy, but because certain kinds of social behavior are necessary if children are going to take part in the discussions that will help them comprehend texts and express themselves orally and in speech, children will need to learn the conventions of turn-taking and keeping comments focused on the topic. The Common Core State Standards include productive participation in discussions in the English Language Arts goals.

Knowledge About Language

Being able to use a language, technically called having *competence* in a language, is different from knowing *about* a language, or what is technically called **metalinguistic awareness** (*meta-* is a Greek affix meaning "about"). You have a lot of metalinguistic awareness of a language you have studied, because much foreign language instruction is typically a study about a language. When languages are acquired in early childhood from being around others, however, we don't typically learn much *about* them. What is to be known about language that is relevant to literacy? The most important aspects of metalinguistic awareness of English for the purposes of literacy are the concept of word and phonological awareness, because we read and write words, and letters of the alphabet (roughly) spell words by their phonemes.

THE CONCEPT OF WORD   The **concept of word** (Morris, 2005) is knowing that a frantically uttered expression such as "MamacomequickYvonneseatingmycandy" is actually made up of the words "Mama, come quick. Yvonne's eating my candy." This is not an easy feat. Even adults can have trouble separating the speech stream into word units. The corresponding aspect of the concept of word that applies to print is knowing that in print, words are indicated by clusters of letters separated by spaces.

Teach It! 4

Language Experience or Group Dictated Story

This authentic writing activity helps emergent literacy learners develop oral language fluency and concepts about print that include print directionality, concept of word, sight word recognition, and phonological awareness.

Not being aware of words in speech puts children at a disadvantage when they are learning to read. Instead of focusing on each word in their minds as they say it, children who do not have the concept of word might scan their eyes across a whole line of text, or they might look at only a single letter, or they might confuse written words with spoken syllables. A child who doesn't have the concept of word and isn't looking at the correct word unit is not likely to have learned to recognize new written words from the activity. But the child who has the concept of word, who looks at the written words at the instant each is sung or read, will likely have made matches between some of the written versions of the words and the spoken versions. That child should be able to recognize some of those words in the future.

PHONOLOGICAL AWARENESS   Beyond the level of words, there are other levels of speech about which emergent readers must be aware. These are syllables, onsets and rimes, and phonemes. Awareness of these smaller units of spoken language is referred to as *phonological awareness*. *Syllables* are the pulses of language. They are the "beats" we hear in *elbow* (two syllables), *love* (one syllable), and *popsicle* (three syllables). As was discussed in Chapter 3, onsets and rimes are the next largest parts of syllables: The *onset* is the beginning consonant sound (if the syllable has one) and the *rime* is the vowel sound plus any consonant sound that follows. In *cat*, the onset is /c/ and the rime is /at/. In *step*, the onset is /st/ and the rime is /ep/. As the smallest speech sounds in language, *phonemes* roughly correspond to individual letters. *Dig* has three phonemes: /d/, /i/, and /g/. *Clam* has four phonemes: /k/, /l/, /æ/, and /m/. (Note that we conventionally represent phonemes with slashes on either side.)

In terms of phonological awareness, there is a range of tasks that children are recommended to perform:

- Clapping out syllables in spoken words (*ba/na/na*)
- Producing rhymes for single-syllable words (*bit—kit; bat—cat*)
- Segmenting single-syllable words into phonemes (*bit = b/ih/t*)
- Breaking off a phoneme from a single-syllable word (*sat → at*)
- Adding a phoneme to a single-syllable word (*b + at = bat*)
- Substituting phonemes in single-syllable words to make new words (*sit → sat; sit → bit; sit → sick*)

A good deal of research (e.g., Adams, 1990; Snow et al., 1998; Wagner, Torgesen, & Rashotte, 1994) has shown that children who are aware that words can be broken into phonemes and can manipulate phonemes will have an easier time matching letters and sounds and learning to read words when they begin to read than children who are not familiar with phonemes. We also know that even short periods of instruction on working with phonemes can improve children's word reading (Blachman & Tangle, 2008).

Check Your Understanding 4.2: **Gauge your understanding of the skills and concepts in this section.**

Print-Based Learning and Emergent Literacy

Now let's look at the print side of things. As we said, children's emergent literacy is partly knowing about language and partly knowing about print. Print awareness includes having an understanding of the following:

- *Concepts about print:* the set of ideas about what print is and how it works
- *The alphabetic nature of writing:* the idea that, in languages such as English, German, Spanish, and Kiswahili (but not Japanese or Chinese), writing works by using units of letters to represent language at the level of phonemes
- *Alphabet knowledge:* the ability to recognize and produce many letters of the alphabet
- *Alphabetic concepts:* an understanding of the rules that relate letters to sounds.

Concepts About Print

New Zealander Marie Clay (1975) offered this account some years ago of a novice teacher giving a reading lesson to a group of beginning readers:

> Suppose the teacher has placed an attractive picture on the wall and has asked her children for a story, which she will record under it. They offer the text, "Mother is cooking," which the teacher alters slightly to introduce some features she wishes to teach. She writes:
>
> Mother said, "I am baking."
>
> If she says, "Now look at our story," 30% of the new entrant group [children who are just beginning reading instruction] will attend to the picture. If she says, "Look at the words and find some that you know," between 50 and 90% will be looking for letters. If she says, "Can you see Mother?" most will agree that they can, but some see her in the picture, some can locate M, and others will locate the word Mother.
>
> Perhaps the children read in unison, "Mother is . . ." and the teacher tries to sort this out. Pointing to said, she asks, "Does this say is?" Half agree that it does because it has s in it. "What letter does it start with?" Now the teacher is really in trouble. She assumes that the children will know that a word is built out of letters, but 50% of the children still confuse the verbal labels word and letter after six months of instruction. She also assumes that the children know that the left-hand letter following a space is the "start" of a word. Often they do not. (pp. 3–4)

As this example shows, there are many **concepts about print** that children must have in place so that in a reading lesson, they can orient themselves properly to a book and direct their attention appropriately. These concepts include knowing the layout of books; knowing what the print and the pictures do; knowing how print is laid out on the page; knowing the terms used in reading instruction, such as "the beginning of the sentence," "the end of the sentence," "the first word," and "the top of the page"; knowing what a word is; knowing what a letter is and that uppercase and lowercase letters are different versions of the same thing; and knowing at least some marks of punctuation. Watch this video depicting concepts about print and answer the question that follows.

 Video Exploration 4.1: Watch the video (https://www.youtube.com/watch?v=AV1HY_TUcuM) and answer questions that reflect the content you have read.

Alphabet Knowledge

Alphabet knowledge is an important part of a child's emergent literacy. Some children learn to recognize most letters of the alphabet before they enter kindergarten, and all are expected to recognize and produce all 26 letters by the beginning of first grade. Knowing the letters does two things for a child: it gives us an idea of how much exposure to print a child has had and it helps that child learn to read (Walsh, Price, & Gillingham, 1988).

Teach It! 6
Big Book Lesson

Using an oversized book, children in this activity are invited to listen and respond to questions aimed at developing their orientation to books, attention to print, and familiarity with the language of books.

Teach It! 13
Working With Names to Teach the Alphabet

This engaging activity helps emergent literacy learners develop knowledge of the alphabet while also learning about their classmates.

Differentiated Instruction

SIOP® Sheltered Instruction Observation Protocol
Emergent Readers

Emergent literacy faces in two directions. In one direction, it focuses on the concepts about reading, writing, and written language that children have acquired at home. The teacher can build on them and make a bridge that connects what children are figuring out for themselves with the formal reading curriculum. In another direction, emergent literacy helps us realize the concepts and abilities that some children have not developed yet—concepts and skills they will need to be successful in learning to read and write. These children will need to:

* Be read to, to boost their vocabulary and their familiarity with books.

* Explore print, as in giving dictations and having someone read them back.

* Learn the letters of the alphabet.

These are critical experiences, but fortunately it is not such a long list. One way to make sure children get these experiences is to recruit and supervise volunteers. The U.S. Department of Education provides funding for college students to be paid from work-study funds to serve as tutors. Many colleges and high schools have service learning classes in which students are required to perform some kind of community service. Student volunteers can offer effective help to young readers who need it. The key to the success of such efforts is the teacher's supervision. Tutoring is far more effective when a teacher assesses the children in advance to see exactly what they need, and orients and supervises the tutors to make sure they provide the right help (Morris, 2005).

Letter-to-Sound Correspondence: Learning Phonics

A child realizes that language is real and comes in units of words, syllables, and phonemes. The child can now produce not just letter-like forms, but also many actual letters. The child has learned to orient himself or herself to books. The child realizes that ours is an alphabetic writing system that works not by showing pictures of things, not by representing syllables, but by matching letters with phonemes. Now what?

Now comes the process of discovering the system by which writing spells words, and letters and clusters of letters represent sounds or groups of sounds. This kind of knowledge is called *phonics*. It is also called *alphabetic knowledge* and *letter-to-sound relationships*. The patterns that relate letters to sounds are complex. They come in layers that are peeled back, essentially in stages, by the child who is encouraged to be an active explorer of written language.

Many of the learning outcomes that have been described up to now were displayed in chart form in Figure 4.1, "Developmental Milestones: Emergent Literacy."

Check Your Understanding 4.3: Gauge your understanding of the skills and concepts in this section.

Comprehensive Strategies to Nurture Emergent Literacy

Moving children along toward literacy—and giving thoughtful extra boosts to those children who have gaps in their awareness of reading and writing—is the teacher's task in the phase of emergent literacy. Teachers use four kinds of strategies here:

* *Comprehensive strategies.* These strategies develop many skills at once, and include reading aloud, shared reading, and shared writing.

* *Strategies to develop specif ic skills.* Some skills should be taught directly, like alphabet knowledge, hearing sounds in words, phonics, and strategies for comprehension.

* *Strategies calling attention to language and literacy.* Teachers who support emergent literacy model clear language, point out key points about language print, and think aloud as they read and write.

* *Environmental strategies.* Young children's literacy is supported in passive ways, too, by having a classroom environment and classroom routines that support reading and writing. A literacy-rich classroom environment includes learning centers that encourage drawing and early writing, literacy-centered play, a reading corner, a classroom library, listening centers, charts and posters, and technology that allows children to guide themselves through a reading experience.

We will begin with comprehensive strategies to develop children's emergent literacy. These are strategies that develop several aspects of emergent literacy at once. They include reading aloud, interactive reading aloud, dialogic reading, guided reading, shared writing, writing workshop.

Reading Aloud

Reading aloud is one of the most useful, active things adults can do to nurture children's literacy growth. Many of the abilities that are considered essential to literacy can be developed as children listen to a book read aloud by a family member or teacher. Watch this video of John Lithgow, actor and author of children's books, explain why he believes reading aloud to children is important; then answer the question that follows.

 Video Exploration 4.2: Watch the video (https://www.youtube.com/watch?v=sonMj03ZJPQ) and answer questions that reflect the content you have read.

Among the main benefits of children being read to are the following:

- *It expands their vocabulary.* As Stanovich (1992) has pointed out, there are words that are more commonly encountered in books—even children's books—than in conversation or from watching television. Listening to books being read aloud helps children learn a literate vocabulary.

- *It develops their ability to comprehend written language.* Research on reading comprehension tells us that it involves component skills that include perceiving main ideas and supporting details, making inferences, venturing predictions and confirming them, and visualizing in the mind's eye what the words suggest. Children have the opportunity to develop all of these abilities from listening to a book being read aloud and discussing it.

- *It encourages enthusiasm for literacy as they participate in the reader's excitement.* When children first learn to talk, parents slow down and exaggerate their speech and their gestures as if to say, "This is how language works. This is how we show excitement and interest. This is the way we soothe each other." Similarly, when adults read books aloud with expression, they have the opportunity to show children how written language conveys the full range of emotions. This not only will make literacy appealing to children but also will show them how to derive meaning from and associate emotions with the language of print.

- *It makes them aware of the structure of stories and of other kinds of texts.* Skilled readers learn to find questions and pursue answers according to the structure of whatever text they are reading. A story shows characters in settings and the problems they have and how those problems are solved. Expository writing frames questions about topics and goes about answering those questions. By reading texts aloud and commenting on them, a careful teacher can help students to become aware of the recurring structures of different texts and use them to guide their comprehension.

Reading aloud two or three times each day should be a regular feature of every classroom from preschool through the primary grades and on through the elementary grades. Even when children are learning to read, it is not until fourth grade that many children's reading ability approaches the speed and fluency with which teachers can read to them. Many children's reading rate will take much longer to develop. Therefore, the teacher's reading aloud is a necessary source of language, of stories, and of information for children.

Here is an important caveat, though: Simply reading aloud is not enough. For children to derive the most benefit from a read-aloud session, the session must be conducted well.

Interactive Reading Aloud

Interactive reading aloud invites participation by children. Teachers do three main things when they read aloud interactively.

Teach It! 1

Reading Aloud

With thoughtful preparation, this comprehensive literacy strategy develops children's awareness of the language and structure of books, builds vocabulary, and enhances comprehension.

1. *Use questions and prompts to guide children's attention as they listen.* As they introduce the story, teachers raise questions and ask children to listen for answers. If they are reading a story, they may ask about the main character, the problem, what the character will do to solve the problem, and what will happen as a result. If they are reading an informational book, they will ask students what they already know about the topic, and then ask children to listen to see what else they can find out. As they read the story, they will ask the children what they are learning, and then ask predictions about what they will find out next.

2. *Think aloud, and point to important parts of the text.* Teachers may call attention to what the picture is showing and what the text is saying. They may talk about words or parts of words such as plural markers or past tense endings.

3. *Invite comments and discussion after reading.* Teachers may ask children to choose their favorite part of a story, or the most interesting thing they learned about a topic, and to say why they chose it. They may ask children to retell what they heard, and ask other children to help fill in details.

Two variations of interactive reading aloud are explained in the sections that follow. The first is Beck and McKeown's Text Talk (Beck & McKeown, 2001). The second is McGee and Schikedanz's Repeated Interactive Reading Alouds (McGee & Schickedanz, 2007).

TEXT TALK.   A set of guidelines for interactive read-aloud sessions, Text Talk includes six emphases:

1. *Choosing rich texts.* Texts with "extended connected content for building meaning" (p. 14) are preferred. These texts that challenge children to infer characters' feelings and motives, use text structure to predict outcomes, and explore issues deeply are used in Text Talk activities because they invite deeper discussions than books that are simpler and more transparent.

2. *Questions that ask children to describe and explain.* Rather than questions that elicit one-word answers or invite simple recall of what happened, teachers ask students to describe what is happening and explain why it is happening.

3. *Questions that build on students' responses.* Students with less experience discussing texts may give answers that are based on past experiences or free associations with the topic, so the teacher must skillfully take first responses and follow up with questions that steer students back to events and issues in the text. The teacher may also scaffold children's responses, asking, "Do you think the character did that because of X or Y? Why do you think so?" The teacher may also think aloud, offering his or her own good answer, and modeling for the children how a competent reader answers the questions the teacher is posing.

4. *Using pictures carefully.* Because many or most younger students are challenged to make meaning from decontextualized language (see above), the teacher should read the text aloud first and ask questions to elicit discussions before showing a picture.

5. *Appealing to background knowledge judiciously.* Asking less experienced students what they already know about the topic of a story may lead them away from exploring the issues in the story; so the teacher keeps reminders of background knowledge closely related to the story.

6. *Explaining vocabulary.* The teacher seeks out five to ten words per lesson that the children may not know, and explains them briefly as the story is discussed, and more extensively afterwards. The teacher makes note of those words, and reminds students of their meanings later on.

REPEATED INTERACTIVE READ-ALOUDS.   McGee and Schickedanz (2007) incorporated parts of the Text Talk approach (see above) into a three-lesson sequence of interactive read-alouds.

1. *First reading:* During the first reading, the teacher not only reads aloud but also calls the students' attention to and explains the key elements of the plot: the setting, the main character, the problem the main character has, and the question of what the character or characters will do to solve the problem. The teacher ends that reading by asking a "why" question that elicits higher order thinking and elaborate explanations from the students. The teacher also explains the meanings of several vocabulary words identified in advance.

2. *Second reading:* Now that the teacher has read the text aloud one time, explaining the key points and word meanings, on the second reading the students are asked to answer questions that look for inferences and explanations. The teacher can also discuss meanings of any words that still appear unclear.

3. *Third reading:* The last time through, the teacher uses illustrations as prompts and asks students to retell what happened—using the illustrations on each page for predicting what will follow. The teacher also asks students to talk about characters, problems, and what the characters did to solve the problems.

CCSS

Helping Young Readers Comprehend Narrative and Informational Text

The Common Core State Standards ask children as young as kindergartners and first and second graders to notice and navigate literary structures and content. They are expected to ask about and explain details in a text, identify genres of texts, follow plot lines and retell stories, identify narrators, describe events from different characters' points of view, perceive messages and themes, explain how the authors' word choices contribute shades of meaning to the text, and compare and contrast different versions of the same story. They should be able to recognize the roles of authors and illustrators, and discuss the meaning that is provided by text and pictures, respectively. (See the Common Core Reading—Literature Standards for Kindergarten, grade 1, and grade 2 <http://www.corestandards .org/ELA-Literacy/CCRA/R>.)

The children who are being asked to meet the standards listed above are the same ones who may just be learning the alphabet and the layout of books, or struggling mightily to pronounce individual words or to read whole sentences without making mistakes. They may well be too busy trying to decipher the printed page to think about themes, characters' points of view, authors' word choices, and the like. But while they are learning to process print, they can learn the skills and concepts from the standards if teachers concentrate on them as they read texts aloud and discuss them with children.

More Response Options for Younger Children

The meanings of books can loom larger in children's imaginations when they are provided with opportunities to respond to the books in various ways. Although children of all ages can talk about what they read (Morrow & Gambrell, 2004), younger children find it most natural to respond to books with their whole bodies: by getting up and moving around, by repeating chants, by acting out parts, and by drawing key scenes. English language learners have more opportunities to participate if meaningful responses to stories are encouraged through drama, music, and art rather than through discussion only.

USE CHANTS A very engaging form of response to a story is to repeat a key phrase or chant every time it occurs in a book. English language learners profit from repeating shorter chants, which become nuggets of remembered language that are useful models of grammar and good for pronunciation practice.

USE DRAMA Many children's books have clear patterns of actions that are easy for children to act out. Some books, such as Michael Rosen's *We're Going on a Bear Hunt* (2003), are already scripted for children to act out. Both have chants and movements that the children will enjoy. *The Three Billy Goats Gruff* is not scripted as a play, but it has simple, repeated actions and chants that are easy for children to practice and perform. The whole story can be rehearsed and staged in a single class period. Single scenes of longer stories can be acted out, too, if time is short.

Acting involves interpretation. You can encourage children to interpret stories imaginatively as they rehearse the dramatizations: "How does the little goat feel when he sees the troll? How might he look at that point? What would his voice sound like?" Props help children get into character. In *The Three Billy Goats Gruff*, horns made of construction paper bring the goats to life, and a robe and a club add to the troll's fierceness.

USE ART Drawing is a favorite way for children to respond to a story. The drawings may be extended by asking the children to leave space at the bottom of their papers and think of one line they want to dictate to the teacher. The children can rehearse reading these lines and then take them home to read to family members.

Dialogic Reading

When working with individual children, one approach called **dialogic reading** helps put the child in the active role as a storyteller and not just as a listener. Dialogic reading has promoted gains in children's language acquisition and growth in understanding concepts about print (Whitehurst & Lonigan, 2001).

Dialogic reading is intended to be used by parents, teachers, and volunteer tutors, for example, college students working in special literacy programs such as America Reads or Jumpstart. In some communities, training in dialogic reading is available through family literacy programs offered by public libraries. The training is supported by 20-minute videotapes (Whitehurst, 1994). Adult readers are taught to read interactively with the child. Two acronyms, PEER and CROWD, are used to remind the adult readers of the steps. PEER is a mnemonic for a strategy used to nurture language development with younger children as they read a book together with an adult. The letters stand for:

Prompt the child to name objects in the book and talk about the story.

Evaluate the child's responses and offer praise for adequate responses and alternatives for inadequate ones.

Expand on the child's statements with additional words.

Repeat—ask the child to repeat the adult's utterances.

For more advanced children, a more detailed form of dialogic reading called CROWD is used. The acronym CROWD identifies five kinds of questions adults ask:

Completion prompts. Ask the child to supply a word or phrase that has been omitted. (For example, "I see a yellow duck looking at __.")

Recall prompts. Here the child is asked about things that occurred earlier in the book. ("Do you remember some animals that Brown Bear saw?")

Open-ended prompts. Here the child is asked to respond to the story in his own words. ("Now it's your turn: You say what is happening on this page.")

Wh- prompts. The adult asks what, where, who, and why questions. ("What is that yellow creature called? Who do you think Brown Bear will see next?")

Distancing prompts. Here the child is asked to relate the content of the book to life experiences. ("Do you remember when we saw a yellow duck like that one swimming in the lake? Was it as big as this one?")

Shared Reading

Shared Reading (Booth & Schwartz, 2004; Holdaway, 1979) is a strategy for guiding the students' attention through the reading process. It requires a "big book"—a book large enough so that all can easily read the print; an easel to place the book on, so the teacher's hands are free for pointing; and a pointing stick.

Seat a group of up to ten children close enough to you so that they can see the text, and also feel a sense of community. With the book on the easel, use your pointer stick (a ruler or something more exotic, like a Harry Potter wand) to point to each word as you read it. But read the words smoothly and fluently, keeping in mind that you are modeling fluent reading.

Big books are large versions of children's books with print and illustrations that can be read by a group of children. While teachers sometimes make big books themselves, many publishers are producing big book versions of simply written picture books, especially those with highly patterned texts that are especially good for emergent and beginning readers.

Big books can be used to show children the layout of books and also to practice reading and rereading text. In a typical lesson with emergent readers, the teacher reads the book twice.

ON THE FIRST READING

- Put the big book on an easel, and call the children's attention to the cover. Point to the title, and have the students read it aloud with you. Ask the students to say what they think the book will be about, given the title, and invite their ideas and predictions.

- Point to the cover illustration, and invite the students to say what they see. When they think of the title and consider the picture, what do they think will happen in the story?

- Open to the title page, and point to the author's name. Make sure the children understand that this is the person who wrote the book. Do the same with the name of the illustrator. Do the children know any other books by either one of them?

- Now turn to the first page of text and read it aloud, pointing to the words as you go. Read several more pages this way, pausing to discuss a picture or to comment on an action.

- Ask the children to make predictions, even predictions about what will happen on the other side of a page. Sometimes rhyming books have a phrase on one page that ends in a word that is matched with a phrase on the next page ending in a rhyming word. You might pause at the page turn and ask the children what will come next. For example, on one page of John Langstaff's *Oh, A-Hunting We Will Go* (1991), from an English folk song, are the words:

> *A hunting we will go*
> *A hunting we will go*
> *We'll catch a fox*

Before turning the page, pause and ask the children to predict what comes next. The text continues:

> *And put him in a box*
> *And then we'll let him go.*

ON THE SECOND READING   Now get the children to help you read the book.

- Go back to the beginning of the book, and invite the children to read it again with you. Using a stylus or something similar, choral-read a page with the children.
- Still pointing to the words, echo-read the next page with the children.
- Silently point to the words in a repeated phrase, and invite the children to read them.
- Finally, invite individual children to come up and read a line of text as you point to the words.

ON THE THIRD READING   Now you may teach a lesson with the text—using the following activities.

- Cover a word with your hand or with a piece of tag board, and ask students to guess it from context, or from context with only the first letter showing, or the first two letters, and so on.
- Write four or five sentences from the text on strips of paper, and have students arrange them in order in a pocket chart.
- Cut apart a sentence and have a student or students arrange the words in order in a pocket chart.
- Pass out word cards and have students match them to words in the text, or with words that begin with the same letter, or that rhyme with them, or that contain the same syllable.
- Pass out cards with lower case letters on them and have students match them with uppercase letters in the text, and vice versa.
- Point to capital letters at the beginnings of sentences and explain why they are there.
- Point out the function of punctuation.
- Ask students to point to words that show how something looked, or how someone felt, or what someone did, etc.

You may have a discussion of the book. Ask the students about favorite parts of the text. You may put questions to them—open-ended questions that connect to the students' backgrounds, and experiences, and even to other books they have read.

Following the reading with the group, leave the big book available for children to read individually and to each other.

Guided Reading

The **guided reading** strategy, developed by Irene Fountas and Gay Su Pinnell (2001), is done with small groups, usually between four and seven children. The children are grouped by their reading level, and the lesson is carried out with a book that is moderately challenging—that is, one in which children can read about nine words out of ten without help. Ideally, the children are seated at a crescent-shaped table with the teacher inside the arc, so he is close to each child.

1. *Preview the Book.* The lesson begins by previewing the book, both to arouse interest and also to pre-teach a few key words the children might need. You may do a picture walk through the text to support the children's understanding. Introduce the book in a way that connects with and builds on the children's prior knowledge. "Hmm . . ." you might say, "This looks like a story that could be about a friendship; see, it says (pointing to the text) *Lost and Found* by Oliver Jeffers (2005) and if we look at the picture, the boy and the penguin are hugging. What do you think it's about?"

Teach It! 11

Shared Reading

In this modified form of shared reading, the teacher provides guided practice in using comprehension strategies as he "thinks aloud" while modeling effective reading.

2. *Teach Vocabulary.* After children have the opportunity to talk with you and one another, you may then shift to looking at some key vocabulary words from the text that you have prepared in advance on word cards. Remember, too many words can overwhelm children, so just do a few, perhaps only two. As you show the words, pronounce them and discuss their meanings. This is an opportunity for word study to begin, but don't focus on that yet. Rather, the next step is to read the story.

3. *Read and Think Aloud.* Read aloud the first page or two, and think aloud about the characters and their situation. Ask questions to engage the students.

4. *"Whisper-Reading."* Once you decide the students know enough to continue reading on the own, invite them to "whisper-read" the text—reading just loudly enough for you to hear and monitor their reading, but not enough to bother their neighbors.

5. *Monitor Children's Reading.* As the children read, younger children—kindergartners and first graders—are invited to point to each word as they read. (They will be asked to stop pointing once their reading becomes less halting.) Listen for children having problems, lean in and offer encouragement, correct reading problems, and invite children to reread a line.

6. *Discuss.* Following the reading, invite the children to have a discussion about what they read, in order to make sure they see that getting the meaning is the purpose of reading. Ask questions that invite deeper thinking and longer responses: "Why did a _____ do _____? What would have happened if _____ had not _____?"

7. *Teach a Skill.* Later, you may go back and teach a lesson about a specific skill, using words or passages from the text.

8. *Display the Book.* Finally, the books may be set out for the children to reread with a buddy, to practice reading for fluency.

Shared Writing

In **shared writing** (Tompkins, 2000), the teacher and the children produce a text together. The text can be inspired in many ways:

- A counting text based on a theme: "One hungry lion, two scared gazelles," etc.
- A story, perhaps based on a children's book, such as *Frog and Toad* or *Corduroy*
- Seasons or months
- Special things about each student

Depending on the children's needs and the teacher's objectives, the teacher can carefully emphasize the spelling, the way the words are arranged on the page, the punctuation, or the choice of words ("Let's use words that make the readers see what we mean!").

Teach It! 56
Shared Writing

With this instructional activity, young children are invited to collectively compose a text while developing concept of word and building phonics knowledge.

Teach It! 57
Sample Writing Lesson

See how this sample shared writing lesson helps develop phonological awareness as it encourages children to listen for phonemes and "share the pen" as they represent phonemes with graphemes.

Writing Workshop

Beginning in kindergarten, many teachers conduct writing workshops three or four days per week. For emergent readers and writers, teachers begin by reminding children of the topics they want to write about. Children who are reluctant to begin writing immediately might draw a picture of their topic. The teacher reminds the students to leave space at the bottom of the drawing for their writing. The children then have a period of 10 to 15 minutes for writing and drawing at their seats. Those who have drawn pictures write captions underneath their drawings. Then, one at a time, they take the page to the teacher and read it aloud to her or him. The teacher writes the words correctly above the child's words and might take this opportunity to show the children how letters represent sounds. During sharing time, children share their works with the rest of the class.

The writing workshop should have a period of time set aside for focused lessons that show students how to handle particular aspects of writing.

Check Your Understanding 4.4: **Gauge your understanding of the skills and concepts in this section.**

Teaching Specific Skills

In addition to the comprehensive teaching strategies described in the preceding pages, teachers need to teach specific skills, too. Often, skills can be taught as part of a comprehensive teaching strategy, such as shared reading, guided reading, or writing workshop. What matters is that the skills be taught systematically, according to a curriculum of concepts and skills that children need at each grade level. Here we describe skills instruction to develop phonological awareness, to teach the alphabet, and to teach phonics.

Teaching Phonological Awareness

Children who are aware of the sound constituents of words have an advantage when it comes to learning to read words because they will be aware of the units of words that are matched with letters. The National Reading Panel (2000) recommends that teachers teach phonological awareness from kindergarten through grade 2. For students with reading disabilities, phonological awareness instruction may need to be continued beyond second grade (O'Connor & Davidson, 2014). This teaching may occupy a short part of each day—six or seven minutes—to yield the 20 hours a year of phonological training that the NRP recommends. Activities to boost phonological awareness can take place at several levels.

LISTENING FOR SPECIAL WORDS From Mary Hohman (2002) comes the suggestion of using "Magic Words." Say a word like *hotdog*, and tell the children that you are about to tell a story that will have the word *hotdog* in it—and that they should clap their hands when they hear the word. Start telling the story. For instance, you could say, "Last summer I went down to the park. I was really hungry, so I walked up to the food counter and ordered a—hamburger. The waitress said 'We don't have hamburgers. I'll have to make you a hotdog.' "

Make up several stories with the word *hotdog*. Then ask the children to choose a new magic word, and then make up a story that has that word in it. The children can take turns making up stories of their own with "magic words" in them, and tell these stories to others.

Next, raise the level of challenge of the magic word game by asking children to listen for two words together. If those words are *ironing board*, for instance, you might say, "My father was ironing his shirt. He was ironing it on the table, but the table got too hot. He was ironing it on the floor, but the floor was too dirty. 'Daddy,' I said. 'I know. Why don't you try ironing on the ironing board that's in the closet?' "

You can also have children listen for one word repeated two times, such as "Short short."

> *"There was a girl named Short. But Short wasn't short. Short was tall. Her friend Gladys was short. One day Gladys asked Short,*
> *'If you were short, Short, your name would match you better.' "* (Temple & MaKinster, 2005)

CLAP OUT WORDS You can make clapping games that range from the simple to the elaborate. An easy game is to ask children to clap their hands to the words you pronounce. Clapping in a sequence adds more challenge: hands together, hands on knees, hands on chest, hands on sides of thighs. Have children clap to the words as you say these words with emphasis:

> *"When—I—go—to—Lu's—big—house*
> *I—like—to—play—with—Lu's—pet–mouse."*

SONGS, CHANTS, AND POEMS   Songs and chants are a natural way to get children to pay attention to rhymes—and also to memorize words, phrases, and sentences that will aid language development. Songs, chants, and poems are also a lot of fun to learn and repeat.

A song like this one invites hand claps and close attention to the rhymes:

> *"Miss Mary Mack*
> *Dressed in black*
> *Silver buckles*
> *Up and down her back."*

Watch this video in which a child and her grandmother perform *Miss Mary Mack* and answer the question that follows.

 Video Exploration 4.3: **Watch the video (https://www.youtube.com/watch?v=hP9V0S51GVo) and answer questions that reflect the content you have read.**

The lyrics to *Miss Mary Mack* are available in book form. Tutors and new teachers are advised to seek out collections of songs, especially those with tapes. The following are good bets:

Beall, Pamela Conn, Nipp, Susan Hagen, & Klein, Nancy Spence. (2002). *Wee Sing 25th Anniversary Celebration*. New York: Price Stern Sloan.

Beall, Pamela Conn, & Nipp, Susan Hagen. (2005). *Wee Sing Children's Chants and Finger Plays*. New York: Price Stern Sloan/Penguin.

Cole, Joanna. (1990). *Miss Mary Mack*. New York: Morrow.

Delacre, Lulu. (2004). *Arrorro Mi Nino: Latino Lullabies and Gentle Games*. New York: Lee and Low.

Graham, Carolyn. (2004). *Let's Chant, Let's Sing*. New York: Oxford University Press.

Greenfield, Eloise. (2016). *In the Land of Words: New and Selected Poems*. Illustrated by Jan Spivey Gilchrist. New York: Amistad.

Jenkins, Ella. (2014). *123's and ABC's*. Washington, D.C.: Smithsonian/Folkways.

Orozco, Jose-Luis. (2009). *De Colores and Other Latin American Folk Songs*. Los Angeles: Arcoiris Records.

_____. (2002). *Diez Deditos and Other Play Rhymes and Action Songs from Latin America*. New York: Puffin.

_____. (2002). *Fiestas: A Year of Latin American Songs of Celebration*. New York: Dutton.

Prelutsky, Jack. (2016). *Read-Aloud Rhymes for the Very Young*. Illustrated by Marc Brown. New York: Dragonfly.

Silberg, Jackie, Schiller, Pam, & Wright, Debbie. (2002). *The Complete Book of Rhymes, Songs, Poems, Fingerplays*. Lewisville, NC: Gryphon House.

All of these are valuable additions to a teacher's personal collection. Also, experienced teachers know many other songs that you can learn from them. Songs for transitions, songs that introduce tasks, songs to celebrate special people—all of these are essential for a teacher's repertoire. When you find a teacher who knows these songs, write them down! And also, bring along a device for recording sound so you can capture the tunes.

AT THE SYLLABLE LEVEL

- Children can clap along to the syllables in their names—"Bet-ty," "Ta-kee-sha," "Da-vid."
- Children can raise their hands when the teacher says a word with one syllable, two syllables, or three syllables.
- When the teacher says "One syllable!" a child must say a one-syllable word; when the teacher says, "Two syllables!" and calls on a child, that child says a word with two syllables; and so on.

AT THE ONSET AND TIME LEVEL

- Children are asked to supply rhymes to complete couplets such as the following:

  Ding, dong, dell
  Kitty's in the _____ (well)
  Ding, dong, dasement
  Kitty's in the _____ (basement)

Figure 4.2 Elkonin Boxes

SOURCE: Elkonin, D. B. "Personality psychology and the preschool age child." In the collection *The personality development of the preschool age child.* Moscow, 1965.

Ding, dong, dimming pool
Kitty's in the _____ (swimming pool)

- When the teacher says a target word, such as *boy*, the children raise their hands when they hear a word that rhymes with it as the teacher reads from a list of words such as "*tea, tock, tack, toy.*"

- When the teacher says a word such as *bat* and then pronounces the sound /*k*/, the children say a new word that begins with the sound /*k*/ and rhymes with *bat*: *cat*.

AT THE PHONEME LEVEL   There are three kinds of tasks that are generally used to increase children's awareness of phonemes: One is *phoneme segmentation. Segment* means to break something into small parts. Phoneme segmentation tasks have children take spoken words and break them into their individual sounds.

- A spoken exercise goes like this: "If I say *dog* /*d*/ /*o*/ /*g*/, you say *cat, ball,* and *foot* the same way."

- The children place letter markers into Elkonin boxes (see Figure 4.2) as they pronounce each letter sound. Then they say the word that is formed by the sounds (Elkonin, 1965).

- Once children begin to learn letter sounds, they can practice pushing tokens marked with letters. For example, given a card marked with three boxes, and the three letter chips, *l, e,* and *t,* the child places each letter into the box, pronouncing its sound at the same time: *ull, ehhh, tuh* and then saying the whole word *let*.

A second way children become aware of phonemes is to combine phonemes into words. For example:

- The teacher asks, "What word do I get if I add the sounds of *ih* and *tuh*? or *suh* and *ay*? or *cuh, uh,* and *puh*?

A third way that children become aware of phonemes is to delete a phoneme from a word and say the word that is left over. For instance:

- The teacher asks, "What word to I get if I take off the sound *suh* from *slot* Or if I take off the sound *duh* from *find*?

Games that work with phonemes can be playful, of course. For example, the children can sing a song that substitutes the vowel sounds:

I like to eat, eat, eat, apples and bananas
I like to eat, eat, eat, apples and bananas.
I like to oot, oot, oot, ooples and bonoonoos
I like to oot, oot, oot, ooples and bonoonoos
I like to oat, oat, oat, oples and bononos
I like to oat, oat, oat, oples and bononos.

Teaching the Alphabet

"Whole-part-whole" is the mantra of many seasoned teachers. It means *begin by showing students how larger chunks of language are used meaningfully. Then call their attention to the parts. Then have them use the parts in the context of the whole.* That suggestion can be applied to teaching the alphabet. Children pay closer attention to the letters of the alphabet after they have come to notice writing as a holistic display; and they learn the letters as they use them when they are trying to write and read messages.

WORKING WITH NAMES   Cunningham and Allington (2003) suggest that teachers call children's attention to the alphabet by focusing on their names. A teacher writes each child's name on a piece of tagboard and puts all of the names in a box. Each day the teacher draws out a name, and calls that child forward and interviews him or her—asking about favorite pastimes, pets, games, and so on. Then the teacher puts the child's name on the bulletin board and explains that this word is a name. The teacher can point to the letters, reading left to right, and have the children count the letters. Now the teacher can call attention to the letter that begins the name. If the name is *Nancy*, the teacher can ask if the children can spot a small letter that looks like the big letter that begins the name *Nancy*. The teacher can ask if other children have Nancy's letter *N* in their name (each child has her name taped to her desk, of course). Each day another child's name is drawn from the box, that child is interviewed, and the teacher calls the children's attention to the letters in this new name. As this activity is carried on day after day, the children are naming more and more of the letters of the alphabet, including the other letters that make up each name, both upper- and lowercase.

ALPHABET BINGO Another way to help children recognize letters of the alphabet is to pass out cards with the letters of the alphabet written on them where the numbers would be written on a Bingo card, as shown in Figure 4.3.

The order of the letters may be scrambled. All upper- or lowercase letters may be used in the beginning, and then a mixture of the two is used, as children are able. The children are given cardboard chips just the size of the cells. As a letter is called out, each child places a chip over that letter. The child may call BINGO! when she has a row of chips arranged up or down, side to side, or diagonally. Alphabet Bingo cards and markers can be made with materials found in the home or classroom. Watch this video that shows an Alphabet Bingo game made by a parent and then answer the question that follows.

 Video Exploration 4.4: Watch the video (https://www.youtube.com/watch?v=8GG8kq8K4VY) and answer questions that reflect the content you have read.

Figure 4.3 Alphabet Bingo

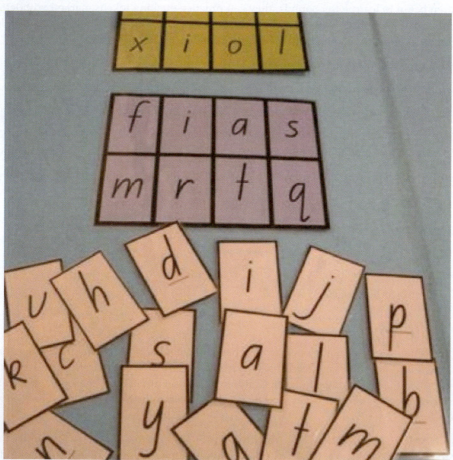

JUMPING LETTERS   From Patricia Cunningham's energetic teaching (Cunningham & Allington, 2003) comes an idea that associates letters with sounds in children's minds. The teacher (or the teacher and the class) thinks of a movement or action that can be paired with each letter of the alphabet. Then the children shout the letters and make the movements: JUMP! for J, LEAP! for L, SING! for S, and so on. The class may go out on the playground to practice these first, to give them an air of excitement, and later the letters may be acted out a little less exuberantly in the classroom. It can be great fun to call out the letter and ask children to perform the action, or demonstrate the action and have children shout the letter.

LETTERS ON THE WEB   There are many fine programs on the Internet that help children learn the alphabet. As you know, such sites can come and go quickly, but as of this writing, the following were good bets.

- "Alphabet Action" Learning Planet shows the letters in order on the page. When the child clicks on a letter, he hears the name of the letter pronounced, and sees a picture of a word that begins with the letter.
- "Mrs. Alphabet" offers songs and chants for every letter of the alphabet, and many other activities.
- "Haunted Alphabet" from Kaboose presents a spooky picture with letters of the alphabet hidden in it. A child clicks on a letter and it is magically transported up to its place in the alphabet. If she clicks on a shape that is not a letter, she hears screechy laughter (which some children will find to be more fun!).

Entering "Alphabet" in a search engine will turn up dozens of activities that can be accessed at no charge, including interactive games children can play on the computer and downloadable worksheets that can be duplicated for the class.

Teaching Phonics

Instruction in phonics, or letter-to-sound correspondences, should begin in kindergarten. Phonics instruction can be a natural part of the comprehensive strategies of guided reading and shared writing, in which the teacher calls attention to the spellings of words, has children predict the letters that spell them, and guides children in reading and spelling words that share the same spelling rimes—(the rime, remember, is the vowel and consonant element that follows the onset: in *bat*, *b-* is the onset and *-at* is the rime).

Check Your Understanding 4.5: Gauge your understanding of the skills and concepts in this section.

Environmental Strategies to Support Emergent Literacy

Environmental strategies for supporting children's emergent literacy are simply the things you want to incorporate into classroom routines and into the physical array of the classroom. The way the teacher talks and models language and the physical classroom itself should demonstrate both the importance of literacy and the way literacy works while also providing many opportunities for children to observe and use written language. There are many ways in which classrooms can be arranged to immerse children in language and print.

Calling Attention to Language and Literacy

Teachers of the early grades are primarily teachers of language. They use language carefully, which means they speak clearly and articulately, and they use interesting vocabulary. They think aloud about words and sentences, calling attention to interesting synonyms and antonyms, to inflectional endings, and to other aspects of language that the curriculum calls out, or that are shown to be necessary by their observations of the children.

PREPARING YOURSELF TO BE A LANGUAGE MODEL   Becoming an enthusiastic and knowledgeable model of language takes more than knowledge of skills; it takes learning a lot about language yourself. If you are still in school, it would be a good idea to take a course in *linguistics for teachers* (such courses are normally part of the preparation of teachers of English to speakers of other languages, or TESOL teachers). Some recommended reading you can do are your own is:

Adger, C. T., Snow, C., & Christian, D. (2002). *What Teachers Need to Know About Language (Language in Education) Language in Education: Theory and Practice*. McHenry, IL: Delta Systems.

Moats, L. C. (2012). *Speech to Print: Essentials for Teachers*. Baltimore, MD: Brookes.

Sacks, D. (2004). *Letter Perfect: The Marvelous History of Our Alphabet from A to Z*. New York, NY: Broadway.

Temple, C., Nathan, R., & Temple, C. (2013). *The Beginnings of Writing* (4th ed.). Boston, MA: Allyn and Bacon.

And, of course, you should read lots and lots of books for pleasure, both children's books and adult books, fiction, nonfiction, and poetry.

A TOUR GUIDE TO WRITTEN LANGUAGE   As models and guides, teachers are tour guides to the details of written language as well as spoken language. With early emergent readers, as teachers read big books or dictated text, they point to each word (to demonstrate the concept of word), they run their hand under lines of print (to indicate the direction in which we read), they point to uppercase and lowercase letters, and they indicate punctuation and what it calls on readers to do.

They point to titles on the covers of books, and the names of authors and illustrators. They lead discussions of pictures and texts and point out when they indicate the same or different things.

COGNITIVE APPRENTICESHIPS   The idea of **cognitive apprenticeships** means that children in school can be considered as understudies or apprentices of skilled language users, readers, and writers—their teachers (Collins, Brown, & Newman, 1987). In an art studio or on a job in the skilled trades, people who are learning a craft work for many years under the direction of people who are more skilled than they are. The skilled master craftspeople or journeymen teach as much by example as they do directly. They learn to slow down their procedures and "think aloud" as they work, so the apprentice can have the richest exposure to skilled practice. In a classroom, a teacher models her own practices in language use, her own thought processes as she reads, and her own decisions as she writes. The idea of cognitive apprenticeships is not so much a teaching strategy as a mindset that a generous and effective teacher can adopt, in order to maximize opportunities to teach children about language and literacy.

Features of the Classroom That Support Literacy

Let's think for a minute about the ways environments support and encourage certain activities. A church might contain quiet space, a lofty ceiling, religious symbols, statues of saints, images of religious narratives embedded in stained glass, writing in Gothic script, and ethereal organ music. All of these were arranged by someone to support quiet meditation and engender what Sigmund Freud called the "oceanic feeling," a feeling of being immersed in something vastly larger than ourselves. A department store has attractive lighting to accentuate the colors of items on display, soft music, walkways that force you to confront item after item, well-dressed and smiling salespeople, and even piped in artificial smells—all carefully orchestrated to put you in the mood to buy something, or, better yet, lots of somethings. How about a classroom? How do you arrange your classrooms to invite and support literacy?

LABELS   Label objects around the classroom with written letters that are readable from far off. Every several days, take time to "read the room" together with the children (Fountas & Pinnell, 1996) as you or a student points to the labels with a pointer or ruler. Remind students to listen for the first sounds in the words, such as in *door* and point out that the first letter in *door* is *D*.

LITERACY PLAY   Make props readily available to support children's dramatic play. Some of these props might include reading and writing. For example, the doctor's office has an eye chart and a pad for the doctor to write prescriptions. Shelves in a grocery store center might have labels (fruit, soup, bread) where the grocer would stock the items, along with pads handy for the customers to use for writing grocery lists.

CLASSROOM LIBRARY   Create a classroom library in a corner of the room. It should have a carpet and comfortable chairs (such as beanbag chairs) for creating an inviting reading environment. Include a space for displaying books so that children can see their covers, and change the books on display every few days to catch the children's attention. Books should accommodate a range of tastes, from informational books with bright illustrations to simple patterned books. On a regular basis, read a book or part of a book aloud and then place it on display in the library corner to entice children to look it over. The classroom library should include books written by individual classroom authors and books written or dictated by the whole class—perhaps books of favorite jokes and riddles, books about animals, and books about the seasons.

CHARTS AND POSTERS   Display on the walls around the classroom posters of children's books and pictures of authors. You can solicit these directly from children's book publishers. Children know authors such as Rosemary Wells, Dr. Seuss, Sandra Boynton, and Mo Willems, and they get excited when the teacher announces that the class has another book by one of these or other authors they know and like. You can also display charts of interesting things, such as volcanoes and maps of the town or neighborhood with the children's street names labeled. You could also include autobiographical posters with each child's name and something special that each child has dictated. Children love to see their own works posted.

CLASSROOM POST OFFICE   Include in your classroom a post office where children can mail letters. Each child could have a mailbox (constructed from three-inch cardboard tubes) for receiving mail. Have children write each other letters at least once a week; the teacher should also make a point of writing something to put in each child's box every few days.

WRITING CENTER   Create a writing center with paper, markers, and pencils. Include magazines as sources of pictures that can be cut out and glued to attach them as illustrations for children's compositions.

DISPLAYING PRINT   Even as you invite children to write inventively, including mock-writing, or read to them and show them print, you also need to show them individual letters and demonstrate how the letters are formed. There are many ways of doing this:

- Alphabet letter cards can be posted around the room, with pictures of objects that feature that letter.
- Games for matching letters, coloring letters, and tracing letters can be laid out for children to play with at center time.
- Magnetic letters and link letters (cardboard letters with edges cut like jigsaw puzzle pieces) can be placed in centers, so children can arrange them to match words printed on tagboard, including their classmates' names. (Note that for beginners, letters all of the same color are preferable to letters of mixed colors.)
- Children can practice writing letters at their desks as the teacher writes a model. They can use large-ruled paper for this or individual slates and chalk. Later, they can practice writing letters with a grease pencil on a transparency film overlaid on sample words with large letters.
- Alphabet strips can be taped to children's desks. A strip of tagboard with the letters of the alphabet carefully printed in lowercase can be attached to each child's desk in front of the pencil tray. Such strips are available commercially, or they can be produced either by the teacher or by an aide.
- The teacher can teach children the alphabet song, pointing to the letter cards on the wall as the children sing the song slowly.
- Children's names can be written on cards and taped to their desks, with the first letter of the first name written in a bright color. Then the children can practice saying, "A is for Ana, B is for Bart," and so on.
- Sandpaper letters on cards can be used in centers for children to trace with their fingers.
- Letter cards can be sent home so that parents can play letter recognition games with the children.
- Alphabet books can be made. Prepare a blank book for the class and print a letter on the top of each page, A to Z. The children think of objects that begin with the sound of that letter and take turns drawing pictures of those objects on the appropriate page.

Teaching Resources

To add to the environmental support for children's emergent literacy, you need books! Books! Books! Some of these you and the children make yourself. Others you can look for at yard sales, or ask parents to donate to the class.

CLASSROOM-PRODUCED BOOKS   Classroom-produced books provide a useful and enjoyable way to showcase children's authorship and to share their works with each other. Single-author books typically are written or dictated by a child (if written, they have corrected text pasted on or written in by the teacher or parent volunteer) and, of course, they are illustrated by the child-author. Composite books are collections that all of the children in a class contribute to. The range of such books is very broad, but for emergent readers, the following are recommended. These can be written by the children themselves (with corrections written in darker ink) or simply dictated. Remember that because the books are intended to be read repeatedly by children, the text should be spelled correctly.

ALPHABET BOOKS   Every child is assigned a letter and writes a word that begins with that letter and draws a picture of it.

COUNTING BOOKS   A group of children are assigned numbers 1 through 10. They draw pictures of 1, 2, 3 (and so on) of something and then write the name of the things (e.g., birds, pennies, cars) next to or under each drawing.

RIDDLE BOOKS   Children contribute individual riddles. The riddle is written on one side of the page and the answer on the other.

JOKE BOOKS   The jokes of five- and six-year-old children are funny, if only for their lack of obvious humor. Individual children can contribute jokes to a whole class book.

CONCEPT BOOKS   Concept books focus on one or a few specific topics, such as kinds of animals, sports, famous people, things to be thankful for, or images we associate with each season. Ideas for topics are limitless.

Check Your Understanding 4.6: Gauge your understanding of the skills and concepts in this section.

Involving Families in Emergent Literacy

The day a child leaves home to enter kindergarten is a poignant one for families. Many parents feel the shock of having well-meaning strangers take over much of their child's upbringing; but for parents who feel "different" from the school because of language, culture, or income, the feeling of estrangement can be particularly pronounced. Kindergarten and first grade are especially important times for teachers to reach out and invite parents to take part in their children's education.

Keeping parents involved in their children's education is important for the children, too. Parental involvement in school is linked to everything from children's academic achievement to good behavior (they will be less likely to be disruptive); and it even reduces the risk that they will use drugs later on (National Center for Education Statistics, 1999. Of course, parents help children's literacy learning at home, too; and the amount of time parents devote at home to reading to their children, telling them stories, and teaching them songs is clearly related to the gains children make in literacy. Likewise, a child's level of reading ability in English is related to the mother's reading ability in English.

But there is good news here, too. Over the last 30 years there have been big gains in the amount of support families give their children in reading—with the biggest increase by far in the poorest families. These increases in parent involvement are the result of enormous efforts by the schools, the public libraries, and even social services—often working together.

For emergent readers, families can be involved in their children's literacy instruction in two ways: in the school and at home.

In the Classroom

First, it is desirable for parents to come into the classroom and take part in activities. They can help move instruction forward by reading to children, taking dictation, and helping to publish and bind books. They can also tell stories, especially family stories; and they can demonstrate family traditions and crafts. In this latter way, they can make their families lives part of the curriculum.

At Home

Family literacy initiatives can also be reinforced at home by sending home to parents materials and ideas for helping develop their children's literacy. Two good examples of home-directed family literacy initiatives are home books and book baggies.

HOME BOOKS   Simple books with very short and predictable texts can be written and sent home for children to read aloud to their parents. Eight-page home books can be made from one sheet of paper, printed on both sides, and assembled with the two double pages stapled one inside the other. Pictures are added to remind the children of what the text says (see Figure 4.4).

The teacher reads the book through twice with the children before they take it home so that they will be able to read it on their own. Instructions go home with the book for parents to read the book with their children and to read it many times, if possible. Home books can go home once a week. They provide useful practice in reading and help children to acquire concepts about print and even sight words.

BOOK BAGGIES   A book baggie consists of a simple paperback book in a bag with an accompanying activity sheet (such as instructions to draw a favorite character, solve a word hunt, or complete an alphabet matching game) and perhaps a recording of the book on tape. Parents are encouraged to read the book with the child and take time to do the accompanying activity. Children should be told how to take care of the book bags when they go home. A book bag may spend several days at a time with each child and then be repacked with a new activity sheet and passed along to a different child.

FIGURE 4.4 A Typical Home Book

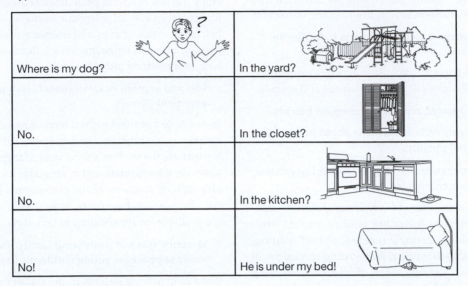

Where is my dog?	In the yard?
No.	In the closet?
No.	In the kitchen?
No!	He is under my bed!

Help with Family Literacy

A parent who was a regular volunteer in a Head Start classroom worried aloud because her child was going into kindergarten the next fall.

"But you can still volunteer in the kindergarten," the teacher pointed out. "They will be happy to have you."

"Me? Suppose they hand me one of those school books to read?" the troubled mother said.

Like this mother, there are parents who do not volunteer to help in school and do not read to their children because they cannot read well themselves. For those parents, the agencies that used to provide adult literacy services are now offering family literacy programs, in which parents who are English learners are taught basic English and parents who need help with reading are taught to read to their children. These programs can be quite successful, since the imperative of helping the children can serve as a motivation for parents to improve their own literacy skills, and the stories they practice to read to their children can be appropriate fare for developing their own reading fluency. Children who do not speak English at home often benefit from participating with their parents in a family literacy program. Watch this video of a family literacy program in action and then answer the question that follows.

 Video Exploration 4.5: Watch the video and answer questions that reflect the content you have read.

For information on programs that offer literacy services to parents, contact the following organizations:

- ProLiteracy (Formerly known as Literacy Volunteers of America)
- The Barbara Bush Literacy Foundation
- The National Center for Family Literacy

Check Your Understanding 4.7: Gauge your understanding of the skills and concepts in this section.

For Review

At the outset of this chapter we stated that when you reached this point in your reading and studying you should be able to:

- **Define emergent literacy.**

Emergent literacy is:

- a period in children's experience between the time when they first notice print and wonder what people are doing when they work with it, and the time when they can read words; and also

- the early informal and formal teaching that children receive in preschool and early kindergarten at the hands of careful teachers who make sure that all children understand what reading and writing are and what they are for, so they can benefit fully from reading instruction.

- **Describe language-based learning as it applies to emergent literacy.**

Language-based concepts include language competence, vocabulary, syntax, and awareness of words and sounds.

- **Describe print-based aspects of emergent literacy.**

Print-based concepts include concepts about print, alphabet knowledge, and phonics.

- **Explain comprehensive strategies to develop general aspects of emergent literacy.**

Many strategies were shared for helping children's general emergent literacy, including reading aloud, interactive reading aloud, dialogic reading, shared reading, guided reading, shared writing, and writing workshop. In addition, "passive" strategies were shared for immersing children in literacy and the language of literacy.

- **Explain specific strategies for developing targeted emergent literacy concepts and skills.**

Strategies for teaching specific aspects of emergent literacy include teaching phonological awareness; listening for special words; clapping out words; teaching the alphabet; using songs, chants, and poems; working with names; playing alphabet bingo, jumping letters, and letters on the web; and teaching phonics.

- **List and explain environmental strategies to support emergent literacy.**

As we noted in this chapter, environments sell. Environmental encouragements and supports for emergent literacy include the teacher's serving as a language model and someone who is interested in language and literacy. They also include features of the classroom—labels, posters, and charts around the room, as well as colorful books that are available for the children to look through and read.

- **Describe ways of promoting family literacy and home support for young children's literacy growth.**

Ways of involving parents in the classroom were shared, and also strategies to extend instruction into the home, including home books and book baggies. Organizations such as the Barbara Bush Foundation are active in the field of family literacy.

For Your Journal

1. Take a moment to review your answers to the questions in the Anticipation Guide that opened this chapter. Has your thinking changed? If so, write about the changes in your journal.

2. Some teachers and literacy experts expect children to learn much of what they need to know about literacy from their own discoveries: from being surrounded by books and charts, being read to, and having chances to read and write on their own level. Others rely less on discovery and plan to teach virtually all the skills of reading. If you could think of these teachers as being placed along a continuum, where along this continuum would you place yourself?

Taking It to the World

1. What are your first memories of reading and writing? Can you remember not being able to read and write? Were you curious about these activities? What things did you do to teach yourself about them?

2. Visit a preschool—a Head Start program, if possible. Ask the teachers what they do to support children's early literacy. How and when are reading and writing used during the day? How have their approaches to supporting children's early literacy changed over the last ten years?

3. To learn about efforts to involve parents in supporting children's literacy, interview an elementary school teacher or administrator. How are parents' ideas and volunteer efforts brought into the classroom? What things are sent home to help parents help their children? What special efforts being made toward increasing family literacy?

4. Continuing with the interview in item 3, how are English learners being supported as they learn to read and write? How is the school working with their parents?

5. Speak with a kindergarten or first-grade teacher about how he or she assesses students' concepts about print and what types of screenings are used to assess students' reading skills.

Chapter 5
Phonics and Word Knowledge

Learning Outcomes

After reading this chapter you should be able to:

1. Describe phonics and word knowledge and explain the difference between the two.

2. Teach children in the logographic phase of word recognition.

3. Define phonemes and graphemes, and explain how they relate to teaching children in the alphabetic phase of word recognition.

4. Explain how onsets, rimes, and phonogram patterns are taught to children in the orthographic phase of word recognition.

5. Differentiate various kinds of morphemes, and teach children in the morphological phase of word recognition.

6. Discuss the importance of teaching students to use word roots and affixes from Latin and Greek sources to recognize and understand words in the derivational phase of word recognition.

7. Teach children to read unknown words in context.

Anticipation Guide

The following statements will help you begin thinking about the topics covered in this chapter. Answer *true* or *false* in response to each statement. As you read and learn more about the topics mentioned in these statements, double-check your answers. See what interests you and what prompts your curiosity toward more understanding.

_____ 1. Teaching children the relations between letters and sounds is all they really need to recognize words.

_____ 2. *Sight words* are words that are not decoded, but that are recognized instantly.

_____ 3. As they learn to read words, children most naturally learn first to read letters, then syllables, then whole words.

_____ 4. *Phonics* is an umbrella term for a variety of explicit, implicit, and systematic ways to show children how the print-to-speech/speech-to-print system works.

_____ 5. Phonogram patterns are closely related to onsets and rimes.

_____ 6. A morpheme is a controlled substance that can only be purchased with a prescription.

_____ 7. A consonant digraph is a single sound—one in which two separate consonant sounds cannot be heard—even though it is spelled with two consonant letters.

_____ 8. Knowing where a word came from can help a person read and understand that word.

_____ 9. A minority of the words in the Modern English language came from Old English.

_____ 10. The English spelling system is so irregular that looking for patterns in it is a complete waste of time.

A Classroom Story

Literacy Activities in a First-Grade Classroom

Maria Gupta plans to show her first-grade students how words are constructed by building them from consonants and vowels. On a digital overhead projector, she places cut-out consonants in one row and vowels in another. She has chosen the letters the children can recognize and name. The children are ready to study ways those letters can combine and spell words.

Poised to begin, she calls the children's attention to the screen. "Class," she says, "here is a way I think you'll find interesting to learn how words are made. Watch me make a word and take that word apart, and make another word!" Ms. Gupta moves the consonant s from the row of consonants. She thinks out loud as she does this, and she continues to think aloud as she moves through the modeled lesson.

"Okay, I'm moving the s. What sound does this letter make?" The children respond with the sssss sound, and she asks for the name of this letter as well. "Correct. I'm putting it down here where I'm going to build a word. But, I think I need more letters to make a word. Now I'm getting a vowel; I'm going to try a, hmm . . . okay, we have sa. I'm going to think of a word that begins with sa; you try, too, and I'll get another letter. I'm going to try t because I may have thought of a word spelled s a t." She moves the letter t beside s and a, and asks the class if they know this word. Many of the children respond correctly, but not all of them. Ms. Gupta says, "Yes! It's the word sat. Let's say all three sounds. We can hear them and then put them together to make sat. Sat is a word!" Ms. Gupta says, "Its nice to learn to make words."

For the next step, Ms. Gupta takes the letters away one by one beginning with the s. She then asks if they can pronounce the at that is left and guides them in deciding together if a word can be made with just two letters. In talk that ensues, Ms. Gupta makes teaching points at each opportunity. For example, she says, "Yes, we can make a word with just these two letters this time because at is a word. But we nearly always need more letters to make a real word in English because we don't have many two-letter words!" Ms. Gupta repeats word building in the same way with other consonants and vowels.

What Is Phonics? What Is Word Knowledge?

Phonics has to do with the relations between **graphemes** and **phonemes**—or to put it another way, between letters or groups of letters, and the sounds they represent. **Word knowledge** is a broader term that includes phonics but also involves knowledge of other aspects of how written words work, such as the morphemes or meaningful word parts out of which they are constructed, their relations to other words, and their histories.

This chapter is about what children need to know in order to read words, and how we can teach them word knowledge. It assumes that the children have reached the point at which:

- They know most of the letters of the alphabet.
- They realize that spoken words can be broken down into smaller units of sound.
- They are curious about the ways that print represents spoken words.

Now they are ready to learn about the English system of spelling, so they will be able to read the words they encounter daily in print, and write the words they want more or less correctly. Fully learning how English words are read and spelled will take some time—years, in fact. Most children can learn the basic letter-to-sound correspondences by the end of first grade, but knowing what to do when you add inflectional endings to words, sorting out homophones and homographs, spelling prefixes and suffixes, and then dealing with morphemes from Latin and Greek sources—well, all of that will take most of the elementary school years.

The relations between letters and sounds in English are somewhat systematic, but they are certainly not simple. In languages spelled with *shallow orthographies* (an **orthography** is a spelling system), where one letter spells one and only one sound, word recognition and spelling are simple and straightforward matters. (Spanish has a shallow orthography: The letter *A* in Spanish spells the sound "ah"' and no other sound; and the "ah" sound is only spelled with the letter *A*.) But over the centuries English has developed a *deep orthography*. The spellings of many of our words don't always have very much to do with their sounds, but rather with the histories of words and their relations to other words. It is not correct to say that in English, simply teaching phonics as the relations between letters and sounds is sufficient. But neither is it correct to say that English spelling has no system. Teaching children to read in English, we may begin by teaching which letters make which sounds, but we cannot stop there. We need to teach layers of word knowledge beyond simple letter-to-sound phonics. Watch this video that explains how word study should be conducted across grade levels and then answer the question that follows.

Video Exploration 5.1: **Watch the video and answer questions that reflect the content you have read.**

Throughout this chapter, we make suggestions for teaching word recognition. But because children develop through phases of word recognition, they need different kinds of instruction at each phase. Over the years as students learn to read and spell words, there are two kinds of developments taking place. One is children's growing awareness of the structure of words. Another is that the words learners encounter at higher grade levels are getting more sophisticated.

Let's look now at phases of word recognition and then methods of instruction that can help children at each phase. Bear in mind that the ages assigned to each phase are approximate, and many children will be found ahead of or behind these estimates.

Check Your Understanding 5.1: **Gauge your understanding of the skills and concepts in this section.**

Words as Wholes: The Logographic Phase

When children are just beginning to notice words around them, they tend to recognize familiar words as whole displays. These children, usually preschoolers and kindergartners, may recognize the word *look* by associating the two O's with eyes. They may identify the same word with different but related names, calling a Crest toothpaste label at one time "Crest" and at another time "toothpaste" (Harste, Woodward, & Burke, 1984). They are not yet reading the letters in the words, but are trying to find any identifiable feature that will help them remember the words, almost as if the words were faces. Frith (1985) and Goswami (2000) called readers in this phase *logographic readers,* which is just a Greek way of saying they are reading words as whole displays (*logo* means "word," and *graph* means "writing"; the term is normally used to describe writing systems such as Chinese, where characters spell whole words).

Children in the *words as wholes* or **logographic phase of word recognition** often give no response at all when faced with words they do not know. They do not yet have a strategy for sounding out words. Marsh et al. (1981) called this phase of word recognition "glance and guess" because children look at a word and call it by the few names of words they know, or say nothing at all. They have no means yet to begin to recognize words by associating sounds with their letters.

Teaching logographic word readers focuses first on having the children amass many words that they can read (Cunningham & Stanovich, 1998; Juel, 1988; Lehr, Osborn, & Hiebert, 2006). To help the children acquire sight words, the teacher may use the strategies of labeling objects around the classroom (the clock, the door, the shelf), doing shared reading, or using the language experience approach. The teacher begins to call children's attention to letters, starting with the consonant sounds that begin words. But the main emphasis is on having children accumulate several dozen sight words—words they can recognize easily—not only to help them begin to read, but to give them the wholes (words stored in memory) from which they can learn the parts (letters and their relations to sounds).

Teaching the Logographic Reader

Children at the logographic phase of word recognition are emergent readers. They are just beginning to recognize words as wholes, so we encourage that. As children learn to recognize several dozen words as wholes, they will pay more attention to the letters that make up those words.

Begin word study at all levels with **whole-part-whole teaching**—that is, by paying attention to words in the context of meaningful sentences before you focus attention on individual words and their parts. The few minutes of extra time that are required to pay attention to the context may well keep some children from becoming confused and will make it more likely that children will apply what they learn from the word study sessions when they are reading words in connected text. Two models of whole-part-whole teaching follow here: the language-experience approach and guided reading.

Teach It! 8

Modified Reading Recovery Lesson

This highly structured lesson reflects whole-part-whole teaching as it supports emergent readers' development of oral language fluency, print directionality, concept of word, sight word recognition, and phonemic awareness.

READING WORDS IN CONTEXT   Children who are getting familiar with words need structured opportunities to focus their attention on the written word at just the instant they hear the spoken word, so they can build a connection in their memories. There are two tried-and-true teaching methods that accomplish this. One is the *shared reading method* (Booth & Schwartz, 2004; Holdaway, 1979), described in chapter 4, and the other is the Language Experience Approach.

THE LANGUAGE EXPERIENCE APPROACH   The **Language Experience Approach**, or LEA (Crawford et al., 1995; Stauffer, 1975), works for people of all ages who are learning to read and need additional support. The LEA is unique in that it uses the student's oral language to teach written language, that is, to teach reading. There are several cumulative steps to take when teaching with the LEA and many variations of it. The following is a step-by-step process we recommend. Use it with a small group or in working with one child.

First Lesson

In the first 20- to 30-minute lesson, complete these three steps.

Step 1: Discussion.   Talk with students about their experiences (e.g., their favorite foods or birthday parties). Respond positively, be curious about their stories, and value their input. Let the children know that you will write down some things from their stories that they can all read together. In later LEA lessons, the discussion topics could be about science or current events.

Step 2: Dictation.   Ask the children what to write, select some of their responses, and write them on large chart paper, an overhead, or a computer screen. Be sure everyone can see your writing. Make teaching points about where to begin writing as you think appropriate. Read each sentence and ask children to read it back to you.

Step 3: Reading the Text.   Now it's time for the children to read their text. But first read it to them again and guide them to watch the words as you run your finger or pointer under them. Then have the children read along with you, and finally they read on their own.

To extend the lesson, give the children copies of the text and have them practice in pairs or alone. Emphasize that this is just practice; give the children time and support to engage deeply in reading their own language.

In this initial two-day cycle of LEA, the first lesson consists of motivation and discussion, dictation and reading, and shared reading, as just described. On the following day, there are several additional steps.

Second Lesson

Step 1: Reading the Text.   Read the text again and prompt careful watching of the words as you point to them. Then have the children read with you. Practice this as much as needed. When reading sounds somewhat fluent, have the children take turns reading on their own. Include everyone. Every child can read, even if it is only a word or two with your support.

Step 2: Reassembling the Text.   Before step 2, make copies of the sentences on sentence strips in the order they appear on the original text. Begin the lesson by having the children look at the whole text and then have them look for the first sentence. As children point out each sentence, put them in a sentence strip holder or adjustable pocket chart one at a time and practice reading them together. Each time, read the sentence and then read the entire text. Again, children can take turns reading individually as they are able. You can also ask children to point at the sentence that tells [fill in blank].

This two-day cycle is repeated once or twice every week with a new theme for each set of lessons. Children will not learn all the words at first, but keep developing new charts for them to maintain interest. Be sure to keep copies available so children can practice. When you notice that children have learned a number of words, you can add a third lesson on sight vocabulary and move on to a three-day LEA cycle.

Third Lesson

Reassembling the Words into Sentences.   Before step 1, cut each sentence strip made for the second lesson into individual words. Place the words in the pocket chart or even on the chalk rail. Place them in a random order and support the children in reassembling the words into sentences. Have the original story nearby so they can refer to it as needed. Build independence by asking children, "If you don't know a word, can you find it in our story? Now read the sentence. Can you read the word?" As sentences are reassembled, guide the reading of the whole text from time to time. Finally, you can implement other word activities. Here are a few ideas:

- Give word cards from the sentences to the children, and ask them to find the words in the text.
- Say, "Here is the word _____ . Find the same word in the text."
- Make a large chart-paper copy of one of the texts with some words left out. Tell the children that some words are

missing and ask if they can identify them. Read with the children, pausing when you come to a missing word. Support them in "guessing the missing word" and write it in.

- Guide the children to write and keep a personal file collection of the words they learn. Begin with a few words and encourage building the collections and game playing with the word cards.

For further support of word recognition, you might color code sentence strips and word cards. Or various colors might be marked on the back of cards. Word cards are inevitably mixed up as children work with them at their desks or tables. They are easily sorted back into word groups of original sentences according to the colors on the reverse side.

Several weeks or even months after the third lesson activities, children will likely show signs of recognizing using letter-sound correspondences in words. This is a signal to add a fourth day to the cycle, one for word analysis using the context of words the children now recognize at sight.

Fourth Lesson

Word Recognition Study. The children read the story, they find words that have the same beginning, and you support their learning to associate letters and sounds using words they already know. Guide the children to draw conclusions, that is, to make phonic generalizations out of their observations of letters and corresponding sounds. Continue to use the written language, the words, sentences, and whole texts that have evolved from the children's oral language dictations. This makes powerful use of their background knowledge and helps them to extend their knowledge of sounds and letters in known words to new words. You can also bring out old LEA charts from time to time for review lessons and practice.

Repeated readings develop fluency and **automaticity** (when children recognize words automatically). As word recognition becomes easier, they are able to focus attention on comprehension (Samuels & Farstrup, 2006).

WORD BANKS   Using either the shared reading method (see Chapter 4) or the language experience approach, you can extend the children's word learning by using *word banks*. Once a student has demonstrated she has learned to recognize a word that is separated from other words, write that word on a piece of thick paper or tag board and give it to her to put into her word bank, a personalized collection of words in a container such as a zipper-close plastic bag or an index card box. Students should practice reading the words in their word banks every day or every other day. They can

- Read the words to partners or to parent volunteers.
- Group the words into categories, such as things, actions, animals, etc.
- Group all the words that begin with the same letters.
- Do "word hunts": look for the same words in children's books.

Try to find time to review each child's word bank every week or 10 days. If there are words the child cannot read correctly, take them out of the word bank and put them in a special envelope inside or beside it. The child can practice reading those words later, and if they are read correctly, the words can go back into the bank.

MORNING MESSAGE   As a technique for getting students to understand written language and focus on words, morning message (Kawakami-Arakaki, Oshiro, & Farran, 1988) gets high marks. Use chart paper or a pocket chart, and write the words in handwriting large enough for all of the children gathered in front of you to see. A typical morning message says

Today is Wednesday, October 17th.
The weather is snowy.
We have art today.
Surprise! Today is Janisha's birthday!

Teach It! 18
Making and Using Word Banks
This personalized collection of known sight words can be used for a variety of activities.

Ask the students what words you should write. If a child says "Today," ask which letter it should begin with. If she volunteers "T," ask if it will be an uppercase or a lowercase T. A child can come forward and write some of the letters for you. The other children can "air write" (make gestures of writing in the air) while one child writes on the chart.

Write some of the words that are often repeated on separate pieces of thick paper. Either tape them to the bottom of the chart or arrange them in a lower pocket of the pocket chart. Invite children to come forward, find the proper word, and either tape it onto the chart (the tape is already placed on the back of the word) or insert it where it should go in the pocket chart. Have the child read the sentence aloud before inserting the word in the sentence; then read the sentence with the word in place.

Next, have all of the children practice reading the lines of print as you follow along beneath the words with the pointer. First, they read the lines aloud as you point, then they choral-read the text, then they echo-read, and then different groups of children are invited to read.

Finally, ask individual children to come forward and point to any words they can read alone (that is, in isolation). Bracket each word with your hands as the child reads it. If he or she is successful, write the word on a small piece of thick paper and present it to the child. That word then goes into the child's word bank for later practice.

LABELING THE ROOM   Each child's name should be printed in big letters on her or his desk. The important items around the classroom should be labeled, too—the blackboard, the clock, the door, the window, the books, science center, the sink—with cards bearing letters 3 inches high so they can be read from anywhere in the room. In time, children can write or trace the labels you prepare. Take time every other day to "read the room": first as a whole class, then in small groups taking turns to read the signs together. Every few weeks, change some signs around (so that the label "sink" is over the door, for instance) and ask who notices anything wrong. Ask the children to move the words to the correct locations.

Words that are used as labels can be put in students' word banks, too, if the students can read them correctly.

Check Your Understanding 5.2: Gauge your understanding of the skills and concepts in this section.

Letter-by-Letter Reading: The Alphabetic Phase

The **alphabetic phase of word recognition** gradually follows the logographic phase. The phase begins when children recognize the **alphabetic principle**; that is, they realize that words can be broken up into smaller sounds (phonemes) and letters can be matched with those phonemes.

After learning to recognize several dozen words as wholes, most children—usually in mid-kindergarten—begin to read words by their letters, but at first not by very many letters. The reader who is early in the letter-by-letter or alphabetic phase might read the first consonant of a word and call it by the name of another word she or he knows that begins with that sound. A word such as *ball* might appear to children like this: *bxxx*. The child might correctly read the word, especially if she is helped by the context (as in "The girl tossed the b_____ ."), but when she sees it alone she might readily confuse *ball* with *bat*, *bark*, or *beep* (Morris, 2005).

As they advance into first grade, most children begin to read more and more of the letters in words. When they attempt to read a word, rather than calling out the name of another word that begins the same way, a child might sound out every letter, even if it means pronouncing something that doesn't make sense. A child might say, "We went to the fire sta-ty-on" instead of "fire station." With practice, students produce fewer nonsense word readings and read words more accurately.

Children are acquiring a growing body of **sight words**, which they can read accurately and quickly without having to decode them. This rapid word identification occurs after a period of sounding out the words, or phonological recoding, as linguists call it. Ehri (1991) suggests that the earlier practice of reading words alphabetically—figuring them out letter by letter—lays down pathways to the memory that makes it easier for children to recognize the words when they see them later. She explains:

> When readers practice reading specific words by phonologically recoding the words, they form access routes for those words into memory. The access routes are built using knowledge of grapheme-phoneme correspondences that connect letters in spellings to phonemes in the pronunciation of words. The letters are processed as visual symbols for the phonemes, and the sequence of letters is retained as an alphabetic, phonological representation of the word. The first time an unfamiliar word is seen, it is read by phonological recoding. This initiates an access route into memory. Subsequent readings of the word strengthen the access route until the connections between letters and phonemes are fully formed and the spelling is represented in memory. (p. 402)

Frith (1985) and Goswami (2000) called readers in the early part of this phase *transitional alphabetic readers*. Those in the later end of the phase they called *alphabetic readers*. In both cases, the important point is that the readers are looking at the relations between individual letters and individual sounds.

Teaching the Letter-by-Letter or Alphabetic Reader (Grades K and 1)

As alphabetic readers, children are beginning readers who have learned several dozen words and are paying attention to the letters in words and associating them with sounds. The goal of our instruction with these children should be to help them notice more and more letters as well as the sounds with which they are associated. It will also help to call students' attention to sounds in words.

Teaching letter-by-letter or alphabetic readers focuses first on teaching children the common letter-to-sound matches—beginning with consonant sounds and then moving on to long and short vowel sounds, and consonant digraphs and consonant clusters. In addition to previously mentioned word study activities, teachers often use shared writing, sound boards, and word walls for this purpose.

SHARED WRITING   Shared writing is a way for the teacher to demonstrate how spoken words are broken into their sounds and spelled with letters, and also to engage children's participation in writing. After sharing a poem or discussing an event that is exciting to the children, the teacher gathers students around an easel and invites them to help him write about what they just heard. First, children agree on a short sentence they want to write, for example, "A firefighter came to school." The children practice saying the sentence several times so that everyone is aware of the words. Then the teacher says, "Now we're going to write the first word, 'A.' Who can tell us what letter we need to write?" A child suggests the letter A. The teacher accepts it and writes it slowly on the easel. Then he says, "We wrote A. Now what's the next word we want to write? Right. It's 'firefighter.' That's a new word, so I'm going to leave space between the word A and the first letter of this new word. [He puts his finger after the A to demonstrate the space.] What is the first sound we hear in 'firefighter'? Right: it's 'fuh.' What letter are we going to use to write the 'fuh' sound in 'firefighter'? Right: It's F. Who can come up and write the letter F for me?" A child comes up and writes the letter. The teacher proceeds in this way, having the children supply the letters they can, and adding the sounds himself that the children do not hear. If a child makes an error in writing, the teacher puts a piece of wide correction tape over the error and helps the children write the correct letter.

Conduct shared writing lessons with the class almost daily when children are in the alphabetic phase of writing. In the meantime, encourage the children to use writing every chance they get.

SOUND BOARDS   A *sound board* (Blachman & Tangle, 2008) is a device for showing students how words are constructed. Sound boards are about the size of a notebook, and are worked with by one child at a time. It is useful to have a dozen sound boards in a classroom or enough for the entire class. They can be used initially for up to six for a group working with the teacher, and another half dozen to have children using in learning centers.

To construct a sound board, cut a piece measuring 11 × 14 inches from a sheet of poster board; then tape three strips of a different color from the board 1-1/2 inches deep across the long side of the board. Now make grapheme cards (cards with letters and letter units) 1 × 3 inches long. Turning them long side up, write letters exactly the same size on the top half only of each card (the bottom half of the card will disappear into the pocket). Prepare cards with consonant letters on them (written with a broad tip marker in black ink) and other cards with vowel letters and vowel teams (written in red ink).

Single consonant cards should include: *b, c, d, f, g, h, j, k, l, m, n, p, qu, r, s, t, v, w,* and **z.** Cards are prepared for **consonant digraphs,** too (a digraph is two letters that spell a single sound). These should include *ch, th, sh, wh, ck,* and *ph.*

Vowel cards should contain *a, e, i, o,* and *u.* Vowel team cards should contain *ai, ay, ey, ee, ea, ie, oo, ou, ow, oi, oy, au, aw,* and *ew.* Vowel-plus-consonant cards should contain *ar, er, ir, ur,* and also *al* (as in *walk, calm,* and *bald*) (after Blachman, 2000).

The top pocket is for storing learned consonants and the middle pocket is for learned vowels. The bottom pocket is for making words. A manila envelope is attached to the back of the sound board for storing grapheme cards.

To use the sound board, put a consonant such as *s* in the bottom pocket. Pronounce its sound. Then put a vowel letter *a* to the right of it and pronounce its sound. Then put a consonant letter *t* to the right of the vowel and pronounce it. Say all three sounds and then pronounce the word *sat.* Now ask the student to repeat the activity, using the same three letters. Take away the letter *s* and ask him to sound the other two letters out and pronounce the word *at.* Then pick up a new consonant letter card such as *p* and pronounce its sound. Put the *p* to the left of *a* and *t* and ask the student to pronounce all three sounds and say the word *pat.*

Sound boards can be used in many ways. To work with beginning consonants and phonogram patterns, you prepare two to four phonogram patterns such as *-ip, -ap, -ick,* and *-ack,* and a set of cards for consonants (such as *l, t,* and *s*) and consonant digraphs (such as *ch, sh,* or *th*). Children can make many words by changing the consonant or consonant digraph before a single phonogram.

WORD WALLS   Word walls (Cunningham, 1995; Cunningham, Hall, & Sigmon, 2007) can provide strong support in children's learning and teachers' systematic instruction. Word walls consist of words that children are learning arranged

Teach It! 19

Word Wall Activities

As children's development progresses, word walls change from picture-word walls to word-only walls like those in the activities outlined here.

alphabetically on the walls of the classroom in ways that allow the words to be easily seen and accessed. Word walls should be interactive, made and used by both the teacher and the children. Much good instruction can spring from various kinds of words on walls, including serving children's self-assessment needs. Here is a brief description of two types of word walls and how they might be used (see also Bear et al., 2007; McGee & Richgels, 2003; Pinnell & Fountas, 1998):

- *A picture-word wall:* Post the words from favorite books, inquiry units of study, and words and pictures with the letters of the alphabet. It is nearly always best if words are put on the wall during the teaching process.

- *A literature-based picture-word wall:* This example can be applied with young children and older children. Picture having read *Lilly's Purple Plastic Purse* (Henkes, 1996) or *Lilly's Big Day* (Henkes, 2006). You introduce the word wall by showing an enlarged picture or colorful sketch of Lilly on the wall with Lilly's name under it. Next, you ask for suggestions about other words children want to add from the book. You write their words in full view, leaving space for the pictures that will come. The children are asked to remember their favorite word. Next, they are asked to draw a picture that depicts or explains their word and to write the word and explanation. The teacher talks the children through some examples of what they might write.

As children's development progresses, word walls change from picture-word walls to word-only walls. Word hunts and word sorts expand the word study. Books are reread to keep a focus on meaningful reading and reading for enjoyment. Imagine the word walls on science and other inquiry work that you can have with middle and upper grades.

SIGHT WORDS Sight word walls contain high-frequency words that are posted as the children encounter them in their reading and in lessons. The teacher should engage children in working with sight word walls regularly (Cunningham et al., 2007). When word walls are used daily in the course of reading, writing, and spelling, they are embedded in authentic literacy practice. This is how you can create and use a sight word wall:

- Add words gradually (about five per week).

- Make words highly accessible by putting them where all students can see them, writing them in large print with big black letters, and using colors for words that are often confused, such as *for, from, that, they,* and *this.*

- Select only the words children encounter most frequently in their reading and the words they use most frequently in their writing. Do not overwhelm them or yourself with too many words. Nothing succeeds like success!

- Practice the words by saying, spelling, and writing them ("do the wall").

WORD WALL CHANTS As the children and the teacher review the words on the word wall, they can use different and engaging ways to spell out the letters and then read the word. Some of the chants can be done with the children at their seats. Here are several suggestions (but you can make up your own):

- *"The cheerleader":* Lead a cheer for the word ("Give me a P!, etc.")

- *"The movie star":* Blowing kisses, like a starlet on awards night as each letter is said, then cheer the word

- *"The chicken":* Flap your arms up and down as you say each letter and crow out the word

- *"The opera singer":* Singing each letter, and finally the word, in an operatic voice

- *"The volcano":* Saying each letter louder and louder, until you shout the word

- *"The nose":* Holding your nose as you say the letters, and then bray out the word

- *"Dribble and shoot":* Dribbling each letter and shooting the word

- *"Pumping iron":* Pretending to hoist a heavy weight as you say each letter; then pretending to put the bar back on the frame as you say the word with an exhausted voice

- *"Boxing referee":* Shaking the hand downward, as if over a fallen boxer, the students shout the letters, and then the word

PICTURE SORTS   Make sets of 1 × 2-inch cards with pictures on them, depicting objects that begin with different sounds. For example, *sun, sail, sand, soda; can, candy, cat, cart, calendar; dog, dart, dish, diaper, diamond; goat, girl, gorilla, guitar, gun.* Place one member of each group side by side on the table. Scramble the rest of the pictures, and then ask a child to name the picture aloud and then place the picture cards one at a time in a column below the appropriate picture. Once children become proficient at this, substitute a card with a letter as the guide card at the top of the column.

Picture cards can be found online and downloaded either for free or for a small charge.

PLASTIC LETTERS   Gather two to five students in front of you. Using sets of plastic letters (some are sold in toy stores with magnetic backs to stick to refrigerators), make a word like *band*. Say the word aloud, and then take the letter *s*. Exaggerate the sound of /*s*/, and tell the students to watch what happens when you substitute the *s* for the *b*. You get *sand*. Demonstrate this several times, and let some of the children make the same substitution. Then hold up the letter *h* and ask who can tell what word we will have when we substitute the letter *h* for the *s* in *sand*. Then follow with *l*. Pairs of children can follow up by playing this game themselves. On other days, you can introduce other phonogram patterns and other beginning consonants.

PUSH IT SAY IT   From Johnston, Invernizzi, and Juel's *Book Buddies* program (1998) comes the *Push It Say It* technique. Here you prepare word cards as follows. One set of cards should be consonants (such as *s, b, c, t, m*), and the other should be phonogram patterns (such as *-at, -it, -op*). To carry out the activity, first demonstrate it to a student, as follows:

1. Put a consonant card and a phonogram card separately on the table in front of the student. Drawing out the consonant sound ("sssss"), push the consonant card forward.

2. Then, drawing out the sound of the phonogram ("aaaaaat"), push the phonogram card forward.

3. Now pronounce the resulting word (*sat*).

Next, provide the student a consonant card and a phonogram card and ask her to repeat what you did.

MAKING AND BREAKING WORDS   Iverson and Tunmer (1993) developed a procedure for "making and breaking words." The procedure is carried out with a set of plastic letters and a magnetic board (available in most toy stores). The procedure can be done one on one, or on an overhead projector (digital or traditional) for the whole class.

Step One: The teacher asks the student to move the letters around to construct new words that have similar spellings and sound patterns. For instance, the teacher arranges letters to make the word *and*. The teacher announces that the letters spell *and* and then asks the student what the word says. If the student seems uncertain, the teacher forms the word again, says its name, and asks him to name the word.

Step Two: As a next step, the teacher scrambles the letters and asks the student to make *and*. Again, if assembling scrambled letters proves difficult, the teacher spreads the letters apart, in the proper order, at the bottom of the magnetic board and asks the student to make the word *and* with them in the middle of the board. When the student has made the word, the teacher asks him to name the word. If the student responds correctly, the teacher scrambles the letters and asks him to make the word again and to name the word afterward. The teacher repeats the procedure until the student is able to assemble the letters and name *and*.

Step Three: As a next step, the teacher puts the letter *s* in front of *and*, then announces what he has just done. The teacher takes a finger and moves the *s* away and then back and says, "Do you see? If I put *s* in front of *and*, it says *sand*." The teacher asks the student to read the word *sand*, and the student runs a finger under it.

Step Four: Now the teacher removes the *s* and points out that with the *s* removed, the word is now *and*. With the *s* pushed aside, the teacher asks the student to make *sand*. If the student correctly makes the word, the teacher asks him to name the word he has made. Next, the teacher instructs the student to make *and*.

Step Five: As a next step, the whole procedure is repeated, making *hand* and *band*. Now the teacher can make *sand*, then *band*, then *hand*, and *and*, asking the student to name each word as it is made. When the student can do so successfully, the teacher scrambles the letters on the board, and puts the letters *s, b,* and *h* to one side. Now the teacher challenges the student to make *and*. If the student can do so, he is now challenged to make *hand, sand,* and *band*. The student is asked to read each word after it is made.

GUIDED READING   As you saw in Chapter 4, guided reading is done with a small group of children or as few as two children to support their progress in reading development, including fluency, comprehension, and word knowledge. The texts used in guided reading gradually become more and more challenging (Fountas & Pinnell, 1996). Even when you want to use guided reading to emphasize word study, it is important to create a meaningful context for the words. Thus,

Teach It! 10

Guided Reading and the Four Blocks Approach

Learn how a Guided Reading format combined with the Four Blocks Approach creates a rich, supportive literacy program.

you begin the lesson with a focus on meaning before proceeding to word study. Detailed steps for Guided Reading are presented in Chapter 4 and in the Teach It! activity above.

Check Your Understanding 5.3: Gauge your understanding of the skills and concepts in this section.

Chunking: The Orthographic Phase

By late first grade and on to the middle of second grade, most children are looking beyond matching one letter to one sound, and are focusing on vowel and consonant combinations, such as -*at*, -*ock*, -*ake*, and -*ight*. Children are able to separate words into *onsets* and *rimes* as Trieman (1985) called them. The **onset** is the beginning consonant sound of a syllable, such as "buh" in *bat*, and the **rime** is what follows the *onset*: the "-at" in *bat*.

Being able to perceive onsets and rimes in spoken words enables children to play with Pig Latin and other rhyming and word games that we saw in Chapter 4. But being able to perceive onsets and rimes also means children in the **orthographic phase of word recognition** can read by analogy. So if they can read *bake* and *take*, for instance, they can also read *rake*, by mentally subtracting the "buh" and "tuh" from those words, sounding our **r** as "ruh," and adding it to "-ake" to get *rake*.

By the way, we sometimes hear the term *phonogram patterns* referring to *rimes*. Technically speaking, a **phonogram pattern** written is the written form of a rime. Onsets and rimes exist in speech, but phonogram patterns are written (*phono-* comes from a Greek word for "sound" and -*gram* comes from a Greek word for "writing"). Whatever we call them, they are the rhyming parts of words like *bake* and *cake*, *dance* and *prance*—clusters of vowels or of vowels and consonants that are found in many words. Wylie and Durrell (1970) scanned a list of 286 spelling or phonogram patterns and identified 37 that each generated at least 10 words. They are:

-*ack*, -*ail*, -*ain*, -*ake*, -*ale*, -*ame*, -*an*, -*ank*, -*ap*, -*ash*, -*at*, -*ate*, -*aw*, -*ay*, -*eat*,
-*ell*, -*est*, -*ice*, -*ick*, -*ide*, -*ight*, -*ill*, -*in*, -*ine*, -*ing*, -*ink*, -*ip*, -*it*, -*ock*, -*oke*, -*op*
-*ore*, -*ot*, -*uck*, -*ug*, -*ump*, -*unk*

Wylie and Durrell's phonogram patterns account for the spelling of at least 500 words. Of course, there are many other phonogram patterns that did not make the 10-word criterion that are useful for students to know: -*alk*, -*ish*, -*eed*, -*eel*, -*eal*, -*eak*, -*oak*, -*old*, -*ow*, and –*y*. You can surely think of many others.

Reading by chunking means not only that children can read letters in clusters, but also that they begin to recognize that some groups of letters such as *bite* have a long vowel sound and some such as *bit* have a short vowel sound, depending on the ways the vowels are marked (in this case, by the presence of a silent E).

Frith (1985) and Goswami (2000) call this phase of word reading *orthographic* (which is a Greek way of saying "writing by the rules") because the children are looking beyond individual letter-to-sound relations to rules that connect larger units of word parts and spelling. (The *orthographic phase* was the last of Frith and Goswami's phases of word recognition. But we have added two more. Read on!)

Teaching the Reader at the "Chunking" Phase: The Orthographic Reader (Grades 1 and 2)

Teaching readers at the chunking or orthographic phase focuses on the common rimes or phonogram patterns. Teachers use word sorts and word wheels for this purpose, and also strategies we saw earlier such as word walls and making and breaking words.

WORD SORTS Word sorting activities include sorting words by spelling or phonogram patterns—for example, words that are spelled like *rock*. Word sorts also may focus on the concepts that words represent—for example, sort all the weather-associated words in one row (*rain, snow, . . .*), and sort all the cooking-associated words in another row (*stove, bowl, . . .*). Word sorting by affixes and words provides sound practice and the kind of hands-on activity that older children appreciate.

Sorting instruction encourages children to see words as objects that they manipulate and own by organizing and classifying them. Jerry Zutell (1999, p. 105) notes, "Organizing objects, events, and experiences into categories and classes is a fundamental way we make sense of the world around us. The act of sorting makes words concrete objects of study."

The first time children do word sorts, it is good to begin with a small-group demonstration. After children have had a lively experience with a text—whether by reading a big book, reading back a dictated story, or reading a trade book—the teacher calls their attention to a small group of individual words. These words are chosen because they share patterns that can be generalized to other words. By *generalized*, we mean that once children have noticed a pattern in one word, they can apply that pattern to help them read other words. For example, the words *sit* and *cub* can be chosen for children who are early orthographic readers, because they introduce patterns that other words share (see below). These words are written on cards of thick paper or tag board. If they will be used in front of a small group of children, use 3 × 5-inch cards.

Now the teacher writes on new cards several words that share the same phonogram patterns as *sit* and *cub*. For example, he writes *fit, bit,* and *kit*; and *tub, rub,* and *sub*.

The teacher then puts the two original cards on the table or in the top pocket of a pocket chart, side by side. He reads both words several times, pointing to each word, to make sure that all of the children can read them. Next, the teacher scrambles the remaining cards. Then, he draws one of the remaining cards—let's say it is *rub*—and holds it up for the children.

"Where does it go?" he asks. "Should I put it in the columns with *sit* or with *cub*?" Note that he doesn't read the word he drew yet.

The children say it goes in the column under *cub*. Then the teacher says, "Let's read down the column. *Cub* and *rrrrrrr*— . . ."

The children say "*Rub!*" The teacher congratulates them, and then he stresses the point that once they could read *cub*, and they saw that the new word began with *r*, they could read it: "*rub*."

Now he invites children to come up one at a time to choose words from the scrambled set and place them under the guide words, *sit* or *cub*. Later the teacher can add another group of words to the sets: *dad, sad, mad,* and *had*.

Watch the teacher and student in this video sort words together and then answer the question that follows.

 Video Exploration 5.2: Watch the video and answer questions that reflect the content you have read.

Group Word Sorts After the children demonstrate that they understand how the activity works, they may practice in pairs. Once the procedures for word sorts have been taught to the class, pairs or trios of students can play word sort games with groups of words that have been prepared in advance. The procedures for the game work the same as in the group lesson just described.

- Prepare groups of words on 1 × 2-inch cards, about the size of a business card.
- Create four to five examples of each spelling pattern.
- Make sure that each student can read at least one word from each group. These words should be used as the guide words. They should be placed at the top of the column, and during the word sorting game, the other words should be placed one at a time underneath them.
- Leave the other cards face up and scrambled.
- Have children take turns choosing a card from the scrambled pile, placing it in the column beneath the guide word, and reading down the column of words.

The Memory Game A memory game can now be used to give children more practice with the patterns. Once the students have sorted the words into their respective columns, they can put the cards face down on the table in front of them, arranged in rows. Taking turns, one student turns over two cards. If they match (that is, if they share the same phonogram pattern), that student gets to keep those cards. They continue playing in turns until all of the cards are paired with other cards and taken off the table (see Figure 5.1).

The Race Track Game Further practice with the patterns can be provided with board games. Groups of cards arranged into patterns make good board games. In the "Race Track" game, a board with fifteen to twenty blank spaces is drawn up (see Figure 5.2). Sets of word cards that share spelling patterns are shuffled and dealt to two to four players. One player

Figure 5.1 The Memory Game

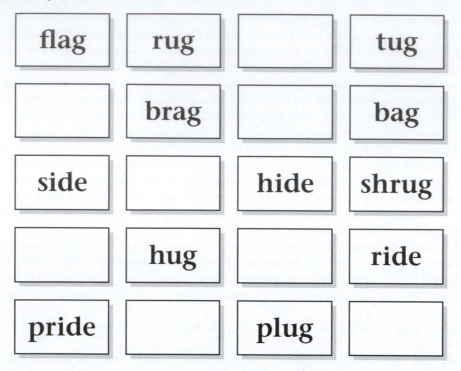

flag	rug		tug
brag			bag
side		hide	shrug
	hug		ride
pride		plug	

rolls one die and moves her marker piece (similar to marker pieces in a Monopoly game) the number of spaces showing on the die. If she is the first to land on a space, she may put down one card on the space. The next player who lands on that same space must put down a word with the same spelling pattern or forfeit a turn. The game continues until all cards are exhausted. Note: It can add a welcome element of chance if you add some wild cards to the stack: "give two cards to the person to your right," etc.

Speed Sorts After children become accurate with word sorts, they can extend their expertise by seeing how quickly they can sort, using speed sorts. This activity supports fluency and healthy competition in a game-like task. (Sixth to eighth graders really like them.) Like so many developmentally appropriate activities, speed sorts build intrinsic motivation and provide that all-important sense of satisfaction!

A speed sort is done as follows:

- Use a timer of some type.
- Children sort as fast and as accurately as they can.
- Children self-assess the sorts with a rubric alone or with another child. If they encounter any uncertainty, they skip the word and later get help with it.

Figure 5.2 Race Track Game for Word Sorts

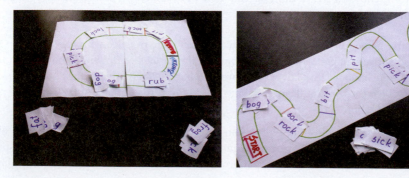

- Children may chart the number of words sorted correctly in a set number of minutes. Once the activity has been taught well, a teacher-made charting sheet aids children's independent charting. Learners thrive on healthy competition with themselves.

Onsets and Rimes for Word Study   The order of words used in word sorts matters. We work in this order:

- ***Start with single beginning consonants.*** For demonstration purposes, we can begin with *m* and *s*. Why those two? Because you can stretch out the pronunciation of the sounds (try stretching out the sound of *t*, if you don't believe us!), and also the two sounds are nicely contrasted. Then you can add *l* and *n* because those, too, can be stretched out. Later, you can add *b, d, f, h, p,* and *t*. Those letters usually represent a single sound each. Choose the most different letters to introduce together. Avoid grouping *b* and *d* because they look similar; and also avoid *d* and *t* because they sound similar. Beginning consonants are introduced with picture sorts, and later you can substitute letters on cards for the pictures.

- ***Then introduce short vowel phonogram patterns.*** Use words with these short vowel patterns:

  -an, -ad, -ap, -at
  -ed, -et
  -it, -ip, -id
  -ot, -ob, -op
  -up, -ub
  -ill, -ell
  -ack, -eck, -ick, -ock
  -ank, -ink, -ump

- ***Now make groups of words with the same short vowel, in different spelling patterns:*** For example, *cap, bad, sack, stab,* and *sank* as a group contrasted with *jump, pup, cut, stub, rut,* and *duck*.

- ***Introduce r-controlled vowels:***
  -ar, ur, -ir, -or

- ***Introduce words with*** *-all*.

- ***Introduce consonant blends at the beginning of words:***
  dr-, tr-, cl-, pl-, st-

- ***Introduce long vowel patterns:***
  -ate, -ake, -ail, -ame, -ain, -ay
  -eat, -eal
  -ice, -ide
  -ool

- ***Introduce patterns with*** *-ook* and *-ull*; and *wa-*.

- ***Then two-syllable words,*** such as *mother, table, kitten,* and *happy*.

- ***Then compound words,*** such as *into, cowboy, steamboat,* and *football*.

- ***Then words with inflectional endings,*** such as *-er, -est, -ing,* and *-ed*.

Word Sorting with Two-Syllable Words   Learners in grades 2 through 4 must learn what happens when syllables meet. This is more of a challenge for spelling than for reading, but readers must be aware of the problems raised by the vowel marking systems of English. For example, the spelling pattern of *bat* is fairly easy to learn. But when *bat* adds the grammatical ending *-ed* or *-ing*, the consonant must be doubled. If it were not doubled, the E or the I would have the effect of marking the vowel in *bat* long, giving it the pronunciation *baited* or *baiting*. Conversely, the final two consonants in *sing* are enough to insulate the vowel from the lengthening effect of *-ing*, so nothing needs be added to its final consonants. And here is an oddity: Because the *x* in *ax* is made up of two sounds, [k] and [s], the X "insulates" the vowel A from the lengthening effect of any following vowel, so we can write *axes* and *axing*. But words that contain a long vowel already do not need to double the final consonant: *dream, dreaming; cool, cooled*.

Children can be taught when and when not to double consonants if endings are added to single-syllable words. To teach children to sort for two-syllable words, begin by making groups of words that double the final consonants before adding the ending *-er* or *-ing*. For example, the guide words might be *batted* and *dreaming*. The "scrabbled" words can be *call, steal, sit, start, run,* and *cut*. Children place each word under a guide word depending on whether the word doubles the final consonant when the ending is added.

Figure 5.3 A Word Wheel

Figure 5.4 Flip Cards

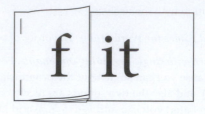

▌ ## Teach It! 16

Word Hunts

This Teach It! activity shows how to construct a word hunt based on a poem to help children make connections between the spelling and pronunciation of words.

WORD WHEELS   On a piece of thick paper or tag board, write a phonogram pattern like *-an, -it,* or *-ock*. Leave space to the left of the pattern. Then cut out a round piece of the same material, and write consonant letters such as *f, s, h,* and *p* (for *-it*) facing outward around the edges of the circle. Attach the circle to the slip of paper with the phonogram pattern using a brad, Children can rotate the circle until a beginning consonant lines up with the phonogram pattern, and then pronounce the resulting word (see Figure 5.3).

WORD HUNTS   Word hunts help children make connections between spelling the words and reading them. This is important because some children do not automatically apply what they learn in word study activities when they are trying to read words in texts. Word hunts also incorporate children's literature, poetry, or other whole texts. Poems that rhyme are especially good fare for demonstrating predictable spelling patterns in writing. Poetry anthologies edited by Jack Prelutsky such as *The Random House Book of Poetry for Children* (New York: Random House, 1983) are good places to start.

FLIP CARDS   Instead of a circle with consonants as in the word wheels, cut out a set of short cards (1 inch × 1 inch), write consonant letters on them, and staple them to a longer card (1 inch × 3 inches) with a phonogram pattern written on it, as shown in Figure 5.4. Children can fold back the short cards to pair up different beginning consonants with the phonogram pattern and then read the resulting word.

Check Your Understanding 5.4: **Gauge your understanding of the skills and concepts in this section.**

Meaningful Word Parts: The Morphological Phase

From first grade up, normally advancing readers enter a phase of word recognition that could be called the phase of reading by *meaningful word parts.* Because those meaningful word parts go by the technical name **morphemes**, we choose to call this the **morphological phase of word recognition**. In truth, it is not strictly a phase, because children can still be learning phonogram patterns (the focus of the preceding orthographic phase) even as they begin to attend to morphemes in words. Also, because some morphemes are encountered earlier than others and some morphemes are more obvious than others, the morphological phase of word recognition stretches over many years. There are three main kinds of issues at play in the morphological phase.

One issue is presented by *compound words* like *fireman* and *birdhouse.* Compound words are made up of two (or more, but usually two) morphemes, each of which could also stand alone as a meaningful word. Readers from late first grade and second grade are recognizing the "small words within the big words," as many teachers put it. Compound words are usually not challenging to understand, but because they add to the length of words, they may make the words daunting to young readers.

Another issue in the morphological phase is recognizing *inflectional morphemes,* such as plural markers and verb tense endings: the difference between *bird* and *birds,* and *want* and *wanted.* These inflectional markers always are attached at the ends of words. They do not change the meaning of words, but rather refine the meaning, as in telling if there is more than one of something, or if an action is happening in the present or already happened in the past.

A third issue is that words can have *derivational morphemes,* too. These are *prefixes* and *suffixes* such as the *un-* in *unkind,* the *-ful* in *helpful,* the *non-* in *nonsense* and also the *-ness* in *happiness.* These morphemes can never stand alone, but they can change either the meaning (as in *kind → unkind*) or the part of speech (as in *happy → happiness*) of the words to which they are attached.

If this no longer strictly sounds like phonics, you're right. As word knowledge advances, many more considerations go into reading and writing words than just letter and sound relations.

Teaching the "Meaningful Word Parts" or Morphological Reader (Grades 3 and 4)

Children in the "meaningful word parts" or morphological phase of word recognition are coping with compound words, grammatical endings, and prefixes and suffixes. There are places for explicit teaching—explanations of how words work—extended exploration of words, and also copious reading for students to learn what they need at this phase.

Teaching readers at the morphological phase, the phase of meaningful word parts, should include explicit instruction about those word parts. Teachers continue to use word sorts, word walls, and making and breaking words and other word-building games. Children also should be encouraged to read a great deal. They need to see many words—thousands of words—used meaningfully in interesting text, and also have their attention called to the structures of words.

Watch this video, in which a teacher uses a word sort to help students examine the structure of words and answer the question that follows.

 Video Exploration 5.3: Watch the video and answer questions that reflect the content you have read.

STRUCTURAL ANALYSIS   **Structural analysis** is the activity of examining the parts of a word to help arrive at the meaning of the whole word. This procedure works when (1) the word is a compound word, or is made up of root words and prefixes and suffixes, and (2) the students understand the meanings of those affixes.

As we pointed out in Chapter 3, English words are built from other words. *Compound words* are built three different ways. Knowing whether to write two words together, like *motorboat,* to join them with a hyphen, like *mother-in-law,* or to write them separately, like *fire truck,* is a challenge for spelling rather than for reading. But readers can find long words like *grandmother* or *grasshopper* to be daunting, so teachers often give the advice, "Find a little word that you know inside that big word," and we hold our thumb over part of the word to focus their attention on the other part of the word.

Make 3 × 5-inch cards with these words on them: *foot, ball, basket, ball, rain, coat, lawn, mower, mother, in, law, ninety, six, ice, cream, desk, top, all,* and *right.* Also, make five hyphens ("–") on cards. Place these in the bottom rows of a pocket chart. Have the students help you assemble words to make compound words. Which ones are joined together without spaces? Which ones are joined with hyphens? Which ones are written separately? For more movement in the classroom, write the words and the hyphens on tablets. Pronounce the words aloud and have teams decide if the students holding the words should stand shoulder to shoulder, have a hyphen between them, or stand apart.

To work with *prefixes and suffixes,* make 3 × 5-inch cards with these prefixes and suffixes on them: *dis-, inter-, re-, un-, under-, -able, -al, -ant.* Place these on the bottom row of a pocket chart. Make another set of cards with these root words: *trust, do, act, depend, believe, stand, nation,* and *consider.* Place these word cards on the next-to-bottom row. Then have the students help you combine root words, prefixes, and suffixes into words that you place on the upper rows of the pocket chart. (As an alternative, you can write the prefixes, suffixes, and root words on small pieces of acetate and have the students build words on the overhead projector.) For follow-up, make a word wall of words with prefixes and another word wall of words with suffixes.

WORD JOURNALS   A useful way to have students record and recall words from word-sorting and word-building exercises is to have them keep a word journal. A word journal is a medium-size spiral notebook, with sections labeled according to the groupings of words it contains. These groupings might contain all the categories into which words have been sorted during word-sorting activities. To record compound words, have the students divide a page with two vertical lines to make three columns. In the left-hand column, they can write compound words that have the parts written together;

in the central column, words joined with hyphens; and in the right-hand column, words written separately. For words with prefixes and suffixes, students set aside half a page each for words with *un-*, *re-*, *inter-*, and *dis-*, *-ant*, *-ful*, and *-able*. They add words to those pages from time to time as they come across them from their reading. The teacher reminds the class to share aloud some of their new entries. These also can be added to the word wall.

Check Your Understanding 5.5: Gauge your understanding of the skills and concepts in this section.

Word Histories and Families: The Derivational Phase

From about fourth grade up, students who read with at least average proficiency can recognize that words like *telegraph*, *telephone*, *biology*, and *biography* contain word parts that they recognize. They may notice that *telegraph* and *graphic* (as in graphic novel) have something to do with each other, which in fact they do: both have the word part *-graph*, from a Greek word meaning "to write." They may notice a shared part in *telephone*, *telescope* and *telepathy*: *tele-*, it turns out, comes from another Greek word meaning "at a distance." Proficient readers may be aware that *sanity* is related to *sane*, *grave* (as in, "a grave look") is related to *gravity*, *sign* is related to *signal*, and *sympathy* is related to *pathetic*. We call this phase *reading for word histories and families,* or the **derivational phase of word recognition**. We say *derivational* because, as you can see, words like we just saw were derived from the same older sources. Word reading at this phase is still further away from a matter of letters and sounds. It combines word recognition and vocabulary knowledge.

Teaching the Reader of "Word Histories and Families," or the Derivational Reader (Grade 4 and Up)

At the phase of derivational reading, the challenges of reading words have to do with:

- Understanding how words are built from historical spare parts from languages that are no longer spoken
- Thinking of relationships between words that have common ancestors
- Reading words whose spellings honor their histories rather than their present-day pronunciation

We use the term *derivational* for this phase because the most common challenge is reading words derived from other words.

Teaching readers at the phase of word histories and families again includes explicit instruction about word families and word histories. Teachers need to make an interesting subject out of the study of words. Students should have ready access to dictionaries with word histories or etymologies. They can be assigned projects in which they research word origins and see how the histories of words relate to their spellings and connect them to other words. Students need to be encouraged to read prolifically, and to talk about interesting words at the same time they discuss other aspects of texts.

WORDS WITH PARTS FROM ANCIENT SOURCES   From grade 4 on, the words children read, write, and spell that come from Anglo-Saxon sources are rapidly replaced by words from Latin and Greek, such as *fortunate, masculine, ignition, sensitive, symphony,* and *microscope* (see Figure 5.5).

Two thirds of the words in the English language are from Old French, Latin, and Greek; and about a fourth come from Anglo Saxon, with other sources accounting for the rest (Finkerstaedt & Wolff, 1973). It is important, then, for word study to continue right through the sixth grade at least, since learning about words in the derivational phase is a different ballgame from the phonics instruction of the earlier grades.

Teach It! 23

Connect Two

For the derivational reader, this engaging prereading activity supports vocabulary growth as it activates students' knowledge of word histories and families and asks them to predict meanings and relationships among key terms.

Figure 5.5 Origins of Words on Graded Spelling Lists

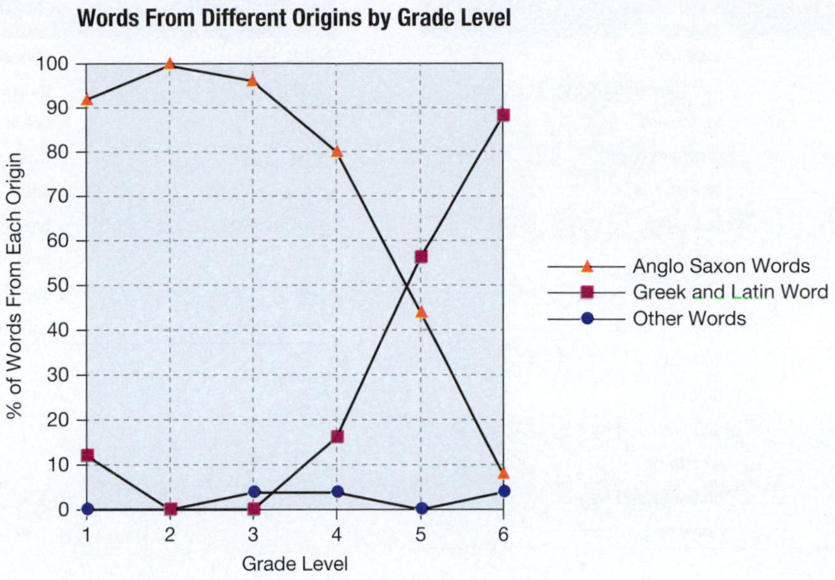

Words From Different Origins by Grade Level

There are four aspects of words from Latin and Greek that teachers and students should be aware of.

- *Ancient stems.* One is the ancient stems themselves, such as *-vis-* (to see), *-miss/mit* (to send), *-grad* (step), and *-path* (to feel or suffer). These stems show up in different combinations to make new words: for instance, *-vis-* gives us *vision, television, revise, supervise,* and *advise. -Miss/mit* gives us *admit, submit, commit, transmit, intermission, mission,* and *remission.*

- *Ancient affixes.* Another aspect is the presence of ancient **affixes**, such as *circum-* (around), *retro-* (back or backwards), *con/com/col/cor* (together [used with Latin stems]), *sym/syn* (together [used with Greek stems]), *in/im/il/ir* (into or not [used with Latin stems]), *ad/al/an/ar* (to or into [used with Latin stems]), *ab-* (from, away from [used with Latin stems], and *a-* (not).

- *Consonant assimilation.* A third challenge that comes up with ancient affixes is **consonant assimilation**, which is the changing of a consonant to match the consonant that follows. When *com-* is joined with *–mit*, it doesn't change: *commit*. But when it's joined with *-relate*, the final consonant changes to match the *r* in *-relate: correlate.* The same thing happens when it joins *-lect* (*collect*).

- *How historic word stems give clues to meaning.* The ancient word roots or stems from Latin and Greek are used again and again in different Modern English words. The stem *bio-*, for example, comes from the Greek word *bios*, meaning "life." It shows up in *biology, biography, symbiotic,* and *biome*. The stem *-meter/metry* comes from the Greek word *metros*, which means "measure." It shows up in *geometry, thermometer, chronometer, psychometric,* and many other words. Knowing what the Latin and Greek stems mean gives a clue to the meaning of unknown English words. For example, if a student knows what *bio-* and *-metry* mean, she may have a general idea that *biometry* means measuring life, which is pretty close to the actual meaning of applying statistical analysis to biological data.

Teach It! 67

Word Origins and Derivations

With a focus on base words and affixes, the language and vocabulary building practices in these Word Origins and Derivations activities help literacy learners in the derivational phase develop a working knowledge of word origins and skills for figuring out meanings of unfamiliar words.

Table 5.1 Prefixes, Suffixes, and Root Words of Latin Origin

Prefix or Suffix	Meaning
con-, com-, col-, cor-	together
ab-	from, away from, by
ad-, al-, ac-, at-	to, toward
de-	down from, off
dis-	lack of, not
e-	out, out of
in-, -il, -im, -ir	into, or not
-ity	state of
re-	back, or again
-ure	state of
pre-	before
-al	characterized by
-tion	a state of
-ary	characterized by
-ist	one who practices

Table 5.2 Roots of Latin Origin

Root	Meaning
-lect, -lege	choose
-ject, -jac	throw
-rupt	break
-tort-	twist
grad-	step
-volt, -volve	turn, roll
-tain	have, hold
-dict	say or tell
-mit or -miss	send

- *Affixes that make derivations.* Students should be able to recognize the affixes that derive one form of a word from another. Sometimes a derivational affix attached the stem is obvious, as in *pure, purity*. Sometimes the stem is a little less obvious, as in *sane, sanity*; or it may be far less obvious, as in *local*, which comes from a Latin word *locus* or "place," which is rarely used.

Teaching students to work with Latin and Greek stems, and also with the affixes that are commonly attached to them, can give them a considerable advantage in understanding vocabulary, especially academic vocabulary.

STRUCTURAL ANALYSIS WITH LATIN AND GREEK PARTS   Make 3 × 5-inch index cards of the Latin and Greek prefixes in Table 5.1.

Display them in a pocket chart for the students. Explain that they came from two languages, Latin and Ancient Greek, that are no longer spoken, but that contribute to most of the words in the English dictionary. Then discuss their meanings.

Then make 3 × 5-inch index cards of the word roots in Table 5.2. Display them in a pocket chart for the students, and discuss their meanings, too.

Have the students help you join prefixes and stems to make words. Discuss what you think the words mean. Then check the meanings in a dictionary to be sure. (Note: Some possible words are *collect, college, elect, object, dejected, eject, reject, conjecture, abrupt, erupt, disrupt, corrupt, revolve, evolve, devolve, contain, detain, retain, attain, contort, distort, retort, torture.*)

Make smaller sets of word cards and have pairs build words with them. Make a word wall on which to display sets of these words. Have students record them in their word journals.

WORD REPORTS   Assign students to teams that will research words that share common roots. Give each team a historical root word, such as *grad-, -meter, bio-, -graph, -tele-,* or *miss-*. Have them look through dictionaries and find all of the words that contain their word root. They may prepare a chart of their findings and present their work to the class.

Check Your Understanding 5.6: **Gauge your understanding of the skills and concepts in this section.**

Helping Students Read Words in Context

When teaching children to learn and recognize words, it is very important to help them connect the words they've studied with similar words they come across while reading various texts. You can help children of all ages become more keenly aware of this in many ways.

Effective teachers know that demonstration and modeling provide a good beginning.

In conducting such demonstrations, model your thinking by thinking aloud and showing the children that this is the kind of thinking they should also do. Imagine yourself reading a text on a large chart or in a big book in view of the children. The conversation goes something like this.

Teacher: Humm. . . . . I'm not sure about this word (silently draw your finger under the word *motorcar*), but it looks like one I know because we did a word sort with *motorboat* in it. And this story is about driving to the store. What do you think, children?

A few children respond that they see *c-a-r* and almost immediately some respond in unison saying, "car!"

Teacher: Nice observation! You saw a little word you knew inside a big word. I like the way you watch carefully and connect words you know with new words. And you are also thinking about what is going on in the story. Good thinking, you used the context!

Once children have been taught through teacher modeling, remind and support them by teacher talk to connect known words to unknown words using everything they already know to learn more and more words. Watch carefully and seize opportunities to affirm children's accomplishments in acquiring word knowledge in their reading.

Word learning strategies discussed in this chapter such as word hunts can also be adapted and expanded. Rather than hunting for the same studied words in books, children hunt for words that are similar to those in a list of known words given to them by their teacher or that they write on their own.

Also, as noted earlier in this chapter, word walls built from social studies, science, or literature units provide words that are similar to studied words. Call children's attention to comparing and contrasting such words to their studied word walls and invite them to find similarities.

A powerful teaching tool for any instruction is your classroom talk and use of language. Often, asking students questions rather than directly telling them something provides strong motivation. Consider a seventh-grade teacher observing a student puzzling over the word *periscope* in a book about submarines. Because in this class they study Greek and Latin roots, the teacher initiates the following conversation.

Teacher: Is there a word you know that looks like this one?

Student: It looks a little like *telescope.*

Teacher: Yes. We've had that one. Do you know any other words that are similar to this one (pointing to *periscope*)?

Student: Well, we also had *microscope* in science the other day.

Teacher: Hmm. . . . what's this book about?

Student: Submarines. Is it periscope?

Teacher: How did you know?

Student: I remembered the scope part. And the "up periscope" I saw in a movie.

Teacher: Great thinking!

Here you saw the teacher guide the student to use multiple cues to figure out the unknown word. As so often is the case, use of multiple cues supports children's literate thinking. Importantly, this teacher's talk attributed competence to the student. This is a wonderful way of building independence and students' awareness that they are in charge of their word learning. Watch this video to see how classroom talk about word meanings can generate excitement and motivate students, and then answer the question that follows.

 Video Exploration 5.4: Watch the video and answer questions that reflect the content you have read.

The Challenges of English Phonics for English Language Learners

English phonics presents special problems to English language learners. Several key differences are listed below.

- In most languages that use alphabets, vowels have one sound only. Different vowel sounds are represented by different letters. Having long and short vowel sounds represented by the same letter, as in English, is contrary to the expectations of speakers of most other languages. Be sure to explain that in English, vowel letters can stand for different sounds, but that there are clues to indicate which sound a letter makes in different environments.

- Speakers of other languages may be puzzled by our labels "long" and "short" for vowels. Actually, the vowels the labels refer to are not long and short at all but *tense* and *lax*, as linguists call them. Some languages really do have long and short vowels: the same vowel sound can be made for a longer time or for a briefer time. Long vowels (long in duration, that is) are often spelled with two vowels in languages that have them, like Saab in Swedish. This may cause confusion for speakers of other languages.

- Speaking of tense and lax vowels, the English language often signals differences between many vowel sounds with the tensing and laxing of the tongue when the sounds are made, such as in *bet* and *bait*. Other languages, particularly Spanish, do not make that distinction. Spanish speakers may thus find the vowel sound in *bait* difficult to distinguish from the vowel sound in *bet*. English also makes a distinction between consonant sounds that are voiced and unvoiced—that is, the vocal cords vibrate the whole time the first consonant in *bat* is made, but the vibration is delayed a bit when the first consonant in *pat* is made. Chinese speakers do not make this distinction, and may have difficulty telling these sounds apart.

- All languages have their own sets of allowable and not allowable sound combinations. Causing difficulty for English speakers are Kiswahili words that allow [ny] and [ng] at the beginning of a word, as in *nyama ya ngombe* ("meat of a cow," or "beef") and words in the Mende language of West Africa that begin with [gb], as in *gbarbartee*, ("turmoil"). In English we find all of the above sound combinations, but only in the middle of a word where two syllables come together, as in *Tanya* and *longbow*, and *tugboat*. In the Spanish language, the consonant combinations [st], [sk], and [sp] cannot begin words, which is why Spanish speakers tend to say "es-school" and "es-sports." Speakers of Spanish will have trouble pronouncing many word-initial consonant blends.

- Students who attended school before coming to the United States may have studied English, but with strikingly different pronunciation from what is spoken here. In East Africa, for instance, what sounds like "way" can be the English word *way*, *were*, or *where*. Be sure to call attention to the American pronunciation of such words.

Check Your Understanding 5.7: Gauge your understanding of the skills and concepts in this section.

For Review

At the outset of this chapter we stated that when you reached this point in your reading and studying you should be able to:

- **Describe phonics and word knowledge and explain the difference between the two.**

Phonics has to do with the relations between graphemes and phonemes. Word knowledge is a broader term that includes phonics but also includes knowledge of other aspects of how written words work, such as the morphemes or meaningful word parts out of which they are constructed, their relations to other words, and their histories. As we saw, it is necessary to focus on teaching not only phonics but also word knowledge, because what children need to know in order to recognize and understand words is much more than a matter of letters and sounds.

- **Teach children in the logographic phase of word recognition.**

The earliest phase of word recognition is when children learn to recognize words as wholes, without sounding them out. This is called the logographic phase of word recognition. Teaching children in this phase employs many methods for exposing them repeatedly to the same words, in meaningful contexts.

- **Define phonemes and graphemes, and explain how they relate to teaching children in the alphabetic phase of word recognition.**

Phonemes are the smallest detectable units of sound, and graphemes are the smallest units of writing—letters, or, in the case of consonant digraphs—two letters that spell a single phoneme. As children ease into the alphabetic phase of word recognition, teachers should call attention to relations between letters and sounds. A host of techniques, including shared writing, "push it/say it," and sound boards are recommended.

- **Explain how onsets, rimes, and phonogram patterns are taught to children in the orthographic phase of word recognition.**

When they reach the orthographic phase, children are reading by onsets and rimes, or phonogram patterns. Onsets are the beginning consonants of a syllable (if any), and rimes are everything that follows. Onsets and rimes are features of spoken language; a phonogram pattern is the written form of a rime. They are important, because relatively few phonogram patterns show up again and again in many words, so if children learn to read by phonogram patterns it expands the number of words they can read. Word sorts and word walls are two good ways to teach children to read by phonogram patterns.

- **Differentiate various kinds of morphemes, and teach children in the morphological phase of word recognition.**

A morpheme is a meaningful part of a word. The varieties of morphemes are root, or unbound morphemes (example: *trust*), inflectional morphemes, which indicate the plural forms of nouns and tense or aspect of a verb (*trusted, trusting*). A derivational morpheme changes a word from one part of speech to another, or changes the word's meaning or part of speech (*distrust, trustworthy*). For students in the morphological phase of word recognition, teachers need to call attention to meaningful word parts, including words within words and prefixes and suffixes. Techniques such as word banks and word building are recommended, as is explicit teaching through mini-lessons.

- **Discuss the importance of teaching students to use word roots and affixes from Latin and Greek sources to recognize and understand words in the derivational phase of word recognition.**

Words with Latin and Greek roots begin to show up in children's reading and writing vocabularies by fourth grade and take on increasing prominence thereafter. Two thirds of the words in the English language come from such roots. The same root may be used again and again, and with the addition of affixes, the possible word combinations are multiplied. In the derivational phase, readers are aware of historical morphemes in words and also derivational relationships among words. Students need to pay attention to historical root words from Latin and Greek, their affixes that may be modified through consonant assimilation, and their derivations one from another. Recommended methods are explicit teaching of roots and affixes, word building, and word linking activities.

- **Teach children to read unknown words in context.**

All of the word study activities explained in this chapter will do little good if students don't use what they learn to read words in real contexts. In this chapter we stressed the role of the teacher as a model reader, thinking aloud to demonstrate how he or she puzzles out the identity of an unknown word when the word is encountered in a real reading context.

For Your Journal

1. Now would be a good time to revisit the Anticipation Guide questions from the beginning of the chapter and answer them again.

2. Imagine a grade level you want to teach or are teaching. Make a list of what you need to know about teaching words. Jot down any related concerns or frustrations you have at this point or anticipate having later.

Taking It to the World

The debate about whole-word versus phonics instruction as ways of teaching children to read has never been as simple as people often make it sound. Virtually all teachers read to children, invite children to write, and give them opportunities to explore meaningful print; and virtually all teachers point out letter-to-sound relationships to children. But there are differences in the amount of emphasis that teachers put on these activities.

Either alone or with a partner, interview two or three first-grade and two or three second-grade teachers about their approaches to teaching reading. What things do the teachers at the same grade level have in common? What aspects of teaching are approached differently?

Ask them also to what extent their reading approaches are left up to their own decisions and to what extent their approaches are guided by reading coaches at the school level or district level.

Chapter 6
Helping Readers Build Fluency

 ## Learning Outcomes

After reading this chapter you should be able to:

1. Define reading fluency and explain its components.

2. Model fluent oral reading.

3. Support children's oral reading fluency.

4. Enable students to practice reading fluency with and without the teacher's guidance.

5. Use performance activities to motivate children to read repeatedly to develop fluency.

Anticipation Guide

The following questions will help you begin thinking about the topics covered in this chapter. Answer true or false in response to each statement. As you read and learn more about the topics mentioned in these statements, double-check your answers. See what interests you and what prompts your curiosity toward more understanding.

_____ 1. Fluency is considered a key area of reading ability by the U.S. government.

_____ 2. Reading fluently consists entirely of reading quickly.

_____ 3. Children who read fluently tend to understand what they read.

_____ 4. Teachers should never model fluent reading for children, for fear of discouraging them.

_____ 5. An average reading rate for a third grader is about 30 words per minute.

_____ 6. Four aspects of reading fluency are accuracy, rate, meaningful phrasing, and expression.

_____ 7. If students practice reading one text quickly and accurately they will become more fluent.

_____ 8. The average fifth grader reads more than half an hour a day.

_____ 9. Setting aside time for children simply to read in school has been shown to boost both fluency and comprehension.

_____ 10. Reading expressively doesn't just sound good; it helps you understand more, too.

A Classroom Story

Volunteer Tutors Help Children Develop Fluency

Katie Flowers directs a tutoring project for a small liberal arts college. The program has worked continuously for 13 years and is very popular with college students. Nearly 100 of them volunteer each term to go out to a local school and work one on one with a first-, second-, or third-grade student who has been recommended by a teacher for extra help.

At the beginning of each semester, the students are given a couple of hours of training. Then they go out to a local school two times each week, both before and after school. Each time the students go out, they follow a lesson plan with five parts. The lesson plan was borrowed from Darrell Morris's Howard Street Tutoring Manual (2005):

1. *Read an easy book to develop fluency.*
2. *Read a harder book to help the children learn new words.*
3. *Do a word study task—phonics or vocabulary.*
4. *Have the child write something.*
5. *Read aloud to the child.*

Katie asks the teachers to fill out feedback forms at the end of each term. Last spring, one teacher reported that over the year a third-grade student progressed from 58 to 153 words per minute. Another teacher reported a big increase in a child's Lexile score on a commercial reading test. These and other comments from teachers attest to the success of the students' tutoring, but they also reveal something else. The teachers' comments nearly all emphasize the aspects of reading that are stressed under the federal No Child Left Behind legislation: phonemic awareness, phonics, word recognition, fluency, vocabulary, and comprehension. Over the past 20 years, these aspects of reading have always been stressed in the tutoring program, just as all of them have been emphasized in Morris's Howard Street model. But Katie realizes she should adjust the emphasis of the tutoring on some of these aspects, at least to make sure the tutoring "stays on the same page" with where the teachers are now placing their emphases.

One area that calls for more attention is reading fluency. Katie sets about making sure her first training session this fall will show her student-tutors how to do repeated reading, readers' theater, and choral reading. She thinks to herself that the tutors and their young charges will need to work in groups some of the time in order to do these fluency activities—and that will bring some welcome variety to the tutoring sessions.

Reading fluency is an important area of children's reading ability. As we will demonstrate in this chapter, if children are to read well, they must read fluently—with appropriate rate, automatic word recognition, expression, and meaningful phrasing. Reading fluency can be taught, and it should be.

Fluency in Reading

"Dance like nobody's watching, . . . sing like nobody's listening." That advice is true whether we are dancing, singing, swinging at a baseball, or reading. Conscious attention to the act itself takes concentration away from the purpose of the activity, and it makes our performance stiff, self-conscious, and not very successful. With regard to reading, it has been demonstrated that those who have to devote close attention to deciphering the words on the page have diminished comprehension—the more they're thinking about pronouncing the words, the less they're thinking about the meaning (Foorman & Mehta, 2002; Perfetti, 1985; Samuels & Farstrup, 2006).

Reading fluency has two parts: effortless efficiency at word recognition and the ability to render the text expressively so that it sounds like it makes sense. Here is the National Reading Panel's (2000) definition of reading fluency:

> *Fluency is the ability to read a text accurately and quickly. When fluent readers read silently, they recognize words automatically. They group words quickly in ways that help them gain meaning from what they read. Fluent readers read aloud effortlessly and with expression. Their reading sounds natural, as if they are speaking.* (p. 22)

Fluency is not just word recognition. Children can score well on word recognition tests without being able to read smoothly, accurately, and with expression in connected text. In between the component skills of word recognition, vocabulary, and comprehension skills and the ultimate goal of successful reading, reading fluency stands in the middle—serving as the organizer that orchestrates those skills and puts them to work in reading text, so that with experience over time, learners will acquire the large vocabularies, the versatility with sentence and text structures, and the background knowledge they need to become successful readers.

Learning to read fluently can be compared with learning to drive a car. Like effortless driving, fluent reading requires the orchestration of many tasks at once. A beginning driver can only focus on one task at a time, but a seasoned driver can change lanes, obey signals, watch for traffic, and choose which route to take, all while carrying on a conversation or listening to a talk show on the radio (but not texting, we hope!).

Drivers learn to drive with some training and a great deal of practice. Readers need practice, too; but most young readers simply don't get enough of that practice. One careful study of fifth graders' reading showed just how scant that practice can be (see Table 6.1).

Table 6.1 Differences in Amounts of Independent Reading by Fifth Graders

Percentile Rank	Minutes of Book Reading Per Day	Words Read in Books Per Year
98	65.0	4,358,000
90	21.1	1,823,000
80	14.2	1,146,000
70	9.6	622,000
60	6.5	432,000
50	4.6	282,000
40	3.2	200,000
30	1.3	106,000
20	0.7	21,000
10	0.1	8,000
2	0.0	0

SOURCE: R. C. Anderson, P. T. Wilson, and L. G. Fielding, in *Reading Research Quarterly, 23*, 285–303 (1988). Reproduced with permission of Wiley Inc.

According to this study, the average fifth grader reads fewer than five minutes a day. That finding prompted one of the researchers to observe, "If you walk into a typical elementary school today, you would have to say that you were among non-readers" (Wilson, 1992). The good news is that 14 minutes of reading per day amounts to a million words read in a year, so efforts to increase children's time spent reading need not change children's lives dramatically to have some results. But such efforts will not soon close the gap between good readers and poor readers. In one year, the top six readers read as much as the bottom six readers would read in 54 years, and the top three readers read as much as the bottom three readers would read in two centuries.

On the positive side, we know that some of children's favorite moments in reading instruction come as they listen to the teacher reading aloud to them fluently and with animated expression, and also when they are able to perform fluent reading aloud brilliantly in front of their classmates (Ivey & Broaddus, 2001). As a second grader who participated in a study of oral reading exclaimed to Martinez, Roser, and Strecker (1999), "I never thought I could be a star, but I was the best reader today."

Fluent reading was itself elevated to star status among the five main emphases in "scientifically-based reading instruction," the approaches sanctioned under the federal *No Child Left Behind* Act in 2003. The implication was reading programs that hoped to receive government funding needed to show that reading fluency was a priority. It also meant that reading experts considered an emphasis on reading fluency to be a best practice in reading instruction.

They still do. Under the Common Core Standards, reading fluency is included in the Foundational Skills for Reading, where the fourth standard in each of grades kindergarten through 5 is the expectation that students will "Read with sufficient accuracy and fluency to support comprehension."

Components of Reading Fluency

Fluent reading consists of four integrated features, according to Rasinski (2003).

ACCURATE WORD RECOGNITION   A fluent reader does not stumble over words but recognizes almost all of them automatically. Accurate word recognition is relative to one's reading level, of course. A text written on a technical subject with many complex and unfamiliar words will be hard for most of us to read with accuracy. For a young student, a text written for older and more advanced readers will be challenging, too.

A REASONABLE RATE OF READING   Fluent readers read quickly enough to process ideas—that is, they don't read so slowly that they have forgotten the beginning of a sentence by the time they reach the end of it. Reading rate, combined with reading accuracy, is often used as a measure of reading fluency. **WCPM**, or *words read correctly per minute*, is a metric for the number of words read in a minute, minus the words read incorrectly. Jan Hasbrouck and Gerald Tindal have calculated average WCPM scores for children at different percentile ranks in every grade level at three different points in the year. Hasbrouck and Tindal's fluency norms are widely used as measures of students' reading fluency. The norms are updated periodically. You can find the latest version by looking up "Oral Reading Fluency Norms" on a search engine.

Bear in mind, though, that there are two more important features of fluency.

MEANINGFUL GROUPING OF WORDS   Grouping words or "**chunking**" is another important aspect of reading fluency. The ways we group or chunk words in a sentence can affect the meaning of the sentence. Consider the sentence, "Poisonous snakes, which should be avoided at all costs, live close to many roadways of Arizona." A fluent reader would read the sentence with pauses for the commas, and the pauses indicate that the phrase "which should be avoided at all costs" refers to all poisonous snakes and not just a few. A disfluent reader who read the sentence without those pauses might draw the conclusion that only some poisonous snakes should be avoided. And that is a dangerous misreading of the sentence. Grouping words intelligently and honoring punctuation are important parts of reading fluency.

EXPRESSIVE READING   Expressive reading is putting correct emphasis or stress on words and adding expression to the reading, so that it "sounds like talk," as many teachers say. Correct emphasis and appropriate expression are actually two different things. Let's consider emphasis first. Putting emphasis on different words can change the meaning of a sentence. For example, read this sentence putting heavy stress on one word at a time:

> THAT is Rachel's old bicycle. (Yes, that one.)
>
> That IS Rachel's old bicycle. (But somebody must have said it wasn't)
>
> That is RACHEL'S old bicycle. (Somebody must have said it belonged to someone else.)
>
> That is Rachel's OLD bicycle. (Not her new one.)
>
> That is Rachel's old BICYCLE. (Not her motorcycle.)

The expressiveness of reading conveys aspects of meaning, too. Consider this sentence:

It snowed last night, and school is cancelled.

1. Read it as if you lived in Florida, where it hardly ever snows.
2. Read it as if you lived in a place where snow was so common school was nearly always cancelled—no big deal.
3. Read it as if you were elated. You get to stay home!
4. Read it as if you were really disappointed—the teacher had something exciting planned.

Together, stress on words and expressive speech are called **prosody**, which is a linguistic term for the "music" of language. Another term for prosody is **suprasegmental phonology**, which literally means the sounds of language in units larger than syllables and phonemes. Research shows that some readers have more knowledge of prosody than others. And those with more awareness of prosody or suprasegmental phonology tend to be better readers with better comprehension (Veenendaal, Groen, & Verhoeven, 2015). If you can teach students to read with proper prosody, you are helping them become better comprehenders.

It's useful for teachers to keep in mind those four aspects of reading fluency: *accuracy, rate, meaningful word grouping,* and *expression*.

Teaching Reading Fluency

How should teachers instruct students to read with fluency? Rasinski, Reutzel, Chard, and Linan-Thompson (2011) recommend that teaching reading fluency include these six emphases:

1. *Model fluent reading.* Teachers should demonstrate both fluent and disfluent reading and discuss the differences, so that children will know what sort of performance they are aiming for.
2. *Provide explicit instruction.* Teachers should demonstrate, discuss, and provide practice in each of the four features of fluent reading described above.
3. *Offer opportunities to read.* As we saw in Table 6.1, children vary tremendously in the amount of reading they do. A goal of teaching should be to give children plentiful opportunities to read, both within and outside of the classroom.
4. *Supply appropriate texts.* Appropriate texts will be accessible to every student—materials that they can read with and without help or with support, depending on the task. They should include a range of genres, with a balance between fiction and informational books. And they should include series books, or at least books by the same author.
5. *Guide students' reading.* Teachers should help students choose books and set goals for their reading. At regular intervals they should engage them in conversations about what they are reading. They should praise students for the aspects of fluency they are practicing, and offer them guidance on the features they need to learn or work on.

6. *Monitor students' reading.* Whether students are reading silently or orally in class, teachers should monitor them to make sure they are staying focused. Monitoring reading means making sure not only that children are participating in reading tasks but also that those tasks require sustained, meaningful reading of texts.

Watch this video in which a literacy expert explains how students become more fluent readers by practicing their oral reading, and then answer the question that follows.

 Video Exploration 6.1: Watch the video and answer questions that reflect the content you have read.

Check Your Understanding 6.1: Gauge your understanding of the skills and concepts in this section.

Modeling Fluent Oral Reading

As a five-year-old, one of the author's daughters loved to pretend-read books. Once she picked up Bill Martin's *Brown Bear, Brown Bear, What Do You See?"* and read, "Wuh, wuh, wuh once . . . thuh, thuh, thuh, there . . . wuh, wuh, wuh, was . . . a buu, buh, buh, bear . . ."

"Annabrooke," I said. "What in the world are you doing?"

She beamed and said proudly, "I'm reading like a first grader!"

The anecdote should make us pause to ask, do our students know what fluent reading sounds like? Many students may not, if most of the reading they hear around them is the word-by-word struggles of other neophyte readers.

Teachers should be careful to provide models of fluent reading for their students. We mean this in three senses. First, teachers should actually demonstrate the concept of fluent versus disfluent reading. You'll find suggestions for how to do this in the Teach It! activity below.

Second, teachers should frequently read aloud to students and entice them with examples of rich language read well. And third, teachers should call attention to the prosody, or the appropriate emphases and expression, of oral reading.

Read Aloud With Expression

When you read aloud to children, you are pointing out for them what is important and interesting in books. You convey enthusiasm and paint events with importance using your voice. Your voice is a marvelous instrument, capable of communicating joy, drama, humor, excitement, and importance. If you do not have very much experience reading to children, or even if you do, it is worth taking the time to become a charming and charismatic reader.

QUALITIES OF VOICE   Have you ever watched a golf coach demonstrate the proper way to drive a ball? The coach will slow down and exaggerate the swing to give the learner time to watch the grip of the hands, the planting of the feet, the rotation of the hips, and the swing of the arms. Reading aloud to children is like that: You slow down and exaggerate the swings of the voice from fast to slow to high to low; you add pauses to create suspense; you read the action as if you were seeing it and the dialogue as if you were hearing it. Listen to a recording of a professional actor reading a children's book. Note the way the actor gives life to characters, creates suspense, moves the story quickly along in spots, and slows it down for dramatic effect in other places. All of these are techniques that you can imitate, and they will add power to your reading aloud.

BRING CHARACTERS TO LIFE   When books have more than one character in them, it helps animate the reading if you read each character's lines in a different voice. Younger characters might get higher voices; older characters lower ones; and wiser characters slower, more thoughtful voices. As a rule of thumb, try to portray personality styles—clever, lazy, humorous, haughty—in the different voices, rather than the character's ethnicity or region of origin—since doing the latter may be offensive to some.

Teach It! 30

Demonstrating Fluent Reading

Learn the components of fluent reading and how to demonstrate them for your students in this activity.

Teach It! 31

Becoming a Model Expressive Reader

See these pointers for developing prosody to become an inspiring, expressive reader.

DEMONSTRATE PROSODY   As we said earlier in this chapter, the prosody or the "musical elements" of sentences are not just engaging to listeners, but meaningful, too. Students should gain control over prosody—that is, placing stresses on certain words, adding pauses in appropriate places, grouping phrases, accelerating and slowing down speech, and varying volume, all in accordance with the meaning and the emotional tone of what they are reading. They can learn these things from teachers who model them well.

How can you become an inspiring model of an expressive reader with command of prosody? Use the suggestions in the Teach It! activity on prosody below.

ENGAGE THE STUDENTS AS YOU READ   When you read a text aloud to your students you should take steps to call attention to your fluent reading. Make sure to point out to students how you:

- Match the emotional qualities of the passages—serious, humorous, exciting, urgent—with your tone of voice.
- Stress the important words in the passages.
- Honor the punctuation—pausing at commas, stopping at periods, and raising your voice at the ends of sentences with question marks.
- Read the dialogues as if people were actually talking.

Your reading will be more successful if you take steps to engage the students as you read. These steps include previewing the text, pausing to raise suspense before important parts of the text, asking for predictions, inviting the students to recite repeated parts of the text with you, and rereading the text to invite the students to recite more of it with you.

Choose Texts for Reading Aloud

Your school librarian, or the local children's librarian, will have good recommendations for read-alouds. There are printed sources you can rely on for suggestions as well. The International Literacy Association annually sponsors the Children's Choices Project, in which teachers across North America ask children to select the books they enjoy most from each year's new publications. *The Reading Teacher* publishes the results. The American Library Association's monthly journal *Bookbird* publishes reviews of books with curricular tie-ins. And the *Hungry Mind Review* publishes suggestions of books that are especially provocative and interesting for young people.

Read books from parallel cultures often. American children are truly fortunate to have books available that reflect the lives of all of our children, from nearly every cultural group and nation. As Rudine Simms Bishop (1999) reminds us, books from parallel cultures can serve as windows and mirrors: as windows into other cultures that are different from the readers' own, and as mirrors of the readers' own culture, to give those readers reflections of their own experience. The best books each year about African American children's experience compete for the Coretta Scott King Award. And the best books about Latino children's experience compete for the Américas Award.

Don't overlook informational books—especially books about science and social studies topics—when choosing books to read aloud. Children enjoy hearing about the real world, too. Informational books for young people are written with as much skill and artistry as fictional works, but listening to them and understanding them exercises different kinds of concentration and comprehension (Duke & Pearson, 2002). The National Science Teachers Association's journal *Science and Children* recommends good titles for children in their field. The National Council for the Social Studies' journal, *Social Studies and the Young Learner*, recommends good books for young readers as well as topics from the social sciences. Finally, articles from the excellent specialized journals on scientific, geographical, and historical topics, such as *Ranger Rick, National Geographic World,* and *Cobblestone,* can make excellent read-alouds as well. Remember, a key to a good read-aloud is that you, the teacher, have surveyed the text, planned how to read it orally, and determined where to put emphasis.

Teach It! 26

Fluency Oriented Oral Reading (FOOR)

This structured oral reading activity offers opportunities to develop fluency using echo, paired, and choral reading of fictional and informational texts.

Extend the Meaning of the Text

After reading a text aloud to the students, you may further engage them with the meaning of the text during follow-up activities. These include dramatizing the students' favorite parts, posing reader response questions, having the students do a free-write, or having them fill out a four-way response chart.

FOUR-WAY RESPONSE CHART   To make a four-way response chart, the students each take a sheet of paper and divide it into four panels. In one panel they write an important quote (younger readers write just a few words) they remember from the text. In another panel they draw a picture of an important character or scene. In a third panel they write about or draw what the text reminded them of or made them think about. In the last panel they write what they liked about the text.

Check Your Understanding 6.2: Gauge your understanding of the skills and concepts in this section.

Supporting Children's Reading for Fluency

There are at least three general approaches to supporting children's reading for fluency:

- Sustained silent reading
- Directed activities, such as repeated reading
- Artistic means, such as readers' theater and choral reading with voice choirs

The Mixed Success of Sustained Silent Reading

In the 1960s, the practice of Uninterrupted Sustained Silent Reading or USSR was introduced to boost the quantity of children's reading. Later (perhaps because of the collapse of the Soviet Union?), the practice was renamed Drop Everything and Read, but the idea was the same: to declare a period of about 20 minutes each day in which everyone in the building—teachers, principal, custodians included—would read for pleasure. There was to be no instruction, no testing, and for the most part little supervision of children's reading during these intervals.

In a report published in 2000, however, the National Reading Panel concluded that there was not enough reliable evidence that supported the benefits of sustained silent reading to justify a recommendation that the practice be used in schools. The Panel did not find evidence that the practice was *not* beneficial, either; but their finding persuaded many policy makers to discourage the use of sustained silent reading, at least during the school day. Independent reading was still assigned after school.

What was wrong with sustained silent reading? Some critics (e.g., Kuhn & Stahl, 2003) worried that many students would not stay on task during sustained silent reading time without monitoring by the teacher, and since the teacher was supposed to read, too, that monitoring would not be available. Others worried that, left to their own devices, students would choose material that was too easy to increase their fluency by much (Shanahan, 2002). As Reutzel et al. (2008, p. 38) put it, "[T]he traditional implementation of SSR (Sustained Silent Reading) has been criticized for the lack of teachers' teaching, monitoring, interacting with, and holding students accountable for their time spent reading." Unless teachers are monitoring them, many students do not actually read during classroom periods devoted to silent reading. Observe the student in this video and then answer the question that follows.

 Video Exploration 6.2: Watch the video and answer questions that reflect the content you have read.

Still, logic (and math) is on the side of sustained silent reading, if it can be done in such a way as to appease the criticisms just mentioned. Given the amount of time children spend reading outside of school (see Table 6.1), just 15 minutes of sustained silent reading per day *triples* the average fifth grader's accomplishment. It amounts to *20 times* the reading done by the least avid five readers and *150 times* that of the two or three least avid readers. That's a lot of bang for 15 minutes of instructional time.

In recent years the practice of sustained silent reading has been redesigned to include monitoring by the teacher and an emphasis on comprehension, and these new practices are showing beneficial results.

Scaffolded Silent Reading (ScSR)

Reutzel et al. (2008) added several enhancements to Sustained Silent Reading in a method called **Scaffolded Silent Reading (ScSR)**. In daily lessons, teachers begin with a mini-lesson in which they demonstrate an aspect of fluent reading. First, the teacher models fluent reading, and then discusses the demonstration, making points about such features as expressive reading, self-correction when she misread a word, meaningful word grouping, or an appropriate reading rate. Then the students read for 15 minutes from a self-selected text on their particular independent reading level (a text at an *independent reading level* is one in which the student reads more than 95% of the words correctly).

Although the readings are self-selected, students must read selections from each of a range of genres of literature: folktales, fables, adventure, science fiction, sports, mystery, biography, historical fiction, autobiography, poetry, and fantasy. Students also are assigned 15 minutes of out-of-school reading each day, which is certified by their parents. The teacher has a five-minute weekly conference with each student in which she monitors the student's fluency and comprehension, and has the student set goals for completing the book. In a study of third graders in four low-income schools, ScSR proved to be as effective in boosting fluency and comprehension as a method that featured repeated oral reading.

Repeated Reading

In **repeated reading**, a child practices reading the same moderately challenging passage repeatedly up to four times until she or he can read it at a predetermined level of speed and accuracy. To carry out repeated reading, select passages of between 50 and 500 words, depending on the reading rates of the children. The passages should come from different sources, but they should be running text and not poetry or lists. Informational text should be mixed in with fiction. Find a text written at each student's *instructional level*—that is, the student should be able to read the text with 90% to 95% accuracy—making one error for each 10 or 15 words. It is important that the text be somewhat challenging, so the student has room to improve. But if the text seems a little too difficult for the student, offer support, such as *echo reading* (you read a line and the child reads a line).

Sit next to the student in a quiet place, and listen as she practices reading the text repeatedly. Keep a copy of the text yourself on which you can mark the student's reading errors. Errors are words that are omitted, or for which other words are substituted, or that are mispronounced. If the student does not say a word, wait two seconds and say the word yourself, and count that as an error. Time the student's reading for exactly 60 seconds, then stop the student, count the total number of words read, and subtract the errors from the total. The child should practice reading the text several times—preferably until she reaches the criterion score for her grade level, outlined in Table 6.2.

Once the child has reached the criterion score, assign her another text of equivalent or greater difficulty to practice reading. From time to time, ask the child to read a passage she has not prepared, and measure the reading rate for an independent comparison.

Keep a record of the child's efforts on a log, such as the one in Figure 6.1.

Table 6.2 Average Reading Rates

Grade Level	Target Number of WCPM
Second half of first grade	60 WCPM
Second grade	90 WCPM
Third grade	100 WCPM
Fourth grade	110 WCPM
Fifth grade	120 WCPM
Sixth grade or higher	140 WCPM

SOURCE: Rasinski, 2003.

Figure 6.1 A Chart for Recording Repeated Readings

Child's Name:				
Name of Passage	Dates Read	Date Ended	WCPM	Comparison Text Rate

Instructions: Record the name of a new text the student is working on, and enter the dates that he or she reads the text. In a separate row, you may enter the date of each day the student reads the same text, and enter the WCPM (words read correctly per minute) attained that day. When the child reaches the criterion score, enter the date of that achievement. Occasionally (at least every two weeks) have the child read a text of similar difficulty that he or she has *not* prepared. Enter the name and date in the first two columns, and enter the fluency score (in WCPM) in the right-hand column.

Differentiating Instruction

English Language Learners

Measures of reading fluency count the number of words read in a period of time and subtract from that number a reader's errors in word reading. Fluency scores may be reported as words read correctly per minute (WCPM) or the reading may be characterized qualitatively on a rubric such as Rasinski and Zutell's *Multidimension Index* (Rasinski, 2003). When fluency assessment is conducted with native speakers, we assume we are testing children's speed and accuracy at reading words, whether the children read words as wholes or decode them. We are also indirectly assessing their understanding of the materials, since being able to follow the syntax of the sentences, the structure of the text, and the meaning of the ideas contribute to the rate and accuracy of reading.

Be aware, though, that English language learners may score poorly on reading fluency measures, but not for the same reasons that native speakers do. English language learners' poorer performance on both rate and accuracy can be caused by difficulties in rapidly pronouncing words in an unfamiliar language (Ockey, 2010). The good news is that such readers may comprehend words that they mispronounce.

The methods in this chapter that provide practice in fluent reading may be challenging for English language learners. The practice of repeated oral reading can be helpful for English language learners, but teachers should take extra care to avoid making it embarrassing. English language learners may read faster silently than they do orally, so practices like Scaffolded Silent Reading are recommended for them.

Guided Repeated Oral Reading (GROR)

Guided Repeated Oral Reading (GROR) is a step beyond repeated reading. The lesson begins with the teacher modeling fluent reading and then discussing what she or he did that made the reading fluent. Then the students are given a section of text written at their independent reading level and asked to read and reread it three to five times. The students may pair up and buddy read (each partner reads a sentence or a paragraph, and the other partner helps with difficult places). Using a fluency phone (see Figure 6.2), made by parent volunteers from PVC pipe, can motivate repeated reading. The student reads the text into the telephone, as if she or he were a news reporter calling in an important story.

The teacher monitors the students' reading and discusses the meaning of the passage with them afterwards.

Figure 6.2 A Fluency Phone

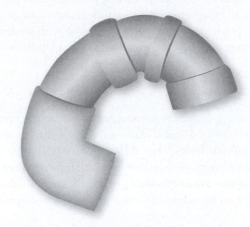

Check Your Understanding 6.3: Gauge your understanding of the skills and concepts in this section.

Practicing Fluency With and Without the Teacher's Guidance

The method of repeated reading requires that the teacher set aside the time to listen to individual students reading. Rasinski (2003) recommends setting aside time each day for repeated reading instruction. If that recommendation is followed, the teacher of a moderate-size class might reach each child for a few minutes each week. What should the students do when they are not with the teacher? Four suggestions are *paired reading, buddy reading, Radio Reading,* and *Fluency Oriented Reading Instruction* or FOOR.

Paired Reading

In **paired reading** (Topping, 1987), a fluent reader is matched up with a less fluent reader. The "more fluent reader" in this method might be a parent volunteer, a tutor from the local university, or even an older student.

The two readers work together on a passage that is chosen at the less fluent reader's instructional reading level. The more fluent reader begins by reading the passage aloud to the less fluent reader. Next, the two read the passage through several times in unison. Then the less fluent reader takes over the reading, while the more fluent reader monitors the partner's reading. The more fluent reader corrects the other's errors by saying the word correctly, and by having the partner reread the sentence in which the misread word occurred. The fluent reader might say, "Read that sentence again and make it sound like you're talking to me."

Labbo and Teale (1990) suggest having a less fluent reader from an older class pair up with a younger reader who needs support and carry out the paired reading procedure. Research shows that the activity can be beneficial to both students.

Buddy Reading

Buddy reading is another way for students to practice reading for fluency without the teacher's devoting time to individual students. At its simplest, two students take turns reading paragraphs of the same text to each other. A more elaborate

Teach It! 27

Paired Reading

This activity contains the steps for a paired reading to do with your students, pairing less fluent readers with more fluent readers to read (and reread) a text together.

version begins with the teacher reading from a big book or a projected text while running his hand under the words and using a fluent delivery. Then pairs of students take turns reading passages from the text (Koskinen & Blum, 1986). How are the pairs formed? In one approach, the teacher divides the students into four groups of readers, from the most fluent (group 4) to the least fluent (group 1). Students from group 4 are paired with students from group 2, and students from group 3 are paired with students from group 1. Some teachers find that students spend more time on task if they are allowed to choose their own partners.

Radio Reading

Any successful strategy to promote reading fluency requires repeatedly practicing reading the same text. A motivator for repeated reading is performance. The strategy of **radio reading** (Nichols, Rupley, & Rasinski, 2009) combines both. The teacher prepares chunks of text at appropriate levels for each student (that is, slightly challenging) and invites the students to reread it repeatedly in preparation for a group performance in which they will read their text aloud as if they were radio announcers. The scripts may be part of the same news show, with each student taking a different part. Only the teacher and each student have copies of the text, so the other students must listen for comprehension.

Fluency Oriented Oral Reading (FOOR)

This strategy combines group instruction with paired study. **Fluency oriented oral reading (FOOR)** (Kuhn, 2004) proceeds in a three-day cycle. The teacher assembles a group of students who are on roughly the same instructional reading level. Copies of the text are provided for the students and the teacher.

Day 1: The teacher fluently reads a passage aloud to the students. The teacher may "think aloud," and call attention to the way he reads the words in groups, and how he provides emphasis with his voice to important words. The teacher may discuss the meaning and invite comments. Then teacher and students echo read the text. They take turns echo reading the entire text.

Day 2: The students pair up and take turns reading the text—each one reading a sentence or a paragraph.

Day 3: The students come back together in the original group with the teacher. Now they choral read the text—that is, they all read the text as if with one voice. The students may take turns reading parts of the text in dramatic fashion, following the ideas of readers' theater.

Check Your Understanding 6.4: Gauge your understanding of the skills and concepts in this section.

Embedding Repeated Reading in Performance

Language education is about more than skill development. Teachers want to cultivate children's appreciation for language and broaden the variety of literature that children can enjoy. So it is recommended that teachers use literary performance as another approach to teaching children to read fluently. Two such activities are readers' theater and choral performance.

Readers' Theater

Readers' theater combines an emphasis on fluency, meaning, drama, and rhetoric, as students practice reading texts aloud and use their voices to convey the meaning of the text. Performing in readers' theater is much like acting on a stage, except that instead of speaking memorized lines, the students read them; and instead of moving dramatically around the stage, the students convey meaning with the sound of their voices and their facial expressions. Readers' theater is most commonly used with fictional works, and when it is, the readers must decide what the characters are like, what is at stake for the characters at each point in the text, and thus how the reading should sound. On the other hand, if the piece is informational or persuasive, the readers must decide what the text is saying, what the important points are, and what kinds of emotions the readers should convey. In either case, students need to practice reading the same passages many times to "get them right." Thus they are doing repeated readings naturally, with the emphasis on meaning.

As they prepare to read a fictional text with readers' theater, players should discuss the setting of the text, who the characters are, and what they are like. Then they should read portions of the text several times in order to read the lines fluently and with the expression that is called for. It helps if the teacher offers coaching, asking the students:

- "What is your character feeling right now? How do you sound when you feel that way? Should your voice be loud or soft? Fast or slow?"

Teach It! 28

Readers' Theater

Learn how to do this engaging activity with your students to cultivate literary and language appreciation while building their reading fluency, comprehension, and confidence.

- "What might your character think about what the other character is saying? How will your character sound, then?"
- "What is going on at this point in the story? How is your character reacting to it?"
- "How is your character changing as the story proceeds?"

As they prepare to read an informational or argumentative text, readers decide what the message of the text is and how they feel about it. Then they decide what points to read with greater emphasis, where to put pauses for suspense, what parts should be said quietly, what parts loudly, and what parts to hammer home. They think about how the beginning and the end of their piece should sound. The teacher's side coaching helps the students make these decisions.

Both the teacher and the other students can offer comments and suggestions after each practice reading.

SELECTING TEXTS FOR READERS' THEATER   Fictional texts for readers' theater can be found in picture books and chapter books, and in the many commercial sets of readers' theater scripts now available. Some of these even have different levels of reading for particular parts so differentiation can occur within the same production. The best choices are those that contain a good deal of dialogue. For example, *White Dynamite and the Curly Kid* by Bill Martin Jr. and John Archambault is written entirely in dialogue. Frances Temple's *Tiger Soup* contains a readers' theater script in the dust jacket. Chris Raschka's *Yo! Yes?* is a simple dialogue between two little boys with a multicultural theme. When using longer books, choose dialogues taken from pivotal scenes in the plot. *Roll of Thunder, Hear My Cry* by Mildred Taylor contains many scenes in which confrontations between people of different races are thoughtfully handled. Kate DiCamillo's *Because of Winn Dixie* contains many poignant encounters between characters. Informational or argumentative texts should be interesting and powerful. News stories of historical events make good texts for readers' theater. So do speeches, such as Martin Luther King Jr.'s "I Have a Dream" speech.

To get the class ready for a readers' theater activity, do the following:

1. Make a photocopy of the text you plan to use for readers' theater.
2. Read through the text and mark the parts that should be read by different readers. Create a code for different readers, such as a capital letter to represent the name of each different character, and a capital N followed by a number for narrator number 1, 2, 3, and so on.
3. Put brackets [ ] around the parts that will be read by each reader, and write in a letter over each section to indicate who should read it.
4. Strike through any parts that do not need to be read. Often "He said," "she replied" and the like can be eliminated without affecting the meaning.
5. The text can be duplicated and distributed with the marks just described—but it will be easier for students to read if you type it out with each character's name by his or her part.

Scripted texts for readers' theater are available in which roles are identified for readers of different levels of fluency. Books containing readers' theater scripts include the following:

Braun, W., & Braun, C. (1995). *Readers' theater: Scripted rhymes and rhythms.* Calgary, Alberta: Braun and Braun Educational Enterprises.

Coleman, M., Farley, J., & Holliday, S. (2001). *Readers theater level 1.* Columbus, OH: McGraw-Hill. (grade levels 2–5)

Crawford, S. A., &. Sanders, N. I. (1999). *15 irresistible mini-plays for teaching math.* New York, NY: Scholastic.

Farley, J., & Sishton, J. (2001) *Readers theater level 2.* Columbus, OH: McGraw-Hill. (grade levels 3–7)

Glassock, S. (1995). *10 American history plays for the classroom.* New York, NY: Scholastic.

Glassock, S. (2001). *10 Easy-to-read American history plays that reach all readers.* New York, NY: Scholastic.

Hoberman, M. A. (2001). *You read to me, I'll read to you*. Boston, MA: Little, Brown.

Haven, K. (1996). *Great moments in science*. Englewood, CO: Teacher Ideas Press.

Pugliano-Martin. C. (2000). *25 just-right plays for emergent readers*. New York, NY: Scholastic.

Pugliano-Martin, C. (1999). *25 Spanish plays for emergent readers*. New York, NY: Scholastic.

Worthy, J. (2005). *Readers theater for building fluency*. New York, NY: Scholastic. (grade levels 3–6)

When you assign roles in readers' theater, you can give all the students roughly equal chances to participate. There can be several narrators. Students can read the lines for more than one character (although if they do, they should read the same characters' lines consistently—and they might develop different voices for different characters). The same script can be read by more than one group, and the "readings" (as in interpretations) can be compared later. Another way to involve more students is to choose different scenes from a longer work, and assign each scene to a smaller group of students.

Choral Reading in Voice Choirs

Choral reading is another performance-oriented way of practicing reading for fluency. As in readers' theater, because students are reading and rereading to get just the right sounds to convey meanings and emotions, the practice of repeated reading is embedded in a meaning-driven activity. Choral reading in **voice choirs** can be done with poetry, speeches, or other texts. When they are choral reading poetry, readers should practice over and over again to get the sounds right. What are the possible variations of sound? Texts may be read:

- By the whole chorus, by individuals, by pairs, or by two alternating sections
- In loud or soft voices
- Rapidly or slowly
- Melodiously, angrily, giggling, or seriously

VOICES IN UNISON   When children chorally read a poem in unison, you can add an emphasis on meaning to the practice of reading for fluency by discussing the circumstances or the context in which it might be said. For example, the following poem, "The Grand Old Duke of York," has a martial rhythm, so you can invite the children to imagine they are a platoon of soldiers marching along a road. From a single vantage point, they are very quiet when they are heard from a distance, then louder as they approach, then very loud when they are right in front of the person, then quieter until they are very quiet. Have them practice reading the poem in unison, going from very quiet to VERY LOUD to very quiet again.

The Grand Old Duke of York (Traditional)

The Grand Old Duke of York
> *He had ten thousand men.*
He always marched them up the hill
> *Then he marched them down again.*
And when they were up they were up.
> *And when they were down they were down.*
And when they were only halfway up
> *They were neither up nor down.*

Watch this video of a class of young learners reading "Humpty Dumpty" together and then answer the question that follows.

 Video Exploration 6.3: Watch the video and answer questions that reflect the content you have read.

POEMS IN TWO PARTS   Reading poems in two parts, or *antiphonally*, allows a sort of call-and-response or dialogue pattern. It is more challenging for two groups of children to read different lines of the same poem while keeping the rhythm intact, and the challenge leads naturally to many repeated readings as the children work to perfect their reading. The repeated reading is desirable, of course, because the practice builds fluency.

"Come Play Catch?" by Bucksnort Trout can be read either by two individual children or by two groups. One group takes the words on the left and the other takes the words on the right. The children should practice reading the poem until they can keep up the rhythm perfectly.

Come Play Catch?

Hey, Cousin Kenny, can you come play catch?
> *Can you catch come, come? Can you come play catch?*

Whatcha say, Cousin Kenny, can you come play catch?
> *Can you come catch, come play catch—huh?*

Hey, Aunt Jody, can you come jump rope?
> *Can you rope jump, jump? Can you come jump rope?*

Whatcha say, Aunt Jody, can you come jump rope?
> *Can you rope jump, come jump rope—huh?*

Hey, Uncle Harry, can you come hopscotch?
> *Can you scotch hop, hop? Can you come hop scotch?*

Whatcha say, Uncle Harry, can you come hop scotch?
> *Can you scotch hop, come hop scotch—huh?*

Hey, gorilla, will you put me down?
> *Will you down, put, put? Pretty please, down, down?*

Whatcha say, gorilla, will you put me down?
> *Will you down put, put me down—huh?*

To add an emphasis on meaning, the teacher can provide a context and roles for the speakers of the two parts. The following traditional poem, "It's Time to Go to Bed," can be read with the left-hand lines spoken by a patient mother to a grumpy child, whose lines are on the right. Then the children can be asked to read the poem several more times, with the mother growing increasingly impatient and the child growing increasingly stubborn. Of course, many other scenarios are possible.

It's Time To Go To Bed

It's time to go to bed.
> *What time is it?*

It's time to go to bed.
> *What time is it?*

It's time to go to bed.
> *I don't want to go to bed.*

You have to go to bed.
> *What time is it?*

You've got to go to bed.
> *I don't want to go to bed.*

You must go to bed.
> *I don't want to go to bed.*
> *I'm not sleepy.*
> *I'm not sleepy.*

It's time to get up.
> *What time is it?*

It's time to get up.
> *What time is it?*

It's time to get up.
> *I don't want to get up.*

You have to get up.
> *I don't want to get up.*

You've got to get up.
> *I don't want to get up.*

You must get up.
> *I don't want to get up.*
> *I don't want to get up.*
> *I'm sleepy.*
> *I'm sleepy.*
> (Preece, 2009)

POEMS IN ROUNDS *Rounds* are songs and poems that are sung or read with the same lines read by different people beginning at different times so the words overlap each other. Reading poems in rounds adds another layer of challenge that requires still more practice—and, as we have said, practice means repeated reading, which leads to fluency. The country poem, "Can you dig that crazy music?" whose author is anonymous, can be said as a round, with up to three parts. When they are performing the poem, have each group begin reading right after the group before it completes the first line. Have each group read the poem through two times fully, going straight without a pause from the last line on the first reading to the first line on the second reading. The second time through, the first group repeats the last line while the second group reads it, and then the first and second group repeat the last line as the third group reads it. It helps if someone claps to keep time.

> *"Can you dig that crazy music?"*
> *Can you dig it, Can you dig it, Can you dig it, Can you dig it?*
> *Can you dig that crazy music?*
> *Can you dig it, Can you dig it, Can you dig it, Can you dig it?*
> *Oh, look. Here's a chicken come struttin' down the road.*
> *Now, now. There's another on a barbed wire fence.*
> *Maaaaaa-ma! Maaaaaa-ma!*
> *Get that son-of-a-gun off my porch!*

Check Your Understanding 6.5: Gauge your understanding of the skills and concepts in this section.

For Review

At the outset of this chapter we stated that when you reached this point in your reading and studying you should be able to:

- **Define reading fluency and explain its components.**

Reading fluency is automatic word recognition at a reasonable rate and with meaningful "chunking" and expression. Its components are accurate word recognition, an adequate reading rate, sensible phrasing, and reading with expression. Reading fluently boosts comprehension: The more naturally and fluently a child reads, the more attention that child will have left over to think about what she or he is reading.

- **Model fluent oral reading.**

Fluency can be learned. Teaching children to read particular texts fluently will carry over to their reading of other texts. Approaches to teaching reading for fluency include modeling fluent reading. Modeling fluency is important not only because children need to understand what the target is but also because an important aspect of

fluency—prosody or suprasegmental phonology—should be modeled by the teacher.

- **Support children's oral reading fluency.**

The chapter shared strategies that the teacher can use to guide students' reading for fluency, and also to have them practice reading with each other. The method of repeated reading has been shown to be effective in boosting fluency rates.

- **Enable students to practice reading fluency with and without the teacher's guidance.**

Strategies such as Buddy Reading and Fluency Oriented Oral Reading can be used with and without the teacher's direct guidance.

- **Use performance activities to motivate children to read repeatedly to develop fluency.**

Embedding repeated reading in performance, such as choral reading of poetry and readers' theater, is a creative approach to having students read and reread for fluency, while also stressing expressive reading.

For Your Journal

1. Review the Anticipation Guide and compare your earlier answers with what you think now.

2. Fluent reading means reading with expression and not just reading quickly. Fluent reading is a

skill that many adults need to work on, especially if we are going to be models for children. Find a well-known children's book with rich language. J.R.R. Tolkien's *The Hobbit* is a good choice, or Kate

DiCamillo's *Because of Winn-Dixie*. Practice reading passages of the book out loud. Then go to the library and check out the audiobook versions of the book. Listen carefully to the professional readers.

3. Choose one reader and listen for two minutes. Then write in your journal: What makes this person's reading so interesting to listen to? How many of the qualities of reading fluency that were described in this chapter are present in the readings? How does the reader group words? How does the reader use intonation—make his or her voice rise or fall at certain points? How does the reader bring characters to life?

4. Finally, try reading the text yourself the way the professional reader did it. Try tape recording your reading, and analyze it the same way you did the professional reader's version. Afterward, decide what aspects of good oral reading you do well. Determine which aspects you want to work on. Write these things in your journal. And be sure to practice.

Chapter 7
The Importance of Vocabulary Development

After reading this chapter you should be able to:

1. Argue for the importance of developing vocabulary.

2. Summarize important research about vocabulary and apply it in the classroom.

3. Describe important components of a strong instructional program for vocabulary development.

4. Develop students' independence in vocabulary acquisition.

Anticipation Guide

The following statements will help you begin thinking about the topics covered in this chapter. Answer *true* or *false* in response to each statement. As you read and learn more about the topics mentioned in these statements, double-check your answers. See what interests you and what prompts your curiosity toward more understanding.

_____ 1. All children begin school with nearly the same level of vocabulary.

_____ 2. One of the most important ways to expand vocabulary is through wide reading.

_____ 3. Teachers should be clear with students that when learning vocabulary terms they should not mix ideas or words from more than one language.

_____ 4. Most vocabulary learning occurs during school years.

_____ 5. Teaching strategies for word analysis benefits most students.

_____ 6. Dictionaries have proven to be of little value in vocabulary development; they are more useful for spelling.

_____ 7. Teachers need to decide on the most useful words to teach directly; it isn't possible to teach all the words children need.

_____ 8. Knowledge of word meanings can be easily tested; you either do or don't know a word.

A Classroom Story

Vocabulary Developed While Studying American History

Ms. Olson smiles, deeply satisfied as she listens to her students use new vocabulary terms as they share their responses to the book she has just read them about Marian Anderson:

Ginny: "I think what's most important about Marian Anderson is that she never gave up; she loved to sing and kept singing even when she had to go to Europe to do it. She was courageous and determined."

José: "I think I'll remember her because she had such an amazing voice heard only once in a hundred years."

Randy: "She was full of trepidation, many times, too! Our country was segregated and people blocked her out. She was scared—full of trepidation. I think that's a great word for her."

It's February, Black History Month, and Ms. Olson is trying a new way to increase her students' interest in the vocabulary associated with their social studies unit while also helping them develop a historical sense of the challenges faced by Black Americans. She has chosen to focus the unit on Black leaders from a variety of fields—politics, sports, and the arts—who have made important contributions to our society while overcoming significant obstacles. She introduces each leader individually by reading aloud from biographies and then helps children extend their understanding of the situations and personal characteristics of these leaders by having them select descriptive words for each.

She has decided to use a timeline as a graphic organizer for the people and events they study, especially because the leaders represent a long span of history. She wants to see if her students will become more conscious of important vocabulary related to the particular historical periods and will retain new words more easily when they can associate them with particular people and events. She has posted a timeline on the side wall of her room with the dates from 1700 to 2000 and has anchored the span with large cards identifying Colonial America, Slavery, Abolitionist Movement, Civil War, Expansionism, and Twentieth Century. She feels fortunate to have collected a set of pictures of several important black leaders, including Harriet Tubman, Frederick Douglass, Booker T. Washington, Jackie Robinson, Louis Armstrong, Marian Anderson, and Martin Luther King Jr., all of which find their place on the timeline. As a way to help students reflect on the impact of each leader, Ms. Olson asks them to select key terms to describe the person and then posts these words on the timeline beside the pictures.

In preparing for the unit, Ms. Olson has reviewed the selection of books she has collected for her class to read both independently and with partners. She has also selected a few to read to her class as a way of focusing discussion on the characteristics of these groundbreaking leaders. She knows the leaders' struggles may not seem real to some of her students. She also wants to use these biographies to focus students' attention on both terms that help define the struggles and words that describe the leaders.

To introduce Marian Anderson's contributions, Ms. Olson reads aloud When Marian Sang *(Munoz Ryan, 2002) and shares the pictures with the class. Then she asks students to turn to a partner and, using their 12-inch voices, decide on a few words that best describe Ms. Anderson. As the partners discuss their ideas, Ms. Olson posts some words above the picture of Marian Anderson on the timeline:* concert, opera singer, spiritualist, segregation, *and* Lincoln Memorial. *These are important words about the context that she will refer to later as they discuss the struggles Anderson faced. After a few minutes Ms. Olson calls the class together to share what words and phrases they had selected as describing Marian Anderson. She writes these on the smartboard:* talented, courageous, stubborn, religious, loved her mother, beautiful, amazing voice, gracious, opera singer, strong, peaceful. *This activity helps the children focus on words that relate to the context of Anderson's life and experiences. To help them internalize these descriptive words she then asks the students to think about how all these words relate to Marian Anderson's life and to vote on the four that they think are most important to post on the timeline by her picture. She explains that they will compare the words to those already posted for earlier leaders on the timeline. She ends the lesson by showing the students another book,* Marian Anderson: A Voice Uplifted *(V. G. Jones, 2008) and suggests if they want to learn more about her life they might like to read the book and others in the class library or go online and find out even more about her.*

Knowing vocabulary is essential to comprehending what one reads (Blachowicz, Fisher, Ogle, & Watts-Taffe, 2006; Davis, 1944). For nearly a century, research has stressed the relationship between vocabulary knowledge and text understanding (Baumann, Kame'enui, & Ash, 2003; Blachowicz & Fisher, 2014; National Reading Panel, 2000; Whipple, 1925). In this chapter we will discuss why attention to vocabulary is so important in the elementary and middle grades and outline what research tells us about vocabulary development. You will also learn about the role teachers play in helping students develop their interest in and knowledge of words, including the decisions teachers need to make about teaching vocabulary and guiding students to become independent learners. With state standards increasing expectations for students building knowledge during the elementary years, there is new attention to **academic vocabulary**, those words needed for success in learning mathematics, history/social studies, and science. This chapter begins with an explanation of what is included in the concept *vocabulary* and provides a summary of important research findings. The majority of the chapter then provides guidelines and examples to help teachers determine how to productively create a balanced and rich vocabulary program for their students.

What Is Vocabulary?

Vocabulary is knowledge of words and word meanings (Lehr, Osborn, & Hiebert, 2006). This is not as simple as it sounds, however, particularly for English, one of the most word-rich languages of all. As Lederer wrote, "English has never rejected a word because of its race, creed, or national origin" (1991, p. 22). The foundation of English is Germanic, but it has a strong Latin influence, and has added and continues to add words from many other languages. While the number of words in any language is difficult to compute, most linguists estimate that English has about twice as many words as Spanish or French. In addition, English is continually evolving and changing; it is reported that Shakespeare himself added nearly 1,700 new terms to the language. English is growing quickly today, too. The editors of the *Oxford English Dictionary* estimate that they add at least 1,000 words each year, although that estimate is considered conservative by many (*Oxford Dictionaries Online* quarterly update, 2013).

Determining the number of words in English or, on a more personal level, the number of words in an individual's vocabulary is difficult because there are so many dimensions of what counts as a word. Do inflected forms, plurals, compounds, and phrasal groups count as distinct words, or are they combined and counted as a single word, as a word family? For example, how many words should be counted for the varied forms of *play* (*play, player, replay, playback*)? Another issue is how to count the varied meanings and grammatical forms of the word: *play a game, play an instrument, attend a play* (at the theater), *make a move or play* (noun), or *be a key player* and *read the playbook*? These considerations make determining vocabulary size challenging, but they also make clear that vocabulary deserves the attention of teachers in helping students understand all that is included in building their word power and recognize why it is important to prioritize the learning of language.

Synonyms and Polysemous Words

An important consideration in thinking about vocabulary learning is that while the purpose of words is to identify and label what we know, there are often several similar words that may label the same basic concept; learners need to differentiate among these words and choose the most precise and appropriate one for their use. Many words have **synonyms**, other terms with nearly the same meaning. Just think of the various ways to describe an action considered *fair*. One might consider using *just, right, honest, objective, even-handed*, or *unbiased*. As this example demonstrates, the same basic concept or meaning can be expressed with various words. Many times the reason for this rich array of options for one concept is that English has adopted words from many other languages, all used for the same concept. (The term *just* as a synonym for *fair* comes from Latin, for example.) In addition, English users keep modifying and refining words to fit particular needs.

English is challenging to teach because often teachers focus on the individual words as they occur in a particular text or topic and neglect to help students think of the larger, more extensive ways the same term may be used. These variations are especially important for English language learners to know, because the same word may have several different meanings. Take the same example of *fair*. It can also be used to describe a light-skinned person or one with a clear complexion. Such **polysemous** words abound in our language. So, while it seems easy to say that the concept *vocabulary* has two parts—the word and the meaning that the word stands for—there is much beneath that statement. This reality makes both teaching and assessing vocabulary difficult. Researchers ask, "What does it mean to know a word?" "Is knowing one meaning of a term adequate?" "Is knowing affixed forms of a term (*fair, fairly, unfair*) considered as a single term?"

Children build their vocabulary knowledge with **incremental growth**, expanding the variety of words they possess, building their familiarity with multiple meanings, and learning appropriate uses for those terms. Sometimes children understand a concept, but do not have precise words to indicate what it is. For example, children may not know the word *interrogate*, but they do know what it is to have someone question them in order to find out if they did something wrong! At other times students may encounter words they are able to pronounce but for which they lack the meaning or concept. Many children will lack both the label and the concept behind the word *ennui*, because few of them will know what it is for a person to be sated over a long period of time to the point where nothing is capable of exciting them. If they do not know the concept, then it is certain that they will not know how to use the term appropriately until they encounter it several times and in several different contexts.

Receptive and Expressive Vocabulary

In addition to consisting of words and their meanings, vocabulary also varies between being either receptive or expressive. **Receptive vocabulary** refers to the words students can understand when they hear or see them, and **expressive vocabulary** refers to the words they can use themselves. And, of course, words can also be received and expressed or produced in speech or in print (*oral* or *written*). Words that can be identified but are not known well enough to be used accurately are also described as part of *passive* (versus *active*) *vocabulary*.

An individual's receptive vocabulary is usually larger than his or her expressive vocabulary, either in speech or in print; that is, most people can understand more words than they feel confident enough to use. This is true, in part, because when one hears terms that are fairly new, those words aren't used in isolation but are embedded in meaningful contexts of talk or prose. The context supports the listener or reader in determining a likely meaning. The more frequently the same term is used in somewhat similar contexts, the more likely it is that listeners will build their own understanding or meaning for that word. And, because words have specific ways they are used in different settings, learning appropriate use and the connotations of meaning in each context takes a significant amount of time and effort. That is one of the reasons that wide reading is so productive; readers can attend to new terms closely, reexamine them at their own pace, and make personal notes.

The relationship between receptive word knowledge and expressive vocabulary is interesting when focusing on written language. Until about fourth grade when the gap is largely closed (Loban, 1976), most students' spoken vocabulary is larger than the number of words they can recognize or use in print. This means that for teachers of the primary grades, teaching vocabulary often is viewed as helping students recognize the printed form of words they already understand in speech. However, even in the primary grades it is also important that teachers expand children's knowledge of unfamiliar words and their meanings. Recent research (Christ & Wang, 2011; Neuman & Wright, 2014) has made it clear that young children benefit when they are introduced to precise words for experiences they have both inside and outside of school. Both hearing and reading words related to units children are studying is important. Children from homes with fewer resources and those from immigrant families profit significantly from preschool and primary programs that prioritize building children's vocabularies by introducing them to a wide variety of new words.

It is important to note that learning words and understanding how to use them develops over time with multiple opportunities to encounter the terms. Students build their sensitivities to language and vocabulary uses by hearing a great deal of elaborated talk and by reading widely in materials that introduce them to new vocabulary and new ways of expressing ideas. Listening and reading enrich receptive vocabulary; speaking and writing provide opportunities for children to deepen their knowledge of terms and explore ways to use them.

Other Dimensions of Vocabulary Acquisition

As children mature, there are many dimensions of vocabulary that deserve attention. Besides knowing words at different levels, oral and written, from receptive to expressive, word learning varies in some other ways, too. Many words have multiple meanings—like *fair*, *bank*, *root*, *staff*, *vessel*, *glass*, *row*, and *star*. Some words are completely polysemous, like the bank of a river and a savings bank (although the meanings were originally much closer). And some words have much closer multiple meanings, like a *glass* window and a drinking *glass*. Sensitivity to the varied meanings associated with words develops incrementally.

Understanding that words have denotations and connotations also develops incrementally. **Denotations** are the literal meanings of the words, and **connotations** are the associations we have for those words. So the word *tyrant* has the denotation of someone who governs with little regard for the governed, and the connotation of a terrible, brutish person. Becoming sensitive to the connotative meanings of words is an ongoing process for students; as they begin to recognize new terms they also need time to explore the connotations those terms have and how they are most accurately used.

Words differ in their degree of formality and informality, as well as their propriety and impropriety. Informal and formal words with roughly the same meaning are "Hi" and "Greetings," and "automobile" and "car." Propriety adds a different dimension and refers to words that are not allowed to be used on the school grounds, or for which our grandmothers sometimes threatened to wash our mouths out with soap. Because language is living, what may be considered inappropriate for one generation or cultural context may be acceptable in another. Staying attuned to language and vocabulary choices is a life-long necessity.

There are many dimensions of vocabulary learning that develop over time. In addition to understanding the components explained in the preceding paragraphs, another major aspect of vocabulary growth is being aware of how each content area has specific words to describe and define its major attributes or processes. For example, learning about how bicycles work requires use of specific words related to their parts, motion, and force (pedals, tires, wheels, tubes, pressure, etc.). Each "content" area or topic to be explored requires attention to the "language" central to it. As children mature, they encounter an increasingly wide range of content with challenging content-specific and academic terms that are new both in speech and in print (Blachowicz, Fisher, Ogle & Lang, 2013).

In the intermediate grades, children also need to expand their understanding of **morphology**, using the meaning-bearing units of words to determine how words are formed and modified by affixes and bases and how Greek and Latin combining forms can be keys to unlocking meanings. Also in these grades, students need to learn more about how language continues to grow and change over time and to become sensitive to our evolving language. With teacher modeling and encouragement, students become more "word conscious" and enjoy playing with and respecting their language.

Vocabulary is defined as words and their meanings, but as is clear from the elaborations above, this is a deep "concept." Children are continually expanding their understandings about the many dimensions of words and how our language functions. Teachers have a tremendous opportunity to nurture children's language growth by understanding these various dimensions of vocabulary. The research review that follows makes clear that being thoughtful about how one approaches vocabulary teaching in the classroom makes a huge difference for children.

Check Your Understanding 7.1: Gauge your understanding of the skills and concepts in this section.

What Does the Research Say About Vocabulary?

Over the last two decades there have been several excellent reviews of the research on vocabulary. Together, they make clear how important attention to vocabulary is and the contribution good vocabulary makes to reading comprehension. Perhaps most importantly, vocabulary knowledge is one of the best predictors of reading comprehension (Kame'enui & Baumann, 2012; Nagy, Anderson, & Herman, 1987). Why this is so may relate to the fact that vocabulary knowledge can be used as a measure of general verbal ability that underlies learning (Terman, 1916). It is also true that the ability to make inferences is a critical component both in reading comprehension and in learning the meaning of new words (Blachowicz & Fisher, 2014; Sternberg & Powell, 1983). Both explanations have strong support in the research literature. In addition, text meanings are conveyed by the words authors choose; to understand these meanings requires knowledge of the words. Children are hampered in comprehending stories and content materials if they lack the vocabulary required to understand both the explicit content and the more subtle connotations particular words convey. Analyzing the word choice of authors and considering alternatives is one of the ways we can interrogate a text and engage in close reading.

The research also makes clear that direct vocabulary instruction is important for students to build the vocabularies they need for learning and success. Attention to vocabulary needs to be given early and continue throughout the grades (Baumann, 2009; Stahl, & Stahl, 2012; McKeown, Beck, & Sandora, 2012). Several components of that instruction have been identified, including creating word-rich environments, modeling interest in words, targeting some words for focused instruction, building word-learning strategies, and raising students' awareness of important words and usages (Baumann, 2009; Blachowicz & Fisher, 2014; Graves, Kame'enui, & Baumann, 2012). Direct instruction is important for children of all ages and needs to include opportunities for children to regularly use the words they are learning both orally and in their writing.

Factors Contributing to Vocabulary Growth

We know that there are great differences in students' vocabularies. One factor contributing to these differences is related to economic conditions in the home. Hart and Risley's (1995) long-term study of vocabulary development in children during the first years of life revealed significant differences that were strongly related to parental income and welfare status. Children in households with lower incomes were exposed to significantly fewer words and to less oral engagement. These conditions affected the children's breadth of vocabulary use as well as their rate of vocabulary growth during these formative years. Hart and Risley found that when these children from lower income homes enter school, they possess only about half the vocabulary of their more privileged peers and thus they begin their school careers at a disadvantage.

Another factor contributing to the size of students' vocabularies is the amount of reading they do (McKeown, Beck, & Sandora, 2012). Keith Stanovich (1992) demonstrated that children who were avid readers had much larger vocabularies than children who did not read as much, even when the children had the same levels of general intelligence. Perhaps a big reason for this is that written language is a far richer source of vocabulary than either speech or television. As Figure 7.1 demonstrates, even a children's book has richer vocabulary than a prime-time adult television show, and even more sophisticated vocabulary than the conversation of college-educated adults. The best way to get a bigger vocabulary is to read widely.

Listen to reading researchers in this video refer to this same research by Hayes and Ahrens/Cunningham, which underscores the importance of reading and being read to, and then answer the question that follows.

 Video Exploration 7.1: Watch the video and answer questions that reflect the content you have read.

Vocabulary Development for English Learners

Research studies have also demonstrated that vocabulary knowledge is a critical factor in the school success of English language learners (Carlo, August, & Snow, 2005; Graves, August & Mancilla-Martinez, 2012). Knowledge of English vocabulary is one of the strongest correlates associated with the discrepancy between the reading performance of native English speakers and English language learners. This correlation remains despite the fact that many English language learners possess a large vocabulary in their native language (Garcia, 1991; Goldenberg, Rezaei, & Fletcher, 2005; Verhoeven, 1990).

Figure 7.1 On the "Richness" of Vocabulary From Different Sources

Richness of Vocabulary from Oral and Written Sources

Comparison of oral language, television, and written language

Hayes and Ahrens (1988) analyzed the difficulty level of these three different sources of vocabulary by finding the average difficulty level of the words used. They found that written language provides a much richer source of vocabulary than does either oral language or television. In fact, the average difficulty of the words in children's books is considerably higher than the language children hear orally.

Adult speech	Rank of median word
College graduates speaking to friends and spouses	496
Expert witness testimony	1008
Television texts	
Popular adult shows	490
Popular children's shows	543
Cartoon shows	598
Printed texts	
Newspapers	1,690
Adult books	1,058
Comic books	867
Children's books	627

These results were based on the analysis of a large set of transcripts of speech, television programs and books. The researchers determined the average frequency for each of the types of sources they analyzed. (The frequency levels for the words were determined from analysis of a large corpus of written English texts. For example, the most frequently occurring word is "the" so that word is ranked number 1; the 10th most frequent word is "it" and the 9,000th word is "shrimp.")

To help English learners accelerate their acquisition of English, direct language and vocabulary instruction is beneficial (Graves, August & Mancilla-Martinez, 2013; Linan-Thompson & Vaughn, 2007). The same components of vocabulary instruction that are important for all children are also true for English learners, but teachers need to be even more intentional and provide strong support for a great deal of practice with the language/vocabulary being targeted.

The impact of readers' vocabularies is most clear in the comprehension of academic content. While most students, including those who are from lower income homes and English language learners, do well with conversational English, it is when they engage in more academic topics that the differences emerge. Cummins (1980) describes these differences as **basic interpersonal communication (BICS)** and **cognitive academic-language proficiency (CALP)**. For learners to be successful in school, they need to become increasingly competent with academic language. This is clearly an ongoing process. Teachers need to be sensitive to the fact that the more dense materials are with content-specific terminology, the more support students will need in making sense of the materials. Stories and literature are much less dependent on specific terms used by authors than are the informational texts used in science, social studies, and mathematics. This reality makes support for English learners even more important in content instruction. (Echevarria, Vogt & Short, 2013; Nagy & Townsend, 2014)

Research and the Common Core

The research on vocabulary development and instruction also undergirds the focus vocabulary receives in the CCSS. The CCSS and most other state-level standards highlight the importance of vocabulary throughout both the reading and the language standards. The most focused attention comes in the Standards for Language under the section for "Vocabulary Acquisition and Use." The three specific standards state that students should be able to:

- determine or clarify meanings of unknown and multiple-meaning words and phrases
- demonstrate understanding of figurative language, word relationships, and nuances in word meanings and
- acquire and use accurately a range of general academic and domain-specific words and phrases.

The anchor standards for Reading also emphasize the importance of a strong vocabulary. The fourth anchor standard states that students should be able to: "Interpret words and phrases as they are used in a text, including determining technical, connotative, and figurative meanings, and analyze how specific word choices shape meaning or tone" (Common Core State Standards for English Language Arts & Literacy in History/Social Studies, Science and Technical Subjects, K-5, p. 10).

The standards expect students to be developing their command of vocabulary for general oral and written uses as well as for academic learning. The assessments derived from the standards also expect students to be able to use vocabulary and to determine specific meanings from the contexts in which they occur.

The CCSS also differentiate two types of academic vocabulary: **general academic vocabulary** and **domain-specific vocabulary**. The first category includes terms that have applicability across several disciplines, like the words *summarize*, *structure*, and *environment*. Within the group of general academic terms there is a subset of "school-specific" words and phrases that describe processes learners need to employ (*compare/contrast, underline, diagram, find supporting evidence*, etc.). These academic terms and their specialized meanings often pose the greatest challenges for English learners (Graves, 2006; Marzano, 2004). The other category of academic terms and phrases are domain-specific, which means they are part of a particular content or topic: *artery, blood vessel*, and *vertebrae* are examples of words that relate specifically to the study of biology.

Vocabulary Instruction

While the demands for vocabulary learning are high, research studies also indicate attention to vocabulary development is valuable for all students (Graves & Silvermann, 2010). Good instruction makes a difference from early pre-primary interventions (Beck & McKeown, 2007; Stahl & Stahl, 2012) throughout the grades (Frey & Fisher, 2009). With the growing recognition of the importance of vocabulary to comprehension and learning, there has been an upsurge of instructional research that confirms the value of a consistent approach to vocabulary instruction. In their summary of instructional research, Blachowicz, Fisher, Ogle, and Watts-Taffe (2006) explain that good vocabulary instruction:

- Takes place in a language and word-rich environment that fosters the **word consciousness**, motivation, and ownership that support incidental word learning.
- Includes intentional teaching of selected words, which provides multiple sources of information and opportunities for repeated exposure, use, and practice.
- Includes the teaching of generative elements of words and word-learning strategies in ways that give students control over their own strategic behaviors.

Check Your Understanding 7.2: Gauge your understanding of the skills and concepts in this section.

Teaching Vocabulary

Teaching vocabulary is an important part of literacy instruction and deserves careful attention and regular effort. Under good instruction, all students can expand their vocabularies and develop generative knowledge about how words and language function. The following section provides principles of good instruction and ideas for classroom practices and is organized around these principles:

1. Motivate students to be open to learning words by promoting a respect for language.
2. Create a language-rich environment in which students can learn words through general acquisition.
3. Teach specific words (during language arts and during specific content study).
4. Teach students strategies for learning new words.
5. Use assessment to monitor students' vocabulary learning.

Promoting Respect for Language

Vocabulary is powerful! Having a word in our vocabulary means we can notice something. Each word is a flashlight that illuminates another corner of our experience (Patterson, 1984). In psychological research, it was demonstrated years ago that we most readily recognize what we have a name for (Brown, 1958). This point was made in a classroom setting by Mary Cowhey (2006):

> *During my first year teaching, I estimate I lost twenty to thirty minutes of instructional time each day dealing with post-recess conflicts, long tearful renditions of who did what to whom, fraught with passionate contradictions and denials . . . The following*

summer I took a workshop in Second Step, a "violence prevention curriculum." . . . I was surprised when some students really couldn't identify emotions such as disgusted, scared, and angry in photos of children. Before I began teaching Second Step lessons, I observed a couple of boys "joking" with some other children. They didn't notice when one of the other children became upset, and continued "joking" even when the other child began to cry. When I intervened, the jokers said "We were just having fun." I asked if they thought Patrick, who was crying, was still having fun. They said yes. (p. 40)

As Mary Cowhey's (2006) example makes clear, having a word in one's vocabulary means that one understands the word and can connect it to experience. Indeed, she goes on to say that her lessons about emotions

. . . explicitly teach children to read facial expressions, body language, and tone of voice to name the emotion being expressed, to recognize cause and effect, and to realize that two people can have very different feelings about the same situation. (p. 40)

But without the word, there is nothing to anchor the experience in consciousness, and nothing to enable one to communicate about it to others.

As the preceding example makes clear, teachers need to take advantage of the myriad opportunities that present themselves regularly in the classroom to help students focus on using the best and most appropriate words for what they are feeling, doing, and learning. Develop students' flexibility with language by regularly asking:

"What's another way of saying that?"

"How else could you explain that?"

"Can you find a way to describe that more specifically?"

"What's another word for that?"

We also have worked with many students who think that learning words is something that happens all at once. They see or hear a word and remember it—they think. Teachers can motivate students to put some effort into retaining new and interesting words by modeling for them that word learning takes intent and practice; adding words to one's vocabulary doesn't happen all at once. When teachers share their strategies for adding words to their own corpus of known words by writing words on word cards, making personal associations with terms, drawing ways to identify meanings of terms, putting them into rhymes, and practicing using the focus words whenever possible, students begin to understand that words don't just float into our receptive or expressive vocabularies without some conscious effort. In elementary classrooms teachers often create word walls where the key words that are being learned are posted so children can see them on a daily basis and refer to them often as they engage in discussion and in writing.

An easy way to make the process of word learning a reality is to have a word of the week that the whole class can be engaged in learning. One outstanding second grade teacher, Judy McKee, kept a commercial word-of-the-day calendar on her desk, and each week she and the children selected one word from the calendar to be the focus of their collaborative word learning that week. After discussing what the word meant, the class, with the teacher's guidance and feedback, would brainstorm how they might use it. They would write the word, compose several sentences in which it was used, and illustrate the word on a large sheet of chart paper kept near the door. Then, during the week the children would get special credit if they used the word accurately in their talking or writing. The children quickly learned the fun of expanding their vocabularies as well as the need to put some conscious effort into reaching the goal. The class became a lively, word-rich setting where parents and others in the school also became more "word conscious" and learned from this group of seven- and eight-year-olds.

Teachers also share their respect for language and help students develop their "word consciousness" when they comment on the special words authors use. Before engaging in a read aloud, teachers should consciously think ahead about a few words they can point out to help build students' awareness of how important the choice of particular words is in enhancing the story or text. For example, after reading the sentence "The terrier bounded up the stairs looking for Charlie," one teacher commented about how the word *bounded* created a clear image in her mind; she emphasized how much better it was to use *bounded* than *ran* or *jumped*. Another teacher, while reading *Sara Plain and Tall* with his class, asked students to periodically close their eyes and visualize what they would say in response to the author's word images. Savoring the word choice of authors and experiencing their impact is a wonderful way to build a love of language and a respect for the power of words.

Children learn to love words and appreciate their impact when teachers read and discuss how our language has evolved and what other languages have helped enrich English. When the class is studying history and other cultures, adding a component of vocabulary study helps children become more thoughtful and inquisitive. What words have entered English from Native American languages? How have the Latin that was spoken in ancient Rome and the more recent French and Spanish languages enriched English? Reading books like *The Timeline History of the English Language* (Judge, 2009) and *Say What? The Weird and Mysterious Journey of the English Language* (Gorrell, 2009) can stimulate interest in our

Teach It! 1

Reading Aloud

Reading aloud supports vocabulary development as it draws attention to language and affords teachers and students the opportunity to explore an author's word choice.

fascinating language, encourage children to think about and ask questions, and build a better understanding of why we write and spell words as we do.

Teachers can also stimulate children's interests in vocabulary when reading stories from other cultures. With a little Internet research, teachers can find information about the language in which the story was first written and can identify a few words or phrases in that language that children can learn. Bringing in some texts in other languages and those written in two languages (see Colorin Colorado, Del Sol Books, and Ashay By The Bay for examples) helps children realize the varieties of ways cultural groups write and express ideas. If there are children whose families speak other languages in the classroom, it is interesting to ask them for those languages' names for characters in well-known folk tales and stories. A key is to keep broadening children's interest in language whenever there is an opportunity.

Creating a Language-Rich Environment

A cornerstone of classrooms rich in language is teachers reading aloud to students from a variety of books just beyond the students' own reading levels. Much of the vocabulary students will want and need to learn can be introduced naturally through the oral reading or "read alouds" by the teacher. When teachers are aware of their students' language development they can select books and articles to read orally that prepare their students to encounter these words in the texts they will be asked to read. Before beginning a unit on water and environmental concerns, teachers who have collected news articles and stories about natural occurrences and problems with water, draught, and pollution of waterways read short selections orally, emphasizing some of the key words and phrases students will be encountering (water cycle, run-off, contaminants, reservoirs). By discussing these terms in their context of current news, students become more aware of their importance and the varied ways they are used. Teachers who then post these words, phrases, and some visuals associated with them add to students' developing awareness of the words and concepts.

Teachers at every grade level can entice students into developing interest in words and language as they read aloud from literature, too. Pausing over interesting terms and phrases, thinking aloud and elaborating on words, exploring the images created by text passages, and savoring particular words are all ways teachers can help students develop interest in words and build their vocabularies. Teachers can also ask students to listen for interesting, beautiful, and curious uses of language and then take time after an oral reading to discuss what students noted. It is useful to write these words and phrases on the board so all students, particularly English language learners, have the advantage of both hearing and seeing the terms. Many teachers also ask students to keep special "Writer's/Word Books"—notebooks in which they write special word uses and phrases they encounter both in the group activities and in their individual reading. This can be the beginning of a lifetime of paying attention to how our language works and noticing the array of options speakers and writers have for expressing their thoughts. The Writer's Books can also be used to collect new words students are learning related to content expectations.

Teachers can do a great deal to build students' interest in words and language by having newspapers, magazines, and books in other languages in the classroom and referring to them periodically. Listening to music from other countries and cultures is another way to develop sensitivity to languages and vocabulary different from our own. Because so many of our academic terms have Latin and Greek origins, it is often interesting to compare forms of the words we use with those

Teach It! 21

"Word Conversations" for Primary Grades

With this activity, teachers select, introduce, and generate questions about key terms, phrases, and concepts their students will encounter in texts that they'll read.

in Spanish and other languages of the students in the classroom. For example, during the political elections in the fall or during school elections, it would be interesting to put terms related to the process on the board and ask students to supply the equivalent terms in their home languages. What would *election, candidate, voting, campaigning,* and *party* look like in Spanish, French, Farsi? Asking the question and taking time to compare languages is another way to expand students' flexibility with words and the ever-expanding corpus of words in English.

In the intermediate and middle grades, students also take great pleasure in word play and jokes. Reading humorous pieces to them and challenging students with riddles and jokes can connect with students' developing explorations of the richness and complexity of language. For example, teachers encourage students' word flexibility with statements like:

Nothing succeeds like success: no—recess.

I've heard of trade schools, and I'd like to.

What's black and white and red/read all over?—(newspaper).

Teachers extend an interest in words when they create bulletin boards devoted to polysemus words, changing word meanings, new terms, and confusing phrases. Finding time for children to share new words they encounter outside of class, whether while reading or listening, can also easily reinforce the importance of having fun with words. Students become co-creators when they add expressions and new words they encounter on their own. It is also fun to encourage students to create their own words for particular items or situations. By using familiar word parts, they can engage in the same process going on all around them. An easy place to start is with new terms for sports and fashion.

The classroom also is enriched when teachers make available books that explore and play with language. Students enjoy reading books like *Bullfrog Pops!: Adventures in Verbs and Direct Objects* (Walton, 2011); *Miss Alaneus* (Frasier, 2007); *Children Around the World* (Montanari, 2004); and *Baloney!* (Scieszka, 2005). In addition, books with puzzles and word games, rhymes and riddles, and magazines that introduce varied topics in inviting formats encourage language exploration. Critical to these classroom collections on language is a good set of dictionaries—all students should have their own and the classroom should contain more adult and larger dictionaries for reference. Making available and teaching students how to use both dictionaries and classroom thesauruses and online dictionaries gives them tools so they can keep

Differentiated Instruction

Creating Acrostics

Getting to know your students is made interesting and enjoyable by asking each student to create an **acrostic** poem of his or her name. Each letter in the student's name is written vertically down the left side of a piece of paper. The students select descriptive words that begin with the letters of their name and then use these terms to create the poem. For example, Diedra created her poem in the following way:

Daring
Interested
Explorer
Doing
Rambunctious
Activities

It is very easy to identify some of the things that Diedra may be interested in doing, given the window on her personality and interests she opens. Each student's poem is distinctive; even those who are shy generally reveal that aspect of their selves, too. Teachers can use this activity as a way to build awareness among a class of the value of selecting words carefully. Involving students in several steps makes it more likely that they will find good terms. Start by brainstorming lots of words that begin with each letter of a person's name. Then give students thesauruses and have them search for additional words that may be even more illustrative of what they want to say about themselves. Model this with your own name if they seem unsure of how to proceed. The dictionary can also be helpful in leading students to just the right words. These resources make it more likely that they will find the best terms to describe themselves. Finally, before the poems are completed, have students check their acrostics with a partner for a final review. The final poems can be read orally, posted in the room, and combined with lists of students' favorite music, books, and activities. It certainly is a good way to focus students' attention on the value of words and the connotations and nuances each word we use contains.

expanding their language on their own (Blachowicz, Fisher, Ogle & Watts-Taffe, 2013). In classrooms with English language learners, some bilingual dictionaries are also important. The whole class can enjoy exploring how different words are expressed in each language and can learn a great deal when the different forms of the words are displayed in the classroom.

Some Web sites also include frames for you to create your own games and crossword puzzles with words children need to review from your instructional program. FunBrain is one; Vocabulary University is good for upper elementary and middle grades. The PBS television series *Between the Lions* has put many word games online; "Surfing the Net With Kids" keeps you up to date with new recommended links for word games.

Play with words is an important component in children's vocabulary development. Don't overlook it!

Teaching Specific Words

As teachers create classrooms where they and their students identify as language "experts" and pay attention to the options that our rich vocabulary makes possible, they also need to help students learn new vocabulary as part of the instructional reading they do daily in class. Both in literature and in other content instruction, specific terms are needed to insure comprehension of text materials. By attending to these terms, teachers are also building the vocabulary knowledge students will need for long-term school success. The less students are stimulated at home with rich oral language contexts, the more important it is that teachers at all grade levels focus on and reinforce vocabulary development.

SELECTING WORDS TO TEACH   Teachers need to identify which words need to be taught—often a challenging task. Then they need to explain the meaning of these terms, provide examples, and develop activities that help reinforce the learning of these words. Finally, teachers must assess students' success in learning the selected words.

Teachers are often unsure about which words they should teach directly. Fortunately, there are good sources of help in making those decisions. Most basal reading programs and anthologies now include a vocabulary strand and highlight some key words that are essential to the selections. Focusing students' attention on a small set of words prior to reading a literature selection will help them notice these words as they read. By focusing on certain key terms, teachers will help students attend to them better and also be able to find out how many of the words students already know. The terms can then be discussed after the reading, and students can practice using them in their own speaking and writing. The same is true in most science, social studies, and other content area curricula. Textbooks often identify key terms that are basic to the content. Teachers can highlight these and ask students to complete a **Rate Your Knowledge chart** (Blachowicz, 1986) especially when they are unsure of students' preparation for a particular topic being studied. Look at the example shown in Figure 7.2 for a Rate Your Knowledge chart that was used as a pre-reading activity.

Figure 7.2 Rate Your Knowledge Chart

These are words we are going to be using during this unit. Mark how familiar you are with them as we begin. Those that are not so familiar are words to put in your learning journal so you can build your understanding of them during our study.

Key Words	New to Me	Have Seen	Know Well
mummy			
pyramid			
scribe			
artisan			
pharaoh			

If we had to teach all of the words children need to learn, we couldn't do it. Nagy and Anderson (1984) put the number of words in "printed school English" at 88,500! And that was just through ninth grade! There is no way to teach 10,000 words a year. Most of these words will have to be learned from experience, especially from reading. But teaching specific words is important, too, and identifying the terms that are central to students' comprehension of content is a starting place for instruction.

Beck and her colleagues have come up with a way of approaching the seemingly enormous task of teaching general vocabulary (Beck, McKeown, & Kucan, 2002). They have identified three "tiers" of words. The first tier includes common, everyday words that most of us know. The second tier of words are those that we encounter frequently in school and in reading and that are used in a variety of situations; knowing these words provides a foundation for many kinds of learning. In the CCSS usage, these are general academic terms and are worth teaching in language arts and reading. The third tier of words includes the specialized vocabulary terms connected to particular content, identified as domain-specific in the CCSS. They have specific meanings that need to be developed as part of learning the content. These terms are only taught as they are needed for specific content understanding.

Marzano (2004) has also developed a useful guide for deciding which content words to teach. He and his colleagues collected all of the academic terms needed for students to be successful with state and national standards and then sorted them by school levels. The Academic Vocabulary List includes key words for 11 subject areas, including science, mathematics, language arts, history, social studies, the arts, and health. These words are then organized according to four levels: level 1 = grades K–2; level 2 = grades 3–5; level 3 = grades 6–8; and level 4 = grades 9–12. These lists provide a good reference for teachers who want to assess and then develop their students' vocabularies for academic reading and learning.

Another important source for words is the students themselves. Some researchers have demonstrated that involving students in selecting the words to be studied is a productive strategy (Fisher, Blachowicz, & Smith, 1991; Haggard, 1982). Students are able to self-select important terms that are similar to and equally valuable to those the teachers select. And, when students self-select terms, their involvement has the added benefit of motivating them to learn the terms more deeply.

BUILDING VOCABULARY WITH READ ALOUDS   Research studies have shown that children encounter the majority of the words they will learn beyond their common conversational vocabulary through reading and listening to books. Across the grades there is clearly value in teachers reading orally from material slightly beyond students' independent reading levels. Making the most of these opportunities for vocabulary development is important. Beck and her colleagues provide excellent guides on how this can be achieved.

When young readers (kindergarten and first grade) are learning new words, Beck and colleagues (2002) suggest that teachers conduct a rich discussion of words that includes these six steps:

1. Contextualize words, one at a time, within a story. For example, with kindergartners, the teacher could use Don Freeman's perennially popular *Corduroy* (1978) as a pretext for introducing the words *insistent, reluctant,* and *drowsy.* The teacher says, "In the story, Lisa was reluctant to leave the department store without Corduroy [her new teddy bear]."

2. Ask the children to repeat the word so as to make a phonological representation of it.

3. Then explain the meaning of the word in a child-friendly way: "*Reluctant* means you are not sure you want to do something."

4. Now provide examples of the word in other contexts: "I am reluctant to go swimming in the early summer when the water is cold."

5. Next, ask children to provide their own examples: "What is something you would be reluctant to do?"

6. Finally, ask the children to repeat the word they have been talking about, to reinforce its phonological representation.

Word conversations are not as easy as they look. Teachers need to do the following:

- Choose books carefully to provide a meaningful context for introducing the vocabulary.
- Think carefully about the words, and formulate child-friendly explanations of the word meanings.
- Plan questions to relate the words to the children's experience.
- Remind the children of the words they are studying, giving them several opportunities to pronounce the words. (See Beck et al., 2002, for further discussion of this approach.)

Teaching Targeted Words

When teaching literature that children read by themselves, teachers are often perplexed about which words should receive particular focus. There are often many words that are important to establishing the characters, setting, and tone, yet these terms are not repeated often in the stories. As Pearson, Hiebert & Kamil (2012) explain, the unknown words in a narrative text are, for the most part, unlikely to be either related to one another or encountered again, whereas the new terms of one topic in a content area are: (1) likely to be encountered many times in the chapter in which they initially occur, (2) likely to be related to one another, and (3) highly likely to be the conceptual foundation for the new ideas in the next chapter or topic (p. 244). This makes the instructional task of developing vocabulary with literature one that requires substantial attention.

It is important to remember, too, that children encounter most of the new words they learn through reading (Nagy, Anderson & Herman, 1985). Clearly, literature is the richest context for encountering new vocabulary and for expanding understanding of how words can be used in different contexts. Most authors include new terms that students benefit from learning; to maximize the possibilities these valuable sources of quality language provide, teachers need to be attentive to giving children many opportunities to learn key words and practice using them regularly.

DEVELOPING VOCABULARY WHEN READING LITERATURE One vocabulary strategy, the **Vocab-O-Gram** (Blachowicz & Fisher, 2014) works well as both a preview of the story and a diagnostic for the teacher. The teacher previews the story and makes a list of the terms that seem most important to understanding the story content and theme. From this initial list the teacher then considers which of these words are important to the characters, setting, problem, solution, and tone of the selection and adds any that may be needed so students have words to describe the basic elements of the story. (This may be thought of as a way to check that students can engage in a close read of the author's structure, too.) With the final list of 10 to 15 terms, the teacher then creates a graphic students can use to sort the terms by categories. One column should be included for words that just don't seem to be clearly identified with the story elements and for those words in- dividual students simply find unfamiliar. (See Figure 7.3 for an example.) The final step in this activity is to ask students to write a sentence or two predicting what they think the story will be about or what they think the plot and theme might be.

Teachers also help students focus on upcoming vocabulary important to the story they will read by leading a group discussion of key terms they have identified. Showing the terms, one at a time, to the group and asking them to pronounce the words and then discuss what they know about them helps students use the words and learn with each other. When children seem insecure with the terms, it is often helpful to have them work with a partner. "Turn to your partner and share what you think this word may mean." If a word is completely new, the teacher can show a picture illustrating the word or make some physical representation that the children can guess. Once they begin to grasp the concept, children

Figure 7.3 Vocab-O-Gram

Before we read the Japanese folktale, see what you can predict about how these terms will be used. Put each term in the box with which you think it is connected. Words: bitterly cold, weaving, reed hats, empty cupboards, New Year's Day, kind old man, stone statues, fortunate, Jizo, guardian god of children, old woman, hungry, no coal, sack of food, thank you, village, gift.

Characters	Setting	Problem
Feeling/Tone	Solution	Other Words

can return to their partners and brainstorm ways they might use the word. In this process the children are also using the word/s orally and focusing attention on them. When terms are new and particularly important, the group may extend their examination of the words by searching for the word/s in the text and writing out the phrases or sentences in which the terms are used. A valuable component in learning these words is to have students keep them in their vocabulary notebooks and create illustrations of them.

Helping students move from recognizing new terms to being able to use them independently takes time. A good way to help students in this learning process is to give each student a word ring, a small flexible ring onto which students can add word cards for the words being learned that week. Tagboard cards that have had a small hole punched are easy to use: On one side, students write the word, and on the other they draw a picture of the word and write a sentence using it with the other words being learned that week. Students keep their own word rings and can review them at any time. Children can look for these words in other materials they read and they can also refer to them in their writing and class discussions.

DEVELOPING VOCABULARY WHEN READING INFORMATIONAL TEXTS Just as teachers need to plan ahead for the best ways to introduce and help students learn new terms needed to comprehend literature, they also need to analyze the informational texts they want students to read to identify the vocabulary needed for both reading and learning about content from oral, visual, and hands-on activities. In fact, it is much more important that teachers think carefully about the vocabulary needed in teaching information because there can be many terms that are essential to comprehending the content. In many schools much of the science and social studies instruction is provided in an activity-based format. This means both teachers and students need to be especially attentive to the language used to describe and explain what is seen and done. It also means that teachers need to think carefully about what vocabulary is central to the concepts they want students to understand and that they will expect students to use in their oral and written responses. As Scott and colleagues (2011) illustrated in their study of the content of fourth- and fifth-grade science and math texts commonly used in schools, there were over 4,000 content-specific terms that experts include in their materials. Whether schools use activity-based or text-based instruction, understanding a significant number of content-specific, or domain-specific vocabulary terms is essential to students' learning.

Learning domain-specific and general academic vocabulary is even more challenging because the same term may have very different meanings depending on the content area. For example, the simple term *operation* means very different things in the fields of mathematics or medicine. The same is true of the terms for tasks we ask of students. In English language arts students are asked to analyze how characters develop, or how specific word choice shapes meaning. In math they may be asked to analyze givens and relationships. In science they may need to analyze and interpret data or analyze alternative explanations. The process of analyzing data is not at all the same as analyzing characters, so in addition to teaching content terms, we must also teach the terms for the processes students need to learn to use.

Identify Key Vocabulary With so much vocabulary essential to children's developing concepts and knowledge as well as their being able to enact procedural and performance skills, it is important to highlight this learning need and help students take charge of their own vocabulary development. One of the easiest ways to collaborate with students in this task is to begin each unit of study by identifying key terms that need to be learned and key outcomes they will need to achieve. Initially teachers can model this process for students by previewing materials to be learned and listing key terms that will be used. They can put these words on a grid and then have each student rate his/her own level of knowledge of the words (which words are known quite well/which have been seen or heard but are not really known/which are basically unfamiliar and new). By doing this activity at the beginning of a unit of study both students and teacher can determine how much time will need to be devoted to learning the words more deeply. The same list can be reviewed at the end of the unit and the class can evaluate their success in mastering the key terms. After the class has become familiar with this way of self-assessing and charting growth, students are generally quite honest in their responses. Some teachers have found it good to add a fourth column: illustrate or give an example. This helps students who tend to rate their knowledge higher than might be accurate. Figure 7.2 is an example of a Rate Your Knowledge Chart from a unit on Ancient Egypt.

Another easy way to highlight the importance of attending to content-specific vocabulary as a unit of study is initiated is to ask students to brainstorm words they think will be important in their reading and learning of the topic. Explain that you want them to brainstorm A–Z words they think they will need. You may divide the class into groups and have each complete the full alphabet list or assign a portion of the alphabet to each of four groups, for example. Group 1 generates a list of words from A to G; group 2 generates words from H to N; group 3 lists words from O to T; and group 4 works with letters U to Z. If the lists don't contain many of the words you know are important, ask students to preview the text materials you have prepared and then create a new list of text-focused terms. This activity could then evolve into a discussion of some of these words and raise students' awareness of important terms that will require their attention. With this kind of preview it is easier to focus students' attention on delving deeper into the meanings of these new words.

Reviewing and Rehearsing Terms Once teachers and students identify the vocabulary to be learned about a particular topic, teachers need to plan and then have students engage in activities that will help them differentiate the important terms and rehearse and practice using these words. Because so many of the important terms in any one content area are often similar, it can be helpful to provide some guidance in the form of graphic tools, especially morphology brainstorming, concept clustering, idea webs, and semantic feature analysis.

Morphology Brainstorming If there are terms with similar Greek or Latin roots or affixes, it is good to guide students to examine these word parts. First, identify a few affixes, roots, or combining forms and introduce or guide students to determine the meaning. Then ask students to find other words with these elements and make a class list of them. For example, in a unit on Ancient Egypt teachers identified several terms that described experts or persons who engage in activities with the combining forms "or," "er" and "ologist": *embalmer, builder, Egyptologist, surveyor,* and *archeologist.* These words were listed and the class discussed how the words were formed and what the parts meant. Then students made their morphology brainstorming lists of additional words they knew, along with some they located in their texts that contained the same combining forms. Using structure as a tool to word learning is important and can be easily incorporated into content lessons.

Concept Clusters/Idea Webs The **concept cluster** activity helps students become familiar with important terms and builds their understanding of what they mean and what terms are associated with the same concepts. Students are given a list of the key terms for the topic/unit they are studying. They then chunk or group the similar terms under the categories that are provided. A more challenging form of this activity is to have the students create their own clusters of terms and create a concept label for those terms that makes clear how they are related. For example, after students have been introduced to the key terms for their unit on weather and climate, they are given a graphic organizer on which they can chunk terms into three categories: Atmosphere, Weather Conditions, and Measuring and Forecasting.

The words they use are: *cyclone, anemometer, exosphere, barometer, troposphere, precipitation, Doppler radar, Celsius scale, nimbus, cirrus, weather satellite, pressure, hurricane, thunderstorm, meteorologist.*

Semantic Feature Analysis **Semantic feature analysis** is a graphic display that focuses on the features that distinguish words in a particular category from one another, such as various types of vehicles or human activities. The teacher creates the matrix either as a model or with students during a unit of study. The students then determine which features each of the terms possesses and finally are able to compare and contrast similar terms.

The semantic feature analysis grid helps students distinguish items based on important attributes. It provides an interesting way to discuss key words at depth, analyzing which features are present and which are not among similar concepts. Whether the chart is used to differentiate simple machines, mathematics operations, or forms of government, teachers can help students refine their understanding of key terms by using this graphic tool. The simple example shown in Figure 7.4 helps young students distinguish between two animals they are studying, sharks and dolphins.

Figure 7.4 A Semantic Feature Analysis

	Bear live young	Have gills	Cold-blooded	Have milk
SHARKS				
DOLPHINS				

Teach It! 24

Semantic Feature Analysis

Through the construction of a matrix, this vocabulary enriching activity helps students analyze features of the topics or concepts they are studying.

Teach It! 66

Cumulative Semantic Map

This activity provides students with a visual resource for examining meanings and categories of related words.

Semantic or Concept Web for Upper Grades   One approach to **semantic webs** is the character/topic web, in which the name of a major animal or object is written in the circle in the middle of the display. Then words that describe the central focal object or character are written as satellites around the name. Examples that illustrate each attribute are written as satellites around the descriptive words. Figure 7.5 depicts a semantic web on dolphins.

Webbed Questions   Schwartz and Rafael (1985) suggest guiding the students' responses to a semantic web and having them offer answers to three **webbed questions** asked about the target word, as shown in Figure 7.6.

What is it?

What is it like?

What are some examples of it?

In their research to determine the effectiveness of various approaches to vocabulary learning, Bos and Anders (1989, 1990) compared the effectiveness of three semantic relatedness techniques (mapping, semantic feature analysis, and semantic/syntactic feature analysis) to definition study with students of various ages and abilities. They concluded that all three of the interactive techniques were more effective than the traditional approach to having students write and study definitions.

Activities to teach content vocabulary should help students realize that word learning is an ongoing process and that knowing a word involves many levels of understanding. With this reality, it is important that students have teacher support in identifying words worth learning and in engaging in activities that help reinforce and refine the developing meanings. Word learning activities should relate words to a meaningful context, to other words, and to the students' own experiences. The suggested activities and others you may try should satisfy these requirements by encouraging:

- making connections (to self, personal stories, and other words and texts);
- collaborating with peers (interpersonal dynamics through all the language arts);
- exploring meaning (using context, asking questions; making statements; interpreting; using higher-level thinking such as application, synthesis, and evaluation); and
- participating as an active reader (summarizing, predicting, confirming, and clarifying).

Figure 7.5 A Semantic Web

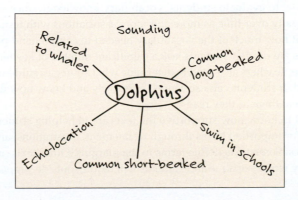

Figure 7.6 Webbed Questions

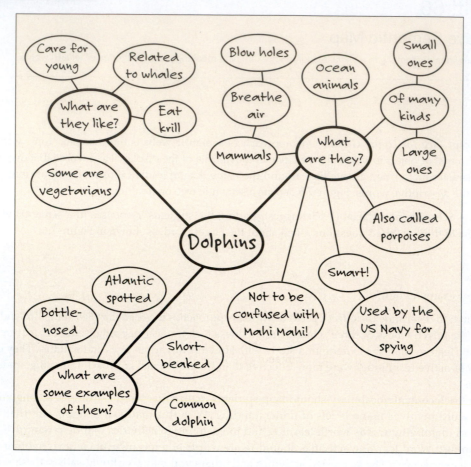

The middle-school literacy coordinator in the following video demonstrates a few of the strategies discussed in this section to support students' acquisition of content-specific vocabulary. Watch this video depicting a social studies lesson with a focus on economics and then answer the question that follows.

 Video Exploration 7.2: Watch the video and answer questions that reflect the content you have read.

Assessing Students' Vocabulary Learning

Teachers have struggled with how to evaluate students' vocabulary knowledge since word learning is not a one-step process. Words are learned gradually over time as more and more associations with terms are experienced. Yet it is also important for teachers to find out how much of the vocabulary needed to comprehend particular texts is known by students before the texts or materials are used. If students lack a significant number of key terms, then more pre-reading and concept building needs to be done. Teachers also need to determine what strategies students possess so they can figure out new terms in context as they read. If students can use context effectively and know how to identify combining forms and affixes, they have good tools to help them as they read.

However, teachers also need to know how supportive the texts are in helping students access new terms. Supportive texts will provide meanings for important terms through restatement, illustrations, and examples. The terms may be identified in bold type or in italics. Some texts define terms in the margins. Other texts or text sections may not provide these scaffolds and key terms may remain opaque and students will require outside support for the vocabulary to become meaningful.

Before asking students to read a text or begin a unit of study, teachers can easily identify students' familiarity with key terms. Several informal activities provide good starting points. Using a Rate Your Knowledge chart of the terms, students can indicate their levels of familiarity with them before reading. As students are completing the activity, teachers can move around the classroom, making an informal assessment of how the students are responding. Teachers can also ask students to "Connect 2–3 of the Terms" and write a sentence using the terms as an initial assessment. The students who struggle to create interesting and accurate sentences can be noted and more vocabulary work can be provided. An alternative activity is to have students sort new terms into concept groups and then to label the groups. Each of these informal activities provides a way for teachers to get an initial assessment of students' familiarity with key terms and concepts needed for learning.

These same activities can be used at the completion of the study, also. Changes in levels of knowledge of terms, ability to write using the terms accurately, and ability to cluster similar terms by concept are what is expected from focused learning. Both students and teachers can compare beginning and ending knowledge levels and evaluate growth together.

If the study permitted focus on particular combining forms or affixes, the same kind of pre–post assessments can be given. Creating an activity in which students are asked to divide several key content words into their parts (prefix, base, suffix) and provide meanings for each is a quick way to determine how comfortable students are in using word parts. Any unfamiliar word part can then be included on a study list—with students searching for other similar words, with groups creating lists of families of terms, etc. At the conclusion of the unit, students can be asked to create a list of related terms, define some unknown terms with the familiar parts, or engage in using the word parts in some creative way.

By focusing assessment on specific terms that are used in the stories, informational texts, or general unit concepts, teachers and students can take the word-learning journey together. Specific targeted words and word-learning tools are valuable to monitor, and the concreteness of the gains motivates students to continue their learning.

Check Your Understanding 7.3: Gauge your understanding of the skills and concepts in this section.

Teaching Strategies for Independent Word Learning

Students also need to develop independent strategies for dealing with the new words they will meet both in school and in other areas of their lives. The goal is that when they encounter unknown words, students can examine the external context for general clues, look at the structure and morphology of the word itself (the internal context) for clues, or consult a reference, if needed. They will also determine if the word is one they want to add to their general vocabulary. If it is, then they will employ a strategy to help them retain the word—by creating a word card, making a personal association and practicing it, or using some other memory device.

Teachers can do a great deal to help students become active language learners. For students to maximize their opportunities to expand their vocabularies, they need to be actively engaged in their own learning. They need to be helped to develop some awareness of how they can learn new words and to explore strategies for attending to words and rehearsing them. It is important that teachers not give the false impression that word learning is the same as memorizing definitions for terms on a list the teacher supplies. Teachers do a big disservice when they pass on this traditional and ineffective approach to word learning. Rather, teachers need to guide students to understand that word learning is an ongoing and cumulative process.

When teachers create a word consciousness in their classrooms and engage students in a variety of different approaches to word learning, students are most likely to notice unfamiliar words when they see and hear them. They are also much more likely to internalize some of the approaches to determining the meanings of unfamiliar words and relating the new terms to others that are associated or similar.

Using Context Clues

One of the most immediate sources of information about new terms students encounter as they read is the context of the text sentence and passage itself. While context does not necessarily help in determining what a word means, it is often very useful. The immediate sentence in which a new term appears, the surrounding paragraph, and visual displays can be useful, and students should learn to mine themas clues to meaning. A starting place for determining what these words mean is to use the surrounding context—the sentence, paragraph, and visual clues in written texts or the meaningful talk one hears. The following sections list several frequently used **context clues** that authors use and to which students should attend.

SYNONYM OR APPOSITIVE   The author provides an additional word or phrase that explains the less familiar one within the same or adjoining sentences. An **appositive** refers to nouns or noun phrases placed close by the word or phrase it renames.

Example: John Brown, the fiery abolitionist, migrated or moved to Kansas.

EXPLANATION   The author provides a definition or elaborates on the term.

Example: Can't you ever stand still? You are so peripatetic; it makes me dizzy the way you are always moving around.

CONTRAST OR ANTONYM   The text includes an **antonym**, a word or phrase that contrasts with the targeted word.

Example: There was an abundance of strawberries, but almost no one to pick them.

GENERAL CONTEXT   No specific synonym or phrase is included, but the meaning is inferred from the surrounding information and familiar content.

Example: It was such a memorable experience! Katie couldn't imagine that all of her friends could have kept the secret of her party from her for so long. And what a festive party, with a piñata and taco bar!

VISUALS   In addition, books frequently contain visuals that help children (and adults) determine the meanings of many terms, especially in content materials where diagrams, illustrations, and maps can provide needed contexts for specific terms. Just as early primary teachers involve students in previewing stories by doing "book walks," students can learn to independently use the rich visual information that generally is part of informational texts if teachers have taken time make them aware of these important sources. Children need to develop the habit of previewing material they are going to read, attending to the visuals, and connecting the visuals to the written text sections. By reading visual information, students have a valuable source of information that can help them understand key vocabulary as they encounter the new words. They can learn to "read" the visual components and relate them to the other parts of the text.

Readers need to learn to use all the resources authors provide as they consider what unfamiliar terms may mean. Because context is often not clear in revealing meanings of terms, it is always good to take advantage of tables of contents, dictionary, and glossary supports. Teachers should help students learn to use these important resources as they read informational/content area materials and can reinforce such use by also having students create these supports when they write their own essays, books, and feature articles.

Showing Relationships Among Terms and Word Parts

In addition to using the external context of the text sentences and visuals to discern the meaning of unknown terms, students need to also use the internal context of words, the meaningful affixes and roots, to determine word meanings. Morphology often provides keys that can unlock meanings of complex terms. The intermediate grades are the years to focus students' attention on how words are formed and modified. Identifying morphemes, particularly derivational morphemes and common affixes, helps students determine word meanings.

Students can develop their vocabulary detective skills by attending to the meaningful parts of unfamiliar terms. For example, students who encounter the word "disrupt" while reading won't be lost if they take the word apart. The meaning of *disrupt* can be deduced from partial knowledge (e.g., *disrupt* = *dis* (apart) + *rupt* (break up). The student can connect

Teach It! 67
Word Origins and Derivations
Through an examination of morphemes and affixes, these language and vocabulary building practices help students determine word meanings by calling their attention to how words are formed and modified.

Figure 7.7 A Connected Word Web

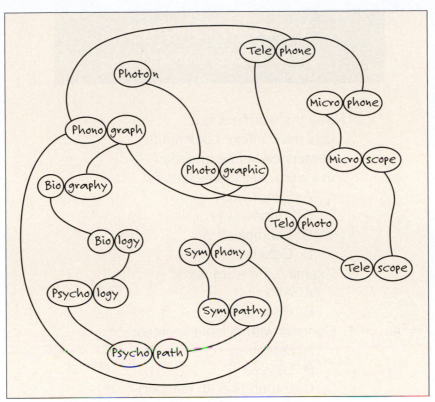

the morpheme *-rupt* to other words they may know like *interrupt* and *corrupt*. Students can take the prefix *dis-* and brainstorm other words with the same prefix—or even the prefix used as a standalone slang word, "Don't 'dis' me." Students who actively use morphology have an important word learning tool.

CONNECTED WORD WEB   A more advanced activity for students in sixth grade and up is to take word parts of historical morphemes (such as *-rupt, -graph,* and *tele-*) and historical affixes (such as *con-, sym-,* and *a-*) and link them together using a **connected word web**, such as the one shown in Figure 7.7.

Students draw circles around the historical morphemes and connect them with lines to the same historical morphemes in other words. Then they do the same with historical affixes. Finally, they try to infer the meaning of unknown words if they know what the historical morpheme and affix mean; and they try to infer the meaning of the historical morpheme and affix if they know what some of the words mean. Students need to learn how to search word histories online or they should have a good dictionary with etymologies (word histories) available to check answers. The more they understand how to use morphemes and combining forms, the deeper their independent word learning becomes.

VOCABULARY DETECTIVE BOOKMARKS   Students can access a variety of clues to the meaning of unknown terms. An easy way to help them remember to do so is to have them create **Vocabulary Detective Bookmarks**. They can design their own and make them personal, but a basic one is shown in Figure 7.8.

In adding new vocabulary terms to their own lexicons, learners start with a kernel of meaning for a new term and then keep expanding their understanding of how that term is used in varied situations. Each time learners encounter the term in print or in oral language, they can check out their own understanding against the new input and then modify their association network for the term.

CONCEPT OF DEFINITION MAP   A graphic format that helps students understand the ways an understanding of new terms is built is the **Concept of Definition Map** that highlights the relations among words and their meanings (Schwartz & Raphael, 1985).

Figure 7.8 Vocabulary Detective Bookmark

> ## *Vocabulary Detectives:*
> ### *Keys for Unlocking Unknown Words*

1. Say the word out loud.
2. Use the context: Look at the sentences before and after the word. Are there clues in
   A. Synonyms?
   B. Antonyms?
   C. Examples?
   D. Details?
3. Examine the word parts:
   A. Affixes
   B. Root words
4. Connect with reliable sources:
   A. Dictionary
   B. Glossary
   C. Expert (friend, teacher)

The new term is listed in the center of the Concept of Definition Map. Above the term, the student indicates the larger class of word to which the new one is related. Then the student elaborates the description of the term with more categorical and semantic information related to the word's definition, along with examples and nonexamples. Some variations of the map also ask students to draw an example of the term. By building this kind of association web around the new term, students can develop a better concept of what word learning entails.

Figure 7.9 Concept of Definition

SOURCE: Schwartz & Raphael in "Concept of Definition: A Key to Improving Students' Vocabulary," *The Reading Teacher 30*(2), 1985. Reproduced with permission of Wiley Inc.

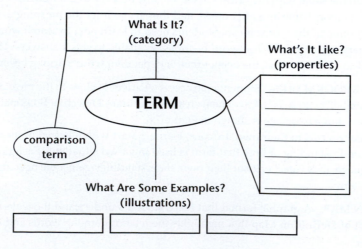

Differentiated Instruction

Visualizing Vocabulary

In a case study focused on using visual enhancements with English language learners and other reluctant readers (Ogle, 2000), struggling, less-than-enthusiastic science students became much more eager learners when their teacher developed a vocabulary card deck for them. Each week there were eight terms to be learned for which students were given 4 × 6-inch note cards. On one side, the students wrote the term and a description based on information from the teacher. On the other side, the students drew what they thought represented that term. During the week, students were given five minutes at the beginning of each science class to test their friends on the word cards. They would show the pictures to another student, who would have to guess what term was being illustrated. The increased motivation and learning were apparent. Students who had barely contributed to class became eager to see if their drawings would elicit the accurate connection for the class terms. José turned out to be a fairly gifted artist, and soon other boys were calling on him to help them more creatively illustrate terms. He also provided suggestions for depicting some of the more abstract concepts. A nearly invisible student became a central resource to the class with his artistic talent, and in the process, the teacher also learned that he had more to contribute about science than she had expected. While he hesitated to speak in class, he didn't hesitate to illustrate ideas. (See Figure 7.10 for an example of a student's word cards.)

NONLINGUISTIC REPRESENTATIONS   Another important tool in word learning is creating visual diagrams or pictures of the targeted terms. Marzano (2004) includes in his six-step process for helping students learn new academic terms the component "Students create a nonlinguistic representation of the new term." After the teacher provides a description of each term to be learned, students first write their own explanation of the term, and then represent the term in a graphic organizer, picture, pictograph, or cartoon form. Students who have experienced this form of representation often prefer the fun of illustrating new words they are learning in their own word notebooks. This is an especially valuable personal learning tool for English language learners and students with nonverbal strengths who can build personal visual associations with new terms.

Figure 7.10 José's Word Cards

Figure 7.11 Concept Ladder

What kind of thing is this?	What is it a part of?	What causes it?
What are the kinds of it?	What are its parts?	What does it cause?

CONCEPT LADDERS **Concept ladders** (Gillette, Temple, Temple, & Crawford, 2012) provide yet another way for children to organize their thinking and to categorize, thus supporting comprehension. The concept ladder shown in Figure 7.11 would be useful in a study on volcanoes and earthquakes. Such a graphic organizer requires students to think deeply about new terms and how they are related. It also helps students think of new terms as having important attributes that distinguish them from other similar terms. The more students play with new words and think of them as related terms the more likely they are to retain those words and use them successfully.

THE FRAYER MODEL Another graphic organizer for laying out words for a concept in relation to other words is the Frayer Model (Buhel, 2001). The Frayer Model directs students to think of essential and nonessential characteristics of a concept as well as examples and nonexamples of it. The model is best used to name a common concept that has many characteristics and examples. That way, the students are able to consider a larger number of words in context. See Figure 7.12 for the general template.

Watch how the Frayer Model is used in the following video, in a middle-school math class, to support students' ability to learn content vocabulary, and then answer the question that follows.

 Video Exploration 7.3: Watch the video and answer questions that reflect the content you have read.

Figure 7.12 Frayer Model

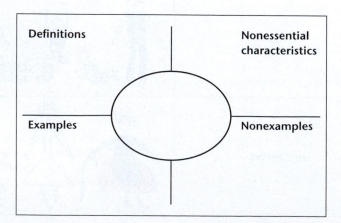

Using Online Sources to Build Vocabulary

Teachers can stimulate students' interest in words by using the online resources on vocabulary Web sites. Some have a new word each day that can be shared; others are great for providing word histories and noting new words that come into our language. There are a number of dictionaries, so terms can be looked up and the definitions and references compared. One of the easy ways to help students explore language is to introduce them to the resources now available on the Web. These tools are particularly useful for English language learners because they can use the online resources to look up words that they don't know in English and get helpful hints on what other sites are useful. There are several fun sources for words listed below.

General vocabulary and interesting information about words:

Wordsmith

Vocabulary.com

Funbrain

Spanish-English dictionaries are available at:

Spanishdict

YourDictionary

My Spanish Dictionary!

This chapter has presented a variety of ways teachers can create classrooms alive with words and attention to the power of language. Activities to teach vocabulary should relate words to a meaningful context, to other words, and to the students' own experiences. The goal is that students develop the habits of inquiring and exploring, making connections (to self, personal stories, and other books), collaborating with peers, expanding meaning (asking questions; interpreting; using higher-level thinking such as analysis and synthesis), and experimenting with new words and ways of expressing ideas and enjoy using language to grow and express themselves and their ideas. The most basic foundation is to help students develop a respect for language and create a classroom full of language—in both play and study.

Check Your Understanding 7.4: Gauge your understanding of the skills and concepts in this section.

For Review

At the outset of this chapter we stated that when you reached this point in your reading and studying you should be able to:

- **Argue for the importance of developing vocabulary.**

Vocabulary is an important component of reading comprehension. Words are labels for concepts, and the more concepts we have, the more easily we can understand both oral and written messages/texts. Words are also complex: many are polysemus and take on different meanings in different contexts. Words have specific denotations and connotations and these can change over time. Because English is evolving and growing, learning about words and developing strategies for understanding written language are important. Students with larger vocabularies have higher comprehension of what they read.

- **Summarize important research about vocabulary and apply it in the classroom.**

Vocabulary is a big divider: Research has made clear that some children come to school with at least twice as many words in their vocabulary as others, and the vocabulary size affects their understanding, not only of text, but of the world around them. With regular and meaningful vocabulary instruction, students' vocabularies grow significantly; such instruction includes attention to both general vocabulary and content area, academic vocabulary.

- **Describe important components of a strong instructional program for vocabulary development.**

There is a vast vocabulary to learn, so teachers must prioritize. Several guidelines for teaching vocabulary were provided in this chapter, beginning with teachers creating interest in words and language use, developing a classroom environment that encourages respect for words, teaching specific words and relationships among them, and teaching students strategies for understanding words and ways to become independent word learners. Across the content areas teachers have multiple opportunities to help students acquire new word meanings and deepen their understanding of how words work. The most basic foundation is to help students develop a respect for language and create a classroom full of language—in both play and study. One way to think about vocabulary that needs to be learned is to use the three tiers model developed by Beck and colleagues. Tier 1 words are the most common conversational words we use daily and are most easily learned by English language learners. Tier 2 words are used in general academic contexts, while Tier 3 words are more specifically related to particular topics or discipline areas. Teachers need to think about the usefulness of words they might teach in relation to these tiers and also to the content they want students to learn. General academic and discipline-specific words are both needed, but may be developed with different intensity. Across the content areas teachers have multiple opportunities to help students acquire new word meanings and deepen their understanding of how words work.

• **Develop students' independence in vocabulary acquisition.**

Involving students in assessing their own readiness for particular units of study (both literature and informational) and taking ownership of learning terms is important so that students become lifelong vocabulary learners. All of this is possible when teachers create classrooms alive with talk and curiosity about vocabulary. Teachers who encourage children's explorations with words and provide tools for them to use give children a good start. These tools include using context clues, both internal and external; understanding morphology, relating terms semantically, and developing the habit of reviewing and practicing using new words.

For Your Journal

1. Review the Anticipation Guide and compare your earlier answers with what you think now.

2. Reflect on how you learn new vocabulary and list 2 to 3 added components that might enhance your own strategy for learning new words based on what you have read.

3. What questions do you have about incorporating vocabulary instruction in your teaching? Share these with a classmate and make notes of the ideas you generate.

Taking It to the World

How much does vocabulary matter to people? Sit down with two or three classmates and make a list of as many ways as you can that vocabulary matters in people's lives. It might help get the conversation going to recall the self-help books published for adults that promise them more successful careers if only they will master a larger vocabulary or the vocabulary items on the SAT test.

Think also of times—in films or in the discourse of our politicians—when having a larger vocabulary is held up as a sign of snobbery.

After making a list of both kinds of situations, try to reach a conclusion. What are the advantages of having a large vocabulary? What caveats should be kept in mind about using the right words at the right time? How will you use these conclusions in your teaching?

Chapter 8

Reading Comprehension, Part I: Making Sense of Literature

 ## Learning Outcomes

After reading this chapter, you should be able to:

1. Explain how students come to understand literature.

2. Utilize general strategies for teaching students to read with comprehension.

3. Teach specific skills of reading comprehension.

4. Demonstrate methods of close reading of fiction.

5. Assess students' reading comprehension.

Anticipation Guide

The following statements will stimulate your thinking about the topics of this chapter. Answer *true* or *false* in response to each statement. As you read and learn more about the topics in these statements, double-check your answers. See what interests you and what prompts your curiosity toward more understanding.

_____ 1. Comprehension, or understanding what you read, is entirely a process of memorizing the details of the author's message.

_____ 2. Comprehension is the aspect of reading that has traditionally gotten the most attention in classrooms.

_____ 3. Comprehension relies on what a reader already knows about the topic of the text. The more you already know, the more you are likely to understand from the reading.

_____ 4. Good readers constantly monitor their understanding, to be sure they are making sense of the text.

_____ 5. Teaching a student to read with comprehension is not at all like teaching athletic skills or skill in art.

_____ 6. Good comprehension lessons have three parts: consolidation, building knowledge, and anticipation, in that order.

_____ 7. Following the structure of the text helps the reader make sense of what is written.

_____ 8. Teaching comprehension is complete once the reader understands the meaning of a text.

_____ 9. Literary aspects like plot, characterization, literal and figurative language, and the characters' point of view may concern teachers of literature, but not teachers of reading.

_____ 10. The Common Core State Standards treat reading comprehension as a single skill: comprehension is comprehension, regardless of the type or topic of the text.

A Classroom Story

Reading for Comprehension in a Fourth-Grade Classroom

The students in Hank da Silva's fourth grade at North Street Elementary School can predict the day's events in broad outline, but not completely. They know that after the morning class meeting, they will talk about their topics in social studies. They have been reading about the settlement of the Great Plains in their social studies text. At the same time, they have been reading Patricia McLachlan's Sarah, Plain and Tall *and Laura Ingalls Wilder's* The Little House on the Prairie. *Mr. da Silva reads to them from* Letters from a Woman Homesteader, *a work of nonfiction told in the form of letters home from a feisty single woman in the 1880s. He has also bookmarked and assigned three Internet sites where students will find information about the settlement of the Great Plains by European Americans.*

The class has written dual-entry diaries every day about their readings. They have also created a Venn diagram comparing what skills people have to have if they move to a new place now compared to what skills people needed in the days of the homesteaders. Figure 8.1 shows what the class has come up with.

This morning, Mr. da Silva is conducting a discussion of a couple of pages of the social studies book. He begins by pointing out that sometimes textbooks do not make their meanings very clear.

"Take right here, for instance," he points out. "The text says, 'Westward expansion gave the new country a constant sense of excitement, of new possibilities.' What do you suppose the author means by that sentence? Let's start with 'Westward expansion.' What do you suppose he means by expansion? *If the author were here, what do you think he would say about that?"*

After lunch, Mr. da Silva has reading workshop. According to the rotation chart on the wall, some students read independently. Today those students are doing something special: They are writing self-assessments about their reading comprehension, which they will later give to Mr. da Silva. A group of six students who are reading Phyllis Reynolds Naylor's Shiloh *meet with Mr. da Silva for a literature circle; each of the six students is conducting a part of the discussion, according to a role she or he has been assigned. Mr. da Silva takes part in the discussion, but he also is taking occasional notes. He writes about how the discussion is going. He writes a note to remind himself to have the students ask more questions of each other in the literature circle rather than just reporting on what they think. He also makes a note that four of the students do not seem to make the connection between the boy's asking the shopkeeper for stale bread to feed the dog he has hidden away and the food that people in the community begin leaving for his father, a mail carrier. In other words, they are not making inferences. In the course of the next week, Mr. da Silva will make a point of reading with each one of these students to see what aspects of reading comprehension they are using well and not so well. In the meantime, he will teach a minilesson on making inferences during reading workshop tomorrow.*

Figure 8.1 What You Need to Live in a New Place

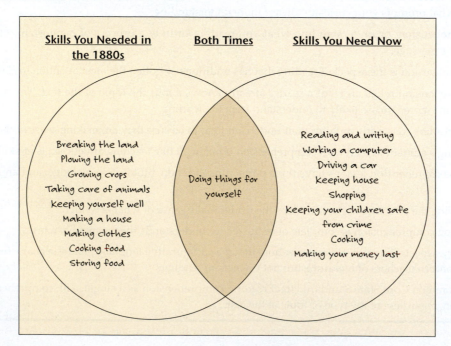

How Students Understand Literature

The goal of reading instruction is for all students to read with comprehension—understanding what they read. Comprehension in reading is also a sort of thermometer measuring the intellectual life of a classroom. True, teaching children to read with understanding is partly a matter of teaching them a special set of reading skills. But it is also a matter of exposing students to literature—both fiction and nonfiction—cultivating their knowledge about a range of subjects, stimulating their habits of inquiry, helping them make connections between ideas, and inspiring in them a broad range of interests. Researchers tell us that reading comprehension has too often been left to chance, as if understanding would happen if only children could read the words. Surveys of reading instruction in elementary schools, from more than thirty-five years ago (Durkin, 1978–1979) and more recently (Pressley, 1999), have found that word recognition instruction is common enough, but it is rarer to find teachers trying to develop their students' comprehension. Reading comprehension *is* heavily stressed in state standards for literacy, and especially so in the Common Core State Standards.

In this chapter, we talk about ways to help students understand narrative texts. Chapter 9 is devoted to teaching readers to understand and learn from informational text. First, we set out some ideas about reading comprehension.

Reading comprehension has two sides to it. On one side we focus on what the reader already knows about the topic of the text, and on his or her strategies to make sense of the text. Because this side of comprehension focuses on the reader's efforts to construct knowledge, we call this the *constructivist side*. The other side of comprehension is the *textual side*. The focus here is on the ways texts convey meaning, including the nuances of vocabulary, the plot or other text structures, the author's point of view, references to other texts, and other literary devices.

Constructing Meaning

A reader is a sense-maker, one who works to construct meaning from a text. Many reading specialists' favorite explanation of how meaning construction works is schema theory, articulated many years ago by Richard Anderson and David Pearson (1984).

SCHEMA THEORY   **Schema theory** (Anderson & Pearson, 1984) holds that readers understand what they read by finding cues in the text that lead them to summon up frameworks of stored knowledge from their memories. These frameworks of prior knowledge have been called *schemas*. Once readers have a schema in mind, they use it to make sense of the other details. There is a complementary relationship between readers' schemas and the details on the page. Noting the details tells them which schemas to evoke, and evoking the schemas helps them to make sense of the details. Consider the following example:

> *Shawn's footsteps slowed as he approached the door to Belinda's apartment. Two children were ahead of him, already knocking on the door. They were dressed in the proper clothing. But Shawn had on his old jeans. Shawn was also embarrassed because he was empty-handed. His mother had been at work when he got home from school, and he hadn't any money of his own.*
>
> *The door swung open, and there was Belinda in a nice dress and a party hat.*
>
> *"Hi," she said. "Come on in."*
>
> *"Hi," he said as he sidled into the apartment, his hands behind his back. Inside, the table was set for the celebration and piled high with the things other children had brought. Shawn avoided the table and slid into a corner.*
>
> *Just then, Belinda's mother shouted from the kitchen, "Get ready to sing, everybody. Here it comes!" She marched ceremoniously in from the kitchen holding forth her beautiful creation, her face brightened by the nine tiny flames.*

If you spent your childhood in the United States, you surely realized that the passage tells of a birthday party. Once you worked that out, you summoned a cognitive scheme that led you to feel Shawn's embarrassment because he hadn't worn party clothes or brought what each of the other guests had piled on the table—a birthday present. You also knew what song would be sung ("Happy birthday to you . . ."), and what it was the mother proudly carried in from the kitchen (a birthday cake with nine candles). How much of what you understood about the passage was actually supplied by the text? And how much information did you yourself supply?

Schema theory is a powerful way of understanding comprehension. It shows us that students' prior knowledge, or their schemas—like the knowledge you just brought to the birthday party scenario—is very important to their reading comprehension. It also shows us that understanding is real activity. Readers do not passively absorb meaning from the page; they construct meaning by trying to make sense of details according to the schemas they already possess in their memories. Watch this video in which a teacher activates her students' prior knowledge before reading a new book and then answer the question that follows.

 Video Exploration 8.1: Watch the video and answer questions that reflect the content you have read.

READER RESPONSE THEORY   Reader response theory is an explanation of what happens when individual readers make meaning from literary texts (Bleich, 1978; Iser, 1978; Rosenblatt, 1978) (see the World of Reading box). As formulated by Louise Rosenblatt, reader response theory suggests that three considerations are involved whenever a fictional text is read meaningfully: the *reader*, the *text*, and the *poem*.

The Reader   The reader brings her background knowledge to the reading. That knowledge includes the meanings she holds for words; her likes, dislikes, fascinations, and fears; her experience with works of a certain style or genre or works by a certain author; and her experiences in the world with certain people, places, and things.

The Text   The text consists of the words put on the page by the author, along with the images, if any, provided by an illustrator. It includes the design and layout of the book—or, if it is an electronic text, it can add audio, links, and other aspects of the presentation to our list of features. The text is, in short, all of the things put in front of the reader or audience to respond to.

Authors, illustrators, and designers of books and other media have a full range of artistry at their disposal in creating a text. Writers select words for their exact meanings, but also for their figurative associations and connotations, as well as their appeal to the senses. Authors create settings and characters, and they roll out events in patterns and plots, depicted from a particular perspective, narrated in a certain style and tone, all working together to drive home a theme. Illustrations may duplicate what the text says, they may show just a few aspects of what is written, or they may create irony by suggesting something very different from or even contradictory to the text.

The Poem   The *poem* is the word used for the meaning of a text that each reader constructs. Readers have knowledge of things in the world, and much of it varies from place to place, culture to culture, and age group to age group. Readers have knowledge of literature in general and some genres and authors in particular. They also have drives, concerns, and preferences. They bring all of this with them when they read a text. But there are always things they don't bring, since readers have gaps, too. They may lack relevant world knowledge, or understand little of the dynamics of literature, or have limited vocabulary. What they bring and what they do not bring to a reading will dispose them to attend to certain aspects of the text, ignore other aspects, and even supply still other aspects of their own. The particular mix of what is in the text and what the reader brings to the text is unique to each reader. And that is what is called the *poem*. (Rosenblatt is using the historical sense of the word *poem*, meaning a "created thing," not necessarily something that rhymes!)

The poem is what comes to mind when you think back on a book you have read. It is not just the author's exact words. It is not just your memories from your own life and your knowledge of word meanings and literary devices that you called to mind as you read. It is a construct that is made of both.

But here is a question: Where should we say the meaning of a particular text resides? Does a text "mean" whatever any reader thinks it means? Or does each text have a particular meaning? Scholars disagree on the answer, and tend to take positions along a spectrum between one position that affords a reader a lot of freedom to make her own meaning and the opposite position that insists there is a fixed meaning to every text that every reader should "get." The way you teach will be influenced by the position you take. If you believe in the reader's freedom to make meaning, you will ask open-ended questions and encourage alternative interpretations of a text. But if you believe a text has a fixed meaning, you will encourage your students to arrive at that meaning, and you will discourage alternative interpretations.

A middle ground is to make sure the students understand the devices texts use to convey or afford meanings. Educating readers about the workings of literature will give them relevant tools to make sense of literary texts.

SCHEMA THEORY AND BACKGROUND KNOWLEDGE OF ENGLISH LANGUAGE LEARNERS   Schema theory and **reader response criticism** both stress the importance to comprehension of what a reader already knows. But learners who come to our schools from other cultures and other parts of the world may either lack relevant background knowledge, or—what may be even more confusing—have different associations for the same referents. A wedding is a happy occasion, right? Not in some parts of India, where a bride may be bartered away by her parents into a miserable subservient role in a family of strangers. Going out to a restaurant is a pleasure, not so? Not in some parts of Morocco, where going out to a restaurant brings scorn on a family because it is assumed that the wife is too lazy to cook. Be careful to look for places in texts where culture-based background knowledge may be essential to readers' understanding, and explain that information as you need to.

The World of Reading

Reader Response in Action

Diane Barone (1992) reports on a second- and third-grade class in which the teacher was having her students record their reactions to each chapter of Roald Dahl's *Danny the Champion of the World* (1998) in a kind of response journal called a **dual-entry diary**. An early chapter in the book describes the cozy days enjoyed by Dahl's protagonist, living in a gypsy wagon with his father. After reading this chapter, a student in the class wrote that he was expecting the woman to come into the story at any time. The teacher was puzzled, because the only woman who had been mentioned in the book was the boy's late mother, who had died in childbirth. But in entry after entry, her student registered his worry that the woman might come into the story on the very next page. As it turned out, this young reader had lived a cozy existence for some time alone with *his* own father—until the father found a female companion. For the little boy, the woman really did come along, and the boy no longer had an exclusive claim to his father's attention.

The boy created a poem out of *Danny the Champion of the World* that was about the almost-too-good-to-be-true bliss of a boy's living alone with his father and his feeling of dread at its loss. The boy's concerns had led him to write responses that seemed bizarre at first. Yet it serves as a good example of how stories can evoke different responses from different people, children included. Teachers need to be aware of this critical piece of information.

As the boy's reading of *Danny the Champion of the World* suggests, there can be striking variations in the interpretations or poems created by different readers. That is why David Bleich (1970) urges teachers to think of literature discussion groups as interpretive communities. *Interpretive communities* are places where readers share their responses to works of literature so that communities of understanding can be formed. The sharing of individual responses not only contributes to a larger understanding of a work, but also promotes students' awareness of each other's thinking. Becoming aware of others' thinking is of particular value when the students come from different social and cultural backgrounds.

It takes special approaches on the teacher's part to set up an interpretive community. Merely asking students to answer literal questions will not do it. Teachers need to create a risk-free environment and to conduct—or let students conduct—discussions that invite personal responses to questions such as, "What did you notice in the text? What did it make you think of? How did it make you feel?"

Textual Factors in Comprehension

Complementing the constructivist side of comprehending fiction, the other side of the issue of comprehension is what the reader should know about the ways literary texts are constructed.

LITERARY TEXTS COME IN *GENRES*   Knowing whether a text is a folktale, a fantasy, or a work of realistic fiction shapes a reader's expectations for what is likely to happen in the work—or at least it should. Readers should be aware of **genres** of literature and be able to explain their features and the way awareness of the genres influences what they expect to happen in a story.

LITERARY TEXTS HAVE *SETTINGS, CHARACTERS, PLOTS,* **AND** *THEMES*   It organizes children's expectations when they recognize that stories introduce characters in a setting. The characters have problems they try to solve and goals that they attempt to achieve over a series of events called a *plot*. The Common Core State Standards express the expectation that children will recognize these elements and be able to talk about them as they discuss stories.

LITERARY TEXTS USE LANGUAGE IN UNIQUE WAYS   Literary texts differ from **informational texts** in striking ways. Literary texts use language that appeals to the senses far more than informational texts. A children's book or poem regularly uses words that suggest sights, sounds, and feelings. Poetry uses words that have sensory qualities—words may be chosen because their sounds reinforce the message being conveyed. Literary writing has distinctive tones: It may be comical, somber, suspenseful, or lyrical, and the choice of words and length and rhythm of sentences all contribute to the tone. Literary language can be either literal (saying things directly) or figurative (saying things by association). It often uses comparisons—similes and metaphors. Finally, although literary texts may tell truths—as in lessons about the human experience—their details do not reliably relate directly to reality. From reading the *Harry Potter* books you can learn truths about destiny, the conflict between good and evil, and the power and limitations of friendship, but you can't use the books as a roadmap that will lead you to an actual Hogwarts School.

Acts of Comprehension

What are key strategies and skills that children and other readers use to comprehend text? Researchers have agreed on several. This list, derived from Pressley and Afflerbach (1995), captures the issue nicely. Comprehending a passage well involves the following:

Engaging prior knowledge

Knowing vocabulary

Visualizing details and events

Following the patterns of texts

Asking questions and pursuing answers

Making inferences

Monitoring comprehension

Noting main ideas from supporting details

Summarizing and rehearsing main ideas

ENGAGING PRIOR KNOWLEDGE   When they begin to read, good readers focus on the topic of the text, decide what they already know about it, and make predictions about what they are likely to learn. As they read, they go back and forth between what they knew about the topic and what they are finding out. When they are finished reading, they might reexamine what they knew or thought they knew and take note of how their knowledge has changed on account of the reading they have done. Not all readers do this fully developed version of engaging prior knowledge and checking new information against it, but readers should at least sense the topic of the reading and be reminded of what they already know about it.

Families can support children's development of comprehension by keeping up their contributions to children's background knowledge and supporting children's voluntary reading. Teachers can remind parents of the importance of taking their children to the library and museums and of putting informative children's magazines on their children's gift lists. *Ranger Rick*, the nature magazine, features enticing photographs of animals in the wild and articles on wildlife that fascinate children ages seven and up. *Cobblestone* magazine features interesting articles on historical topics that appeal to children ages nine and up. *National Geographic World* features highly illustrated articles on everything from undersea exploration to mountain climbing, and *Sports Illustrated for Kids* follows teams and players and talks about the basics of the sports.

For general reading, including stories to read, *Cricket* magazine for children ages eight and up and *Ladybug* for slightly younger children feature work that makes good reading by well-known and aspiring children's authors. *Highlights for Children* also features stories and interesting informational articles, as well as riddles and games.

KNOWING VOCABULARY   Knowing the words in a text is an issue both in comprehension and in word recognition. As an aspect of comprehension, vocabulary items can be considered building blocks of understanding. It is possible to understand a text without knowing all the words, by making inferences from the context surrounding the unknown word. But making such inferences ties up concentration that might otherwise be used to comprehend the larger meaning of the text. Whether by making important information unavailable or by distracting attention, a shortage of vocabulary makes comprehension harder. A good reader has a vocabulary available that is nearly equal to the vocabulary she or he encounters in reading.

Reading experts tend to agree that in order for a student to read a text without help, she must recognize and know the meanings of all but three or four words out of a hundred. If you have studied a foreign language in high school or college, you will know what a stiff challenge it must be for our English language learners to achieve that level of vocabulary knowledge. Teachers should explain all of the words they can (English language learners aren't the only ones who need it), but that won't be enough. Make sure English language learners have bilingual dictionaries at the ready, and encourage them to use them.

VISUALIZING DETAILS AND EVENTS   In creating works of fiction, authors take pains to describe events so the reader can visualize them and be drawn into the scene, or in Langer's term, "step into the **envisionment**." Here is the beginning of Frances Temple's (1996) *The Beduins' Gazelle*:

> *Halima sat with her chin resting on her knees, close enough to touch her kinspeople, yet with her mind far away. The singsong of the storyteller's voice lulled her. The lanterns threw a soft glow on the dark wall of the tent, on the red and brown embroidered cushions, on the familiar faces of the listening women and children. Halima played with her bangles, her mind drifting with the story.* (p. 1)

Teach It! 68
Visualization

This activity, in which students are encouraged to envision or record images—as words or pictures—created in response to what they are hearing or reading, enhances comprehension.

The author's appeals to sights, sounds, and touch lead a competent reader to create an image of the scene in a Bedouin's tent in North Africa, where the events of the novel will soon unfold.

FOLLOWING THE PATTERNS OF TEXTS   Texts come to us in genres, which are a combination of purpose and pattern. The narrative or story genre, for instance, has the purpose of relating fictional events in an entertaining or edifying way that usually evokes an emotional response. Stories follow structures or patterns called **story grammars**. A story usually introduces a main character and other characters in a setting and engages that character in an initiating event that leads the character to set a goal; then there might follow a series of episodes in which the character makes attempts to reach the goal. Each attempt has an outcome, and then follows a consequence, the state of affairs at the end of the story (Stein & Glenn, 1979). As we discussed in Chapter 3, research and experience have shown that even by the time they are in first grade, listeners and readers use their knowledge of story grammar both to understand and to produce their own stories.

Of course, texts have other kinds of structures, too. Patterns such as lists, taxonomies (hierarchical lists), descriptions, comparisons, and cause-and-effect and problem-and-solution explanations guide readers' understanding. Persuasive essays use the structure of claims, reasons for the claims, and evidence to support the reasons.

Text on the Internet has a sort of concatenated structure; that is, items are linked to other items, sometimes items within items like a Russian doll, or in the form of a web of connections. Readers can click on a term within an entry and be taken at once to a new entry that explains the term. While reading the new entry, readers might be invited to click on another term within that entry and be taken to a new entry explaining that term. So an entry on mammals might allow readers to click and go to an explanatory entry about elephants. There they might be invited to click and go to another entry or even a whole new Web site on Tanzania because that country is home to many elephants. The challenge to the reader, of course, is to keep in mind the topic of the original search and the questions that guided that search.

Reading by the pattern can help to guide the reader's understanding below the surface events toward the deeper logical structure of the text. Readers who know how to follow the patterns of text when they read learn to raise questions and search for answers according to the way the text reveals its contents. When they are reading a story, readers can identify the problem that the character has and try to anticipate the solution to the problem. When they are reading a problem-and-solution explanation, readers can identify the problem and look for solutions.

When working with the English language learners in your classroom, it helps to know that text patterns can differ by culture. The stories most often read in the United States and Canada have predictable plot structures: A character has a problem, and the whole story is a series of attempts to solve the problem and reach a resolution. Such patterns are less common in the books children read in Argentina, or even France—where the goal of the writer is to be wildly imaginative—and predictability is considered a failing. North American children's literature often features realistic fiction—stories about children who might have once lived, even though they were invented by authors. But realistic fiction for children—like literature of any kind for children, for that matter—is rare in most of the world. Books that are popular with children in North America are rarely didactic; that is, they don't overtly teach moral lessons, and if there are lessons to be learned, it is left to the reader to infer them. Stories for children in most of the world, though (and these are oral stories, more often than not), far more often do teach moral lessons, and these lessons are stated explicitly, so there is little room for children to make inferences. To be able to comprehend the books they are presented in American schools, readers from other cultures need to learn the "rules of the game" those books are playing. Otherwise, our books may be as baffling to English language learners as a game of rugby is to an American football player or a game of cricket is to a baseball player.

ASKING QUESTIONS AND PURSUING ANSWERS   As they come up with ideas related to the topic of the text, good readers make predictions about what they will find out. Then they monitor what they are learning from the text to see whether those predictions are being confirmed. When good readers read a story, they can follow the outlines of the plot to generate predictions and experience satisfaction or surprise as those predictions are confirmed or refuted by what happens. In fact, authors count on readers' acts of prediction to evoke emotional experiences of suspense, surprise, and completion as patterns of events raise expectations and sometimes thwart and sometimes satisfy them.

MAKING INFERENCES   When readers have to work out for themselves information that is not directly supplied by the text, they are making inferences. Fiction writers often leave gaps in the text (Iser, 1974) that must be filled in by the reader's inferences, and readers experience the activity as engagement. Even young readers make inferences. For example, kindergarten children enjoy listening to Harry Allard and James Marshall's ever-popular picture book *Miss Nelson Is Missing* (1977), about a too-sweet school teacher who is replaced by a very mean substitute teacher. Most young children, but not all, can infer the substitute teacher's identity from the next-to-the-last page of the book. There, the illustration shows (but the text does not mention) an ugly black dress hanging in the sweet teacher's closet underneath a box with the word WIG written in upside-down letters.

MONITORING COMPREHENSION   Good readers are aware when a text is making sense, and they realize when it does not. Perhaps they misread a word, or they assumed the text was going to say something that it does not. Then the breakdown in their comprehension leads them to go back and make a "repair." They reread the misinterpreted word or reconsider where the argument is going so that they again have the feeling they are understanding the text. Comprehension monitoring, then, assumes that readers think on two planes: They think about what the text means, and they are also aware of their own understanding or lack of it.

In the case of fictional or poetic texts in which there is figurative language or symbols, or irony to be navigated, the reader has more interpreting to do.

NOTING MAIN IDEAS AND SUPPORTING DETAILS   Readers who are aware of the argument of the text can distinguish main ideas from small details. Consider, for example, a child reading this passage from *Charlotte's Web*:

> *On foggy mornings, Charlotte's web was truly a thing of beauty. This morning each strand was decorated with dozens of tiny beads of water. The web glistened in the light and made a pattern of loveliness and mystery, like a delicate veil. Even Lurvy, who wasn't particularly interested in beauty, noticed the web when he came with the pig's breakfast. He noted how clearly it showed up and he noted how big and carefully built it was. And then he took another look and saw something that made him set his pail down. There in the center of the web, neatly woven in block letters, was a message. It said:*
> *SOME PIG!*
> *Lurvy felt weak. He brushed his hand across his eyes and stared harder at Charlotte's web. (White, 1952/1980, p. 77)*

There are many details in this passage about the way the spider's web looked. But a reader who gets the main idea will focus on the fact that the spider has written words, they describe her friend Wilbur the pig, and they have been noticed with great surprise by Lurvy, the farmhand. The child who has been following the plot of the story will realize that Charlotte's writing is a possible solution to the main problem of the book because it is meant to impress Wilbur's human owners so they will spare the little pig's life.

Readers who distinguish main ideas do so by following the argument of the text. They understand the problems the text is setting out to solve, and they are aware when information is significant in providing answers to questions or solutions to problems posed by the text: Such information is a main idea.

SUMMARIZING AND REHEARSING MAIN IDEAS   Once they identify main ideas, good readers might slow down, reread the passage that contained them, and rehearse the ideas so that they will remember them later (Pressley & Afflerbach, 1995). Following the reading, the readers might retell the main ideas to themselves, or they might reread important passages aloud to a friend. Good readers might reread the key passages in the text to make sure the main ideas were stated the way they remembered them. In this way, good readers hope to store the main ideas in memory and learn from the reading.

Check Your Understanding 8.1: Gauge your understanding of the skills and concepts in this section.

Teaching for Comprehension: General Strategies

Reading comprehension has many aspects, as we saw earlier in the chapter. But there are some general recommendations that can organize most lessons for comprehension. Think of a comprehension lesson as a meal, with an appetizer to get you started, a main course for nourishment, and a dessert to top it off. Similarly, when teaching comprehension, you want to begin by preparing students to make sense of what they will be reading (that's the appetizer), guide them in making sense of the text (that's the main course), and reflect back on what they learned from the text (that's the dessert—or perhaps you'd call it the after dinner conversation).

We call these three phases of the lesson **anticipation**, in which students are prepared to understand; **building knowledge**, in which they are guided to inquire and make meaning; and **consolidation**, in which they reflect back on, discuss, and otherwise do something with what they learned so they can make the new knowledge their own. Together, we call the three phases the ABC model.

The ABC model offers instructional choices for guiding comprehension—for activities to be used before reading (in the *a*nticipation phase), during reading (in the phase of *b*uilding knowledge), and after reading (in the phase of *c*onsolidation) after Vaughn and Estes (1986) and Steele and Meredith (1997). The ABC model is flexible. Within its three parts or phases, the teacher can make many choices. So, eventually, can the students, because they need to internalize the pattern of thinking captured by this model and use it when they read independently.

Strategies for the Anticipation Phase

Before they read, students should think about the topic, then recall their prior knowledge about it. If they don't have very much prior knowledge about the subject or if their thoughts about it are disorganized, the teacher might want to spend some time telling the students more about the topic and organizing their thinking about it. Readers should wonder how their present knowledge about the topic might relate to the text they are about to read. If they are to read an informational text, what do they still want to know about the topic that they might learn from this text? If it is a fictional text, what other works do they know by this author or in this genre? What does their prior knowledge lead them to expect from this reading? This preliminary phase of the lesson is what we call the *anticipation phase*.

Teaching goals in the anticipation phase are designed to prepare the students to read with comprehension. We want them to do the following:

- Connect the topic (or the genre, or the author) of the text they are about to read with their prior knowledge.
- Raise questions about the text they are about to read and set purposes for reading.
- Know the vocabulary they will need to make sense of the text.

Several teaching approaches can be used to achieve these goals.

FOCUSING QUESTIONS Questions that make a connection between what the students already know and what the reading will cover are valuable ways to prepare for a reading. In keeping with the goal of encouraging principled knowledge, it is advisable to steer questions toward the main ideas of the passage.

For example, a group of fifth graders are reading Pam Conrad's *Pedro's Journal* (1992), a fictional account of Columbus's historic voyage. Before the students begin reading the first chapter, the teacher asks, "If you were about to sail three ships across the Atlantic Ocean in 1492, at a time when nobody knew for sure what was on the other side of the ocean, what three pieces of advice would you give yourself?"

The students might discuss the question as a whole group, or use the think/pair/share procedure. Doing so activates thoughts and ideas that will help them make sense of and appreciate what they will encounter as they read the book.

THINK/PAIR/SHARE Focusing questions can be still more effective when a mechanism has been provided for all students to consider and answer them. Think/pair/share (Kagan, 1997) is a cooperative learning activity in which the teacher puts an open-ended question to the class, preferably by writing it on the board. Children are given two minutes to respond to the question individually. (Often they are asked to do this in writing.) Next, each child turns to a partner, and they share their answers with each other. Finally, the teacher calls on two or three pairs to share their answers with the class. Then the class begins reading the text. In a think/pair/share activity, every student—even in a class of 30 or more students—is motivated to think about the topic and to discuss it with someone else.

ANTICIPATION GUIDE Anticipation guides are used with fiction or with informational text. In using an anticipation guide (Vaughn & Estes, 1986), the teacher prepares a set of questions with short answers (usually true/false answers) that tap important aspects of the topic of the text. The questions are distributed to children on a worksheet, and the children are asked, individually or in pairs, to answer the questions as best they can before reading the assigned text. After reading the text, they return to the questions at the end of the class to see how their thinking has changed. Figure 8.2 provides an example of an anticipation guide for *Pedro's Journal*.

PAIRED BRAINSTORMING When factual information will be shared, older students can be asked to make personal lists of the facts they know or think they know about the topic of the reading (Vacca & Vacca, 1986). After two minutes, they turn to a classmate and combine their lists. The teacher can make a master list of the class's ideas and post them on the board or on a piece of newsprint so that the students can compare them with the ideas they have after they have read the text.

Figure 8.2 Anticipation Guide for *Pedro's Journal*

Instructions: Before reading *Pedro's Journal*, answer these questions *true* or *false* on the left-hand side. After reading the book, enter new answers on the right-hand side.

Answer Before   *Answer After*

_____   1. Columbus was well liked by his crew.   _____

_____   2. Columbus prepared his ships to sail in front of the wind.   _____

_____   3. Columbus's captains were very loyal to him.   _____

_____   4. The first people Columbus met lived in a city.   _____

_____   5. Columbus was very respectful of the people he met.   _____

_____   6. Columbus seemed very interested in finding gold.   _____

TERMS IN ADVANCE   A teacher may display a set of key terms that will be found in a reading and ask students to ponder their meanings as well as the relationships between the terms. The students are asked to predict how this particular set of terms might be used in the passage they are about to read. For example, if they are going to read *Miss Nelson Is Missing*, the terms might be as follows:

kind teacher	*mean substitute*	*police inspector*	*return*
misbehave	*make faces*	*homework*	*disguise*

Strategies for the Building Knowledge Phase

Once students have had their expectations raised for what they are about to read, they are ready for activities that will help them construct meaning from the text or build their knowledge. As they read, students need to compare their expectations with what they are learning from the text. They should be able to revise their expectations or generate new ones as the text reveals more information, raises more questions, or plants more clues. They also need to think about what they are reading and be able to identify the main points. They will need to reflect on what the text means to them personally and fill in any blanks in the text—that is, to make inferences about what the text says. Finally, they should be able to question the text, to argue with it. We call this phase of the lesson *building knowledge*. Several strategies for helping students to build knowledge are described next.

THINK-ALOUDS   A **think-aloud** is an activity in which a skilled reader reads aloud a passage of text and talks through her cognitive processes as she makes sense of the text. Think-alouds are patterned after coaching in sports, or the teaching of a craft. When a basketball coach teaches dribbling and shooting, she gathers the players around and then shows them how she dribbles and shoots. Then she guides and corrects them as they practice doing the same thing. When a potter shows apprentices how to throw down the clay at the center of the wheel, poke his thumbs into the whirling mass and pull up the sides, he does that many times in front of the students. Then he guides and critiques their practice. The same technique of offering demonstrations and then guiding students' practice can be used in teaching reading with comprehension, too, as a teacher reads a page out loud to a group of students and then verbalizes what is going through his mind, phrase by phrase. Think-alouds work best when the teacher is well prepared. Since the purpose of a think-aloud is to describe processes that are carried out automatically and unconsciously, it is not easy to find words for these processes. It is advisable to (1) choose in advance the passages to use for think-alouds, (2) determine the comprehension processes that the children still need to understand, and (3) practice in advance how you will explain those processes.

READERS' WORKSHOP   A readers' workshop combines a think-aloud with guided practice. The teacher typically begins with a brief demonstration of a skill in comprehension or other type of skill. The demonstration is followed by a discussion of the skill, with the goal of making the students able to verbalize the strategy that the teacher has used; for example, finding a main idea and the details that support it, making judgments about a character from the details that are provided, or deciding on the meaning of a phrase of figurative language. The teacher then asks individual students or pairs of students to read a passage or section of text aloud, using the newly taught skill. The students may read for self-selected books, and older students may keep a journal of their responses as they read. The teacher monitors their reading,

Teach It! 50

Know-Want to Know-Learn (K-W-L)

Appropriate for fictional and informational texts, this pre- and post-reading activity develops comprehension through responses to questions regarding what students already know and want to learn about a topic, and finally, what they learned from reading the text.

and, as the students present to the others what they have read and how they responded, the teacher discusses with the students their success in using the skill.

GUIDED READING   The guided reading procedure (Fountas & Pinnell, 1999) provides an excellent opportunity to teach comprehension. Guided reading proceeds in three steps.

1. *Prepare the children to read with understanding.* Begin with some of the following preliminary activities.
    - *Preview the text.* Show them the cover illustration, the title, and some of the pictures inside. "Think aloud" and speculate on what the text might be about. You may discuss the author and the kinds of books she or he writes.
    - *Introduce the genre.* Depending on whether the book is a folktale, a biography, a tall tale, or a work of realistic fiction, you may expect different things to happen in the text.
    - *Go over vocabulary.* Tell the students that they will meet some interesting words in this text. Name them one at a time. If the schedule allows, do a *word conversation* to introduce each word.
    - *Teach other skills.* Depending on your objectives for this lesson, teach a brief focused lesson on the skills you want the students to practice. For example, if you want the students to pay attention to the plot of the story, you can prepare them to fill out a *story map* such as the one found in Figure 8.4. Show the whole group how to fill out a story map, and later have them fill out a story map themselves after they have read the story.
    - *Read the story to them.* If the story is challenging for some of the students, you may choose to read it aloud to them first. If you have a big book version of the text available, they can read along with you.
    - *Begin a K-W-L (Know-Want to Know-Learn), a DRA (Directed Reading Activity), or a DRTA (Directed Reading-Thinking Activity),* strategies that will be explained in detail later in this chapter. Comprehension strategies that ask children to discuss what they know and what they think they will find out can be introduced now.

2. *The students read the text.* The students may read the text on their own or in pairs. A number of useful strategies for having them read with a purpose follow here.
    - *If you are conducting a DRA, a DRTA, or a K-W-L,* they read to an assigned stopping place and have questions to guide their search for information.
    - *They may buddy read,* that is, take turns reading paragraphs or pages.
    - *They may use the paired reading/paired summarizing technique* (Crawford et al., 2005). That is, one student reads a paragraph aloud and summarizes it. The other student asks questions about the passage that both answer. Then they change roles with the next paragraph, and so on.
    - *They may read with text coding* (Crawford et al., 2005). That is, the teacher helps students think of a set of four to six questions or issues they wish to track as they read the text. For example, if they are reading a passage about acid rain, they may be asked to look for passages that say where it occurs (W), others that say what its sources are (S), others that describe the chemical reactions that make it happen (CR), others that talk about the damage it does (D), and still others that talk about possible preventions of the problem (P). As they read, the students pencil in the letter indicating which kind of information they have found.

3. *The group reviews what they have learned.* After the students have read the text, the teacher brings them back together to discuss the text and to consolidate what they have learned.
    - *Discussions can use many of the formats described in this chapter.* These methods include Sketch-to-Stretch, shared inquiry, dual-entry diaries, Save the Last Word for Me, and dramatization.
    - *Revisiting the skills you introduced.* Assuming you began the lesson with certain skills in mind—understanding characterization, following the plot, getting the main idea, and so on—you will revisit those skills now. Have the students or pairs of students explain how they read and what they discovered, and make sure everyone understands and can carry out the practice you introduced.

QUESTIONING THE AUTHOR   The Questioning-the-Author technique, designed by Isabel Beck and her colleagues (Beck et al., 1997), rests on the realization that readers sometimes fail to understand what they read, not because they are incompetent, but because the authors haven't made their meaning sufficiently clear. When students listen to their peers reading their works aloud in a writing workshop, they don't hesitate to say, "I don't know what you mean right there. Help me understand." Yet when young readers come across unclear passages in a published text, they often assume that the problem is theirs for not understanding, rather than the author's for not writing clearly. This focused reading technique encourages students to question what they don't understand in a text.

To prepare to conduct the Questioning-the-Author procedure, choose a portion of texts that will support an engaged discussion of 20 to 30 minutes. Read through the text in advance and identify the major concepts that the students should glean from the text. Plan frequent stopping points in the text to devote attention to the important ideas and inferences in the passage. Write some probing questions to be asked at each stopping point to motivate discussion.

Conducting the Questioning-the-Author lesson then proceeds in two stages:

Stage 1. Preparing the Students' Attitudes. Begin the discussion by reminding students that comprehension often breaks down because authors don't tell readers everything they need to know. Things may be unclear. Ideas may have been omitted or hinted at but not stated. A good way to comprehend is to think of questions you would ask the author if she or he were present and imagine what the answers might be. Because the author is not present in the classroom, the class will attempt to answer for the author.

Stage 2. Raising Questions About the Text. Now have the students read a small portion of the text. At a preselected stopping point, pose a question or query about what the students have just read. Early in the text, initiating queries might be:

- What is the author trying to say here?
- What is the author's message?
- What is the author talking about?

Later in the text, follow-up queries might include:

- So what does the author mean right here?
- Did the author explain that clearly?
- Does that make sense with what the author told us before?
- How does that connect with what the author has told us here?
- But does the author tell us why?
- Why do you think the author tells us that now? (from Beck et al., 1997)

As you ask these questions, ask several students to contribute ideas. Prod the students to clarify their thoughts, to elaborate on their ideas, to debate each other's ideas, and to reach a consensus opinion.

THE DIRECTED READING ACTIVITY   In the Directed Reading Activity, a teacher poses a question to the students before they read a section of the story, and asks them to read the section to find the answer. The teacher's questions are meant to guide the students' attention to the important part of the story. An early question might ask about the setting. Another might ask about the main characters and the problem they face. Another might ask about the characters' attempts to solve the problem. And another might ask about the outcome of those attempts and their consequences—how things turn out for the characters in the end.

Questions can address more subtle features of the text, too, such as asking students to identify the way the author lets you know what kind of person a character is, or to explain how an author foreshadows something that will happen later, or to infer what a character's motives are or how one character feels about another.

In a single day's reading, the teacher usually breaks the text into about five sections, and will choose the stopping points in advance. More stops may break up the flow of the story, but fewer stops may not direct the students' attention to all of the important places in the story.

Once students gain skills at identifying characters, their main problems, and their efforts to solve them, they may be ready to move on to the Directed Reading-Thinking Activity. Many teachers continue to use the Directed Reading Activity, however, in order to help students develop key aspects of comprehension.

THE DIRECTED READING-THINKING ACTIVITY   The Directed Reading-Thinking Activity (Stauffer, 1975), or DRTA, uses the dynamic of prediction and confirmation to create interest and excitement around a reading assignment, provided

Teach It! 33

Directed Reading-Thinking Activity (DRTA)

This activity supports comprehension through the process of predicting that involves recalling and reorganizing prior knowledge as the story unfolds.

the text is a work of fiction with something of a predictable structure. The DRTA is normally done with a group of six to ten students; this size is large enough to yield a range of predictions but small enough for everyone to participate. It is advisable that the students be roughly matched for reading ability, because all students must wait for the slowest one to finish reading each section.

The DRTA can be used by itself, or it can follow one of the activities we introduced in the anticipation phase. Some teachers precede the DRTA with the terms-in-advance procedure or with the anticipation guide.

The teacher prepares for a DRTA by choosing four or five stopping places in the text, yielding more or less same-sized chunks of text. The stops should be placed right at points of suspense, places where the reader has been given some information and is wondering what is going to happen next (in other words, where the commercial break would be placed in a television thriller). One of these is normally right after the title.

In a DRTA, the questions are worded in an open-ended way. The teacher asks, "What do you think will happen? Why do you think so?" More specific questions from the teacher would take some of the initiative for making predictions away from the children, and the point here is for children to learn to ask their own questions about what they are reading.

There are a number of ways to scaffold a DRTA to make it more accessible to students. One is to read the text aloud instead of having the students read it. This variation of the method goes by a different name: the *directed listening-thinking activity*. Another is to think aloud yourself. If the predictions are slow in coming or seem to be going too wide of the mark, the teacher can offer a choice. For *Miss Nelson Is Missing*, the teacher might say, "I'm wondering if Miss Nelson has gone away to teach in another school where the kids are better behaved, or if she'll come back to her same class. Which one do you all think will happen?" Finally, in third grade and above, instead of a teacher-directed activity, a DRTA can be done by individual students or pairs of students.

Strategies for the Consolidation Phase

By the time they enter the consolidation phase, the students have gone through the text and have begun to comprehend it. They need to go further, though, and apply the meaning in order to convert it into useable knowledge. They need to summarize it and be able to interpret and debate the meaning while applying it to new situations and creating new examples of it.

Students need to practice higher-order thinking with the issues from the text. After they read, students should be able to think back over the material and summarize the main ideas. They should compare what they found out with what they thought about the subject when they first approached the reading. If the ideas are not transparent, students should be able to interpret them. If the text is evocative in some way, students might be able to make personal responses to the ideas, such as applying them to the way they normally think or to the realities of their own lives. Students should also be able to test out the ideas—using them to solve problems or think up other solutions to the problems posed in the text.

DUAL-ENTRY DIARY   The **dual-entry diary** (Berthoff, 1981) is a kind of journal students use to record responses to readings. To make a dual-entry diary, the students draw a vertical line down the middle of a blank sheet of paper. On the

CCSS

Common Core State Standards for Discussing Literature

The Common Core State Standards treat students' ability to participate in a discussion of literature as a language skill rather than an aspect of their reading comprehension (CCSS Speaking and Listening: Comprehension and Collaboration, Standards 1, 2, and 3), which means that a single lesson will have objectives for developing students' comprehension of a text and other objectives for helping them learn to discuss ideas from the text. The teaching strategies that follow in this section are useful for developing students' ability to participate in discussions of literature.

Teach It! 34

Dual-Entry Diary

This activity invites students to select and comment on text passages as it prepares them to participate in discussions of literature.

left-hand side, they write a passage or draw an image from the text that affected them strongly. Perhaps it reminded them of something from their own experience. Perhaps it puzzled them. Perhaps they disagreed with it. Perhaps it made them aware of the author's style or technique.

On the right-hand side of the page, they write a comment about that passage: What was it about the quote or image that made them choose it? What did it make them think of? What question did they have about it?

There are a number of ways in which these journals may be treated next. Students can exchange them and comment on each other's quotes. The teacher can take them up (a few each day) and comment on them. Or the children can bring them to a discussion group in which they are reading a common book and offer their comments to the discussion.

SAVE THE LAST WORD FOR ME   Save the Last Word for Me (Short, Harste, & Burke, 1996) provides a framework for a small-group or whole-class discussion of a text. The procedure is especially good for encouraging children to take the lead in discussing their reading. The steps of the strategy are as follows:

1. After being assigned a reading to do independently, students are given note cards and asked to find three or four quotations they consider particularly interesting or worthy of comment.

2. The students write the quotations they have found on the note cards.

3. On the other sides of the cards, the students write comments about their chosen quotations. That is, they say what the quotations made them think of, what is surprising about the quotations, and why they chose them.

4. The students bring their quotation cards to discussion groups. The teacher calls on someone to read a card aloud.

5. After reading the quotation on his or her card, the student invites other students to comment on that quotation. (The teacher might need to help keep comments on the subject of the quotation.) The teacher also may comment on the quotation.

6. Once others have had their say about the quotation, the student who chose it reads his or her comments aloud. Then there can be no further discussion. The student who chose it gets to have the last word.

7. That student can now call on another student to share his or her quotation and begin the process all over again. Not all students will be able to share their quotations if the whole class takes part in the activity, so the teacher will need to keep track of who shared quotes and make sure other children get chances to share their quotes the next time.

LITERATURE CIRCLES   **Literature circles** (Short & Kauffman, 1995), **grand conversations** (Eeds & Wells, 1989), and **book clubs** (Raphael et al., 1995) are all terms for literary discussions in which students' curiosity about the text is allowed to play a directing role.

Students in such discussions typically have read the same work; that work might be a short text they have already read or heard, or it might be a longer work that is discussed while students are still in the middle of it. The choice of texts for literature circles is critical because not all works are equally successful in evoking interested responses. Those that are successful often have a core mystery, elements that invite more than one interpretation, and a clear connection to issues that matter to the students.

These discussion groups may at first be conducted with the whole class at once until students have grown familiar and comfortable with the procedure. Then they may be conducted in smaller groups of four or five students meeting

Teach It! 36

Save the Last Word for Me

This comprehension-building activity invites students to select and respond to text passages they find particularly interesting or meaningful.

simultaneously. Literature circles are conducted several times a week. Early in the year, they might last no more than 20 minutes, but as students gain experience and confidence talking about literature, they might run for up to 40 minutes, not counting the time it takes to read the text. Everyone is free to offer comments and questions in literature circles, and students are reminded that they are free to address their comments and questions to other students and not always to the teacher.

The role of the teacher in a literature circle is mainly to be a spirited participant; however, Martinez (in Temple et al., 2014) points to four additional roles teachers play:

1. *The teacher is a model.* The teacher might venture her or his own questions or responses to get a discussion going. The teacher is careful to speak as one seeking insights and not as a lecturer. The teacher's statements might begin, "I wonder about . . ."

2. *The teacher helps students learn new roles in a literature circle.* Although all students know how to have conversations, they might need reminding about ways to participate in conversations in a classroom. These include rules such as the following:
   - Sit in a circle so that everyone can see each other.
   - Only one person speaks at a time.
   - Listen to each other.
   - Stay on the topic.

3. *The teacher moves the conversation forward.* Without dominating the discussion, the teacher might invite other students to comment on something one student has said. The teacher might ask a student to clarify an idea. Or the teacher might pose an interesting open-ended question that she or he has thought about in advance. (Such interpretive questions are discussed in the section on shared inquiry later.)

4. *The teacher supports literary learning.* Lecturing about literature is not an adequate substitute for having students think and talk about it; nonetheless, it helps if teachers supply students with concepts and terms they can use to give form to ideas they are trying to express or insights they are struggling to grasp. A student might notice that there is a point in a story where tension is highest because the main question in the story is about to be answered. The teacher tells the student that this is a *climax.* Researchers have noted that students' discussions go deeper when they have literary terms available to them (Hickman, 1979, 1981).

When conducting cooperative learning activities, the teacher might need to assign students particular roles to play in a group. Over time, when individual students learn to play the many roles of encourager, timekeeper, facilitator, recorder, and summarizer, they eventually learn all of the aspects of a good participant in a group because a good participant may practice most of these roles at once.

Literature circles often function better when students have particular roles to play. Also, by performing designated roles, students may exercise the many tasks that are carried out by an effective reader and discussant of literature. Table 8.1 outlines roles that students may play in a literary discussion (Daniels, 1994, 2001).

Five suggestions make the use of these roles more successful:

1. Teach the roles to the whole class, one at a time. The teacher might read or tell a story, then introduce one of the roles—for example, the connector. The teacher might then call attention to a connection between something in

---

Table 8.1 Roles in a Literary Discussion Group

- *Quotation finder:* This student's job is to pick a few special sections of the text that the group would like to hear read aloud.

- *Investigator:* This student's job is to provide background information on any topic related to the text.

- *Travel tracer:* When characters move from place to place in a text, this student's job is to keep track of their movements.

- *Connector:* This student's job is to find connections between the text and the world outside.

- *Question asker:* This student's job is to write down (in advance of the discussion) questions for the group to talk about—questions he or she would like to discuss with the others.

- *Word finder:* This student's job is to find interesting, puzzling, important, or new words to bring to the group's attention and discuss.

- *Checker:* This student's job is to help people in the group do their work well by staying on the topic, taking turns, participating happily, and working within time limits.

- *Character interpreter:* This student's job is to think carefully about the characters and to discuss what they are like with the other students.

- *Illustrator:* This student's job is to draw pictures of important characters, settings, or actions so that the other students may discuss the pictures.

- *Recorder:* This student's job is to take brief notes on the main points raised in the discussion.

- *Reporter:* This student's job is to report on the group's discussion to the teacher or to the whole class.

the text and something in real life. Then the teacher will invite several students to do likewise. Over several days, many of the roles can be introduced in this way before students use them in an extended discussion.

2. Encourage students to ask questions from their roles rather than to say what they know. For example, the character interpreter might invite the other students to construct a character map or a character web about a character and venture his or her own ideas only after the other students have shared their own.

3. Choose only the most useful roles for a particular discussion. Sometimes four or five roles are sufficient.

4. Rotate students through the roles. Each student should play many roles over the course of several discussions. The accumulated experience of playing many of these roles adds dimensions to each student's awareness of literature.

5. Be careful not to stress the roles more than the rich discussion of the literary work. Having students carry out the roles is a means to the end of sharing their insights about a work. Once the conversation is under way, the teacher should feel free to suspend the roles and let the conversation proceed.

Watch this video of students engaged in literature circles for *Mufaro's Beautiful Daughters* and then answer the question that follows.

 Video Exploration 8.2: Watch the video and answer questions that reflect the content you have read.

SKETCH-TO-STRETCH   An ingenious device for having students of all ages respond together to a literary work is Sketch-to-Stretch, from Short et al. (1996). After the students have read and thought about a poem or a story, they are invited to draw pictures that symbolize what they believe are the main ideas or central themes of the piece. One student shows his or her drawing to a group of students, and they interpret the picture, saying what they think it means and how its images relate to the literary work. After the other students have had their say, the student who drew the picture is invited to give his or her own interpretation of the picture.

SHARED INQUIRY DISCUSSION   The Great Books Foundation developed the shared inquiry method to accompany their literature discussion program (see Plecha, 1992), which has been conducted in thousands of schools and libraries for more than 30 years. **Shared inquiry** is a procedure by which the teacher leads a deep discussion into a work of literature. It is best done with a group of eight to ten students, to maximize participation but allow for a diversity of ideas. The procedure follows these steps:

1. Before the discussion takes place, choose a work or part of a work that encourages discussion. Such a work should lend itself to more than one interpretation (not all works do this well) and raise interesting issues. Folktales often meet these criteria surprisingly well.

2. Make sure that all of the students have read the material carefully. (The Great Books Foundation insists that students read material twice before discussing it. But in our experience, a reading using some of the comprehension methods just described can make the students very aware of the contents of the reading selection.)

3. Prepare four or five discussion questions. These should be what the Great Books Foundation calls *interpretive questions*, and they have three criteria:
   a. They are real questions, the sort you might ask a friend after watching a provocative film.
   b. They have more than one defensible answer. (This criterion guarantees a debate. If it is not met, the discussion won't be a discussion but a "read my mind" exercise.)
   c. They must lead the discussion into the text. (A question such as, "Why was the giant's wife kinder to Jack than his own mother was?" leads the children to talk about what is in the text first, even though they might then comment on what they know from experience. A question such as, "Have you ever done anything as brave as Jack?" leads the discussion away from the text and out into 25 different directions.)

4. Write the first question on the board, and ask the students to think about the question and then briefly write down their answers. (If the children are so young that writing answers is laborious, allow plenty of time before calling on anyone. This allows them time to think about their answers.) As you invite students to answer, be sure to ask reluctant speakers to read what they wrote as well. Encourage debate between students, pointing out differences in what they say and asking them and other students to expand on the differences. Press children to support their ideas with references to the text or to restate ideas more clearly. However, avoid correcting a child or in any way suggesting that any one answer is right or wrong. Finally, do not offer your own answer to the question. Keep a seating chart of the students' names with a brief record of what each one has contributed. When the discussion

Teach It! 44

Dramatizing a Story

This engaging activity brings students closer to the story by allowing them to experience the events and action as they happen.

of a question seems to have run its course, read aloud your summaries of the students' comments and then ask whether anyone has anything to add.

5. Once the discussion gets going, follow the children's lead and continue to discuss the issues and questions they raise.

Even when they don't use the whole approach, many teachers use aspects of the shared inquiry procedure in conducting book discussions. For example, they might ask students to write down ideas to bring to a discussion, or they might take notes during the discussion, or they take care to draw out the students' ideas and not dominate the discussion themselves.

DRAMA IN RESPONSE TO STORIES   James Moffett (1976), a brilliant teacher of the language arts, pointed out many years ago that forms of literature differ in the degree to which they move closer to or further away from actual events. An essay about human nature is *abstract* (the word comes from two Latin morphemes that mean "drawn away from"), far removed from actual events. A story is more concrete, getting closer to events. Still, by putting events into story form, an author summarizes them, compresses actions, and leaves out much of what might really have happened. Drama, however, is live action: It is nearly as close to the real events as we can get because it plays the events out in real time for us so that we can see, hear, and feel them as they unfold. Here is Moffett's shorthand way of stating these points:

- Drama shows what is happening.
- A story tells what happened.
- An essay tells what happens.

Dramatizing a story, or a part of a story, can be a very effective way for children to unpack its meaning. Dramatization should be done after the children have read or heard a story and have had a chance to air their first thoughts about it.

The teaching approaches that we have considered up to now encourage discussions of stories or enactments of them. It is also useful to lead students in activities that teach them particular aspects of stories.

Check Your Understanding 8.2: Gauge your understanding of the skills and concepts in this section.

Teaching for Comprehension: Specific Skills

The teaching strategies that were presented in the previous sections are lively and natural ways to invite students to think about and comprehend what they read. But there are times when teachers need to work on individual aspects of comprehension. The Common Core State Standards name several of them. The CCSS expect students in the elementary grades to be able to:

1. Recognize main ideas and understand how details support them.
2. Perceive the theme of a work, and be able to summarize the work.
3. Identify, describe, and compare characters, settings, and main events in stories, along with the details by which they are developed.
4. Have a robust understanding of the language used in literature, including literal and figurative language, and metaphors and similes.
5. Recognize different genres of literature, and be able to follow their structures to arrive at or construct the meanings of literary works.

CCSS

Common Core State Standards and Aspects of Comprehending Literature

Many teachers consider it a successful class if all of the students are engaged in a story and are eager to talk about it. The Common Core State Standards remind us that there are different levels of quality to students' talk. Students should be able to talk about characters, setting, plots, themes, and genres. They should be able to talk about the main ideas and details of a story, and also about the craft that produced it and its structure (CCSS Comprehending Literature: Key Ideas and Details, Standards 1–3; Craft and Structure, Standards 4–6).

6. Understand the point of view from which a story is told, and the points of view of different characters within a story, and the difference in the point of view of the characters or the narrator and the reader.

7. Recognize, in an illustrated text, the relative contributions the written words and the illustrations make to the meaning.

8. Compare and contrast different versions of the same story, or different works by the same author or illustrator.

Individual aspects of comprehension can be developed in any of three ways, or a combination of them:

- Developing the skill in the context of a more global activity
- Engaging in a game or other exercise that practices that skill
- Using a graphic organizer

Common to all three is that the skill should be clearly demonstrated, expressly named, and discussed so that students are conscious of it, and given guided practice. If the latter two approaches are used, the skill should soon be practiced in a holistic reading and discussion activity, and not left as an isolated piece of learning.

Comprehension in Context

Many of the aspects of comprehension just listed can be developed using the teaching strategies described earlier in this chapter, so long as conscious attention is paid to the aspect you want to develop.

Take for example, the skill of perceiving the theme of a work and being able to summarize the work. The teacher can demonstrate and explain that skill and provide guided practice in using it, in the context of the following strategies that were presented earlier in this chapter: Readers' Workshop, Guided Reading, and the Directed Reading Activity. The teacher can also use Think-Alouds to demonstrate the skill.

Games and Other Focused Activities

The dynamics of a game played with a group can motivate students to use a skill. Here are several games devised to teach comprehension skills.

STORIES AND THEMES In order to teach students to find themes to stories, prepare a set of very short stories that clearly illustrate themes. Or, use a selection from Aesop's Fables with the ending proverbs removed—you can easily locate Aesop's fables online. Write out a set of theme statements for the stories, or collect the morals from the fables. (For the purpose of this exercise, theme statements and morals to fables are close enough to be used interchangeably.) Divide the class in half. Project a short story or fable, and have a person from Team A read it aloud. Then project the list of theme statements or morals. After conferring with each other, Team B members must select the appropriate theme statement or moral. Be sure to take a minute to discuss why the theme statement or moral fits the story. Then have a member from Team B read aloud the next story, and ask Team A to choose the most suitable theme statement or moral.

STORIES AND SUMMARIES Use the same game structure as Stories and Themes. Have one team read aloud a short story. Have the other team choose the most appropriate summary from a set that you have prepared ahead of time. After each turn, discuss what made that an appropriate choice of a summary.

CHARACTERS AND DESCRIPTIONS Using the same game structure as above, prepare a set of sentences that name actions that a character does. Prepare a set of adjectives that describe personalities. Team A reads the list of actions. Team B must choose from the list the adjective that best describes the character who performed those actions.

Figure 8.3 A Language Chart

Books by William Steig	What Was the Problem?	What Was the Solution?	How Were Things Different at the End?
Sylvester and the Magic Pebble	Sylvester got turned into a rock.	His parents found the magic pebble and wished him back to his old self.	Sylvester was happy to be normal.
Caleb and Kate	Caleb got turned into a dog.	Kate said the magic words and changed him back.	Caleb and Kate were glad to be together.
The Amazing Bone	Pearl was going to be killed by a wolf.	The bone said a charm and shrank the fox.	Pearl was glad to be home with her family.

MAIN IDEAS AND SUPPORTING DETAILS   Before reading a book aloud to the class, choose two or three main ideas from the book. Write each of these ideas on a strip of tagboard. Find two or three sentences from the book that provide supporting details to each main idea and write those, too, on tagboard. After reading the story, explain what a main idea is and what supporting details are, by using examples (other than the ones you have prepared on tagboard). Then have the class form two groups; mix up the supporting details, and distribute them to the two groups. Hold up a main idea, and invite the children to come forward and hold up the supporting details cards they think fit with it underneath. Do the same for the other ideas until all cards have been used.

Graphic Organizers

Several graphic organizers have been developed that help develop specific skills of comprehension.

THE LANGUAGE CHART   Created by Hoffman and Roser (1992), a Language Chart guides students to compare several different stories, works by the same author, or works illustrated by the same artist. At the same time, it leads to thinking about themes, characters, and plots. To use a Language Chart, you might choose three or more books with features in common and construct a language chart as a means of comparing them. The language chart lists titles of books in one column (the *X* axis) and lists questions about themes, characters, plots, or styles in one row. After each book has been read, the teacher or a student leads a discussion about each question, and then uses the students' answers to fill in the box at the intersection of the book title and question, as shown in Figure 8.3.

STORY MAPS   The *plot* of a story is a way in which authors organize places, people, actions, and consequences to make all of those things meaningful for the reader. The elements of a plot are as follows:

- *The setting:* the time and place the story happened
- *The main characters:* the persons the story is about
- *The problem:* the challenge the main character faces, which it is his or her goal to solve
- *The attempts:* the effort or series of efforts the character makes to solve the problem, along with their outcomes
- *The solution:* the attempt that finally pays off in solving the problem or the event that otherwise puts an end to the action
- *The consequence:* how things are for the characters at the end, including what the events of the story meant for them

You can help students use the plot consciously in understanding a story by using a *story map*, a chart that invites them to identify the keys parts of a story (see Figure 8.4).

The process builds their responsiveness to the structures of story plots. For students younger than second grade, it might be preferable to use a simpler version of a story map consisting of only the setting, the characters, the problem, and the solution.

Figure 8.4 A Story Map

Setting	Characters	Problem	Attempts	Solution	Conclusion
In . . .	there was	who wanted	so she . . . , but . . . And she . . . but . . .	Finally, she . . . and . . .	In the end . . .

Figure 8.5 A Character Cluster for *Miss Nelson Is Missing*

CHARACTER CLUSTERS   A way to link attributes, including descriptions, actions, and feelings, to a person so that a character is created is the **character cluster**, which is a semantic web with the character's name written in the middle, main features of the character written as satellites around the character's name, and examples of those features written as satellites around the features. Figure 8.5 contains an example of a character cluster.

CHARACTER MAPS   When characters in stories interact with other characters (which is most of the time), students need some way of keeping track of them and their relationships with each other. **Character maps** are graphic organizers that guide students' thinking about relationships between characters. In a character map, you write the names of two or more

Teach It! 42
Story Maps
These graphic organizers enhance children's text comprehension by familiarizing them with story grammar as they identify and sequence key story elements and events.

Figure 8.6 A Character Map for *Roll of Thunder, Hear My Cry*

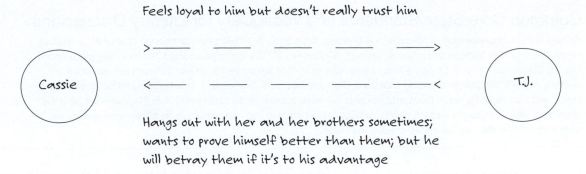

characters in their respective circles. The circles should be spaced widely apart on the page. Then draw arrows between the characters. Along the arrow that points from Character A to Character B, write about how Character A feels about Character B. Along the arrow that points from Character B to Character A, write about how Character B feels about Character A (see Figure 8.6).

Check Your Understanding 8.3: **Gauge your understanding of the skills and concepts in this section.**

Close Reading

The Common Core State Standards call for students to exhibit a careful understanding and to have the ability to explain fine points of literacy texts. That call has been met with the revival of an old practice of literary analysis called *hermeneutics* (from a Greek word meaning "finding out") or **close reading**. Close reading is the intense exploration and examination of a piece of text, usually a short piece of text, for the purpose of unearthing the many aspects of its meaning as well as its stylistic and rhetorical features. The method is meant to be used with a text whose meaning is not obvious. "Stylistic" aspects of the text include the inferred reasons behind author's word choices, tone, and other artistic devices. "Rhetorical" aspects of the text include the structure of the text, including the plot, but also flashbacks, allusions, and other literary tricks of the trade.

Close reading is more concerned with the text's meaning than with the reader's response to it (Hinchman & Moore, 2013). The Common Core State Standards' push for close reading that is beginning even in the lower grades is less concerned with eliciting the reader's responses, feelings, or even enjoyment than with developing investigative skills—and making sure readers to have experiences with rich and challenging texts.

Six Close Readings

Close reading almost always requires rereading a text several times, asking different questions each time. For starters, you can use the six readings of one passage we explain below. We think you will agree that quite a bit more meaning comes to light than through a single reading.

FIRST READING: GET THE GIST.   On the first reading, we ask students to retell what the passage said. They should summarize the passage in a few important words in everyday language, answering questions, such as What's going on? or What happened?

SECOND READING: GET THE IMPORTANCE   On the second reading we ask students to explain why the passage matters. For example, we can ask what the passage tells us about the setting and the character—about her or his situation, concerns, and goals. What are we learning about the character's main goal, so that we can predict what might come next in the text?

THIRD READING: GET THE STRUCTURE.   We can begin with the structure of the story. How does the passage function in the story? Why does the author tell us these things now? Is the passage introducing an idea, supporting an idea that has already been introduced, making a transition to a new idea? Then, taking a closer look, we can ask the students to unlock the

CCSS

Common Core State Standards and Vocabulary for Literary Discussions

As part of the comprehension of literature, the Common Core State Standards include having vocabulary to discuss characters and their feelings and motives, settings, and actions (CCSS, Comprehending Literature: Key Ideas and Details, Standards 2 and 3). Students should also have control of literary terms, so that they can talk about an author's craft (CCSS, Comprehending Literature: Craft and Structure, Standard 5). Teachers should be careful to model and also explicitly teach the words students will need in order to discuss stories from the inside out (as if the characters were real people and the events actually happened) and from the outside in (as if they were writers and were interested in the way the author created the work).

sentences. What or who is the subject of a challenging sentence, what is the action, and what (or who) if anything is the receiver of the action? Where are the describing passages, and what are they saying about what they describe? What are the "glue" words that link one idea to another? What relation do they signal between ideas? What are the transition words that shift attention from one assertion to the next? It may happen that when you ask these questions you will find that many students fail to understand sentences that we assumed they did, especially if the sentence has imbedded clauses or uses the passive voice.

FOURTH READING: GET THE WORDS.   Next we ask students about the most unusual words in the passage. How can they puzzle out a key word's meaning if they didn't already know it? We ask the students to note each word's literal meaning—its denotation. We ask the students to note the word's connotation, too: the suggestion, or value judgment it makes. (Is it a positive or negative or neutral way of describing something? Is it derisive or flattering?) We can ask the students to note the word's sensory side, too: How does it sound—smooth, jerky, crunchy, violent, nerdy? Why was this word chosen instead of alternatives? What does the word choice say about the speaker's feelings, attitudes, and mood, or about the author's intentions? There are other questions we can ask about words, too. How does the dictionary define the word? What are the origins of the word?

FIFTH READING: GET THE STYLE.   Next we can ask about the style of the text. Is it meant to be humorous, exciting, mysterious, evocative, authoritative, or something else? How do the students know? What effect does the author seem to be striving for? How does she or he achieve the effect? If the author were advising us as writers so that we could write a passage like this one, what would she say? What did the author have to know in order to write this passage, especially to write it the way he did?

SIXTH READING: COMPARE TO OTHER PRESENTATIONS.   Finally, we can ask the students to relate this text to other texts. How does it remind us of other works by the same author? By the same illustrator? About the same topic? How does it compare with versions of the same folktale, or with other tales of the same genre (quest story, hero story, fable, or tall tale)? How is the tale similar to other tales from the same culture? How does it contrast with similar stories from a different culture? How is the movie version like and unlike the book?

A Close Reading of *Tom Sawyer*

To illustrate these six readings in action, let's apply them to the opening page of Mark Twain's *Tom Sawyer*. Table 8.2 provides a discussion.

> "TOM!"
> No answer.
> "TOM!"
> No answer.
> "What's gone with that boy, I wonder? You TOM!"
> No answer.
>   The old lady pulled her spectacles down and looked over them about the room; then she put them up and looked out under them. She seldom or never looked THROUGH them for so small a thing as a boy; they were her state pair, the pride of her heart, and were built for "style," not service—she could have seen through a pair of stove-lids just as well. She looked perplexed for a moment, and then said, not fiercely, but still loud enough for the furniture to hear:
>   "Well, I lay if I get hold of you I'll—"

She did not finish, for by this time she was bending down and punching under the bed with the broom, and so she needed breath to punctuate the punches with. She resurrected nothing but the cat.

"I never did see the beat of that boy!"

She went to the open door and stood in it and looked out among the tomato vines and "jimpson" weeds that constituted the garden. No Tom. So she lifted up her voice at an angle calculated for distance and shouted:

"Y-o-u-u TOM!"

There was a slight noise behind her and she turned just in time to seize a small boy by the slack of his roundabout and arrest his flight.

"There! I might 'a' thought of that closet. What you been doing in there?"

"Nothing."

"Nothing! Look at your hands. And look at your mouth. What IS that truck?"

"I don't know, aunt."

"Well, I know. It's jam—that's what it is. Forty times I've said if you didn't let that jam alone I'd skin you. Hand me that switch."

The switch hovered in the air—the peril was desperate—

"My! Look behind you, aunt!"

The old lady whirled round, and snatched her skirts out of danger. The lad fled on the instant, scrambled up the high board-fence, and disappeared over it.

His aunt Polly stood surprised a moment, and then broke into a gentle laugh.

[Source: http://www.pagebypagebooks.com/Mark_Twain/Tom_Sawyer/CHAPTER_I_p1.html].

The Common Core State Standards require that students be able to answer questions like the ones listed above, and to do so will require more than one reading of a passage. To guide close reading requires careful preparation by the teacher as well.

The Common Core State Standards for reading comprehension do not require that students have and evoke background knowledge about a topic they will read about. The emphasis is placed squarely on what students can understand from reading the text alone. While as a teacher you may find it helpful to explain to the students who Mark Twain was and when he wrote, to help students meet the Common Core State Standards, it will be wise to challenge them to construct as much meaning as they can from the text alone.

Check Your Understanding 8.4: Gauge your understanding of the skills and concepts in this section.

Table 8.2 A Close Reading of *Tom Sawyer*

Get the Gist	Tom's Aunt Polly is looking for Tom, who is hiding from her because he ate jam without her permission. He escapes by tricking her, but in the end she thinks what he does is funny.
Get the Importance	The passage introduces Tom as a mischievous boy who lives with an older aunt who is strict with him, but likes him and is amused by him.
Get the Structure	The passage starts off the book with a mystery: where is Tom? Who is this old woman? Why is she calling Tom? We meet the characters in action see something of their personalities, and their relationship.
Get the Words	Aunt Polly uses many colloquial or "country" expressions that may be typical of a rural woman in the late 1800's: "What's *gone* with that boy, I wonder?" "Well, I *lay* if I get hold of you I'll—" "I never did see the *beat* of that boy!" What IS that *truck*?" We can mostly tell the meanings of these expressions from the context, though. "Jimpson" weed is put in quotation marks because that is Aunt Polly's name for Jimson weed. Aunt Polly must have gotten more of her learning from word of mouth than from reading. About the author's word choice: he sometimes uses exalted language that contrasts humorously with the lady's country expressions: ". . . she lifted up her voice at an angle calculated for distance and shouted . . ." The switch hovered in the air—the peril was desperate—"
Get the Style	The author starts right in with the action and no introduction, which has the effect of showing us as much as telling us. Tom is never described other than by his actions. We are introduced to Aunt Polly by her speech patterns, and by the author's insightful descriptions of her foibles (the glasses she wears for show). As we already noted, he sometime uses elegant language to describe simple humorous events.
Compare to Other Presentations	The writing seems remarkably fresh and lively for a book published 150 years ago. The book can be compared to film versions—an animated version of *Tom Sawyer* came out in 2000 with country music stars supplying the voices (among them Waylon Jennings, Lee Ann Womack, and Hank Williams, Jr.)

Assessing Comprehension

We have seen in this chapter that reading comprehension is a complex activity that includes readers'

- Prior knowledge and their willingness to use it to generate questions about what they are reading.
- Willingness to seek answers to questions and construct meaning.
- Ability to follow the pattern or structure of the text.
- Facility in making mental images of what is described in the text.
- Perception of main ideas and how details support those main ideas.
- Ability to make inferences—merging textual clues and background knowledge.
- Metacognition—thinking about their understanding and rereading to repair their understanding when it fails.
- Ability to connect the meaning to other texts and to issues outside of the text.

There is no simple way to measure all that. The most thorough approaches to the assessment of comprehension are observations of the reader's attempts to comprehend. In addition, you may wish to use a more quickly administered device, recognizing that it will yield an incomplete picture of a reader's comprehension.

Approaches to assessing comprehension include the following:

- *Observational assessments:* You observe and assess students' comprehension behaviors as students demonstrate them in real reading tasks.
- *Self-assessments:* You ask students to observe and critique their own use of comprehension strategies. Self-assessments have the advantage of teaching students to be mindful of reading strategies and to be deliberate about their use when they read.
- *Quantitative assessments:* Periodically, you might gather data that allow you to compare students' performance against some standard, such as grade-level expectations.

Observational Assessments

One kind of observational assessment is simply to keep a folder for each student into which you place observations that you write down every few days. The observations consist of whatever strikes you as being worthy of note: for instance, a student can provide background knowledge on a topic or cannot; a student makes predictions that honor the plot of a story or offers random predictions; a student makes a straightforward inference or fails to; a student states a main idea or says something else when asked to.

A more systematic way of making observational assessments is to keep a checklist of reading behaviors—in this case, comprehension behaviors. Schedule an eight- to 10-minute period every other week to read with each child, individually or in a group of no more than four, and record observations on a checklist such as the one shown in Figure 8.7.

Student Self-Assessments

Having students assess the strategies they use to understand and respond to a text is a good way to make them purposeful and self-directed readers. You may engage students in creating a **rubric** to use to assess the strategies they used to read a text with understanding. The items on the rubric should come from the students, but you might remind them to include items such as surveying the text in advance to see what it was about, setting questions and purposes before reading, checking from time to time to make sure they are understanding, looking up unfamiliar words, summarizing what they understood, and the like. You might also have students write a letter to students who will read the work in the future, explaining how they went about understanding it (Wilder, 2016). Watch this video about the importance of teaching students to self-monitor for reading comprehension and then answer the question that follows.

 Video Exploration 8.3: Watch the video and answer questions that reflect the content you have read.

Quantitative Assessments

Teachers and students also need to know how well students are reading in comparison with their grade-level group. Teachers and grade-level teams can focus attention on aspects of teaching that need improving, but only if they have

Figure 8.7 Observing Comprehension

Student's name: _____ Date: _____

Material read: _____ Level: _____

1. Before reading

a) The reader appeared to be familiar with the topic (or the author or the genre) of the text before reading.

No prior knowledge shown	Some prior knowledge shown	Much prior knowledge shown

b) The reader raised questions about the content of the text before reading.

Did not produce questions, even when prompted	Asked some (vague) questions when prompted	Volunteered intelligent questions

c) The reader was able to make predictions about what was coming in the text.

Did not produce predictions, even when prompted	Made imprecise or illogical predictions	Consistently made logical predictions

2. During reading

a) The reader read aloud with animation that honored the meaning of the text.

Read without meaningful inflections and word groupings	Sometimes showed meaningful inflections and word groupings	Consistently showed meaningful inflections and word groupings

b) The reader knew the vocabulary in the text.

Did not appear to understand many key words, and made little effort to learn what they mean	Did not appear to understand some key words, and made occasional effort to learn what they mean	Knew most key words, and often used context to approach the meanings of unknown words

c) The reader continued to ask questions and make predictions.

Did not produce predictions, even when prompted	Made imprecise or illogical predictions	Consistently made logical predictions

(Continued)

Figure 8.7 Observing Comprehension (*Continued*)

d) The reader found answers to questions or confirmed predictions.

Found answers to some questions, but mostly when the answer closely matched the question	*Rarely found answers to questions, even when prompted*	*Actively pursued answers to questions, often without prompting*

e) The reader was able to make inferences.

Rarely made inferences even with supportive questions	*Made more obvious inferences*	*Consistently made inferences, and picked up on subtle nuances*

f) The reader monitored comprehension.

Frequently misread words in the text without self-correcting	*Occasionally misread text and made some self-corrections*	*Rarely misread text and reliably self-corrected*

g) The reader perceived main ideas or claims and the details that support them.

When asked, did not distinguish between more and less important statements	*Did restate some main ideas when asked*	*Consistently restated main ideas, and could provide support for them from the text*

3. After reading

a) The reader could retell or summarize the text.

The retelling had major gaps	*The retelling was fairly complete*	*The retelling was complete, and the reader summarized the main points*

b) The reader identified themes in texts.

Did not offer thematic statements when asked (for example, to choose a title for a chapter)	*Sometimes, but inexactly, could answer questions about "the main thing you learned" from the text*	*Consistently made appropriate statements about the main meaning or theme of a text*

evidence that tells them where the strengths of their instructional program are as well as the areas in which they need improvement.

Several kinds of assessment devices are available. For the purpose of getting a close look at readers' strengths and areas of need, probably the most informative are **informal reading inventories.** Informal reading inventories must be administered one at a time, so they are time consuming. But the fact that they yield both quantitative results (in terms of reading levels) and detailed portraits of most areas of students' reading abilities makes them worth the investment of time.

Informal reading inventories (IRIs) are thoroughly discussed in Gillet, Temple, Temple, and Crawford's *Understanding Reading Problems* (2012).

Although teachers can make their own IRIs, most teachers prefer to use commercially available ones. Here are some recommended informal reading inventories:

Temple, C., Crawford, A., & Gillet, J. (2008). *Developmental literacy inventory: Emergent reading through high school.* Boston, MA: Allyn and Bacon.

Leslie, L., & Caldwell, J. (2017). *Qualitative reading inventory-6.* New York, NY: Pearson Education.

Silvaroli, N., & Wheelock, W. (2003). *Classroom reading inventory.* New York, NY: McGraw-Hill.

Check Your Understanding 8.5: Gauge your understanding of the skills and concepts in this section.

For Review

At the outset of this chapter we stated that when you reached this point in your reading and studying you should be able to:

- **Explain how students come to understand literature.**

Reading comprehension is using the knowledge we already have to understand the new information we find in the text. It is an active process in which we seek after new knowledge and make meaning in the process. Responding to literature, too, is an active process in which we bring our own expectations and associations to the words the author has strung along the pages of the text.

The advent of the Common Core State Standards has reminded us that fully comprehending fiction requires some specialized knowledge of aspects of literature, including characters, settings, plots, and themes, as well as the knowledge of literary concepts and terms for discussing those characteristics.

Comprehension has several components: knowing the vocabulary of a text and being able to follow the text's structure, visualizing it, making predictions about it, summarizing its meaning, getting the main ideas in it, making inferences within it, interpreting it, arguing with it, and monitoring one's comprehension of it.

- **Utilize general strategies for teaching students to read with comprehension.**

To support students as they seek to understand what they read, there are teaching techniques we can use before, during, and after the reading or during the phases of a lesson that we have called *anticipation, building knowledge, and consolidation.* In the anticipation phase, we remind students to think of what they already know about a topic, raise questions about what they are about to read, and otherwise prepare for reading. In the building knowledge phase, we guide students in using strategies to set expectations and meet them and to clarify meanings. In the consolidation stage, we have a host of methods for having students think back over what they have gained from the reading, respond to it, interpret it, critique it, apply it, and debate it.

- **Teach specific skills of reading comprehension.**

There are separate sets of Common Core State Standards for literature and informational text, and both sets name quite specific skills. In the case of fiction, students should be able to recognize main ideas; perceive themes; speak knowledgeably about characters, settings, and main events; examine the language use; recognize and read appropriately in different genres; understand the points of view from which a story is told; compare narratives presented in different media; and compare and contrast different versions of the same story. In this chapter we approached these aspects of understanding literature in three ways: developing the skill in the context of a more global activity, using a game or other exercise that practices the skill, and using graphic organizers.

- **Demonstrate methods of close reading of fiction.**

Close reading is an in-depth investigation of the meaning of a text, usually done through several rereadings. In this chapter we outlined suggestions for six readings: Get the Gist, Get the Importance, Get the Structure, Get the Words, Get the Style, and Compare to Other Presentations.

- **Assess students' reading comprehension.**

In this chapter we discussed three different categories of assessments. Observational assessments are structured ways of observing and drawing conclusions about students' comprehension behaviors as students demonstrate them in real reading tasks. Self-assessments are occasions for students to observe and critique their own use of comprehension strategies. And quantitative assessments are done periodically to allow you to compare students' performance at comprehension against some standard, such as grade-level expectations. One method of quantitative assessments is the use of informal reading inventories.

For Your Journal

1. Return to your answers to the Anticipation Guide that opened this chapter. Look at the items for which your answers remained the same. In your journal, explain how you came to know the answers. Look at the items where your answers changed, and explain how your thinking has changed.

2. This chapter explained how reading comprehension of fiction and response to literature work. Chapter 9 focuses on teaching students to comprehend and learn from informational text. What do you think the main differences are between teaching students to comprehend and respond to fiction and teaching them to do this for informational text?

3. Recall the vignette of Hank da Silva's classroom that began this chapter. He used a combination of strategies for teaching students to read with comprehension. Think of a class you have taught or might teach. Describe the combination you might choose from the reading comprehension strategies you have seen in this chapter. How would you make them work together?

Taking It to the World

1. When they observed skilled teachers teaching reading comprehension, Michael Pressley and his colleagues (1996) found that they usually taught their students to do the following:

   - Make predictions of what was to come in the text based on their prior knowledge
   - Generate questions about issues in the text
   - Seek clarification about confusing parts
   - Form mental images of what they read
   - Relate what they already knew to what they are reading in the text
   - Make summaries of what they have read

   Alone or with a group of your fellow students, observe three reading lessons in a primary grade school. Do these six activities capture what the teachers are doing by way of helping the children read with comprehension? Do they do other things as well, such as encouraging students to make inferences or debate about what they read?

2. Go to a school, and practice a shared inquiry lesson. Make sure you use a text that has a core of mystery to it (many folktales work fine), and prepare your questions carefully according to the criteria given on those pages. Before you put the questions to the children, though, write out your own best answers to your questions. How do the students' answers compare to yours? Are you surprised? If so, what surprises you and why?

3. Using the same text as in your shared inquiry lesson, try dramatizing a story with your classmates. Then try the activity out in an elementary school. What different insights about the text come to light when you dramatize it rather than discuss it?

Chapter 9
Reading Comprehension, Part II: Understanding and Learning with Informational Texts

 ## Learning Outcomes

After reading this chapter, you should be able to:

1. Describe the particular components of informational texts.

2. Explain how readers comprehend informational texts.

3. Help students identify and use features of informational texts.

4. Identify teaching frameworks that support learning with informational texts.

5. Foster students' independent reading and learning.

Anticipation Guide

The following statements will help you begin thinking about the topics of this chapter. Answer *true* or *false* in response to each statement. As you read and learn more about the topics in these statements, double-check your answers. See what interests you and prompts your curiosity toward more understanding.

_____ 1. There has been a big shift from fiction reading to informational reading by adult readers in the United States.

_____ 2. Primary children get too confused with the different formats of nonfiction texts, so instruction in using nonfiction should wait for third grade and above.

_____ 3. Elementary students need to be challenged to engage in both close reading and reading of complex texts.

_____ 4. One of the best ways to show students how to read informational text with comprehension is to read an informational text yourself and discuss it with your students.

_____ 5. Having prior knowledge helps students to comprehend, but one kind of prior knowledge is about as useful as another.

_____ 6. Students who have had an extensive introduction to a topic are likely to be more motivated to learn about it than are those with only superficial knowledge.

_____ 7. Just as stories have a "grammar" that readers can follow to understand the story, informational texts have recognizable structures.

_____ 8. Reading strategies for informational texts are the same as those for fiction.

_____ 9. Informational texts have so many different structures that there is little point in teaching students the parts of an informational text.

_____ 10. When it comes to teaching vocabulary, teachers should stress only the words the authors of the text prioritize.

A Classroom Story

Reading to Learn in a Primary Classroom

Teacher Debbie Gurvitz likes to introduce her first- and second-grade students to informational reading through integrated units of study. In the spring, she develops an expanded science unit that involves a real problem-based inquiry. It serves as a way of expanding students' reading skills in nonfiction and of teaching some science standards. Recently, Ms. Gurvitz focused the unit on pond life and the relationship between the quality of the water for animals and the human community. To introduce the unit, she invited a naturalist from the local nature preserve to speak to the students. When the naturalist showed the students some of the animals from the pond, they became fascinated with the mutant frog he included. "Wow, that's weird!" "That doesn't look like the frog I have at home. Who did that to it?" "What happened?" The children's questions came naturally and quickly. Garth, one of the first graders, expressed the feelings of the whole group when he said, "Ms. Gurvitz, we really have a problem!"

Ms. Gurvitz took her lead from the children and helped them to focus their study of the natural environment on the frog problem. They began by framing the problem—exploring what facts and information they already knew and identifying the questions they had. On a large piece of chart paper they made a list of what they knew about frogs. She helped them write questions for research; these also filled a sheet of chart paper and were hung on the wall. As a result of these discussions, she divided the class into smaller groups that searched for information to help solve the problem. In this case, it was a very real problem. Scientists do not understand why so many frogs in the area are being born with strange-looking body parts. This created an authentic study full of the kinds of ambiguities that are found in most scientific research.

Ms. Gurvitz was careful to make sure she could locate the kinds of reading texts the children could read. She wanted some that would be at an independent level for all the children and some that would be good instructional-level texts for her guided reading groups. After collecting the books, she leveled them to ensure that she could accommodate the whole class with appropriate materials.

In considering the language arts and reading objectives she wanted to address, Ms. Gurvitz focused instruction on helping students find answers to questions they posed. She wanted them to learn to use the table of contents and the index in books to locate the information they needed. She knew this would be a good opportunity for them to learn to make decisions about what sections of a text they would read and to gain control over information searching as contrasted with fictional reading. She also wanted the children to learn to make notes about what information they were collecting so that those notes could guide their reporting. To do this, she made copies of the **Amazing Fact Sheet** *(see Figure 9.1) and put them in a shoe box on the inquiry table so students could take one whenever they wanted to save some interesting or important information.*

As she introduced this way of making notes, Ms. Gurvitz used one child as a model. Side by side at the smartboard, she and Andrew made a note card of the information he wanted to remember.

"Andrew, what do you want to write?" Ms. Gurvitz asked.

"It says that frogs lay lots of eggs in water," Andrew replied.

Ms. Gurvitz encouraged him, "So, can you write that on your Amazing Fact Sheet?" Andrew began to write and the other children watched. When he tried to write "water," he hesitated.

"What is giving you trouble with that word?" Ms. Gurvitz asked. "Can you find it written somewhere?"

Figure 9.1 Amazing Fact Sheet

AMAZING FACT SHEET

An amazing fact about frogs is that

_____

_____

Found in (provide the source of your information)

_____

Written by _____ p. _____

Reporter _____

With that nudge, Andrew turned to the book again and located the word; without any further help, he finished his writing. Ms. Gurvitz reminded him to list the book title, the author, and the page that contained the fact on his note. Finished, he then signed the note on the Reporter line.

Ms. Gurvitz praised his efforts: "Good work, Andrew."

She concluded the mini-lesson by reminding the children that when they found interesting information, they should write that on an Amazing Fact Sheet and put it in the Amazing Facts Box on the counter. Each morning, Andrew and other children read their cards during the morning share time and used them to build their knowledge.

To be human is to be a learner. Young children, like those in Debbie Gurvitz's classroom, are full of questions, so many that parents and teachers are sometimes amazed by the depth and breadth of children's curiosity and their knowledge. With so much information available on the Internet and also in newer children's books and magazines, there seems no end to resources from which children can learn.

However, to use these resources successfully children need guidance and support. They need to learn how resource materials are organized and how to locate the sections that contain answers to their questions. They need materials they can read and view that are targeted to their knowledge and skill levels. They will encounter a high number of unfamiliar terms that are specific to the topic they are researching and need to learn how to determine the meanings and uses of these new words and phrases. They will also be challenged to learn to use both the written and the visual information in nonfiction materials.

Now that reading informational materials has become a major part of literacy stimulated by the CCSS and the recently developed individual state standards, it is important that teachers think carefully about what students need to know and be able to do to be successful across this broader range of reading materials. Many teachers have spent most of their literacy lives immersed in fiction. The twenty-first century, however, is the time the field of education and society in general are becoming part of an informational world. It is time for all of us to delve deeply into the varied forms of information available.

In this chapter we identify some of the major differences between fiction and **informational texts** and suggest ways teachers can provide instruction so students can comfortably navigate and learn from the wide range of interesting and informative nonfiction texts. While it has always been true that many students prefer reading and learning about the world around them and about history, informational materials have only in the past decade made their way into the center of instructional programs. And, even then, many of the informational articles included in core reading programs are brief and not substantial enough for students to develop fully their skills and interests in reading nonfiction. Children need to have regular opportunities to read from books, magazines, online resources, and visual documents. They need teachers' help in becoming familiar with the variety of ways authors/illustrators convey their ideas, in learning how to use both text and visual sources together to construct their understanding, and in learning to attend to vocabulary and learn new concepts.

Characteristics of Informational Texts

The reasons we read informational texts are usually different from those we have for reading fiction and poetry. We want to learn something new, understand something better, or explore a new perspective on a topic of interest. In schools, many of the books students use for these purposes are textbooks in social studies, science, and mathematics. Students need to learn how these texts are structured and how to use the resources they contain successfully. They also need to become familiar with the much larger corpus of informational materials that can be read during content instruction, especially in integrated units of instruction like the example in the opening vignette, and for personal interests. These resources include a wide variety of distinct types of information from magazines, books, pamphlets, and comics to visuals and Internet sites.

External Features

One of the most obvious differences between informational texts and fiction is in the way they are structured. Compare a story or fictional book with an informational article. Which has a table of contents you will refer to while reading? Which has headings and subheadings within each chapter or article? Which includes a variety of illustrations, maps, or photographs? These attributes, and many more, are referred to as the *external features*.

External features help readers understand how the information in the text (article, Web site, or book) is organized and provide resources to help readers understand what is most important. These aids include the following:

Table of contents

Chapters

Headings and subheadings

Illustrations (e.g., maps, graphs, diagrams, pictures, cartoons)

Captions

Index

Vocabulary noted in italics or other graphic ways

Glossary of terms

References

Children's books, even those for early primary grades, now include many important features that make navigating these materials easier and that reveal the way the author has prioritized and organized the content. Most important is the table of contents. In addition, books generally include a glossary and an index. The chapter titles are worth some attention because they are often key indicators of how the author has organized the information. Within each chapter, there is likely to be a further breakdown of information with headings and subheadings designed to guide our reading to important content or main ideas. Many books and articles also highlight key vocabulary with italic or boldface type or in marginal notes that provide explanations of the terms. A well-organized informational piece includes several of these external features that help us locate the part of the text we want to read when we have particular questions we want answered. In addition, because timely, accurate information is important, readers need to be aware of both the copyright date and the author's qualifications.

Books for very young readers are just now beginning to include these features. Books included in a classroom library should be screened so they are well constructed and contain a table of contents and chapter divisions. Pages should be numbered because it is hard to locate and return to information without some pagination as a reference. The illustrations in books for young readers are also important. Often the color photographs are stunning, but they do not support or extend the written text information. Some books now display graphics in a wide variety of places on the pages and often on two-page spreads. They need to be clear and the captions should be connected to images so young readers know how to match them. Sometimes the captions are beneath the picture; at other times, they are beside or even above the illustrated material. Only by carefully studying the individual pages and mapping the positions of text, graphics, and captions can their relationships be determined. Then their appropriateness for children can be evaluated and instruction planned if there are potential confusing features.

Visual and Graphic Information

A very attractive feature of most informational articles and books is the visually presented information. Some **visuals** are included basically to draw attention to the text, but in most cases the visuals are integral to the information that is developed. **Graphic** books are also becoming more and more available on content topics. Think of an informational book you have recently read or a children's book such as *Face to Face with Manatees* (Skerry, 2010) or *The Manatee Scientists* (Lourie, 2011), with their amazing photographs, informational sidebars, maps, drawings, and journal features.

More than ever before, good informational books, textbooks, and magazines use pictures and visuals to enhance engagement and help readers understand the concepts. Much of the information, in fact, is presented in the pictures, graphs, diagrams, maps, cartoons, and their captions. One textbook editor explained that because children are more attracted to visual arrays, whenever possible publishers transform as much of the content as possible into visual formats: diagrams, maps, charts, tables, and pictures. The authors and publishers assume that students will read both the narrative and visually presented information together and integrate the ideas presented.

The ability to interpret visual displays and integrate them with verbal text, however, is not a natural skill for children. In fact, several research studies have documented the difficulty children have in using both types of information in their reading and learning (Denton et al., 2015; Liebfreumd, 2015). For example, Jian (2016) concluded after studying fourth-grade students' eye movements when reading short science texts with diagrams that the students did not know how to combine information from the two types of sources. Her eye movement analysis showed that children read and reread the three paragraphs of text without referring to the two diagrams; they also examined and reexamined the two illustrations but never connected or looked between the two types of information as they were reading. This finding confirms other research (Moore & Scevak, 1997;) Roberts, Norman, Duke, Morsink, Martin & Knight, instruction about how to read visuals nor how to integrate visual and verbal sections related to the same ideas. Yet, as Moline explained, "Our second language, which we do not speak, but which we read and write every day is visual. . . . Visual literacy is not a cute new toy for children to play with; it is the means by which we manage in the everyday world." (2011, p. 9) To comprehend informational materials children need to be able to interpret a wide range of visual displays in their texts from diagrams, flow charts, and equations to maps and cartoons.

The Structure of Web Sites

Internet sites have an external structure just as informational print texts do. The organization is different from print, but has some of the same elements. With the increased use of Web sites, it is important that students also know the basic structure and functions of the parts of these resources and learn how to distinguish reliable sources from others. A key to deciding if a Web site is worth reading is knowing who has created it. This information is located on the initial page of each site and is required by law. It may be under the heading, "About Us" or "Home." This is an important first step in surveying a Web site. It is like looking for the author, illustrator, and publisher of a book. Additional information about the site can often be found in the section on Sponsors and in links that are provided. Students also need to learn how the content is structured and organized on each site. This can be challenging; successful use may depend on the depth of students' prior knowledge about the content and on the questions they formulate.

Internal Organization

Another key to reading and learning from informational materials is becoming familiar with the **internal organization**, the way the writer has organized the ideas. As readers of narrative stories, we have learned—often first by listening to stories our parents read to us—that fiction has a predictable pattern. We read to find out who the characters are, what problem they encounter, and how they go about resolving it. Then we savor their victory at the end. No similar single pattern characterizes informational texts; however, there are clearly discernable structures that are important to help students identify. Even very young children are often quite able to recognize and use some of these patterns (Langer, 2011). The most common ways of organizing ideas in informational texts include the following:

- Description (main ideas and details)
- Compare/contrast
- Problem/solution
- Cause/effect
- Sequence of events

The last internal structure, sequence, is often the easiest to discern because it is most like the structure of narrative stories. Some research has indicated that children do well with the more complex organizations, too, so all types should be represented in materials for children. In dealing with these structures, a complicating factor is that often these organizing structures are mixed within a single article or text; for example, in describing how a simple machine works, a text may insert a problem that can be solved with the machine and shift the structure to a problem/solution frame.

Density of Vocabulary

One of the major differences between informational texts and stories is the central role vocabulary plays in them. One author likened content textbooks to dictionaries with elaborated definitions of terms (Newkirk, 2012). In their analysis of the most widely used fourth- to fifth-grade science and social studies textbooks, a group of experienced teachers identified over 6,000 words that were conceptually difficult or unfamiliar for students. In reflecting on the challenge for young readers in dealing with these enormous vocabulary demands, Scott concluded, "the sheer volume of the task of learning new words is overwhelming" (2012, p.184). Not only do informational texts and textbooks contain many new terms but also a significant number of these terms identify the key content to be learned. In addition, these words are often used in very precise ways despite the fact that many are polysemous; thus students can easily fail to attend to the way the terms are used in the particular context and not fully comprehend the concept.

Most informational texts include a large number of both Tier 2 and Tier 3 words. In addition, the vocabulary often is not just single words, but includes complex phrases. Particularly in science, there are many such complex phrases (*solar cell, solar system, solar energy*) that cannot be understood by knowing the common meaning of the individual terms (Hiebert & Cervetti, 2012). In social studies texts the problem of polysemy is also a challenge; however, it more often occurs with common terms used in specific ways (i.e. selection of candidates, amend, argue).

CCSS

Comprehending Informational Text

Grade 1: Standard 10. With prompting and support, read informational texts appropriately complex for grade 1.

Grade 2: Standard 10. By the end of year, read and comprehend informational texts, including history/social studies, science, and technical texts, in the grades 2–3 text complexity band proficiently, with scaffolding as needed at the high end of the band.

Many texts now highlight the words and phrases that are considered most important, which provides support for readers. Some explain or provide meanings for the terms in marginal notes or in footnotes. Others include a glossary so that readers can check their understanding. These resources are not generally available in the literature children read and so deserve attention and instruction from teachers.

Expectations Within Current Standards

The CCSS make the inclusion of informational text reading an important part of the responsibility of elementary teachers from kindergarten forward.

Anchor Standard for Reading, Standard 10 states that students: *Read and comprehend literary and informational texts independently and proficiently.* Within the Informational Text Standards for K–5, the standards for first and second grade are shown below, and each subsequent grade has a similar, appropriate expectation.

The current focus on knowledge standards (science, math, and social studies) and measuring what students learn each year puts pressure on teachers to cover more content. This means that students are asked to read more and remember what they are taught. In this climate of rising expectations, students who have read widely possess the background knowledge that enables them to remember new material and deepen their knowledge schemata. Instead of diminishing, the demands on learners as readers are increasing.

Another implication of the current accountability climate for teachers is that the assessments of students' reading abilities are now balanced between reading for literary purposes and reading to learn. These assessments reflect the fact that for students to be successful as readers throughout schooling and life, they need to read for a variety of purposes from a variety of materials. Reading fiction for pleasure is only one of many forms reading takes. More important for school success across the curriculum is the ability to read informational texts and learn from them (CCSS, 2010; Ogle & Blachowicz, 2001). The more content information, prior knowledge, and vocabulary students possess, the more successful they will be as readers and learners.

Instructional Implications and Priorities

Clearly, elementary teachers need to conceptualize their reading instruction so that it introduces children to a broad range of quality reading materials; for most teachers this means putting more emphasis on informational reading than was their own experience as students. It also means guiding children to attend to both the ways informational resources are organized and the content of what they read, to think of the important ideas and the supporting details in a single text, and then to compare and contrast the information in several texts. Teachers can build these habits in students in a variety of ways.

1. Read aloud to students regularly from interesting, high-quality informational books and articles. Develop a collection of high-quality informational books, magazines, and articles that can be expanded each year. As you build your collection, school and community librarians are good resources to consult in selecting outstanding books. Also helpful are the annual lists of recommended trade books compiled by the National Science Teachers Association and the National Council of Social Studies. More extensive recommendations are available from the School Library Association, especially their annual Notable Children's Books, and from resource books and chapters (Knoell, 2010; Temple, Martinez, & Yokota, 2014).

2. Include some author studies that focus on writers of informational materials—and there are many. Think of the interests primary grade children develop exploring the books of Donald Crows, Lois Elbert, Gail Gibbons, and Seymour Simon; intermediate level readers love books by Jim Arnosky, Ruth Heller, Jim Murphy, and Joanna Cole; and middle grade readers find intriguing the content of authors like Mark Aronson, Russell Freedman, and Walter Dean Myers.

3. Whenever possible, read from more than one author on the same topic. When you find magazine articles connected to some of the books you use, copy or print them out and put them inside the texts. Put sticky notes containing the

titles of similar books inside books you read. Then when you read orally, share from at least two or three (include poetry, too) and "think aloud" about style, focus, and the information they contain.

4. Help students develop engaged reading by modeling and thinking aloud as you read from short, well-written informational texts. As you read aloud, show the text on a visualizer so students can follow along as you read. Highlight key terms, underline new ideas, write questions in the margins, and engage students in responding to the author's ideas. With such engaging experiences with short mentor or model texts, students can easily be led into reading a variety of other materials alone, with partners, or in small groups.

5. With the adoption of the CCSS, there is an increased interest in developing integrated curriculum units. In fact, that is what is suggested in the PARCC guides to curriculum. When elementary and middle reading programs are constructed in units with broad themes (some focused on content in social studies and science), students can experience a range of texts on the same topic or theme and deepen their understanding of the variety of ways authors express ideas and convey information. With longer units, teachers can introduce several genres, develop strategies for students' reading and thinking, and differentiate the instructional support students need. This type of content-based unit structure is being implemented in many schools and districts across the country (Guthrie & Ozgungor, 2002; Ogle & Lang, 2011; Overturf, 2015; Pearson, Cervetti, & Tilson, 2008), and many example units are available through state departments of education and the Achieve and PARCC Web sites. Many publishers have supported this focus of instruction by making collections of materials on a single topic or theme available, and others have created short, highly visual informational books for young readers at a range of reading levels. By integrating instruction, teachers can develop both literacy and content and also improve learning in both areas (Pearson et al., 2008).

Through thoughtful planning, teachers can provide a broad range of materials and instruction about reading them that makes students comfortable negotiating a variety of text types. Because purpose has such a powerful effect on individual reading habits (Duke, Caughlan, Juzwik, & Martin, 2012), it is important to provide opportunities for many purposes, from learning new information to performing tasks to recreating experiences and representing them in new ways. Fortunately, resources that meet these varied purposes and needs are readily available now. In an electronic environment where we have access to a world of information, students must learn to use this source of informational materials as they engage in inquiry and write their own articles and reports (Biancarosa, 2012). Reading across texts, comparing authors and ideas, and evaluating materials are important priorities. Students' abilities to read, write, and think critically are necessary, especially with the range of unedited ideas available on the Internet. Today's elementary and middle school classrooms can become alive with the kinds of experiences that help students develop these skills.

Check Your Understanding 9.1: Gauge your understanding of the skills and concepts in this section.

Understanding How Readers Comprehend Informational Texts

Learning from reading is an active, ongoing process that can be described by what we do before, during, and after engagement with a text. Just as we do with instruction in reading literature, we follow the simple **ABC framework**—Anticipating, Building Knowledge, and Consolidating Learning—in reading to learn. We begin by anticipating what we want and need to learn from the text. Then, we build knowledge while reading and engaging with authors. Finally, we consolidate the new ideas with what we already knew, sometimes adding depth and sometimes modifying our thinking. This ongoing process is also a recursive one. That is, with each new set of ideas we read, we rethink what we know, ask new questions, set new purposes, and build on the ideas that are freshly learned. Some essential aspects that undergird teaching active reading include the following:

- Activating schemata or prior knowledge
- Assuming a metacognitive orientation
- Setting one's own purposes and asking questions
- Actively seeking information and making notes so that it can be retained for connecting and organizing ideas
- Forming interpretations of what is read
- Consolidating new information and ideas

- Analyzing and evaluating the sources and adequacy of information
- Creating a synthesis and representation of the learning that can be shared
- Reaching conclusions about and finding applications of what has been learned

Reading is a complex process that involves orchestrating these various facets of comprehension. **Close reading** refers specifically to careful attention to all aspects of how an author creates meaning, identifying the ideas, then analyzing and critically evaluating what an author writes. Such reading involves initially focusing on the ideas developed by authors (key ideas, details, and examples), then shifting attention to the structure and techniques used by the writer, and finally to thinking critically about how these ideas and points of view compare and contrast with those of others.

Teacher modeling is an important part of developing students' abilities to orchestrate the skills and foci needed for close or analytic reading. Teachers can assist children in thinking more deeply and analyzing how authors succeed in communicating ideas and supporting their points of view and arguments. This focused, intense scrutiny of texts is only done with short segments of text when there is a desire or need for such analysis, especially when readers are trying to better understand how texts work.

These modeled lessons need to be complemented by lessons focused on helping students deal with individual strategies: finding main ideas; connecting these ideas with details; recognizing how vocabulary is introduced and developed; identifying techniques authors use to construct their texts; summarizing texts; and then comparing and contrasting different texts for ideas and points of view. The way teachers introduce learning tasks to students and provide them with instructional tools to use as they learn will determine to a great degree students' success at becoming strong at comprehension. Planning carefully across each year, beginning with initial assessment of what students already know and can do and then structuring good teaching and guided practice activities that build on this knowledge, will lead both teachers and students to success.

The Importance of Background Knowledge

Reading is always an active, constructive process during which students need to activate what they know to make sense of text. Readers comprehend by having the details in the material they are reading lead them to evoke relevant knowledge schemata. Then they use these **schemata** to give meaning to the details and, ideally, to understand the meaning of the whole passage. There are at least four kinds of **background knowledge** that readers need in order to comprehend well. The first is knowledge of the vocabulary. The second is knowledge of text structure. The third and fourth deal with content knowledge, both topical and principled.

VOCABULARY   One of the most important tools in understanding a text is having a grasp of how the key terms are used in a specific content area. Vocabulary represents the knowledge of words and their meanings. In reading, the issue of vocabulary knowledge ranges between word recognition and comprehension. In word recognition, children may labor to recognize a word in print, but once they recognize it, they may or may not know the spoken word and its meaning. Obviously, a reader must know the meanings of most of the words in a text to be able to read it successfully. When reading informational texts, the demands of learning the academic terms can be enormous. Given this reality, it is important that students learn strategies to identify important terms, know how words are formed, and understand how to use context to determine meaning (Blachowicz, Fisher, Ogle, & Watts-Taffe, 2013; Nagy & Townsend, 2011).

KNOWLEDGE OF TEXT STRUCTURE   The **text structure** is a little like the grammar of a sentence. Because you understand the grammar of a sentence such as "The man bit the dog," you know who was bitten and who did the biting. In the same fashion, if you understand the structures of stories, you know how to follow a plot. If you can understand the structure of explanations, you know how to find the questions and get the answers to them. If you understand the structure of persuasive writing, you know how to spot the claim and weigh the support for it (Duke et al., 2012; Goldman & Rakestraw, 2000). The more you know about the way informational articles and texts are generally organized, the more you will be able to predict and read actively. This knowledge of text structures also helps you retain what you read, because you can organize the ideas into major categories for memory. Watch this video, in which a teacher gives her students an introduction to text structure, and then answer the question that follows.

 Video Exploration 9.1: Watch the video and answer questions that reflect the content you have read.

TOPICAL CONTENT KNOWLEDGE   The term **topical content knowledge** represents a fairly shallow level of knowledge, consisting of little more than a passing familiarity with the subject of the reading. For example, assume that while reading, a little girl is faced with a scientific passage about ducks. If she has seen a Donald Duck cartoon (and realizes that the character of Donald is based loosely on a real duck), she will have some topical knowledge about ducks. She will realize ducks have beaks, two wings, and two webbed feet and that they make quacking sounds. This amount of knowledge will not help much when reading a scientific text about ducks, but at least it will help her picture what is being talked about.

PRINCIPLED CONTENT KNOWLEDGE   In contrast to topical content knowledge, **principled content knowledge** entails a deeper kind of understanding. It consists of familiarity with the topic as well as an understanding of its parts, its causes and effects, and other issues related to it (Gelman & Greeno, 1989). For example, readers who have learned about geese and know something about the lives of migratory aquatic birds will have principled knowledge with which to understand a scientific passage about ducks. Readers with principled knowledge are better prepared to understand challenging passages than readers who have only topical knowledge. Their curiosity is likely to be deeper, and their expectations will conform more closely to the unfolding presentation of information in the text. The reader with topical knowledge, by contrast, might recognize isolated parts of the information in the text, but will be less prepared to make sense of the flow of information or the more important ideas in the text.

The Teacher's Role in Guiding Instruction

The choices teachers make in determining instructional focus and the kind of guidance they provide greatly influence the way students think as they read and make a difference in the kinds of knowledge students gain about the subject matter in the curriculum. Too often, content reading becomes frustrating for both students and teachers. To prevent this, teachers need to take care to focus instructional time on the most important aspects of comprehension development. As we already noted, a key is to ensure that students have an understanding of how the content or text they are reading is organized. This framework provides a structure within which students can distinguish key ideas from those of lesser importance. During instruction, teachers have several important tasks. These include modeling and guiding engagement with text, teaching skills and strategies, eliciting students' own interests and motivation, and providing adequate time for students to explore ideas and concepts in depth.

DEVELOPING PRINCIPLED KNOWLEDGE   The kinds of knowledge students gain about the subject matter in the curriculum are very important. In reading to learn, the content-specific information needs attention, something that is not a priority when reading fiction. A key to comprehending a text is having the ability to link ideas presented within and across sentences to create a sense of a whole text. Teachers influence students' knowledge formation in two important ways: by the questions they ask and by the depth of study they encourage with their students.

The Questions Teachers Ask   The ideas to which you call children's attention by means of your questions or comments influence the course of the children's thinking about what they read and study. You can direct students' attention toward important ideas or trivial ones. When reading a story, it makes a difference whether you dwell on minor details or ask questions that call attention to the deep structural elements of the story: the character's problem, goal, conflicts, and solutions to problems or the author's message or theme in the story. When reading informational text, it matters whether you call attention to minor details or to important ideas such as chronological development, cause and effect, or hierarchical relationships between ideas. It is important, too, that you draw students' attention to the important concept-carrying vocabulary and help them use these terms as they learn the new content.

The Depth to Which Teachers Lead Children to Study a Topic   You can encourage children to gain deeper knowledge about topics by staying with subjects for more than brief periods. You also can enhance children's understanding by looking at topics through many different disciplines. For example, look at a historical phenomenon such as immigration through fictional works in addition to the social studies text. By seeing phenomena through the eyes of fictional participants, students have more possibility of connecting with, visualizing, and interpreting the concept. Lengthy discussions, especially those that make connections between the subject of study and the children's own experience, also make it more likely that children will form deep, principled knowledge about a subject (Allington & Johnston, 2002).

Teach It! 47

Anticipation Guide

This before-reading activity offers an opportunity for developing comprehension by tapping into and organizing prior knowledge around important ideas.

SKILLS AND STRATEGIES   In addition to some background knowledge with which to understand text, readers need skills and strategies. **Skills** are processes that readers use habitually. **Strategies** are the processes by which they use their skills under conscious control. Teachers need to know what skills and strategies students possess and consciously develop a strong repertoire of both in all students.

When children first learn to read, they may be taught to perform comprehension activities consciously as reading strategies. For example, when they come across a word they do not know, the teacher might urge them to read to the end of the line to get a sense of the meaning of the sentence, and then go back and guess the meaning of the unknown word. This strategy is known as the *reading ahead/reread activity*. Later on—possibly much later on and after continued support from the teacher—when the readers habitually use the context to figure out unknown words, the behavior has become a skill.

When students are working with difficult material, however, or when they want to be especially careful in their reading, skilled readers often employ some reading strategies consciously (Pressley & Afflerbach, 1995). For example, even when their reading skills are adequate for comprehending a section in a social studies text, readers might consciously choose to apply the strategy of summarizing and rehearsing main ideas to remember them for a discussion the next day.

INTEREST AND MOTIVATION   Performing acts of comprehension takes some effort, and exerting effort takes will. No wonder children are more likely to take the trouble to do what they need to do to understand what they read when the topic is interesting to them. This fact, although not always honored in school curriculum offerings, has been recognized for the better part of a century (Beane, 2002; Dewey, 1913; Guthrie & Davis, 2003). But readers may be interested in a topic in different ways, and these differences have consequences. In the opening vignette, as Ms. Gurvitz began her unit on the pond, she had a naturalist speak with the children and show them samples of the frogs that were deformed. This piqued their interest.

Readers might be interested in a topic because it has been presented in an engaging way—with exciting illustrations or dramatic writing and exclamation points. Or they might be interested because they have some reason to find out more about a topic and they want to know more about the line of inquiry the text is following. For example, because you want to know how to help your present or future students read with comprehension, you might find this text of particular interest. You likely don't need movie poster-like illustrations to draw you into the ideas presented here. If you pick up the Sunday magazine in your newspaper, however, it might take an interesting picture with a curiosity-provoking caption to get you interested in reading about something that is new to you.

These individual *motivations* for learning correspond to the kinds of prior knowledge readers have about a topic. Readers who have principled knowledge about a topic tend to be interested in adding to and deepening that knowledge, whereas readers with shallower, topical knowledge might not be motivated automatically to learn more about something through reading. Research has shown (Alexander, 1998) that readers with these different kinds of background knowledge notice different things in a text. Readers with only topical knowledge might focus on flashy or exotic details to the exclusion of main ideas and arguments, whereas those with principled knowledge might do just the opposite.

THE "MATTHEW EFFECT": ASPECTS OF COMPREHENSION ARE INTERRELATED   What we have just considered as separate aspects of comprehension—prior knowledge, strategies and skills, and interest—are in fact interrelated. Although it is true, as Duffy and Roehler (1989) and others have shown, that children can profit from being taught to carry out comprehension strategies, it is also true that reading comprehension develops as a conglomerate of achievements (Alexander et al., 1994). For example, engaging prior knowledge can be helped along by teaching; however, for this teaching to be successful, children must have some prior knowledge of the topic to call on. Moreover, children are more likely to have deep enough interests in the topic to use the strategies of applying prior knowledge, making predictions, arguing with the text, or finding main ideas, unless their prior knowledge is deep and principled. To carry this point further, if their prior knowledge about a topic is deep and principled, then their interest in the topic will also extend below the surface to main ideas and structures of argument.

The process is cyclic and is an example of what researcher Keith Stanovich (1986) called the **"Matthew effect"** in reading, a term derived from a passage in the gospel of Matthew about the rich getting richer and the poor becoming poorer (see Figure 9.2). The more you know, the easier it is to learn more; the more quickly you develop early literacy skills, the faster your reading accelerates as you can read more. When young readers have deep and principled knowledge, they will have deep interest; if they have deep interest, they will use thoroughgoing strategies of comprehension; and if they use thoroughgoing strategies, they will gain more principled knowledge.

The cycle works the other way, too. A reader might lack deep knowledge, not habitually use thoroughgoing reading strategies, or have only superficial interest in the topics being read. These factors may interact to prevent satisfactory comprehension. The best teaching for comprehension, then, includes attention to all these aspects:

Figure 9.2 The Matthew Effect in Reading Comprehension

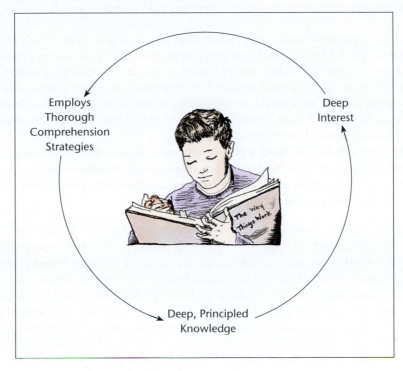

- Creating a learning environment in which students can become immersed in a topic over time and explore it deeply
- Guiding students' attention to the way the texts they read are organized
- Helping students develop principled knowledge by encouraging them to consider ideas deeply, and pointing them toward the main ideas and the underlying structures and issues
- Teaching thoroughgoing, powerful strategies for comprehending and remembering and then supporting and reinforcing these strategies until they become habituated into skills
- Engaging children in deep discussions of what they read and getting them to think about, write about, and respond to what they read so they will understand issues deeply and extend their curiosity to other meaningful topics in their world
- Focusing their attention on the vocabulary of the topic or area so they develop a more precise way of thinking and differentiating ideas
- Encouraging students' questions and taking their inquiry seriously, weaving their deep-seated interests into the very fabric of the school day

Student Engagement

Although the teacher's role in developing a thoughtful class is critical, students play equally important roles as learners. Right from the beginning of the school year, teachers need to take time to observe how students approach learning. What is their level of **engagement**? How involved and aware are students of what learning entails? They need to be active—and interactive—if they are going to be successful learners. People learn best when they do so strategically. That means taking charge of their own reading with a clear purpose. Just as in reading fiction, students need to be actively engaged while reading and learning from nonfiction and other content materials. Because content material is usually dense with ideas to be learned, the following strategies are especially important.

ANTICIPATING   Students need to anticipate—to ask what they want to learn from the reading. They do this by first assessing what they know, what the task demands are, and what needs to be accomplished. For young students, this initial orientation is modeled in the K-W-L framework discussed later in this chapter. As students begin their engagement with a new topic, watch them and discuss with them how they begin. Do they skim through the material and activate what they know and make connections with the text? Do they look closely at diagrams or pictures and think about their meaning?

Once students have assessed their starting point in learning, they then need to develop a plan for how to proceed in order to accomplish their goals. This includes knowing that there are options for how to proceed. Students too often think that all they can do is read and then reread. Instead, they need to know they can use a variety of tools to guide their acquisition of knowledge. They are going to want to make notes when they encounter new information that is important or use some form of marginal notation if they can keep the materials. Stick-on notes serve wonderful purposes in helping students keep track of what they want to learn. These notes can be grouped later to chunk information in a way that will give the student a more coherent sense of what is to be learned.

Some students learn best when they can create a graphic network of ideas or draw diagrams of what they learn. Being active during the process of learning is essential. It takes little time to check whether students are using active strategies when they read informational material that is full of important concepts and main ideas. (Several strategies that support students' active engagement are discussed later in the chapter.)

BUILDING KNOWLEDGE   Students build knowledge as they deal with the ideas they are reading about. That means **monitoring** what they are thinking and learning, asking questions as they go, and creating summaries of ideas for themselves. Some students like to think aloud, others make notes in the margin or on sheets of paper, some prefer drawing key ideas to represent the text's main ideas, and some like to share with another person what they are getting out of a text as they read. Teachers need to model each of these approaches to building knowledge. Asking students to put stick-on notes in their text material as they read is an easy diagnostic of how they attend to important elements of these texts.

Students also enjoy hearing what classmates think is most important from what they have read, so group sharing at the end of a reading period can be very productive. Teachers also can create large bulletin board displays or butcher paper matrices on which students can post what they think is most important and interesting in what they read. These then can serve as ongoing records of students' growing knowledge. As teachers expand the options for engaged reading and help students practice these strategies frequently, they will become better equipped to make decisions about which strategies work best for them in particular situations.

CONSOLIDATING WHAT THEY LEARN   As students continue to build their knowledge and understanding as a result of reading, they also consolidate what they are learning. That means going back and thinking again about how the ideas fit together and what they mean. Students can create a new graphic representation of what they have learned. They might write an outline and then elaborate on it in a summary, or they might want to talk to someone about the ideas they have gained. If students are using a textbook or a guide from a teacher, they can return to the questions or talk about the main objectives. If students are going to retain important ideas, they need to do something actively with them—by summarizing or extending what the authors have presented.

Most elementary students need sustained teacher guidance and support to develop the habit of rehearsing what they are learning. Several graphic organizers discussed later in this chapter can help students to organize their thinking and provide good visual reviews of content. If they transform the ideas they are learning into a new form, students have a greater chance of remembering them (Cain, Oakhill & Bryant, 2004). Simply asking the question "What did that mean to me?" helps students to stay active metacognitively. Strategies for working together to read, question, and reflect can be used with even the youngest students, who can learn to work in pairs and ask each other what they have learned (Pressley, 2002).

Finally, good readers engage in evaluation of both the materials they read and their accomplishments. If the text seems unclear or lacking in information, they might decide to read other sources to clarify ideas or to confirm accuracy and currency. Good readers also assess the achievement of their own purposes. Returning to their questions or categories that were unclear, good readers make sure they understand and have met their own purposes. They know that learning takes effort.

Those students who are not confident learners often feel disadvantaged when there are intense content expectations. You can help them to realize that they can learn new material, but it is a process that takes time and active involvement on their part. It is essential to give insecure learners and second-language learners models of process learning and time to rehearse and clarify ideas. They need to understand that reading a text once is never enough if the material is new and important. Studies of effective fourth-grade teachers (Allington & Johnston, 2002) revealed that they often help students to engage in rehearsing the same materials many times as a tool to their learning. Regularly modeling and reinforcing a process of anticipating, building knowledge, and consolidating learning will create active, confident readers (Pressley et al., 1998).

COLLECTING BOOKS FOR READING ALOUD   Teachers model good reading for their students. One way teachers can insure that students will develop an interest in and familiarity with informational books is to build a collection of texts that you can read to your students. You probably remember some special books that teachers read to you. You may also remember teachers who read aloud to you from the newspaper or current magazines. Begin collecting informational materials you can share with your students. Find good biographies and autobiographies that you can use to entice students into reading about real people and events. (For example, Barack Obama has written a very accessible autobiography, *Dreams From My Father: A Story of Race and Inheritance*.) Locate books about special holidays like the Mexican Day of the Dead, the Muslim religious month of Ramadan, and the American holidays of Halloween and Fourth of July. With increasingly diverse student populations in our schools, all students can learn about important traditions. These make good read-aloud texts.

If you read magazines like *National Geographic* and *Smithsonian,* start making a file of good articles that you can read to students to entice them into expanding their own interests. As you visit schools, talk with teachers about the magazines they bring in to share with their students and start making a list of resources that can deepen what you can bring to your future students. Reading aloud to students from informational texts is an important part of building students' familiarity with these resources and expanding their interests.

Check Your Understanding 9.2: Gauge your understanding of the skills and concepts of this section.

Teaching Students to Use Features of Informational Texts

Reading informational texts involves navigating a variety of types of materials with many different features and levels of density. Successful reading of these texts in order to learn requires that readers develop specific strategies to use with textbooks, magazines, trade books, newspapers, primary documents, and Internet sites. For example, one strategy not appropriate with fiction involves dropping in and out of texts. When looking for specific information, readers of informational texts will notice that they don't have to start on the first page and read to the end of the material. Rather, by using the table of contents and index, they can find a pertinent section without reading the whole text. Or they might be able to skip parts that are less essential to their purposes. The first thing they might observe about informational material is that it is organized differently from fiction both internally and externally, which makes searching text quite easy. Watch this video in which a teacher and students identify text features that will help them read their textbooks more quickly and easily, and then answer the question that follows.

   Video Exploration 9.2: Watch the video and answer questions that reflect the content you have read.

Kindergarten and first-grade teachers can do a great deal to introduce children to the special way informational magazines and books are structured so that they do not overlook the richness of these resources. When introducing a new informational text or textbook, it is useful to do a picture and visual walk through the text. Each new text deserves attention because there are so many different formats and ways or organizing text.

CCSS

Knowing Features of Informational Text

Because of the increased focus on informational text reading, students need to develop their abilities to use the features of informational texts that will help them build their understanding. The CCSS standards for informational reading elaborate on the development of these skills and place much of the focus for this instruction in the primary grades. See Standards 5 and 6 for first and second grades below.

First grade, Information Reading Standard 5.   Know and use various text features (e.g., captions, bold print, subheadings, glossaries, indexes, electronic menus, icons) to locate key facts or information in a text efficiently.

6. Name the author and illustrator of a text and define the role of each in presenting the ideas or information in a text.

Second grade, Information Reading Standard 5.   Distinguish between information provided by pictures or other illustrations and information provided by the words in a text.

6. Identify the main purpose of a text, including what the author wants to answer, explain, or to be comfortable with the features that help them navigate these materials.

Figure 9.3 Nonfiction Book Checklist

Title _____	
Author _____	
Nonfiction Book Checklist	
_____ 1. Table of contents	Something I liked about this book:
_____ 2. Index	
_____ 3. Photographs	
_____ 4. Realistic, accurate illustrations	
_____ 5. Maps	
_____ 6. Diagrams	
_____ 7. Captions—bold lettering	Something I learned from this book:
_____ 8. Glossary—words and definitions	
_____ 9. Page numbers	
_____ 10. Other	

Write Informational Book Reports

A good way to reinforce the special nature of informational books is to have first- and second-grade students complete nonfiction book reports using the checklist shown in Figure 9.3 that is part of a four-sided "booklet" a team of primary teachers created. By having a checklist of features, children develop a habit of using these features regularly. In addition, the book report asks students to tell what they liked, what they learned, and what would make the book better, and then to draw a picture that reflects the main idea of the book (adapted from D. Gurvitz).

Preview Informational Texts

Intermediate-grade teachers also can have children preview expository texts they are using both as textbooks and as other resource materials. Students have fun when teachers prepare scavenger hunts that can be completed by using text features like the table of contents, index, and glossary. For example, a partner scavenger hunt based on the book *Hurricane* (Haselhurst, 2005) included the following:

1. Which chapter gives information on how to prepare for a hurricane?
2. Where is information that clarifies the differences between hurricanes and tropical cyclones?
3. On which pages are there maps of hurricane paths?
4. Where is the term *debris* defined?
5. How is the book organized to help keep your interest and help you learn?

At the beginning of the year, it is always good to refresh students' use of all the ways information is available. Reading aloud to students from magazines and books and periodically stopping to consciously think aloud about ideas and questions that come from the reading provide further opportunity to focus children's attention on illustrations, captions, and other presentations of information. Viewing a transparency or visual of the first one or two pages in a chapter or article with the class lets you talk with the students about what they do when they navigate a page of informational text. In fact, informational texts are similar to the computer programs with which many students spend a great deal of leisure time. Students can have fun exploring the similarities and differences in materials presented in these two formats. After such a comparison, encourage students to add diagrams and other visuals or links from their textbooks to other sources. They can become active in making materials more accessible. Rather than feeling overwhelmed by texts, students need to develop confidence in using texts and in going beyond single texts when these are not clear.

Teach It! 55

Using the Table of Contents to Predict

This activity helps students prepare for content learning and supports comprehension as they become familiar with and anticipate the ways informational text is structured and organized.

Predict Tables of Contents

Intermediate-grade students should begin to anticipate how informative expository material is organized. By third grade, most students should be able to predict what might be in the table of contents of an animal book (e.g., description, habitat, food, family). Before studying regions of the earth in fourth grade, some students should be able to identify possible topics that will reoccur with each region studied (e.g., plants, animals, geography, human life). Fifth graders need to know that biographies have some common topics that are used to organize information (e.g., early life, education, hardships, accomplishments). Teachers can model this prediction of content topics by leading a discussion as the class begins a topical study asking what areas or categories of information the students think will be included in what they learn. Beginning with biography is easiest: When studying great leaders, what topics do students anticipate will be included? Children's ideas generally include when the person lived, their early life, family, problems the person overcame, education, and accomplishments. From there, students can be guided to think of categories important to each of the topics they study as an initial step in reading and learning content. One way to assess students' developing awareness of these expert ways of organizing content information and then using it to prepare for reading and learning is to have them create a possible table of contents alone or with a partner. In this way, teachers can help students to think more deeply and to begin to develop principled knowledge.

Create Chapter Graphic Organizers

At the middle-grade level, teachers can have students identify and use the external structure of chapters in textbooks and magazines to make notes. They skim through the chapter and create a **chapter graphic organizer** or map of the chapter with the title in the center and each of the main headings on one spoke of their spider map (see Figure 9.4).

Figure 9.4 A Chapter Graphic Organizer

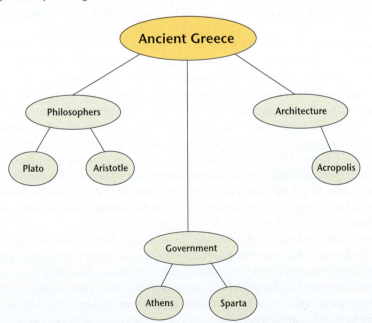

Teach It! 48

Graphic Organizers

Graphic organizers provide an ongoing visual for student learning: they can be used before, during, and after reading and can be formatted to align with the organization of the text under study.

This graphic organizer is then used while students read to help them understand how the information is related. This mapping of the text can also be used as an interactive guide for reading. The students can brainstorm what they know about each section before reading; write those ideas on the map; highlight the areas that are least familiar and that will require slower reading, note making, and possible rereading; and then make notes on their map of new information as they read. This active engagement helps students to focus and retain information as they read.

Jigsaw Text Sections

Another strategy teachers employ to help students utilize the external structure of articles and chapters is to have a chapter read using a type of **jigsaw** cooperative learning strategy. The class first previews the text and identifies the major sections, which the teacher writes on the board. Then the class is divided into teams, with one team assigned to each major section. Each team of students reads and creates a visual report of the key ideas of their one section of the text. Because many of the informational chapters and articles have such a heavy load of information, asking students to learn just one section from reading makes it manageable. Each group then reports on their section. Serving as "teachers" for the rest of the class both enhances the students' engagement in reading and creates a shared environment for learning.

Use Visual and Graphic Information

There are several ways to guide students' use of the visual and graphically presented information in the texts they use to learn new content. First, assess how students attend to pages of busy text. Informally ask students individually to describe how they read a **two-page spread** in a book or magazine they will be reading. As they share, make notes of their approaches. Where do they start? Do they read the visually presented information? When do they read it? Do they integrate the visuals and the running text? Do they read captions on graphs and pictures? Are they aware of how they approach reading when the materials are presented in a variety of formats? Do they integrate these different sources in notes they make or in summaries they create?

Questions such as these can help you to assess students' engagement with text materials. From this assessment, you can develop your instructional focus. A good starting point is modeling how to approach busy text by doing **think-alouds** such as the following with groups of students. Make a transparency or copy of one or two pages of text. Using an overhead projector or visualizer, demonstrate how you survey the page, noting the different layout of information and graphics and raising questions that are stimulated by the text. Start by looking at the title of the chapter or section and note the way the sections are marked—with boldface print or words in capital letters, for example. Then, focus on the visuals, such as pictures, diagrams, or notes in the margins. Ask, "Why did the author/s use this cartoon? What is its role in this section? Let's see, the caption says . . . Oh, yes, I bet it is an example of …" By covering up the text on the projected pages, students can be led to survey the graphic information. From this survey, students can reflect on the content they think is being emphasized and what questions they believe will be answered in the next page or two. In this way, the importance of using the visually presented material may become clearer to them. In fact, sometimes this kind of preview can reduce the actual reading time considerably

After teacher modeling, students can apply their own skill in attending to the visual features by drawing arrows between visuals and the narrative text that is connected to them. This can be done with acetate pages placed over the text or by having photocopied pages of the text on which students can draw the arrows. Many teachers find that helping intermediate-grade students associate the visual and verbal components of texts is challenging and yet very worthwhile. If children are having trouble with these tasks, it can be more enjoyable to start by practicing with nonacademic materials such as creating origami figures or doing magic tricks from books or articles that use visuals to reinforce the steps in the processes to be enacted.

CCSS

Comprehending Non-Textual Information

According to CCSS Information Standard 7, students should be able to:

Third Grade: Use information gained from illustrations (e.g., maps, photographs) and the words in a text to demonstrate understanding of the text (e.g., where, when, why, and how key events occur).

Fourth Grade: Interpret information presented visually, orally, or quantitatively (e.g., in charts, graphs, diagrams, time lines, animations, or interactive elements on Web pages) and explain how the information contributes to an understanding of the text in which it appears.

Fifth Grade: Draw on information from multiple print or digital sources, demonstrating the ability to locate an answer to a question quickly or to solve a problem efficiently.

When teachers take time to think aloud about how to approach the mixed types of presentations in informational texts, students begin to think metacognitively about their own approaches to texts. Adults use many of these strategies automatically when appropriate. Students, by contrast, often need to hear another person's thinking before they understand how active they need to be as readers.

Use the Organization of Internet Sites

Web sites have an external structure that is important for students to understand. Just as they may find it useful to draw the layout of a page of a printed textbook, they also can learn a great deal about Web site layout by sketching the various sections on two or three Web pages and then comparing them. Most important is identifying the major sections usually presented across the top of the site or down the left side. See Figure 9.5 for a general frame for this evaluation.

Web sites are often selected by teachers or through adult supervision. However, it is also good to teach students how to identify good Web sites themselves. A step that precedes going to the Web site itself often comes as students use a search engine (AolKIDS, Yahoo Kids, Google Safe Search, Safe Search App, Ask Kids, etc.) to locate possible sources online. The URLs tell a great deal about the site authors and can help in the selection of a good Web site. Sites that are government or university sponsored are generally more reliable than those that come with a ".com" address. Teachers can help students in site selection by writing a sample set of URLs on the board as students begin the study of a particular topic where they will use online sources. For example, as students in one class began researching information about the building of the Statue of Liberty, their teacher wrote the URLs and sources for the following Web sites on the board and asked which ones they thought would provide the best, most reliable information:

1. National Parks Service
2. NYCVP: Official Home of New York City Vacation Packages
3. The Statue of Liberty-Ellis Island Foundation (SOLEIF)
4. Wikipedia
5. *New York Daily News*, with stories written by subscribers

In the discussion that followed, students thought about the impact of site sponsors and promoters on the information presented; these insights helped the class become more critically aware of how to look for information. The teacher followed up this initial part of the search for sites by showing students how they could also cross-check information by using encyclopedias that are online or checking print sources and textbooks that are edited before being made public.

Once a few Web sites are selected, students need to learn to navigate the sites themselves. The organization of Web pages varies considerably, and the best formats keep evolving. Some have key categories and options listed in ways that

Figure 9.5 Analyzing Internet Sites

Home	About Us	Connect	How to …	Programs

make them easy to use; others can be cluttered and take several steps to navigate. Taking the time to walk through Web site structure using an LCD projector and to "think aloud" about how to scan the various parts of the visual layout can be very helpful to young users. Research by Leu and others (2007) indicates that all too often, students don't explore Web sites in enough depth to take advantage of the resources that are available. Knowing how material is organized and which categories are the most general are important keys to using Webs sites. So, too, is interpreting the visually presented information. Students can use some of the same methods for looking at Web pages that they use for scanning and interpreting pictures and visuals in texts.

Developing Students' Understanding of Internal Organization

External features of informational texts are easy to identify and help students use in their reading. More challenging is identifying the internal structure or organization of texts so readers can think like content experts and organize the ideas they are learning. Differentiating main ideas from significant details and less important information is a major focus of comprehension and needs to be taught over several grades. The internal organization helps in this process; readers need to think about what is most important: Did the author focus on the problem and solution, create a description, or did she try to compare and contrast? When students attend to the organization of ideas, they have a tool that helps them determine the importance of ideas within a text and remember them.

The varying patterns can make predicting and organizing ideas more difficult for novice readers; therefore, it is all the more important that teachers provide guidance so students can learn to identify these internal structures. As they do, their ability to write informational pieces and reports more effectively also will improve. Here again, graphic organizers can help students recognize the underlying organization of texts. Figure 9.6 shows some simple models.

COMPARE TEXTS   One way to introduce internal patterns of texts is by collecting several books on the same topic and guiding students to compare their internal structures. By introducing the reading of the book in this way, you engage the students to think in terms of the big picture about what an author is trying to accomplish in a text. An easy way to create varieties of texts is to download articles from online encyclopedias and Internet articles and compare their organization. This can be a starting place for contrasting and comparing longer articles and books. By comparing and contrasting two to three texts on the same topic, you can help students understand how point of view and perspective influence writing. This is also one of the expectations of the CCSS informational reading standards.

WRITE TEXTS   A good way to help students apply their knowledge of text organization is to have them write their own books using the structure of one they have studied. For example, during a unit on insects, third-grade students used Brown's (1949) *The Important Book* as a model for their writing. Each student wrote about his or her chosen insect and used the book structure as a guide. They took the text's predictable pattern,

The important thing about _____ is that _____. They have _____, _____, and _____, but the important thing about _____ is _____,

and wrote about insects. One child had studied bees and wrote, "The important thing about a bee is that it stings. It is true that a bee has two pairs of wings and collects honey, but the important thing about a bee is that it STINGS!" Each child used this same pattern to write about his or her insect and the teacher then collected the pieces into a class book, *Important Insects*. This experience helped students focus their attention on simple, predictable text structures. Later, the teacher introduced other, more standard structures used by authors of informational books they were reading. With this concrete experience in writing, the students were more attuned to organization and the structure of ideas.

ATTEND TO VOCABULARY AND CONTENT-SPECIFIC TERMINOLOGY   A key to learning content material is to give attention to vocabulary that conveys key concepts. Again, the differences between reading for pleasure and reading to learn are dramatic. When one reads for oneself, unfamiliar vocabulary can be ignored. In fact, good readers attend only to information that they know is helpful in comprehending. As a result, they skip unfamiliar terms. In reading to learn, however, this practice can hinder comprehension. The unfamiliar terms are often exactly what the reader needs to attend to. Therefore, you need to help students develop the habit of attending to key terms that are content carriers. There are three important components to vocabulary learning in content materials:

- Words the authors prioritize (e.g., with boldface, italics, marginal definitions, or illustrations)
- Teacher-highlighted key new terms
- Students' own monitoring of what words are new and need to be learned

Figure 9.6 Graphic Organizer Models

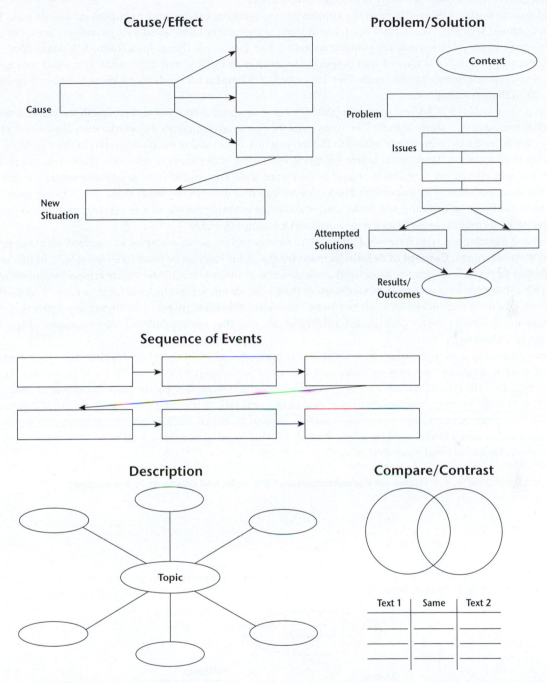

The first place to start in attending to vocabulary is by noting what the authors have already indicated as important through highlighting, putting words in italics, and adding boxed definitions or illustrations. Without teacher guidance, students often overlook these aids. Because authors often assist readers by highlighting these terms, helping students to preview material to find these indicated words can be a great support to later reading and learning.

Teachers can help students note key words, too, by creating a list of key terms and then giving students some activities to focus their attention on these terms. One easy way to do this is to ask students to **Connect Two** (or three) of the terms and create new sentences using them. Even if the students do not know much about the words, they can have fun anticipating what they mean. Working with partners to create new sentences gives children a chance to use the words orally, too, thus increasing their awareness of the words both visually and orally. A more sophisticated activity is to ask students to chunk new words into categories and then label the groups and justify them to the class. The children now are attuned to these words and will definitely notice them as they read.

In addition to noting key words from the subject matter, teachers can be alert to important words from the text that are not content specific. Words from academic discourse that are not limited to a single subject area, but are also not much used in everyday speech are sometimes called *Tier Two words* (Beck, McKeown, & Kucan, 2002; Kucan, 2012). For example, *cotyledon* is a word that is specific to biology or botany; and *differentiate* is a word that is used in many contexts, but not normally in speech. Tier Two words are helpful for students to know because they are often encountered in their reading.

The Web site *WordSift* will let you paste in a passage of text and have it scanned to distinguish the easier words from the more challenging ones—many of them Tier Two words. The program highlights the words; then, if you click on one, it will display a semantic map with words related to the target word. It will also show photographs of the words.

Students need to follow their initial search for terms with some active ways of retaining them. You can model this process by keeping a list of key terms on the board or on a word wall. This list can include both the words you introduced and ones the students identify as important. Then students can find more examples of these words being used in other places in their reading and listening and build a more elaborate meaning for the words. Asking students to draw their own images of the terms also helps to lock new words and meanings in place.

Elaborating associations with new words through drawings and personal examples will help students to retain the words and their meanings. **Concept of definition maps** for the terms can also be used (see Figure 9.7). In this way, students learn that terms have meanings, associated examples, and attributes. Specific terms are critical in content learning. Marzano (2004) has provided an excellent summary of the key academic terms students need to know and use to meet the content standards in each of eleven academic areas. Some school districts are now identifying key terms that students should know and be able to use for each grade level. This is one way they are highlighting the importance of specific academic language in learning.

With the importance of vocabulary in informational materials, students need to develop their own metacognitive control over what words are new to them, and they need to develop ways to retain those particular terms and their meanings. Individual vocabulary notebooks and word cards are good tools for students to use to rehearse and practice these words. Making new vocabulary a part of the oral talk of the classroom is an essential component in this process. Some teachers employ a reward system to encourage usage, such as giving students points when they hear and note a new word being used by a fellow student. This highlights oral as well as written vocabulary recognition and provides an internal incentive as well.

Check Your Understanding 9.3: Gauge your understanding of the skills and concepts in this section.

Figure 9.7 Concept of Definition Map

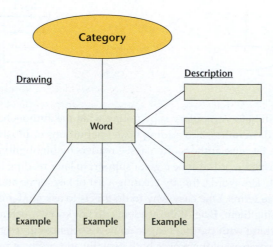

Differentiated Instruction

Reading Comprehension: Understanding and Learning with Informational Texts

Many students who speak languages other than English in their homes do very well with conversational English, and teachers may be unaware of the need to provide specific instruction when it comes to the academic vocabulary necessary for content area reading and learning. Yet this is an area deserving particular attention. Research studies have highlighted the fact that there is a great difference between conversational English and academic English competence. Teachers can do a lot to help English language learners be successful in this area of academic learning by focusing on vocabulary development.

Begin by assessing students' depth of understanding of key academic terms. For example, if the unit in social studies is about the westward movement of European pioneers across the continent, then terms like *pioneer, covered wagon, wagon train, trails, obstacles,* and *hardships* will probably be needed. These are terms that students would not encounter in normal conversational contexts. They are academic terms needed for this particular unit of study. In a similar way, as a unit in science on light is initiated, teachers highlight terms that will be used and check to see if academic terms like *opaque, translucent, transparent, reflection,* and *refraction* are familiar to students. Because these are words not used in regular conversational English, they need to be highlighted and taught specifically.

It is often helpful to English language learners to make a list of key terms and then compare them with the same terms in their home language. Because there are many Latin-based cognates used in English, this can make the learning task much easier. For example, the science terms can be listed on one side and the Spanish terms on the other.

Opaque	opaco/a
Reflection	reflexión
Refraction	refracción
Translucent	translúcido/a
Transparent	transparente

English language learners will be much more successful if teachers focus on key academic terms and provide them with extended opportunities to practice these words and phrases. It is in academic English that these English language learners deserve our help.

Teaching With Informational Texts

As students become familiar with the structure of informational text, they can use that knowledge to engage actively with the authors of those texts and think about learning new content. There are some basic frameworks for instruction and supporting strategies teachers can use that provide rich contexts for learning that afford ample opportunities for students to apply these skills and use them on their own. These frameworks and strategies have been developed separately, but often work well when used together. Here are few basic guidelines worth remembering:

1. Model and reinforce the importance of previewing informational material carefully and then rereading. There is an overwhelming amount of information in a good text and one reading is not sufficient. Take time so students can connect the new information with what they already know or think they know.

2. As the class is studying a new topic, use it as an opportunity to do a close read with your students from an important but somewhat challenging article or chapter section.

3. Build the habit of students underlining (their own books) or putting sticky notes on important ideas and information. This habit can also be extended by making notes or graphic outlines of important information. It is the practice of reading with a pencil and paper at one's side.

4. Develop in students the habit of using all the visual information available as they read—making the connections the authors and illustrators provide for readers.

K-W-L

Until students are able to take control of their learning by finding their own questions and level of knowledge, it is unlikely that they will retain much of what is studied. Motivation and personal interest are foundational to students' focusing their cognitive efforts. Therefore, the time spent activating personal and class interest is important.

Students become much more engaged in reading when they and their interests are the starting point for new inquiry and learning. **K-W-L** (Ogle, 1986, 1991) is a group process in which the teacher models and guides active engagement with informational texts. It uses the knowledge and information students bring to help each other build a better starting place for learning and for sharing the results of their reading. The adept teacher weaves together what some class members know (either topical or principled knowledge) and stimulates questions for all to pursue as they read to learn. The process also helps students who lack confidence in both reading and writing because the teacher is the first one to write on the board. This permits children to see the written forms of key terms they will encounter later in the text. It also models what the students will write on their own guide sheets or in their learning logs (see Figure 9.8).

What We Know   The teacher and students begin the process of reading and learning by brainstorming together what they know (the *K* in K-W-L) about the topic. The teacher guides students to probe their knowledge statements and find conflicting or partial statements of what they know. For example, as a group brainstorms what they know about the desert, one student says, "Nothing much lives there." Another volunteers, "That's not true! I know lots of insects live there. I just read a book about tarantulas." The teacher can encourage more student engagement by continuing the thinking: "Does anyone else know something about what lives in the dry, barren lands of the desert? Can anyone frame a question that may help us find out more?"

Another student chimes in, "We'd better find out what animals can survive there with little water or food." The teacher writes on the blackboard, overhead, or computer what the students ask as their own questions and what they volunteer they think they know, writing down their ideas just as the students say them (see Figure 9.9).

The teacher does not correct or evaluate, but encourages and stimulates students to think broadly about what they bring to the study. Through this brainstorming process, some questions or uncertainties generally surface. The teacher's role is to help students activate their knowledge and develop interest in the topic. Some basic rules are established at the beginning:

- All ideas are acceptable.
- Say what first comes into your mind. These ideas will be checked and edited or revised later.
- Listen to each other, but do not judge the quality of ideas.
- The goal is to get as many different ideas out as possible in the time allotted.

As ideas are voiced and written down, they might seem random and unconnected. At this point, you need to make a decision. If the group is engaged and ready to think a little more deeply, ask the students to think of ways in which the experts organize information on this topic. This move to a deeper level of thinking (to principled knowledge) can begin by first focusing on categories of information about which the children already have some intuitive knowledge. You can initiate reflection: "Look at what we listed in the 'Know' column. Are any of these items connected? For example, I see three items about animals that live on the desert. I also see some plants. Can you find other items that go together in a category? What are the basic categories of information we are likely to need to use?" In this case, the categories might be those shown in Figure 9.10.

The teacher might also begin simply by asking students to step back and think about the topic generally: "If you were going to write a table of contents on this topic, the desert, what would you include?" The ideas that students volunteer can be listed at the bottom of the "Know" column.

Teach It! 46
Paired Brainstorming

As a pre-reading activity, paired brainstorming activates students' prior knowledge of a topic and invites them to pose questions.

Figure 9.8 K-W-L Guide

SOURCE: K-W-L Guide, D. Ogle (1986), from "K-W-L: A Teaching Model That Develops Active Reading of Expository Text," in *The Reading Teacher, 36*(6), 564–570.

1. K – What We Know	W – What We Want to Learn	L – What We Learned and Still Need to Know

2. Categories of Information We Expect to Use:

A.   E.

B.   F.

C.   G.

D.   H.

3. Where We Will Find Information:

1.

2.

3.

4.

Figure 9.9 What We Know About Deserts

WHAT WE KNOW

Lots of snakes
Sand and windy
Cactus
Road Runners
Tarantulas
Hot weather
No water
No rain
Gila monster
Lizards
Bats
Phoenix
Sun City
Oil under the ground
Utah and Arizona

Figure 9.10 Categories of Information

Categories of Information:

A. animals   C. location   E. physical features
B. climate   D. plants

What We Want to Know   With a variety of ideas being shared, the teacher can easily ask what the students want (the *W* in K-W-L) to know. Again, it is the students' responsibility to think of real questions as you write down what they say. These questions form the second column on the worksheet or board. If students are not familiar with the process of generating their own questions, you might need to model some questioning at the beginning. You might be able to extend comments made by class members into questions.

For example, if the class is beginning a unit on the desert region and someone has listed cactus as a plant in the desert, you can extend this by suggesting, "I wonder whether there are any uses people make of cactus in the desert?"

You can write this in the "We Want to Know" column and continue to guide students to find questions, suggesting, "Is there anything else we might want to learn about the animals that live in the desert? Do we have to be careful of any of them? If we were hiking, should we watch out?"

This process puts the students right in the center of any new study. Rather than beginning with a text and previewing it, the students and the teacher become active listeners and recorders. This group-focusing effort helps students think about the range of ideas that they and others already have on the topic. It should also help them make new connections and become intrigued by what they don't know. Listening to each other can stimulate new vocabulary and associations; the writing done by the teacher often helps more reluctant readers begin to make associations between oral language and the written forms of words they will encounter as they read.

Once the students have discussed the topic, they are more ready to begin their own reading. It might be useful to have students write down on their own worksheets or learning logs the pieces of information they individually think they know and the questions they want to know more about. In this way, both the group and the individual are respected. You could have students work in pairs to do both the writing and reading because this is more stimulating and supportive of some children who lack confidence in writing and taking risks.

What We Learned You can diagnose from this discussion what texts will be most useful to the students. It might be that what you thought would be adequate turns out to be inappropriate. Rather than reading the planned text, the class can collect other materials and even write some of their own materials as needed. This is where the Internet can come in handy as a resource. Look up a few sites and bookmark them for the class. If the text or texts in the classroom and school library are appropriate, students can read and make notes on their own about what they learn (the *L* in K-W-L)—both answers to their questions and unexpected information they think is interesting and/or important. Many teachers create large bulletin boards with sections for the "What We Know," "What We Want to Learn," and "What We Learned" sections of the K-W-L project. Students can keep adding information and questions to the class chart as they study. Small index cards work well for this kind of class activity. You can also make photocopies of material or graphics that students find and want to have shared.

Watch this video in which a teacher begins a KWL chart by asking students what they know about coral reefs, and then answer the question that follows.

 Video Exploration 9.3: Watch the video and answer questions that reflect the content you have read.

K-W-L+ After years of working with students in content areas, teachers know that even with motivation and engagement, students will not remember much of the new information the first time they encounter it. Therefore, the "plus" in ***K-W-L+*** (Carr & Ogle, 1987) extends this learning process by asking students to do more reorganizing of what they have learned by making a semantic map or graphic organizer of the key information (see Figure 9.11). Students select the major categories and list facts under those categories, thus rethinking what they are learning.

Figure 9.11 K-W-L+ Semantic Map

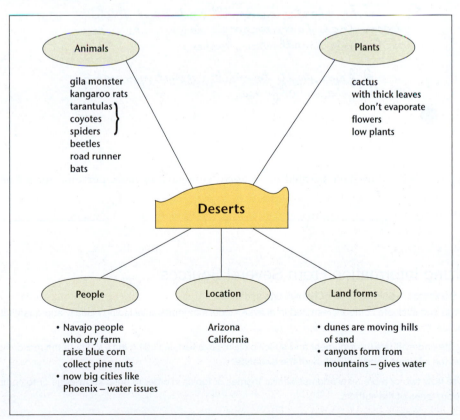

Figure 9.12 K-W-L+ Essay

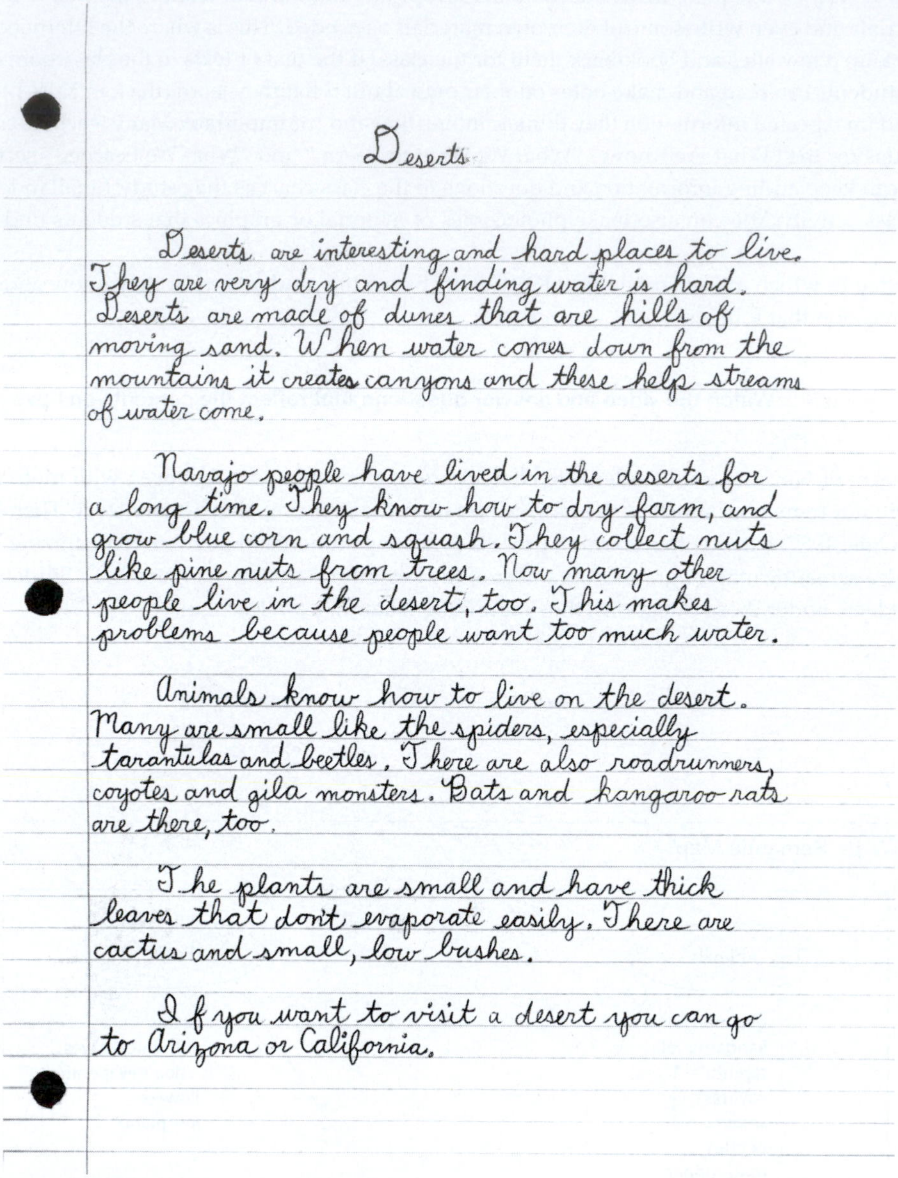

> ### Deserts
>
> Deserts are interesting and hard places to live. They are very dry and finding water is hard. Deserts are made of dunes that are hills of moving sand. When water comes down from the mountains it creates canyons and these help streams of water come.
>
> Navajo people have lived in the deserts for a long time. They know how to dry farm, and grow blue corn and squash. They collect nuts like pine nuts from trees. Now many other people live in the desert, too. This makes problems because people want too much water.
>
> Animals know how to live on the desert. Many are small like the spiders, especially tarantulas and beetles. There are also roadrunners, coyotes and gila monsters. Bats and kangaroo rats are there, too.
>
> The plants are small and have thick leaves that don't evaporate easily. There are cactus and small, low bushes.
>
> If you want to visit a desert you can go to Arizona or California.

Finally, they write what they have learned in an essay, summary, or more personal form (see the example in Figure 9.12).

CCSS

Synthesizing Information From Several Sources

Reading Standards 7–9, Integration of Knowledge and Ideas

7. Integrate and evaluate content presented in diverse media and formats, including visually and quantitatively, as well as in words.

8. Delineate and evaluate the argument and specific claims in a text, including the validity of the reasoning as well as the relevance and sufficiency of the evidence.

9. Analyze how two or more texts address similar themes or topics in order to build knowledge or to compare the approaches of the authors.

The cognitive activity needed to use ideas they have been learning in a new written format deepens memory and provides an additional opportunity to consolidate their learning. Engaging actively in this variety of learning gives the students a sense of how they can become active learners on their own, even when the teacher is not present. Reorganizing and rehearsing new knowledge and connecting it with what was previously known establishes for students the effort needed in learning and reinforces their personal self-esteem because they possess a productive process for school tasks. This whole process prepares students for the expectations contained in the CCSS that call for "integration of knowledge and ideas" (Standards 7–9).

I-Chart

Using multiple sources of information is an important way to help students find texts that meet their own levels of knowledge and interest, discover answers to their own questions, and compare and contrast authors' points of view. It encourages the critical thinking so needed in the world today. Yet many students have a difficult time using more than one source effectively. Hoffman (1992) has developed a very useful tool in the **I-Chart**, which helps students take important questions, select three to four sources of information they want to use to explore those questions, and then come to their own conclusion about the questions they framed initially (see Figure 9.13).

Once students have used the K-W-L process to activate their knowledge and interest, they select some key questions for more in-depth research that they can do together. The class or small groups can decide on the questions they want to concentrate on and write these on the chart. Then the best sources of information to answer the questions are selected, usually with teacher help and guidance, and they are also listed across the top of the chart. This simple framework establishes that multiple sources are needed when seeking answers to questions.

The practice of summarizing the information and answering their own questions scaffolds the process of inquiry well. Using the I-Chart establishes a simple framework for a systematic search for information. The chart also includes a column for interesting information, that is, pieces that do not fit the basic questions but still are relevant to the students' inquiry. This often becomes an important way to take notes on ideas that can be shared with the class later—ideas that are full of potential for more reading.

Figure 9.13 I-Chart

Questions	What We Know	Text 1	Text 2	Text 3	Summary
1.					
2.					
3.					
Interesting new info/ New questions					

Involving Students in Self-Assessment

As children move into the intermediate and middle grades, they should be involved in monitoring their own growth as readers. Having students maintain reading logs helps them become more self-conscious about their reading habits, preferences, and strategies. Asking them to keep a record of all the books and articles they read along with their responses to the pieces is an easy starting place. Periodically, it is helpful to ask all students to record their responses to particular texts. In this way you can compare how students respond and what focus they reflect. Asking students to share their responses with each other is a good way to stimulate a discussion of the various ways readers attend to and construct meaning from texts. Reading logs can provide an ongoing record of engagement and help teachers know if students need to be encouraged to expand their range of readings. Some students tend to stay in one genre or with very easy books.

Another way learning can be made visible to students is to have them keep samples of texts that they have marked with marginal notes or sticky notes during the four quarters of the school year. They can return to earlier text notations and analyze changes. If students are engaged with several units and reading many informational texts over the course of the year, there should be changes in depth and range of responses they can look for. For example, students can track the number of times they make comparisons across texts, as well as the times they question authors' inferences, ask questions of a text, and visualize ideas presented. The K-W-L sheets can be a good component of this kind of activity, too. Students can evaluate the quality of their questions, the extent to which they fulfill their desires to learn new content, and the graphic organizers and summaries they create.

Both the KWL+ and the I-Chart are frameworks that prepare students for the expectations contained in the CCSS that call for "integration of knowledge and ideas" (Standards 7–9). When students engage in inquiry, they read and integrate information from varied sources, they analyze different text structures and note the ways authors use evidence, and, finally, they synthesize and write what they have learned.

K-W-L and the I-Chart are frameworks through which teachers can engage students personally and cooperatively in thinking about their relationship to a content area to be studied and in setting a course for learning. The frameworks do not show students how to actually engage with the text as they read it, however. That is where good instruction can help students as they work with interesting texts. Several ways teachers can guide students in reading carefully and with good comprehension follow. In addition, it is good to visit the CCSS standards as you consider how you can help students develop text comprehension. The "key ideas and details" is the first section of the CCSS. See the CCSS box below.

Shared and Close Reading

Primary students need many opportunities to be guided by their teachers in thinking as they read texts with many ideas and combined types of information. The teacher-guided practice of shared reading was developed for use with big books; however, it also works well when teachers use the large-size news magazines (*Time for Kids*) that can be put on easels. The teacher draws students' attention to the text features, the visuals, and information about the authors. Then, depending on the reading abilities of the students, the teacher either reads most of the text or involves students in reading small sections. The first read is followed by second and third reads, with students taking over more of the reading as well as the rereading of important portions. This practice permits teachers to model key comprehension strategies and then listen as students copy the same moves.

CCSS

Close Reading of Informational Text

Anchor Reading Standards 1–3, Key Ideas and Details

1. Read closely to determine what the text says explicitly and to make logical inferences from it; cite specific textual evidence when writing or speaking to support conclusions drawn from the text.

2. Determine central ideas or themes of a text and analyze their development; summarize the key supporting details and ideas.

3. Analyze how and why individuals, events, and ideas develop and interact over the course of a text.

When a large text isn't available, teachers can develop close reading by using the same news magazines or articles from children's magazines. By showing the text on a visualizer, the teacher can guide students in reading deeply for key ideas and arguments, along with locating supporting information and examples in the text. Instructions to find important ideas and either underline them or have the teacher mark them can focus students on careful reading. Ask students questions like:

"What did you think was most important in this paragraph?"

"What information does the author give to explain?"

"Can you draw lines to connect the ideas/examples that fit together?"

"What questions do we need to ask?"

CLOSE READING EXPANDED   Comprehension of many informational texts requires much more attention than does understanding of fiction. Most of us know the importance of using a highlighter or making notes as we read to make sense of materials assigned in courses we take. Carefully monitoring understanding, making notes, and rereading are essential when reading challenging informational texts. In the intermediate and middle grades, children need to develop tools they can use when confronted with texts about unfamiliar topics that are also dense and include new vocabulary. Among these tools are text marking, "reading with a pen in hand" and making 2-column or T notes. All of these are designed to help students achieve the first goal of close reading—*understanding what the text says*.

The second component of close reading is **analytic reading**. The purpose of this focus is to not only make sense of the content but also develop an *understanding of how the language and structure the author uses contribute to and create the intended meaning*. With informational texts this often includes attention to the external features, the sections of text identified with headings, the diagrams and illustrations that accompany the verbal text, and highlighted vocabulary. From thinking about the writing also comes the query, "What lead did the author use to attract us to this topic and increase our motivation to read further?"

A third component of close reading of informational text involves both *evaluating* the content, how it is presented and what evidence supports the conclusions, and *comparing* the approaches and media used by different authors/authorities. This kind of reading is easily developed when students are engaged in extended units of study, reading different authors and using various types of sources (print, visual, and digital).

In the organization of the CCSS, these three components are represented in the three sections of the standards: Key Ideas and Details, Craft and Structure, and Integration of Knowledge and Ideas. This structure also reflects the long-standing approach to reading explained by Great Books developer M. Adler. In their classic explanation *How to Read a Book* (1972) VanDoren and Adler explain that nonfiction/informational reading involves three readings or three stances: the structural stage, the interpretive stage, and the critical stage. More recently, Shanahan (2016) has also explained close reading using this basic framework, calling for three readings: In the first, students focus on what the text says; in the second, they focus on how the text works; and in the third, they focus on evaluating the text—comparing it with other texts or thinking about its implications. Beck and Sandora (2016) develop their interpretation of close reading by identifying two basic stages of reading: understanding the gist and analyzing the grist (the more valuable or deeper comprehension). They contend that the first kind of surface reading must precede close reading for deeper comprehension. "Surface or gist comprehension comes first and allows one to go on to close reading, which then enables deeper or deeper comprehension" (p. 5).

Obviously there are different interpretations of what close reading entails, but it is clear that comprehension requires thoughtful attention by readers and that all facets of comprehension are not developed at once. Readers need to focus on the key ideas and details to make sense of the author's intended meaning. Then, as they revisit a complex text, analyzing how the author uses language and organizes the presentation, the intended meaning and point of view can be more clearly understood. Integrating ideas from the text with what else is known, evaluating the content, and then using the new ideas and information going forward are all parts of competent reading.

The CCSS imply that these three aspects of reading occur in sequence, and generally they do. However, when working with disciplinary materials, expert historians and scientists begin their reading of texts from a different perspective. Historians first check the source of the text, asking who wrote this, when was it written, and what was the problem being addressed (Ogle, in press; Weinberg et al., 2012)? Scientists often begin by reading the title and any summary or abstract, and then attending to the charts showing the data analysis (Purugganan. & Hewitt, n.d.). They do not read a text from start to finish as readers of narratives do. Therefore, while the components of competent reading are well represented in the CCSS, they are implemented in different order depending on the type of texts and the purpose for their use.

GETTING STARTED IN ELEMENTARY GRADES Close reading is an important concept in the current way of thinking about reading instruction. Guiding students to employ some of the strategic thinking and language associated with these activities and assessments that focus on close reading of texts therefore needs to be part of instructional programs. Using the three-part framework of the CCSS provides a good structure within which teachers can plan focused coaching to help students develop the habit of reading carefully. Lessons that analyze short sections of texts, or that use short texts are particularly helpful for this type of analytic thinking and reading. Many example texts are included in Appendix C of the CCSS documents and in many online sources.

The starting point is for teachers to explain to students the importance of reading some texts several times, particularly those that are challenging and have been determined to be important to content acquisition: A single reading of these texts is not adequate. Modeling by the teacher of how an adult engages in reading and thinking while showing students a copy of the text or while reading it orally helps provide a real example of the benefit of this slower, reiterative attention to text segments.

For primary grade children, the teacher can guide students in a two-level picture and story walk through the text, noting how the illustrator communicates ideas and how the subsequent pictures connect with earlier ones. For example, in the book *Redwoods* by Jason Chin (2009) the illustrations show a boy learning about the redwoods by reading a book as he moves from the subway into the forest. The teacher notes the use of the books and guides, "I wonder why the boy is always reading?" Later she comments, "Now he is reading a different book on how to climb big trees. It seems the boy is learning everything from what he reads; let's see if that's what the author is trying to do here."

Following this picture walk the teacher begins reading the book, thinking aloud and asking children what they notice:

"What is the big idea on this page?"
"Why do the redwoods grow so tall?"
"I was surprised by the way the author used the phrase 'well suited' to refer to what the trees get from the environment."
"What questions does the page raise in your minds?"
"What words does the author use that help us create images of the trees in their environment?"
"How does the author demonstrate the phrase 'big round masses along its trunk'?"
"The author helps us understand the meaning of 'epiphytes' with this picture."
"What do you think the author wants us to think will happen next? Why?"

After participating in this type of shared reading of the text, teachers can write some of the major questions that can guide students' thinking on the board and ask students to share their own thinking with a partner or by writing ideas and questions on sticky notes as they read. In the intermediate and upper grades teachers need to continue to provide modeling of the thinking involved in reading more complex and demanding texts. Readers need to focus on the ideas developed by authors (key ideas, details, and examples) and the structure and techniques used by writers, and they also need to think critically about how these ideas and points of view compare and contrast with those of others.

Teachers can also develop different aspects of close reading when they have texts that make such foci natural. For example, during a science unit on space, some students read the short book *Exploring Space* (Jerome, 2005). The teacher wanted students to think about the author's craft and guided them to preview the text; then she asked them to begin by silently reading the introduction, which recounts the tense landing of the lunar spacecraft *Eagle*. Next the teacher reread the introduction orally and asked students to think about why the author would choose this example to begin the book. She paused and commented, "I think the author wants to make us feel the excitement and danger of space travel. What a good lead to make me want to read more!" In this way the teacher was inviting students not only to think of the content and visualize the event but also to think of the author's craft as a writer.

Focusing on students' ability to think more deeply and making connections across texts was a natural follow-up to reading this text. The teacher had a collection of short books on space exploration and asked students to compare the tables of contents of three books and write down the topics in each book. Then students were asked to create a list of topics they wanted to include in the informational book they would write on space exploration. In this way the children began to understand how much content there is on a particular topic and how one book can only provide a segment of that content. The importance of reading several texts and comparing authors' approaches and content became a reality; in addition, it helped students think of their own interests and point of view in approaching topics and writing about them.

FORMATIVE DIAGNOSIS   The best way for teachers to determine how to focus close reading activities is to begin with some informal diagnosis of how students are reading. One easy way to do this is to have students engage in a "Think Aloud" while reading a piece of text. Simply tell students that you are going to ask them to stop at a particular point in the text and tell you what is on their mind at that time. It is easier to do this on an individual basis, but small groups also work. At first, teachers may need to model this for students. Many younger students are in such a habit of reading for speed that they cannot tell the meaning of what they have read. Others may focus on the last sentences or ideas in a text and not put them in a larger, meaningful context. Some read by constructing a meaning across sentences and paragraphs, they but may not prioritize the main ideas. It is helpful to ask students how they clarify points that are unclear as they read. Note if they reread at the point of difficulty or if they have to start at the beginning and reread the whole text. Note if they use visual and graphic displays to help figure out content. Are they able to pronounce unfamiliar words with the help of the text supports? From short diagnostics it is then possible to prioritize where to focus more intense guided close readings. Periodic lessons targeting underdeveloped mental activities and strategies can help students develop into stronger readers.

Most teachers have found that using a short, challenging text with a small group of students can help them focus on those important aspects of content and how authors develop meaning. Turning parts of the process of thinking about the texts over to the students periodically helps them develop theses habits when reading independently.

SUGGESTED FOCUSING QUESTIONS   In getting started, it is good to consider some basic questions that others have already been asking. For example, for

Main Idea and Details:

1. What is the author trying to say in this section?
2. What is the main thing that grabs my attention? Why?
3. What is the key point being made?
4. What is the purpose of this example?
5. What evidence or details support this idea?
6. Why did the author write _____?
7. How are these points connected?

Craft and Structure:

1. What does the word _____ mean in this passage?
2. What words are most important in this section in explaining _____?
3. How does the author's choice of these words affect the meaning?
4. What figurative language (metaphors, similes, personifications) helps make this clearer?
5. What does this sentence mean, and how does it fit with the paragraph or section?
6. Why do you think the author included this information or example?
7. How else could this be organized to make it clearer?
8. How do the illustrations, map, or other visuals affect your understanding of the content?
9. What was the author's purpose in this section?

Integration and Evaluation:

1. What information or reasons does the author give to support the main thesis or point?
2. Are the sources up to date? Does more recent research or theory confirm this presentation or perspective?
3. How does this information compare to other texts and online sources?
4. How could the author have developed this to make it easier to understand?
5. Where else can you use this information or perspective?
6. How credible is this author? What questions are still unanswered?

TRANSFER TO INDEPENDENT READING   Remember that the goal of close reading is for students to develop the habit of asking these questions and analyzing texts as they read independently. Just as doing a "Think-Aloud" can serve as an initial diagnostic of students' reading strategies; it can also help teachers monitor whether students are actually applying some of the questioning that has been modeled during instruction. In addition, it is helpful to ask students to respond on a copy of a short text by making marginal comments and marking up with ?, !, underlining, arrows, etc. the text as they read. Students generally enjoy these activities, and they provide a written record for teachers of what has been internalized and what still requires more instructional focus.

Most content materials require close reading if the content is to be learned. Yet, research indicates that students don't have strong backgrounds in this type of intense reading. For some students, using the image of reading like a detective is helpful. Their roles are not just to absorb what is in a text they must read, but rather to engage actively in figuring out what the text means and what clues the author has provided to how that meaning was constructed. They need to use the clues from the way the text is structured both internally and externally. They need to be smart and use their own prior knowledge of the topic and similar content. They need to be regularly asking questions and thinking beyond the confines of the particular text, sometimes testing their ideas and seeking added resources in the process as they proceed to develop their understanding.

Developing the habit of close reading comes with these teacher-led group activities, followed by gradually releasing the responsibility to students, putting charts of ways to question texts and monitor comprehension on the walls, and then having students read with partners, implementing their own careful reading together. As students realize how much there is to think about and connect, they appreciate the time it takes to reflect on the texts and share their ideas and questions with one another. This practice also helps students gain comfort with the more academic vocabulary they encounter throughout most informational materials.

Partner Reading Routines

Paired reading/paired summarizing and PRC2 are other classroom reading activities that support students' engagement with short texts and provide a setting for gradual release to the students. In **paired reading/paired summarizing**, students join a partner and they read a text together; then, they divide the text into chunks of one or two paragraphs. The first student reads a chunk aloud as the other student reads along silently. Then, the first student summarizes what the passage said. The second student then asks questions about the passage to probe its meaning. Both students attempt to answer the questions. The students exchange roles for the next passage. As in the implementation of most routines, students will play their roles more effectively if the teacher first demonstrates what is meant by making an effective summary and by asking good questions, and gives students a chance to respond to some examples.

A more extensive routine for partner reading, Partner Reading and Content, Too (**PRC2**), has been developed for students who need added supports in reading and learning with content texts. Teachers model and guide students in learning how to preview short texts, ask questions that lead to good discussion, engage in shared dialog around the information in the text, and share what they have learned with their classmates. Partners who read at approximately the same level share in reading a short informational book, two pages at a time. Each partner is responsible for asking questions and leading discussion on the page he/she reads orally. After their 20 minutes of reading together, they record any vocabulary they want to learn and write a key idea they gained on a sticky note to be shared with the class. By engaging in PRC2 for a few weeks, whole classrooms of students deepen their content learning and gain confidence using the academic language and concepts orally. This PRC2 format works well in both classrooms with English learners and those with monolingual students (Ogle & Correa, 2010).

REQUEST PROCEDURE   The **ReQuest** procedure (Manzo, 1969) is best suited for use with informational texts. In this procedure, two students read through a text, stop after each paragraph, and take turns asking each other questions about it, which the other student must try to answer. It helps if the teacher serves as a partner when the technique is first introduced. Because one goal for teaching comprehension is to develop principled knowledge of the topic, the teacher's questions serve as valuable models of ways to inquire about the important ideas in a text.

For an example of the ReQuest procedure in action, assume you have assigned the students in the class to pairs. Amalia and David are reading a text together. After they both read the first paragraph silently, Amalia asks David three good questions about that paragraph. She asks questions about main ideas. She asks questions that probe beneath the surface. She asks what importance some item in this paragraph might come to have later in the text. David answers those questions as well as he can. After David has finished answering Amalia's questions, they both read the next paragraph. Now it is David's turn to ask Amalia questions about the new paragraph, and Amalia has to answer them. When both students

Teach It! 54

ReQuest Procedure

This activity and its variations help students develop principled knowledge and offer opportunities for practice in asking higher-order-thinking questions.

have brought to light the information in that paragraph, they read the next one, and Amalia gets the first turn at asking David several good questions about that paragraph, and so on.

The ReQuest procedure can be used well with a whole class, too. One way to do this is for the class to read one or two paragraphs from the text. Then, the students pause and close their books, and take turns asking the teacher all the questions that come to mind. Following that, they read a new paragraph and the roles are reversed: The teacher asks the students several good questions, taking care to model not just factual questions, but also those that probe concepts and implications. After several such exchanges, the teacher might shift the activity to ask students to predict what the rest of the assignment will be about and state why they think so (Vacca & Vacca, 1996). Another variation for a whole-class use of the ReQuest procedure is to assign students to teams of three and have them take turns asking and answering questions.

Metacognitive Graphic Organizer

In contrast to the partner and group approaches that help students read and reflect on the content they are learning, it is also important to encourage students to reflect individually as they read and respond to texts. One tool that focuses students' thinking and writing is the metacognitive graphic organizer. Although several variations that are helpful for intermediate and middle grade students are available (Radcliffe, Caverly, Hand, & Franke, 2008), the key to the metacognitive graphic organizer strategy is that students create their own graphic organizer as they preview a chapter of text *and* use this visual as a guide for their reading. The term **metacognition** refers to the process in which learners are self-aware of their own learning needs and can monitor and adjust to the demands of the text.

Students place the title of the chapter or article in the center of a sheet of paper and then add the major headings from the chapter as they survey the material. After doing this, they return to the text and look at the visual information in charts, diagrams, and the like. They put key ideas from these visuals on the graphic where appropriate under the headings. They can add subheads if necessary to make the flow of the text clear. Once the author's structure and visuals are clearly framed, students return and do the metacognitive check by asking themselves and marking which sections are familiar (✓), which are unknown or unfamiliar (?), and which seem interesting (+). Sections that seem most necessary for the course, if that is the purpose of reading, can be highlighted with an asterisk (*). In this way, readers create a personal guide for reading and study. Then, while reading, students can make additional notes on the outline or on sticky notes.

When they have finished reading, students review the graphic and the notes they made and decide whether to revise the graphic, add to it, or write some extended notes to rehearse the important ideas. The final step of note-making is designed to encourage student reflection and learning. What an individual student does depends on how much detail needs to be absorbed to achieve the learning goal. It might be that the actual organization of the text is different from what the student initially drew and requires creating a revised text graphic. Or it might be that there are many new ideas, and the student needs to write a summary explaining the meaning of the ideas. Students monitoring their own learning can adjust this final stage of learning to their own needs to retain the content.

Teach It! 49

Metacognitive Graphic Organizers

In this activity, students become self-aware of their learning processes and needs as they create their own graphic organizer while previewing a text/chapter.

Personal graphic guides are very helpful to many students. They combine attention to the text with attention to the learner at the same time. In longer chapters, they help students maintain their focus on how all the ideas and sections fit together. They also provide a great tool for review and rehearsal later.

Reciprocal Teaching

One of the most researched strategies for engaged reading of informational text for intermediate and middle students is **reciprocal teaching**. Developed by Palincsar and Brown (1986) to help less able readers handle the demands of expository texts, reciprocal teaching includes four different strategies that students learn to use. Teachers first model each of the strategies and then turn their role over to the group of students. The students apply what they are learning by becoming teachers for their classmates and guiding the continued reading of small portions of text. The four basic strategies are as follows:

1. Summarize what has just been read.
2. Think of two or three good questions about the passage.
3. Clarify any ideas or information that was not clear.
4. Predict what you think will be in the next part of the text.

In conducting a reciprocal teaching exercise, decide in advance how large the chunks of text will be that the students will read before you engage them in thinking about that portion. The text units should be short enough that the students can discuss each in five to seven minutes. Tell the students you will be the first discussion leader and that they should pay attention to how you conduct the discussion, and not just focus on answering the questions.

Model reading a short section of text and creating a summary of the main ideas. Depending on the group and the amount of time needed to teach each of the four strategies, you might spend several sessions on a single strategy, or you might model more than one at a time until all four strategies become part of the readers' response to each paragraph or segment. Students learn to ask good questions about the text through this process. They also learn to identify problems that hinder comprehension—vocabulary items that are unfamiliar, for example, or references that are confusing, or other unclear aspects—and ask questions to clarify these problems posed by the text. Finally, they learn to make predictions about where the text is leading. Students then assume the teacher role for each segment of text so that by the end of a class period, many students have had the opportunity to lead their fellow students in considering the meaning of a common text. You can create a visible chart of the four strategies to help students understand the process. This becomes a guide for students when they lead the discussions.

This form of guided and shared reading has been effective in helping less able readers make sense of dense text material. The combination of good interactive strategies with group-oriented teaching and a shared learning approach helps students maintain interest in and focus on the material they are studying.

It is not easy to generate increased interest or to give students a sense of power when dealing with difficult and dense reading material. Both reciprocal teaching and the teaching strategy Questioning the Author (Chapter 10 includes a detailed discussion) give teachers and students supportive formats that deepen their personal engagement with texts and provide much preferred alternatives to round robin reading, a still overused way to have students read content texts.

AN EXAMPLE OF RECIPROCAL TEACHING   George Mead and five of his fifth-grade students are reading a short informative text on crocodiles and alligators. Mr. Mead is still modeling the reciprocal teaching process with these troubled readers because they have had only a few experiences with the process. He has decided in advance that this text is best read in units of paragraphs. These students are very unconfident about their abilities as readers and the text is dense.

Mr. Mead announces that he will be the discussion leader for the first paragraph. He advises students not only to pay attention to the paragraph and participate in the discussion but also to observe carefully how he conducts the discussion.

Teach It! 52

Reciprocal Teaching

This structured small-group activity provides opportunities for students to actively build comprehension of informational text as they practice summarizing, questioning, clarifying, and predicting.

They know that each of them will play the role of the discussion leader when the next paragraphs are read. Mr. Mead has prepared a chart that lists the steps that are taken after each paragraph is read. He refers the students to the chart to help them follow the procedure he is using as he leads the discussion. Mr. Mead asks everyone to read the first paragraph silently. When they are finished, he gives a verbal summary of the paragraph and looks around at the students to ask if they would summarize the passage in the same way or if they have something to add. Next, Mr. Mead formulates a question. He takes care with the question because in addition to eliciting students' ideas, he is demonstrating the art of questioning for them. He asks, "What are the easiest ways to tell the differences between alligators and crocodiles?" He draws out the students' ideas on this question and affirms their suggestions. When Matt volunteers that the shape of the mouths might be easier to notice than either how their teeth fit together or whether the animal has sensory pits, especially if one was coming at you, he gets a nod.

Next, Mr. Mead attempts to clarify parts of the paragraph that are unclear to the students. He notes that the word *crocodilian* is used for the whole group of reptiles that includes crocodiles, alligators, and caimans. He asks whether someone can clarify when to use *crocodilian* and when to use *crocodile*. As the students try to differentiate the uses of the terms orally, Mr. Mead knows that they are becoming more familiar with these words in both their reading and their speaking. To help them as they clarify, he writes the words on the board as one student explains that *crocodilian* should be above the other three words, *crocodile, caiman,* and *alligator,* because they are all examples of this group of reptiles. Then Mr. Mead goes on to make a prediction, suggesting that the text will probably tell how these different reptiles survive. Finally, he assigns the next section of the text.

After that paragraph is read, Mr. Mead takes another turn as discussion director to make sure the students fully understand how to carry out the steps in conducting a discussion before it becomes their turn. Mr. Mead often refers to the chart as he conducts each step in the discussion. He knows that if the students do not clearly understand how to follow the procedure, he will have to intervene later, which will undermine the students' autonomy and confidence. Before the third passage is read, Mr. Mead points to the student on his left and asks her to lead the next discussion. After that student has had her turn, the role of discussion leader passes to the student on her left, and so on.

Questioning

Before we close this section on teaching for content learning, it is valuable to address the role of questioning for both teachers and students. Asking and answering questions are major parts of the life of schools. Each of the active strategies described here requires both teachers and students to become good at asking important and thoughtful questions. Questioning is an important active thinking activity that learners use while reading and trying to make sense of text. It is a central part of comprehension for students and teachers. Therefore, it is valuable to spend time both in analyzing the questions you ask and in developing students' sensitivity to what constitutes good questions and good questioning. A starting place is to discuss with students what role questioning plays in learning and what they think good questions are. Direct the discussion to include the realization that some questions ask for very specific and direct information (e.g., "What was the pharaoh's role in religion?"), some for more abstract interpretations or conjectures (e.g., "What effect did the caste system have on how people treated each other?" or "What similar situation have we had in our country?"), and some are very personal (e.g., "What do you think?" or "How does this make you feel?").

You also need to record yourself during class discussions and to analyze periodically how you use questioning. Traditionally, and continuing into today, many teachers have used questions to find out how well students have comprehended what they read. The teacher asks the student a question, the student answers, and the teacher gives some evaluative feedback. Researchers refer to this form of school dialogue as **I-R-E** (initiation, response, evaluation) and conclude that the process helps teachers test students more than it aids student comprehension (Mehan, 1979). To encourage students to ask good questions and engage in metacognitive self-monitoring, you need to model good thinking when sharing ideas out loud and questioning students.

You can use questioning to model the process of thinking before and during reading. Begin a lesson or introduce a story by asking students what they already know about a topic. This kind of questioning activates students' own thinking. Most teachers use questions to help students connect ideas, consolidate what they have read, and reflect on ideas. However, you can ask much more thoughtful and reflective questions by first considering how you want to focus students' reflections about what they have read. Think about how you can involve students in reflecting together to deepen their responses to questions you or the texts pose.

Many educators focus on the nature of the process of constructing meaning and argue that questions should ask students: "What do you predict will happen?" "What else could have been done?" and "What does this remind you of?" They argue that the reader–text interaction should be the focus of attention and that questions should derive from those

The World of Reading

Using Taxonomies in Questioning

As we take time to consider the role of questioning in learning, we need ways to categorize and analyze the nature of our questions. There are some commonly used frameworks that can be used to help us in this activity. The most widely used is probably one developed by Benjamin Bloom and his colleagues in the 1950s and revised in 2010. Bloom's **taxonomy** was not initially created for use by teachers, but was developed as a taxonomy of educational objectives to measure school goals and assessment. However, teachers saw its value and have used it as a tool to help them reflect on their classroom questioning patterns. The taxonomy has seven levels of questions: memory, translation, interpretation, application, analysis, evaluation, and synthesis.

In research studies of classroom talk, it is not uncommon to see analyses of the levels of teacher questions. In some descriptions of reading comprehension and reading assessment, Bloom's seven levels have been chunked into three or four levels. For example, one common way of describing reading is by thinking of literal, interpretive, applied, and critical levels of comprehension to define kinds of questions in relation to text.

Raphael (1986) has helped students to think about sources of information for questions they are to answer by creating four categories:

- *Right there:* Questions that can be answered directly from the text
- *Think and search:* Questions that require more than one piece of information from the text
- *Author and you:* Questions that go beyond the text
- *On your own:* Questions that rely on the reader

The whole strategy is called Question-Answer-Relationships (**QAR**) and provides very practical definitions that make it easy for students to become more involved in both planning their strategies for responding and becoming aware metacognitively of the range of responses they need to be able to make to the text.

Taxonomies provide a helpful language to think about questioning and the kinds of thinking we want to help stimulate in students. Some teachers keep the levels of questions in their teacher manuals or put them on the bulletin boards so that both they and students are more aware of the need to go beyond the literal or memory level. Other teachers do not like to use taxonomies to evaluate comprehension. Rather than conceiving of them as a hierarchy, these teachers see taxonomies as an array of options that are available to use as appropriate.

interactions. Do readers connect and respond personally to what they read? Can they establish a purpose and fulfill their own purpose? This focus leads to another range of questions about text construction or engagement. Some students never seem to connect text to their own lives or to the reality around them. Thinking of this dimension of questioning can be helpful in planning for activities so that students see school learning as part of their own world.

Because the process of asking and answering questions is a critical part of teaching and evaluation, some focused attention to questions is necessary. By considering the nature of the questions they ask and the questions in the materials they give students, teachers can make the questions as valuable as possible. Modeling and attending to questioning provides the context for students to become more aware of their own questioning and encourages them to develop questioning skills that are useful to their own learning. Guiding students to analyze the questions they ask during the routines of Paired-reading/Paired Summarizing, PRC2, and ReQuest takes their attention and metacognitive reflection to a deeper level and provides settings for them to practice asking quality questions.

Check Your Understanding 9.4: Gauge your understanding of the skills and concepts in this section.

Classrooms That Develop Independent Learners

Ample resources exist for teachers to develop students' competence and confidence in reading to learn from informational texts. Planning instruction so this actually happens means not only focusing on your own class but also collaborating with other teachers so the routines you develop get reinforced with all teachers and across the grades. It also involves organizing instruction so there is a gradual release of responsibility from teacher to students, giving them opportunities to become secure in their own strategies. This last section suggests some options for ways to strengthen instruction for independence through instructional organization and use of student-directed research projects, and computer-based technology. It also addresses the importance of including English learners more fully in the classroom.

Organizing Instruction

As teachers take seriously the importance of helping children use informational materials confidently, the greatest challenges are finding the time and structuring the learning experiences properly. Two general approaches are often used. The first is to think of teaching reading as finding a balance between the reading of fictional literature (for literary purposes) and the reading of informational material (to learn). The second approach is to create integrated units of instruction and combine standards and strategies for more than one area: combining reading, writing, and oral language, or combining both literacy and content (social studies and science) in units. If your school has basal readers, check to see that there is a balance of literary fiction and nonfiction and informational selections. Many of the newer basal reading programs include more varied selections, as publishers are recognizing that students need to become familiar with these texts. You also need to provide experiences in integrated content units so students learn the value of using a range of informational resources in their learning. Within both approaches teachers can incorporate more time for students to engage in research projects, either conducted alone or in groups.

Engaging in Research

An important part of study reading is learning to conduct research and write reports. This skill has often been left for the middle grades, where teachers demonstrate a semi-formal approach to research. However, the new CCSS include research as an ongoing part of the task of informational reading, with the expectation that students will engage in several short research projects each year. In kindergarten and the primary grades, the focus is on shared research and writing projects; by the intermediate grades, students should be able to identify their own interests and conduct research on their own and then share it with others in written and oral forms. It is clear that when primary-grade teachers engage students in informational reading and research, the process can be scaffolded so that by the time students reach the middle grades, they are already confident in the skills that permit them to conduct good research. Think back to the activities that have been described already. Research requires the following:

- *Asking good, researchable questions.* Learning to narrow one's topic is a basic skill that needs to be developed. When children use K-W-L and I-Charts, they become experienced in finding good questions.

- *Locating good sources of information.* Integrated units that are framed around students' questions develop their abilities to find the materials they need and to locate within the texts the sections that will answer their questions.

- *Making notes of important ideas.* Children who get in the habit of writing Amazing Fact Sheets have already learned how to make good notes. The use of graphic organizers and journals also helps students build good note-making skills.

- *Critically evaluating information.* Students who have regularly read several texts on the same topic know the importance of evaluating the sources of information they use and cross-checking them for accuracy and currency. They learn to check the authors of Web sites for their expertise and biases. They also know that textbooks and encyclopedias are good, reliable backup sources for their use.

- *Organizing information.* When students learn to chunk ideas as part of the K-W-L process, when they cluster new vocabulary, and when they learn to look for and use internal text organization in their reading and writing, they develop skills in organizing ideas into interesting and coherent texts. The more writing they do throughout the elementary grades, the more confident they will become in creating interesting and meaningful texts.

- *Presenting information visually and graphically.* Students who have studied how authors and illustrators present visual information and weave it together with the connected texts are more able to create their own. The computer tools and digital cameras that schools possess make this task an exciting one for young students.

Look back over the different strategies that help to engage students actively as learners across the content areas. All of these taken together prepare students to be active, thoughtful learners. With this foundation, doing research and writing reports and even creating a more formal research paper are not difficult.

As we think of learning new material and conducting research, writing becomes an essential part of the ongoing literacy curriculum. When children write regularly, they develop their skills and fluency as writers. Regular writing, just like regular reading in a variety of genres for a variety of audiences and purposes, creates confident and capable learners. The more students can engage in their own inquiry on topics and questions of their choosing, the more they will want to write and share what they learn. The more they write, the more comfortable they will become with informational texts and the more able they will be to consider alternative ways authors can present information to connect with their readers. These experiences also prepare them for the focus of most of the writing they will be asked to do throughout their schooling: reports, summaries, and expository and persuasive essays.

Involving English Language Learners

Research projects and integrated units provide an open framework in which teachers can involve students at all levels of language competence in classroom learning experiences. Because the unit model provides for a range of materials and activities, students with little English can participate using resources in their own language and can begin their learning in their first language. Helping English language learners to create vocabulary lists with words in both English and their first language makes their participation in the general classroom activities more possible.

Teachers and other students can often gain from the English language learners' knowledge about the topics of study. Often, their experiences have been rich in the content of focus. For example, students from South America might have personal experiences with some varieties of frogs we consider exotic and might have a sense of their value that is different from the sense of urban dwellers in North America. Children from North Africa can contribute much to the study of civilizations that have derived from ancient Egypt or of studies of deserts. All children bring with them their experiences, language, and folktales and stories that can enrich any unit of study. Think of the potential resources represented by diversity in the classroom, and seek out what your students and their families can bring to each other.

During the development of the units, English language learners also can participate in ways that go beyond verbal learning. They can take major roles in creating the visual displays and the graphic representations of the topics, as in the development of the murals of the frog issue. If some dramatic presentation of content is part of the unit, these students can build their English skills by memorizing parts and participating in group presentations.

Using Computer Resources

Units of instruction provide an ideal place to introduce the use of computer resources. A number of excellent Web sites exist that can be resources to learning. With the help of the instructional media or technical support team in a school, specific and appropriate Web resources can be bookmarked for a class and students can participate in learning from these resources. Many also contain great visual content, so students with limited English proficiency can learn in easy ways.

The computer also makes the development of reports easier for all. Digital cameras make it possible to dress up reports (e.g., by importing pictures of direct explorations during science units) and clip art and free photographs available on the Web help students create impressive reports. By the middle grades, many teachers help students create podcasts and movie trailers as part of their research reporting. The ease with which corrections can be made on the computer gives students more freedom to compose their own reports and not fear misspelled words or poor handwriting. Students take great pride in producing reports with great graphics and high-quality print that reflect their best work. Knowing that their work can be turned into high-quality products serves as an incentive to many students. For primary students, the support of parent helpers or older-grade aides in the classroom can make the computer accessible and not consume all of the teacher's time.

Teachers can build a strong reading to learn curriculum in both of these ways—by creating a balance between fiction and informational material in the reading block of the day or by integrating reading to learn instruction with content units. Our experience has been that for new teachers, it is easier not to do all the instruction through integrated blocks initially, but to first be sure there are resources for the range of reading and learning needs of students in your class. It is critical to pay attention to what students bring with them in terms of their skills and strategies for reading informational texts and to provide instruction so they can develop increasingly sophisticated knowledge of how to read to learn using a variety of materials and for a variety of purposes. Reading to learn from science content is different from reading to learn from social studies materials and mathematics. All are different from reading that is taught as if a selection of text were sufficient just to be read and enjoyed. The world of informational content is large and well worth exploring and making one's own.

Check Your Understanding 9.5: Gauge your understanding of the skills and concepts in this section.

For Review

At the outset of this chapter we stated that when you reached this point in your reading and studying you should be able to:

- **Describe the particular components of informational texts.**

The components of informational texts include the external features that support students in understanding the organization of information and prioritization of ideas, the visual and graphic features, the density of ideas, and the internal organization of texts. Internet sites are another type of informational text with their own structure. All of these texts require attention to specific vocabulary terms and phrases.

- **Explain how readers comprehend informational texts.**

For students to be successful they need to have adequate background knowledge including vocabulary, knowledge of text structures, and both topical and principled content knowledge. Students' engagement also depends on their motivation and sense of purpose in reading and learning.

- **Help students identify and use features of informational texts.**

Teachers at all grade levels can assist students in identifying and using text features. Primary grade teachers can lead students in picture/visual walks as they introduce new books. Students can then use a book report guide to assess which features are present in their book. By writing informational books and articles with these features, students come to understand their importance and use. In the intermediate and upper grades students can create graphic organizers of chapters using the headings for each section; they can also jigsaw the reading of longer texts section by section. Students learn to identify internal organizational patterns by comparing and contrasting books on the same topic. They can also use the table of contents and headings to discern basic organizations and write their own articles using different patterns. Teachers can identify the academic vocabulary within informational texts and students can "connect two" or chunk new terms. At upper levels they can create concept of definition maps for important words.

- **Identify teaching frameworks that support learning with informational texts.**

In planning instruction, teachers keep in mind the ABC's of teaching: Activate students' prior knowledge, Build new knowledge, and help them Consolidate learning. The KWL and KWL+ frameworks focus on engaging students in learning by building on what they know and want to learn. The I-Chart is a powerful tool for students to use to extend their study using several texts to answer their own questions. Active reading strategies that help students comprehend the texts they use include teacher-guided close reading, paired reading/paired summarizing, PRC2, ReQuest, and reciprocal teaching.

- **Foster students' independent reading and learning.**

Teachers can create extended learning opportunities within a core reading framework, but more deeply when they create integrated units of instruction—either within the language arts or across reading and content areas. Engaging students in research projects using multiple sources of information, including the Internet and computer resources requires them to use good reading skills. English learners also gain when teachers use longer units of instruction. Visual and graphic information is helpful for all students, but particularly those learning English.

For Your Journal

1. Review the Anticipation Guide and compare your earlier answers with what you think now.

2. Keep a record of all the reading you do for one or two days. Note the material you read, the time you spent, and how you engaged yourself in the materials, including what you thought and felt as you read. Try to remember your school experiences, and write about what kinds of materials you were taught to read. What tips did you learn for reading and comprehending informational material?

Taking It to the World

1. Most children are curious about the world around them. Yet sometimes teachers get very busy meeting all the curricular demands and overlook students' interests as a natural connection point to content. Visit a school library or a public library and become familiar with some of the excellent magazines available for young readers. Sit down and talk with some children about which of the magazines they enjoy most. Then, see whether the library has a service that permits you to search the magazines by topic so you can use articles in the future as you develop your own teaching units and extend readings on key topics in the curriculum.

2. Try out your skills in eliciting from students what they know about a topic and helping them articulate good questions to extend their knowledge. The K-W-L process is an easy way to start. Ask a teacher to allow you to teach a lesson with a small group of students around some topic of current interest, such as an item in the news or some community event. Have two or three short texts with you so you can read to the students to help them answer their questions after the first two steps in the K-W-L are complete. Keep a copy of the chart you create so you can reflect on the students' knowledge and interests after the session.

Chapter 10
Critical Thinking and Critical Literacy

 Learning Objectives

After reading this chapter, you should be able to:

1. Define critical thinking and critical literacy, as well as the "New Literacies."

2. Examine the intriguing aspects of literature that may systematically invite discussions.

3. Discuss the structural features of persuasive texts.

4. Use teaching strategies to guide students to think critically about works of literature and persuasive writing.

Anticipation Guide

The following statements will help you begin thinking about the topics of this chapter. Answer *true* or *false* in response to each statement. As you read and learn more about the topics in these statements, double-check your answers. See what interests you and what prompts your curiosity toward more understanding.

_____ **1.** Even primary grade children can think deeply about texts if they are asked good questions.

_____ **2.** Critical thinking is the process of reasoning and reflecting in order to decide what to believe or what to do.

_____ **3.** Critical literacy is concerned with the social or political purpose of messages and the contexts in which they are understood.

_____ **4.** The structures of stories are usually very different one from another, to keep them from being boring.

_____ **5.** To find ways stories influence readers, don't look at just one story, but at many—the effects of stories accumulate.

_____ **6.** Engaging students in deep discussions of stories and essays is an excellent way to meet many of the Common Core State Standards.

_____ **7.** A *Socratic Seminar* is a form of debate only practiced by the Cincinnatus Society of Ohio.

_____ **8.** Good arguments usually consist of claims, reasons, and evidence.

_____ **9.** It is not good to teach children to be skeptical of some things they read. It will make them bitter people if done too early.

_____ **10.** Fortunately, all arguments students read before they reach high school will be logically formed and honest.

A Classroom Story

Suppose *Beauty* Had Been Ugly?

Midge Burns' combined class of second and third graders has just finished listening to her read Marianna Mayer's version of Beauty and the Beast.

"I'm wondering about something," says Mrs. Burns. Second grader Connie smiles. It is April of the year, and Connie knows Mrs. Burns always begins an interesting discussion with those words.

"Suppose Beauty had been ugly. Do you think the Beast should have married her?"

"That would be sort of no fair if he wouldn't," says Abigail, looking unsure.

"What do you mean?" asks Mrs. Burns.

"I mean, the Beast shouldn't expect Beauty to love him if he's not willing to love her . . . I mean . . ."

"They're both ugly, so they should get along," says Daniel.

"I think there's a something like a moral to the story," says Michael.

"And what's that?" asks Mrs. Burns.

"I think it's saying 'Don't judge the book by the outside . . .'"

"Don't judge the book by its cover," offers Phillip.

"That's right," says Connie. "They called her Beauty, but that just meant she was kind and gentle and she looked out for other people. 'Cause you don't marry people just 'cause they look good.''

"Then let me ask you something else," continues Midge Burns. "Suppose Beauty had been a boy in this story, and the Beast had been a girl." (A whoop goes up from the children.)

"That would be a problem," says Laurinda.

"Why is that?" asks Mrs. Burns.

"I saw it on TV that the girls asked boys to the prom. I don't think that's right. Besides, suppose the woman in the story was older than the man?" Laurinda clearly looks troubled.

"Why do we care?" demands Michael. "We don't know how old Beauty or the Beast is. The story doesn't say. But you should be free to marry whoever you want."

"My Mom says it's not OK for a girl to ask a boy to marry her. That's what my Mom says. I'm not sure if that's true," says Harriet.

"It doesn't matter," repeats Michael. "But I'll tell you what bothers me. In these stories, the guy marries this woman he doesn't even know."

"That's true. And I wish the woman would say, 'How can I marry you? I don't even know you. I don't even know what your attitude is,'" says Connie.

"I know," says Harriet. "In these stories, the people are marrying complete strangers. They don't even know if they change their underwear . . ."

CCSS

Common Core State Standards and Good Discussion

The children in this vignette exercised many of the skills called for in the Common Core State Standards. They asked and answered good questions, they discussed the theme of the story, they drew on evidence from the story to support their own interpretations, they thought deeply about the motivations of characters in the story, and they (vehemently!) distinguished their own take on the events from the apparent perspective of the author. In the process, they addressed Reading Standards for Literature, Standards 1, 2, 3, and 6; and Speaking and Listening, Standards 1 and 2. Not bad for one discussion! In subsequent lessons, they can do still more. They can compare Mayer's retelling of "Beauty and the Beast" with the Disney film. They can also compare it to the Russian version, "The Snot-Nosed Goat" (from the Afanas'ev collection of Russian Fairy Tales) and to the Appalachian version, "A Bunch of Laurel Blooms for a Present" (from Marie Campbell's *Tales of the Cloud Walking Country*).

Critical Thinking and Critical Literacy

In this example Midge Burns is inviting her students to practice critical thinking.

We know that she's encouraging critical thinking because of several things she does:

- *Her questions take a critical attitude.* Not only do the questions flow from the assumption that students are capable of coming up with their own responses, but they also imply that the meanings suggested by the text can be scrutinized and challenged, and possibly rejected in favor of better ideas.

- *Her way of conducting the discussion shares the responsibility for making meaning.* The teacher spreads responsibility for making meaning by expecting the students to provide ideas. And while she sometimes says things to help students express themselves more clearly, she doesn't position herself as the authority on the meaning.

- *She treats the meaning-making as a social activity.* She encourages students to interact with each other, sometimes to build on each other's ideas and other times to critique them, but at all times to work toward more sophisticated thinking.

- *She has thought hard about the text herself.* She has examined the text for the issues it raises that might be important to the students and the attitudes and assumptions it conveys. Even though she doesn't plan to share her own insights, she has constructed a general idea of ways the discussion might go.

The students are thinking critically, too. We can see that because they:

- *Offer insights and not just recycled facts.* They are aiming to think through what the text might mean, and what they can do with the meaning.

- *Behave as if they feel free to question and to doubt.* They don't passively accept the suggestions made by the text.

- *Follow the ramifications of ideas.* They "try ideas on for size" in real life, and they make connections to other things they have read and heard.

- *Offer support for their assertions.* They advance ideas, and support their ideas with evidence.

- *Listen carefully to each other and build on each other's ideas.* They don't just passively agree, though; they are willing to question each other's assertions, and venture alternatives.

Defining Critical Thinking

Philosophers usually define **critical thinking** as a process of reasoning and reflecting that is done in order to decide what to believe or what course of action to take. Critical thinking is usually done in response to something—a problem we are facing in life, something we read, or an argument we hear (Fisher, 2001). But a philosopher's definition can miss a lot of what children and teachers do when they think critically in classrooms. Young critical thinkers like those in Midge Burns' class do several things well.

- They read or watch or listen as if the meaning of the text were the starting point in their pursuit of greater awareness and not the end point. They ask not only "What does the text mean?" but also "What can I *do* with the meaning?"

- They make meaning by constructing interpretations of what they hear and read and supporting those interpretations with evidence from the text.

- They use reading and discussions of reading as opportunities to learn what their classmates think, even joining their ideas with those of others to create more sophisticated insights.

- They look below the surface of texts, and use their knowledge of literary structures and genres as they construct meaning and venture interpretations.

- They hold texts up to scrutiny, sometimes questioning their messages and the purposes of those behind the messages.

Defining Critical Literacy

When readers examine the social, political, and cultural purposes and values that the texts they read reflect, they are using **critical literacy**. Critical readers may ask who is behind the text and why the argument is being made. They may ask whose voices are missing from the text. They may "talk back" to the text, and construct different readings of it. When they ask these kinds of questions, they are becoming "text critics" (Freebody & Luke 1990). Critical readers learn that texts are powerful tools that can be used to influence readers. That is why teachers like Midge Burns help students examine the unstated value messages behind texts.

Even preschool children encounter persuasive messages. Saturday morning television shows abound with advertisements designed to make children want to buy things. Children shower arguments on each other, sometimes primitive, sometimes not. Although some adults might wish to hold off on discussing persuasive messages with children—especially dishonest messages—more and more teachers are deciding that children should learn to understand and—if necessary—to protect themselves from such messages in the elementary grades. The Common Core State Standards require students to follow and critique arguments and informational presentations, and also to create logical arguments in writing. In the rest of this chapter, we will first take a broad view of how texts work—beginning with narratives, then going on to informational and persuasive texts, and finally considering what happens when students read several texts on the same topic, sometimes even texts from different genres. Then we will present teaching strategies for guiding students' reading and thinking about different kinds of texts for different purposes. Some of the strategies may encourage critical thinking; others may encourage critical literacy. In this chapter, as in real classrooms, we will often mix the two. Watch this video in which students talk about how they will engage in critical literacy when thinking about the Vietnam War, and answer the question that follows.

 Video Exploration 10.1: Watch the video and answer questions that reflect the content you have read.

Critical Thinking and "The New Literacies"

"New Literacies" is a term that applies to making meaning from non-print forms of communication, forms that are emerging so rapidly we have to call these practices "literacies" instead of "literacy" because new media may require new reading and writing strategies.

In the previous generation, television and radio stations in America were required by the Federal Communications Commission (FCC) to address at least two sides of every controversial issue they raised. But in 1987, the "Fairness Doctrine" was abandoned, and since then commentators with unapologetically partisan agendas have been allowed to say almost anything they want on the air, however groundless, and even call it "news." Similarly, material that was put in print and shared with the public came mostly through mainstream media that screened the material for fairness and accuracy. But with the rapid growth of the Internet as a source of information, material can now reach the public without any filtering. Books, magazines, and newspapers are mostly still accountable for what they publish, and they are screened for accuracy before they are released to the public. But texts on the Internet are mostly unedited and, while they may look "authoritative," they are often filled with strongly biased and misleading information. This state of affairs requires that students learn to apply their own filters. As Leu and his associates (2010) explain,

> Whereas critical evaluation is important when reading offline information, it is perhaps more important online, where anyone can publish anything; knowing the stance and bias of an author becomes paramount to comprehension and learning. Determining this in online contexts requires new comprehension skills and strategies. For example, knowing which links take you to information about who created the information at a site (and actually choosing to follow these links) becomes important. So too, is knowing how to check the reliability of information with other information at other sites. Students do not always possess these skills. In one study (Leu et al., 2007), 47 out of 53 higher performing online readers in 7th grade believed a site designed to be a hoax was reliable (Save the Endangered Pacific Northwest Tree Octopus: <http://zapatopi.net/treeoctopus/>), despite that most students indicated in an interview that they did not believe everything they read online. Moreover, when told the site was a hoax, a number of students insisted it provided accurate and reliable information. (p. 4)

Leu and his colleagues have taken the lead in arguing that teaching students to read must involve teaching them the "new literacies" of online reading. In the twenty-first century, the dominance of the Internet, of ebooks, iPads, and other devices as information sources and as communications facilitators makes their argument strong. These literacies are not static; in fact, it seems that there are new forms of Internet literacies emerging regularly. That is why Leu chooses to call them "literacies" and not "literacy." Some options like Twitter, YouTube, Snapchat, and Instagram stimulate more student-to-student exchanges and help students create their own visual and verbal messages. There is a nearly overwhelming amount of information available on the Internet; it is important that students learn to navigate the Web and use it for many different purposes. Schools bear responsibility to provide guidance for students, particularly since students from less affluent families still may lack regular access at home to the Internet.

CCSS

Common Core State Standards and New Literacies

The Common Core State Standards call for students to be able to interpret information from digital sources (Comprehending Informational Text, Standard 7), and they require that students be able to distinguish between the author's point of view and their own (Comprehending Informational Text, Standard 6) although the standards don't point out the need for extra care in judging the reliability of Internet-based texts.

In describing the necessary functions teachers can help students develop for online literacy, Leu (2010) includes five essentials:

1. Identifying important questions
2. Locating information online
3. Analyzing information (sources and content)
4. Synthesizing information
5. Communicating information

Leu and colleagues (Coiro & Dobler, 2007; Leu et. al., 2013) explain that while those skills just listed are similar to the literacy skills required to read print on paper effectively, literacy functions work differently when the information is online. In fact, some students who do very well comprehending online materials have been very poor at comprehending in traditional text tasks. The reverse is also true.

It is important that teachers help students learn to think deeply and comprehend whether they are reading printed text on paper or viewing text online. Online literacy is more interactive and more engaging for many students. The strong use of visual information may support comprehension in distinct ways. Clearly, the new literacies that have come with new technology warrant the attention of those of us who are concerned with children and young people's literacy.

Check Your Understanding 10.1: Gauge your understanding of the skills and concepts in this section.

Looking Critically at Works of Literature

Even the most familiar stories, such as "Cinderella," "Beauty and the Beast," or "Jack and the Beanstalk," may be influencing young readers' and listeners' attitudes and beliefs in subtle ways. Here, we will pay attention to two kinds of influence fictional texts have on readers. The first point is that fictional texts often relate symbolically to people and actions in the real world. A single text, or more likely, a collection of texts, may have the effect of conveying specific attitudes toward certain groups of people, certain actions, or certain values. The second point is that the structure of a particular text may lead the reader toward a certain attitude about characters and events, and these same attitudes may carry over into readers' beliefs about the real world.

Watch this video in which a teacher encourages her students to share the opinions that they formed while reading and answer the question that follows.

 Video Exploration 10.2: Watch the video and answer questions that reflect the content you have read.

The Web of Narrative and "the Way It Is"

Anthropologists sometimes look at the many stories or other texts that are circulated in a society and note that they constitute a common story, a sort of web of narrative. This may be called the *mythos*: whether it is a story or a series of stories, or even a series of advertisements or a string of video games, the collection of texts become familiar and understandable because they say the same things again and again. The *mythos* may consciously or unconsciously relate to a kind of logic of "the way things are." Anthropologists may call this unspoken understanding of the social order the *logos*, a tacit understanding of "how things are" and "how things work" (Rappaport, 1999). For example, traditional fairy tales spin a narrative web that portrays males as active heroes who go on quests, and females as passive creatures who wait to be rescued and become prizes to be won by the bold masculine heroes. Male heroes often strive aggressively or violently against those who are cast as foes. Females use extreme kindness and self-denial to achieve what is necessary—not their goals, because in traditional stories females are often punished if they have goals—but to have things turn out well.

Although they are "just stories," through much repetition the web of narrative normalizes a certain understanding of "the way things are." In traditional stories told in European and American culture, "the way things are" is that only aggressive males and self-denying females have things turn out well. The winners, usually males, are solitary figures who triumph over others, and have no sympathy for those who stand in their way.

Of course, the *mythos*—that is, traditional Western stories taken as a whole—teaches a *logos* that may be far out of touch with society as it is today. For instance, can you imagine having a class of boys and girls—or teaching in a school faculty of men and women—who behaved that way? This is a big reason children need to think critically about stories.

Dramatic Roles

A closer look at the structure of individual narratives shows how a story shapes readers' reactions to it. From experience hearing and reading stories and watching media, readers construct what has been called a *story grammar* (Mandler & Johnson, 1977; Stein & Glenn, 1979): a set of rules that help them make sense of who is doing what and the meaning of the characters' actions.

One version of a story grammar assigns roles to characters (Souriau, 1955; Temple, Martinez, Yokota, 2018, in press). A character in a story may be the hero or the protagonist, the person whose needs give rise to the actions in the story and with whom readers most strongly sympathize. Another character may serve as a rival, a person against whom the hero competes to get what he wants. Yet another character may be the helper, who supports the hero. Readers sense who is playing what role, and their loyalties are directed accordingly: They cheer the hero (and may forgive his or her aggressiveness), they spurn the rival (and afford her or him little sympathy), and they appreciate the efforts of the helper (but don't give him or her much consideration beyond what she does for the hero).

The French drama critic Etienne Souriau (1955) represents characters' roles by means of Zodiac symbols. The first four roles are common to nearly all stories:

- ♌ *The Hero* is the character whose desire and need drives the story forward.
- ☉ *The Goal* is the hero's main need or desire.
- ♂ *The Rival* is the person or force that works against the hero, and stands between the hero and her or his goal.
- ☾ *The Helper* is a person or persons in a story who helps the hero along the way, as he or she works to achieve the goal.

The last two roles appear only occasionally in stories:

- ☊ *The Beneficiary* is the person, the people, or some other entity who benefits or is intended to benefit from the main character's actions in the story, and receive the goods.

Often, but not always, the Beneficiary is the Hero herself.

- ♎ *The Judge* is the person or power who decides if the hero or someone else will receive the benefits.

In simple stories, characters may play roles consistently throughout the story. In "Jack and the Beanstalk," Jack is the Hero, the Giant is the Rival, and the Giant's wife is Jack's reluctant Helper. But in more sophisticated literature, characters may go from playing one role to playing another. John Reynolds Gardiner (1980) shocks his young readers when the Rival, Stone Fox, turns into the Helper at the last minute in the eponymously named book. In *Because of Winn Dixie*, Dunlap and Stevie Dewberry and "old pinch-faced" Amanda Wilkinson go from being Rivals or at least unfriendly strangers to Helpers. In *Because of Winn Dixie*, the various characters Opal befriends are the Beneficiaries of her socializing grace, but only after they have played the role of Judge, too, and accepted the idea of becoming a community.

Teach It! 43

Character Clusters and Character Maps

These activities provide a visual for enhancing comprehension as students identify roles and traits of story characters and examine relationships among them.

Common Core State Standards and Characters' Perspectives

CCSS Standard 6 for Reading Literature asks that students understand the effect of characters' points of view on the way events are portrayed. Dramatic roles are a sturdy device for helping students retell a story from different characters' perspectives. It can be fascinating to put another character in the protagonist's role and ask what she or he wants (and why), who opposes her, and who helps, and why.

Students can use dramatic roles to take different perspectives on a story. They may take a character who seems to be playing one role and think how the story would seem if they imagined that character playing a different role. For example, in "Jack and the Beanstalk," suppose the Giant's wife were the hero; that is, suppose we saw things from her perspective. What is her goal? Who is her rival? Exploring these questions can lead us to think of even seemingly transparent stories in strikingly new ways. It also may make students more empathetic people in the long run.

Characters as Stand-Ins for Other People

Characters in stories have special meanings for us in our own lives. For example, we can say the story of "Cinderella" is about what happens when a deserving but overshadowed young person like Cinderella competes for recognition against overprivileged people like Cinderella's haughty stepsisters. Kate DiCamillo's *Because of Winn-Dixie* is about what happens when a troubled child (Opal), who is searching for community, reaches out to the people around her, who are also suffering and lonely, but powerless in their isolation.

Cinderella and Opal are like many other people we know. We speak of "Cinderella" sports teams, who have these same attributes of being deserving but overlooked until one day they burst into glory. And many a youngest child, feeling that other siblings get all the breaks, has identified with Cinderella. Opal in *Because of Winn-Dixie* reminds us of Maniac Magee (in Louis Sachar's book by that name) because Maniac, too, is a kid who lacks a normal support group and who ultimately creates community. In real life they both remind us a little bit of other peacemakers, like Mother Teresa and Martin Luther King Jr. But they also remind us of some children in dysfunctional families, who must do more than their fair share to make things right for the others in their surroundings.

Check Your Understanding 10.2: Gauge your understanding of the skills and concepts in this section.

Thinking Critically About Texts Other Than Stories

In this section we will discuss two approaches to understanding messages that may be designed to persuade readers and listeners. One is to look at arguments, and the other is to subject messages to systematic doubt.

Examining Simple Arguments

When faced with a message that seeks to persuade us or even inform us, students can learn to look closely at the ways in which the arguments are made. Teachers can help younger students approach arguments in a simple way. Let's assume students are given a piece of persuasive writing such as the following.

> *Dogs make better pets than cats. There are two good reasons. First, dogs are good companions. Second, they guard your house and keep you safe.*
>
> *Dogs make good companions because dogs are friendly animals. The ancestors of dogs hunted in groups, so they had to learn to get along with others. The ancestors of cats hunted alone, though, so they never had to learn to get along with others.*
>
> *Dogs protect your house because they want to protect the place they live. They are friendly to people and other dogs they know, but they want to keep strangers away—at least until they know them. Cats won't protect your house. They mind their own business when people come around.*
>
> *Wouldn't you rather have a cuddly dog than a snobby cat?*

Figure 10.1 Looking at Arguments

What are you saying?	Dogs make better pets than cats.
What are your reasons for saying it?	First, dogs are good companions. Second, they guard your house and keep you safe.
What evidence do you have?	Dogs make good companions because dogs are friendly animals. The ancestors of dogs hunted in groups, so they had to learn to get along with others . . . Dogs protect your house because they want to protect the place they live. They are friendly to people and other dogs they know, but they want to keep strangers away . . .

Students ask these questions:

- *What are you saying?* What claim or suggestion is the message making?
- *What are your reasons for saying it?* What reasons does the message give about why we should accept that claim or suggestion?
- *What evidence do you have?* What evidence does the message give that would make us believe each reason?

With regard to the example, we can answer the questions as in Figure 10.1. A good argument will make clear claims, with clear reasons, and ample evidence to support each reason.

Examining More Complex Arguments

Of course, most arguments are more subtle than the one we just considered about dogs and cats. Take the following one, about fracking.

Fracking is a modern way of extracting natural gas from deep underground pockets. The word fracking is short for "hydraulic fracturing." Here is an argument in favor of fracking.

Fracking is a good idea for many reasons. First, the energy needs of the United States are going up every year and more energy sources are needed to meet the demand. Second, fracking makes it possible to extract natural gas that could not be reached by other means. Third, because fracking is often done in rural areas with limited employment opportunities, fracking is bringing much-needed jobs where they didn't exist. Fourth, the energy industry is one of the most profitable industries in the United States. Fifth, fracking companies are good neighbors: they make contributions to local libraries and schools. Sixth, it's exciting to see those big trucks roll through town loaded with complicated equipment—surely those fascinating machines will get more kids interested in science.

To examine this more complicated argument, we would follow the same three steps, but in more detail:

1. What is the argument saying, or what is the *claim*?
   a. Is the claim stated clearly?
   b. Is the claim worded in such a way that it can be negated?
2. What reasons are offered to support the claim?
   a. Are the reasons *relevant*? Do they seriously support the claim?
   b. Are the reasons *sufficient*? Does more need to be said to support the claim?
3. What evidence is offered to support each reason?
   a. Is the evidence *representative*? Does it point to isolated events or can it be demonstrated to be true in most cases?
   b. Is the evidence *verifiable*? Can it be shown to be true?

Let's hold this argument up against those criteria.

1. What is the *claim*? *The claim is that fracking is a good idea.*
   a. Is the claim stated clearly? *Not very. We might ask, "Is fracking a good idea compared to what?" Or, "Do the benefits of fracking outweigh the risks?"*
   b. Is the claim worded in such a way that it can be negated? *Not completely. Fracking may be a "good idea" in the sense that it is a breakthrough in petroleum engineering—hats off to the team that thought it up! But saying fracking is*

a "good idea" ignores the trade-offs between benefits and risks, which is the more relevant question. Without knowing exactly what the author is arguing, it is not possible to say if the argument is valid or not.

2. What *reasons* are offered to support the claim?

   a. Are the reasons *relevant*? *Some reasons are relevant, but many are not. It is relevant to say that America's energy needs are expanding (though that's not sufficient—we'll get to that). It is relevant to say fracking taps gas supplies that were not accessible before. It is relevant to say fracking may bring employment to areas that need jobs. It is not relevant to say that energy is a big industry; and it is only marginally relevant to say that fracking companies may offer charity to local libraries and schools, or that seeing complicated machinery will increase children's interest in science.*

   b. Are the reasons *sufficient*? *It is not sufficient to say that fracking will meet America's energy needs. We deserve to know how fracking compares to other energy sources. We also need to consider what environmental risks are associated with fracking—and they are many—before agreeing that it is a good solution to America's energy needs. Also, the argument suggests we should keep finding more sources of energy, but ignores the need to conserve: to use less energy.*

3. What *evidence* is offered to support each reason?

   a. Is the evidence *representative*? *That fracking reaches gas that wasn't accessible before has been demonstrated repeatedly. It is true. The statement that fracking companies contribute to schools and libraries is hearsay—it may happen from time to time, but no evidence is presented that schools and libraries are frequently helped by fracking companies.*

   b. Is the evidence *verifiable*? Can it be shown to be true? *The statement that seeing trucks loaded with sophisticated gear will interest children in science is pure conjecture. It can't be considered to be true.*

Examining Arguments That Don't Persuade Fairly

Many texts don't argue fairly, of course. To understand how misleading arguments work, more tools are needed. Students can be led to ask four questions such as these to look below the surface of misleading arguments:

- *What's missing?* A statement may seem perfectly OK with its claims and reasons and evidence—until we realize what it has left unsaid.

- *Is this for real?* Are there "facts" in the text that we might have reason to doubt?

- *What's in the words?* What loaded words are used? "Loaded" words are terms that pass judgments without making arguments.

- *Who cares?* Texts often argue as if all readers wanted a state of affairs that we don't necessarily value.

For an example of these questions being asked of the topic of dogs and cats, see Figure 10.2.

Figure 10.2 A Further Look at Arguments

What's missing?	The argument about dogs and cats doesn't mention that dogs are more costly to keep and are sometimes aggressive toward innocent people.
Is this for real?	What proof, beyond simply saying so, does the text offer that dogs have always been gregarious and cats have always been solitary?
What's in the words?	Using the word "snobby" to describe cats is unfair because it goes beyond the evidence. The text hasn't proved that cats believe themselves too good to spend time with others, as the word "snobby" suggests.
Who cares?	The text assumes that everyone wants a companionable pet. But many readers may prefer their pets to be more independent and to require less frequent attention.

CCSS

Common Core State Standards: What If the Informational Books are Biased?

The Common Core State Standards require that by fourth grade, half the texts that students read be informational, and that proportion increases to 55 percent by eighth grade. Students as early as grade 2 should be able to identify the purpose of a text (Comprehension of Informational Text, Standard #6).

That standard is not as simple as it may seem. Many adults have been appalled by the trend to politicize science in recent years. In the area of climate change, sophisticated campaigns have been launched to counter the consensus finding of climate scientists that human beings cause global warming and that global warming threatens life on the planet. Children wishing to read up on global warming might come across Holly Fretwell's *The Sky's Not Falling: Why It's OK to Chill About Global Warming.* They would have to do a little research to find that according to the *Los Angeles Times* (Simon, 2007), the publisher of *The Sky's Not Falling* (who also published *Help! There Are Liberals Under My Bed!* and other such titles for children) expressly solicited manuscripts that would argue that humans are not causing the planet to heat up. (The winner of the bid turned out to be an economist who works for a think tank that fights environmental protection laws.) The book was commissioned as a rebuttal to a children's book version of Vice President Al Gore's Academy Award–winning documentary *An Inconvenient Truth.* Laurie David and Cambria Gordon's *The Down-to-Earth Guide to Global Warming* (2007) presented Vice President Gore's summary of scientific consensus on the subject.

Regardless of whether children's books are commissioned by big business or by the political left or right to interpret the world for children with a particular slant, it is likely that as more informational books come into schools, more politically motivated discourse will come along with them. Identifying the purpose of many of these texts will not always be easy. Teachers and children will need to develop their critical literacy so that they can be clear on who is saying what, and why.

Examining Arguments That Don't Look Like Arguments

Many of the messages children see in a day are intended to persuade them. But few of them take the form of well-formed arguments, with claims, reasons, and evidence (see Figure 10.3).

There are four "scans" (based on Alan Luke and Peter Freebody's [1999] "Four Resources Model" of reading) that we can give such texts to figure out what they are and how they work, what they mean, what we will do with them, and what they're doing and why they're doing it.

1. ***What kind of text is this? How does it work?***   On the first scan, we try to determine what kind of text we are looking at. Is it a story, a piece of information, an advertisement, or something else? We should be alert to texts that pretend to be one thing, but turn out to be something else: entertainment that is selling something, and so on.

Figure 10.3 Persuading Without an Argument

Stay ahead of the pack
On a Bronwyn bike

Once we know what it is, we can also ask how it works. Each type or genre of text has its own code, its own set of rules. A story has a plot (characters, setting, problems, solutions, and consequence). A persuasive essay has logic (claim, reasons, and evidence). An informative piece has its structure of presentation (cause and effect, steps in a procedure, chronology, taxonomy, comparison and contrast). An advertisement has its rhetorical strategy (an ideal situation that can be attained by Joe or Jane Average if she or he will only consume a certain product). Once we are aware of those rules, we can use them to decipher its meaning.

2. *What does this text mean?*   Texts can have meanings on many levels. Once we identify the meaningful parts of a text, we can ask what associations those parts bring to mind. We can ask how those parts work together to create meaning. And we can generate one or more readings for the text.

3. *What can I do with this text?*   Once we have arrived at some meanings of the text, we can choose what to do with it. There are many ways to read a text. We can read to be entertained. We can read to be informed. We can read to be persuaded, or to have our views reinforced. If we decide to be critical, we can ask what effects the text is trying to have on its readers. In some cases, readers decide to take direct action—they may write letters to advertisers, they may speak for change at a school or community meeting, or they may create a civic project to bring about change.

4. *What is the text trying to do, and why?*   Once we adopt a critical stance to the text, we can ask what the text is trying to do to us. We can ask about the motives of those who wrote it. We can decide whose views and interests are advanced by the text, and whose views and interests are left out.

Asking about the simple advertisement for Bronwyn bikes that began this section, we might see responses like those in Figure 10.4.

Figure 10.4 Four Ways of Looking at a Questionable Text

1. What kind of text *is* **this? How does it work?**	This thing looks like an advertisement. Advertisements work by showing an idealized person who looks like a mirror image of the reader. Since the person in the image is exaggeratedly happier and more successful than the reader, the reader wants to know how he or she can be like that idealized person. Then the reader notices that the idealized person is using the product being advertised, and is led to conclude that by using the product he or she too will be as happy and successful as the person in the image. Bingo!
2. What does this text mean?	Associations? The boy on the bicycle in front looks like he is in competition with them, and he is winning. They look frustrated, which confirms this interpretation. Since the lead boy's bicycle is shown more clearly and colorfully than the other clunkers, the advertisement suggests that the bicycle is the key to the boy's success and happiness. The caption confirms this. Thus the meaning of the whole advertisement seems to be that if you buy this bicycle, you will stay in front of the other boys who are your competition. But maybe the boy on the lead bicycle is trying to escape from the boys behind him. That's another possible reading of the advertisement. Either way, discerning readers may decide that the text is setting up an unhappy division between the boy in front and the boys behind him. Hmm. A more expensive bicycle may help you get ahead of your friends. But it may also keep you from having friends.
3. What can I do with this text?	Readers might be persuaded by the advertisement, and hound their parents to buy them a Bronwyn bike. Or they may choose to question the advertisement, and reject its message.
4. What is the text trying to do and why?	The text is trying to persuade readers to buy a Bronwyn bicycle. Surely the people who paid for the advertisement want to sell bicycles. Whose voices are left out? People who worry about consumerism being pushed onto children. Also, people who would like information about products, and not just imagery.

Reading Web Sites

The set of questions Luke and Freebody (see above) developed are excellent to use when reading Web sites. In addition, when using Web resources, a preliminary step needs to include asking the question of who sponsors a site and what their authority and purpose is. Too many students approach Web information in the same way they approach printed texts: If it is there, it must be true. Even when Leu et al. (2007) informed students about the inaccuracies in a site, they continued to respond that "if it is there, it must be right"—a real call for our action in giving more attention to critical literacy.

These questions about site sponsorship also are connected to the purposes for which one seeks information. If I want to get a range of ideas for how to clear my garage of spiders, I may try some sites that are from government health offices and some that are from individuals or from blogs. Then the authorship may be varied. If I want to learn more about the relationship between Ponce de Leon and Christopher Columbus, I am going to want only reliable sources, not speculation or opinions. Then the URLs I use should end in ".edu," or be from a reliable, student-oriented search engine like "Ask." The democratization of the Internet means that even elementary students need to learn to think critically about what they are seeing and reading online. Before asking, "What does this text mean?" it is helpful to ask, "Who is sponsoring this site and why?" Beginning with this question makes students better and more productive learners. They can decide if they will read further, and can more easily respond to the question, "What is the text doing and why?"

Online formats are becoming more varied all the time. It is good to help students identify the variety of forms of online communication they will encounter. Some elementary classrooms use discussion formats so students can share their ideas with other students in distant locations; some connect students to adults for book discussions (e-bookchats). These are good ways to help students develop their persuasive abilities. Asking questions of the sources of these communications and knowing whose voices are being expressed is foundational. The more students use online exchanges, the more they become aware of how differently we can respond to the same issues and texts; it can whet their appetite to listen more actively for varied perspectives and interpretations.

Comparing Texts on the Same Topic

Different texts may take different approaches to the same topic without expressly arguing with other texts. For example, a health textbook warns preteens not to get hooked on consumerism, particularly when it comes to clothing and cosmetics. An article in a magazine that is largely sponsored by the clothing and cosmetics industry shows preteen girls how to buy just the right products in order to look glamorous. For younger readers, a book chapter may emphasize a live-and-let-live approach to all living things, including bees and spiders. Another book chapter may warn of the dangers of spider bites and bee stings.

With fictional works, different stories may show the same issue in very different lights. Many of the books of Roald Dahl, such as *Matilda*, *The Witches*, and *George's Amazing Medicine* show adults as oppressive despots, and they delight in the child protagonist's triumphing over them. Other works, such as Vera Williams' *A Chair for My Mother* or Kate DiCamillo's *Because of Winn Dixie,* show adults as so preoccupied with their own problems that they are largely helpless, and the child protagonist makes generous and heroic efforts that bring comfort to the adults as she grows in her awareness of adults' emotions and motives. Such different works don't explicitly argue with each other. Nonetheless, children may be confused by their differing messages if teachers don't help them make sense of the differences.

Check Your Understanding 10.3: **Gauge your understanding of the skills and concepts in this section.**

Teach It 51

What? So What? Now What?

With this activity, students organize facts and opinions as they prepare to engage in persuasive writing and/or speaking.

Teaching Strategies for Critical Thinking

Now that we have surveyed some ways of thinking through how texts do their work, it is clear that readers have a choice: They can read texts actively or passively. They can take control of the understandings they derive from the experience of reading them, or they can allow the text to have the effect on them that the author intended, almost without realizing it. Teachers can make the difference in the ways students approach texts. In the following sections we will share techniques for helping students read while engaging their critical faculties. The chart in Figure 10.5 will relate teaching strategies to the descriptions of critical thinking and how texts work that we have just described.

General Strategies to Encourage Discussion and Debate

This section includes several teaching strategies for encouraging discussions that will lead students into critical thinking and critical literacy.

THE DISCUSSION WEB   The discussion web is a cooperative learning activity that involves all students in deep discussions of readings. The discussion web proceeds with the following steps:

1. The teacher prepares a thoughtful binary question— a question that can be answered "yes" or "no" with support. For example, in discussing "Jack and the Beanstalk," a binary discussion question might be "Was Jack right to steal from the giant?" For Louis Sachar's book *Holes,* the question might be "Did Stanley succeed in the end because of his personal qualities, such as being strong and good, or was it because the luck of his family finally changed?"

2. The teacher asks pairs of students to prepare a discussion web chart that looks like the one in Figure 10.6. Those pairs of students take four or five minutes to think up and list three reasons each that support both sides of the argument.

3. Next, each pair of students joins another pair. They review the answers they had on both sides of the issue and add to each other's list. Then they argue the issue through until they reach a conclusion, that is, a position they agree on, with a list of reasons that support it.

4. At the conclusion of the lesson, the teacher calls on several groups of four to give brief reports of their position and the reasons that support it. The teacher can invite groups to debate each other if they took different sides of the argument.

Figure 10.5 Matching Strategies to Purposes in Critical Literacy

A View of Critical Thinking and How Texts Work	Corresponding Strategies for Teaching
Establishing *purposes* and identifying *authorship* and *credibility*.	Developing purpose-setting questions and plans. Checking site sponsorship.
Responding and Articulating a Position in Relation to the Text	The Discussion Web Debates Value Line

Looking Closely at the Structure of Texts
Structure of folk and fairy tales
     Mythos and *logos*
     The Hero Cycle
Informational and persuasive structures
Propaganda techniques
Visual and graphic components
	Graphic overview of text structure
	Analysis of text arguments and evidence
	Evaluating a Web page
	Creative Dialogue
	Reading for structured opposites
	Matrix of story comparisons

Thinking Critically about Literature and Informational Texts
     Examining Arguments
     What If the Text Doesn't Persuade Fairly?
     What If an Argument Doesn't Look Like an Argument?
	Analyzing propaganda tools
	Anticipation/Reaction Guide
	Questioning the Author
	Socratic Seminar

Figure 10.6 Discussion Web

**Was it wrong for Jack
to steal from the giant?**

1. In pairs, list 3 or 4 reasons to support a "yes" answer to that question, and 3 or 4 reasons to support a "no" answer. Write those reasons in the spaces provided.

YES!   NO!

_____   _____
_____   _____
_____   _____
_____   _____
_____   _____
_____   _____

2. Now, each pair joins another pair. First, share all of your reasons to support a "yes" and a "no" answer. Then, discuss the question to reach an answer you can agree on. Write it in the space provided.

Conclusion:

_____
_____
_____
_____
_____
_____

DEBATES With students in third grade and up, it is often useful to follow the discussion web activity with a debate. The purpose of the debate is not to declare winners and losers, but to help the students practice making claims and defending them with reasons, even when others defend different claims. Working with claims, reasons, and arguments and debating ideas without attacking people—these are key elements in critical thinking.

To have a debate, you need a binary question (that has a yes/no answer). Since the discussion web we saw above also uses binary questions, you can follow the discussion web with a debate. Here are the steps:

1. Think of a question you think will truly divide the students' opinions, and put the question on the board for all to see. If you are not sure the question will divide the students roughly equally, ask for a show of hands for opinions on each side of the issue before going forward.

2. Give students an opportunity to think about the question and discuss it freely.

Teach It! 39

Discussion Web

Promoting thoughtful discussion and interpretation of shared literature with peers, this activity asks students to consider both sides of an argument.

3. Ask students to divide up: Those who believe one answer to the question is right should go stand along the wall on one side of the room, and those who think the other answer is right should stand along the wall on the other side. Those who are truly undecided (that is, after thinking about it, they believe that both sides are partially right or neither side is right) should stand along the middle wall.

4. Explain or review the two ground rules:
   a. Don't be rude to each other. (You might have to explain and demonstrate what this means.)
   b. If you hear an argument that makes you want to change your mind, walk to the other side (or to the middle). Here is a hint to the teacher: As the debate proceeds, you can model the behavior of changing sides with a pantomime, by looking thoughtful for a moment after someone offers a good argument and moving to that student's side.

5. Give the students on each side three or four minutes to put their heads together and decide why they are on that side. Ask them to come up with a sentence that states their position. Then ask them to appoint someone to say that sentence.

6. Begin the debate by asking one person from each side (including the undecided group) to state that group's position.

7. Invite anyone on any team to say things (counterarguments or rebuttals) in response to what the other team has said or give more reasons in support of their own side.

8. Monitor the activity to make sure the tone stays away from negative attacks. Ask for clarification. Offer an idea or two as necessary from the devil's advocate position. Change sides. Encourage the students to change sides if they are persuaded to.

9. When the debate has proceeded for ten or fifteen minutes, ask each side to summarize what they have said.

10. You may follow the debate with a writing activity: Ask each student to write down what he or she believes about the issue and why.

To see a debate in action, watch this video in which students prepare to debate the issue of a school dress code and answer the question that follows.

 Video Exploration 10.3: **Watch the video and answer questions that reflect the content you have read.**

VALUE LINE   A cooperative learning activity that is an extension of the debate procedure is the value line (Kagan, 1994). The value line is well suited for questions that have more than two good answers, and students might have a range of answers along a continuum. Here are the steps:

1. Pose a question to the students on which answers may vary along a continuum. For example, after reading Beverly Cleary's *Ramona and Her Father*, you might ask the children, "Do you think Ramona's parents really understand her?"

2. Give the students three minutes to consider the question alone and write down their answers.

3. Now stand on one side of the room and announce that you represent one pole, or extreme position, on the argument. You might say, "Yes, I think Ramona's parents understand her perfectly, 100 percent of the time." Invite a student to stand at the other end of the room to represent the other pole of the argument. The student might say, "No, I don't think Ramona's parents understand her. Not at all. Never."

4. Now invite the students to line up between the two of you in places along the imaginary value line between the two poles of the argument. Each stands at a point in the line that reflects his or her position on the question. Remind the students to compare their views with those of the students immediately around them to make sure they are all standing in the right spots. After hearing others' answers, some students might elect to move one way or another along the value line.

Teach It! 40

Debate

This activity provides an opportunity for students to work with claims, reasons, and arguments as they learn to debate ideas without attacking those with different points of view.

Teach It! 41
Value Line

This engaging activity provides an opportunity for students to develop critical thinking skills as they learn what their classmates think and practice making arguments.

5. Students may continue to discuss their responses with peers on either side of them.

6. Identify three or four clusters of students who seem to represent different views on the question. Invite them to prepare a statement of their position and to share it with the whole group.

7. As an option, the formed line may be folded in the middle so that students with more divergent views may debate their responses with their peer on the opposite side.

8. You might want to follow this exercise with a writing opportunity in which students write down what they think about the issue and why. In this way, the value line serves as a rehearsal for writing an argumentative or persuasive essay.

Strategies That Look Under the Surface of Narratives

In the chapter on comprehending fiction (Chapter 8) we looked at devices such as story maps that help students understand stories. Here we go deeper and look at ways to see what stories might mean and what they might be arguing for in subtle ways.

BEHAVIOR AND REWARDS. People who worry about violence in the media point to the number of violent acts that not only go unpunished but also win for the perpetrators what they wanted. Critics correctly worry that this is a formula for influencing viewers:

> *"The characters commit X deed, and get what they want.*
> *Therefore, young viewer, you should commit X deed to get what you want."*

But there is a more subtle formula at work in literature that children read, especially the traditional literature, where different types of characters get different results for different kinds of actions.

In stories like "Cinderella" or "Beauty and the Beast," for example, it is clear that men get different rewards than women do for the same actions. Consider the chart in Figure 10.7.

You get the idea. The "yes-yes-yes's" are all successful: They're the males who go after what they want. So are the "No-no-yes's": They're the females who don't go after what they want. The ones who fail, and who are often horribly punished, are the "No-yes-no's": The females who go after what they want. That's a no-no in Western folktales.

Constructing a chart like this with students can be a helpful exercise—but only if there is plenty of time for the students to question whether these patterns make sense in their own lives.

CCSS
Common Core State Standards and the Structure of Arguments

CCSS Standards 2, 5, and 8 for Reading Informational Text require that students follow the structure of arguments (main ideas plus support, plus the logic of proof). The first writing standard asks that students as young as first graders be able to state an opinion and support it with reasons. The Discussion Web, Debates, the Value Line, and similar strategies are excellent ways to help students understand arguments and to prepare them for writing argumentative essays.

Figure 10.7 What They Wanted and What They Got

	Male?	Actively sought what they wanted?	Got what they wanted?
Beauty	No	No	Yes
Beauty's sisters	No	Yes	No
Beast	Yes	Yes	Yes
Cinderella	No	No	Yes
Cinderella's sisters	No	Yes	No
Cinderella's prince	Yes	Yes	Yes
Sleeping Beauty	No	No	Yes
Sleeping Beauty's prince	Yes	Yes	Yes
Snow White	No	No	Yes
Snow White's stepmother	No	Yes	No
Snow White's prince	Yes	Yes	Yes

READING FOR STRUCTURED OPPOSITES   A useful way of interpreting stories is to look for their contrasts, ask what things are similarly contrasted in other stories, and then find parallel contrasts and tensions in our own lives (Levi-Strauss, 1970). A method for doing that is called *reading for structured opposites*. A folktale works very well for introducing this method and could be taught like this:

1. Ask the students to think of the two characters in the story they are reading who are most unlike each other or most opposed to each other. For example, if the story is "Jack and the Beanstalk," the two characters might be Jack and the giant.

2. Write the names of those two characters at the heads of two columns (see Figure 10.8). Ask the students to come up with contrasting descriptive words about these two characters. That is, ask for a word that describes one character; then ask for an opposite word that describes the other character.

To take "Jack and the Beanstalk" as our example, those characters might be Jack and the giant, obviously. Let's begin with them. What words would we use to describe each of them? Each of these columns—a bundle of features with a name at the top—can be called a *category*. We will do more with the categories in a moment.

Figure 10.8 Looking at Relations Between Characters Horizontally

Jack	The Giant
Young	Old
Poor	Rich
Small	Huge
"Plucky"	Dull
Seems weak	Seems strong
"On his way up"	"Over the hill"

Figure 10.9 Looking at Relations Between Characters Horizontally and Vertically

Others Like Jack	Jack	The Giant	Others Like the Giant
David	Young	Old	Goliath
Marty (in *Shiloh*)	Poor	Rich	Judd Travers (in *Shiloh*)
Peter Pan	Small	Huge	Captain Hook
Robin Hood	"Plucky"	Dull	Sheriff of Nottingham
	Seems weak	Seems strong	
	"On his way up"	"Over the hill"	

The dynamics between these characters can be called a *relationship*. In this case, it's a relationship of rivalry—Jack wants what the giant has, and the giant wants to keep what he has and eliminate Jack as a threat (eat him, if possible).

Now who else do we know who could occupy the same *category* with Jack, or occupy the other category with the giant—paradigms that are partially defined by their relationship with the other—in this case, the rivalry of the young, poor, underprivileged one who is on his way up, and the older, bigger, richer one who is desperately clinging to his or her privilege? We will nominate a few and write them in the outer columns to the left of Jack and to the right of the giant (see Figure 10.9).

Wow. It now seems that Jack and the giant are actually more than mere characters in a story. They are bundles of features with names attached—characters who remind us of other characters. Who are other candidates who share these paradigms, and occupy the same categories with each other? (See Figure 10.10.)

There. You may have noticed that in exploring the contrasted characters and their characteristics in this story—in both their categories and their relationships—we have explored text-to-text relationships and text-to-life relationships.

QUESTIONING THE AUTHOR   In the Questioning the Author teaching strategy, also called QtA (Beck, McKeown, & Kucan, 2002), the teacher does three things.

First, the teacher reminds students that authors are people like themselves, with their own ideas, experiences, foibles, and prejudices. When authors communicate with audiences, they sometimes tell readers exactly what they need to know; but often, they take too much for granted and leave out needed explanations. Or they may slant their message to suit their own beliefs, without inviting the reader to disagree. In classrooms where students write and share their works with each other, students are not surprised when their peers make points that aren't clear, or state positions with which they disagree. They find it natural to question their peer-authors at those times. The teacher tries to evoke that same confidence in questioning an author when students are faced with the work not of a peer, but by a published author.

Figure 10.10 Comparing This Story to Others

Others Like Jack in Real Life	Others Like Jack in the Arts	Jack	The Giant	Others Like the Giant in the Arts	Others Like the Giant in Real Life
Serfs	David	Young	Old	Goliath	Nobles
Slaves	Marty	Poor	Rich	Judd Travers	Owners
People	Peter Pan	Small	Huge	Captain Hook	Tyrants
Workers	Robin Hood	"Plucky"	Dull	Sheriff of Nottingham	Sweatshop managers
Children		Seems weak	Seems strong		Bullies
		"On his way up"	"Over the hill"		

The second step is to ask the students to have an imaginary dialogue with the author, and ask about things that are not clearly stated, points where more information is needed, or claims with which they disagree. Here are some basic questions students might ask:

- What is the author trying to say here?
- How can we restate this idea, in words we all can understand?
- Why is the author telling us this now?
- What does the author want us to believe? Why?
- What is the author's point of view?
- How might someone with a different point of view have explained this point?

The third step, which is usually combined with the second, is to invite the students to provide the answers they might expect an author to supply to their questions. A group of students is usually able to do this, because their collective ideas may be more comprehensive than their individual ideas.

SOCRATIC SEMINAR   With students in late elementary and middle school, nearly any topic to be interpreted or explored from different points of view can be used in the Socratic Seminar. The purpose of the Socratic Seminar is to empower students to conduct discussions on their own. The teacher provides a structure that usually leads to successful discussions, but after modeling the process by leading the first few discussions, the students are the ones who ask the questions and conduct the discussion. A Socratic Seminar is not a debate. The ideas offered do not compete with each other. Rather, they often build on each other to reach a mutually constructed and deeper understanding of an issue. Asking good questions and developing ideas in concert with others is good practice in active learning and critical thinking. Taking responsibility for preparing the questions and conducting the discussion intensifies the experience for the students.

Socratic Seminars are done with the whole class. If the group is larger than 12 (and it usually is), a fishbowl arrangement is used. That is, between eight and twelve students sit in a circle conducting the discussion, and the other students array themselves around that group, close enough to hear the discussion.

The Socratic Seminar requires no particular resources other than a text or a topic that students can discuss. It helps if the seating is treated flexibly; that is, either the chairs are moved into a circle, or students sit so they can face each other in a circle. The seminar itself usually takes 40 minutes. Twenty minutes or more will be needed to introduce the idea, and then students will need time to prepare for the seminar.

To conduct the Socratic Seminar, the teacher first immerses students in an interesting topic. The topic can come from literature, social studies, art, science, or any topic about which there are layers of understanding, different interpretations, or diverse implications. One of the easiest ways to introduce the Socratic Seminar is to discuss a piece of literature that the whole class has read. A seminar is also productive midway through a unit of study in which students have acquired a significant amount of information on a topic or theme.

The teacher prepares the students to formulate questions for discussion. The Socratic Seminar requires that everyone discuss good questions. Eventually, students may formulate the questions, but for the first couple of sessions, the teacher may prepare them and use his or her questions to model for the students the kinds of questions that are preferred. A suggested approach to formulating questions worthy of deep discussion is Grant Wiggins's and Jay McTighe's (2005) concept of essential questions. Essential questions usually:

- Lead into the heart of a topic and its controversies
- Invite many answers from different perspectives
- Invite rethinking of old knowledge in a new light
- Lead to discovery and "uncoverage" vs. "coverage"
- Encourage deeper interest in the subject; students keep on questioning
- Are framed in a provocative and enticing style

In practical terms, you may use the following set of suggestions:

A Socratic Seminar is a time to have a good discussion. To have a good discussion, you bring up things you are curious about, things you think are important. To have an even better discussion, you ask your classmates questions—but real questions— questions you don't know the answer to. Those can serve as guidelines. To prepare for a Socratic Seminar, you should plan some real questions—that ask about things you are interested in, that you think are important. And the questions should be real in the sense that you don't already know the answers ("Read my mind" questions are not allowed!).

Figure 10.11 Questions About Stories

Questions That Focus *In* (on the article or topic)	**Questions That Focus *Out*** (toward the world outside the text or topic of study)
1. If the question is about a story, you can ask about: A character's motives. ("Why did she agree to do that?") The relationships between characters ("Do you think he is a good influence on her?") What is going to happen (if we haven't finished reading it yet). Why the author wrote the story. ("What did this author want us to see or to understand?") What the action had to do with the setting. ("Can you picture this story happening anywhere else? Why not?") Why the author used certain words, or a certain style of writing. ("Why do you think the author said it that way?") Something the author has done particularly well. ("What do you think is the best feature of this story?") 2. If it is an informational topic or work of nonfiction, you might ask: What are we learning from this that we didn't know before? Is this argument convincing? What other points of view have we learned about? Is there more to be said about this topic?	1. If the question is about a story, you can ask about: Whether the characters made good choices. ("Would you have done what he did? What is another way to solve that problem?") Whether the behavior pictured in this story should serve as a model for us in real life. ("Is that the way boys should really behave with girls? Suppose she was your sister?") The consequences of the actions. ("What do you suppose happened to each one of those characters after the story was over?") About connections to other stories and to real life. ("What other stories does this remind us of? Who or what does this remind us of in real life?") 2. If it is an informational topic or work of nonfiction, you might ask: Do we think this is true? How do we know? What is the most important idea? If we believe what this text says, what should we do?

Often these questions point in either of two directions, as we see in Figure 10.11. The teacher explains the ground rules for the seminar. Following are some suggestions:

- Be prepared to participate
- Don't raise hands—just find a good time to speak and jump right in
- Invite others in the circle into the discussion
- Refer to the texts or other resources that have been studied
- Make comments that are appropriate, respectful, and focused
- Listen to and build on one another's comments
- Be sure it's OK with others before you introduce a new question

Ground rules are introduced at the beginning of a seminar. It is best if the group is reminded of them often. If a student does an excellent job of adhering to a ground rule, the teacher may point that out, since positive reinforcements will make students feel more responsible than criticisms will.

Participating students (between eight and twelve of them) sit in a circle. The other students gather around what is called the "fishbowl" (so called because their discussion will be observed by the others—see the next section for instructions).

The teacher may invite a student to ask a question and have the other students respond. The other students share their thoughts about the question, and also refer both to each other's answers and to the material being discussed.

When the responses to a question seem to have run their course, another student may raise a new question, or an aspect of an old one. It is considered polite for that student to ask if anyone had more to say about the previous question first, and to wait for any more responses before raising a new question.

After the teacher gives the signal (usually after five minutes), students who are observing from outside the group may "tap into" the group. That is, one student at a time approaches a student in the circle, and taps that student gently on the elbow. Then the new student takes that student's place in the discussion group. The new student should respond first to what the group has been talking about before introducing a new question. From time to time the teacher can invite a student to sum up the positions that have been heard, and ask if there are more ideas.

Following the Socratic Seminar, students are asked to evaluate their participation. They can be asked to write responses to questions such as:

- What did you learn from this seminar?
- How did you feel about this seminar?
- How would you evaluate your own participation in this seminar?
- What can you do to improve your participation in the next seminar?

The teacher "debriefs" the discussion by reviewing the ideas and arguments that came to light. Or she may ask each student to write a journal entry or a personal essay, writing down what he believes about the issue and why.

For future Socratic Seminars, students can be asked to bring "Entry Sheets" on which they have written at least three questions for the others to answer, as well as their own thoughts on those questions. Another device for structuring the seminar would be to pass out small pieces of paper to each student, have them write their name and their class period on it, and ask them to write a short entry each time they offer a question or a response to one. These can be given to the teacher at the end of the class period to keep track of the students' participation.

Reading to Follow Arguments

Students from fourth grade and up are ready to look at the ways persuasive texts and media make arguments. When they are given guidance, they can become quite expert at asking about evidence for perspectives they read and view.

PRODUCING ARGUMENTS   One good way to prepare students for this kind of thinking is to have them produce arguments of their own—and a lively way to do that is to:

- Engage students in issues.
- Ask each student to take a position on the issues.
- Have students debate with others from their position.
- Ask students to write about their position.

A graphic organizer such as the one in Figure 10.12 may be used to help students form their brief position essay.

ANALYZING ARGUMENTS IN TEXTS   After the students can confidently write out their own arguments according to this structure, they are ready to outline the arguments of others. Note that it is best to begin with short, simple, and clearly structured arguments such as the essay on dogs and cats found earlier in this chapter. Teachers may write their own sample essays to give students practice, making sure those essays (1) state a claim clearly, and (2) offer two or three reasons for the claim, (3) support each reason with evidence. It is advisable to use the words *reason* and *evidence* right in the essays, to help students identify them.

Figure 10.12 Structuring an Argumentative Essay

I think . . .	
because . . .	
Evidence for that is . . .	
Also because . . .	
Evidence for that is . . .	

Figure 10.13 A Graphic Organizer for Arguments

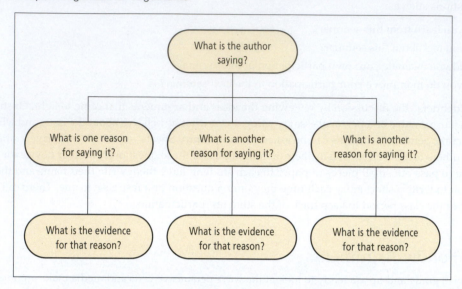

Then the students take notes about the essay in a graphic organizer, such as the one in Figure 10.13.

Once the arguments are laid out this way, the teacher and students can discuss whether the reasons logically support the claim, and whether the evidence really supports the reasons.

To go further in analyzing arguments, you may employ the questions we set out earlier in this chapter.

1. What is the argument saying, or what is the *claim*?
   a. Is the claim stated clearly?
   b. Is the claim worded in such a way that it can be negated?

2. What reasons are offered to support the claim?
   a. Are the reasons *relevant*? Do they seriously support the claim?
   b. Are the reasons *sufficient*? Does more need to be said to support the claim?

3. What evidence is offered to support each reason?

   a. Is the evidence *representative*? Does it point to isolated events or can it be demonstrated to be true in most cases?
   b. Is the evidence *verifiable*? Can it be shown to be true?

When you and the students are examining an argument that seems to be making a dishonest presentation, you can pay attention to one or more of these features:

- missing information (MI)
- loaded words (LW)
- faulty assumptions about what the world needs (FA)

The students can locate and mark places where these problems occur, underlining the offending phrases and putting the corresponding letters in the margins near the problem phrases.

WORDS AND THEIR CONNOTATIONS   For an exercise on loaded words—words that carry judgments that have not been justified—teachers sometimes use an exercise like the following. Students are shown a chart with rows of words divided into three columns. In the middle column goes the most neutral word. In the left-hand column goes a negative word—a word with negative connotations—and in the right-hand column goes a positive word—a word with positive connotations (connotations are the other things a word means beyond its literal meaning, especially the value judgments a word conveys). The students may fill in the blanks in a chart like the one in Figure 10.14, and later create charts of their own.

Figure 10.14 Words and Their Connotations

Negative	Neutral	Positive
Shack	House	Palace
Cowardly	Cautious	Prudent
Sluggish	Slow	Guarded
Oversized	Large	
Fat		
		Confident
	Casual	

Looking at Arguments That Don't Say They Are Arguments

Not all of the messages that seek to persuade people state their claims clearly or offer reasons supported by evidence about why we should accept those claims. So it can be valuable for students to learn how to do a little detective work before they let themselves be persuaded by something they read, see, or hear. The graphic organizer in Figure 10.15 is adapted from Luke and Freebody's "Four Resources Model of Reading" (Luke & Freebody, 1999). Teachers may practice asking the question about a simple text first—even a text as simple as a stop sign. Then the class can move on to another kind of text, such as an advertisement.

Strategies That Compare Multiple Texts With Common Themes

We make comparisons all the time: between sports teams, restaurant menus, and music to listen to. How do we compare texts, especially when they are addressing similar issues in different ways?

COMPARING TEXTS   Primary as well as upper grade teachers introduce students to the value of reading multiple texts and thinking of how texts function when they create thematic and inquiry units. These units usually begin by posing some question for exploration like, "How should we treat the insects in our environment? Should we use insecticides and try to kill them or are there some that are useful to us?" or "How important is it to share with others what we have?" Teachers collect an array of materials that are accessible to students (at their reading levels and that capture their levels of interest and knowledge). These materials represent a range of genres and formats so students can compare and contrast how authors present ideas and information.

CCSS
Common Core State Standards and Word Connotations

Standard 4 of the Common Core State Standards for both Reading Literature and Informational Text asks students to understand literal and figurative language, and also to understand vocabulary from the different academic disciplines. Although the standards don't acknowledge it, under figurative language, the choices of words often have value associations (*patriots* are good people, *terrorists* are bad people, but in some contexts the words could apply to the same person). We can use the term *nominal assumptions* for those occasions where we choose a word with a value attached to it, but without defending the value judgment. Teachers who promote critical literacy will have to go beyond the Common Core State Standards in this instance.

Figure 10.15 Looking Critically at Messages

1. What is this?	Decide what kind of message this is.	
	Then decide how we should read it.	
2. What does it mean?	Now, list some of the words or images in the message that caught your eye—What do they make you think of?	
	Next, say what you think the whole message means.	
3. What is it for?	Decide what you can do with this text.	
	Say what you think others may do with it.	
4. Who is behind the message?	Explain what you think the text is trying to do.	
	Say who you think might want the text to do that, and why.	
	Then say whose point of view you think is left out.	

Watch this video to see how readers think critically about coral reefs as they write about them and answer the question that follows.

 Video Exploration 10.4: Watch the video and answer questions that reflect the content you have read.

USING DIFFERENT INFORMATIONAL TEXTS Many classes begin their inquiries with a group K-W-L with the teacher creating a chart of what the students think they already know about the topic. During the discussion that ensues, the teacher also helps students generate questions that will guide their initial inquiries. Once the students have embarked on their reading, viewing, and searching for information, the teacher can bring them back together to formulate key questions that can then be put on the class Inquiry Chart (Hoffman, 1992). The teacher also selects some of the best texts for students' use in this class activity. Small groups of students can take turns examining the texts and recording what they learn from the authors. The groups can either record their information and ideas on 8 × 11-inch record sheets or put what they learn on sticky notes to be included on a large class I-Chart.

As students read from different sources of information, their awareness of how authors have to select and leave out information grows. The ways authors explain ideas and provide visual information also vary considerably. Students attend to these characteristics and teachers can guide them to make comparisons about which texts are most useful and which could use revision to be more "considerate" to them as readers. See an example of an I-Chart that the teacher used as students completed their unit in Figure 10.16. As part of the culmination of this unit, groups of students wrote their own books and took time to consider the structure, ways they would present information, and the themes they wanted to communicate. The children developed a deeper understanding of the relationship between texts and readers throughout this process.

Children are often amazed by the amount of partial information and misinformation contained in some of the documents. As one group of second graders exclaimed, "These two books are confusing—one says there aren't brown recluse spiders in the middle part of the country; the other says they can be found everywhere in dark, damp areas. One makes spiders sound like they are really helpful; the other tells about a woman who almost died when a brown recluse bit her while she was rocking in her chair and shows an ugly picture of an arm of someone bitten."

READING MULTIPLE VERSIONS OF THE SAME STORY   Another way to help young students understand how texts function in social contexts is to read and examine several texts written by different authors using the same basic story. One of the easiest to use is the Cinderella tale. Almost any library will have several versions of this tale that can be explored. Teachers can read some tales to students and have them chart the similarities and differences in the tales, their structure, their characters, the challenges faced, the ways the problems are solved, and the underlying message the author seems to want readers to accept. For example, after reading the classic French version of Cinderella, students who read *The Rough-faced Girl* (American Indian tale) and *Mufaro's Beautiful Daughters* (West African tale) can discuss the different challenges the girls face and ways they are able to overcome their hardships. The pictures

Figure 10.16 Inquiry Chart

Topic:	Guiding Question 1	Guiding Question 2	Guiding Question 3	Guiding Question 4	Other Interesting Facts and Figures	New Questions
WHAT WE KNOW						
Source 1						
Source 2						
Source 3						
Summary						

Figure 10.17 "Stone Soup": A Single Story from Multiple Perspectives

Title	*Stone Soup* M. Brown, 1947	*Stone Soup*, T. Ross, 1987	*Nail Soup*, Zemach, 1964	*Group Soup*, B. Brenner, 1992	*Stone Soup*, Muth, 2003
Characters					
Setting Genre					
Problem					
Resolution					
Theme or Lesson Learned					

or drawings are also worth examining critically to see how the context and characters are represented. Children may want to create their own illustrations or locate others online or in other books. Figure 10.17 shows an example of how one first-grade teacher helped her students think deeply about different versions of the folktale "Stone Soup". This activity led students to analyze the major story elements and then compare the ways the authors developed the basic story theme in a variety of settings.

Check Your Understanding 10.4: Gauge your understanding of the skills and concepts in this section.

For Review

At the outset of this chapter we stated that when you reached this point in your reading and studying you should be able to:

- **Define critical thinking and critical literacy, as well as the "New Literacies."**

We defined *critical thinking* as a process of reasoning and reflecting that is done in order to decide what to believe or what course of action to take. Critical thinking is usually carried out in response to something—a problem in real experience, something we read, or an argument we hear. *Critical literacy* is the practice of examining the social, political, and cultural purposes and values that texts reflect. Critical readers may "talk back" to the text, and construct different readings of it. We defined *"New Literacies"* as making meaning from non-print forms of communication, forms that are emerging so rapidly we have to call these practices "literacies" instead of "literacy" because new media may require new reading and writing strategies.

- **Examine the intriguing aspects of literature that may systematically invite discussions.**

We explored the ways narratives promote cultural values, the ways the dramatic roles characters play shape readers' attitudes toward those characters, and how characters in books may represent templates for understanding people in the real world.

- **Discuss the structural features of persuasive texts.**

We looked at the structure of arguments and also at the ways communications might persuade when they are not formally shaped as arguments.

- **Use teaching strategies to guide students to think critically about works of literature and persuasive writing.**

We presented several methods for guiding students' critical reading of works of fiction and persuasive texts.

For Your Journal

1. Review the Anticipation Guide and compare your earlier answers with what you think now.

2. This weekend, turn to a children's television channel and watch an hour of shows aimed at children—say, between the ages of 4 and 9. Better yet, divide up this assignment with several classmates so you can cover several different shows for more hours. Takes notes on the advertisements you see. What are they selling? How are they selling it—with reasons, images, or other devices? Decide what you would need to teach children so they could respond rationally to such advertisements.

Taking It to the World

Survey the debates among politicians reported in the news, and choose one issue. Identify the positions of the two or more opposing sides. What arguments—that is, reasons plus evidence—are made in support of each side?

Chapter 11
Teaching Children to Spell and Write

 ## Learning Outcomes

After reading this chapter you should be able to:

1. Explain the phases children pass through as they learn to spell and assess them.

2. Use best practices to teach children to spell.

3. Explain and teach a five-stage writing process.

4. Support children's writing in different genres.

5. Assess children's writing.

6. Teach writing to learn.

Anticipation Guide

The following statements will stimulate your thinking about the topics of this chapter. Answer *true* or *false* in response to each statement. As you read and learn more about the topics in these statements, double-check your answers. See what interests you and prompts your curiosity toward more understanding.

_____ **1.** Being a poor speller can make a student a disfluent writer.

_____ **2.** When we speak of a writing process, we mean a process by which many successful adult writers as well as schoolchildren produce written compositions.

_____ **3.** The goal of writing instruction is to teach children to write everything once and write it correctly.

_____ **4.** Children can help each other learn to write.

_____ **5.** It is generally better for teachers to assign writing topics than to let children choose their own.

_____ **6.** Children need different levels of support as they learn to write. Some children flourish in the open atmosphere of the writing workshop, but others need more explicit guidance.

_____ **7.** It is important for teachers to write in front of children and demonstrate writing as a studio craft.

_____ **8.** The difference between editing and revising is that editing is done only by professional writers.

_____ **9.** There is no such thing as different levels of support teachers give to writers at different ages. Writing is a sink-or-swim affair.

_____ **10.** Learn first; then write about what you know. Writing about what you haven't learned yet is a waste of time.

A Classroom Story

The Writing Process in a Third-Grade Classroom

At West Street School in Geneva, New York, Anne Bergstrom is trying a new approach to her third graders' study of African geography. The school's experience has corroborated what the National Assessment of Educational Progress has found: Not only do elementary students need to know more geography, but they also need to know how to think with geographical information. So this spring, because their student teacher from last fall, Sarah Barry, is studying in Dakar, the capital of Senegal, Ms. Bergstrom has arranged to conduct an inquiry lesson on Senegal via the Internet.

In the fall, the students located Senegal on a map and discussed its tropical climate and its history as a slave state and as a colony of France. They researched and read material about Senegal from the National Geographic Web site. They also did their best to make sense of the U.S. State Department's Web-based information. In December, the students thought of questions they wanted Sarah to investigate, wrote them on a piece of chart paper as part of a K-W-L chart (see Figure 11.1), and sent them to Sarah in an e-mail.

Sarah wrote the students an e-mail from Senegal and asked them how they wanted her to find answers to their questions: "Who do you want me to talk to? What do you want me to ask?" The students took turns writing e-mails to Sarah on the classroom computer. But Sarah realized that there are fascinating things about Senegal that the students did not know to ask about. So she sent them occasional transmissions that she called "mysteries," intriguing photographs with questions attached. The students took turns writing to Sarah about the mystery; they sent guesses or questions they wanted to ask her. In a way, Sarah became an extension of the class, their remote-control anthropologist.

In the spring, Ms. Bergstrom had the students prepare write-ups of what they had learned. The students used the writing workshop to focus on their topics, write a first draft, revise their drafts, edit them, and prepare them for publication. Later, the class collaborated on a joint composition: the script for a class play about aspects of life in the West African country of Senegal, which they performed for an audience of the whole school.

Even preschool and kindergarten children are eager to write—that is, if we accept making communicative marks on paper as "writing." As we saw in previous chapters, writing down ideas word by word and sound by sound helps young learners take a close look at the language they speak and the system of print that represents it. But emphasizing writing has other advantages, too:

- Writing makes students more observant, both of their own inner experiences and of the outside world.
- Being writers makes students closer readers of other writers. Young writers are sensitive to language and style, and can feel like "workers in the same vineyard" as Cynthia DeFelice, Kate DiCamillo, Steve Jenkins, and other admired authors.
- Writing makes students more reflective as they record an idea, examine that idea in print, and maybe come up with a further idea.

Figure 11.1   The First Questions We Have

The First Questions We Have

1. Do they go swimming?
2. What is the population?
3. Do they know about King's fight for freedom?
4. How do they talk?
5. What do they eat?
6. How hot does it get?
7. What are their houses made of?
8. What do they do in their spare time?
9. Was it a slave trading place?
10. What do they celebrate?
11. What games do they play?
12. What kinds of animals do they have?
13. What are their religions?
14. How do people treat each other?
15. What kind of jewelry do they wear?
16. Does anyone have piercings or tattoos?
17. Do they trade? What do they trade with other countries?
18. Does everyone have a job?
19. Are there homeless people?
20. How do they dispose of trash?
21. Do they brush their teeth, and if so, with what?

- Writing builds community. As students work hard to capture and communicate their thoughts and experiences, and as they listen to their classmates' efforts to do the same, students reveal themselves to each other and come to better understand each other.

- Applied to literature and to other subjects in the curriculum, writing responses and other kinds of inquiry also serve as a powerful learning tool.

In this chapter we will present many ways teachers can help children learn to write. We begin by talking about spelling—how it is learned and how it is taught. Then we will look at different levels of instruction and support for children's composing. We will explore the well-known "writing process," a set of activities through which writers often create works. We will look in more detail at many ways of teaching and supporting writing in different genres, too—narrative, poetry, journals, and the nonfiction genres of persuasion, description, and explanation. Finally, we will present ways of teaching students to use writing in order to learn in the disciplines.

Spelling Development and Assessment

Children can and should be taught to spell correctly. But in the beginning, children do not need to be able to spell in order to communicate on paper. Many teachers of preschool and kindergarten children encourage their students to organize and communicate their ideas by making scribbles and drawing on paper. Over time, children gradually add both learned and invented spellings to their graphic productions.

Stages of Spelling Development

One of the most fascinating discoveries of the past century in the literacy field has been about children's ability to recognize the ways in which letters represent sounds in print and their inclination to experiment with their own spellings. The discovery of **invented spelling** followed naturally from what was learned about the ways children learn spoken language: Children see people around them communicating in some medium (in this case, print); decide to try out their own versions of that communication; organize their versions according to rules or patterns that are logical, though incorrect by adult standards; and gradually, bit by bit or phase by phase, modify their strategies so that they grow closer and closer to the versions they hear and see adults using.

Sure enough, children appear to go through phases as they experiment with invented spellings for words (Bear et al., 2007; Gentry, 1989; Schlagal, 1989; Temple et al., 2012). Progress through the phases depends on three things: children's own developing concepts of how the English spelling system works (what we call their word knowledge), the levels of challenge that system presents to them as they move through the grades, and, of course, what and how they are taught. How do we describe children's spelling development? Different writers label the phases differently. The labels we will use here are from Temple, Nathan, and Temple (2012) and they were inspired by the work of Henderson (1990), Gentry (1989), Schlagal (1989), and Ganske (2003). The phases we will use in this book are the *prephonemic phase*, the *early phonemic phase*, the *letter name phase*, the *orthographic phase*, the *morphological phase*, and the *derivational phase.* To correlate our phases of spelling development with other writers' phases, see Table 11.1.

Table 11.1 Comparing Descriptions of Spelling Development

	All Children Read	Schlagal, 1989[1]; Bear et al., *Words Their Way*[2]; Ganske, *Word Journeys*[3]
Mid kindergarten	Prephonemic	Emergent
End of kindergarten	Early Phonemic	
Mid first grade	Letter Name	Letter Name
End of second grade	Orthographic	Within-Word Pattern
Late second grade through fourth grade	Morphological	Syllable Juncture
Early fourth grade through adulthood	Derivational	Derivational Constancy

Learning a system of spelling phases is worthwhile for teachers, because looking developmentally at children's progress through phases of invented spelling reveals a great deal about children's knowledge of words; this is important to understand in order to help them learn to read (Hauerwas & Walker, 2004).

The Prephonemic Phase of Spelling

When children first begin to write, they often fill entire pages with a lot of unconnected letters (see Figure 11.2).

Although what the child has written has no meaning, he or she has demonstrated the **prephonemic phase of spelling**. It is a kind of writing that uses letters without regard to their sounds. In this phase, children write down letters at random or possibly with some early notion of how they might represent ideas.

Children at the prephonemic phase of spelling know how to make many letters (and often many more pseudo-letters). They know what writing looks like, and they might know how it is arrayed on the page. But children at this phase have not yet discovered the **alphabetic principle**: the understanding that spelling represents words by relating written letters to spoken phonemes. If this is the case, then much reading instruction in which children are expected to learn to recognize words by being exposed to them will not be effective yet. Neither will phonics instruction that focuses on learning particular letters and sounds, which requires an understanding of the fundamental idea that words are real, they consist of phonemes, and those phonemes are represented by letters.

The Early Phonemic Phase of Spelling

Figure 11.3 represents the work of a child in the early phonemic phase of spelling.

This child has used letters to represent some of the sounds in words but not all of them. That is why we call this the **early phonemic phase of spelling**: The child is just beginning to represent words by their phonemes. Children at this phase typically represent only the first and last and possibly a middle consonant in the word. They usually leave out vowels unless the whole word is a vowel, such as *A*. Children who spell in the early phonemic phase sometimes spell the first sound in a word with a sensible choice of a letter, then add random letters to make the word longer and hence make it look like a word (Ferreiro & Teberosky, 1982). But note carefully what we mean by a sensible choice. When children do use letters to represent sounds, rather than to use letters for sounds in conventional ways, they spell intuitively, matching as best they can a letter with a letter name that sounds closest to the sound they want to spell. Thus, for example, they are likely to choose the letter *H* to spell /*ch*/, and the letter *Y* to spell /*w*/.

If children are spelling in the early phonemic phase, we know that they have discovered the alphabetic principle. They are not yet very proficient, however, at breaking words into phonemes and matching them with letter sounds. Matching

---

Figure 11.2 Prephonemic Spelling

SOURCE: Temple, C., Nathan, R., Burris, N., & Temple, F. (1993). *The beginnings of writing* (3rd ed.). Boston, MA: Allyn & Bacon.

Figure 11.3 Early Phonemic Spelling

SOURCE: Temple, C., Nathan, R., Burris, N., & Temple, F. (1993). *The beginnings of writing* (3rd ed.). Boston, MA: Allyn & Bacon.

Teach It! 12

Phonemic Segmentation with Elkonin Boxes

For children in the early phonemic phase of spelling, this instructional activity is particularly effective: It engages learners kinesthetically and provides a visual to help them segment phonemes.

---

letters to sounds contains at least four operations: (1) making the word hold still in the mind, (2) breaking it down into phonemes, (3) matching each phoneme with a letter, and (4) writing down that letter. All of these steps may be difficult for a beginner.

Determining the number of sounds children can represent in their spelling yields important diagnostic information. Bear in mind Ehri's hypothesis that a child's memory for storing images of written words for later recognition consists of a number of "slots" (Ehri, 1991, 1997a). A child with more memory storage "slots" for word recognition will store a more complete memory of that word and will recognize it more accurately when she sees it written down.

Examining a child's invented spelling can yield clues to his or her ability to segment words into phonemes. A child who writes *HK* for *truck* (that is, the early phonemic speller) shows a limited ability to segment phonemes in words. When it comes to recognizing words in print, that child will try to say the word on the basis of very shallow processing, typically looking at the first letter and calling out a word he or she knows that begins with that letter. Because the child does not yet focus on all of the letters and phonemes in the word (Morris, et. al., 2000), he or she can easily confuse the words being read with other words that share one or two of the same letters.

The Letter Name Phase of Spelling

At a slightly more advanced phase, a child offers spelling like that in Figure 11.4.

This child is in the **letter name phase of spelling**. Here, Iuliu represented all or nearly all of the phonemes in a word, but he did so intuitively. He made logical judgments when he chose a letter to represent a sound, but that logic still diverged quite a bit from the conventions of English spelling. For instance, Iuliu wrote *H* for the /č/ or "ch" sound in *Charlie* and *much*, probably because the letter name "aitch" contains that sound.

Children use names of the letters of the alphabet as if they were building blocks of sound out of which words could be constructed. In the case of some sounds, the letter name strategy results in spellings that look conventional; in others, the spellings can look bizarre. Especially in these cases, examining children's letter name spellings gives us a window into the ways children think about words and also into the eccentricities of the English spelling system.

- *Spelling most consonants.* As the sample in Figure 11.4 demonstrates, many consonant letters are spelled intuitively in ways that look conventional. Note the spellings of *L* in *Charlie*, the *S* in *so*, and the *M* in *much*. The names of these letters are close enough to their corresponding phonemes to make the letter name strategy successful or nearly successful.

- *Spelling nonintuitive consonants.* Young children often spell the sound of /w/ as in *went* with the letter *Y*. In such cases, they choose the *Y* for the sound of its name. After all, the letter name for *W* ("double U") doesn't sound at all like /w/, but the name of *Y* ("wye") is a good fit, so this choice of *Y* for the /w/ sound is not surprising for the child who is using the letter name strategy.

- *Spelling digraph consonants.* Young spellers are troubled by the spellings of digraphs, since they do not know about the conventions for spelling them. Note the invented spelling of the *CH* digraph in spelling the /č/ sound in *HOLE*

Figure 11.4 Letter Name Spelling

"Charlie, I like you so much."

(Charlie) and *MOH (much)*. In both cases, the letter *H* was chosen because the name of that letter sounds closest to the phoneme that is usually spelled by *CH*. The letter *H* is often used by children in the letter name phase of learning to spell the sounds of /š/ *("sh")* and /č/ *("ch")*.

- *Spelling **Ns** and **Ms** before stop consonants.* In spellings like *YUTS* for *once* and *AD* for *and*, letter name spellers often leave out *Ns* and *Ms* when they come before other consonants, especially before what are called *stop consonants* (so called because they briefly stop the flow of air through the mouth) such as /p/, /b/, /t/, /d/, and /k/. The problem is not that children don't know how to spell the /n/ and /m/ sounds. It is rather that they are used to feeling the consonants produced in the mouth as they sound out the word in order to spell it (Read, 1975). When *Ns* and *Ms* are pronounced before stop consonants, you cannot feel them in your mouth, because your tongue goes to the same position to form the stop consonant anyway. Say the words *wet* and *went* aloud, and you will see what we mean: The activity of the tongue in the mouth is the same in both cases. What is different when *N* or *M* is present is that the whole syllable is pronounced through the nose. The omission of *N* and *M* in this position is prevalent in the spellings of kindergarten and first-grade children and in older children who are advancing slowly as spellers.

- *Spelling word-final **R, L, M,** and **N**: "syllabic sonorants."* Spellings such as *FLEPR* for *Flipper* shows another common feature of children's letter name spelling. Unstressed syllables ending in *R, L, M,* and *N* often lack vowels when they appear at the ends of words. Thus it is common to see *TABL* for *table*, *LEDL* for *little*, and *BIDM* for *bottom* in the writing of children in the letter name phase of spelling. English has a convention that all syllables must be spelled with vowels. Even though children in the letter name phase represent most vowels, they leave them out of these words, presumably because they expect every letter they write into a word to be clearly sounded, but in these syllables, no distinct vowel sound is heard (Read, 1975).

- *Spelling long vowels.* As Iuliu's spelling of *U* for *you* in Figure 11.4 demonstrated, long vowels in words usually "say their names"; that is, the sound to be spelled sounds much like the name of the letter we would use to spell that sound.

- *Spelling short vowels.* Spelling short vowels presents problems to letter name spellers. Short vowels do not sound very much like the "long" vowels spelled by the same letter. There are no vowel letter names that have short vowel sounds, so the speller must choose the letter name that is the best fit with that short vowel. This in practice is the long vowel sound that sounds the most like, or is produced in the mouth in the manner most like, that short vowel sound. This principle explains the spelling of *O* for the short vowel /uh/ in *much*. It also explains why children write *A* for /ĕ/ in *bet* and *E* for /1/ *("ih")* in *bit*.

Children who are letter name spellers represent nearly all of the phonemes (the smaller speech sounds) in words. But they represent those speech sounds intuitively, using a letter name strategy, rather than conventionally, using the kinds of spellings for sounds that are seen in books. Letter name spellers' ability to segment words into all of their phonemes gives them many corresponding "slots" in word memory storage for the parts of the words they see in print. Letter name spellers are usually beginning readers who are making progress acquiring sight words.

Letter name spellers have a means at their disposal to write many words, and children enjoy this freedom to create. Their spelling ability is still limited, of course. Because they spell words by relating letters to their individual sounds, they are not yet taking advantage of onsets and rimes and phonogram patterns. Nor are letter name spellers yet aware of the conventions for marking vowels "long" or "short."

Research shows that the practice of invented spelling is good for kindergarten and first-grade children. Children who are encouraged to invent spellings learn to recognize more words than children who do not use invented spelling. But children should not persist in letter name spelling much beyond the end of first grade. To help them make progress, teachers need to be careful to remind children that invented spelling is "temporary spelling"; it is the way that they can write some words before they learn the way words are spelled in books. Teachers also need to be careful to give students correctly spelled material to read and to take opportunities to call children's attention to standard spelling patterns in print.

The Orthographic Phase of Spelling

Children in the **orthographic phase of spelling** are beginning readers who are becoming aware of conventional spellings for sounds. They are learning phonogram patterns (onsets and rimes) and are trying to master the marking systems for long and short vowels, although not always correctly, as seen in Figure 11.5.

Orthographic spellers may be keen observers of the English spelling system, and the difficulties they face in spelling correctly often reflect the eccentricities of the system. For example, orthographic spellers may write *LUV* and *ABUV*. The correct spellings, *love* and *above*, thwart their expectations.

Figure 11.5 Spelling in the Orthographic State

SOURCE: Temple, C., Nathan, R., Burris, N., & Temple, F. (1993). *The beginnings of writing* (3rd ed.). Boston, MA: Allyn & Bacon.

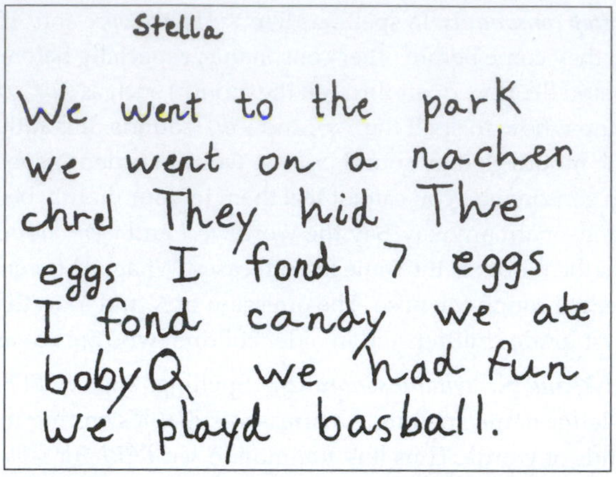

> Stella
>
> We went to the park
> we went on a nacher
> chrel They hid The
> eggs I fond 7 eggs
> I fond candy we ate
> boby Q we had fun
> We playd basball.

Children who spell in the orthographic phase show us that they have learned many things about the way the English writing system works, and this knowledge can help them both in writing and in reading. These children show a grasp of common onsets and rimes in their writing, indicating that they should be able to use knowledge of these patterns to read unfamiliar words. Children who are aware of onsets and rimes can use the strategy of reading by analogy. For example, if they encounter the unknown word *sill*, they can recognize its similarity to the known word *pill* and will read *sill* by mentally taking away the /p/ sound and substituting the /s/ sound in front of the -*ill* rime. Such reading by analogy leads to more rapid and accurate deciphering of words than does puzzling out words letter by letter.

Spelling in the orthographic phase presents challenges that many students never move beyond. A student who has learned to spell *gate*, for example, might still be unsure how to spell *great, bait, straight,* or *eight*. It will take a habit of studying words carefully plus an act of memory to master these challenges. Both are encouraged by good teaching.

The Morphological Phase of Spelling

Children in the **morphological phase of spelling** are able to spell in stable and correct ways grammatical endings and prefixes and suffixes—items that linguists call *bound morphemes*. Also, with regard to suffixes, the speller is able to consistently spell some inflectional word endings such as -*s* or -*ed* that have alternate pronunciations, depending on the sounds in the syllable to which they are attached. (Compare, for instance, the pronunciation of -*s* in *wants* and *slows*, and the pronunciation of -*ed* in *wanted, slowed,* and *hiked*.)

Spellers in this phase have learned the common patterns of spelling such as the phonogram patterns and the rules for marking vowels long or short. But the spelling system of English reflects more than sounds. There are grammatical endings and prefixes and suffixes that must be spelled in certain ways, even when they may be pronounced differently from one word to another. Also, when grammatical endings and prefixes and suffixes are attached to other words, they often have the effect of marking a vowel long or short in the root word, which is another complication for a learner to take into account.

The child who wrote the piece in Figure 11.6 shows some of the difficulties posed by the morphological phase. Note his spelling of *chewed*. Note also, the effect of his South Texas accent on his spelling!

The Derivational Phase of Spelling

Moving still further away from the expectation that letters simply spell sounds, learners encounter the **derivational phase of spelling**, in which spellings must honor the origins of words and their relationships to other words. Some words are derived from other "living" words, and others are derived from common ancient sources (hence the name "derivational"). Many words that are found from fourth grade up, such as *photograph, sign, doubt,* and *bomb* don't have a very obvious connection between letters and sounds because their letters relate not so much to sounds as to word histories—or to other words from which they are derived.

Figure 11.6 The Struggles of the Morphological Phase

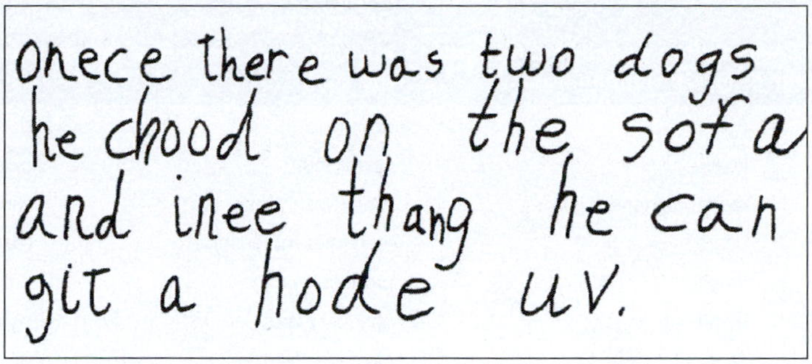

When children reach the most advanced phase of word knowledge, they can recognize meaningful chunks of words called *morphemes*, and use them not just for spelling and reading but also as a clue to word meanings. In the derivational phase of word knowledge, children think of words in family relationships, and use their awareness of these relationships to write and read words.

For example, recognizing the relation between *photograph* and *photography* helps a student spell the reduced vowels in both words, because the reduced and unrecognizable second *O* in *photograph* is stressed and identifiable in *photography*. Likewise the *A* in the next to last syllable of *photography* is stressed and recognizable in *photograph*. But beyond the help with spelling, recognizing the morpheme *photo* and associating it with the meaning "light" helps unpack words like *photosynthesis*, "coming together with light."

Some words defy simple spelling-to-sound relationships because of spelling changes that happened over the centuries. For example, many words from Anglo-Saxon with *O* before following consonants pronounce that vowel as a short *U*: *brother, mother, son, love, cover*. It turns out the letter *O* was written in for the original letter *U* in many of those words by scribes in the tenth and eleventh centuries, to make them easier to read when they appeared in the Gothic script (Scragg, 1974). Medieval scribes also gave us the *B* in *doubt* (originally it was spelled without the *B*) to make the word resemble the related Latin word *dubere*. Children are unlikely to discover these things, but it will certainly help if their teachers know them and talk about them.

There are words that sound the same like *deer* and *dear*, *bare* and *bear*, and *waist* and *waste*, but have different meanings. They are called **homophones** (from *homo-*, meaning "the same," and *phone*, meaning "sound"). There are other words that have the same spellings but have different meanings, like *lead* ("I will lead you to your table") and *lead* ("I put a lead weight on the line"). They are called **homographs**. Sometimes homographs are pronounced the same, but still have different meanings, as in "sock someone in the arm" and "put on a sock." Several homophones and homographs are shown in Table 11.2.

Homophones can be funny. Fred Gwynne's *The King Who Rained* and Peggy Parish's *Amelia Bedelia* still delight readers after many decades. Their humor hinges on homophones.

English contains many "loan words" from different languages, and most of them are pronounced according to the rules of the original languages: *taco, filet, wiener, fuselage, macho, chassis, chic*, and *wiki*.

Assessing Spelling Knowledge

Children's knowledge of spelling develops in two ways. One way is the level of words they can spell. For instance, we would expect a second-grade child to be able to spell *train, queer*, and *float*, but not *conceive* or *profitable*, while a sixth grader

Teach It! 67

Word Origins and Derivations

For learners in the derivational phase of spelling, this activity supports advancing word knowledge through an examination of morphemes, affixes, spelling patterns, histories, and "family" relationships among words.

Table 11.2 Homophones and Homographs

HOMOPHONES. These are words that are spelled differently, pronounced the same, and have different meanings.		HOMOGRAPHS. These are words that are spelled the same, but have different meanings. Some homographs are not pronounced the same.	
too	two	dove (bird)	dove (from "dive")
new	knew	close (shut)	close (nearby)
red	read (past tense)	wind (twist)	wind (breeze)
deer	dear	read (present tense)	read (past tense)
there	they're	produce (verb)	produce (noun)
him	hymn	conduct (verb)	conduct (noun)
cent	sent	discharge (verb)	discharge (noun)
reel	real	relay (verb)	relay (noun)
Some homophones are phrases.		**Some homographs are spelled the same and pronounced the same. They still have different meanings.**	
I scream.	ice cream	show (verb)	show (noun)
depend	deep end	shift (move)	shift (work period)
will he	Willy	sock (verb)	sock (noun)
		bank (for money)	bank (of a river)

should be able to spell the harder words. Another way children's spelling ability develops is that they work their way through stages of spelling knowledge, and each stage is a way of thinking about the ways written words are structured.

USING WORDS FROM SPELLING TEXTBOOKS   Commercial spelling and language arts programs normally provide lists of words children are expected to learn every week. Those lists are arranged at difficulty levels according to their grades. Publishers use various means to level words, including surveys of children's writing and studies of the vocabularies of textbooks and trade books.

If you are using a spelling series, or if you are teaching grade-level-based spelling lists every week, it is important to find children's instructional level in spelling. The range of spelling abilities of a typical classroom of children is very wide. If students in a typical classroom were asked to spell words they had not yet been taught, their scores might range from less than 10% to more than 90% (Morris, Nelson, & Perney, 1986). But if the lowest scoring spellers were taught words at their instructional level of spelling instead of words at their grade-placement level, teachers might be able to fill in the foundational spelling concepts the students are missing and that they need for further learning; in the long run, these students would actually make more progress toward learning to spell the harder words. This was exactly what Darrell Morris and his colleagues (Morris et al., 1995) found in an experimental study.

The instructional level of spelling is found by testing children on spelling words they have not been taught and finding the grade level of words where the children score from 50% to 75% (Henderson, 1990). To assess children's spelling ability for grade-level placement, construct a spelling inventory, consisting of 20 randomly chosen words from each grade level in grades 1 through 6 of the spelling program. (These lists are usually found as an appendix in the teacher's guide.) You can test a whole class by beginning with the words one year below grade level and calling out the words as the children spell them. Then call out the correct spellings, or display them on an overhead transparency, and have the children mark their own errors. Call out words from higher-level lists and have the children continue to spell words until they misspell 50% of the words. Children who score 50% spelling errors can stop. After you look over their papers, you can go back and privately ask some children to spell words from easier lists if they did not reach the instructional level on the first list you called.

ASSESSING SPELLING QUALITATIVELY   Students work their way through stages of spelling development that reflect how they think about the structure of words. Those stages are described in Table 11.3. The student's spelling level suggests ways that she or he can be taught to spell.

To assess a child's level of developmental spelling, you can administer a list of words that are arranged to elicit invented spellings at different levels. A typical list of such words is found in Figure 11.7.

Developmental spelling inventories with full explanations are available in *Words Their Way* (Bear et al., 2007), *Word Journeys* (Ganske, 2003), and *The Developmental Literacy Inventory* (Temple, Crawford, & Gillet, 2009). As all of these

Table 11.3 Stages of Invented Spelling

Stage	Also Known As	Examples	Typical Age
Prephonetic	Preliterate	bumpy = R4TSX	Preschool and kindergarten
Early phonemic	Early phonetic	bumpy = BP	Kindergarten and early first grade
Letter-name	Phonetic	bumpy = BOPE	Early to mid-first grade
Common patterns	Transitional, within-word pattern	bumpy = BUPPY	Late first to mid-second grade
Syllable juncture		batted = BATID	Mid-second grade through third grade
Derivational constancy	Conventional	photograph = FOTOGRAF	Fourth grade and above

SOURCE: Bear, Invernizzi, Templeton, and Johnston (2000); Gentry (1981); Henderson (1990); Schlagal (1989); Temple, Nathan, Burris, and Temple (1993).

Figure 11.7 Words to Elicit Different Levels of Invented Spelling

SOURCE: Temple, Crawford, and Gillet, *Developmental Literacy Inventory: Reading and Spelling from Emergent to Mature Levels.*
© 2009. Reprinted by Permission of Pearson Education, Inc.

1. lit	6. peeked	11. spacious	16. physician
2. chap	7. sailed	12. design	17. biographical
3. rock	8. shove	13. brilliance	18. sympathetic
4. truck	9. sitter	14. traction	19. adjournment
5. lend	10. batted	15. doubting	20. collegial

publications make clear, improving children's spelling knowledge enhances their word knowledge, especially if they are taught to use what they learn in the context of writing and reading.

Check Your Understanding 11.1: Gauge your understanding of the skills and concepts in this section.

Teaching Children to Spell

Spelling instruction should address three goals:

1. "survival words"— students should be taught the correct spellings of words they use often in their writing

2. students should be taught words that contain features they are trying to master

3. students should be taught ways to generalize from spelling words students know to spelling new words

Teaching frequently used words is done a couple of ways. One is by using Word Walls, in which words that students use regularly in their writing are copied onto index cards and arranged either alphabetically or in semantic groups on the wall. Words chosen for Word Walls should be those that many children use, but struggle to spell correctly. They may be high-frequency words, but they may also be words related to units children are studying and writing about in science, social studies, and other subjects. (See the discussion of Word Walls in Chapter 5.)

Another way to teach frequently used words is to keep a log of commonly used words that individual children struggle to spell. These words are recorded in the student's own *spelling dictionary*, which is made from a small spiral-bound notebook, with pages labeled with alphabetical headings.

A third way to teach frequently used words is to collect them and add them to students' weekly spelling lists. Many commercial spelling programs set aside four or five locally chosen words for the students to learn. Students may nominate words themselves, or you may choose them based on your observations of their needs.

Teaching words that contain features children are trying to master is the basis for most current commercial spelling programs. There is an economy in teaching children words that share not only the same phonogram patterns, such as *pitch, stitch, hitch,* and *itch,* but also the same spelling features, such as the *-tch* consonant cluster in the previous words and also in *latch, match, crutch, Dutch, Scotch,* and *botch;* as well as the *-dge* consonant cluster in *badge, ridge, budge,* and *hedge.* Of course, there are many other such features. Basal spelling programs teach groups of such words, and so do guides to teaching spelling and word knowledge such as Bear, et. al.'s *Words Their Way* and Ganske's *Word Journeys.*

The need to teach correct spelling should be taken seriously. It is true that children can invent spellings for most words they write. And inventing spellings form an important part of children's learning about the way words are written and read (see Temple et al., 2013). But inventing spellings for words takes considerable effort. As Steve Graham and Karen Harris (2005) have demonstrated, not having many spellings available in memory is a handicap that impedes students' fluency in writing. Teachers should teach students to spell correctly. It's an important part of teaching them to write.

Learning to spell is more than accumulating words. Students learn concepts about English spelling or *orthography* and advance through stages, or layers of strategies, as they learn to spell words. But students also learn to spell more and more sophisticated words as they go through the grades, and words can be classified according to the grade level at which they are first found in appreciable numbers.

Common Approaches to Teaching Children to Spell

There are some techniques for teaching spelling that every teacher should have in her or his "toolbox." They include the test-retest method; the multisensory method; the method of grouping words by spelling patterns; teaching six different syllable types; and teaching morphemes, or meaningful units of words.

USE THE DIFFERENTIATED TEST-RETEST METHOD Depending on the grade level, choose 10 to 20 words per week for students to learn. If you assign students to groups by spelling level, you can call out words for students in Group A, B, and C to spell, or you can test the groups at different times. In either case, call out the words on Monday, then pass out lists of words and have students correct their work. They should study the words they did not spell correctly, using the multisensory procedure described in the next section. Test the students on the words again on Wednesday, and if they miss more than one word out of five, test them again on Friday.

USE THE MULTISENSORY STUDY METHOD For the words that students need to learn, it helps if they use a multisensory approach for studying new words. Multisensory teaching engages more senses as the name implies, having students look, read, say, and touch as they study. To use the multisensory method, instruct the students to:

1. Look at the correctly spelled word. Say the word aloud.
2. Name the letters one at a time, touching each letter with a pencil eraser as you name it.
3. Cover the correctly written word and write it on another piece of paper.
4. Uncover the word and check your spelling.
5. Repeat these steps as necessary.

LEARN WORDS BY SPELLING PATTERNS Monosyllable English words are made up of *onsets* and *rimes.* The *onset* is the consonant (or consonant blend or consonant digraph) that comes at the beginning of the word, and the *rime* (that is the correct spelling) is the vowel and what may come after it. Rimes are sometimes called *phonogram patterns,* and examples are *-at (fat, sat, hat)* and *-ick (sick, pick, tick).*

When students are learning words, call their attention to any words that share patterns with other words. Play word sort games and construct word walls with groups of words that share phonogram patterns. Record them in a notebook, one pattern per page; and encourage students to add new words to each group as they encounter them.

TEACH SYLLABLE TYPES Besides teaching onsets and rimes, it will help to teach students about the six types of syllables in English words (Blachman & Tangel, 2008; Moats, 2009). Learning syllable types is especially helpful when spelling words containing more than one syllable. The types are:

- *Closed syllables.* Closed syllables are found in single-syllable words like *cat* and *dog.* Sometimes a consonant cluster may close the syllable, at in *pick, bridge* and *patch.* In words of more than one syllable such as *better* and *summer,* the middle consonant is doubled to keep the vowel in the second syllable from lengthening the vowel in the first syllable (*sumer* would be pronounced "soomer" and *beter* would be pronounced "beater").

- *Syllables with vowel + consonant + silent e.* A common way of marking a vowel long is to have a vowel followed by a consonant followed by a silent *e,* as in *cake, Pete, bike, spoke,* and *duke.* A *y* or *i* functions like a silent *e* in words of more than one syllable, as in *lazy*, *spiky*, *poky*, and *Lucy*. As we noted above, spellers have to be careful to double the middle consonant when they add endings with *e, i,* or *y* to closed syllables to prevent those endings from lengthening the preceding vowel.

- *Open syllables.* We know that some single-syllable words like *so, hi,* and *my* have long vowel pronunciations. These are called *open syllables.* Open syllables are important to notice when they occur in words with more than one syllable, such as *table, ladle, motor,* and *rival.* The vowel is long even though a syllable beginning with a consonant follows it.

- *Syllables with vowel teams.* English has an abundance of words with vowel teams, and the pronunciations of the teams can vary a lot. The old standby rule, "When two vowels go walking, the first one does the talking" applies to many words with vowel teams, like *team, soak,* and *bait.* But it fails with words like *thief, bread,* and *broad*; and is of no help in *caught* and *tough.* When vowel team spellings generalize to many words, they are worth studying in groups with word sorts and word walls. The rare ones must be learned as exceptions.

- *Syllables with R-controlled vowels.* The vowel sounds in words like *word, car, warm, purr,* and *perfect* is neither long nor short. These vowel sounds are called *R-controlled,* and should be learned as separate patterns. Note that vowels that follow *w* have unusual pronunciations, too: as in *wad* and *swamp.* Their spelling must be learned a special cases.

- *Syllables with a consonant + le.* A syllable with a consonant + *le* has the effect of marking the vowel long in a preceding open syllable, as it does in *idle* and *stable.* If it follows a closed syllable, it acts like a double consonant and preserves the short sound of the preceding vowel, as in *dribble, stubble,* and *fiddle.*

TEACH MORPHEMES   As we noted in the chapter on linguistics, morphemes are meaningful units of words. They may be *free morphemes* like *run,* or *inflectional morphemes* like the *s* on *runs* (it tells you the number of the subject of the verb *run* or that the noun *runs,* as in baseball, is more than one). They may also be *derivational morphemes* like the *y* in *runny,* which turn one word into another and change its grammatical function, too.

Beginning spellers sometimes have trouble spelling inflectional morphemes, because their spelling stays the same even though their pronunciation changes. For example, the plural marker S keeps the same spelling even though the letter S has different pronunciations in *dogs* and *hats*; and the past tense marker –ED has three different pronunciations in *slowed, hiked,* and *wanted,* but only one spelling.

But derivational morphemes present greater challenges, especially from about third grade on, when over half of the words in the English language turn out to be derived from other words (Stahl & Nagy, 2006). The effects of morphemes like *dis-, un-, inter-, mono-,* and many others are more important to vocabulary than to spelling. Morphemes like the varieties of *in-* and *com-* do create spelling issues, though, when they are *assimilated* to the consonants that follow them. (*Assimilated* means change their form to match.) Let us explain. *In-* from Latin means "into" or "not." Before a word that starts with M or P, though, it turns into *im-,* as in *important* and *immature.* Before a word that begins with R, it turns into *ir-,* as in *irreversible.* And before a word that starts with L, it turns into *il-,* as in *illegal* or *illegible.* Better informed spellers know to look for the presence of *in-* in the meaning of a word as a clue to whether the consonant N, M, R, or L will be doubled. Spellers must be careful with the similar sounding prefix *e-* meaning "away" or "out of." So *immigration* doubles the M because it has *im-* + *migration.* But *emigration* does not double the M because it is made up of *e-* + *migration.*

Com-, from Latin meaning "with" or "together," behaves much the same way, as in *commit, connect, collect,* or *correct.* *Ad-,* from the Latin meaning "to" or "toward," also assimilates differently when following L, C, or S, as in *allow, accord,* and *assert.* Be mindful that another Latin prefix, *ab-,* means "from," "away from," or "by," so *abuse* does not double the first consonant. The Greek prefix *a-* means "not," so when it is attached to *pathetic* in *apathetic* the P does not double. The best advice is to keep a good dictionary in the classroom, one with etymologies or word histories, and take the time to look up words with the students. If you cultivate their curiosity about words and their histories, students are likely to become better spellers.

Check Your Understanding 11.2: **Gauge your understanding of the skills and concepts in this section.**

A Writing Process in Five Parts

A model of the writing process was put forward over 30 years ago by Pulitzer Prize–winning journalist and writing teacher Donald Murray (1985) and language arts specialist and researcher Donald Graves (1982). That model is now used widely both within schools and in other areas to describe what people do when they write, and also to guide teachers of writing. According to their writing process model, thoughtful writers may go through five steps or phases as they produce their works: rehearsing, drafting, revising, editing, and publishing.

Rehearsing

The process of rehearsing entails preparing to write by gathering information and collecting one's thoughts. Student writers think of what they might like to write about, they survey what they know about the topic, and they begin to plan a way to write about it. Several strategies are available that can teach students to rehearse their ideas before writing:

- *Brainstorming and clustering.* Children can jot down in list form their ideas about a topic before embarking on writing about it. As a more elaborate version of the brainstorm, they create a graphic organizer, such as a cluster or semantic web, with the topic listed in the center connected to "satellites" around it (see Figure 11.8).

- *Interviewing each other to find the story.* Students can interview a partner. Regardless of whether a writer has already prepared a cluster, it often helps if another student asks questions about the topic to help him or her "find the story." The student asks questions such as the following:
  "Why did you choose this topic?"
  "What most interests you about the topic?"

  The student also asks questions about details, things the writer might not realize other people will want to know.

- *Making class collaborations.* When introducing a new kind of writing, such as a poem or a fairy tale, it might be best to ask the students to compose one work together before writing on their own. This is especially helpful for younger students. The teacher can contribute as well to help steer the work in positive directions. If the students have difficulty beginning, offer them a series of choices:
  Where does the story take place? In a big city or a small village?
  Who should be the main character? A young girl or an old magician?
  A young girl? Okay. Then who can describe her? And what is her problem?

- *Researching the topic.* Students are often able to write stories or papers about personal experiences off the tops of their heads, but when they are writing about the real world beyond themselves, they will soon run

---

Figure 11.8 A Cluster

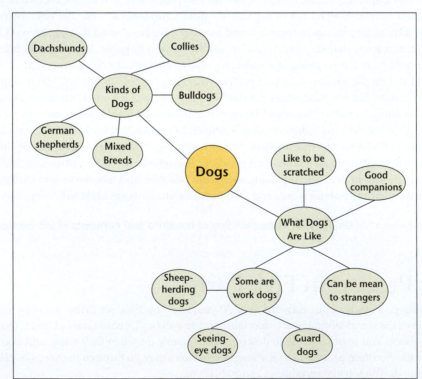

out of things to say unless they collect information about their topic. They might need to read up on it or interview experts about it, or they might observe carefully and collect details about it. Lucy Calkins and her colleagues in the New York City Writing Project (1994) suggest having students keep notebooks for gathering observations.

Drafting

Drafting involves setting ideas out on paper. Drafting is tentative and experimental. Students write down their ideas so that they can see more of what they have to say about their topic; often their best ideas do not occur to them until they begin committing thoughts to paper. The phase of drafting is not the time to be critical about spelling and handwriting. Such mechanical concerns are better dealt with later; this is the time for students to focus on getting their ideas onto the page.

Young writers are not in the habit of writing more than one version of a paper. Proficient writers, however, know that good writing is rewriting. Teachers can encourage students to think of writing as drafting in a number of ways:

- Stamp the papers DRAFT or have students write their drafts on the blank backs of recycled office paper. Both measures make it clear to everyone that these versions of papers are not final.

- Have the students write on every other line. This leaves room for them to add material they think of later on.

- Show students how to use arrows, carets (^), and stapled-on sections to indicate on a draft how it should be rewritten. Unless they are shown, students will not know how to physically mark up and modify a draft and use it to plan the next version of the paper.

- Remind students not to worry too much about spelling, handwriting, and mechanics at the drafting stage. A large advantage to writing more than one draft of a paper is that it frees writers to concentrate on their ideas at first and then worry about form and correctness later. This should be explained to students at the start, and the treatment of their early and later drafts should be consistent with it. Be careful, however, that you do not encourage students to be messy. Bromley (1999) advises against calling an early draft of a paper a "sloppy copy."

Revising

After their thoughts have been written out in draft form, students need to think about stating their ideas more clearly. Most students need to be shown ways that writing can be improved: by having clear beginnings, middles, and ends; by finding a topic and sticking to it; by showing and not telling; and other techniques. Teachers can teach these points through focused lessons (discussed later) and help young writers internalize them by means of conferences. Teachers use two main kinds of conferences in teaching writing.

TEACHER-LED CONFERENCES   Conferences allow the teacher to assist students in clarifying their writing and also to model ways to ask helpful questions that will encourage other struggling writers—their peers. The teacher needs to ask questions that teach, pulling solutions from the students themselves and always respecting the students' ownership of their writing. The teacher asks students questions to help them focus on areas to improve their writing, and provides checklists of things to watch out for.

PEER CONFERENCES   Once the teacher has modeled the process, students can hold conferences with each other. Because many conferences will be going on in the room at one time, it helps if students understand their tasks clearly. The teacher can put together a checklist of good questions to ask as the students review their works-in-progress with each other, such as the following:

- Did my opening lines interest you? How might I improve the beginning?
- Do I need more information anywhere? That is, where could I be more specific?
- Do you ever get lost while reading my draft?
- Do I stay on topic?
- Do I come to a good conclusion?

Editing or Proofreading

Once a paper has been drafted and revised, it needs to be reviewed for mistakes. Naturally, proofreading is held off until the last version because whole paragraphs might be cut or added in the revising stage. The habit of proofreading must be taught. It consists of three things:

- Caring that the paper is correct
- Being aware of particular errors
- Knowing how to set those errors straight

A caring attitude toward writing is probably best developed by publishing what students write. Students are most likely to care about correctness once they realize that writing is not simply done for a grade, but that their works must pass the scrutiny of others, who will be distracted from their ideas if the papers are marred by flaws in spelling, grammar, and handwriting.

Children should be made aware of errors through focused lessons that demonstrate one or two errors of writing at a time. Focused lessons treat errors that one or more students are actually making in their writing. Areas in which children make errors might include the following:

- Beginning each sentence with a capital letter and ending it with terminal punctuation (a period, a question mark, or an exclamation point)
- Making each sentence express a complete thought, avoiding sentence fragments and run-on sentences
- Spelling correctly

After clearly teaching students to be aware of different kinds of errors and how to repair them, the next step is to get the students to proofread their own work. Give them a checklist to guide their proofreading, such as the one shown in Figure 11.9. Each point on the checklist should be carefully introduced, explained, and practiced before students are sent off to use it on their own. Several versions of the checklist might be introduced during the year as new points for correction are added to the students' repertoires. Once the checklist has been introduced, students should practice using it with a partner to go over each other's papers before they are ready to use the checklists by themselves.

Figure 11.9 A Proofreading Checklist

1. Did I begin each sentence with a capital letter?

2. Did I use capital letters for other words that need them?
   --Names of persons or places
   --Names of days of the week, months, and holidays
   --Titles of books, TV shows, movies, or songs
   --Names of bands, brands, sports teams, and businesses
   --People's titles (Mr. Juarez, Mrs. Jones, President Lincoln)

2. Did I end each sentence with the right punctuation?
   --a period (.) if the sentence makes a statement
   --a question mark (?) if the sentence asks a question
   --an exclamation point (!) if the sentence sounds excited or angry
   --quotation marks (" ") if the sentence shows someone talking

3. Did I use apostrophes (') correctly?
   --plurals (more than one) *don't* need apostrophes
   --possessives (show someone owns something) *do* need apostrophes

4. Does every sentence express a complete thought?

5. Did I keep from joining two sentences with a comma?

6. Did I indent for each new paragraph?

7. Did I check the spelling of words I was unsure of?

Publishing

Publishing is the final stage of the writing process, and it actually drives the whole endeavor. The prospect of sharing what they have to say with an audience makes many students want to write, rewrite, and smooth out and refine, especially if they have seen other students' work received with appreciation and delight. Publishing also lets students see what others are doing. A good idea is contagious; and anything from an interesting topic to a plot structure, to a way to use dialogue, to the habit of taking risks with spelling may be shared from one student to another through the process of publishing. How refined should published works be? Not all writing that is published in the classroom has to be perfect. Age level matters here. If they are to be kept in the classroom community, younger children's publications may be less than completely perfect; if they are going "public" such as out in the hallway, that writing should be corrected up to your grade level standards. Watch this video, which addresses how to integrate spelling into the writing process, and answer the question that follows.

 Video Exploration 11.1: **Watch the video and answer questions that reflect the content you have read.**

Different Levels of Support for Writing

The writing workshop model assumes students are capable of a fair amount of self-direction and that they understand at least the rudiments of how ideas are put down on paper. It is true that children as young as kindergarten age can participate in writing workshops in some fashion. But teachers find that many young writers—and not just the youngest—sometimes need more explicit support as they learn to write. As teachers adjust the explicitness of their instruction and the fullness of their guidance according to the needs of the learners, they practice "gradual release of responsibility" (Pearson & Gallagher, 1993). The **gradual release of responsibility** model, as elaborated by Regie Routman (202), has the teacher providing high levels of direct teaching and support to beginners and giving more freedom to perform on their own to students who have largely learned the target skills. Figure 11.10 shows examples of the kinds of activities that are conducted at each level of writing support.

Figure 11.10 Gradual Release of Responsibility in Writing Instruction

SOURCE: After Routman, 2013

Demonstrated Writing	Interactive Writing	Guided Writing	Independent Writing
I do. You watch.	*I do. You help.*	*You do. I help.*	*You do. I watch.*
Students mostly observe Teacher mostly demonstrates and explains The **teacher's** level of control	Students add to teacher's lesson Teacher controls the activity	Students create within guidelines set by teacher Teacher structures the activity; students create	The **students'** level of control Students create independently Teacher is observer and resource
Typical Activities			
Modeled writing Focused lesson	Shared writing Interactive writing	Writing Frames Form Poems Graphic Organizers	Writing workshop Independent writing

Teach It! 4

Language Experience or Group Dictated Story

In this authentic writing activity, the teacher records student responses during a discussion about a shared experience (e.g., field trip) or a topic under study.

Although some of the activities at the more highly supported end of the scale are intended for young children, it is not the case that only younger writers need more support and only older writers need less. At one time or another, writers of all ages can use both support and freedom to create.

SHARED WRITING In shared writing, the teacher not only models acts of writing but also engages students in composing the writing. When shared writing is used, the topic needs to be one that both the teacher and the students are familiar with and are excited about. Such a topic might be a shared experience such as a field trip, a story that everyone is reading, or a topic that is under investigation by the class. Completion of a K-W-L chart offers a natural occasion for shared writing. Another kind of shared writing activity is group dictation. Here the writing activity is preceded by some kind of activity that excites the students and stimulates talk about it. The teacher leads a discussion and helps students find things to say, asks the students to offer comments about the topic, and then writes these down on a piece of chart paper. The teacher might lead the students to sound out some of the words and to offer spellings for them.

INTERACTIVE WRITING By using interactive writing you can help emergent and beginning readers and writers explore the writing system in its details. Developed by Moira McKenzie at the Ebury Street Centre for Language in London, the method has been incorporated into Fountas and Pinnell's guided reading program because "Interactive writing provides an authentic setting within which the teacher can explicitly demonstrate how written language works" (Fountas & Pinnell, 1996, p. 33).

Interactive writing works very much like taking a dictated account except that the teacher and the children "share the pen." The procedures follow these steps:

1. The teacher and a group of six to twelve students share an experience and agree on a topic. The topic might be a retelling of a story or a poem or a song, the daily news, or an idea that the class is studying.

2. The students offer a sentence about the topic. The teacher has the students repeat the sentence many times and even count the words to fix them firmly in their minds.

3. The teacher asks the students for the first word, and then pronounces that word slowly, writing its letters.

4. The teacher asks for the next word and invites a child up to write the whole word, a few letters, or a single letter. The teacher fills in letters the students miss. Each time a word is added, the whole text is read back by the students, with the teacher pointing to the words.

5. To help the students orient themselves to the text and add letters, the teacher might write blanks where the letters should go.

6. The teacher uses correction tape to paste over letters that are poorly formed.

7. The teacher instructs the class about words and print as the lesson progresses, reminding students about words they know or almost know and spelling patterns they have seen before, and prompting them to leave spaces between words and to add punctuation.

GUIDED WRITING When teachers instruct students about how to create a particular pattern of writing or use a particular strategy, or compose a sample piece as a group, and then ask individuals or pairs of students to produce their own writings according to the form or the strategy, they are guiding student writing. Guided writing is used when students can handle the rudiments of writing—making letters and spelling words—but still need to know some strategies for organizing their ideas on the page.

Many types of the writing lessons described in the next section on writing in the genres lend themselves to guided writing. For example, the form poems of *cinquains* and list poems can be done as class collaborations and then individually by students as guided writing activities.

WRITING FRAMES   Steering young writers' composition in certain productive directions is the job of writing frames. Even professional writers use them. Margaret Wise Brown's *The Important Book* is essentially a writing frame that she uses over and over. On each two-page spread she writes, "The important thing about _____ is _____. It has _____. And it _____, and _____. But the important thing about _____ is _____." Of course, she fills in the blanks with a topic word, descriptive words, and actions. Judy Allen's *Are You a Spider?*, like her *Are You a Butterfly?*, *Are You a Ladybug?*, and *Are You an Ant?*, begins with the question posed by the title, and then proceeds with, "If you are . . .," and then supplies descriptions of how these creatures look, how they are born, how they grow, where they live, what they eat, and what or who their enemies are. Of course, these same frames can be introduced to young writers by reading one of the books to them. Then the children can be given handouts with the repeated phrases filled in but the details left blank.

Writing frames are often used as a way of scaffolding writing tasks for English language learners and other students who find writing to be a special challenge. English language learners can be helped by sentence starters, too.

INDEPENDENT WRITING   Types of independent writing include writing in journals, self-initiated writing of all kinds, and writing done in writing workshops. It is important that students of all ages have regular chances to write independently. Doing so allows children to exercise many of their ideas and strategies for writing—from letter formation to the direction of print on a page, to spelling, to the use of illustrations, to the arrangement of ideas in a composition. Good writing ideas are contagious. If you observe students who have spent extended time in writing workshops, you will see that many more ideas emerge from these students and are passed from student to student than the teacher would have had time to think up and teach them during more structured writing time.

Some students will produce writing on their own, but many will not. That is why the writing workshop is so valuable: It combines teacher example and direction with encouragement of children's peers to get them writing. What about students who find writing difficult? See the suggestions in the Differentiated Instruction box.

The Writing Workshop

A popular approach to teaching children to write is the writing workshop, in which students are shown how to use the writing process and are given regular opportunities to produce many kinds of writing. Teachers who teach writing successfully work three elements into their teaching:

- *Time.* Writing workshops should be scheduled at consistent intervals so students know when they will have opportunities to write. When students know that they will have these opportunities regularly, they are more likely to collect ideas during their daily lives that they can write about during writing workshop.

- *Emphasis on communication.* It matters a lot whether students are writing for the teacher (to demonstrate skill or to get a grade) or writing because they want to say something to people who will be interested in hearing it. When writing is real communication, students may engage more of their powers of expression. Students should have opportunities to choose their own topics or—when the topics are assigned—to decide on their own approach to a topic. When conferences are conducted to help students improve writing, their ownership of the work—that is, what they mean to say—must still be respected, with freedom left for them to choose the advice they will follow as they seek to refine a work.

- *Demonstration and direct instruction.* Teaching writing is a studio craft, with attention to the process of creating. The teacher should demonstrate every phase of the process so that students will know how writing is done. The teacher should also teach skills of writing, from organization to correct punctuation, but this should be done in the context of writing for communication so that students will actually come to use them.

How often writing workshops are conducted and how much time they are given varies from one teacher to another. Figure 11.11 shows one plan for managing the time in a writing workshop. This writing workshop lasts an entire 60-minute class meeting, perhaps three days a week, with time set aside for five distinctive activities.

SENSE-OF-THE-CLASS MEETING   Assuming that the students are already engaged in writing tasks, the period begins with a brief sense-of-the-class meeting (Atwell, 1986) to find out who is working on what writing topic. Students keep a list of writing topics in a journal or a writing folder; if they do not have a work in progress, they should have a topic ready to be written about. By finding out and recording several interesting things about each child at the beginning of the year, the teacher can have a lively suggestion available if a student comes up empty.

Differentiated Instruction

Helping Struggling Writers

The writing workshop is a wonderful forum for many children's creativity, but it has not always served all children well. There are some students for whom the self-direction afforded by the writing workshop seems almost tantamount to neglect, particularly children whose home culture and language differ significantly from those of the school (Delpit, 1996). One explanation of the difficulty is offered by Collins (1998), who points out that writing is a secondary form of discourse normally based on speech, which is the primary form of discourse. If the kind of discourse a child sees in books and is expected to produce with a pencil fairly closely resembles the kind of discourse that is spoken, then the task of learning to write is largely one of discovering or acquiring the relations between speech and writing—that is, to figure out the strategies that enable us to put down on paper what we say in speech. The kind of writing workshop described earlier should serve this child well, for as Collins (1998) tells us,

> When literacy activities involve language forms and functions that are close to one's primary discourse, they can be achieved through a balance between acquisition and learning which favors acquisition. The typical writing workshop shows this balance in favor of acquisition, owing to its pronounced student-centered methods, including student-generated topics and genres for writing, multiple drafts to gradually improve writing, and supportive feedback from teachers and peers. When literacy activities involve ways of using language substantially different from one's primary discourse, the balance shifts in favor of learning. (p. 6)

As you might recall from the discussion of language acquisition and language learning in Chapter 3, *learning* refers to formal, teacher-directed, explicit instruction. *Acquisition* means learning by discovery and inference from being immersed in writing activities. Moving the balance toward learning means explicitly teaching students what they need to know to carry out the processes of writing. Struggling writers do not need to be taken out of writing workshops and given skill sheets to fill out. It is still possible for teachers to teach students strategies for writing that they can use to express themselves to an audience of their peers (Harris & Graham, 1996).

Strategies are explicit procedures. Strategies relate to every aspect of writing, from choosing a topic to deciding which parts of the topic to include and which to leave out, to organizing ideas on paper. Strategies may be taught in two ways. One is by means of focused lessons. In a focused lesson, the teacher makes it very clear to the students when and how to use a particular technique in writing, whether it be a beginning + middle + ending organization for a paper or the way to punctuate dialogue. Another means of teaching a strategy is using writing guides or graphic organizers. For struggling writers, having a graphic organizer to follow, such as a story map or an outline for a persuasive essay, helps to make the writing strategy explicit. When the students understand the steps to the strategy, the teacher gives them guided practice using the strategy and provides feedback on their use of it. After they have learned to use the strategy, they will no longer need to use the graphic organizer.

FOCUSED LESSONS   The goal of writing workshops is to encourage students to write about things they care about for real audiences and to improve their writing so that it communicates more and more effectively. It is essential to give students time, models, and opportunities to write. But students also need careful instruction on all aspects of writing—from how one carries out the writing process to proper punctuation. Focused instruction helps children in the rehearsal and drafting stages by showing them strategies for writing, and it helps them in the revising and editing stages by giving them criteria or working standards for making their writing better.

Figure 11.11 Daily Schedule of a Writing Workshop

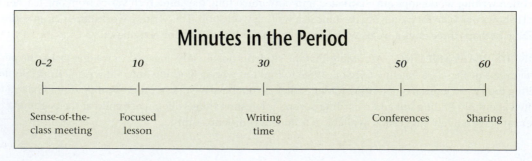

Focused lessons may relate to any aspect of writing, from mechanical issues such as spelling and punctuation to word-choice issues such as showing, not telling, to write vividly and clearly, to composition-related issues such as ways to write strong introductions and closings. Focused lessons also may highlight the writing process itself, showing students how writers get ideas and narrow them, how writers put ideas into words, how writers go back and make the work better, and how writers share their work and learn from their peers' comments.

The goal of all focused lessons is for students to internalize the main points and use them while they are reviewing their peers' papers and their own. In other words, the writing teacher tries to work himself or herself out of a job. It is important to conceive of focused lessons not as teaching about writing in the abstract, but rather as providing guidance to the children's own writing and editing processes.

Focused lessons can follow a four-part model for teaching skills in context: demonstration and immersion, attention to detail, guided practice, and independent use. In the writing workshop, focused lessons use those four parts in the following ways.

1. *Finding a text that demonstrates a point or skill you want to teach.* For example, if you want to show children how to write vivid beginnings to stories by jumping right into the action, read the beginning of *Charlotte's Web*:

    > "Where's Papa going with that axe?" said Fern to her mother as they were setting the table for breakfast.
    >
    > "Out to the hoghouse," replied Mrs. Arable. "Some pigs were born last night."
    >
    > "I don't see why he needs an axe," continued Fern, who was only eight.
    >
    > "Well," said her mother, "one of the pigs is a runt. It's very small and weak, and it will never amount to anything. So your father has decided to do away with it."
    >
    > "Do away with it," shrieked Fern. "You mean kill it, just because it's smaller than the others?" (White, 1952/1980, p. 1)

2. *Sharing the example and calling students' attention to the skill it demonstrates.* E. B. White could have begun his story by describing the setting and the characters, but he didn't. He started right in with the action. He decided to have Fern ask that question, hear that terrible answer, and get upset. After just these few lines, it is evident that the main problem of the story will be saving the little pig's life, and readers will want to know what can be done to solve this problem.

    You might ask the students how the beginning made them feel and what it led them to expect. What advice do they suppose E. B. White gave himself that made him begin the story that way? Discuss this example until the point is clear that a good way of beginning a story is to start right in with action that shows readers a problem and makes them care what will happen in the story.

3. *Providing the students with guided practice using the skill.* Ask the students to take out a draft of a story they are writing. Have them rewrite the beginning of the story so that it starts right in with action or dialogue that leads the reader right into the main problem of the story. Have the students pair up and take turns explaining to a partner the changes they made to their paper.

4. *Encouraging students to use the skill in their independent writing.* So that the points taught in the focused lessons enter students' repertoire of writing skills, you might add each point to a writing rubric or editing checklist or to your guidelines for good writing. You can also add that point into rubrics used to evaluate students' writing or into the checklists they use to edit their own and each other's drafts.

WRITING TIME   During much of the writing workshop, all of the students are writing. This is quiet time. The teacher writes for the first five minutes as well, to help establish an atmosphere for quiet independent work. For the next ten minutes, the teacher might move around to individual students, to encourage them as they write. Nathan and colleagues (1988) advise that the teacher go first to those who appear to be having trouble writing.

CONFERENCES   After the students have written for a designated amount of time, a period of conferences begins. The teacher can conduct a conference for the whole class, with one student, or with a small group.

Students may confer with a partner or with a small group. Conferences were discussed in detail earlier. Students who wish to continue writing during this time may do so.

SHARING   The last 10 minutes of the workshop are reserved for sharing. The teacher should choose students to share who are far along in a draft or whose work displays an interesting issue. Different students should share each time because only one or two can normally share in a 10-minute period. Some teachers extend sharing time to get in three students a day; that way, every student gets to share every other week. Watch this video about how a teacher establishes a sharing-friendly community of writers and then answer the question that follows.

 Video Exploration 11.2: Watch the video and answer questions that reflect the content you have read.

MODIFYING THE WRITING WORKSHOP FOR ENGLISH LANGUAGE LEARNERS   English language learners can benefit from instruction using the writing workshop approach, with certain modifications.

- During the rehearsal phase of writing, help them brainstorm English vocabulary they are likely to need, and write these words on the board.

- Allow them to write a first draft in their first language.

- Keep a bilingual dictionary handy, and encourage English language learners to use it as they create finished drafts of their works. Then allow time for them to look up key words using their dictionaries.

Check Your Understanding 11.3: Gauge your understanding of the skills and concepts in this section.

Writing in Different Genres

A writing *genre* is a form or pattern of writing related to a purpose. Different kinds or genres of writing pose particular challenges to writers. The main genres of writing include the following:

- *Journals* are personal accounts of events or ideas whose purpose is to record experiences and help writers remember them and think about them deeply.

- *Stories* are fictional accounts of characters in settings who attempt to overcome problems. The purpose of stories is to provide outlets for writers' inventiveness and to entertain others.

- *Poems* are compositions that capture and convey emotions and insights while taking liberties with sentence and paragraph construction.

- *Expository accounts* are intended to be careful descriptions or explanations of things in the world.

- *Persuasive essays* convey writers' views of real issues in their lives and attempt to influence their readers' views.

These genres include important subtopics: A play is a kind of story; a song is a kind of poem; an observation report in science is a kind of expository account, as are biographies and autobiographies; and an advertisement is a kind of persuasive essay. They may also be mixed with each other; sometimes writers describe or explain to persuade readers or to tell them a story. Often writers write novels in blank verse—that is, poetry that doesn't rhyme, such as Jacqueline Woodson's *Brown Girl Dreaming* (2014).

Journals and Other Personal Writing

Journal writing consists of jotting down thoughts, feelings, and impressions that are close to the writer; the intended audience is the writer herself or himself. Such writing usually comes fairly naturally to young writers because it has few formal demands. Nonetheless, the kind of personal expressive writing found in journals is important for students to use because it serves as a sort of playground or laboratory for the imagination (Britton, 1970). Students may begin working with ideas in journals that they later turn into more formal pieces.

DUAL-ENTRY DIARY   Journals have other important pedagogical uses, too. Response journals are used to encourage students to reflect on their reading and their learning. A simple but powerful approach to response journals is the *dual-entry diary* (Barone, 1992; Berthoff, 1981). In a dual-entry diary (DED), students are asked to divide the page down the middle with a vertical line. On the left-hand side, they record phrases that they found striking, important, or puzzling. On the right-hand side, they write comments on the passages. DEDs can be used to respond to literature or a host of other topics. After the students have written their DEDs, the teacher may write comments in them or may ask the students to share their entries in a discussion group.

DIALOGUE JOURNALS   In this form of response writing in journals, students are assigned to pairs by the teacher. After they have read a part of a book or participated in some other learning event, they write their impressions of it in their

Teach It! 34

Dual-Entry Diary

This activity invites students to select and comment on interesting or puzzling text passages as it prepares them to participate in discussions of the texts they are reading.

journals. Later, they have written conversations with each other. One makes a comment in writing and ends with a question for the other. The other answers the question, makes a comment as well, and writes another question for the partner, and so on.

Stories

Most students enjoy writing stories, and because they are surrounded by stories, they find it natural to do so. Yet the structure of stories is fairly complicated, so some instruction in writing stories is helpful. There are many ways to show students how to write stories.

IMITATING AN AUTHOR   In the genre study approach, you might read the children several stories by the same author and then ask them to write a similar story. For example, second- and third-grade children delight in writing their own episodes about Amelia Bedelia (Parish, 1992), James Marshall's character Fox (Marshall, 1994), Russell Hoban's character Frances (Hoban, 1995), or Mo Willems' Pigeon (Willems, 2003).

STORY MAPS   Outlines that guide students to write stories part by part are called story maps. Story maps are used in reading instruction as devices for calling children's attention to the parts of a plot. In writing, story maps like the one shown in Figure 11.12 can be used as frameworks for planning out a story.

In a map such as the one shown in Figure 11.12, students fill in the blanks on the right-hand side of the chart. If they are using the map for planning, after the students have filled in the chart, they write the story out, adding details and whatever other twists occur to them as they write.

DIALOGUE STORIES   A simple but effective pattern for structuring stories is the dialogue story. Students can be shown an example of a dialogue story, such as John Archambault and Bill Martin Jr.'s *White Dynamite and the Curly Kid* (1989). Then ask the students to write their own story in dialogue form. As a rehearsal step, have two students make up an oral story together and each write their own version of it later.

Figure 11.12 A Story Map

There was a person . . .
who wanted . . .
So she . . .
but . . .
(and she . . .)
(but . . .)
And then she . . .
And finally, . . .
So . . .

Teach It! 64

Form Poems

With this activity, children develop awareness of how form and meaning shape each other in poetry as they collaborate with classmates to create a poem.

Poems

Styles of poems range from those that put an emphasis on form to those that stress ideas and let form take care of itself. Following are three different approaches to writing structured poems. Even though the form is tightly prescribed, children write poems that are lively and surprising with these frameworks to support them. To teach children to write a form poem, follow these steps:

1. Show the students an example of a well-written poem that follows the form. (You might need to write this yourself or save it from a previous class.)

2. Have the students help you create a poem as a group. Discuss each choice they make so they understand the process well.

3. Have individuals or pairs write their own poems.

4. Share several of the poems, and discuss their qualities. Also call attention to the ways in which the poems followed the structure.

5. Make a wall chart in which you feature several of the students' poems; also outline the procedures for writing a poem with the structure in question.

ACROSTICS   Acrostics can be used simply, as when they spell a person's name. Students write a name in capitals vertically down the left side of a page and then go back and insert a word that begins with each letter. Here is one:

Persistent
Energetic
Never dull
Native of the mountains—
Yes, you will like this person.

On a more ambitious level, students can create acrostics with whole phrases, rhymed or unrhymed, but still have the first letter of the first word of each line spelling a word when read from top to bottom:

Alicia lived through long, cold days
Like an old unnoticed stone
Off the path, far from the crowds
Never seen,
Ever.

In their wonderful book, *Ways of Writing with Young Kids*, Sharon Edwards and her colleagues (2003) explore many ways of using acrostics. A particularly interesting way is to have a poet read her acrostic aloud to the class twice: first as a poem, with attention paid to the sounds, the images, and the tone, and then to uncover the mystery word that is spelled by the poem.

CINQUAINS   Christmas tree–shaped poems that look like the following are called *cinquains* (after the French word *cinq*, for "five"):

Harry
Young, charmed
Studying, flying, surviving
Ron Weasley's best friend
Wizard

Cinquains are surprisingly useful means of encouraging students to think about a concept. They follow a simple pattern:

- The first line names the topic.
- The second line contains two describing words.

- The third line has three action words ending in -*ing*.
- The fourth line is four feeling words, which may be written as a phrase.
- The fifth line is a one-word synonym for the name in the first line.

LIST POEMS   Throughout the ages, many fine poems have been developed around the idea of lists. Take this medieval prayer, for example:

From Ghoulies
And Ghosties
And long-legged Beasties
And Things that go bump in the night:
Good Lord, deliver us.

Writers can use the idea by listing all of the things that are:

—dark

—lonely

—round

—scarce

The effect is heightened when writers include in their list both concrete and abstract things. For example,

A pebble in the pond
a policeman's beat
the moon's halo
subway tokens
surprised eyes
a ghost's mouth
and the world—
are round.

Expository Writing

Expository writing includes texts that describe or explain. Focused lessons that share good examples from literature and encourage their imitation can help young writers create expository works. Graphic organizers serve as valuable tools for helping children to write descriptive and explanatory prose. A number of graphic organizers are popular with children from second grade up and have been discussed at various points in the book. As you might recall, graphic organizers are important learning aids in comprehension (see Chapters 8 and 9) as well. This reinforces an important theme of this book about the close connection between the teaching/learning of reading and writing.

CLUSTERS   Clusters, also called semantic webs, are linked circles that show relationships between ideas. The writer starts by naming the topic of the writing in a circle in the center of the page and then writes subordinate topics in satellite circles around the main circle. Aspects of each subordinate circle are written in still more satellites (see Figure 11.13). After the details about a topic have been set out in the form of a cluster, the writer can refer to them in writing out an essay.

Figure 11.13 A Cluster, or Semantic Web

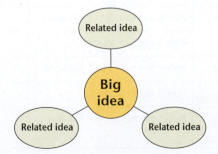

Figure 11.14 A Venn Diagram

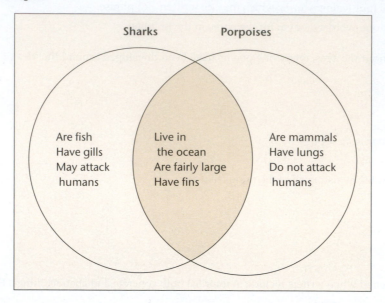

VENN DIAGRAMS   Venn diagrams are helpful planning aids when writers want to compare and contrast two items, and they consist of two interlocking circles. In the outer left-hand circle is listed everything that is true about Topic X but not Topic Y. In the outer right-hand circle is written everything that is true about Topic Y but not Topic X. In the overlapping part in the middle is written everything that is true about both Topic X and Topic Y. (See Figure 11.14 for an example.)

DESCRIPTIVE ESSAY FRAMES   Frames provide boxes that prompt writers to collect and organize their thoughts before writing out an essay; in this way, they can lend structure to a piece of writing. Like all writing frameworks, though, they should be used sparingly: They can become a crutch to be relied on too much and they may take the place of the student's own voice and originality. Figure 11.15 shows one example of a frame for structuring a descriptive essay.

CAUSE-AND-EFFECT CHARTS   When students plan to write about cause-and-effect chains, they can organize their ideas before writing using a cause-and-effect chart. A cause-and-effect chart can have few or many boxes. Causes are listed in separate boxes on the left-hand side of the chart and effects are listed on the right. Several causes may contribute to a single effect, which may simultaneously be the cause of several other effects. The chart in Figure 11.16 shows the many causes of air pollution and their related effects.

Figure 11.15 A Framework for a Descriptive Essay

I'm going to write about . . .		
Here is a word that describes my topic:	Here is one example of that word	
	Here is another example	
Here is another word that describes my topic:	Here is one example of that word	
	Here is another example	
Here is another word that describes my topic:	Here is one example of that word	
	Here is another example	
This is how I feel about my topic:	Here is the reason I feel that way	

Figure 11.16 A Cause-and-Effect Chart

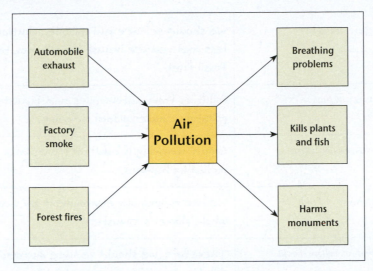

PERSUASIVE ESSAYS   There are many ways to help students produce arguments and shape them into persuasive essays. A popular procedure for helping students formulate their ideas for a persuasive essay is the K-W-L strategy (Ogle, 1986), discussed in Chapter 9. By constructing a K-W-L chart, students consider what they already know about a topic, formulate questions that say what they want to know about it, and later list what they learned about the topic.

Having done this activity, you can then construct a new chart labeled like the one in Figure 11.17 that will guide the students to think about and take positions on actions that should follow from those findings.

After the students have completed the chart, they might think about ways to use their entries in an argumentative essay. One way in which the essay can be structured is to enter the information into another kind of format, like the one shown in Figure 11.18.

Writing should be integrated into the reading program early and children should write every day. How can we accomplish these two goals?

MIXING GENRES: RAFT   A writing-to-learn strategy that calls attention to genres even as it mixes them up is the RAFT procedure, developed by Carol Santa (1988). RAFT is an acronym for **R**ole, **A**udience, **F**ormat, and **T**opic.

Once a *topic* has been established in a lesson, students are invited to adopt different *roles* of people or other characters who have a stake in the issue. For example, if the topic is protecting dolphins, the roles might be fishermen, conservationists, the state wildlife protection people, and (with a little imagination) the dolphins themselves. Once each student (or teams of students) has chosen a role, the student decides who the *audience* is—the people or characters to whom the message will be addressed. For example, conservationists might want to send a message to fishermen on the topic of protecting dolphins. But now the question is what *format* the message might use. Conservationists could write persuasive letters,

Figure 11.17 What? So What? Now What?

What?	So What?	Now What?
Pollution from automobiles and industrial pollution causes global warming.	Global warming is bad for plants and animals, including humans.	We should reduce automobile pollution by driving less and reduce industrial pollution by using less fossil fuel.

Figure 11.18 Framework for a Persuasive Essay

What do you believe should be done about _____?_	We should reduce automobile pollution by driving less and reduce industrial pollution by using less fossil fuel.
What is one reason why that should be done?	Pollution from automobiles and industrial pollution causes global warming.
(What is a second reason why that should be done?)	Global warming is bad for plants and animals, including humans.
(What is a third reason why that should be done?)	We are ruining our environment by warming the whole planet's climate.
So, say again what you believe should be done about _____._	Therefore, we should reduce automobile pollution by driving less and reduce industrial pollution by using less fossil fuel.

editorials for the local newspaper, billboard advertisements, or catchy jingles, to name just a few formats. Once the four aspects of the RAFT are decided on—the Role, the Audience, the Format, and the Topic, the students create their works.

As an added twist, Alan Crawford (Crawford et al., 2005) suggests using *Reciprocal RAFT*, in which the original messages are distributed to students in the class, who then adopt the role of the audience and respond to the messages.

Teaching Students to Write in Genres: Descriptive Writing

Writing expert Lucy Calkins (1994) suggests that teachers immerse students in genre study, in which they read several published works written in a particular genre and then try their hands at writing in that genre. The format for teaching lessons of genre study is basically the same as that for focused lessons.

In the following sample lesson, teacher Paul Darion has decided to immerse his students in descriptive writing.

- *Share a sample of the writing form.* To demonstrate descriptive writing, Mr. Darion selects the opening paragraphs from Frances Temple's *Tonight, By Sea* (1995) and makes copies of them for his students. He plans to call the students' attention to the author's skill at writing vividly. In this case, the writer has carefully observed a process and shown it to the reader, step by step, and has put the reader in the picture by naming sights, sounds, smells, and tactile sensations.

Common Core State Standards

Writing Position Papers

The Common Core State Standards ask that students—beginning in kindergarten and with increasing sophistication as they progress through the grades—be able to write position papers on a host of topics. Position papers often take the form of (1) stating a position, (2) stating two or three reasons for it, (3) supporting each reason with evidence, and (4) restating the conclusion. Active class discussions and graphic organizers can bring out positions for students to take and provide structure for their arguments. But it is important to give students much practice in actually writing out their position papers, too (CCSS Foundational Standards, Text Types and Purposes, 1).

Teach It! 61
Descriptive Writing

This engaging activity provides an opportunity for young writers to practice descriptive writing as they become more familiar with the genre.

- *Call attention to the features of the writing form.* Mr. Darion reads the passage aloud as the students read along. Then he invites the students to say aloud what they experienced in reading the passage. He invites one student to retell the process of lighting a fire. Then he invites several more students, one at a time, to name a detail the writer has given and say whether that detail is a sight, a sound, a smell, or a feeling. Mr. Darion has also decided to pass out different colored pencils and ask students to use different colors for words that appeal to different senses. This part of the lesson ends with the students saying aloud how the writer achieved vivid descriptive writing: "Descriptive writing names things exactly, and uses words for sights, sounds, smells, tastes, and feelings."

- *Provide guided practice in using the writing form.* Sometimes, the next thing Mr. Darion does is to have the students observe something carefully in the classroom and describe it in writing. Today, however, he pulls out a mystery bag he created beforehand. It is nothing more than a paper bag containing an object (such as a chess piece, a spark plug, a sewing thimble, or a Christmas tree light bulb). Mr. Darion invites the students, one at a time, to reach into the bag and touch the object. The students then describe it on paper, with the understanding that they must thoroughly describe the object before they name it.

- *Make a poster explaining how to write in that genre.* Mr. Darion has the students create a poster that names the kind of writing, provides an example of it, and includes a graphic organizer that makes clear the instructions for writing in that form or genre. The students will now be able to refer to the poster as they complete their own writing.

- *Encourage the students to write in that genre during their independent writing.* Mr. Darion reminds the students of what they know about descriptive writing and encourages them to describe things carefully with words that appeal to the senses. The term *descriptive writing* enters the students' vocabulary, and the reminder to "use words that name sights, sounds, smells, tastes, and feelings" is commonly heard among the students themselves.

Kneeling in the sand, Paulie shredded dry seaweed and fluffed it into a heap between the three black cooking stones, half forgetting that she had no food to cook. She broke palm fronds over the seaweed, then propped two pieces of driftwood with their tips just above the palm. Raking the sand together with her fingers, she built up a ring around the outside of the stones, careful to make room for the air to blow in and give life to the fire, a little and not too much.

Paulie leaned back, still kneeling, circling her upper arms in her hands to warm them. Night had come. The tree frogs stopped singing all at once.

"You got matches, Uncle?"

Paulie's uncle was washing in seawater from a bucket, pouring it down his back to get off the sweat and the sawdust, rinsing his arms.

"All the matches gone, Paulie."

"Go see if you can borrow a coal," her grandmother said. Sitting on the steps of her house, a cloth around her thin shoulders, Grann Adeline leaned toward the fire as if it were already lit. She frowned, slapped at a mosquito on her ankle. "Go on, girl. Ask sweetly and somebody bound to give you an ember."

Paulie wandered down the sand path. The small houses clustered under the trees were mostly dark. She could hear voices talking softly, a baby crying. A thin dog came out and sniffed at the backs of her knees. Paulie looked for the glow of a cook fire, smelled the breeze for one. She could feel the sea air, and hear the waves coming in, but it seemed like nobody was cooking.

Source: From Tonight, by Sea, *by Frances Temple. Scholastic Inc./Orchard Books. Copyright © 1995 by Frances Temple. Reprinted by permission.*

Check Your Understanding 11.4: **Gauge your understanding of the skills and concepts in this section.**

Assessment of Writing

Various parts of this chapter have focused on teaching children to revise and edit their own work. Revising and editing are basic forms of assessment of children's writing. Assessing students' writing and providing ongoing feedback are critical in encouraging students to write. However, in assessing students' writing, keep in mind some valuable principles:

- Not everything should be assessed. Most of children's writing should be for communication and should not be graded.
- Assessment should teach; that is, children should learn about writing from the assessment.
- The criteria for assessment should be explicit and clear.
- Children should be involved in their own assessment.
- Assessment should show strengths and progress as well as needed improvements.

Using Rubrics

Rubrics are detailed presentations of quality criteria. They address several aspects of writing at once, and they explain clearly what constitutes a good job. Rubrics may be constructed by the teacher or by the students and the teacher together. They should be closely connected to the qualities of writing that have been stressed in the focused lessons as well as any checklists that have been used to guide the students' revising and editing. Students should be fully aware of the meaning of each criterion (aspect of quality) on the rubric before they produce the work that will be assessed. Watch this video of a teacher developing a rubric with her fourth-grade students to assess personal narrative and answer the question that follows.

 Video Exploration 11.3: Watch the video and answer questions that reflect the content you have read.

Following are the steps for using rubrics:

- Choose four to eight qualities of writing to assess. (Consider having the children suggest qualities of good writing.)
- Make sure the qualities of writing you assess have been carefully explained.
- Describe good work according to each quality. You may also describe fair and poor work.
- Share the rubrics with the students before they write the works that will be assessed.
- Use the rubrics often so that students learn what they mean and are able to use their criteria to guide them when they write.

Whatever assessment tools you use to evaluate children's writing, it is important to use the same terms in your instruction as you use in evaluation. For example, if you evaluate children's use of written dialogue, you must be sure you have carefully taught them how to do it (Spandel, 2012). Use the same terms in your instruction such as "dialogue"; avoid switching to "write like talking marks" or other terms and phrases that will confuse the children. And make sure your writing lessons and writing workshops are filled with teacher-to-children, teacher-to-child conversations about writing and writing terms.

SIX TRAITS WRITING EVALUATION   The Six Traits model for writing assessment meets all of the principles just identified. Developed by Vicki Spandel and her associates (1996, 2000) at the Northwest Regional Education Laboratory, the Six Traits model seeks to direct teachers' and students' attention to six aspects of writing: ideas and content, organization, voice, word choice, sentence fluency, and conventions.

1. *Ideas and content* amount to the quality of having something to say and saying it clearly to the reader. They include having found out something about the topic before writing about it and having an original point of view. They can include providing details that lend an eyewitness feel to the paper.
2. *Organization* refers to the paper's having a beginning, a middle, and an end. It may include supporting main ideas with details, sticking to the topic, and making clear transitions from one point to another.
3. *Voice* describes the quality of reaching for words that express ideas well, even when this means writing words one has not been taught to use or to spell. A paper with a well-developed voice approaches the writer's oral fluency and expressiveness.

4. *Word choice* is the quality of showing the writer's meaning with precise words and specific details, and using fresh ways of expressing ideas, avoiding clichés.

5. *Sentence fluency* means a reader can easily read the work aloud. There are sufficient numbers of sentences to convey the meaning, and the sentences are varied in their length and form.

6. *Conventions* include spelling, capitalization and punctuation, and grammatical correctness. In later grades, conventions may refer to allocating separate ideas to separate paragraphs.

Children of different ages and levels of development naturally will be more or less advanced in their performance within each trait. Spandel and her associates have listed behavioral descriptors at four levels of development:

- *Exploring writers* are young writers who are experimenting with the whole enterprise of making meaning with graphic communication. Thus, within the trait of ideas and content, exploring writers might use pictures and scribbles to express ideas.

- *Emerging writers* are still young writers, but they have advanced to the point at which they are starting to work the features of conventional writing into their graphic productions. Thus, within the trait of ideas and content, emerging writers may use pictures or both pictures and mock writing in such a way that a reader might be able to guess an approximate meaning.

- *Developing writers,* through a mix of their own inventions and discoveries and overt teaching, can produce written messages that convey clear meaning, with the beginnings of formal organization and attention to some of the conventions of spelling and capitalization. Thus, within the trait of ideas and content, developing writers create stand-alone messages that are more readily decipherable. Their works show some attention to detail.

- *Fluent/experienced writers* express meanings more eloquently in print and take advantage of many features of fluent writing within all six traits. Thus, within the trait of ideas and content, fluent writers create works that show advancing mastery of qualities of writing, including the ability to say things clearly and in fresh and interesting ways, honoring more and more of the conventions of writing.

SIX TRAITS RUBRIC If you use a Six Traits Rubric (see Figure 11.19), be sure your students are familiar with the rubric that will be used to judge them. Read the rubric together and have it available in the classroom. It is sad to say, but often true that children end up hating to write because they have not been given a fair chance to learn well and to prepare for assessment. High-quality instruction/assessment will help you avoid mistakes that can be tragic. Your students will be judged all their lives by their writing.

Spandel's text on Six Traits writing assessment (Spandel, 2013) includes many examples of student writing at various grade levels that correspond to each trait, such as word choice, sentence fluency, and punctuation. Direct "how to do it" teacher guidance is provided that shows appropriate instruction to use, for example, if a student overuses words such as "things," writes a series of choppy sentences, or doesn't use adequate punctuation.

Work Sampling

Another effective approach to evaluating writing is work sampling. One way to sample work is to choose representative pieces of each child's writings at intervals during the year, but at least once per month. Sit down with the child and discuss the improvements you both see. Ask the child to take the lead in pointing out the improvements. If the child needs help, you might comment on the following:

- The length of each piece
- Organization: sticking to a topic and saying interesting things about it
- The appearance of new features, such as description or dialogue
- Attempts to write in a new genre, such as persuasion or description
- Attention to mechanics, such as spelling, punctuation, and handwriting

Before ending the conversation, ask the child to set goals—writing improvements to make in the next month. Write these down, or have the child write them, with a copy for yourself and a copy for the child. Provide regular reminders of the goals.

Check Your Understanding 11.5: Watch the video and answer questions that reflect the content you have read.

Figure 11.19 A Rubric for Assessing Writing: Six Traits Writing Evaluation Sheet

---

Ideas and Content:

Clear ideas. It makes sense.

The writer has narrowed the idea to a manageable topic.

Good information—from experience, imagination, or research.

Original and fresh perspective.

Details that capture a reader's interest. Makes ideas understandable.

Organization:

A snappy lead that gets the reader's attention.

Starts somewhere and goes somewhere.

The writer continually makes connections within the work.

Writing builds to a conclusion.

The writer creates a memorable resolution and conclusion.

Voice:

Sounds like a person wrote it.

Sounds like this particular writer.

Brings topic to life.

Makes the reader respond and care what happens.

The writer has energy and is involved.

Word Choice:

Words and phrases have power.

Word pictures are created.

Thought is crystal clear and precise.

Strong verbs and precise nouns.

Sentence Fluency:

Easy to read aloud.

Well-built sentences.

Varied sentence length. Some long sentences, some short.

Conventions:

Looks clean, edited, and proofread.

Free of distracting errors.

Easy to read.

No errors in spelling, punctuation, grammar and usage, capitalization, and indentation.

Writing to Learn

Writing can be used to boost learning in at least five ways:

1. *Writing requires students to make their thoughts explicit.* Fuzzy thinking leads to fuzzy writing (vague, unfocused, disorganized) and vice-versa. When students learn to read back and reflect on what they write, they have a tool for sharpening their thinking. In the meantime, teachers can reflect with individual students about their writing, and help them clarify their thoughts. As the Brazilian educator Paolo Freire (1976) noted nearly half a century

ago, writing can raise our consciousness by enabling us to enter into a dialectic (a sort of creative argument) with our own thoughts.

2. *Writing can lead students to surprise themselves, by expressing thoughts they didn't know they had.* Donald Murray (1982) considered drafting—writing out ideas in an unrestrained fashion—as a means of discovering what you know about a topic. The point is, students often don't know what they know about a topic until they write about it. Of course, writing that will be made public must be revised and shaped for clarity and elegance. But in the early stages of writing, or when writing in a journal, composing constitutes a sort of laboratory for the mind and the imagination.

3. *Writing commits students to ideas.* In a class discussion, some students may be timid and unwilling to state their own views, or they may simply agree with someone else's strongly stated opinion. But teachers can ask students to individually write down what they think about a topic or their questions about it, and insist that they read their own comments aloud instead of deferring to others.

4. *Writing guides inquiry.* Whether the assignment is a brief position paper or a longer research project, teachers can assign formats to guide students' thinking and expression.

5. *Writing calls attention to language.* The act of writing makes explicit many aspects of language that otherwise don't often come to consciousness. Spelling, word choice, sentence grammar, paragraph structure, and larger patterns of the organization of ideas are all laid bare when written down.

Virtually all of the ideas already presented in this chapter are means of using writing to help students learn. A few additional ideas are given below.

ENTRANCE CARDS   The topic of the next day's class is announced in advance. Students are required to write at least one good question about the topic on an index card, and bring that card as a ticket for admission to the class discussion. The teacher may collect the cards and read the questions randomly, or call on the students to read their questions aloud. Optionally, the questions may be worked into a K-W-L chart.

EXIT CARDS   At the conclusion of a class, students can be given four minutes to fill out an exit card with answers to three questions:

1. What is the most important thing you learned today?
2. What is one question you have about the topic?
3. What is one comment you want to make about today's lesson?

The teacher collects the cards and reviews them before the next class. He or she may choose to open the next class with answers to the questions. In any case, having students name the most important thing they learned from the class leads them to mentally review what happened in the class, and reading students' answers to the questions gives the teacher a window into what the students took from it.

LEARNING LOGS   Learning logs are daily journals the students keep. They provide a way for students to make explicit their thoughts about what they learned (or think they learned) in a class.

Often they take the form of "Write a letter to _____ (an absent class member) and explain exactly how we solved the problem we studied today." The teacher reviews the journals periodically to see what the students are understanding and where their difficulties are.

Other learning logs may be structured with questions to guide students' responses. The teacher can ask what students' favorite part of the lesson was, what the hardest part was, how they felt about it, what would make the lesson more productive for them, or what they were doing to understand the material.

I-SEARCH PROJECTS   As a way of guiding inquiry and making it more personal, writing teacher Ken Macrorie (1988) developed the I-Search procedure. The I-Search procedure follows the format given in Figure 11.20, with variations to make it less sophisticated for younger students.

Figure 11.20 Writing an I-Search Inquiry

What you want to know

(Write this section at the very beginning of your project.) Tell us the question you want to find out about. Say what you already knew about this question when you began your search. Tell us why you cared about or were interested in this question.

How you will find out

(Write about these questions when you begin your search.) What will you do to find answers to your question? Who will you talk to? What will you ask them? What will you read? What Internet sites will you visit?

(The teacher usually specifies what kinds of sources the student is expected to use.)

What did you learn?

What are three or four major things you found out? State your findings one at a time, and support each one with examples, stories, or arguments that will help the reader understand how you arrived at those conclusions. Try to connect your findings with your original questions.

Lessons for the writer

In this part of the paper, tell the story of your investigation and what you learned in the process. Did other questions occur to you in the course of the investigation? Did some sources turn out to be more useful than others? Did you discover new sources of information as you went along? If so, how? Did you find trends of agreement in your sources? Were there any disagreements among them? How did you decide what to conclude?

References

At the end of the paper, write out the references you consulted, using the form your teacher tells you to use.

Check Your Understanding 11.6: Gauge your understanding of the skills and concepts in this section.

For Review

At the outset of this chapter we stated that when you reached this point in your reading and studying you should be able to:

- **Explain the phases children pass through as they learn to spell and assess them.**

The first aspect of writing dealt with in the chapter was spelling, and we saw stages or levels of strategies that students typically use as they learn to spell: *prephonemic, early phonemic, letter name, orthographic, morphological,* and *derivational*. Because the words children are challenged to spell gain complexity as children advance through the grades, one way of assessing spelling development is to sample the spelling of words from different grade levels. Because children use different strategies for spelling as they gain maturity and experience, another way to assess spelling development is to examine the spelling strategies children use.

- **Use best practices to teach children to spell.**

Spelling instruction should address three needs: teaching "survival words"—words students will use often in their writing; teaching words that contain features children are trying to master; and teaching ways to generalize from spelling words students know to spelling new words. In this chapter we shared methods for teaching children to memorize spellings. We also shared means of teaching syllable types and morphemes in words.

- **Explain and teach the five-part writing process.**

The writing process involves phases of rehearsal, drafting, revising, editing, and publishing. Variations of it can be used with children from the early grades. Children need different levels of support in learning to write. In this chapter we used the model of the "gradual release of responsibility" to guide us from teacher-centered modeling, to scaffolded productions by children, to independent writing.

- **Support children's writing in different genres.**

The products of writing are arranged into genres. Genres include expressive writing such as journals, stories, poems, expository writing, and persuasive essays. Suggestions were given for helping students write in each genre.

- **Assess children's writing.**

Children's writing does involve correct mechanics—spelling, punctuation, appropriate capitalization, and paragraphing. Assuming that the point of writing is communication, assessment of writing should include issues like composition, clarity, organization, voice, and attention to audience. Two general approaches to assessment were described in the chapter: rubrics and work sampling.

- **Teach writing to learn.**

Writing is a powerful tool for teaching students to think, analyze, and remember. Tools for teaching writing to learn include entrance and exit cards, learning logs, and research papers.

For Your Journal

1. Review the Anticipation Guide and compare your earlier answers with what you think now.

2. Try out the writing process for yourself with the assistance of a partner, although you can do this activity alone.

   - Make a list of five topics you might write about. These should be topics you might share with children in grades 1 though 5.

   - Ask yourself or have a partner ask you what interests you about each topic. Find your story!

   - Write a draft of your paper. Write for eight minutes without stopping.

   - Read back over your paper, or have a partner read it, and consider areas you need to revise.

   - Write about this writing experience in your journal, reflecting on what happened in the process, how you felt about writing this way, and if it was different than previous writing you've done.

3. In helping children learn to write, where do you think the proper balance can be found between the need to encourage children to feel ownership for their writing and take initiative for their learning and the need to teach them to write better—that is, more coherently and correctly?

Taking It to the World

1. The writing process described in this chapter—rehearsing, drafting, revising, editing, and publishing—is often described as the way professional writers create. But is it? Find and interview at least two writers. If possible, look for writers of fiction and poetry as well as writers of nonfiction. Ask them what they do when they write. (*Hint:* Don't mention the writing process or talk about the steps. See whether they mention those themselves.) Compare your notes with those of your classmates. Do the writers do similar things as they write? Does the process they use seem to depend on whether they are writing fiction or nonfiction? Do their processes resemble the process described in this chapter?

2. The writing workshop described in this chapter is widely regarded in the educational literature as a valuable development. Many teachers use the workshop approach successfully and many children seem to have internalized the steps of the writing process, but maybe not as many as reading the literature might suggest. Visit an elementary school, and ask the teachers whether they use writing workshops with their children. If so, how often? What do they like about it? Does it work for all students? If not, what modifications must they use for the children who struggle? If they don't use the writing workshop, why don't they? What approach to writing instruction do they use?

Chapter 12
Assessing Literacy

 ## Learning Outcomes

After reading this chapter you should be able to:

1. Define reading assessment and explain why we assess students' reading.

2. Use different approaches to assessment.

3. Understand the most frequently used terms for assessment.

4. Be able to assess emergent readers.

5. Be able to assess beginning readers and beyond.

6. Understand other uses of assessment, including the assessment of teachers and English language learners.

Anticipation Guide

The following statements will stimulate your thinking about the topics of this chapter. Answer *true* or *false* in response to each statement. As you read and learn more about the topics in these statements, double-check your answers. See what interests you and prompts your curiosity toward more understanding.

_____ 1. Assessment of literacy is done at different times and for different purposes. At the beginning of the year, screening assessment is done, followed by diagnostic assessment for those who need it. All during the year all students are subjected to monitoring assessment, and at the end of the year, most face outcomes-based assessment.

_____ 2. High-stakes assessment has so alarmed and angered the American public that it probably won't be around by the time this book makes it into print.

_____ 3. The concepts of validity and reliability are not just of interest to researchers; teachers also need to be concerned with the validity and reliability of the instruments they use.

_____ 4. Informal assessments are only given on weekends, preferably at a cookout with everybody dressed in old clothes.

_____ 5. An important piece of information yielded by assessment concerns children's independent, instructional, and frustration reading levels.

_____ 6. It is usually harder for a child to read words in the context of a meaningful passage than it is to read them off lists.

_____ 7. The online management and reporting of children's assessment data are becoming something of an industry in the United States.

_____ 8. All assessment should be done using scientifically tested instruments.

_____ 9. Readability measurement is an exact science. It is possible to pinpoint precisely the level of challenge any piece of text will pose to any reader.

_____ 10. Assessment is for children. There is no earthly reason why teachers should ever assess themselves.

A Classroom Story

Assessment Drives Teaching Decisions

John Samuels teaches a diverse group of first graders at a small elementary school in a farming community. Of his 27 students, 7 speak Spanish at home. The parents of 8 of the children (including two of the Spanish-speaking families) are scientists at a nearby agricultural experiment station. Some children are from families of farm workers, and others are from families on public assistance. John believes very strongly that his job as a teacher is to help all of his children be as well prepared as possible for a happy and successful life.

At the beginning of the year, John, the school's reading teacher, and the three other first-grade teachers in his school administer a screening test of early reading abilities to the entire first grade. They test the children's letter knowledge, their concept of word, their phonemic segmentation and phonics skills (through an invented spelling task), and their recognition of both environmental print and decodable words. The results for John's class are given in Table 12.1.

John and the other three teachers look through all of the scores together. They decide that the top scoring readers in John's groups are probably beginning readers already. The middle group still needs a moderate amount of support in emergent literacy skills and concepts. The group with the lowest scores will need special intervention to help them profit from reading instruction during the year.

During the first two weeks of the school year, John gives further diagnostic tests to his students. The children with the lowest scores have their concepts about print assessed as well as their awareness of phonemes in words. The early screening already showed him which letters of the alphabet each child still needs to recognize and be able to produce, and their other scores suggested that they will need a holistic introduction to reading, with frequent sessions of listening to read-alouds, lots of dictation and shared book reading, and shared writing. They will need the whole sequence of systematic phonics instruction.

But John is also a good "kidwatcher." He observes the children carefully as they participate in his early lessons. He is pleased to see them singing along to "Down By the Bay" and smiling as they clap along to the rhythm. He watches to see whom they interact with on the playground.

He has already visited with their families before school started. The parents want their children to learn, and they make it clear that they are counting on his suggestions for ways to help their children. One of the fathers and two of the mothers are unemployed. They seem skeptical when John suggests that they might come into the classroom to help out, but John thinks at least the father and one of the mothers can be persuaded.

John finds time to read a simple book with each of the top- and middle-scoring children, and he keeps a running record of their abilities. He has learned to be a little skeptical of test scores, and he watches carefully to see if their performance in a real reading task lives up to what the test predicted. He is "roaming around the known," as Marie Clay (1993) puts it. Soon he has determined a reading level for each child and is ready to place the children in their first group for guided reading.

As he makes running records of the middle-scoring children's reading, he finds levels of books they can read at the instructional level, too. He notes they have developed some sight vocabulary and are developing some phonics skills. They are not fluent

Table 12.1 Scores of First Graders on the Early Reading Screening Inventory

Student	Alphabet Knowledge (%)	Concept of Word (%)	Invented Spelling* (%)	Word Recognition (%)
High-scoring group				
Janice	100	100	92	80
Ephraim	92	100	88	75
Ignacio	98	100	90	80
Topaz	96	90	92	82
Middle-scoring group				
Peter	70	80	65	50
Carla	65	88	60	55
Laticia	68	80	70	60
Low-scoring group				
Juana	52	40	35	20
George	55	45	30	24
Alexia	40	40	20	10
Amanda	30	30	16	5

*Includes phonemic segmentation and early phonics.

readers—they read word by word, without inflection. He will see if he can match them up with tutors from the nearby college's service learning project.

Assessment is an essential part of doing anything well, including the teaching of reading. The topic of assessment is getting more attention in reading instruction now than ever before. With the current emphasis on "research-based reading instruction," educators are paying more and more attention to how children are learning, what works and what doesn't, and why.

What Is Assessment and Why Do We Assess?

Assessment in reading entails gathering, tabulating, and interpreting information to determine how well a student reads. Assessment covers everything from informal observations of a student's reading to the use of commercial tests. Assessment practices include:

- Deciding what we need to know about a child's or group of children's reading.
- Deciding what measures will tell us what we want to know.
- Gathering and tabulating, or summarizing, information with those measures.
- Interpreting the information.
- Making decisions about what to do next, based on the new information.

There are different purposes for assessment and also different audiences for the information that assessment brings to light.

1. *We assess to guide our instruction.* We may assess to:

   - *Identify reading levels (independent, instructional, and frustration)* so we can place students in materials at the right level.
   - *Investigate children's readiness or prior knowledge* before starting instruction. Many aspects of learning to read and write are developmental, and in order to give the right instruction, teachers need to know where learners are in their development. For example, emergent readers need to develop the ability to segment phonemes and also develop a concept of word before more advanced phonics lessons will make sense to them.
   - *Locate children's strengths and areas of need* so we can steer our instruction toward appropriate targets. There are many aspects of children's literacy development, and if there are some aspects in which they are not progressing adequately, we need to locate these so we can offer specially tailored help. For example, a child may have learned many sight words, but have low reading fluency. We need to know that, so we can work on the student's fluency.
   - *Identify children's literacy strategies* so we can strengthen appropriate ones and direct a child away from inappropriate ones. For example, good readers preview texts and set purposes for reading to help them understand better. Does each child know how to do this? Some immature readers look only at the first letter of a word and guess any word they know that begins with that letter. We can direct that child's attention to more letters and letter combinations in words.

2. *We assess to make sure our instruction is succeeding.* Some approaches work better than others with individual children, or with whole classrooms of children. We assess to:

   - *Find out if a teaching approach or set of materials is working for a child.* For example, to build reading fluency, teachers may use "buddy reading" or a computer program. But does the child know how to take advantage of these activities? Or in teaching word study, the teacher wants each child to study words that are right at his or her level of development of word knowledge. Is this the case? In guided reading, we want children to read some texts that are moderately challenging and some texts that are easier. Is each child placed with the right materials?
   - *Find out what strategies seem best suited to whole groups of students.* Research shows that schools that are most effective in helping all children learn to read and write are those in which teachers monitor how well instruction is working, and then use this information as they work with other teachers to find ways to improve instruction (Cunningham & Allington, 2015; Taylor, et al., 1999). Teachers may monitor a host of factors, from classroom routines and management strategies to teaching methods, to materials, to ways of working with instructional aides and parent volunteers, to ways of assessing children.

3. *We assess to give feedback to students and their parents.* Findings from assessments should be communicated to children and their parents, so both can work toward the children's success. We assess to:

   - *Show students what they are doing well and what they can do better* by communicating information in a way that helps them become aware of those strategies they are using successfully; this can point the way toward improvements.
   - *Help students set goals for better performance* and monitor their progress toward meeting those goals.
   - *Help parents understand how their children are performing* in learning to read and what they can do to help.

4. *We assess to make sure all students are meeting state standards for learning.* The federal No Child Left Behind law that passed in 2002 mandated that every child in America be tested in reading from grades 3 to 8, with tests developed by the individual states. Beginning in 2014, new tests developed by the Partnership for the Assessment of Readiness for College and Careers (PARCC) will assess students' achievement of the Common Core State Standards—at least they will in the states and territories where the CCSS have been formally adopted. Because the standards-based tests have significant consequences, many teachers are giving more frequent assessments throughout the year to monitor their students' progress toward meeting the standards on which their state tests are based.

5. *We assess to make decisions on the placement of students in special instructional services.* All children in the United States are entitled by law to special education services as they need them, and they are also entitled to special support to learn the English language, if necessary. Parents may request that their children be screened for such services, but teachers may also identify students who need more support than what is likely to be available to them in the regular classroom. In either case, special screening is called for, including specialized tests that are normally administered by school psychologists. But the teacher's own observational records and assessment results play a useful role in these decisions.

6. *We assess ourselves as teachers or as teachers-to-be.* We make sure our professional knowledge is up to date, and that our practices are serving our students as best they can. We assess our professional knowledge, both to keep ourselves current and to meet teaching licensing requirements.

Check Your Understanding 12.1: Gauge your understanding of the skills and concepts in this section.

Approaches to Assessment

With the many different purposes for assessment comes a variety of means to measure and investigate children's reading and writing abilities. These range from the formal to the informal, or from the more precisely measured and quantifiable (scores that can be counted with exactitude) to the more holistic and qualitative. Precise tests that yield quantifiable scores may seem more trustworthy and serious, but since they focus on a limited set of predetermined factors measured during an hour or two that are plucked randomly out of a child's life, they are also bound to miss a lot. On the other end of the spectrum we have holistic observations of what a young reader and writer is actually doing, often over a longer period of time. But many of the judgments may be based on the teacher's perspective, so they may be more richly informative, but also less reliable.

Formal Assessments

On the formal end of the spectrum we have standardized or norm-referenced tests, standards-based tests, and curriculum-based measurement.

NORM-REFERENCED TESTS   Standardized or **norm-referenced tests** of reading compare children's performances with those of large numbers of other students. For example, tests such as the Stanford Achievement Test and the California Achievement Test report children's reading performances in comparison to those of other students at their grade level. The tests are given under rigorously controlled conditions so the results will be comparable. Norm-referenced tests are typically used, along with other data, to inform decisions about placing a child for special reading services. But these tests traditionally have lacked an obvious connection with any school curriculum, so it is difficult to tell what aspect of a school's instruction has contributed or failed to contribute to a child's performance.

STANDARDS-BASED TESTS   **Standards-based tests** have emerged in recent years as individual states have set standards for achievement in reading and other subject areas at each grade level, as they have been required to do by the federal Every Student Succeeds Act and are now required for the many states that have adopted the Common Core State Standards.

Standards-based tests are meant to assess each student's performance on the standards set by the states. Students may be promoted to another grade or held back, depending on their performance, and schools may suffer sanctions if they do not make "adequate yearly progress." Standards-based tests are sometimes called *high-stakes tests*, because a child's performance on such a test can determine whether she or he is promoted to the next grade, and the performance of many children can determine if a school is rated as achieving or underachieving.

CURRICULUM-BASED MEASUREMENT (CBM)   As the term *high-stakes testing* implies, by the time a student takes a standards-based test, it is usually too late for the teacher to do anything more for the student that year. To make sure that children are making good progress toward meeting the standards measured on the high-stakes tests—and indeed, to better teach children to read—many educators are turning to the practice of curriculum-based measurement (Fuchs, Deno, & Mirkin, 1984; Shinn, 1989), a set of practices and instruments that have been borrowed from the special education field. These measures are normally based on the skills students are expected to acquire according to the state standards for learning, but they have the advantage of being administered repeatedly— sometimes as often as weekly—throughout the school year so the teacher can still take corrective action as needed. Curriculum-based measurements are very brief samples of behavior, deliberately so because a teacher may have to test 25 or more children individually several times during the year. To test oral reading, for instance, a teacher may have a student read three passages aloud for one minute each and average the speed and accuracy of the reading. Nonetheless, even such brief measures of oral reading have been shown to predict students' later performance on different states' high-stakes standards-based tests. Although curriculum-based measures have many uses, among the most promising is that they facilitate continuous monitoring of a student's performance in reading throughout the year, to ensure that both the student's learning strategies and the teacher's instruction are working well.

Curriculum-based measurements may be designed by the teacher or they may be purchased commercially. For grades 5–8, Timothy Rasinski and Nancy Padak (2005) offer a series of Three-Minute Reading Assessments: Word Recognition, Fluency, and Comprehension. Many states are using DIBELS, the Dynamic Indicators of Basic Early Literacy Skills, and studies have shown scores on DIBELS predict later performance on the standards-based tests of some states, including Arizona (Wilson, 2005), Florida (Buck & Torgesen, 2003), North Carolina (Barger, 2003), and Oregon (Shaw & Shaw, 2002).

DIBELS was created with public funds, and it is available for free on the Internet. However, for a fee, the providers of DIBELS offer an electronically based data management and reporting service that keeps track of each child's scores on each part of the test, follows the child's progress on each of several indicators over time, and makes available a number of verbal and graphic ways to display results.

The Developmental Reading Assessment (DRA) is published by Pearson. Based on the model of an Informal reading inventory, the DRA provides a range of assessments for screening, diagnosis, and monitoring. For a fee, the DRA enables teachers to manage the test scores online and perform a number of tracking, comparing, and reporting functions.

Less Formal Assessments

Somewhere in the middle of the spectrum are informal reading inventories and running records.

INFORMAL READING INVENTORIES   Informal reading inventories (IRIs), developed over 70 years ago by Emmett Betts (1946), are comprehensive measures of students' reading ability. IRIs are administered to individual children to create diagnostic profiles: a picture of individual readers' word recognition, reading fluency, comprehension, and overall reading levels. In contrast to standardized reading tests, IRIs have not been normed by elaborate field testing with hundreds or thousands of children. Hence they are called "informal" reading inventories.

IRIs are created from samples of grade-level texts, either taken from basal readers at ascending grade levels or written by the test authors and matched to grade levels according to readability formulas. IRIs consist of lists of words and text passages of graduated levels of difficulty—usually from early first grade or preprimer through grade 8 or higher.

Teachers may create their own IRIs, but many good ones are commercially available, including the Qualitative Reading Inventory (Leslie & Caldwell, 2005) and the Classroom Reading Inventory (Wheelock et. al., 2011,). The Developmental Literacy Inventory, written by some of this book's authors (Temple, Crawford, & Gillet, 2009), combines an Informal Reading Inventory with assessments of emergent literacy.

RUNNING RECORDS   Developed by Marie Clay (1993) to support her Reading Recovery Program, **running records** are teacher-made assessment devices administered to individual students to monitor their fluency, word recognition accuracy,

Figure 12.1 Running Record Sheet

Name: _____   Date: _____

School: _____   Teacher: _____

Analysis of Errors and Self-Corrections

Information used or neglected [Meaning (M), Structure or Syntax (S), Visual (V)]

Easy:

Instructional:

Hard:

Text Titles	Running Words Errors	Error Rate	Accuracy	Self-Correction Rate
Easy (100%–95%)		1:	%	1:
Instructional (94%–90%)		1:	%	1:
Hard (89% and lower)		1:	%	1:

Teacher Observations:				
Analysis of Errors and Self-Corrections				
			Information used	
Page	E	SC	E	SC
			MSV	MSV

and reading levels. Running records are usually carried out in the first two grades with younger readers, with whom they may be used every month or more frequently, both for diagnostic testing and for monitoring.

The teacher chooses simple texts that he or she suspects are at several difficulty levels for the child: one moderately challenging, one easy, and one more challenging. Clay suggests that an easy book would be one that the child has read before with the teacher, and of which the child can read more than 95% of the words. A moderately challenging text would normally be one that the child had seen before but not studied with the teacher, and whose words the child can read with 90% to 95% accuracy. A difficult text would be one the child had not seen, and whose words the child could read with 80% to 89% accuracy.

The teacher's role is to observe carefully and record what the child says as she or he reads the book. It is best to construct a form for recording the student's performance, like the one shown in Figure 12.1, but in a pinch you may sit close enough to the child to see the words as they are read, and make notes on a piece of paper.

The running record shown in Figure 12.1 allows the teacher to observe the following:

- The error rate
- The self-correction rate
- The kinds of miscues (incorrect word identifications) that the child makes: visual, structural, or meaning-based
- Other behaviors, such as the direction in which the student reads, the number of repetitions of words, and so on.

The characterizing of miscues as *meaning-based, structural, or visual* is intended to bring to light the kind of information a child is tracking in a text. Clay writes:

> **Meaning:** *Does the child use meaning (M)? If what he reads makes sense, even though it is inaccurate, then he is probably applying his knowledge of the world to his reading.*

> **Structure:** *Is what he said possible in an English sentence (S is for syntactically appropriate)? If it is, his oral language is probably influencing his responding. If it is not . . . [he] is paying close attention to detail, or to word by word reading. . . .*

> **Visual information:** *Does he use visual information (V) from the letters and words or the layout of print? [In a footnote, Clay adds, "Whether the child is relating visual information to sounds (phonological information) or to orthography (information about spelling) is a refinement of using visual information not distinguished in this analysis at this time."]* (Clay, 1993, p. 31)

A running record is a quick way to verify that a particular book is written at a child's instructional or independent reading level. It should be supplemented, though, by other kinds of assessments when you need more detail on a child's word knowledge (see Chapter 5). Running records are used most often with beginning readers; however, when children reach a level of reading where both fluency and comprehension become issues—and teachers are rightly becoming concerned about both of these even with young readers—you will want to use measures for those aspects of reading, too. Many teachers follow a running record with a retelling task (i.e., the child is asked to retell what he or she just read, and the teacher may tick off items from a pre-prepared list of main ideas and details).

Observational Assessments

On the less formal end we have observational assessments, sometimes called "Kidwatching," and portfolios—both of which may be made more reliable with the help of rubrics.

Sheila Valencia and her colleagues (Valencia, Hiebert, & Afflerbach, 1993) popularized the idea of the **authentic assessment** of literacy. Authentic assessment addresses the problem that most assessment methods have students carry out contrived tasks that are not always representative of what they do in purposeful reading and writing. Contrived tasks may not yield the full picture, including what they have achieved, how they think about literacy, how they habitually read and write, their interests and motivations, preferences, strategies, or likes and dislikes. Authentic assessment thus involves both informal and structured observations (sometimes called *kidwatching*) and work-sampling, including portfolios. Authentic assessment also includes the use of rubrics.

Teach It! 34
Dual-Entry Diary

The Dual-Entry Diary serves as an authentic assessment as it captures how a student is thinking about and responding to a topic under study.

KIDWATCHING   **Kidwatching** is a term coined by influential literacy educator, Yetta Goodman (Goodman, 1985; Owocki & Goodman, 2002), to refer to a host of observations, ranging from observations quickly captured on sticky notes to home visits, to more formal assessments.

Kidwatching Is Informed   Teachers learn more from observing children in the daily life of the classroom if they know a good deal about language and literacy processes, as well as how children talk, read, think, investigate, and interact with each other and the world.

Kidwatching Is Nonjudgmental   Teachers record events or pieces of language as they occur, without filtering them through judgments. Planning what to do on the basis of the collected evidence will happen later, preferably after many different kinds of information have been collected. Here is an example of one kidwatcher's observation:

> Notes on Erin (11/19) age 5-$\frac{1}{2}$ in the library corner: Erin is turning the pages of Fruits Good to Eat in order, at a regular pace. She gets to the page with a pineapple on it, looks at it closely, turns to Robin, and asks, "Is this a pineapple?" Robin replies, "I think so, but let's ask Ms. B." They come to me. I ask Erin what she thinks, and she says, "I think so, but what does this say [pointing to the print]?" When I ask her what she thinks, she says, "I think it says pineapple because that's in the picture and there's a p." (Goodman, 2006)

Note that this kind of written observation is also called an *anecdotal record.*

Kidwatching Uses Diverse Sources of Information   Goodman (2006) writes, "Kidwatchers use a variety of tools to document their observations, including informal conversations, formal interviews, check sheets, observation forms, field notes, portfolios, and home visits." Using many sources of information, including not only the teacher's observations but also the child's and the family's points of view, as well as more formal assessments, allows teachers to make small adjustments—and sometimes larger ones—to instruction and classroom procedures.

PORTFOLIOS   **Portfolios** are collections of children's works gathered according to the objectives of the teacher's instruction. They may be maintained by the teacher as a way of keeping a diverse collection of artifacts related to a child's progress in learning to read and write. But usually they are maintained in collaboration with each child. The teacher and the child should decide in advance the sorts of items that should be kept in the portfolio. These might include:

- Lists of books read
- A reading journal
- Repeated reading score sheets
- Written works chosen as indicative of the child's best work and range of work during a particular time period
- A list of topics for the child's writing
- Learning logs
- Running records

Periodically—at least once a month or once each marking period—the teacher schedules a conference or interview with the child. Ahead of the conversation, both the child and the teacher should look through the portfolio to find signs of progress and areas that need work. During their conversation, the child describes what he or she has learned during this period and sets goals for improvement during the next period. The teacher may ask questions to find out what things the child likes and doesn't like to read, what strategies he or she is using in reading, and aspects of the reading instruction that might be changed. The teacher makes suggestions to help the child learn.

Portfolios can also show parents and other members of the community the work that is done in school each day. Watch this video showing how one school displays students' writing and answer the question that follows.

 Video Exploration 12.1: Watch the video and answer questions that reflect the content you have read.

RUBRICS   According to Andrade (2002),

> *A rubric is a scoring tool that lists the criteria for a piece of work, or "what counts" (for example, purpose, organization, details, voice, and mechanics are often what count in a piece of writing); it also articulates gradations of quality for each criterion, from excellent to poor.*

 Rubrics have the advantage of allowing teachers to observe and evaluate an authentic performance, such as a child's oral reading, or a piece written for a real purpose other than testing. They also have the advantage of pointing out to the students the aspects of reading and writing that we consider important. Especially when rubrics are shared with a student before he or she carries out a task, the rubrics tell the child what the important tasks are, and how to do them well.

Rubrics may be already designed by educational experts, such as the Multidimensional Fluency Scale for measuring reading fluency and the Six Traits rubric for evaluating writing. Rubrics may also be developed by teachers, or even by the students themselves. When students participate in designing a rubric, they may become more strategic in reading—that is, they have a better idea about how they should try to perform.

It helps to think of a rubric like a chart. Each row names an important aspect of performance on a task, and the boxes under each column provide descriptions that range from unsatisfactory to satisfactory to excellent performance on that aspect.

 Check Your Understanding 12.2: **Gauge your understanding of the skills and concepts in this section.**

Terms Used in Testing

Students' performance on norm-referenced tests are usually reported in three ways. First, they are given **raw scores**, which simply report the number or the percentage of items on the test they answered correctly. Raw scores mean little, though, without the understanding of how a particular child's score compares with those of other children in the same age group. Therefore, scores are presented in two additional ways. **Percentile scores** are based on a 99-point scale, and they tell a child what percentage of the children in a comparison group received a lower score than his. **Stanine scores** may also be used to report performance on a test, especially when they are also used to eliminate the fine distinctions reported in percentiles that don't mean much. Stanine scores are reported in whole numbers on a 9-point scale. The spread of scores represented by each number is based on a *normal curve of distribution*. Scores of 4, 5, and 6 are average. Scores of 1, 2, and 3 are below average. Scores of 7, 8, and 9 are above average. **Grade-equivalent scores** are just what they sound like: indications of what grade-level material an average reader would read at an instructional or independent level based on her performance on this test. Thus if a fourth grader's grade equivalent score on a reading test is 7.5, that means he scored the way an average seventh grader would have scored on the material in that test. (But that doesn't mean the child is ready to be promoted to seventh grade; just because he read material on a test intended for fourth graders like an average seventh grader would doesn't mean that he will be able to read seventh-grade materials like an average seventh grader.)

Tests are often described in terms of their validity and reliability. **Validity** refers to the extent that the tests measure what they claim to measure. Because all tests take a sample of a child's performance and claim to generalize from that sample to the child's more global level of performance, it is important to know if the test really does tell you what it says it does.

Educators often speak of different kinds of validity.

- *Content validity* is the degree to which a test measures what it says it does. If a test of reading comprehension asks students to answer questions about a passage after reading it, that test can be said to have content validity because answering questions is a reasonable demonstration of comprehension. But if the test asks students to locate all the words in a passage beginning with *B*, it would not have content validity as a test of comprehension.

- *Predictive validity*, also called *assessment-criterion relationship validity* (Gronlund, Linn and Davis 2000), refers to the power of the test to predict the student's future performance on related tasks. Predictive validity is of great importance with screening assessments and monitoring assessments because a key purpose of those measures is to use students' present performance on early reading tasks to predict their future reading ability. Note, too, that the predictive validity of a test may depend on when—that is, with what age child—it is used. For example, a test of phoneme awareness given to five-year-olds is not a very good predictor of future reading performance (Snow, Burns, & Griffin, 1998). The same test given in first grade may have greater predictive validity because a greater number of six-year-olds versus five-year-olds display some phonemic awareness.

Reliability has to do with the likelihood that the results of the test are stable and dependable; that is, if the same test were given to the same child by two different people, or on two different days, would the results be similar? There are different ways reliability is used.

- *Test-retest reliability*, in which the same students are given the same test within a short interval, to see if the results are similar

- *Split-half reliability*, in which samples of a student's performance on different items of the same test are compared with each other
- *Inter-rater reliability*, in which an instrument such as a rubric is used by different raters to assess the same student, and the results are compared

The terms *validity* and *reliability* are usually applied to standardized tests, but they are worth considering regardless of the kind of assessment being done. Since 2002, the federal No Child Left Behind Act has required that assessments be scientifically validated, which means that assessment instruments must have demonstrated validity and reliability. But a caution is in order—many valuable ways of collecting and making judgments about children's reading and writing do not have demonstrated validity and reliability. Informal observation of students' reading is one; all types of informal reading inventories are another.

- *Formative assessment* is done while instruction is going on, in order to see how well the instruction is working.
- *Summative assessment* is done after instruction is completed to see what the instruction accomplished.

We need to assess and monitor many things with respect to what children are learning about literacy.

Check Your Understanding 12.3: Gauge your understanding of the skills and concepts in this section.

Assessing Emergent Readers

Emergent readers are usually preschool, kindergarten, and first-grade children who are developing concepts about language and print and knowledge of the alphabetic writing system that form the foundation on which later reading is built. Children develop all these concepts at different rates and to different extents. Giving children special, finely tuned intervention early on can help many of them avoid reading failure and enable them to make progress as readers and writers. Assessment of children's early literacy is essential. So what do we need to know? Effective early literacy assessments focus on several areas.

- *Concepts about print.* The more developed holistic sense children have of what literacy is about, the better they will be able to focus their attention on the details they must understand in order to read. Without an orienting sense of what literacy is and what books are for, early literacy instruction may be confusing for some children.
- *Knowledge of the alphabet.* Children must know many letters of the alphabet to begin to develop the ability to read. Knowledge of the alphabet is an indicator of the amount of print exposure they have had (the more letters they know, the more print they are likely to have seen). But knowing letters is also important in itself because the more letters they know, the more successfully they can explore how print and speech go together. There is a difference between letter identification and letter retrieval. Because some readers with disabilities have difficulty naming letters quickly (Katzir & Pare-Blagoev, 2006), a number of assessments of early literacy include a timed letter identification task.
- *Awareness of sounds in language.* Writing represents spoken language, and in English, writing represents language at the level of words, onsets and rimes, and phonemes, as we saw in Chapter 3. The problem is that in speech, children can use language without thinking about it; but when they learn to read and write, children must be conscious of words, rimes, and phonemes. Those aspects must be real for young learners, because they will need to think hard about the relations between units of spoken language and units of print.
- *Knowledge of some words.* Virtually all children in America are exposed to print before they begin formal reading instruction. Many of them learn to identify some words: their own names, names of fast food restaurants, words from favorite book titles. The number of words they can identify while still prereaders is a sign of emergent literacy.
- *Listening comprehension.* Children need to have receptive language developed to the degree that they can follow books read aloud to them by the teacher and also comprehend texts themselves when they become readers. Some, but not all, emergent literacy assessment instruments include measures of listening comprehension.
- *Knowledge of letter-to-sound correspondences (phonics).* Children need to develop ideas about the relations between letters and sounds to learn to read. Children's understanding of letter-to-sound correspondences can be assessed beginning in kindergarten and continuing through first grade. (Phonics knowledge will continue to be assessed in beginning readers and in older struggling readers.)

Contemporary assessment of early literacy, then, tracks the development of concepts about print, awareness of sounds, awareness of letters, knowledge of words, and (sometimes) listening comprehension.

Measures of Emergent Literacy

Teacher-made measures of emergent literacy can be fashioned after the Early Reading Screening Inventory (Morris, 2003) and the Print Concepts Assessment (after Clay, 1993). The Early Reading Screening Inventory, as the name implies, has been widely used to identify young readers in early first grade who will need additional help to learn to read. Other emergent literacy assessment programs are in use around the United States, some of them promoted by individual states. The Phonological Awareness Literacy Survey (PALS) is provided to school districts in Virginia and is widely used elsewhere as both a screening and a monitoring tool. The Illinois Snapshot of Early Literacy is promoted by that state as a screening tool. The Texas Education Agency developed the Texas Primary Reading Inventory with versions for kindergarten through third grades, which can be administered as a screening, diagnosis, and monitoring tool.

At the University of Oregon, the Dynamic Indicators of Basic Literacy Skills (DIBELS) was developed with a federal grant and is available to teachers for free online. This test, which can be used as a screening, diagnostic, or monitoring tool, begins with a preschool version that assesses initial sounds or onset fluency. At the kindergarten level are added tests of phonemic segmentation fluency, letter naming fluency, and nonsense word reading fluency. These continue through first grade, where an oral reading fluency measure is also added, and continues through third grade. These are called fluency tests because children's responses are timed, and the speed of the child's responses is noted in addition to accuracy.

Below we will look first at the assessment of children's concepts about print. Next, we will look at assessing alphabet knowledge and concept of word. Then, we will turn to assessing children's ability to break speech down into small units (phonological awareness) and finally, to assessing word recognition.

Assessing Print Concepts

Marie Clay's Concepts About Print Test measures:

- Book orientation knowledge.
- The knowledge that print, not the picture, contains the story.
- Principles involving the directional arrangement of print on the page.
- Children's understanding of important reading terminology such as *word, letter, beginning of the sentence,* and *top of the page.*
- Matching upper case and lower case letters.
- Understanding simple punctuation marks.

Assessment of print concepts can be done with a simple illustrated children's book, so long as the child being tested has not seen it before. Marie Clay's Concepts About Print Test has two specially made books (*Sand* and *Stones*), but teachers can get much of the flavor of the procedure with a book of their own choosing. Here are the steps:

1. *Knowledge of the layout of books.* Hand the child a book, with the spine facing the child, and say, "Show me the front of the book." Note whether the child correctly identifies the front.

2. *Knowledge that print, not pictures, is what we read.* Open the book to a double spread with print on one page and a picture on the other. Then say, "Show me where I begin reading." Watch carefully to see if the child points to the print or the picture. If the pointing gesture is vague, say, "Where, exactly?"

3. *Directional orientation of print on the page.* Stay on the same set of pages, and after the child points at some spot on the printed page, say, "Show me with your finger where I go next." Then observe whether the child sweeps his finger across the printed line from left to right or moves it in some other direction.

Then ask, "Where do I go from there?" and observe whether the child correctly makes the return sweep to the left and drops down one line.

Note that a correct direction pattern is like this:

If the child indicates some other directional pattern, make a note of it.

4. *Knowledge of the concepts of beginning and end.* Turning now to a new page, say, "Point to the beginning of the story on this page" and then "Point to the end of the story on this page." Observe whether the child interprets both requests properly.

5. *Knowledge of the terms top and bottom.* Turning to another pair of pages that have print on one page and a picture on the other, point to the middle of the printed page and say, "Show me the bottom of the page" and then "Show me the top of the page." Then point to the middle of the picture and say, "Show me the top of the picture" and then "Show me the bottom of the picture." Note whether the child responds accurately to all four requests.

6. *Knowledge of the terms word and letter.* Now hand the child two blank index cards and say, "Put these cards on the page so that just one word shows between them" and then "Now move them so that two words show between them. Now move them again so that one letter shows between them" and then "Now move them so that two letters show between them." Make note of the child's response to all four requests.

7. *Knowledge of uppercase and lowercase letters.* Find a page with both uppercase and lowercase versions of at least two letters. Point to a capital letter with your pencil and say, "Show me a little letter that is the same as this one." Next point to a lowercase letter and say, "Now point to a capital letter that is the same as this one." Repeat this procedure with other pairs of letters.

8. *Knowledge of punctuation.* Turn to a page that has a period, an exclamation point, a question mark, a comma, and a set of quotation marks. Pointing to each one in turn, ask, "What is this? What is it for?"

It is advisable to make up a record sheet that provides for the quick recording of information yielded by the assessment.

Assessing Alphabet Knowledge

When testing students' alphabet knowledge, ask them to recognize all of the letters of the alphabet in both uppercase and lowercase. We also ask them to write all of the letters once each, without specifying uppercase or lowercase. The letters are always presented in a scrambled sequence so that the children cannot use serial order as a cue to identifying a letter.

For a Letter Recognition Inventory, prepare a sheet of randomly arranged lower- and uppercase letters (see Figure 12.2). That is the version to show to the student. Prepare another copy to use as a record sheet. As you proceed from left to right across the line, point to each letter and ask the child to identify it. Enter on the record sheet only a notation of what letters were misidentified or unnamed. Then, call out the letters slowly and ask the child to write each one. Score a letter correct whether it is written in uppercase or lowercase.

Assessing the Concept of Word

To assess a student's concept of word, follow this procedure designed by Morris (1998).

Teach the student to memorize the poem shown below orally, *without showing her the written version.*

My little dog Petunia

Is a very strange dog.

She bellows like a mule

But she leaps like a frog.

Figure 12.2 Alphabet Recognition Assessment—Student Version

R	M	P	G	F	A	Z	S	T	N	B	I	W
Q	O	K	X	C	U	L	V	J	D	Y	E	H

+++

r	m	p	g	f	a	z	s	t	n	b	l	w
q	o	k	x	c	u	l	v	j	d	y	e	h

+++

Figure 12.3 Concept of Word Assessment

Concept of Word Assessment

Student: _____ Grade: _____

Teacher: _____ School: _____

Date: _____ Examiner: _____

	Voice-Pointing	Word Identification
My little <u>dog</u> <u>Petunia</u> 　　　　 1　　 2	_____	_____
Is a <u>very</u> <u>strange</u> dog. 　　 1　　 2	_____	_____
She <u>bellows</u> <u>like</u> a mule 　　 1　　　 2	_____	_____
But <u>she</u> leaps like a <u>frog</u>. 　 1　　　　　　 2	_____	_____

Voice Pointing: _____ (of 4)

Word Identification: _____ (of 8)

Total Concept of Word (Voice-pointing plus word identification): _____ (of 12)

++

Once the student can recite the words from memory, show her the written poem and explain that these written words say the poem just learned.

Now, read through the poem at a slow natural rate, pointing to each word with your finger as you read it. Explain that you want the student to read the poem the way you did, but one line at a time.

Ask the student to say the first line, pointing to each word as she says it. On the record sheet shown in Figure 12.3, enter a score of 1 under *voice-pointing* if she points to every word in that line correctly, and a score of 0 if she incorrectly points to any word in that line. Next, ask the student to point to the word *little*. Enter a score of 1 under *word identification* if she points to it and 0 if she does not. Now ask her to point to the word *Petunia*. Enter a score of 1 under *word identification* if she points to it and 0 if she does not.

Now go to the second line and repeat the process, testing first the student's voice-pointing and then the student's word identification. Award a score of 1 if the student points to every word just as she says it, and a 0 if the student makes any errors. Then ask her to point to *very* and then to *strange*. Award a score of 1 for each word the student correctly points to, and a 0 for each error. Repeat these instructions for lines 3 and 4.

Assessing Phoneme Awareness

Phoneme awareness—the awareness of speech sounds at the phoneme level—can be indicated in many ways. They include comparing phonemes, isolating them, adding them, deleting them, and separating them. Here we will demonstrate phoneme segmentation.

Figure 12.4 Words for the Yopp-Singer Phoneme Segmentation Test

Words for the Yopp-Singer Phoneme Segmentation Test

Student: _____   School: _____

Date: _____   Examiner: _____

1. dog (3) _____   12. lay (2) _____

2. keep (3) _____   13. race (3) _____

3. fine (3) _____   14. zoo (2) _____

4. no (2) _____   15. three (3) _____

5. she (2) _____   16. job (3) _____

6. wave (3) _____   17. in (2) _____

7. grew (3) _____   18. ice (2) _____

8. that (3) _____   19. at (2) _____

9. red (3) _____   20. top (3) _____

10. me (2) _____   21. by (2) _____

11. sat (3) _____   22. do (2) _____

Score (number correct) _____ /22 Percentage score: _____

PHONEME SEGMENTATION   The Yopp/Singer test of phoneme segmentation is done as follows. You say:

> *Today we're going to play a word game. I'm going to say a word, and I want you to break the word apart. You are going to tell me each sound of the word in order. For example, if I say old, you will say o-l-d. Let's try a few words together.* (Yopp, 1988, p. 166)

You follow with three more demonstration words: *ride, go,* and *man.* Praise the child if she is right, and correct her if she is wrong. After the trials, read the 22 words to the child, and have her break each word apart as it is read. You should give praise or correction after each word. Note that the number of phonemes or separate sounds in each word is given in parentheses after the word. Score each word "1" if the child separately pronounces all of the phonemes in the word, or "0" if she does not. The words are shown in Figure 12.4.

ASSESSING PHONEMIC AWARENESS BY MEANS OF INVENTED SPELLING   Another way to observe whether a first-grade child has phonemic awareness is to ask him to spell words that he does not already know. When a child is asked to spell unknown words, he must rely upon his *invented spelling,* the inner capacity to forge connections between letters and sounds. Children have an amazing intuitive ability to invent spellings, and we can learn much about their word knowledge by looking at their invented productions.

A procedure for testing phonemic segmentation (after Morris, 2005), then, is to have the child spell the list of words in Figure 12.5 as you call them out. Then you can count the number of phonemes the child reasonably attempted to represent. (Guides to scoring each word are presented in parentheses.)

Explain to the child that you are going to ask him to spell some words you know he doesn't know how to spell. He will have to figure out the spellings as best he can. After you call out each word (at least twice, and as many more times as he requests), ask him to try to spell each sound in the word. If he says he can't, ask him to listen to the way the word

Figure 12.5 A Spelling Test of Phoneme Awareness

A Spelling Test of Phoneme Awareness

bite   (three phonemes: BIT = 3 points; BT = 2 points, BRRY, etc. = 1 point)

seat   (three phonemes: SET or CET = 3 points; ST, CT = 2 points)

dear   (three phonemes: DER = 3 points; DIR or DR = 2 points)

bones   (four phonemes: BONS or BONZ = 4 points; BOS or BOZ = 3 points)

mint   (four phonemes: MENT or MINT = 4 points; MET or MIT = 3 points; MT = 2 points)

rolled   (four phonemes: ROLD = 4 points; ROL or ROD = 3 points)

race   (three phonemes: RAS, RAC, or RAEC = 3 points, RC or RS = 2 points)

roar   (three phonemes: ROR or ROER = 3 points; RR = 2 points)

beast   (four phonemes: BEST = 4 points; BES or BST = 3 points; BS or BT = 2 points)

groan   (four phonemes: GRON = 4 points; GRN = 3 points; GN = 2 points)

TOTAL: _____ / 35 points, for 35 phonemes represented.

Figure 12.6 Word Recognition for Emergent Literacy

Word Recognition for Emergent Literacy

First List	Second List
bed	and
sad	good
ride	you
pin	the
pole	one
tub	come
got	is
duck	said
ball	play
rule	look

Figure 12.7 Word Identification Response Sheet

Word Identification Response Sheet

Student: _____   School: _____

Date: _____   Examiner: _____

Decodable Words

bed _____

sad _____

ride _____

pin _____

pole _____

tub _____

got _____

duck _____

ball _____

rule _____

Total _____/10

High-Frequency Words

and _____

good _____

you _____

the _____

one _____

come _____

is _____

said _____

play _____

look _____

Total _____/10

++

---

begins. What sound does it start with? Ask him to write down a letter for that sound and letters for any other sounds he can hear. If the student is not sure how to spell a sound, ask him to write a little dash (—).

After reading all 10 words (fewer if the test seems too arduous for a particular child), count the number of reasonable letters the child wrote for each word and compare that to the number of phonemes in the word. A child who consistently writes three or four letters that show some reasonable connection to the sounds in the word appears to be able to segment phonemes. Assuming the child is making an effort, if he writes nothing or strings together many letters indiscriminately we assume he is not yet able to segment phonemes. And if he writes one or two reasonable letters per word, we assume he is just beginning to segment phonemes. You can calculate a score for phonemic segmentation by scoring each word according to the guide at the right of each word and then comparing the total number of points the child receives to the total possible number of points.

Word Recognition

Emergent readers can often recognize a few words. The following assessment of word identification (after Morris, 1998) tests both high-frequency words and decodable words.

Show the student the lists of words in Figure 12.6 and ask her to identify them.

Mark the student's answers on a response sheet such as the one shown in Figure 12.7. Award the student one point for each word she can name correctly.

"Roaming around the Known"

How accurate are all of these measures? According to Snow et al. (1998), the correlations between the component measures listed earlier in this section and children's later success in learning to read are in the 30% to 50% range. Scores in this range suggest that the factors are important in reading, but there is a very real chance that a child will be more or less successful in learning to read than these tests predict. With these limitations in mind, prudent teachers avoid making important decisions about children's education on the basis of one of these tests alone. Many use the practice of following the testing with **"Roaming around the Known"** (Clay, 1993); that is, taking the findings from the assessments as suggestions only, and teaching the child for several days to see how she or he responds to actual instruction—in other words, teaching with the idea that the assessments may very well be wrong.

Check Your Understanding 12.4: Gauge your understanding of the skills and concepts in this section.

Assessing Beginning Readers and Beyond

Beginning readers are starting to read words in connected text. Just as it is important to know that they have their emergent literacy concepts and abilities in place, it is also critical to know if each child is making progress in all aspects of beginning reading. These aspects include word recognition—including having a sight vocabulary stored in memory, decoding skills so that the child can read a word he didn't know before, and the ability to use context to help identify words. Children's reading fluency—their accuracy, rate, and intonation—needs to develop apace as well. Their vocabulary should be growing by thousands of words each year, and they will need to learn vocabulary from reading. Comprehension is the ultimate goal of reading, and we want to know how this ability is growing, too. As we saw in Chapters 6 and 7, comprehension is a complex of many factors including having and using world knowledge, getting main ideas, making inferences, having metacognition or cognitive monitoring—that is, knowing if the text is making sense—and following the patterns of different kinds of fictional and informational texts to construct meaning. We also care about what kind of text and how much of it they read. But one measure that combines all of these factors is their reading levels.

Reading Levels: Independent, Instructional, Frustration

It is possible to measure students' *reading levels*, the levels of text they can read for different purposes. To talk about reading levels implies two things: that texts have levels of difficulty and that readers have levels of ability. To speak of levels of difficulty of texts implies that some are written on a first-grade level, some on a second-grade level, and so on. These levels of difficulty are referred to as **readability**, and we will say more about that later. When we speak of the reading levels of individual readers, it helps to ask what the reading task is: Will they be studying a book in a group under the teacher's supervision, reading a textbook for homework, or reading for pleasure? Depending on the answers to those questions, it is proper to speak not of one reading level but three: the independent level, the instructional level, and the frustration level.

INDEPENDENT READING LEVEL   If the student is to read material on his or her own, without the support of a teacher or other more skilled readers, then the material should fall within the student's independent level of reading ability. In material written at the student's **independent reading level**, the student should encounter no more than three or four unknown words in a hundred and should enjoy nearly total comprehension.

Books that fall within students' independent level include those that students choose to read for pleasure and textbooks they use independently for homework. Regardless of a student's grade placement, if the books are above the student's independent level, then the student should be given easier books or should be offered support for reading such as buddy reading, study guides, or recorded text. Conversely, teachers sometimes have to prod students to read more challenging material that falls within their independent level.

INSTRUCTIONAL READING LEVEL   In the classroom, teachers often work with students using material that is moderately challenging for them so they will learn from the supported practice. Material used for this purpose should fall within the student's instructional level of reading ability. Such material presents the student with unknown words at a rate of up to one in ten, and language and concepts that are not fully comprehended—at least not at first. The intention is that with guided practice in materials written at the instructional level, students will learn the unknown words and come to comprehend the once-challenging language and concepts. The **instructional reading level** corresponds to what Russian psychologist Vygotsky (1976) called the *zone of proximal development*, the area of moderate challenge that is just at the threshold of a reader's growing abilities. It is here that teachers most often practice scaffolded instruction, providing temporary support, including teaching strategies that will help the student learn on his or her own in the future.

Again, a particular student's instructional level often falls above or below that student's grade placement level. Because of the value of working in moderately challenging materials when teaching a student to read, it is very important to locate a student's instructional level wherever it may fall.

FRUSTRATION READING LEVEL   If the material is too challenging—that is, if it contains more than one unfamiliar word in ten, and language and concepts that substantially resist comprehension—the material is said to be written at the student's **frustration reading level**. The frustration level is not actually a reading level because students do not practice successful reading there. It is used instead to define the limits of a student's instructional level. Teachers can assign reading material during closely supervised instructional tasks that approach, but do not cross into, the frustration level.

As the name implies, frustration level text is so challenging to a student that the effort it takes to read it is burdensome and disagreeable. Students may actually progress faster in learning to read and learning to spell when they are placed in instructional level text, even though that is easier than frustration level text.

Students' reading levels are often determined by administering an Informal Reading Inventory. When an IRI is used, it will normally tell you how many errors a student can make in each part to be classified as independent, instructional, or frustrated at that level. If an IRI is not used, you can still get a rough idea of a student's reading level if you know the reading levels of several short texts. Have the child read a passage of at least 150 words. Mark each reading error as an *omission* (leaving out a word), a *substitution* (reading a word other than the word supplied in the text or misreading the word in the text), or an *insertion* (adding a word or words that were not in the text). Each counts as one error every time it occurs. *Proper names* that are misread count as one error, regardless how many times they are misread. *Reversals* (reading two words in the wrong order) count as one error. Repetitions do not count as errors, and neither do self-corrections or long pauses.

Using those criteria, here is how the scores are interpreted:

Independent level: 97% to 100% of the words are read correctly.

Instructional level: 90% to 96% of the words are read correctly.

Frustration level: Fewer than 90% of the words are read correctly.

These criteria are taken from Betts (1946).

Teachers must consider the difficulty level of each book they select for classroom use. Watch this video in which a teacher asks students if the book they are about to read, *The Diary of Anne Frank*, is at their independent reading level, and answer the question that follows.

 Video Exploration 12.2: Watch the video and answer questions that reflect the content you have read.

Reading Levels, Readability, and Text Complexity

Applying the concept of reading levels that was just presented, a teacher might assess a particular third-grade student and find that his independent level is second grade, his instructional level is third grade, and his frustration level is fourth grade. For this information to be useful to the teacher, we must assume that reading material is available that is written at the second-, third-, and fourth-grade reading levels. This assumption is safe to an extent, but not entirely. First, we should note a text may be worded simply but contain a complex idea. Consider, for example, the philosopher Descartes' famous dictum, "I think, therefore I am." One readability measure, the Flesch-Kincaid, rates the readability level of that sentence as late second grade—yet a reader would have to be a considerably more advanced thinker to appreciate the meaning. Or imagine that two different third-grade readers with roughly the same reading abilities read a text about a game of basketball. If one is a passionate player and follower of the game, that student will surely understand the text far better than the other student, who may have no experience with the game at all.

The Flesch-Kincaid readability measure we mentioned considers the surface features of the text: the grammatical complexity of the sentences and the sophistication of the vocabulary. Grammatical complexity as measured by readability instruments is usually assumed to correlate with the number of words in the sentences. The sophistication of the vocabulary is often assumed to correlate with the number of syllables in a word—though more powerful readability measures such as the Lexile system compare words in a text against a dictionary of words rated by levels.

One of the simplest readability devices for English was developed by the late Edward Fry. Fry's procedure is to take three separate 100-word samples from a work to be studied, count the number of sentences in each sample to the tenth place, and then count the number of syllables in each sample. The sentence counts and syllable counts are averaged, and the results are plotted on a graph to yield the readability of the text—in this case, the level of reading ability required to read the text at one's instructional level. (You can find examples of the Fry Readability Graph via any search engine.)

Other popular readability formulas are Flesch-Kincaid (which is folded into most versions of Microsoft Word [go to *Tools → Spelling and Grammar → Options → Check Readability Level*]), Dale-Chall, and SMOG ("Simplified Measure of Gobbledygook").

The **Lexile Framework** has rapidly become a widely used system for establishing a text's readability level (Lennon & Burdick, 2004). The Lexile system, developed with federal funds by Metametrics, Inc., measures both readability of text and reading ability of readers. Readability measures are based on semantic (word-based) and syntactic (sentence-based) features of the text. The semantic score is calculated from the frequency or commonality of the words in the text and the length of the sentences. A computer program compares the words in a particular text to a dictionary that has a score for the frequency with which each word is typically encountered ("the" would be a common word; "Zoroastrianism" would be an uncommon one). The syntactic score is based on the average length of sentences in the text, and the two factors together yield a Lexile score of between 200 (for a very easy text) and 1700 (for a very challenging one). The Lexile Framework is also used to assess a reader's ability to read a text. Using Lexile scores to match readers with books can be more accurate than establishing a child's reading ability in grade equivalents, and then matching the reading score with the readability score of a book. Students with a Lexile score of 300, for instance, would be expected to read with 75% comprehension a book with a Lexile score of 300. Information about the Lexile Framework is available online. Reading difficulty of text is now measured in grade equivalents, Lexiles, Reading Recovery levels, Fountas and Pinnell levels, and others (see Table 12.2).

Table 12.2 Comparing Readability Levels

Several different systems provide ratings of the difficulty levels of texts. Readability formulas such as the Fry, the Dale-Chall, and the Flesch-Kincaid report scores in terms of grade-level equivalents. Most informal reading inventories report results as grade-level equivalents, also. Recently, other systems have proliferated. In addition to Lexiles, which range between 200 and 1700, Reading Recovery (Clay, 1993), Fountas/Pinnell (2005), and Developmental Reading Assessment or DRA (from Pearson Education) provide fine gradations of difficulty for readers in the primary grades. This chart shows how scores from the different systems compare to each other.

Grade Level	Informal Reading Inventory Scores	Fountas/Pinnell Guided Reading Levels	Reading Recovery Levels	Lexiles	Dra Levels
K		A	A, B		A
			1		1
		B	2		2
	Pre-primer 1	C	3		3
1.1	Pre-primer 2		4		4
	Pre-primer 3		5		
		D	6		6
			7		
		E	8		8
1.2			9		
	Primer	F	10		10
		G	11	200–299	
			12		12
			13		
	Grade 1	H	14		14
			15		
		I	16		16
2	Grade 2	J	18	300–399	20
		K	19		
		L	20	400–499	28
		M			
3	Grade 3	N	22	500–599	30
		O, P	24	600–699	34
					38
4	Grade 4	Q, R, S	26	700–799	40
5	Grade 5	T, U, V	28	800–899	44
6	Grade 6	W, X, Y	30	900–999	
7	Grade 7	Z	32	1000–1100	
8	Grade 8	Z	34		

Source: After Salt Lake City School District, 2006.

Figure 12.8 Three Factors of Text Complexity

SOURCE: http://www.corestandards.org/ELA-Literacy/standard-10-range-quality-complexity/measuring-text-complexity-three-factors/; http://www.corestandards.org/assets/Appendix_A.pdf

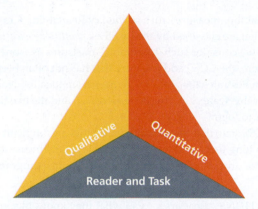

But are these readability measures that are based on grammatical complexity and vocabulary enough? The examples of Descartes' dictum and the basketball text demonstrate two other sources of challenge: the complexity of the ideas in the text, and the reader's familiarity with the content. Together, the three aspects of the surface features (grammatical complexity and sophistication of the vocabulary), the conceptual density of the text, and the reader's familiarity with the material make up what is called **text complexity**.

The authors of the Common Core State Standards argue that the ability to successfully navigate complex text is at least as important to a reader's overall reading skill. Even if teachers do an excellent job teaching comprehension strategies, the CCSS authors claim, students will not gain the reading competence they need unless they regularly read challenging texts.

The CCSS authors also are concerned that traditional ways of measuring readability—the *quantitative measures* just described—are too superficial to capture the real complexity of texts. Therefore the CCSS have added *qualitative* and *reader and tasks measures*.

The graphic depicted in Figure 12.8 shows three aspects of text complexity that are promoted by the Common Core State Standards: *qualitative*, *quantitative*, and *reader and task* factors.

QUALITATIVE FACTORS According to the CCSS, qualitative factors affecting text complexity are:

- *Levels of meaning*, in the case of literary texts, and *purpose*, for informational text. For example, a literary text may tell a story directly and simply, it may tell it satirically, or it may tell it in the voice of an unreliable author. An informational text may clearly inform, or it may have other agendas, too, such as informing and persuading at the same time.

- *Structure.* In the case of literary texts, structure is found along a spectrum from a linear narration (on the simple end) to a story told with flashbacks or from many characters' points of view (on the complex end). A literary text may state its themes explicitly, as in a fable by Aesop, or implicitly or ambiguously. With an informational text, the structure may be simple and familiar, such as a paragraph that states one topic directly, followed by paragraphs explaining that topic, followed by a conclusion. Alternatively, it may be unfamiliar, such as a legal document, or complex, such as a text that makes its points indirectly by implication, contains many counter-examples, or compares two or more items in non-parallel terms; the text may also contain graphics that are either readily understandable or complex.

- *Language conventionality and clarity.* The language may lie along a continuum with concrete, literal, common, and familiar language on one end and figurative, lyrical, ambiguous, misleading, technical, or archaic language on the other.

- *Knowledge demands: Life experiences.* Especially in literary texts, texts lie along continua ranging from single simple themes, descriptions of familiar events, and a narrator with a perspective similar to that of the readers, to the opposites of all of those features.

- *Knowledge demands: Literary knowledge.* Again in the case of literature, texts lie along continua ranging from familiar conventions and genres, with few allusions to other works of literature or other cultural references, to the opposites of all of those features.

- *Knowledge demands: Content or discipline knowledge.* In the case of informational texts, the texts will lie along continua ranging from dealing with everyday topics in familiar formats with few references to other texts or bodies of knowledge, to the opposites of all of those features.

QUANTITATIVE FACTORS   Readability measures such as the Fry Readability Graph, the Flesch-Kincaid measure, and the Lexile system, all described earlier, are classified by the CCSS as *quantitative measures* of text complexity. The CCSS recommend that among other factors, we consider such "countable" measures as word and sentence length in determining the complexity of a text. But even here, the CCSS add a feature that has not often been measured, and that is *cohesion*. Cohesion refers to the ways the text orchestrates the reader's journey from idea to idea. Signal phrases such as "First, let us consider . . . " "The main reasons for this were . . . " "In conclusion . . . " and the like tie sentences and paragraphs together and make the logic of the text easier to follow.

Although the authors of the CCSS state that the quantitative factors are "difficult if not impossible for a human reader to evaluate efficiently, especially in long texts, and are thus today typically measured by computer software," as of this writing neither the Lexile system nor any other readily available computer program measures cohesion along with the other quantitative factors.

READER AND TASK CONSIDERATIONS   Readers vary in what they know, like, or are curious about with respect to a work, author, topic, or genre; and also about the culture of the author or the setting, the author's gender or political orientation, and many other factors that constitute readers' "background" and "taste." What the readers must to do with a text, here called the "task," also affects how complex the text may turn out to be. Do we expect readers to be able to simply say they have read it, or do we want them to be able to summarize it, compare it to other texts or to a video, examine the author's word choices, or judge the degree of relevance of each paragraph to the overall argument?

Somewhere between a readability formula and a comprehension test is the cloze procedure (Bormuth, 1968; Taylor, 1953). The cloze procedure tests a reader's ability to read a particular text at the independent, instructional, and frustration levels. Thus if you are fairly sure of the difficulty level of the text, you can use the cloze procedure to get an idea of the reader's independent, instructional, and frustration levels. And if you are fairly sure of the reading ability of the group of people who take the test, you can use their performance on the cloze procedure to get an indication of the readability level of the text.

To conduct the cloze procedure, select a passage of more than 260 words. Leave the first sentence intact. Then go through and mark out every fifth word thereafter until you reach 50 words marked. Then leave the sentence after the fiftieth word intact. Retype the passage, and replace every word you marked with a blank of equal length. Have the students read the passage and fill in the blanks. Cloze tests are scored as follows:

Independent level: 60% to 100% correct (30+ words)
Instructional level: 40% to 59% correct (between 20 and 29 words)
Frustration level: Below 40% correct (fewer than 20 words)

Word Recognition

Word recognition has several aspects to it:

- *Sight vocabulary.* These are the words a reader has stored in memory—words that can be recognized instantly. Sight words are learned from reading. Words that may initially be decoded or figured out from context become sight words after repeated exposures.

- *Decoding ability.* Young readers frequently encounter words they do not have stored in memory. One way they can read them—which the National Reading Panel and the No Child Left Behind Act have indicated is the most important way—is to decode the word, or work out its identity by matching its letters and its sounds. Children differ in their ability to decode, and a task of assessment is to measure their ability to do it.

- *Identifying words from context.* When unrecognized words occur in meaningful texts, readers have two other ways besides decoding to figure out what they are. One is the syntax of the sentence. For example, if we read, "Give me the _____," we can be pretty sure that whatever fills that blank is a noun, or something that can function like a noun. But suppose the text said, "It was midnight. The safe cracker had opened the safe and taken the money. Just as he reached the door, the lights went on and a voice said, 'Stop. Now turn around slowly. Give me the _____.'" Now we would probably guess that the missing word was not only a noun, but *money*, because the meaning of the text limits our choices to that word. Both of these examples go under the name of *using context to*

Teach It! 25

Repeated Reading

In this fluency building activity, repeated reading also provides teachers with a snapshot of how a student is progressing across a school year. Information gleaned from this ongoing assessment can then be used to inform instruction.

---

support word identification. However, Marie Clay's *running records* procedure keeps track of each kind of context support by distinguishing *structural cues* from *meaning-based cues.* Both of those are distinguished from *visual* or graphophonic cues.

ASSESSING WORD RECOGNITION AND PHONICS   There are several ways to assess word recognition. Assessments of reading fluency in the repeated reading task measure students' accuracy in word recognition. If you know the reading level of the book, and you know the student's accuracy score on at least a 100-word passage (the score, in percentages, is derived by dividing the number of errors by the total number of words), you can compute the student's level of word recognition in terms of grade-equivalents as follows:

Independent level: 97% to 100% correct

Instructional level: 90% to 96% correct

Frustration level: Below 90% correct

Word recognition rates can also be measured by means of an Informal Reading Inventory. Many IRIs measure word recognition in three ways. First, they give a measure of a child's *sight vocabulary,* the words a child has stored in memory and can recognize instantaneously. They do this by "flashing" (exposing very briefly between two index cards) words from a list.

Second, they give a measure of a child's *decoding.* They do this by giving a long exposure of any words the child could not recognize instantly, and allowing the test administrator to compare the difference between the "flashed" and the "untimed" scores. The difference in favor of the untimed score demonstrates the power of the child's decoding ability because it shows how many words he could not recognize instantly, but could sound out given the time to do so.

Third, IRIs also give a measure of children's power to recognize words in context. The child reads aloud words from a text passage as the teacher listens carefully and records and scores the errors. The percentage scores of words correctly read in context are interpreted using the same criteria used in the fluency measure.

Some tests, including DIBELS and the Woodcock-Johnson-III Basic Reading Battery, assess phonics knowledge by testing children's reading of nonsense words, like *VAJ, KOL, NAK,* and the like. The advantage to having children read nonsense words is that we are assured they have never seen them before, so the words must be read by pure decoding. The disadvantage is that, because they are nonsense words, the children don't have the normal self-correction to them that comes from arriving at a word they know in their speech. Another disadvantage is that some of the nonsense words do not conform to English orthography. For example, DIBELS uses *doj, ol,* and *huf,* even though these spellings are not allowable in English; that is, there are no single-syllable words in Standard English that are spelled that way.

Another test of phonics knowledge is done by means of children's spelling. The assessment inventories built into Kathy Ganske's (2000) Word Journeys have children spell challenging words, and then give teachers advice on (1) analyzing the spelling error to assign the child to a probable level of invented spelling and (2) pinpointing the aspect of phonics knowledge that the child needs to learn.

WORD RECOGNITION INVENTORY   Word recognition inventories are part of informal reading inventories. They have two parts: a display list, which is shown to the child one word at a time, and a recording sheet for the child's answers.

To administer a word recognition inventory, you have two options. You can simply point to the words one at a time and have the child read them, putting a checkmark on the recording sheet for each word that is correctly identified. You may record what the child says when she misreads a word if you want to study those errors later. Count the number of words read correctly, and multiply by five points to yield a percentage score.

As an alternative, you can hold two index cards over the word and briefly expose the word (for about a quarter of a second) to the child. If she reads the word correctly, place a checkmark in the "flashed" column of the record sheet and go on to the next word. If the student fails to read the word correctly, record whatever she says in the "flashed" column and then open up the cards to expose the words. If she now reads the word correctly, place a checkmark in the "untimed" column; if not read correctly, record whatever the student says, or enter a zero if she says nothing. Calculate the scores for both columns by multiplying the words correctly identified by five points.

The scores can be used to identify the child's independent, instructional, and frustration levels, as follows:

Independent level: 90% to 100% correct
Instructional level: 70% to 89% correct
Frustration level: Below 70% correct

An example of a Word Recognition Inventory is found in Figure 12.9.

Figure 12.9 Informal Word Recognition Inventory

Display List

station	type	yourselves	study	quit
ought	damp	midnight	easier	alive
doesn't	elbow	motorcycle	headache	moment
coach	mystery	insect	match	range

Record-Keeping Chart

Grade 3	Flashed	Untimed
station		
ought		
doesn't		
coach		
type		
damp		
elbow		
mystery		
yourselves		
midnight		
motorcycle		
insect		
study		
easier		
headache		
match		
quit		
alive		
moment		
range		
Total Errors:		

0-2 errors = Independent Level
3-6 errors = Instructional Level
7 + errors = Frustration Level

Table 12.3 Common Errors by Spelling Stage

Level of Word Knowledge	Target Word	Typical Error	Description of the Error Type
Logographic Reading	plant right	*Larry. He has L.* _____	Student typically looks at one letter and calls out any word it reminds her of.
Alphabetic Reading	plant right	*pal?* *rye gut?*	Student reads through words one letter at a time, making a sound for each letter. Early in the phase, only a few letters are read.
Orthographic Reading	plant right	*pl, pl, -ant, plant!* *ruh, ruh, -ight, right!*	Student begins to see words as clusters of onsets and rimes.
Morphological Reading	ticked surprising unfed	*tiked, tick-ed, ticked!* *surprise, surprising!* *oonfd, oonfeed, unfed!*	Student begins to recognize prefixes, suffixes, and grammatical endings—and to see that they have consistent spellings even when they have different pronunciations.
Derivational Reading	assign	*assigg—No, assign!*	Student recognizes that the target word is derived from a familiar word.

WORD KNOWLEDGE LEVELS BY ERROR TYPE Once you have become accustomed to thinking about children's development through phases of word knowledge, you can observe their reading errors and estimate a child's level or phase of word knowledge. This can be done in a structured way. Ask a child to read 100 words of text written at her instructional level—that is, a piece of moderately challenging text of which the child misreads about one word in 10. Then write down the errors, with the target word (the word the child was attempting to read) next to each error. Compare the errors to the responses in the chart in Table 12.3.

If half of a child's errors fall within a phase, according to the chart, this is a reasonable indication that the child is reading words using strategies from that phase.

Assessing Reading Fluency

Reading fluency has moved from being a neglected skill (Allington, 1983) to an area of intense interest. In *Put Reading First,* Armbruster, Lehr, and Osborn (2001) define reading fluency this way:

> *Fluency is the ability to read a text accurately and quickly. When fluent readers read silently, they recognize words automatically. They group words quickly in ways that help them gain meaning from what they read. Fluent readers read aloud effortlessly and with expression. Their reading sounds natural, as if they are speaking.* (p. 22)

Assessing reading fluency is most simply measured by counting the number of words children read per minute minus the errors. This yields a measure called *words read correctly per minute* (WCPM), which is calculated using this formula:

$$\frac{(\text{Total words read, minus words read incorrectly}) \times 60}{\text{Reading time in seconds}} = \text{WCPM}$$

Thus, for example, if a third-grade student reads 125 words in one minute but makes five reading errors, we would calculate her fluency rate of WCPM as:

$$\frac{(125 - 5) \times 60}{60} = \frac{120 \times 60}{60} = 120 \text{ WCPM}$$

For a third grader in the middle of the year, that would be a normal reading rate (see Table 12.4).

Reading fluency consists not only of speed and correctness but also of reading with expression and proper phrasing. Zutell and Rasinski (1991) developed the Multidimensional Fluency Scale to help teachers observe several dimensions of fluency at once.

These factors are expression and volume, phrasing, smoothness, and pace. The scale is a rubric to guide teachers' judgment. To carry out the procedure, the teacher selects a passage of at least 100 words that should be written at the student's grade level or a year below. The student reads the passage and the teacher records it. The teacher then plays the recording back and evaluates the student's reading for each of the factors of accuracy, phrasing, smoothness, and pace.

Table 12.4 Oral Reading Fluency Norms

Grade	Percentile	Fall WCPM*	Winter WCPM*	Spring WCPM*
2	75	82	106	124
	50	53	78	94
	25	23	46	65
3	75	107	123	142
	50	79	93	114
	25	65	70	87
4	75	125	133	143
	50	99	112	118
	25	72	89	92
5	75	126	143	151
	50	105	118	128
	25	77	93	100

*WCPM is words correctly read per minute.

The 50th percentile for upper grades is 125–150 WCPM.

SOURCE: Republished with permission of The Council for Exceptional Children, from *Teaching Exceptional Children*, by J. Hasbrouck and G. Tindal, 1992, 24, p. 42 © 1992 by The Council for Exceptional Children; permission conveyed through Copyright Clearance Center, Inc.

Reading fluency consists not only of speed and correctness but also of reading with expression and proper phrasing. Zutell and Rasinski (1991) developed the Multidimensional Fluency Scale to help teachers observe several dimensions of fluency at once. (The scale is readily available on line by typing "Multidimensional Fluency Scale" into a search engine).

The measured factors are expression and volume, phrasing, smoothness, and pace. The scale is a rubric to guide teachers' judgment. To carry out the procedure, the teacher selects a passage of at least 100 words that should be written at the student's grade level or a year below. The student reads the passage and the teacher records it. The teacher then plays the recording back and evaluates the student's reading for each of the factors of accuracy, phrasing, smoothness, and pace.

Teachers can use many texts to assess students' reading fluency. Watch this video explaining how to select a text to assess fluency and answer the question that follows.

 Video Exploration 12.3: Gauge your understanding of the skills and concepts in this section.

Assessing Vocabulary

Vocabulary development is recognized more and more as a critical variable in learning to read. But how do we know how many words a child knows? As we saw in Chapter 4, it depends on what we mean by "know." Does the child have a vague idea what the word means? Can the child understand the word when reading it or hearing it, but not when using it? Does the child know all of its meanings? These questions show what a complicated thing it is to assess vocabulary. Vocabulary has often been assessed as part of an IRI and other reading tests. But since the advent of No Child Left Behind

Teach It! 26

Fluency Oriented Oral Reading

This structured oral reading activity offers opportunities to develop dimensions of fluency such as expression, phrasing, and smoothness using echo, paired, and choral reading of fictional and informational texts.

and Reading First, and continuing with the Every Student Succeeds Act, teachers are being called upon to assess children's vocabulary knowledge more or less systematically.

When states specify that teachers use scientifically based tests of vocabulary—that is, tests with proven validity and reliability—the choices are rather limited. A group commissioned by the U.S. Department of Education to approve assessment instruments for use with federally funded programs yielded a very short list of approved instruments for assessing vocabulary at the points of screening, diagnosing, monitoring, and outcomes-based assessment.

According to the *Final Report: Analysis of Reading Assessment Instruments for K–3*, one instrument, the *Peabody Picture Vocabulary Test-III*, was approved for all purposes for levels kindergarten through grade 3. This test costs well over $400, and is administered by school psychologists. Other tests such as the *Expressive One-Word Picture Vocabulary Test*, the *One-Word Picture Vocabulary Test Revised*, the *Texas Primary Reading Inventory*, and the *Expressive Vocabulary Test* were approved for limited applications in certain grades. Recently, however, the U.S. General Accounting Office has questioned the propriety of some of the procedures the Department of Education uses to decide what materials and approaches are to be allowed for federal support. Vocabulary development is included among the Foundational Reading Skills of the Common Core State Standards.

Teachers who wish to construct their own vocabulary tests would still do well to follow the advice of Barone, Hardman, and Taylor (2006) and create devices that ask children to:

- Select the meanings from a set of possibilities when a target word is given.
- Select a target word from a set of possibilities when a meaning is given.
- Classify words into categories.
- Tell which word from a group of words does not belong.
- Use visual and contextual clues to understand difficult words in sentences.
- Choose the correct word meanings, an antonym, or a synonym from a set of possibilities.
- Show an understanding of root words, prefixes and suffixes, historical morphemes, or grammatical endings.
- Choose correct meanings for homophones (words that sound the same but have different meanings: *read a book; a reed in a pond*) and homographs (words that are spelled the same but have different meanings: *lead the way; a lead pipe*).
- Complete a sentence with a correct word choice from alternatives.
- Demonstrate dictionary skills.

Assessing Comprehension

Reading comprehension consists of several abilities. Students' prior knowledge (sometimes called world knowledge) is needed to contextualize the new information they gain from the text. And students need to read actively, using their prior knowledge and clues from the text to set purposes and raise questions to answer while reading. They need the ability to find main ideas and supporting details and recall them later. They also need to be able to make inferences to construct meanings when ideas are not explicitly stated. They need to be able to follow the patterns of different kinds of texts, both fictional and informational, as guides to constructing meaning. And they need to keep building their inventory of vocabulary. They must do all this while reading aloud and silently.

That is a lot for a teacher to assess! In practice, when teachers want to observe this many factors, they often rely upon IRIs because they provide comprehensive measures.

ASSESSING COMPREHENSION WITH AN INFORMAL READING INVENTORY IRIs allow teachers to assess comprehension by using meaningful text passages written at ascending levels of difficulty. Questions are asked before and after the reading, and the child's behaviors are closely observed during reading.

Before reading a passage on an IRI, students may be asked a set of optional questions to ascertain what they know about the topic, to get an indication of the extent of their *prior knowledge* about the topic. Some examples, all taken from Temple, Crawford, and Gillet (2009), are in the following paragraphs.

After they have read the passage, students are asked a series of questions of different kinds. Some questions may also ask a student to summarize a main idea that has been stated in the text. For example, in a second-grade passage, the text says:

Jan lives in the city. The city has many big buildings. People work in some of the buildings. People shop in other buildings. Some buildings have apartments. . . . There are many cars, trucks, and buses in the city. They make a lot of noise. Many people walk on the street. Some people ride on the bus. There are many people on the bus.

The question asks: *What did this story say that it was like in the city?*

Some of the questions require the recall of important details. For example, the text says: *In Israel, the birthday girl or boy gets a beautiful crown of flowers. The mother places the royal crown on her child's head.* The question asks: *According to this passage, in what country does the birthday child wear a crown of flowers?*

Questions may require that readers make inferences to construct meaning where ideas are not stated explicitly. In narratives, some inferences require that the readers infer motives for behavior. For example, in a sixth-grade passage, the text says:

"Cast near the trunk. Watch out for the branches."
"I know, Dad," said Paco. But his first cast landed on top of the trunk. Without commenting, his father paddled the canoe to the other side of the dead tree, pried the lure from the bark, and gently tossed it into the water.

The question asks: *How did Paco feel about his father's advice? How do you know?*

When the text is informational, inference questions can require readers to derive an answer by applying logic to pieces of information that are given, although the answer to the question is not explicitly stated. For example, in a middle school–level passage the text says:

Industries like the textile industry have had to shut down because of increased competition. They could no longer compete in the global economy. Increased competition often leads to lower prices for consumers. But lower prices can sometimes cause lower profits for industries.

The question asks: *From what the article said, do you think you pay more or less for a shirt now that we have a global economy?*

Questions may assess *vocabulary*, too. One kind of vocabulary knowledge is the knowledge of words and their meanings that is stored in memory. Another kind is the ability to infer word meanings from context. As an example of assessing words and meanings stored in memory in a second-grade passage, the text says, *Jan lives in the city. The city has many big buildings. People work in some of the buildings. People shop in other buildings.* The question asks, *When the text said "People shop in other buildings," what does "shop" mean?* As an example of assessing a child's ability to infer vocabulary meaning from context, in a fourth-grade passage the text says, *The wings quiver as they slice through the turbulent air.* The question asks: *In the sentence, "The wings quiver as they slice through the turbulent air," what does "turbulent" mean?* A student who did not already know that the word meant "stormy" or "stirred up" might infer the meaning from the context because it is obvious that *turbulent* refers to air that an airplane is flying through, and it is a condition that makes the wings of the airplane tremble.

For the purpose of scoring, correctly answered questions are counted as a percentage of the total number of questions the child is asked. The scores are interpreted as follows:

Independent level: 90% to 100% correct
Instructional level: 70% to 89% correct
Frustration level: Below 70% correct

Most IRIs contain both narrative and informational texts, so teachers can assess reader success in dealing with all of the factors just mentioned in different patterns or genres of text. For example, the inference question we saw before from the narrative passage about Paco fishing with his father relied upon the reader's prior knowledge of relationships between parent and child to make a successful inference. The inference question regarding the informational passage about globalization, however, requires the reader to consider information about a generalized situation (cheap labor brings down prices on consumer goods) and to draw a conclusion about the way it affects the reader personally (how much he will pay for a shirt).

IRIs also allow teachers to assess students' listening comprehension in contrast to their reading comprehension. In the case of developing readers, listening to a text is usually easier than reading it—the activity of recognizing written words and constructing understanding from them is less practiced than listening to speech and constructing meaning from it. In reading assessment, testing listening capacity offers an indication of readers' potential for comprehending a text, and may serve as a goal against which their reading comprehension of a text can be measured.

OTHER MEASURES OF COMPREHENSION   IRIs afford a great deal of insight into a reader's comprehension, but they do so at a high cost of time. Also, they must be administered to one child at a time, and completing one with a child in third or fourth grade can take an hour. They are most useful for diagnostic testing, to identify strengths and weaknesses of a child's reading ability to guide instruction. Even when a full IRI is not administered, questions of the type just described can be made up by the teacher and used with any text passage, of course. Many teachers include a variety of questions like these during informal observations. For the more frequent testing that's used to monitor children's progress in learning to read, teachers rely on other, quicker means of assessing comprehension. These include oral retellings and fluency measures.

After a child has read a passage, the teacher asks the child to give an *oral retelling*—that is, to retell the passage in his own words. The teacher then makes a mental calculation of how much of the information from the text the child retold. For a slightly more exact way of evaluating the retellings, teachers may use a retelling checklist, which is a list of pieces of information contained in the text, prepared in advance. The teacher checks off the pieces of information that the child retold and then computes the score as a percentage of the whole list of items.

Another way of assessing reading comprehension is to use a structured observation procedure. The teacher sits alone with a child and has the child read a passage aloud. The teacher may ask the student questions before, during, and after the student reads. A checklist for guiding observations may then be used, such as the one shown Figure 12.10.

Measuring Attitudes and Interest

It has long been noted, and was very eloquently affirmed (Allington, 2005), that children learn to read by reading. Children differ enormously in the amount of reading they do, and as Stanovich (1992) has pointed out, those who read more benefit enormously in increased vocabulary, increased world knowledge, better spelling, and even greater measured intelligence. Somewhere between reading ability and the amount of reading that actually gets done is the will to read, a positive attitude toward reading, and a deep interest in books and reading. Where that motivation and interest is lacking, we have a problem. Teachers would do well to assess students' attitudes toward reading.

Surveys can look into children's general attitude toward reading. The Elementary Reading Attitude Survey (McKenna & Kear, 1990) is one widely used instrument that reveals how students are feeling about reading and reading instruction in general. This instrument can tell if a school or a classroom is succeeding in promoting an interest in reading among groups of children, as well as an individual child's attitude. It has also been used in research to track the attitudes toward reading of large groups of students over time.

Reading interest inventories are intended to discover individual students' interests and preferences, and to help teachers and librarians match them up with books and learning experiences they will enjoy.

Differentiated Instruction

Differentiated instruction begins with good assessment. Teachers use different kinds of assessments for different purposes at different points in the year. Commonly, schools administer assessments in these four "moments" or phases of instruction: *screening assessment, diagnostic assessment, monitoring assessment,* and *outcomes-based assessment.*

SCREENING ASSESSMENT   *Screening assessment* indicates which students are where they are expected to be, which are above grade level, and which need additional support. Before instruction begins at the start of the year, teachers may administer screening measures to determine which children are at risk for reading difficulty and may need more support during the year. The screening instruments they use are as economical as possible, because they may be given to an entire class or an entire grade. So they typically examine only a few key aspects of literacy, just enough to identify the children who need extra attention.

DIAGNOSTIC ASSESSMENT   If children have been identified by the screening tests as needing special help, the diagnostic instruments take up where the screening instruments left off. *Diagnostic assessment* indicates how strong each student is in different aspects of reading and writing development. They not only indicate that the child needs to know more letters of the alphabet but also show which ones; not only that she is a struggling reader but also that she is weak in comprehension, especially in making inferences. Individual diagnostic instruments may test specific skills, such as a test of phonemic segmentation or a test of reading fluency. Others are more comprehensive and test many areas of reading ability, such as an Informal Reading Inventory.

Figure 12.10 Observing Comprehension

Student's name: _____ Date: _____

Material read: _____ Level: _____

1. Before reading

a) The reader appeared to be familiar with the topic (or the author or the genre) of the text before reading.

No prior knowledge shown	*Some prior knowledge shown*	*Much prior knowledge shown*

b) The reader raised questions about the content of the text before reading.

Did not produce questions, even when prompted	*Asked some (vague) questions when prompted*	*Volunteered intelligent questions*

c) The reader was able to make predictions about what was coming in the text.

Did not produce predictions, even when prompted	*Made imprecise or illogical predictions*	*Consistently made logical predictions*

2. During reading

a) The reader read aloud with animation that honored the meaning of the text.

Read without meaningful inflections and word groupings	*Sometimes showed meaningful inflections and word groupings*	*Consistently showed meaningful inflections and word groupings*

b) The reader knew the vocabulary in the text.

Did not appear to understand many key words, and made little effort to learn what they mean	*Did not appear to understand some key words, and made occasional effort to learn what they mean*	*Knew most key words, and often used context to approach the meanings of unknown words*

c) The reader continued to ask questions and make predictions.

Did not produce predictions, even when prompted	*Made imprecise or illogical predictions*	*Consistently made logical predictions*

(Continued)

d) The reader found answers to questions or confirmed predictions.

Found answers to some questions, but mostly when the answer closely matched the question	*Rarely found answers to questions, even when prompted*	*Actively pursued answers to questions, often without prompting*

e) The reader was able to make inferences.

Rarely made inferences even with supportive questions	*Made more obvious inferences*	*Consistently made inferences, and picked up on subtle nuances*

f) The reader monitored comprehension.

Frequently misread words in the text without self-correcting	*Occasionally misread text and made some self-corrections*	*Rarely misread text and reliably self-corrected*

g) The reader perceived main ideas or claims and the details that support them.

When asked, did not distinguish between more and less important statements	*Did restate some main ideas when asked*	*Consistently restated main ideas, and could provide support for them from the text*

3. After reading

a) The reader could retell or summarize the text.

The retelling had major gaps	*The retelling was fairly complete*	*The retelling was complete, and the reader summarized the main points*

b) The reader identified themes in texts.

Did not offer thematic statements when asked (for example, to choose a title for a chapter)	*Sometimes, but inexactly, could answer questions about "the main thing you learned" from the text*	*Consistently made appropriate statements about the main meaning or theme of a text*

Based on diagnostic assessment, students will have different kinds of instruction designed for them. They will be assigned different levels of books for guided reading. They will be given different groups of words for word study and possibly will be placed in different points in the sequence of phonics instruction. The teacher will construct focused lessons on aspects of comprehension—on setting purposes for reading, summarizing, visualizing, making inferences, understanding vocabulary from context, learning new information, and interpreting the text. The students will be placed in groups that read different levels of text for fluency practice. They will be placed at their instructional level of spelling words to learn, even if that falls a year above or below their grade-placement level. The assessment picture will be rounded out by other information gained from interviews with the students to determine the topics they are interested in, the kind of reading they most prefer, the conditions they need to help them learn. Watch this video in which a teacher gives a diagnostic assessment by asking a student to write the sentences that she dictates, and then answer the question that follows.

 Video Exploration 12.4: Watch the video (https://www.youtube.com/watch?v=XOYASXJf4zY) and answer questions that reflect the content you have read.

MONITORING ASSESSMENTS   Once courses of instruction have been established for all students, they are given periodic monitoring assessments. Unlike the daily observations, these are more formalized and done on a schedule. The results may be shared with other teachers or with the reading specialist, and provide guidance for determining whether the present plan of instruction should be followed or if different strategies should be tried to improve a student's learning. In addition, the teacher should practice kidwatching by making a habit of selecting a small number of children every day and asking individuals how they are working, what exactly they are doing when they read and write, what they appear to be interested in, what kinds of tasks they are succeeding in, when they work best, and when they get off task—with the goal of learning how the teacher can help each one be successful in this class.

Sometimes called formative assessments because they occur while work is in progress, monitoring assessments are used once the teacher has a plan for instruction for a group of children to make sure the instruction is working and each child is making adequate progress. Reading First schools and many school districts may require that monitoring assessments use formalized instruments. If so, you must find an instrument with several alternative forms for each level. Informal assessments may consist of records of children's repeated reading scores, records of the numbers and levels of books read, and collected writing samples. Of course, teachers may observe other important behaviors that a test would miss: a child's favorite subjects, who her most productive workmates are, and her difficulties with concentration and how they are best handled.

Monitoring assessments are best done at regular intervals—every month or every quarter for most students, but more often for students who seem to have more difficulty learning. It is advisable that monitoring assessments be designed with the end-of-year assessments in mind. Because of No Child Left Behind, nearly all children in American public schools are now tested at the end of their third through their eighth years, so the monitoring assessments should see how much progress children are making toward meeting the standards embodied in those tests, while changes in instruction can still be made.

OUTCOMES-BASED ASSESSMENTS   Late in the year come the outcomes-based assessments, which are based on the state learning standards—for most states, the Common Core State Standards—for each grade level. This is a serious accountability event. While the daily informal assessments and the periodic monitoring assessments focus on children's development as readers, writers, and learners in general, these assessments also have one eye on the outcomes of instruction. Two large scale assessments—one called PARCC (for Partnership for Assessment of Readiness for College and Careers) and the other called Smarter Balanced—are being administered to students in grade 3 and up in some 25 states between them to measure what the students know about reading and writing. Other states have developed or are developing their own tests.

Outcomes-based tests are also referred to as grade-level reading standards-based assessments because the desired outcomes of a year's teaching are reflected in each state's learning standards. Yet another more general term, *summative assessments*, may be applied to them, because they come at the conclusion of or the summation of the period of learning that is being assessed. Standards-based assessments are used to test the skills that are named on the state's standards for learning in literacy.

Check Your Understanding 12.5: Gauge your understanding of the skills and concepts in this section.

Other Uses of Assessment

Assessing most readers for different purposes and at different levels of development and with different tools has been our focus through most of this chapter. Of course there are other types and uses of assessment as well. In the remainder of this chapterwe will consider ways that teachers may assess themselves and others may assess them. We will also consider ways of assessing English language learners.

Teacher Self-Assessment

As new entrants to a profession, beginning teachers must have the professional knowledge they will need to be successful in the classroom. Experienced teachers, too, have the obligation as professionals to keep abreast of developments in the field of literacy and other domains of knowledge that impact their classroom and to continually perform teacher self-assessment activities.

Donald Schön (1983) developed the influential model of the *reflective practitioner*, a professional who is able to learn from experience and create his or her own practical knowledge and skill. This model is still useful today. Professors in your teacher education classes undoubtedly encourage you to observe as closely as you can individual children and whole classrooms, to sense patterns and find possibilities for action.

Becoming a reflective practitioner is not a solitary activity, however. As Taylor and Pearson (2005) noted, in "schools that beat the odds," where students outperform what is predicted for them, teachers come together to share information about their students, about teaching, and about what works in their schools.

Following is an example of a second-grade teacher's observation/assessment discussion with her team teachers:

> *I worked with Michele today. She is putting extra vowels in some words and leaving needed vowels out in others. Today, she spelled chin as CHIAN and cream as CREM; this is a pattern for her. I looked it up in a textbook, and this means that she is using but confusing vowel- and consonant-patterned words. Easy to see, but now what? She is on the verge of getting it but needs help. Here is what I am thinking. First of all, I don't think she can read the words she is trying to spell—chin and cream are not known words for her. I need to step back to a point at which she can succeed. What do you think? Give me some feedback.*

This teacher received suggestions from the team on increasing assessments of Michele's understanding of the words she attempts to spell. They also suggested she give Michele more opportunities to write. Someone suggested word sorting by patterns—*chin, pin, tin, in.* They made a deadline for her to try some of these suggestions and report back to the group.

Teachers benefit from comparing and contrasting their ideas with those of others and from using multiple assessment measures. If the opportunity for collaboration does not exist in your school, you should create it with at least one other teacher. With teachers in your school, create regular meetings to talk shop before or after school, at planning times, or during working lunches.

Because of their many variables, teaching and learning are always in flux. Assessment helps to make order and sense of teaching and learning. For direction and planning, you will learn what children know on a daily basis. When physicians prescribe medication, they are following a routine that is grounded in research on groups of people. In addition, however, physicians tell patients, "Get back to me if this doesn't help within three days, and call me if you have any serious side effects." Modern medicine is wonderful, and much of its success depends on knowing what generally works and on the individual's responses. There is no silver bullet in either the practice of medicine or the practice of education. However, we have good evidence about more successful medical and teaching practices that we must use to improve.

Professional organizations have had their say about the assessment of teachers, too. The International Literacy Association (ILA) and the National Council for the Accreditation of Teacher Education (NCATE) jointly published a set of Standards for Reading Professionals (2006) that outlines what a committee of reading educators believes teachers of reading should know.

The ILA/NCATE standards have been incorporated by many schools of education to guide their curricula. James Zarrillo has written a self-administered guide based on the standards entitled *Are You Prepared to Teach Reading?* (2010). It includes a sample written test at the end of the book.

Professional Assessment of Teachers

In more and more states, teachers' professional performance is being measured in ways that go beyond long-used paper and pencil tests such as PRAXIS and individual states' teacher competency tests. In many states, college graduates seeking teaching certification are now asked to submit portfolios related to their teaching, along with videos of live instruction of students in classrooms. Student teachers may be asked to show evidence that they had a positive impact on the students they taught. Practicing teachers also are having their performance evaluated in new ways that include measures of their impact on students' learning as demonstrated in performance on tests, observations, and other ratings of professionalism.

Programs of the professional assessment of teachers still vary from state to state and sometimes from school district to school district (for a comprehensive review, see Doyle and Han, 2012.) By now, programs for assessing teachers' knowledge and competence in reading instruction are being administered in most of the United States. Prominent among them is the edTPA program, developed by SCALE, the Stanford Center for Assessment, Learning, and Equity.

Assessment of English Language Learners

The federal No Child Left Behind law of 2001 mandated that all states annually test English language learners' English Language Proficiency (ELP), and that they include their scores reporting school-wide achievement in reading, mathematics, and science. Years later, states were still scrambling to come up with valid and reliable assessment procedures for their English language learners (Wolf et al., 2008). The newest federal education law, the Every Student Succeeds Act or ESSA, continues to insist that students' reading proficiency be tested annually.

The Common Core State Standards are keeping up the pressure that the No Child Left Behind Act placed on schools. While the promoters of the CCSS suggest that English language learners receive extra support, they also make it clear that these students should meet the same standards as everyone else:

> The National Governors Association Center for Best Practices and the Council of Chief State School Officers strongly believe that all students should be held to the same high expectations outlined in the Common Core State Standards. This includes students who are English language learners (ELLs). However, these students may require additional time, appropriate instructional support, and aligned assessments as they acquire both English language proficiency and content area knowledge.

Meeting the standards will be a challenge, though, since English language learners as a group (and they are, admittedly, a heterogeneous group), currently score nearly 20% lower than average on tests of reading and mathematics (NAEP, 2011).

Research on the use of wide-scale reading and content area tests in English has revealed that culturally and linguistically diverse students' performance is adversely affected by the fact that, because such tests are designed for monolingual speakers of (Standard) English and do not take into account minority students' linguistic and cultural background, they are often linguistically and/or culturally biased (Abedi, 2002; Garcia, 1991; Pomplun & Omar, 2001; Stevens, Butler, & Castellon-Wellington, 2000). For example, one of the factors that negatively affects minority students' performance is their lack of familiarity with the passage topics and vocabulary of test questions. If they were given the opportunity to respond to test questions in their home language or if the questions were posed to them in their first language, English language learners might demonstrate much greater comprehension of the test passages than is indicated by their answers on a standardized test (Garcia, 1991).

English language learners tend to perform better in science and mathematics than in reading, a difference that may be attributed to the higher language demands of reading tests compared to science and mathematics tests. Nevertheless, the linguistic complexity of test questions adversely affects these learners' performance even on mathematics tests (Abedi, 2002).

Such findings raise a serious question about the validity of standardized tests when used with culturally and linguistically diverse students. Do these tests really measure what they claim to measure, that is, reading comprehension or knowledge in the content areas, or do they measure students' proficiency in academic English and familiarity with mainstream American culture? Admittedly, it is hard to devise test questions even in science and mathematics that do not require knowledge of the language of the test, just as it is virtually impossible to design a reading comprehension test that is culture-free. Nevertheless, the question remains, and can be asked not only of standardized tests, but of classroom assessments as well.

What can be done to reduce the linguistic and cultural bias of tests? First and foremost, English language learners must be included in the design and piloting of these tests (Abedi & Lord, 2001). Then, testing accommodations must be provided for them. Research has shown that the one accommodation that narrows the gap between English language learners' test performance and that of other students is the linguistic modification of test questions with excessive linguistic demands; other accommodations increase scores for *all* students (Abedi, 2004; Abedi, Hoffstetter, & Lord, 2004).

To avoid linguistic bias when assessing English language learners' listening or reading comprehension, teachers can use close-ended or limited-response formats that make minimal demands on students' expressive skills (e.g., illustrations of possible answers that students need to choose from), and which allow teachers to determine whether students understand what they read even though they cannot express their understanding orally or in writing. If teachers speak the students' first language, they may also choose to allow English language learners to answer comprehension questions in that language.

More often than not, teachers assess their English language learners' literacy skills and development using assessment instruments that have been devised for monolingual English children. While understandable, this practice may be problematic because it ignores certain characteristics of bilingual children's knowledge and development and thus yields inaccurate assessment information.

For example, if an English language learner's vocabulary is assessed using an English vocabulary test, the results will indicate the child's vocabulary knowledge *in English* as opposed to her overall vocabulary knowledge, since bilingual children often know different words in each of their languages (Fernandez et al., 1992). Similarly, using running records or informal reading inventories with English language learners may lead to misleading conclusions about children's reading ability if, for example, pronunciation errors are marked as miscues. Such errors may be due to phonological or orthographic differences between English and a child's first language, and they do not necessarily indicate that the child does not recognize or understand the mispronounced words.

Assessment results yielded by fluency measures such as the DIBELS should also be interpreted with caution. Because English language learners often struggle with the pronunciation of English words (even when they know their meaning), their fluency rates often lag behind those of native speakers, even though they may have good comprehension (Lems, Miller, & Soro, 2010). The reverse may also be true, in that some students may be misidentified as good readers based on their scores on fluency measures, when in fact their comprehension of the text may be low (Samuels, 2007).

When assessing English language learners' spelling, teachers may benefit from being familiar with some of the ways in which English language learners' spelling development differs from that of monolingual English children (adapted from Helman & Bear, 2007):

- English language learners progress through the same stages of spelling development as English-speaking children; however, because they are also learning the language as they are learning to read and write, their progress through the stages takes longer than that of their monolingual English peers.

- Some of the misspellings of English language learners may be standard developmental errors, while others may mirror phonological and orthographic differences between English and the students' first languages. For example, spelling *hot* as *hat* may be due to the fact that the vowel sound in *hot* is represented by the letter *a* in a child's first language. Consonant sounds that do not exist in learners' first languages are also likely to be misspelled (e.g., *than* may be spelled as *van* or *dan* by speakers of many languages).

- Presumably because of the system of sounds in their first language, English language learners often do more sounding out than native English speakers, which results in certain words being spelled with more letters than expected. For example, the first vowel sound in *blade* is perceived as a diphthong (a combination of two vowels) and represented by two letters (*ei* or *ey*) in Spanish, which may account for a Spanish-speaking child's spelling the word *lady* as *leidy*.

- Because of the differences between the English vowel system and that of other languages, and because internalizing the English vowel sounds takes a long time, there is greater variability in the vowel substitutions that English language learners make as compared to native English speakers. For example, a Spanish-speaking child may spell the word *dirt* as *dart*, *dert*, or *durt*, substituting Spanish vowels for the English vowel in *dirt*, which does not exist in Spanish.

- Grammatical morphemes (e.g., the past tense ending *-ed* or the plural ending *-s*) may be omitted in English language learners' spelling before the grammatical structures that the morphemes represent become part of children's oral language.

To sum up, when assessing English language learners' literacy skills, teachers need to be very clear about what it is that they want to find out, aware of the ways in which these students' literacy development may differ from that of monolingual English children, alert to possible cross-linguistic influences, and careful in interpreting and using the assessment results. This is particularly important in situations where students are considered for special education services. Those English language learners who are poor readers and writers because of their limited English proficiency can easily be labeled as having a learning disability, even though what they need is not special education, but oral language development and literacy instruction that match their level of English language proficiency.

While standardized tests often fail to reveal the progress made by English language learners in developing English language and literacy, the insights yielded by ongoing assessments and captured in teacher observations, samples of student work, and student portfolios can be extremely useful in documenting such progress. These insights should be shared with the students, their parents, other teachers, and school staff and administrators when making program placement decisions for English language learners. Unlike standardized tests, they will often show that English language learners *are* making progress even though their test scores may not demonstrate it. Moreover, ongoing assessments are likely to be much more useful than standardized tests in helping teachers make informed instructional decisions for their English language learners.

Check Your Understanding 12.6: Gauge your understanding of the skills and concepts in this section.

For Review

At the outset of this chapter we stated that when you reached this point in your reading and studying you should be able to:

- **Define reading assessment and explain why we assess students' reading.**

Assessment means deciding what we need to know about children's learning, considering what means we will need to use to get the information and possibly designing our own, collecting the information, and interpreting the information to help us make instructional decisions to help the students. Teachers have always used assessments for many purposes, but in recent years the emphasis on assessment has intensified, beginning with the federal No Child Left Behind Act, and continuing with the Every Student Succeeds Act. Teachers may assess children at four "moments": for screening, for diagnosis, for progress monitoring, and to assess outcomes. Measures of students' literacy are becoming more uniform across the United States and U.S. territories via the Common Core State Standards.

- **Use different approaches to assessment.**

Several kinds of assessment instruments are available to teachers. Standardized or norm-based tests compare children to other children; and standards-based tests look at their accomplishment of curricular standards. Curriculum-based measurement takes brief snapshots of learning, usually for monitoring purposes, and these are closely tied to the outcomes that are desired at the end of the year. Informal assessments such as the Informal Reading Inventory, the Reading Miscue Inventory, and running records reveal a rich array of information about children's reading.

- **Understand the most frequently used terms for assessment.**

Among those are the validity of an assessment device (the extent to which the test measures what it claims to) and its reliability (the extent to which the findings of the text are stable).

- **Be able to assess emergent readers.**

Assessments are done of various aspects of emergent literacy, including print concepts, language awareness, and letter knowledge. Devices and procedures for assessing those aspects were shared, including the Concepts About Print Test and the Early Reading Screening Inventory.

- **Be able to assess beginning readers and beyond.**

Once children begin to read, we can assess reading levels (independent, instructional, and frustration) as well as their word recognition, fluency, vocabulary, and comprehension. The readability of texts can be assessed by means of a readability formula or the cloze procedure.

- **Understand other uses of assessment, including the assessment of teachers and English language learners.**

Teachers and teachers-to-be are now expected to pass competency tests, most of which are derived from and coordinated with the Common Core State Standards. Laws in force in most states require that English language learners' literacy also be measured at regular intervals.

For Your Journal

1. Now that you have read the chapter, return to the Anticipation Guide at the beginning. What differences are there in how you would answer those questions now?

2. Choose a grade that you would like to teach, or that you do teach. First, describe what aspects of reading and writing you would want to test for in your screening and diagnostic assessments. Second, explain which instruments you would use and why.

3. Go online and find your state's standards for literacy at your chosen grade level. Read the information about the outcomes-based assessments given. Then, for each set of abilities and concepts that they list, describe the way you would monitor students' progress toward achieving those outcomes.

Taking It to the World

The Common Core State Standards were adopted by 45 states in short order, but in the past few years some have withdrawn their adoption. Some states have since framed their own standards that are patterned after the CCSS. If your state did not adopt them, or has rescended its adoption, find the arguments out why. If your state is among the great majority that did adopt them, what steps are your schools taking to meet the standards?

Chapter 13
Integrating Language and Literacy Instruction Across the Grades

 ## Learning Outcomes

After reading this chapter you should be able to:

1. Integrate the teaching of print concepts and phonological awareness with meaningful reading and writing instruction.

2. Plan and implement contextualized phonics instruction for alphabetic and orthographic readers and spellers.

3. Plan and implement contextualized spelling instruction for morphological and derivational readers and spellers.

4. Teach grammar in context to support reading/listening comprehension and writing development.

5. Develop students' awareness of text structure by teaching signal words and the use of headings and subheadings in informational texts.

Anticipation Guide

The following statements will help you begin thinking about the topics covered in this chapter. Answer *true* or *false* in response to each statement. As you read and learn more about the topics mentioned in the statements, double-check your answers. See what interests you and prompts your curiosity toward more understanding.

_____ 1. Teaching foundational skills in context means teaching them as they come up in the context of classroom conversations.

_____ 2. The "part" in a whole-part-whole lesson is the stage of the lesson where the teacher draws students' attention to the way spoken or written language works.

_____ 3. English has six basic types of spoken and written syllables.

_____ 4. Spelling rules are also called phonogram patterns.

_____ 5. The short vowel in a closed syllable is often "protected" by a double consonant.

_____ 6. The word *innocent* contains an assimilated prefix.

_____ 7. Knowledge of grammar supports reading comprehension.

_____ 8. "Mentor texts" are texts that teachers have kept from their own school days.

_____ 9. Signal words are the signs used for words in sign language.

_____ 10. The way information is organized in a text can be easily gleaned from headings and subheadings.

A Classroom Story

Literacy Activities in a First-Grade Classroom

It's October. Nineteen children are looking at books while Ana Lopez sets the nonfiction big book, Bread, Bread, Bread *(Morris & Hevman, 1989) on the easel. Her students come from diverse backgrounds, but all the children can connect meaningfully with this information book. There are actual photos of people making and eating bread—including Mexican tortillas, Indian naan, French baguettes, and other types.*

Ms. Lopez speaks to a small group of children who are not scheduled to participate in this lesson. She offers them a choice of two literacy activities: They can work on creating a poster for a science project or work in the classroom interest center. Once they are settled, Ms. Lopez motions to the other children to join her on the reading rug. She asks them to look at the pictures first, and then whisper their ideas about the book to one another. Now actively involved, children in the larger group whisper and then talk with Ms. Lopez about bread.

Before she reads the book, she points out the author and illustrator names and has the children repeat them. She also asks that they pay attention to the pictures and decide if they depict real people and if they show something meaningful. As she reads the book aloud, she uses a long pointer to indicate each complete word (emphasizing that the groups of letters separated by a space are words) while she encourages the children to read with her.

Ms. Lopez pauses from time to time to spark comprehension-supporting discussions—sometimes about the book and other times about the writing. She says, "I really like the way this author talks about making bread. Who is this author? Let's see that name again." Ms. Lopez prompts pointing out the author's name as the children read it together. Ms. Lopez points out that this book tells us the chronology, that is, the steps to follow in making bread. "Do any of you know something about making bread?"

One child says, "I like the way it smells!"

"Oh yes, and I like the way you are listening! Does anyone else have something to say?" says Ms. Lopez. Several children raise their hands and again engage in conversation. Next, the children who didn't get a turn at speaking are invited to whisper what they know about bread making in one another's ears. Everyone is included!

By drawing the children into talking about the meaning of the text and the nature of the written presentation, Ms. Lopez is teaching good reader behaviors and encouraging the children to think, comprehend, and relate personally to books. She also shows the children that she is interested in what they know or are thinking. She and the class discuss the photos showing people all over the world making bread. The point of this discussion is that the photos sometimes tell more than or the same thing that the words say.

After reading, children are encouraged to identify words they know. Ms. Lopez points out that some words begin with two-consonant blends, such as /br/ in bread, *and asks the children to sound them out. As the lesson continues, Ms. Lopez points out that some words with consonant blends are repeated, such as "bread, bread, bread." She asks the students to find other words that are repeated. A child responds, "I see the word* eat. *And we saw it before, too."*

"Excellent word watching!" Ms. Lopez responds. "Now let's see if we can spot the word eat *repeated throughout the story."*

The teacher draws the children's attention to the fact that the vowel team **ea** *is often pronounced as in* eat *(a long vowel), but that sometimes it is pronounced as in* bread *(a short vowel). Then, the children do a word sorting activity, placing word cards in one of two columns depending on the pronunciation of the vowel team* **ea**.

As Ms. Lopez brings the lesson to a conclusion, the children move into dramatic play as they pretend to make and eat bread. Then, they return to their seats and write the sequence of steps for making bread in their journals.

In the previous chapters of this textbook we have described a host of strategies for teaching reading and writing at different stages of literacy development. We have consistently argued that the ultimate goal of reading instruction should be comprehension, and that the goal of writing instruction should be for students to express their ideas clearly through written texts. We have also suggested, however, that an exclusive focus on the meaning of texts is not enough for students to achieve these goals; and that effective literacy instruction also needs to include attention to **language form**—such as phonemes, morphemes, sentence structure, and text structure. The dual instructional focus that we propose, on making meaning from and through text, *and* on developing students' awareness of formal aspects of language, is consonant with the Common Core State Standards. The CCSS not only include specific language standards, but also address many of the reading, writing, speaking, and listening standards that require instruction to develop students' **metalinguistic awareness**.

That being said, let us hasten to add that we do not see language instruction as an end in itself, nor do we advocate a return to memorized grammar rules, sentence diagrams, or decontextualized grammar drills. On the contrary, we concur with current scholarship (e.g., Derewianka, 2013; Gartland & Smolkin, 2016; Myhill and Watson, 2014), which argues that language instruction needs to be integrated into the language arts curriculum in ways that enhance students' reading comprehension and written expression. For example, one objective for teaching grammar that Derewianka (2013) proposes is that students should understand how different meanings are created through the use of different grammatical forms, so that they can control and shape those meanings more effectively when speaking or writing. Myhill and Watson (2014) make the same point when they explain that it is not enough for students be able to define a particular grammatical structure, such as the passive voice. Rather, students need to understand how a passive construction changes the way information is presented; and, most importantly, they need to understand why an author would choose a passive over an active construction. If students are to develop such understandings, then language must be taught in context. This means that they should encounter a new language pattern/rule in a meaningful text. Then, you should help them to notice the pattern and/or derive the rule based on the text. Finally, you should provide students with opportunities to practice using the new pattern/rule in their own writing.

In Chapter 5 we introduced the whole-part-whole teaching model and explained how it can be used to teach word knowledge in the context of reading meaningful texts. We also described several lesson structures based on this model (reading aloud, shared reading, the language-experience approach, and guided reading), both in Chapter 4 and in Chapter 5. In all these lesson structures, the first part of the lesson focuses on the meaning of the text (the "whole"), the second focuses on some formal aspect of language that is well represented in the text (the "part"), and the third focuses on meaning again (the "whole"). In this chapter we will give you additional suggestions for teaching the "part" (print concepts, phonological awareness, and phonics) as you are using this model. We will also show you how the ABC model that, in Chapters 8 and 9, we proposed you should use to develop students' comprehension of narrative and informational texts can be adapted to include a focus on morphology, grammar, and text structure.

Teaching Print Concepts and Phonological Awareness in Context

From the earliest stages of literacy instruction, children should learn that the ultimate purpose of reading is to understand what texts say, and that the ultimate purpose of writing is to communicate ideas. To this end, as Dahl and colleagues (2001) argue, foundational skills such as print concepts and phonological awareness should be taught in context; that is, they should be integrated with classroom reading and writing activities whose goal is to engage students with the meaning of texts. The whole-part-whole lesson structure lends itself easily to such integration.

Figure 13.1 is an example of a lesson scenario that uses the whole-part-whole model with Eric Carle's book, *The Very Hungry Caterpillar* (1987), and integrates the teaching of certain print concepts with reading, writing, and vocabulary instruction as well as with content learning.

You will notice how, during the picture walk and the interactive read-loud, the teacher focuses the students' attention on the meaning of the text (the "whole") by activating their prior knowledge of the topic, by teaching new words and concepts that are key to understanding the text, and by asking students to make predictions and confirm or disconfirm them based on the text. Her questions as well as her use of visuals prompt and support the students in identifying, retelling, and connecting the main topic and the key details in the text.

During the shared writing activity, the focus of instruction continues to be on meaning (describing the first two stages in a butterfly's life cycle), but a secondary focus on form (the "part") is added. More specifically, the teacher draws students' attention to the capitalization of the first word in a sentence. At the same time, her pointing to the words as she reads the sentences that she and the students have jointly produced reinforces the concept of word and print directionality.

In the writing activity that concludes the lesson, the focus is on meaning (the "whole") again, with students being asked to write a sentence about each stage in the life cycle of a butterfly. During the same activity, with the teacher's support, the children will also apply what they have learned about print directionality, concept of word, and use of uppercase letters at the beginning of a sentence.

Instead of instruction on the use of uppercase letters, the "part" in this lesson might consist of having students clap out the syllables in the words *egg, cocoon, butterfly,* and *caterpillar,* or of asking students to identify the sounds that these words begin with and the letters that represent those sounds. You may also use one of these words as an entry point to teaching a new letter (*e, c,* or *b*) and its associated sound, and then give students some practice with both, using Elkonin boxes or a sound board activity (see Chapters 4 and 5).

Watch the following video, in which a teacher combines science and language arts instruction into one lesson, and then answer the question that follows.

 Video Exploration 13.1: Watch the video and answer questions that reflect the content you have read.

Figure 13.1 Whole-Part-Whole Lesson Scenario: The Life Cycle of a Butterfly

Whole (Focus on Meaning):

A. Introducing the Reading and Teaching Key Vocabulary Through a Picture Walk:

Ms. Collins shows a picture of a butterfly and tells the class they will read a story about how butterflies are born. She has the class repeat the word *butterfly*. She places a picture card of a butterfly on the board, and under it she places a card with the word *butterfly* written on it. To activate students' background knowledge, she asks, "What do you know about butterflies?" "How do you think butterflies are born?" After the students have answered the questions, Ms. Collins says: "We are going to read a book to find out."

Ms. Collins reads the title and the author (*The Very Hungry Caterpillar*, by Eric Carle), points to the picture of the caterpillar on the front cover, has the class choral read the title, places a picture card of a caterpillar on the board (to the left of the butterfly) and a word card with the word *caterpillar* underneath. (By the end of the picture walk, the pictures will be arranged in a circle.) Ms. Collins asks, "Is a caterpillar a butterfly?" "How do you think they are related?" The students make predictions. Ms. Collins says, "Let's look at some of the pictures to find out."

Ms. Collins shows the picture of the egg: "Where did the egg come from?" "What will happen to it?" The students make predictions. Ms. Collins shows the picture of the little caterpillar: "Where did the caterpillar come from?" "What will happen to it?" The students make predictions. Ms. Collins shows the picture of the big, fat caterpillar: "What happened to the caterpillar?" "What does he look like?" "What will happen next?" After acknowledging students' predictions, Ms. Collins shows the picture of the cocoon: "Where is the caterpillar now?" "He is in this cocoon." Ms. Collins has the class repeat the word, and places the picture and the word card *cocoon* on board, between the caterpillar and the butterfly. Then she asks, "How do you think the caterpillar will come out of his cocoon?" The students make predictions. Ms. Collins says, "Let's read the story to see if our predictions were correct."

B. Interactive Read-Aloud

Ms. Collins reads aloud the first two pages; then she asks, "What happened?" "What was there first?" "What happened to the egg?" "How was the caterpillar when he came out of the egg?"

Ms. Collins reads aloud the next 12 pages, showing the pictures to the students and pausing to ask questions such as, "What did the caterpillar do after he came out of the egg?" "What does he look like after one week?" "What will happen next?"

Ms. Collins reads aloud the next page, and then asks, "What did the caterpillar do next?" "What is a cocoon?" "How long did he stay in the cocoon?" "What did he do then?"

Ms. Collins reads aloud the last page, and asks, "Finally, what came out of the cocoon?"

Ms. Collins directs the class to look at the pictures on the board, which are now arranged in a circle, and says, "Let's try to retell the story now." "What was there first?" "What happened next?" "What happened then?" She points to the pictures as the students answer. Then, she says, "Where do you think the egg came from?" "What will the butterfly do next?" "So, the process begins again. This (pointing to the circle) is the life cycle of a butterfly (writes *The Life Cycle of a Butterfly* in the middle of the circle and has the class repeat). A cycle is a process that goes on in a circle. Now, let's see if we can write a sentence about each stage in the life cycle of a butterfly."

Part (Focus on Skills):

C. Shared Writing Activity

Ms. Collins asks, "So, what happened first?" She writes *First* on the board, then asks the students to dictate a sentence. She writes it on the board. She asks, "Why is the F in *first* in uppercase? Because the first letter in the first word of a sentence is always in uppercase." Ms. Collins reads the sentence, pointing to each word. Then, the students choral read it as Ms. Collins points to each word. She invites individual students to come up and read it while pointing to each word. She asks the students to point to various words.

Ms. Collins then asks, "What happened next?" She writes *Next* on the board, then asks the students to dictate a sentence. She invites students to come up and write some of the words in the sentence on the board. "Why is the N in *next* in uppercase?" Ms. Collins reads the sentence, pointing to each word. Then, the students choral read it as Ms. Collins points to each word. She invites individual students to come up and read it while pointing to each word. She asks the students to point to various words.

Figure 13.1 Whole-Part-Whole Lesson Scenario: The Life Cycle of a Butterfly **(Continued)**

Whole (Focus on Meaning):

D. Writing Activity

Ms. Collins prompts the class to describe the remaining stages in the life cycle of a butterfly orally. Then, the students receive a handout with pictures of the stages in the life cycle of a butterfly at the top and are asked to write one sentence under each picture. As she helps the students with their writing, Ms. Collins reminds them to capitalize the first word in each sentence.

Check Your Understanding 13.1: **Gauge your understanding of the skills and concepts in this section.**

Teaching Phonics in Context

The whole-part-whole lesson structure can be used to teach phonics in context as well. The phonics skill taught in a lesson should be well represented in the text that the students are reading, so that multiple readings of the text can serve both to lead to better comprehension and to give students practice with the skill. For example, Colin and Jacqui Hawkins's books for Shared Reading (*Pat the Cat's Big Book, Jen the Hen's Big Book, Mig the Pig's Big Book, Tog the Dog's Big Book,* and *Zug the Bug's Big Book*) are funny rhyming stories with appealing illustrations that children will love to talk about. At the same time, each book contains several examples of CVC (consonant-vowel-consonant) words featuring the same rime (e.g., *cat, hat, mat, rat*), which allows the teacher to highlight the rime and to give students practice reading words that contain the rime as they read an engaging text.

Phonics Instruction for Alphabetic Readers and Spellers

The Common Core State Standards require that phonics instruction begin in kindergarten, with children gradually learning one-to-one letter-sound correspondences, and thus transitioning from the logographic stage of word recognition to the alphabetic stage. By the end of first grade, children should be able to decode regularly spelled words, including words that contain digraphs, as well as final *-e* and common vowel teams representing long vowels.

Blachman and Tangel (2008) propose that children will progress faster through the alphabetic stage of word recognition if they are made aware of the basic syllable patterns of written English in the course of the phonics instruction that they receive. The six basic types of syllables identified by Blachman and Tangel (2008) are:

- *Closed syllables* (as in *it, hat, went, spot,* or *bunch*). They are syllables that contain only one vowel letter followed by one or more consonants, and in which the vowel letter is pronounced as a short (or lax) vowel.
- *Final "e" syllables* (as in *ate, bite, eve, bone,* or *cute*). These syllables contain only one vowel letter followed by one consonant and by the letter "e." In such syllables the final "e" is silent (not pronounced) and serves only to mark the fact that the preceding vowel letter should be pronounced as a long (or tense) vowel or as a diphthong. Classroom teachers usually tell their students that when a word ends in "e," the vowel inside the word "says its name."
- *Open syllables* (as in *she,* or in the first syllable of words such as *silent, label, locust,* or *stupid*). These are syllables that end in one vowel letter that is pronounced as a long (tense) vowel or as a diphthong.
- *Vowel team syllables* (as in *plain, seed, cheat, boat, scoop,* or *scout*). These syllables contain two vowel letters pronounced as a long (tense) vowel or as a diphthong.
- *Vowel + r syllables* (as in *star, herd, bird, short, fur*). In these syllables the vowel letter is followed by "r" and has a different pronunciation than in any other type of syllable.
- *Consonant + le syllables* (as in a<u>ble</u>, app<u>le</u>, nim<u>ble</u>, bott<u>le</u>, cud<u>dle</u>). As the examples show, such syllables never stand alone as words. They are the second, unstressed syllables of two-syllable words. They consist of a consonant followed by "le," and, because they are unstressed, they are pronounced with a reduced vowel (a schwa).

Teach It! 56

Shared Writing

Following the whole-part-whole model, in this instructional activity, the broader focus is on the "whole" or meaning, with a secondary focus on "parts" such as capitalization, print directionality, concept of word, and phonics.

These are by no means the only types of written syllables that English has, but they are the most common. Teaching the pronunciation of the vowel letter(s) in each type of syllable is likely to speed up children's progress through the alphabetic phase of word recognition because, once they have become aware of a syllable pattern, they will be able to generalize it to reading and spelling other syllables that conform to that pattern. It will also ease children's transition to the orthographic phase of word recognition, where they go beyond matching phonemes to individual letters, vowel teams, or digraphs, and begin to learn more complex spelling patterns.

Phonics Instruction for Orthographic Readers and Spellers

In Chapter 5 you learned how, at the orthographic phase of word recognition, children begin to use their knowledge of onsets and rimes in spoken words to read words containing spelling patterns that they know and that represent rimes. We called those spelling patterns *phonogram patterns*. You also learned that at this stage of reading development, children use their knowledge of phonogram patterns to read "by analogy." Thus, if they have learned the pronunciation of the phonogram pattern *-ight* they will be able to read *light, might, sight, bright,* and *slight* simply by decoding the onset of the syllable. Practicing onset and rime (or phonogram pattern) awareness through word sorts, word wheels, and other activities described in Chapter 5 is particularly beneficial when the pronunciation of a phonogram pattern diverges from that of the basic syllable types we described above. The phonogram pattern *-ight* is a case in point. Syllables containing it look like closed syllables—in which the vowel letter should be pronounced as a short/lax vowel; yet, the letter *i* is pronounced as a diphthong in *-ight*. To take another example, in most vowel team syllables, the vowel team is pronounced as a long/tense vowel or a diphthong, but it is pronounced as a short/lax vowel in words such as *bread* and *spread*, or *look* and *book*.

In addition to phonogram pattern practice, children at the orthographic stage of word recognition and spelling development also benefit from being made aware of certain spelling rules that they can understand if they have learned about the basic types of written syllables. Such awareness will provide significant economy in their learning to read and spell, since it will allow them to generalize the rules to new words—which, according to the Common Core State Standards for Language, they should be able to do in second grade.

SPELLING OF WORD-FINAL /K/   One such rule is the spelling of the word-final /k/ sound in one-syllable words. The sound /k/ is sometimes spelled *k* at the end of a word, but in certain words it is spelled as *ck*. To help students understand when the /k/ sound is spelled *ck* in word-final position, have them analyze the words in each of the columns of Table 13.1 and answer the question "When is the sound /k/ spelled *k*, and when is it spelled *ck* at the end of a syllable?"

With your guidance, they should come to the following conclusions:

1. The sound /k/ is spelled *k* at the end of vowel team syllables, as in *peak*.
2. The sound /k/ is spelled *k* and followed by a silent e in final "e" syllables, as in *lake*.
3. The sound /k/ is spelled *k* at the end of vowel + *r* syllables, as in *pork*.
4. The sound /k/ is spelled *k* at the end of closed syllables when it is preceded by another consonant sound, as in *risk*.
5. The sound /k/ is spelled *ck* at the end of closed syllables when it is immediately preceded by a vowel sound, as in *duck*.

THE "FLOSS RULE"   Another rule that students at the orthographic stage of reading and spelling development should be aware of is the "floss rule" (Moats, 2010). The word *floss* actually follows this rule, which is that when an /f/, /l/, /s/ (or /z/) sound immediately follows a short vowel sound at the end of a closed syllable, it is spelled with a double "ff," "ll," "ss," or "zz." To help students to discover this rule, have them analyze the words in Table 13.2 and answer the question, "When is *f, l, s,* or *z* doubled at the end of a one-syllable word?" Help them notice that the doubling only occurs in closed syllables.

SPELLING OF /tʃ/   One more rule that you may wish to teach is the spelling of the sound /tʃ/ in words such as *chip, peach,* and *pitch*. More specifically, you may want your students to understand when to spell the sound /tʃ/ as *ch* and when to

Table 13.1 The Spelling of Word-Final /k/

When is word-final /k/ spelled as -ck?				
beak	stake	shark	ask	rack
week	bike	jerk	desk	speck
shook	woke	lurk	junk	sick
steak	duke	irk	honk	duck
hawk	eke	pork	risk	rock

Table 13.2 The Floss Rule

When is word-final *f*, *l*, *s*, or *z* doubled?				
staf	cliff	scoff	stuff	
call	well	spill	doll	dull
class	mess	kiss	toss	fuss
jazz	fizz	buzz		
How are these words different from the ones above?				
leaf	beef	roof	seal	bail	soil
safe	life	pale	tile	pole	mule
scarf	surf	curl	swirl	girl	

Table 13.3 The Spelling of the Sound /tʃ/

When is the sound /tʃ/ spelled *tch*?			
charm	each	arch	watch, catch
cheek	screech	perch	etch, switch
chop	brooch	porch	notch
chuck	touch	church	clutch

spell it as *tch*. Should that be the case, then let your students analyze the words in the columns of Table 13.3. They should discover that /tʃ/ is always spelled *ch* in word-initial position; it is also spelled *ch* in word-final position unless it occurs at the end of a closed syllable, in which case it is spelled *tch*.

DOUBLING OF THE CONSONANT IN WORDS CONTAINING A CONSONANT + LE SYLLABLE   The doubling of the initial consonant of consonant + *le* syllables is also governed by a rule that you may want your students to discover. Have them analyze the words in the columns of Table 13.4 and determine when a word that ends in a consonant + *le* syllable has a double consonant. With your help, they should conclude that the initial consonant of such a syllable is doubled only when it immediately follows a short/lax vowel in a closed syllable.

What we're proposing that you do with activities such as those described above is that, instead of telling your students the rule, you engage them in analysis of language samples and help them to discover patterns. This is a highly useful skill—one that, once developed, students will be able to continue to use to discover patterns at other levels of language organization, such as morphology, syntax, or discourse.

These language discovery activities can be the "part" of your lessons. The children should have encountered the spelling pattern that you want them to become aware of in the first phase of the lesson, as they read the text for comprehension (the "whole"). When you think that a satisfactory level of comprehension has been achieved, refocus students' attention on the spelling pattern (the "part"), and lead them to analyze the language samples so they will notice the spelling pattern and, with your help, come up with a rule for it. Then, have the class do a Word Hunt using the text they have read to find other words that follow the rule they have discovered. Finally, have them write a meaningful text in which they can apply the new spelling rule, thus returning to the "whole."

The Four Blocks Approach

The Four Blocks Approach proposed by Cunningham, Hall, and Sigmon (2007) is another instructional structure that can be used to teach phonics in context. The four blocks are four reading periods that occur during the school day, with specific activities taking place within each block such that children will get reading, word study, and writing instruction each day. The four blocks are: (1) guided reading, (2) self-selected reading, (3) working with words, and (4) writing. We will describe each block below.

Table 13.4 Doubling of the Consonant in Words Containing a Consonant + *le* Syllable

When do words ending in a consonant + *le* syllable contain double consonants?				
noodle	able	circle	mumble	bubble
feeble	idle	hurdle	simple	paddle
beetle	cradle	turtle	uncle	wiggle
poodle	noble	sparkle	handle	kettle

Teach It! 10

Guided Reading and the Four Blocks Approach

Learn how to use the Guided Reading format combined with the Four Blocks Approach to teach phonics in context, creating a rich, supportive literacy program in this activity.

1. GUIDED READING   For 30 to 40 minutes, with teacher guidance, children read various texts and are taught reading strategies. The lesson focus is also on developing prior knowledge; oral language; word identification including guessing with letter/sound relationships and sensible word meanings in the sentence; vocabulary; self-confidence; motivation; and critical thinking. There is no doubt that small-group reading instruction is superior to whole-class instruction. For this reason, it is critical that your students manage their behavior well in centers! Within guided reading periods, children often engage in shared reading—the teacher reads aloud first, children read the same text with the teacher in unison, and they take turns reading to one another while the teacher listens to selected individuals reading alone. Children read a big book or sets of the same little books. Following instruction, children read with their partners (often two children who read at somewhat different levels, but who are compatible enough to read together) and the teacher watches partners closely, intervenes to stress use of strategies, and encourages. Next, the group comes together again for discussion. The children or both the teacher and the children usually write, or draw and label something about their reading.

2. SELF-SELECTED READING   The goal of self-selected reading is to share different kinds of texts, albeit paper or electronic, and build motivation. The teacher encourages, provides developmentally appropriate books, and "coaches" selected children's reading. Children read with help as needed and confer with the teacher individually. They also select and use a reading comprehension strategy listed on a wall chart. This block lasts about 30 minutes. Watch this video in which Dr. Junko Yokota, professor of language and literacy, tells teachers how to select good books for children's independent reading and then answer the question that follows.

 Video Exploration 13.2: **Watch the video and answer questions that reflect the content you have read.**

3. WORKING WITH WORDS   For about 30 minutes, the teacher and the children engage in various word-related activities, such as reading both familiar words on the word walls and the new ones that are added weekly (approximately five), and which come from the texts the students are reading. The teacher coaches through reviews of the words found in the unit of study. Children sound out the words, look for patterns in words, and discuss and practice the words' spelling patterns. The teacher points out word patterns according to children's literacy development. The children practice reading and writing words, and sorting them with games and word cards.

4. WRITING   A mini-lesson occurs in writing workshop. It begins each writing period, which lasts 45 to 60 minutes, depending on how young children get along in an extended time period. Goals vary depending on the grade and children's learning needs; for example, first graders may focus on having every sentence make sense and using capital letters and punctuation to begin and end sentences, respectively. In addition, the writing block focuses on spelling. Children write during the mini-lesson, on their own and with partners. This is an easy block to teach on multiple levels. Children write books, stories, and information pieces; illustrate their writing; and have conferences with the teacher for individual instruction. The word wall helps children to find words they need and to work on spelling. Writing time concludes with sharing writing in the author's chair. Be aware that different teachers use different formats and structures for writing workshops. What is important is that all writing workshops include the basic essentials—time to write, writing and spelling instruction, strong support, and a warm and inviting work environment.

Teach It! 19

Word Wall Activities

These displays provide a resource for helping children become familiar with the spelling patterns of words they encounter in the texts they are reading and writing.

Teach It! 60

The Writing Workshop

Learn how the writing workshop format provides the "basic essentials" listed above, supporting young learners as they become familiar with the writing process: rehearsing, drafting, revising, editing, and publishing.

Cunningham and Allington (2003) provide some basic guidelines to consider in using four blocks teaching:

- Long-term planning for four blocks teaching is organized around units of study such as inquiry units in science, math, and social studies; four blocks teaching also contributes greatly to integrated curriculum. Short-term planning is laid out in both daily and weekly descriptions. This is the time when some of the arts and media may also be integrated into the already integrated curriculum.

- Oral language is not a formal part of the four blocks, but many conversations take place during all four blocks that help ensure that CCSS speaking and listening objectives are met.

- Four blocks teaching does not eliminate the need for interventions such as Reading Recovery; it is not an add-on and it can be used with other approaches such as response to intervention (RTI).

- Volunteers and paraprofessionals may help support four blocks teaching.

- Finally, it is fine to do whole-class instruction as well; for example, reading big books, or combining reading with music, movement, and song. Whole-class lessons take place as time permits during the four block day.

Check Your Understanding 13.2: Gauge your understanding of the skills and concepts in this section.

Teaching Morphology in Context

As children move on from the phase of orthographic reading and spelling to the morphological phase of word recognition and spelling, they encounter new challenges—multi-syllable words that contain inflectional and derivational morphemes. The Common Core State Standards require that in first grade, children read words with inflectional endings; that in second grade, they decode words with common prefixes and suffixes; and that by fifth grade, they use combined knowledge of all letter-sound correspondences, syllabication patterns, and morphology to read and spell multisyllabic words.

Spelling Instruction for Morphological Readers and Spellers

In Chapter 5 you learned how to use **structural analysis** to teach students how to examine the parts of a word (roots, base words, and affixes) to arrive at the meaning of the whole word. In this section we will show you some spelling rules that apply to multisyllabic words that contain suffixes and prefixes. As you will see, many of these rules build on students' prior knowledge of syllable types.

CONSONANT DOUBLING BEFORE A SUFFIX   Often, but not always, the last consonant of a base word is doubled when an inflectional or a derivational suffix is added to the word. To help your students understand when to double the consonant and when not to double it, have them examine the words in Table 13.5. With your help, they should come to the conclusion that the last consonant of a base word should be doubled if the suffix added to the base word begins with a vowel.

Table 13.5 Doubling of the Last Consonant of a Base Word Before a Suffix (I)

When is the last consonant of the base word doubled before a suffix?				
sad	sadder	saddest	BUT	sadness
sin	sinner	sinning	BUT	sinful
wet	wetter	wettest	BUT	wetness
hot	hotter	hottest	BUT	hotly
star	starry	starred	BUT	stardom

Table 13.6 Doubling of the Last Consonant of a Base Word Before a Suffix (II)

When is the last consonant of a base word doubled before a suffix that begins with a vowel, and when is it not doubled?		
pat	patting	patted
bud	budding	buddy
beg	beggar	begged
scar	scarring	scarred
BUT		
sweet	sweeter	sweeten
cheer	cheered	cheering
long	longer	longest
hard	harder	hardest

This is not the entire rule, though, because the doubling of the consonant depends not only on the letter/sound that the suffix begins with, but also on the structure of the base word. To help your students realize that, have them analyze the words in each column of Table 13.6.

Lead them to notice that the consonant doubling occurs when a suffix beginning with a vowel is added to a base word *only* if the last consonant of the base word is preceded by one (and no more than one!) vowel letter. Use your students' knowledge of syllable types to help them see that

- consonant doubling only occurs with closed syllables and vowel + *r* syllables
- the purpose of the consonant doubling is to preserve the pronunciation of the vowel in those types of syllables

Without the double consonant, the vowel would have a different pronunciation. Finally, your students should learn that the doubling of the last consonant of the base word before a suffix that begins with a vowel occurs only if the last syllable of the base word is stressed. To help them notice that, have them analyze the two sets of words in Table 13.7.

CHANGE OF *Y* TO *I* BEFORE A SUFFIX   When a suffix is added to words ending in -*y*, the letter *y* sometimes (but not always) changes to *i*. When the change happens and when it does not depends on whether the -*y* at the end of the base word is preceded by a consonant or by a vowel. Help your students to discover this rule as they analyze the first two groups of words in Table 13.8. Then, help them to discover the exception to the rule (i.e., that -*y* never changes to *i* before the suffix -*ing*) by looking at the third group of words in the table.

DROPPING OF SILENT -*E*   When a suffix is added to final "e" syllables, the *e* is sometimes preserved and sometimes dropped. As your students will discover if they study the words in the two columns of Table 13.9, this depends on whether the suffix begins with a vowel or with a consonant. Once the students have figured out the rule, you may wish to ask them why the silent -*e* is preserved or dropped.

The Common Core State Standards call for third-grade students to learn how to use conventional spelling for adding suffixes to words, and how to use spelling patterns and generalizations, such as position-based spellings, syllable patterns, and ending rules, in writing words. As we have suggested previously, students should encounter these patterns in the texts that they read, be helped to discover the rules, and then practice using them in their reading and writing. A good place for reinforcing and practicing such rules is the editing stage of the writing process.

Table 13.7 Doubling of the Last Consonant of a Base Word Before a Suffix (III)

How are the words in parts A and B different?			
A.			
edit	editing	edited	editor
alter	altering	altered	alteration
travel	traveling	traveled	traveler
B.			
admit	admitting	admitted	
occur	occurring	occurred	
rebel	rebelling	rebelled	

Table 13.8   Change of Word-Final *y* to *i* Before a Suffix

Study the words in parts A and B below. When does word-final *y* change to *i* before a suffix?		
A	**B**	**C**
beauty—beautiful	play–playful	cry–crying
happy—happiness	pay—payment	fly–flying
easy—easily	joy—joyful	party–partying
study—studied	pray—prayer	study–studying
silly—sillier	key–keyed	
family—familiar	stay—stayed	
Now, study the words in C. Can you discover the exception?		

Table 13.9 Dropping of Silent -e Before a Suffix

Study the words in parts A and B below. When is the silent -e dropped before a suffix?	
A	**B**
lame—lamely	blame—blaming
rude—rudeness	rose—rosy
use—useful	brave—bravest
base—basement	shake—shaker
shame–shameless	secure—security

Spelling Instruction for Derivational Readers and Spellers

According to the Common Core State Standards, starting in third grade, students should also begin to decode words with Latin suffixes and, in grades 6–8, they should be able to use their knowledge of Latin and Greek affixes, roots, and word parts to infer the meaning of unknown words from context. This is because, as we explained in previous chapters, starting in fourth grade, students encounter more and more academic vocabulary that comes from Latin and Greek. Therefore, knowledge of the meaning of Latin and Greek morphemes can hugely support reading comprehension, vocabulary acquisition, and spelling development for students at the derivational phase of word recognition.

ASSIMILATED LATIN PREFIXES   In Chapter 3, we briefly mentioned *assimilated prefixes*—prefixes of Latin origin whose pronunciation and spelling were adjusted to match the pronunciation and spelling of the root of the word. For example, in words such as *import, impossible*, or *imbalance*, the form of the original prefix was *in-* ("not"). However, because it is easier to pronounce an /m/ than an /n/ before a /p/ or a /b/ (since /m/ is a bilabial consonant, just as /p/ and /b/ are), the prefix came to be pronounced /im/ and spelled *im-*. In phonological terms, the final consonant of the prefix was "assimilated" to the pronunciation of the first consonant of the root—hence the term assimilated prefixes. The assimilation was not complete, though, since /m/, /p/, and /b/ are still distinct sounds.

With other words, the assimilation was actually complete, in that the ending consonant of the prefix changed into the beginning consonant of the root. The phonological assimilation is reflected by the spelling of such words—they have double consonants that occur at the junction of the prefix and the root in academic words of Latin origin such as *accredit, collaborate, illegal, oppress*, or *support*. Thus, the word *accredit* contains the Latin prefix *ad-* ("to, toward") and the Latin root *cred* ("belief"), with the form of the prefix having been changed to *ac-* to match the initial consonant of the root. The word *collaborate* comes from the prefix *com-* ("together"), changed to *col-* to match the beginning of the root *labor* ("work"). *Illegal* contains the prefix *in-* ("not"), assimilated to the root *leg* ("law"). The word *oppress* is made up of the prefix *ob-* ("down, against"), which was assimilated to the root *press* ("to push"). And, the word *support* comes from the prefix *sub-* ("under, below"), assimilated to match the root *port* ("to carry"). Table 13.10 contains a list of the Latin prefixes that have undergone assimilation, with their original form and meaning in the first column, examples of words in which they have been added to a root that begins with the same consonant that they end with in the second column, and examples of words in which they have been assimilated in the third column.

INSTRUCTIONAL SUGGESTIONS FOR DEVELOPING MORPHOLOGICAL AWARENESS   Teaching the meaning of affixes and roots, explaining the phenomenon of assimilated prefixes, and engaging students in structural analysis to infer the meaning of unknown words have been shown to improve students' vocabulary knowledge and reading

Table 13.10 Assimilated Latin Prefixes

Original form of the Latin prefix	Words in which the prefix has been added to a root beginning with the same consonant	Words in which the prefix has been assimilated to the root
ad- (="to, toward")	addict, addition, address	accredit, affect, aggravate, allocate, annihilate, appeal, assimilate, attract
com- ("with, together")	commit, common, community, commute	collaborate, collect, college, connect, correct
in- ("in, into; not")	innate, innocent, innovate, innumerable	illegal, immature, immigration, irresponsible
ob- ("down, against")	–	occasion, offer, oppose, oppress
sub- ("under, below, secondary")	–	succeed, succumb, suffer, suggest, suppress, support, surrender

comprehension as well as their spelling (Carlisle & Katz, 2006; Deacon & Bryant, 2005; Nagy, Bernihger, & Abbott, 2006; Nunes, Bryant, & Bindman, 2006). Moreover, such instruction has been proven to be effective not only with native speakers of English but also with English language learners (Kieffer & Lessaux, 2010).

Kieffer and Lessaux (2010) identified four principles for good morphology teaching, all of which support the claim we made at the beginning of this chapter—that language should be taught in context. They are as follows:

1. *Morphemes should be taught in the context of rich vocabulary instruction.* This means that morphological analysis should be performed on words that the students have encountered in a variety of meaningful oral and print contexts. It also means that classroom instruction provides multiple opportunities for deep processing of word meanings and for practice in using the words that contain newly taught morphemes.

2. *Using morphological analysis should be taught as a cognitive strategy.* Teaching morphological analysis as a cognitive strategy means teaching it as a strategic tool for reasoning while interacting with and making meaning from texts. To perform morphological analysis, students must follow a series of steps. First, they must recognize that they do not know the word. Next, they must analyze the word for morphemes that they recognize (roots, prefixes, suffixes). Then, they should hypothesize a meaning for the word based on the word parts. Finally, they should check the hypothesized meaning against the context.

3. *Instruction should introduce word parts systematically and with opportunities for reteaching and practice.* The teaching of morphology needs to be planned in terms of scope and sequence. More specifically, while teachers should begin to develop children's morphological awareness as early as in kindergarten, according to the Common Core State Standards, they should begin to do so with high-frequency, "transparent" morphemes (i.e., morphemes whose meanings are obvious), such as the suffix -er or the prefix un-, and gradually introduce morphemes with less obvious meanings. Also, previously taught morphemes should be revisited, especially when encountered in new contexts in which they may have a different meaning than the one students have already learned. For example, the prefix in- may mean "not," as in "inevitable," or "in/into," as in "intake."

4. *Instruction should be explicit but situated in meaningful contexts.* In order to teach morphemes explicitly but also in meaningful contexts, teachers must plan to illustrate the new morphemes with examples from the texts that students are reading, and that are related to the topics being taught.

Morpheme analysis can be a useful strategy for close reading, and thus be integrated within the building knowledge phase of a lesson. Take, for example, the paragraph from Steinbeck's *Travels with Charlie* in Figure 13.2 (a text exemplar for grades 6–8 included in Appendix B of the Common Core State Standards).

Figure 13.2 Text for Integrated Morphology and Vocabulary Instruction

STEINBECK, John. *Travels with Charley: In Search of America.* New York: Penguin, 1997

I soon discovered that if a wayfaring stranger wishes to eavesdrop on a local population the places for him to slip in and hold his peace are bars and churches. But some New England towns don't have bars, and church is only on Sunday. A good alternative is the roadside restaurant where men gather for breakfast before going to work or going hunting. To find these places inhabited one must get up very early. And there is a drawback even to this. Early-rising men not only do not talk much to strangers, they barely talk to one another. Breakfast conversation is limited to a series of laconic grunts. The natural New England taciturnity reaches its glorious perfection at breakfast.

The last sentence of the paragraph ("The natural New England taciturnity reaches its glorious perfection at breakfast.") would be a good candidate for close reading, because it concludes the paragraph-long description of small New England towns and summarizes the author's perspective on New Englanders. Understanding the sentence and the irony in it hangs on knowing the word *taciturnity*, whose meaning can be explained by teaching the base words *tacit* ("done without words; silent") and *taciturn* ("not talkative"), and then by asking students to infer the meaning of *taciturnity* based on their knowledge of the noun suffix *-ity*.

As this example suggests, reading comprehension can and should be supported by activities aimed at developing morphological awareness, and such activities should be integrated with vocabulary development activities. This conclusion is based on recent research (e.g., Goodwin, Gilbert, & Cho, 2013; Yap, Balota, Sibley, & Ratcliff, 2012) showing that for morphological knowledge to positively affect decoding and comprehension, students must have knowledge of the base words themselves, in addition to knowledge of affixes.

Check Your Understanding 13.3: **Gauge your understanding of the skills and concepts in this section.**

Teaching Grammar in Context

The Common Core State Standards for language clearly require that students demonstrate command of the conventions of Standard English grammar, and lay out grade-level benchmarks that students must attain. The question for teachers is, therefore, not *whether* they should teach grammar, but *how* they should do it.

As we explained at the beginning of this chapter section, current scholarship on language instruction strongly argues that grammar teaching, just like the teaching of any other formal aspect of language, should be integrated with reading and writing activities, such that as students learn grammar, they also become aware of how grammatical choices affect the meaning of texts. Gartland & Smolkin (2016) present three principles that should inform grammar instruction:

1. Integrate grammar instruction into the overall language arts curriculum. This means that grammar instruction should support students' listening and reading comprehension, as well as their speaking and writing.

2. Develop clear objectives for grammar instruction that help students to link grammatical form with meaning.

3. Experiment with specific classroom activities that allow students to see how grammatical choices impact the meaning of texts.

In the remainder of this section, we will show how grammar teaching can help students to link grammatical form with meaning such that it will support comprehension and production of oral and written texts. We will also give you suggestions for classroom activities that you may want to use to include grammar in your reading and writing instruction.

Teaching Grammar Through Conversation to Support Reading/Listening Comprehension

As with any other formal aspect of language, students should encounter the grammar structures that you want them to learn in context, that is, in the texts that they read or listen to. The context illuminates the form, the meaning, and the use of grammatical structures; therefore, you can use it to engage your students in conversations about a particular grammar structure present in the text so they will discover how it works. Let's look at an example.

GRAMMAR TEACHING IN THE LOWER ELEMENTARY GRADES   A class of first graders is reading or listening to a text in which they encounter the sentence "It is 5 p.m. and it is dark outside." After engaging them in several comprehension activities during the building knowledge phase of the lesson, to the teacher decides focus their attention on this particular sentence and asks them why it was dark outside. Based on their prior knowledge and their understanding of the text, they will probably say that it was wintertime. The teacher then asks them how they know that (in wintertime, it is dark outside at 5 p.m.). Then, she writes on the board: "It is 5 p.m. but it is dark outside" and asks the children if this sentence means the same thing as the previous one. Why or why not? Why do you think it is dark outside? Is it because it is wintertime? If it is not wintertime, what might be going on? How do you know? She continues the conversation, helping students to compare the two sentences and to realize that the only difference between them is the use of the conjunctions *and* and *but*. She leads them to conclude that *and* is used to add expected information to a sentence, while *but* is used to add unexpected information.

How is this conversation different from traditional grammar instruction? One significant difference is that instead of telling students a grammar rule and expecting them to memorize it, the teacher draws attention to a grammatical structure

Figure 13.3 Passive Voice Text

ALIKI. *A Medieval Feast.* New York: HarperCollins, 1986.

> Preparations for the visit began at once. The lord and lady of the manor had their serfs to help them. **The manor house had to be cleaned, the rooms readied, tents set up for the horsemen, fields fenced for the horses. And above all, provisions had to be gathered for the great feast. The Royal Suite was redecorated. Silk was spun, new fabric was woven. The Royal Crest was embroidered on linen and painted on the King's chair.**

(the conjunctions *and* and *but*, in this example), and asks questions that help students to figure out how the structure is used and how it affects the meaning of the text. In the course of such a conversation, therefore, the teacher is not imparting grammatical knowledge; rather, the students are constructing it as they work in their zone of proximal development (Vygotsky, 1982) with the teacher's assistance. The teacher's questions help the students to use what they already know and can do to construct a generalization (rule). Having constructed the rule themselves, students are more likely to remember it than if it had been taught to them by the teacher.

To give students practice using the rule they have discovered, the teacher provides pairs of sentences pertaining to the text they have read, and has them connect those sentences using *and* or *but*. Then, as a consolidation activity, she has them write a summary of the text, and asks them to use the two conjunctions as necessary.

GRAMMAR TEACHING IN THE UPPER ELEMENTARY GRADES   Another way in which the teaching of grammar through conversation differs from traditional grammar teaching is that the conversation is not limited to the rule for forming a particular grammatical structure (such as, "add *-ed* to form the past tense"), but, as we have shown above, it also includes discussion of the effect of the structure on the meaning that the text conveys. For another example, let's look at the text in Figure 13.3, taken from Aliki's *A Medieval Feast*.

The bolded sentences contain verbs in the passive voice and could be used to teach this grammatical structure. But, what exactly is there to teach, and how would you go about it?

One way to do it would be to rewrite the passive sentences as active sentences (with the subject "the serfs"), and have students analyze and compare them to the bolded sentences in the original text. This would lead students to come up with the rule for turning an active sentence into a passive sentence. Then, they could discuss how the meaning of a passive sentence is different from that of its active equivalent. With the teacher's help, the students should come to the conclusion that the passive voice is used when the doer of the action is deemphasized or unknown, and when the action itself is emphasized by the speaker/writer. By contrast, the active voice is used when the doer of the action is emphasized. Finally, the class should discuss why the author chose to use the passive voice instead of the active voice in the bolded sentences.

The best place for conversations focused on a particular grammar structure is at the end of the building knowledge phase of a lesson, after the students have already comprehended the text. At that point the students can engage in close reading of a short section (one or several sentences) so they will become aware of how the grammar structure contributes to the meaning of the text as a whole.

This doesn't mean that all close readings should focus on grammar, or that all lessons should include grammar instruction. Nonetheless, when the opportunity arises, that is, when you spot a sentence/passage in the text that you want your students to read that clearly illustrates a grammatical structure, use that sentence/passage to teach grammar! Be a "sentence stalker," as Jeff Anderson (2005) says; be on the lookout for "mentor texts" (Anderson, 2005) that you can use to teach your students how grammar works in context! Figure 13.4 includes some sample mentor texts and the grammar structures you can teach as you use them.

Teaching Grammar to Support Writing Development

Several authors (e.g., Anderson, 2005; Kolln & Gray, 2013; Saddler, 2012) suggest that grammar should be taught in conjunction with writing because, as Kolln and Gray (2013) explain, students who are aware of the grammatical choices available to them are better equipped to control the rhetorical effects of their writing. Also, being able to apply their grammatical knowledge to their own writing is likely to make students see grammar less as something taught for remedial purposes (to fix run-on sentences or agreement errors, for example) and more as a toolkit they can use to make the meanings they intend to make clearly and effectively.

TEACHING GRAMMAR THROUGH WRITER'S WORKSHOP   Anderson (2005) argues that grammar teaching should be built into the writer's workshop and that it should begin with students' reading or listening to a **mentor text**—a short text

Figure 13.4 Grammatical Structures Illustrated by Mentor Texts

1. The Modal Auxiliary *Would* to Express a Repeated Past Action

Once there was a tree. . . and she loved a little boy. And every day the boy would come and he would gather her leaves and make them into crowns and play king of the forest. He would climb up her trunk and swing from her branches and eat apples. And they would play hide-and-go-seek. And when he was tired, he would sleep in her shade.

Silverstein, Shel. *The Giving Tree*. New York: Harper & Row, 1964.

2. The Relative Pronoun *That*:

This is the house that Jack built.

This is the malt
that lay in the house
that Jack built.

This is the rat
that ate the malt
that lay in the house
that Jack built.

This is the cat
that chased the rat
that ate the malt
that lay in the house
that Jack built.

[Traditional. Public domain.]

3. The Past Perfect

I wiped my hands on my apron and went to the window. Outside, the prairie reached out and touched the places where the sky came down. Though the winter was nearly over, there were patches of snow everywhere. I looked at the long dirt road that crawled across the plains, remembering the morning that Mama had died, cruel and sunny. They had come for her in a wagon and taken her away to be buried. And then the cousins and aunts and uncles had come and tried to fill up the house. But they couldn't.

MacLachlan, Patricia. *Sarah, Plain and Tall*. New York: HarperCollins, 1985.

4. Adverbs

Gradually the fawn stopped struggling, as if it understood that I was there to help. I put my arms around it and pulled. It barely moved. I pulled again, then again. Slowly the fawn eased out of the mud, and finally it was free. Carefully I carried the fawn up the bank to its mother. Then, quietly, I returned to the raft.

LaMarche, Jim. *The Raft*. New York: HarperCollins, 2000.

that clearly illustrates one aspect of the writer's craft. Then, the teacher and the students engage in conversation about the text, with the teacher asking questions that lead the students to notice how a particular sentence structure or convention (e.g., use of commas) is used in the text, and providing grammatical concepts and terminology that the students need in order to articulate their observations. Following the analysis of the mentor text, the teacher instructs the students to take out a free-write they have done and play around with it, imitating the structure or convention they have just discussed. Finally, the students share their modified freewrites, and the teacher engages the class in discussion of the modifications they have made and of the effects of those modifications. Thus, the teacher exposes students to additional examples of the new structure used in context and provides opportunities for students to use the new terminology as they critique their peers' work.

For example, as part of a unit in which students learn about point of view, they also learn about pronouns, and practice reading and writing texts in the first, second, and third person. To teach students how to avoid vague pronoun references, Anderson (2005) has his students read a triple-spaced copy of a paragraph from Roald Dahl's *Boy: Tales of Childhood*. He explains that pronouns stand for nouns, and that the noun that a pronoun refers to (the *antecedent*, or the *pronoun referent*) has to be easy for the reader to see. Then, the students read Dahl's paragraph and highlight all the pronouns, after which they draw arrows from each pronoun to its antecedent. Finally, the students take out a draft they have been working on and do the same thing (highlight the pronouns and draw arrows to the antecedents), checking it for vague pronoun references.

In his book on sentence writing, Saddler (2012) presents a host of practice activities that teachers can use to help their students learn how to write effective sentences—from simple sentences to compound sentences, to complex sentences, to paragraphs. One such activity, which could easily be included in a writer's workshop, is the "Artist Study." In this activity, the students are presented with a passage from a book that they are currently reading, and that contains particularly well-written sentences. The students are asked to decompose the passage into simple sentences, and then recombine those into a passage that has a different number of sentences than the original one. The last step is for students to compare their passage to the original, and discuss the two in terms of their effectiveness.

TEACHING GRAMMAR THROUGH THE WRITING PROCESS   Weaver (2008) proposed a framework for teaching grammar throughout the writing process that could easily be adapted to make room for practice activities such as the one described above, and that is built upon the gradual release of responsibility model (Pearson & Gallagher, 1983). These are the steps of her framework:

1. Share a model from literature.

2. Create another example (teacher and students together).

3. Have students create another example in small groups or pairs, and share their work. Discuss as a class and clarify as needed.

4. Have students create another example individually and share their work.

5. Ask students to use the newly taught grammar structure in their own writing.

6. Have students provide peer-feedback and/or provide feedback yourself.

7. Have students revise their papers.

8. Supply students with a checklist for the editing stage that includes the grammatical structure taught.

9. Have students write their final draft.

10. If needed, go through the process again with a different piece of writing.

Watch this video in which a teacher instructs her class in how to edit their writing for grammar and then answer the question that follows

 Video Exploration 13.3: **Watch the video and answer questions that reflect the content your have read.**

Steps 2, 3, and 4 in this framework would allow for some additional practice activities. Step 1 should include a discussion of the model with the class, as well as any grammatical explanations that might be necessary—which brings us to the question, "How much **metalanguage** (language about language, or grammatical terminology) should we use and teach?"

Weaver (2008) claims that "most of the grammatical terms used in traditional grammar books are not really needed to explain grammatical options and conventions . . . (or) for writers to use the language effectively and appropriately" (p. 27). She goes on to say that "patterns are usually much easier to grasp than terms and rules, and examples often clarify better than detailed explanations" (p. 27). We agree that grammatical competence means being able to use grammar rules effectively, not just recite them; students need to be exposed to examples of grammatical structures used in context so they will notice patterns and then arrive at grammatical generalizations (rules) themselves, with the teacher's help. Nonetheless, we believe that a certain amount of metalanguage is necessary for students to be able to express and remember those generalizations. Learning grammar is like learning anything else—when we learn new concepts, we need words for them.

Check Your Understanding 13.4: **Gauge your understanding of the skills and concepts in the section.**

Teaching Text Structure

As you read in Chapter 3, *text structure* refers to the ways in which ideas are organized and linked within paragraphs or longer texts. Examples of text structures include the story grammar common to many narrative texts, and descriptive, comparison/contrast, or cause/effect structures often encountered in informational texts. Children first become acquainted with the structure of narrative texts, but, as they read more informational texts, they need to develop awareness of how such texts are organized, too. Authors of informational texts organize the ideas they present to facilitate comprehension by the readers. Therefore, students having awareness of text structure supports reading comprehension by helping them to identify key ideas and supporting details, anticipate what's to come, and self-monitor comprehension during reading (Fletcher, 2006; Meyer, 2003; Snyder, 2010). Additionally, scholars have proposed that teaching students about connectives that signal the logical relationships between and among ideas in a text will help them not only see the logic of texts better but also write well-organized, cohesive texts themselves (Akhondi, Malayeri, & Samad, 2011).

The Common Core State Standards view knowledge of text structure and signal words as an aid to reading and writing, which is why expectations for students to develop such knowledge are spelled out in the reading and writing standards. More specifically, starting in third grade, students are expected to be able to describe the overall structure (e.g., chronology, comparison, cause/effect, etc.) of informational texts that they read, and to use appropriate transition words (i.e., signal words) to link ideas in the texts that they write.

The inclusion of specific standards for text structure and signal words within the Common Core State Standards for reading and writing also suggests that, like all language instruction, the teaching of these features of texts should be embedded within overall meaning-focused reading and writing activities. As with any formal aspect of language, students should be prompted to notice the structure of a text and its related signal words as they read the text for comprehension purposes, that is, during the building knowledge phase of a lesson that uses the ABC model; and, they should practice using the structure and the signal words as they produce oral and/or written texts during the consolidation phase of the lesson.

Teaching Signal Words to Identify Text Structure

One way to help students understand how a text is organized is by having them complete a graphic organizer, such as those we showed you in Chapter 9, that provides a visual representation of the text structure. For example, if you are teaching a unit about transportation and your students are reading a text that compares and contrasts two means of transportation, such as the text about helicopters and airplanes in Figure 13.5, you may want them to complete a Venn diagram to identify the similarities and differences between the two.

After you discuss these with the class, ask the students where in the text they found the similarities and where they found the differences, and lead them to notice that the former were mentioned in the first paragraph and the latter were described in the second paragraph. Then, ask them how they knew whether a particular feature was common to the two machines, and help them to notice the words and phrases used to signal similarities and differences.

To give students guided practice using the signal words typically encountered in texts with a comparison/contrast structure, you can rewrite the text as a series of simple sentences and ask them to connect the sentences using the signal words identified in the text. Alternatively, you can provide them with a cloze text in which they need to fill in the missing signal words (see Figure 13.6).

Finally, as part of the consolidation phase of your lesson, you can ask students to write a similar text comparing and contrasting two other means of transportation that they have researched, such as trains and subways, or cars and buses. If students are using the writing process when writing such a text, have them complete a Venn diagram at the rehearsing stage and use it to write the first draft. Then, before they revise their draft, remind them, in a mini-lesson, how a comparison/contrast text is structured and what words and phrases they can use to signal similarities and differences.

Figure 13.5 Text with Comparison/Contrast Structure

Airplanes and Helicopters

Both helicopters and airplanes are flying machines. They are made of the same materials and have similar controls. Like airplanes, helicopters are operated by highly trained and highly skilled pilots.

Helicopters and airplanes are more different than similar, though. For example, airplanes have long, slender bodies with wings, while helicopters have round bodies and propellers. Airplanes can travel extremely fast. By contrast, helicopters are rather slow. Unlike airplanes, which take off horizontally and can move in a forward direction only, helicopters take off vertically and can move in any direction. Airplanes need a lot of space for takeoff and landing, whereas helicopters can take off and land on a space as small as the roof of a building.

Figure 13.6 Cloze Text with Comparison/Contrast Structure

Airplanes and Helicopters

_____ helicopters and airplanes are flying machines. They are made of _____ materials and have _____ controls. _____ airplanes, helicopters are operated by highly trained and highly skilled pilots.

Helicopters and airplanes are more different than similar, though. For example, airplanes have long, slender bodies with wings, _____ helicopters have round bodies and propellers. Airplanes can travel extremely fast. _____, helicopters are rather slow. _____ airplanes, which take off horizontally and can move in a forward direction only, helicopters take off vertically and can move in any direction. Airplanes need a lot of space for takeoff and landing, _____ helicopters can take off and land on a space as small as the roof of a building.

Using Headings and Subheadings to Identify Text Structure

In some expository texts, the way information is organized is not necessarily signaled by connectives, but rather by headings and subheadings (which, in Chapter 9, we listed among the "external features" of informational texts). For example, the introductory section of the text about telescopes in Figure 13.7 (an informational text exemplar included in Appendix B of the Common Core State Standards as suitable for grades 4–5) explains why telescopes are necessary, defines telescopes, explains how they work in general, and discusses the etymology of the term *telescope*. The second section, whose heading is "Kinds of telescopes," distinguishes between optical and non-optical telescopes. The following section, bearing the subheading "Optical telescopes," provides more details on one of the two types of telescopes presented in the previous section. More specifically, it classifies optical telescopes into three categories, depending on how they gather and focus light: refracting, reflecting, and catadioptric telescopes. Finally, the last section of the text provides extensive detail on refracting telescopes under that very subheading.

Figure 13.7 Expository Text

FROM Ronan, Colin A. "Telescopes." Reviewed by William A. Gutsch. The New Book of Knowledge®. Copyright © 2010. Grolier Online.

Telescopes

You can see planets, stars, and other objects in space just by looking up on a clear night. But to really see them—to observe the craters on the moon, the rings around Saturn, and the countless other wonders in our sky—you must use a telescope. A telescope is an instrument used to produce magnified (enlarged) images of distant objects. It does this by gathering and focusing the light or other forms of electromagnetic radiation emitted or reflected by those objects. The word "telescope" comes from two Greek words meaning "far" and "see."

Kinds of Telescopes

There are many different types of telescopes, both optical and non-optical. Optical telescopes are designed to focus visible light. Non-optical telescopes are designed to detect kinds of electromagnetic radiation that are invisible to the human eye. These include radio waves, infrared radiation, X rays, ultraviolet radiation, and gamma rays. The word "optical" means "making use of light." Some telescopes are launched into space. These telescopes gain clearer views. And they can collect forms of electromagnetic radiation that are absorbed by the Earth's atmosphere and do not reach the ground.

Optical Telescopes

Different types of optical telescopes gather and focus light in different ways. Refracting telescopes, or refractors, use lenses. Reflecting telescopes, or reflectors, use mirrors. And catadioptric telescopes, or catadioptrics, use a combination of lenses and mirrors. The main lens or mirror in an optical telescope is called the objective.

Refracting Telescopes. A refracting telescope is typically a long, tube-shaped instrument. The objective is a system of lenses at the front end of the tube (the end facing the sky). When light strikes the lenses, it is bent and brought to a focus within the tube. This forms an image of a distant object. This image can be magnified by the eyepiece. This consists of a group of small lenses at the back of the tube. A camera can replace or be added to the eyepiece. Then photographs can be taken of celestial objects. For many years, these cameras used film. Today most are equipped with charge-coupled devices (CCD's). These devices use semiconductor chips to electronically capture images. CCD's are similar to the devices in home digital cameras and video camcorders. However, the CCD's used by astronomers are usually extremely sensitive to light.

Figure 13.8 Graphic Organizer for Expository Text

Network Tree

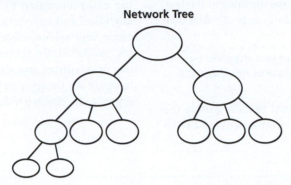

With such a text, having students read the headings and subheadings as a first activity of your building knowledge phase of the lesson will give them a quick understanding of what topics are presented in the text and how the information is organized. To help them visualize the relationships among the topics, you may wish to create a graphic organizer with the class as they read the text the first time (see Figure 13.8 for an example of a graphic organizer suitable for an expository text such as this) and fill in just the topics. For a second reading, the students' task could be to add details to the graphic organizer.

At the consolidation phase of the lesson, you may want students to research non-optical telescopes and add that information to the graphic organizer in preparation for writing their own expository pieces on non-optical telescopes. As they draft and revise their papers, ask them to use headings and subheadings following the model of the original text. This way, you will have integrated the teaching of text structure with reading, writing, and content instruction.

Check Your Understanding 13.5: **Gauge your understanding of the skills and concepts in this section.**

For Review

The Common Core State Standards require that students develop sound knowledge of how language works at all its levels of organization (phonology, morphology, syntax, and text structure) and that they can use this knowledge to learn to read and write increasingly complex texts. In this chapter, we showed you how language instruction can be integrated with literacy instruction to support reading and writing development. At the outset of this chapter we stated that when you reached this point in your reading and studying you should be able to:

- **Integrate the teaching of print concepts and phonological awareness with meaningful reading and writing instruction.**

To do that, teachers can use a whole-part-whole lesson structure, in which students are first engaged in comprehending a text, then helped to notice a print concept or a phonological pattern present in the text, and finally asked to use the newly taught concept or pattern in their own writing.

- **Plan and implement contextualized phonics instruction for alphabetic and orthographic readers and spellers.**

Knowledge of the six basic types of written syllables can help children advance through the alphabetic phase of

word recognition and spelling development. It can also help them learn spelling rules that orthographic readers and spellers need to be aware of. To help students acquire such knowledge, teachers can use the whole-part-whole model or the Four Blocks approach.

- **Plan and implement contextualized spelling instruction for morphological and derivational readers and spellers.**

At the morphological and derivational phases of reading and spelling development, students need to develop morpheme awareness and knowledge of word etymologies. They also need to learn additional spelling rules that apply when affixes are added to roots or base words. If developed in the context of meaning-focused reading and writing activities, awareness of morphemes and word etymologies will support reading comprehension as well as vocabulary and spelling development.

- **Teach grammar in context to support reading/ listening comprehension and writing development.**

Starting in kindergarten, teachers can engage students in discovery activities so they will figure out how a grammatical structure works in a text—how it is formed, how it is used, and how it affects the meaning of the text. Students can use such understandings to better their own writing.

- **Develop students' awareness of text structure by teaching signal words and the use of headings and subheadings.**

Because authors of informational texts organize the ideas they present to facilitate comprehension by the readers, awareness of text structure supports reading comprehension by helping students to identify key ideas and supporting details, anticipate what's to come, and self-monitor comprehension during reading. Additionally, teaching of signal words and of the use of headings and subheadings will help students not only see the logic of texts better but also write well-organized, cohesive texts.

For Your Journal

1. Review the answers to the Anticipation Guide at the beginning of this chapter section. What answers would you give to those questions now that you have read this chapter?

2. Choose one of the texts in Figure 13.4. How would you teach the grammar structure it features so that your students would understand how to form it, what it means, and when it should be used?

3. Read the text "Telescopes" in Figure 13.7. What cohesive devices does it use to link ideas to one another?

Taking It to the World

Interview a staff member in the admissions office of your college or university. Ask her or him what language problems are most common in essay applications (e.g., spelling, grammar, punctuation, text coherence) and which of those weigh more heavily in an admission decision.

Chapter 14

Models and Strategies for Teaching ESL and for Teaching Reading in the Mother Tongue

 ## Learning Outcomes

After reading this chapter, you should be able to:

1. Describe advantages and disadvantages of teaching in the mother tongue with a later transition to English language instruction versus teaching in English only from the beginning.

2. Explain how communicative approaches to teaching English as a second language are more effective and faster than traditional approaches.

3. Implement highly effective second language instructional strategies that result in the development of students' oral communication (listening comprehension and speaking) abilities.

4. Select appropriate strategies for teaching English language learners to read.

5. Coordinate the role of a mother-tongue-speaking paraprofessional and a teacher who speaks only English in classrooms with many English language learners.

Anticipation Guide

The following statements will help you begin thinking about the topics of this chapter. Answer *true* or *false* in response to each statement. As you read and learn more about the topics in these statements, double-check your answers. See what interests you and what prompts your curiosity toward more understanding.

_____ 1. English language learners can learn English in one year.

_____ 2. It is a waste of instructional time to teach a child to read in the child's mother tongue.

_____ 3. Phonics is the most important component of reading for an English language learner.

_____ 4. Children should always be grouped by level of English proficiency for English as a second language (ESL) lessons.

_____ 5. Children who first learn to read in Spanish or another language have to start over when they learn to read in English.

_____ 6. The teacher should always immediately correct the grammatical errors of English language learners.

_____ 7. Children who have learned to read in their mother tongue have little difficulty learning to read in English.

_____ 8. English language learners should always respond in complete sentences.

_____ 9. Some adolescent English language learners are not able to read in any language.

_____ 10. Students are not learning English if they are not speaking.

_____ 11. Children cannot learn to understand and speak English unless they learn the grammar first.

A Classroom Story

A Bilingual Teacher in a Bilingual Classroom

Ms. Ortega is a certified bilingual first-grade teacher. Her 23 students speak Spanish as their first language, and their English proficiency ranges from several who have no English at all to a few children who are at a low-to-intermediate level. Her children are ready to learn to read in Spanish, and she is well prepared to teach them. The Spanish reading program she uses is parallel to the English language program used in other classrooms in her school, but it is not a direct translation. She also has a wealth of children's literature in Spanish.

Ms. Ortega begins her morning business in English. "Good morning, boys and girls." "Good morning, teacher," they respond, politely and respectfully addressing her by her title. After several weeks of school, the children can greet their teacher, respond to the roll and lunch count, and understand most classroom routines in English. Morning business is followed by a 40-minute ESL lesson that is characterized by simple dramatized commands, questions, many gestures and smiles, and much laughter.

After recess, the children have whole-class shared reading activities in Spanish with big books. In smaller groups, they dictate language-experience chart stories in Spanish, read them, put the sentences in order, illustrate them, read to each other, and play word games with vocabulary they have used. Independently and in pairs, they will take turns "reading" big books to each other and reading language-experience stories to family members at home.

Some of the children are beginning to associate sounds with letters they recognize, and Ms. Ortega has begun to teach brief focused phonics lessons related to elements that have emerged from their language-experience charts and for which they have demonstrated phonemic awareness in language play activities. They also work in the more structured Spanish reading program with anthologies of stories and some expository text. The program includes more systematic and explicit activities designed to introduce the relationships between sounds and letters in Spanish several weeks into the school year and after they have developed a basic sight vocabulary.

The children in Ms. Ortega's classroom are indeed fortunate. They are in a full bilingual program with a highly qualified teacher who has appropriate instructional materials. She addresses them in English in the parts of her program where they are ready to understand. She consistently devotes 30 to 40 minutes of instructional time each day to ESL, focusing on listening with nonverbal or simple responses at the beginning, with more emphasis on production later.

Her Spanish reading program is analytic or whole-part-whole, with children learning about letter/sound correspondences in the context of words they already recognize. The plentiful authentic literature in her classroom provides for a strong focus on comprehension and motivation.

The vignette also displays how Ms. Ortega presents the elements of the four blocks framework: guided reading and writing, self-selected reading, and working with words (Cunningham, Hall, & Sigmon, 2007). She demonstrates reading to her students in the **shared reading** activities with big books. She works with words in the brief focused phonics lessons that emerge from meaningful reading and writing activities. She provides guided practice both in the shared reading of big books and in the dictation and reading back of dictated language-experience charts. The children extend their reading practice in reading shared books to each other and language-experience charts to family members. They will soon begin to write in Spanish as an outgrowth of their LEA activities.

The purpose of this chapter is to examine the teaching of reading in the mother tongue and also the teaching of ESL as it relates to the teaching of reading and writing. The audience for the chapter is threefold: bilingual teachers who will teach reading and writing in a language other than English, teachers of English language learners whose mother tongue instruction will be conducted by a paraprofessional or other staff members under the teacher's supervision, and all teachers of English language learners who teach ESL.

Options for Teaching the English Language Learner

There are two basic categories of instructional programs for teaching English language learners. These categories are presented in terms of the generic K–8 school program for them; the specific questions of second language and reading instruction are treated later in the chapter. In Figure 14.1, you will see the various structures that can be applied in English only programs and in full bilingual programs.

Teach Them in English

English-only options for teaching English language learners exist in several forms and for many reasons. In some cases, the numbers of children who have a non-English language in common at a grade level are small, and it is not feasible to

Figure 14.1 Model Program Structures for Meeting the Needs of English Language Learners.

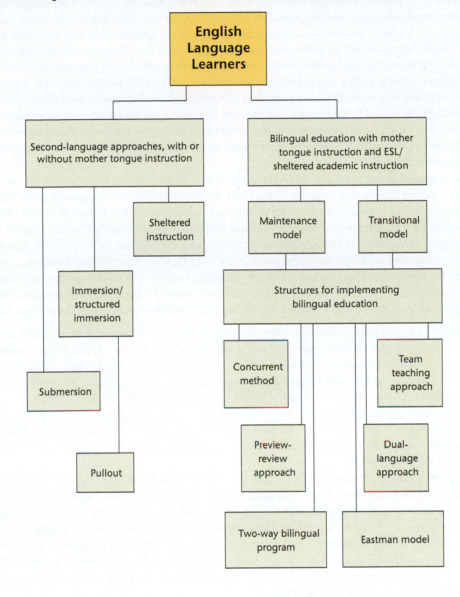

offer a program of mother tongue instruction. A lack of trained teachers and mother tongue instructional materials may exacerbate this situation. Political considerations constitute another reason for providing only English language instruction, such as in California and Arizona, where statewide ballot propositions largely discourage or make difficult the use of mother tongue instruction and mandate the use of what is characterized as structured immersion in English. But there are many limitations in teaching English language learners only in English, as you will see.

IMMERSION INSTRUCTION   One approach to second-language acquisition is **immersion instruction**, sometimes called *structured immersion*. Immersion instructional programs are focused on intensive English instruction during the first year, although it is well documented that children need more than one year to master enough English to learn academic subjects and reading in English (Thomas & Collier, 1997).

ESL instruction is the most important element in an immersion approach to teaching English language learners. Their academic instruction in reading, mathematics, science, and social science is also conducted in English, although English language learners gain little from this instruction. They do not understand or speak English, nor can they read in English at a sufficient level of comprehension. In some cases, support in the mother tongue is provided by a paraprofessional or parent volunteer. For example, that adult might sit down with the English language learners to assist them in understanding a lesson the teacher taught earlier in English and in completing independent work.

SUBMERSION INSTRUCTION   What is often called a *submersion* approach is a variation on structured immersion, and it is truly a sink-or-swim approach. Although most educators do not advocate its use, the submersion approach is often observed as the default methodology in working with English language learners. Non–English-speaking children are simply thrown to the mercies of a teacher, classmates, and instructional materials in English, with no concessions to their language or cultural needs. This sometimes occurs for political reasons. But many times it is simply a reflection of the school's inability to respond to the needs of a small number of non–English-speaking children who have a less common mother tongue.

Lambert (1975) contrasted additive and subtractive education programs for second-language learners. In **additive program**, children add a new language and its accompanying culture to their mother tongue and culture, along with a positive self-image. Stritikus (2006) concluded that additive programs view linguistic and cultural diversity as an asset to be valued.

In *subtractive program*, English and its accompanying culture are substituted for the mother tongue and culture, often leading to low self-esteem, low academic achievement, increased dropout rates, and other negative consequences. Immersion programs are of the subtractive type.

Several major principles guide teachers' understanding of how to provide the best context for learning in general and for learning in a second language. Cummins (1986, 1989) describes two levels of language proficiency that demonstrate the need for high-level proficiency in the second language before academic instruction is provided in the second language. He describes **basic interpersonal communications skills (BICS)** as those that permit English language learners to carry on a simple conversation in the new second language, and they appear to be proficient. But a higher level of language proficiency, **cognitive academic language proficiency (CALP)**, is required for the student to learn to read in the second language or, for example, to learn the commutative principle of addition in mathematics. Cummins concludes that a threshold of language proficiency in the mother tongue must be reached for the student to attain academic proficiency in the mother tongue and later in a second language. This threshold is seldom met in programs of immersion in English.

PULLOUT APPROACH   In the most common pattern for providing English language instruction, the teacher in the self-contained classroom provides all instruction, including ESL. Another common pattern is the pullout program. ESL teachers have their own classrooms, and for periods of 40 to 60 minutes, they pull children out of their self-contained classrooms for ESL instruction and then send them back. In semi-departmentalized and departmentalized intermediate or junior high schools, usually at the fifth- or sixth-grade level and above, one or two teachers might have responsibility for teaching ESL to all English language learners.

Unfortunately, not every teacher is well prepared—or perhaps prepared at all—to teach ESL. One advantage of a pullout program is that a specialist can be very effective in providing this important instruction and will usually have high-quality materials for this purpose.

The pullout approach also has several disadvantages. Children miss instruction in the regular classroom, depending on the hour during which they are absent. English language learners are singled out as "special" or "different" when they leave for ESL instruction, which often has negative consequences. Pullout programs are usually organized according to homogeneous groups in that the ESL teacher will pull beginners from several classrooms for a period of instruction, then intermediate learners from several classrooms, and so on. Even in the self-contained classroom, the teacher should consider teaching the English language learners as a single group, regardless of their proficiency. As you will see later in this chapter, there are advantages to having children at several levels of English language proficiency during ESL/language development lessons, including capable English speakers.

SHELTERED ENGLISH INSTRUCTION, SDAIE, AND SIOP®   **Sheltered English instruction** is a very powerful scaffolding approach for working with English language learners, but it is an intermediate approach. It is designed to follow an initial second-language acquisition program that takes students from non–English speaker status to that of intermediate speaker of English. In California, sheltered instruction is sometimes called Specially Designed Academic Instruction in English (SDAIE) (CATESOL, 1992).

A more recent model of sheltered instruction is called the **Sheltered Instruction Observation Protocol (SIOP®)** (Echevarria, Vogt, & Short, 2013; Vogt & Echevarria, 2015). SIOP is designed to help English language learners meet grade-level CCSS and ELS/ELD standards in California. The emphasis is on teaching academic language to make academic content comprehensible to students.

Sheltered (scaffolded) instruction is therefore an important second-language component of all education programs for English language learners, whether they have been in bilingual education or in an English immersion program. It constitutes, however, a submersion approach when used, or misused, with beginning speakers of English. We examine sheltered English instruction in more depth later in this chapter, but first watch this video in which Dr. MaryEllen Vogt describes sheltered English instruction and the SIOP model and then answer the question that follows.

▶ **Video Exploration 14.1:** Watch the video and answer questions that reflect the content you have read.

Common Core State Standards for English Language Learners

The Common Core State Standards in English Language Arts that have been referred to throughout this book also apply to English language learners. The groups responsible for the standards, the National Governors Association Center for Best Practices and the Council of Chief State School Officers, write:

"[We] strongly believe that all students should be held to the same high expectations outlined in the Common Core State Standards. This includes students who are English language learners (ELLs). However, these students may require additional time, appropriate instructional support, and aligned assessments as they acquire both English language proficiency and content area knowledge."

Teach Them in the Language They Already Speak

The *Lau v. Nichols* decision (see Chapter 2) did not mandate bilingual education as a remedy, but school districts soon found that it was one of the few ways to ensure that English language learners had equal access to education, that is, education in their mother tongue while they learned English. In most bilingual education programs, children learn to read and write, and also to study the other subjects of the academic curriculum—mathematics, social science, and science—in their mother tongue. Simultaneously, they learn English as a second language, a process that typically takes two to five years or more (Thomas & Collier, 1997). As the result of a transition process called *positive transfer of skills*, children can then do in English what they have learned to do in their mother tongue (August et al., 2006; Baker & Sienkewicz, 2000; Cummins, 1981).

The underlying principles of bilingual education are as follows:

- Teach English language learners to understand and speak English as a second language.
- Teach the academic subjects, including reading and writing, in the mother tongue while the children are in the process of learning to understand and speak English; in that way, they don't fall behind in their academic subjects.
- Transition the children from mother tongue academic instruction to English language instruction in a sheltered mode when they have attained an intermediate level of English; this is accomplished through positive transfer of skills.

Because of the lack of instructional materials and a shortage of trained bilingual teachers in many languages, non–Spanish-language bilingual education programs are less common and usually are limited in scope.

In *Preventing Reading Difficulties in Young Children*, Snow, Burns, and Griffin (1998) endorsed the efficacy of teaching children to read in the mother tongue wherever possible before teaching them to read in English. A major five-year developmental study conducted by Thomas and Collier (2002) provides additional evidence to support this point of view. Although many mother tongues were represented in their study of over 210,000 students in five school districts in Texas, Oregon, and Maine, most of the students were Spanish speaking. Thomas and Collier found that one-way or dual-language bilingual enrichment programs that were 90:10 or 50:50 (the ratio of mother tongue instruction to English instruction) were the only programs in which students reached the 50th percentile in both languages and in which there were the fewest dropouts. Children whose parents refused bilingual education programs, because they insisted on English-only instruction, had much lower achievement. The strongest predictor of English language achievement in the study was the amount of formal mother tongue instruction. Thomas and Collier found that the highest achievement in bilingual education programs was associated with those that offered a natural learning environment in school, with rich oral and written language in both the mother tongue and in English, problem solving, group student activities, media-rich learning, challenging thematic units, and use of the students' bilingual and bicultural knowledge to access new knowledge.

In a major meta-analysis of studies about the language and literacy development of language-minority students, The National Literacy Panel on Language-Minority Children and Youth published a report in 2006. Their conclusions paralleled those of the National Reading Panel (2000):

- Phonemic awareness, phonics, fluency, vocabulary, and text comprehension instruction were major factors in the development of literacy; more focus, however, should be placed on working with particular phonemes that do not exist in the students' mother tongues.

- Although language-minority children were able to keep pace with their English-speaking classmates in the development of word recognition skills, they fell behind in comprehension and writing because of the lower level of English language proficiency among these students.

- Children's oral proficiency and reading ability in their mother tongue can be used to facilitate the development of literacy in English as a result of the positive transfer of skills, a finding similar to that of Snow et al. in *Preventing Reading Difficulties* (1998) cited earlier.

- There is a hierarchy of skills in English that must be attained before children can be successful in reading comprehension in English, and individual differences among children are a significant factor in this development; in addition, for language-minority children in special education programs, developing sight word reading and holistic learning strategies might be more effective in teaching them to read and write.

- Most assessment tools used with language-minority children are not effective in measuring their individual strengths and weaknesses; there is little evidence of the effect of sociocultural variables on the development of literacy, except for the positive effect of home language experiences.

TRANSITIONAL VERSUS MAINTENANCE MODELS OF BILINGUAL EDUCATION   There are two underlying philosophies about how to conduct programs of bilingual education: transitional and maintenance. In the more common *transitional model*, children learn English as a second language. They learn their academic subjects, including reading and writing, in their mother tongue, and they make the transition to English language academic instruction in a sheltered mode when they have reached an intermediate level of English, usually between the late second grade and early fourth grade. The major goal of the transitional program is to produce a monolingual, monoliterate, and monocultural child who temporarily uses the mother tongue as a vehicle for learning. Children in transitional bilingual programs usually continue their academic studies only in English after the onset of transition to English, although they sometimes receive continuing support in their mother tongue from a paraprofessional, as needed.

In the *maintenance model*, the process is the same up to the point of transition. After the children begin academic instruction in English, they continue to receive periodic lessons in their mother tongue in all subject areas. The major outcome of the maintenance program is a bilingual, biliterate, and bicultural child who is able to function easily and comfortably in two languages and cultures.

STRUCTURES FOR ORGANIZING PROGRAMS OF BILINGUAL EDUCATION   Within the transitional and maintenance models, there are several structures for grouping children and for assigning teachers and paraprofessionals that can be used in either model.

Concurrent Method   One approach that is often used intuitively is called the *concurrent method*. The teacher says everything twice, once in the children's mother tongue, perhaps Hmong, and once in English, assuming there is only one non-English language in the classroom and the teacher is bilingual. When the teacher is not bilingual, a bilingual paraprofessional may fill that second role, basically serving as an interpreter. It is a time-efficient approach with an uncomplicated structure. It is also very ineffective. English language learners begin to tune out the English, which they cannot understand well or perhaps at all, and they listen only to their mother tongue. If they do learn some English as a part of the process, they learn it in terms of their mother tongue. The outcome is a compound bilingual child with two interdependent language systems. The result can be a lifetime of unconscious translation from one language to another, a process that takes precious time, especially on examinations such as the SAT, the GRE, or the important high-stakes tests that are now required in almost all states. This approach also promotes *code switching*, the unconscious mixing of vocabulary and syntactical structures from two languages.

Team Teaching   The team-teaching approach is quite different. Two teachers, one bilingual, the other usually not, work together in the same classroom. They work independently, but when they teach, each teaches the entire class. The primary advantages of this approach are to provide outstanding language and cultural models to the children and to reduce the number of proficient bilingual teachers needed.

Dual Language   The dual-language model resembles the team-teaching model in that there are two teachers, one bilingual, the other usually not, but in separate classrooms. The monolingual English-speaking teacher teaches English as a second language and academic instruction in English for those in the two classrooms who are ready for it. The bilingual teacher teaches the academic subjects to the English language learners in the mother tongue and also teaches the other language as a second language.

The advantages of the dual-language model are that both teachers are working in a language of comfort to them and the children are learning English and their academic subjects from teachers who are good models. Unlike the concurrent method, they are not learning English in terms of their mother tongue, but rather are developing as coordinate bilinguals with two independent language systems. The major disadvantage is that the English-speaking and non–English-speaking children are rarely working together because their needs are very different. It is important for English language learners to associate with English speakers because they learn English from those children as well as from their teacher. They can avoid the fossilization or stopping-in-place that can occur when children are separated from native and capable English-speaking peers. It is also important for groups of children from different languages and cultures to associate with each other to avoid ethnic, linguistic, and cultural isolation.

Preview-Review Mode The preview-review model is very complex, but it resolves some of the shortcomings of the other models. It works best for intermediate English speakers. Two teachers work together as in the team-teaching and dual-language models: one bilingual, the other usually not. The bilingual teacher provides a preview of the lesson to the group in the mother tongue, and the other teacher then teaches the main body of the lesson to the group in the new second language, English. The bilingual teacher then reviews the lesson in the mother tongue after the main body of the lesson.

Eastman Model The Eastman model (Krashen & Biber, 1988) of the Los Angeles Unified School District also effectively alleviates the problem of isolating students from each other at the elementary level. Spanish-speaking students are organized for mother tongue instruction in reading, the language arts, and academic areas of the curriculum during the morning, along with a program of ESL. English-speaking students are similarly organized for reading and academic instruction in English in the morning. In the afternoon, Spanish-speaking students are mainstreamed with English-speaking students in art, music, and physical education, which are conducted in English. As Spanish-speaking students gain English proficiency after two or three years, they begin to receive sheltered academic instruction in English in the more concrete areas of the curriculum, such as mathematics and science. Because of many abstract concepts in social studies, such as liberty and democracy, English is often introduced later.

Two-Way Bilingual Education The two-way bilingual education program has a different goal from mainstream bilingual education. It is used where two language groups of parents want their children to learn—and learn in—another language. Usually, one group of children will be native Spanish speakers learning English as a second language and academic subjects in Spanish. But another group of English-speaking students is in the classroom because their parents want them to both learn Spanish and study various subjects in Spanish. The program goal is additive in that each group learns the language and culture of the other group. The Eastman model is an effective organizational structure for conducting a two-way bilingual education program.

Check Your Understanding 14.1: Gauge your understanding of the skills and concepts in this section.

Major Principles of Second-Language Acquisition

Teaching ESL is the underlying base of programs established to meet the academic needs of English language learners. It is the major element of the full bilingual education programs in which the mother tongue is used for academic instruction while children develop sufficient proficiency in English to benefit from academic instruction in English later.

Regardless of whether children learn to read and write in their mother tongue, they clearly must learn to speak and understand English. In fact, it is not possible to address literacy for English language learners without considering the close links that must exist between the teaching of reading and writing and the teaching of ESL. Those links are rooted in the constructivist or whole-part-whole approaches that underlie effective practice in both.

Constructivist Versus Reductionist Models of Instruction

At this point, we examine the contrast between constructivist and reductionist models of instruction. A **constructivist view** of instruction focuses on the construction of meaning, using what the child already knows and combining it with new knowledge, concepts, and skills to be integrated. It is learner centered and highly contextualized; these are important factors in working with students from diverse backgrounds, who are often at risk of failure. The factor of background knowledge is well recognized as being a key to success in reading and writing, especially in reading comprehension. English language learners have no lack of background knowledge, but there is often a discontinuity between the background knowledge they have and the knowledge assumed by the texts they will use in learning to read and reading to learn. Within the constructivist view, language acquisition is embedded in function. Skills are taught in a meaningful context, not in a rigid, artificial, isolated, and fragmented way. There are several approaches to second-language instruction that reflect the constructivist view; they are in the communicative category.

The foundation for communicative approaches to second-language acquisition is based on concepts, theories, and hypotheses that have converged around the interaction of constructivist notions about making meaning, including

Vygotsky's (1978) zone of proximal development. Conversely, **reductionist** or **behaviorist** models are skills-based and focus on the disassembly or fragmentation of curricular elements so that isolated skills and concepts can be mastered within a linear paradigm. Traditionally, most students have studied a second language, whether English or a foreign language, using such grammar-based approaches as the grammar-translation and audiolingual methods. These are reductionist or skills-based approaches that move learners from part to whole.

Communicative-Based Approaches

The results of research have changed educators' conceptions of how a second language is acquired and how this acquisition is best promoted in the elementary and secondary classroom. There has been a major paradigm shift away from these grammar-based approaches to language learning and toward those called *communicative*, which are also consistent with meaning-based or constructivist approaches to literacy (Crawford, 1994; Crawford, 2003).

THE INPUT HYPOTHESIS   Several important hypotheses underlie current practice in most **communicative approaches to second-language acquisition** (Krashen, 2004). In his input hypothesis, Krashen concludes that growth in language occurs when learners receive **comprehensible input,** or input that contains vocabulary and structure at a slightly higher level than what they already understand. The input hypothesis reflects Vygotsky's zone of proximal development. The context of the input provides clues to maintain the integrity of the message. According to the input hypothesis, a grammatical sequence is not needed. The vocabulary and structures are provided and practiced as a natural part of the comprehensible input that the child receives, much as the process occurs with infants acquiring their mother tongue. Krashen (1981) relates the input hypothesis to the silent period, the interval before speech in either the mother tongue or second language in which the child listens to and develops an understanding of the language before beginning to produce language.

Krashen's (1991) updated input hypothesis includes what he calls comprehensible input plus 1, or CI + 1. It is a part of language that students have not yet acquired, but that they are ready to acquire. The CI + 1 is a new element to be learned in what the teacher has already made comprehensible. It is contextualized, not isolated, and it may include academic language or other new elements, such as a new language structure.

ACQUISITION-LEARNING HYPOTHESIS   In his acquisition-learning hypothesis, Krashen highlights the difference between the infant's subconscious acquisition of the mother tongue and the conscious learning of a second language of the secondary student of French in a classroom. Students acquire language subconsciously, with a feel for correctness. Learning a language, by contrast, is a conscious process that involves knowing grammatical rules. The infant, of course, is almost always successful in acquiring communicative competence, whereas the secondary school foreign language learner is often not (Crawford, 1994; Crawford, 2003).

Gee (1992) elaborates Krashen's concept of acquisition by adding a social factor reflecting Vygotsky's "zone of proximal development" and also the concept of approximation. He describes acquisition as the subconscious process of practice in social groups, benefiting from exposure to language models, in a process of trial and error. Formal instruction is not needed. Gee's concept parallels how babies and infants learn their mother tongue at home.

NATURAL ORDER HYPOTHESIS   According to Krashen's (2004) natural order hypothesis, grammatical structures are acquired in a predictable sequence, with certain elements usually acquired before others. He concludes that the orders for first- and second-language acquisition are similar but not identical. He does not, however, conclude that sequencing the teaching of language according to this natural order or any grammatical sequence is either necessary or desirable.

MONITOR HYPOTHESIS   Krashen's (2004) related *monitor hypothesis* describes how the child's conscious monitor or editor serves to make corrections as language is produced in speaking or writing. Several conditions are necessary for the application of the monitor:

- Time to apply it, a situation that is not present in most ordinary oral discourse, especially in classroom settings
- A focus on the form or correctness of what is said, rather than on the content of the message
- Knowledge of the grammatical rule to be applied

These conditions serve to illustrate why so few children or adults learn to understand and speak a foreign language in a grammar-translation or audiolingual foreign language course in the secondary school or university.

AFFECTIVE FILTER HYPOTHESIS   In his affective filter hypothesis, Krashen (2004) concludes that several affective variables are associated with success in second-language acquisition. These include high motivation, self-confidence and a positive self-image, and, most important, low anxiety in the learning environment. It is therefore important that teachers avoid high-pressure instruction and especially humiliation of students who are acquiring English.

Other Basic Principles

Results from research have led to other major changes in educators' conceptions of how a second language is acquired and how this acquisition is best facilitated in the classroom, one of which is the obvious similarity between primary- and second-language acquisition. In both, primary- and second-language learners form an incomplete and incorrect **interlanguage** (Selinker, Swain, & Dumas, 1975), with most children moving through similar stages of development in this incomplete language.

APPROXIMATION AND CORRECTION   The role of correction is also similar in both primary- and second-language acquisition. *Approximation* is a related process in which children imitate more proficient English speakers in all of the dimensions of language, oral and written, and test hypotheses about it. Approximation underlies oral and written language in that children are acquiring new understandings and skills within the context of authentic wholes. Children demonstrate behaviors in which they approximate the language behavior of their English models, growing closer and closer to their levels of proficiency. In his view of successive approximation, Holdaway (1979) describes the process as one in which Vygotsky's adults and more capable peers, that is, teachers and proficient English-speaking students, use information in the output from children's responses to construct, adjust, and finally eliminate the scaffolding that facilitates progress in learning.

Terrell (1982) and Krashen and Terrell (1983) conclude that correction should be viewed as a negative reinforcer that will raise the affective filter and the level of anxiety among English language learners. When errors do not interfere with comprehension, correcting them has no more place in the ESL program than it does when infants acquire their mother tongue. Caregivers might expand incorrect or incomplete forms, such as "me go" or "Kitty gots four feets," and say "Yes, you go" or "Yes, Kitty has four feet." There is little evidence, however, that this expansion has any positive effect. Errors are signs of immaturity, not incorrectness; they will disappear naturally as a part of approximation in the developmental process of language acquisition (Crawford, 1994; Crawford, 2003).

These similarities between primary- and second-language acquisition are not consistent with either the grammar-translation or audiolingual approach. Children learning their first language do not rely on grammatical rules or on systematic acquisition of vocabulary. With its emphasis on early production instead of a silent period, on correct production instead of an acceptable though immature and incomplete interlanguage, and on grammatical sequence instead of function and communicative competence, the audiolingual approach bears little resemblance to the way primary or second languages are successfully acquired.

AGE OF ACQUISITION   Finally, age is an important factor in second-language acquisition. Collier (1987) examined the relationship between the age of English language learners and their acquisition of a second language. She found that those who entered the second-language acquisition program at ages 8 to 11 were the fastest achievers. Those who entered the program at ages 5 to 7 were the lowest achievers, and they were one to three years behind children from 8 to 11 years of age. Children who entered at 12 to 15 years of age had the most difficulty acquiring the second language. She projected that they would need from six to eight years of classroom instruction to reach age-level norms in academic achievement.

Collier (1989) later analyzed other research on age and academic achievement in the second language and found that children who had academic instruction in the mother tongue generally required from four to seven years to reach national norms on standardized tests in reading, social studies, and science and as little as two years in mathematics and language arts, including spelling, punctuation, and grammar. She also found that children from ages 8 to 12 who had at least two years of schooling in their mother tongue in their home country needed from five to seven years to reach the same levels of achievement in second-language reading, social studies, and science and two years in mathematics and language arts. Young children with no schooling in their mother tongue in either the home country or the new host country needed seven to 10 years of instruction in reading, social studies, and science. Adolescent children with no ESL instruction and no opportunity for continued academic work in their mother tongue were projected, for the most part, to drop out of school before reaching national norms, regardless of whether they had a good academic background or interrupted schooling.

Check Your Understanding 14.2: Gauge your understanding of the skills and concepts in this section.

Instructional Strategies for Second-Language Acquisition

The implications of Krashen's hypotheses and of related similarities between first- and second-language acquisition are that approaches to second-language acquisition should do the following:

- Provide comprehensible input
- Focus on relevant and interesting themes instead of grammatical sequences
- Provide for a silent period without forcing early production
- Avoid correction
- Maintain a low level of anxiety

There are approaches to second-language acquisition that meet these criteria. The communicative approaches most appropriate for elementary and secondary classrooms are the total physical response method and the natural approach.

The Total Physical Response Method

Asher's (1982) **total physical response (TPR)** method is an important communicative approach in the initial stages of second-language acquisition. The TPR method provides for comprehensible input, a silent period, and a focus on relevant content rather than on grammatical form. The focus of TPR is on physical responses to verbal commands such as "Stand up" and "Put your book on the desk." Because little emphasis is put on production, the level of anxiety is low.

Lessons can be given to small groups or an entire class. In the beginning, the teacher models one-word commands. This is done first with a few children to introduce new vocabulary and structures, then with the entire group, then with small groups of children, and finally with individual children. For example, the teacher says, "Sit," and then models by sitting down. Later, the teacher issues the command without modeling. As the children's levels of language increase, the teacher begins to use two- and three-word commands, such as "Stand up" and "Bring the book."

The children demonstrate their understanding by physically carrying out the commands. The order of commands is varied so that the children cannot anticipate what will be next. Old commands are combined with new ones to provide for review. Whenever the children do not appear to comprehend, the teacher returns to modeling. After a silent period of approximately 10 hours of listening to commands and physically responding to them, a child then typically reverses roles with the teacher and begins to give those same commands to other children. It is important for the teacher to maintain a playful mood during classroom activities.

The TPR approach can be extended to higher levels of proficiency by using the technique of nesting commands. The teacher might say the following:

Jamal, take the book to Svetlana, or close the door.
Noriko, if Jamal took the book to Svetlana, raise your hand.
If he closed the door, stand up.

A high level of understanding is necessary to carry out such commands, but no oral production is needed. Parents of young children will recognize that their infants can understand and carry out such commands long before they begin to speak themselves.

Watch this video to familiarize yourself with the Total Physical Response Method (TPR) and see how it can be used in the classroom. Then, answer the question that follows.

 Video Exploration 14.2: Watch the video (https://www.youtube.com/watch?v=1Mk6RRf4kKs) and answer questions that reflect the content you have read.

The Natural Approach

Terrell's (1977) original concept of the **natural approach** provided for three major characteristics:

- Classroom activities were focused on acquisition, that is, communication with a content focus leading to an unconscious absorption of language and a feel for correctness, but not an explicit knowledge of grammar.
- Oral errors were not directly corrected.
- Learners could respond in the target language, their mother tongue, or a mixture of the two.

Krashen and Terrell (1983) later added four principles that underlie the natural approach to language acquisition:

1. Comprehension precedes production, which leads to several teacher behaviors: teacher use of the target language, a focus on a theme of interest to the children, and maintenance of the children's comprehension.

2. Production emerges in stages ranging from nonverbal responses to complex discourse, with children able to speak when they are ready and speech errors not corrected unless they interfere with communication.

3. The curriculum consists of communicative goals, with topics of interest comprising a thematic syllabus, not a grammatical sequence.

4. Activities must result in a low level of anxiety, a lowering of the children's affective filter, which the teacher accomplishes by establishing and maintaining a good rapport.

Terrell's (1981) natural approach is based on three stages of language development: preproduction (comprehension), early production, and emergence of speech.

Ms. Ortega, the teacher in the bilingual classroom in the chapter-opening vignette, uses the natural approach. The curriculum of her ESL program is made up of themes that are supported by large-format posters and charts, big books, and concrete objects in the classroom. She also uses the four blocks approach to organizing her reading program (Cunningham et al., 2007), but her program is a five blocks approach. She has added ESL as an important fifth reading/language arts area of the curriculum.

THE PREPRODUCTION STAGE   In the **preproduction stage**, topical, interesting, and relevant comprehensible input is provided by the teacher in a close parallel with Asher's TPR approach. The teacher speaks slowly, maintaining comprehension with gestures. Children may respond with physical behaviors, shaking or nodding their heads, pointing at pictures or objects, and saying yes or no. It is important that input is dynamic, lively, fun, and comprehensible. Crawford (1994) provides an example in which the teacher uses a pet turtle and says,

> This is a turtle. It is four years old. Is it green? Who wants to hold it? [Hands to child.] Who has the turtle? Does Tran have the turtle? Yes, he does. Does Rosa have the turtle? No, she doesn't.

This basic input can be repeated with other objects in the classroom, such as large-format posters and illustrations (Crawford, 1994). Crawford suggests that each child in the group be given a different illustration, and the teacher provides input:

> Who has a picture of an airplane? Yes, Olaf, you do. Is the airplane large? Olaf, give your picture to Zipour. Who has a picture of a boat? Yes, Nicole has a picture of a boat.

These examples include three primary preproduction techniques of using TPR strategies, TPR strategies accompanied by naming objects, and pictures.

The required responses include movement, pointing, nodding or shaking the head, and using the names of other children in the group. Remember that nodding the head for an affirmative response and shaking it for a negative one are not appropriate in all cultures; it is the converse in Albania, for example. Children might also have to learn these nonverbal behaviors. Because the emphasis at this stage is on listening comprehension, verbal responses in the mother tongue are also acceptable. This might be a problem if the teacher cannot understand the children's mother tongue, but children usually find a way to help the teacher understand.

Classroom props allow for relevant expansion of this and subsequent stages of the natural approach (Crawford, 1994; 2003). Any manipulative or concrete object is helpful, including flannel boards and puppets. Large colorful illustrations, such as those in big books, are also very helpful. Sources of free color illustrations include calendars (outdated or otherwise), travel posters, large posters available from textbook and trade book publishers, and colorful illustrations in the annual reports of many large corporations, which are often available on request through announcements in major business magazines.

THE EARLY PRODUCTION STAGE   In the **early production stage**, the child begins to produce one-word utterances, lists, and finally two-word answers, such as "big dog" and "in house." Some of the latter, such as "me want" and "no like," are grammatically incorrect or incomplete. According to Crawford (2003), teachers should view these responses as immature, not incorrect. In the presence of good models, these errors will disappear in time, just as they do among infants developing their mother tongue at home.

Several types of questions can be used to elicit one- and two-word responses that are within the reach of children as they move into the early production stage:

Question Format	Illustrative Question
Yes/no	Do you like hamburgers?
Here/there	Where is the picture of the cat?
Either/or	Is this a pen or a key?
One word	How many dogs are there?
Two words	What fruits are in the picture?

As in the preproduction stage, these strategies should be integrated into activities that permit a variety of responses, ranging from physical responses from those not ready for production, to brief oral responses from those who are. As the children begin production, conversations should increasingly require one-word responses. Within the same conversation, the teacher can address questions calling for longer responses to those children who are ready. Teacher questions and commands here are in italics, and student responses are in brackets [ ]:

> *Kjell, show us your picture. What is in Kjell's picture?* [A sandwich.] *Yes, it is a sandwich. What is on the sandwich?* [Ketchup.] *Is there an apple on the sandwich?* [No. Laughter.] *What else is on the sandwich?* [Meat, mayonnaise.] *How does it taste?* [Good.] *What do you like with a sandwich?* [Cookies. Soda.] *I like chips with mine.*

THE EMERGENCE OF SPEECH STAGE   During the **emergence of speech stage**, children begin to produce structures that are richer in vocabulary, longer and more complex, and more correct. This production proceeds from three-word phrases to sentences, dialogue, extended discourse, and narrative, strategies that are also helpful in teaching Standard American English to speakers of African American Vernacular English. At this stage, Terrell (1981) recommends such activities as games, group discussions, preference ranking, skits, art and music, radio, TV, pictures, readings, and filling out forms. An example of a chart that incorporates **preference ranking** is provided below by Crawford (1994) (see Figure 14.2). After surveying the children about their preferences for pizza toppings and recording them, the teacher uses the survey results in Figure 14.2 to ask questions at different levels, each directed at a particular student and designed to elicit a response that reflects that student's stage of English language development. Teacher questions are in italics, and student responses in brackets [ ]:

> *Does Sofik like pizza?* [Yes.] *What kind of meat does Sofik like?* [Sausage.] *How many like tomato on their pizza?* [Four, Margarita, Sofik, Nguyen, and Petra.] *How much does Abdul like pizza?* [He doesn't like it.] *Which children like the same kind of pizza?* [Sofik and Petra.] *Is there a topping that no one likes?* [Yes.] *What is it?* [Anchovy.] *How do we know?* [Nobody wants anchovy.]

Not only is the chart a valuable source of comprehensible input, but the process of gathering the data for the chart is also. In addition, children begin to read each other's names and the words for popular foods in English.

Wordless picture books can also be used as a stimulus for the production of language at the emergence of speech stage. In an article that addresses struggling upper-grade readers, Ho (1999) describes strategies that will also be very effective for English language learners. After a brief book talk with the teacher, a small group of students creates a short text for a wordless book. One student member of the group records the text, although a paraprofessional or parent volunteer might fill this role when the students' writing abilities make this difficult. This is of even more value when two or three groups of students independently create their own text and then share it with the other groups.

Figure 14.2 Second-Language Preference Ranking Chart

Name	Favorite Pizzas					
	Cheese	Sausage	Pepperoni	Tomato	Anchovy	Mushroom
Margarita	X			X		X
Sofik		X		X		
Abdul						
Nguyen	X		X	X		
Petra		X		X		X

Planning and Teaching Natural Approach/TPR Lessons

Teachers will not be able to find student textbooks designed to teach English as a second language using the natural/TPR approaches. Lessons can be planned according to the suggestions below, and, with practice, teachers soon learn how to teach these lessons with minimal advance preparation.

PREPARING TO TEACH   Using the demonstration lesson in the next section as a model, you can organize your natural/TPR approach lessons following these steps:

Step 1: Select a theme or topic.

Step 2: Select a **conversation poster** or other stimulus for the lesson, such as a walk around the school, a science experiment, a reading aloud of the first half of a story, students' clothing, or any other subject of interest. The sequence of conversation posters doesn't matter.

Step 3: Write one or two aims for the lesson; you can include a grammatical element, but you won't teach it as grammar. You don't need to mention the tense or part of speech. Focus on correct usage, not on knowledge of the grammar.

Step 4: Choose several vocabulary words from previous lessons to review.

Step 5: Choose a few questions and commands from previous lessons to review.

Step 6: Based on your theme, the aims of the lesson, and the needs of the students, choose a few new vocabulary words and one or two new commands and questions to introduce. Prepare a strategy to introduce them.

Step 7: Then prepare model questions and commands for the main part of the lesson. You will need three or four for each of the three groups in your class—preproduction, who will respond with gestures; early production, who will respond with one or two words; and emergence of speech, who will respond with complete sentences, although they will be short and often not perfectly correct. You will then be mixing and recombining review vocabulary, questions, and commands with new ones to generate more opportunities for the students to respond. About twice each week, try to integrate a **nested command** into the lesson for students at the stages of **emergent literacy** and emergence of speech. About once a week, and on another day, try to integrate a preference ranking activity into the same stages.

Step 8: Using vocabulary, questions, and commands from your lesson plan, quickly review what they have been learning at the end of the lesson. Natural approach lessons ordinarily are about 30 minutes in length.

A MODEL NATURAL APPROACH/TPR LESSON PLAN

Topic: THE OUTDOOR MARKET
Objectives:

- The students will be able to compare sizes (comparative, superlative).
- The students will be able to form and use -*ing* endings (gerunds).

[Note that the grammatical terms are not taught, but the correct usage of the elements is taught with examples from the poster.]

Instructional materials: a conversation poster depicting an outdoor market, with stalls selling different kinds of goods, such as clothing, kitchen items, tools, people who are vendors, people who are shoppers.
[Note that all vocabulary terms used in the lesson are present in the conversation poster.]

Vocabulary review (from previous lessons): flowers, purse, tools, pink, bald

---

Figure 14.3 Other Suggestions to the Teacher

- There is no fixed sequence for themes in a thematic curriculum. You can select any topic for any lesson.
- Conversation posters are large-format, four-color pictures, large enough to be seen from anywhere in the classroom, or they can be projected onto a screen. They should contain sufficient detail to be used many times at higher and higher language levels throughout the school year.
- A variety of stimuli should be used to keep students interested—conversation poster one day, hats the next, an illustrated read-aloud story the day after that, and so on.
- The questions and commands for teaching the lesson should not be used in the exact order of the lesson plan. The teacher should skip around, combining and recombining vocabulary, questions, and commands in different orders.
- The teacher should direct appropriate commands and questions to each student or to small groups of students according to their proficiency.

Review of command and questions structures taught previously:

- Point to….
- Where is….?
- Who is wearing….?
- Raise your hand if….

New vocabulary for this lesson:

- Comparative and superlative terms: big, bigger, biggest
- Gerunds made from verbs: sleeping, selling, laughing, pushing

New command and questions structures:

- How many….?
- Who has….?
- What are they?
- Name them.

Questions and commands for students at preproduction stage: (responding with gestures, yes/no)

- Point to the man who is sleeping.
- How many men are wearing hats?
- Is the little boy with his mother happy? Is his mother happy?
- Who has the warmest coat?
- If the coat is green, raise your hand. If it is orange, point to the clock. (nested command)
- How many men are smiling? How many women are smiling?

Questions and commands for students at early production stage: (responding with one to two words, yes/no)

- How many people are sleeping at the market?
- I see three of something for sale. They are different colors. What are the colors?
- Listen to both parts of what I say. If the woman with the purse is wearing glasses, raise your hand. If the sleeping man doesn't have a watch, stand up. (nested command)
- I see three of many things for sale. What are they?
- Which bucket is the biggest?

Questions and commands for students at emergence of speech stage: (responding with phrases and simple sentences)

- Why is the man sleeping?
- How many sharp tools do you see? What do you do with sharp tools?
- What do you think is in the big box that the man is pushing on the cart? Why do you think so?
- Why do you think the little boy is smiling?
- Do you think that the lady looking at the sweater will buy it? Why, or why not?

Integration with other subject areas: mathematics—counting

TEACHING THE NATURAL APPROACH/TPR LESSON Using the demonstration lesson as the model, you can follow these steps for teaching the lesson:

Step 1: Quickly review vocabulary, questions, and commands from previous lessons. You can use the previous lesson plan as a model for this.

Step 2: Then introduce the new vocabulary, questions, and commands. Use the conversation poster, dramatization, objects in the classroom, or other resources. Don't worry if everyone doesn't learn them immediately. You have the entire lesson to repeat them. When you introduce a new vocabulary word, don't insist that the students repeat the word after you three times. Your purpose is to have them remember the meaning of the new word—they will learn to

Figure 14.4 Other Suggestions to the Teacher

- Teach new vocabulary, questions, and commands in the context of language, not in isolation.
- Use only the language of instruction in the lesson. You are a teacher of English, therefore speak only English. No Spanish should be used by the teacher.
- Maintain students' comprehension by repeating, dramatizing, modeling, speaking more slowly. Find a way to help them understand.
- Remember that only some of what the teacher says is written in the lesson plan. The teacher must mix and recombine the review vocabulary, new vocabulary, review commands and questions, and new commands and questions, repeating all lesson elements many times, but in many different combinations.

say it later in the lesson or in another lesson. Remember to use your knowledge of students' stages—preproduction, early production, and emergent speech—to plan what to say to each student. Call on everyone to respond together early in the lesson as you teach new elements. As they learn the new elements, start calling on the girls, then the boys, then those in the first row, the second row, those wearing blue, those who had cereal for breakfast, and finally individuals according to their stages of language development.

Step 3: Now begin to use the elements of your lesson plan in the preceding lesson. Be sure to use the appropriate category of question or command according to the students' stages.

Step 4: When you have used them all, begin to mix one question type with a different vocabulary word, then a command type with yet another vocabulary word. Mix and recombine the vocabulary, questions, and commands. Some can be repeated several times. Keep the lesson lively and keep it moving quickly. Make the lesson humorous wherever you can. Avoid correcting students' errors—call on someone else, and then come back to the student who made the error so that they can try again based on what the other student said (Figure 14.4).

Grammar as Part of the Curriculum?

According to Crawford (1994), teachers who would advocate teaching the first-person present indicative tense to a 7-year-old English-speaking child in a primary school classroom would be incredulous at the suggestion that a parent teach the same concept to a 3-year-old at home. Of course, both children can use the tense correctly, neither as the result of formal instruction. It is clear that second-language acquisition programs should be based primarily on content, not on grammatical sequence.

A communicative second-language curriculum is usually organized around a set of themes to ensure the introduction of new vocabulary and concepts of interest and utility to the children. Needed language structures emerge and are acquired naturally within the context of thematic lessons. Some communicative curricula include grammatical sequences as a subcategory.

Terrell (1981) suggests that the initial content should be limited to ensuring that students understand the following:

- Commands for classroom management
- Names of objects in the classroom
- Colors and description words for those objects
- Words to describe people and family relationships
- Descriptions of children and their clothing; school areas and activities
- Names of objects in the school that are not in the classroom
- Foods, especially those eaten at school

Later in the acquisition process, topics of interest to children would include the children's families, their homes and neighborhoods, their favorite activities, and experiences they have had. They also enjoy discussing their preferences about food, colors, television programs and films, and other aspects of their lives.

Building Vocabulary

As noted earlier, introducing vocabulary in context is very important. Giroir et al. (2015) describe strategies for developing the vocabulary of English language learners through **read-alouds** with both narrative and expository text. Comprehensible input is provided, and carefully selected text is linguistically and culturally relevant.

AT LOWER GRADE LEVELS Louie and Sierschynski (2015) provide a thorough approach to vocabulary development for English language learners using wordless picture books in a close viewing mode, analogous to close reading later. It is consistent with concepts underlying Krashen and Terrell's use of communicative strategies in the natural and TPR approaches to teaching second language. There is a focus on text structure based on sequencing in wordless books as students develop a narrative in English for a story. In their recommended four-step process, students look at peritextual features, such as the book cover and title, and then examine illustrations from several points of view, perhaps focusing on one character. They then analyze the text based on the teacher's questions about the author's purpose and how that purpose was carried out. In the last step, students author their own texts for repeated reading and analysis. The **language experience approach** would be useful here.

Hansen et al. (2015) recommend using "perfect pairs" of wordless books (that are related in some way) for this approach to academic vocabulary development. This relationship could be a fictional book paired with an informational text, which in turn can support CCSS goals, or two fictional books reflecting similar story lines, but from different languages and cultures. This could extend students from wordless books into books with text at higher grade levels or higher levels of English language achievement. Serafini (2014) extends this concept and adds that it is not important whether students can correctly pronounce or read the words encountered in these books.

In addition to building a working vocabulary for everyday communication, English language learners also need to develop the academic language necessary for working and reading in the content areas of the curriculum. Nagy and Townsend (2012) point out the efficacy of morphological word study of words with Latin and Greek roots. These words are particularly useful to Spanish-speaking English language learners, as their own language contains many words with roots of the same origins. In addition, words with these origins tend to reflect the higher levels of vocabulary found in academic language. According to Montelongo and Hernandez (2013), there are more than 20,000 cognates among academic vocabulary words in English and Spanish. A useful list can be found in Coxhead's (1997) academic word list.

Collins (2005) found evidence that read-alouds were also a potent aid to the development of vocabulary among young English language learners, especially when rich explanations about new words were provided. In a related study of read-alouds done by parents at home and teachers at school, Roberts (2008) found that read-alouds in either the mother tongue or English produced vocabulary gains among preschool children. We can add that when these read-alouds are done with big books, illustrations provide an important context to the process.

AT UPPER GRADE LEVELS Wessels (2011) shared a vocabulary development strategy for English language learners called *Quilts* that builds on the three-part ABC lesson planning structure that underlies this book. Within the anticipation, reading to build knowledge, and consolidation phases, the strategy focuses on assessing background knowledge, connecting known vocabulary to new vocabulary (perhaps across languages), providing for practice, ensuring multiple exposures to new vocabulary, and addressing higher-level knowledge.

In the anticipation phase of the lesson, the teacher provides a sheet of chart paper folded to create boxes. In groups of three to four, the children write the word for their group in their mother tongue or English in a box. Then they write something about the word, or if they can't do that, they illustrate its meaning with a drawing. They discuss the word within their small groups.

In the reading-to-build-knowledge phase of the lesson, they stop reading when they encounter one of their words and, referring to the quilt, discuss their reactions to the word. In the consolidation phase of the lesson, the students write a definition of the word on a sticky note and put it on the quilt. They then discuss the new words as a larger group. The quilt remains available for future referral.

At higher grade levels, Manyak et al. (2014) propose a valuable model with practical principles that promote word-meaning learning for English language learners, as a further support for them in the CCSS mode. In their model, they: (1) present new words not in isolation, but in context (perhaps a word in italics within a phrase from the text, as in: the *gigantic* ship); (2) provide what they characterize as a "kid-friendly" definition, such as "really, really big"; (3) give several examples of the word in other contexts; (4) ask students to provide examples of uses of the new word; (5) show a visual image that illustrates the word and ask students to connect the image to examples of the word; and (6) ask them to make an application by providing a question that requires the use of the new word.

Before reading, teachers should chunk the text, selecting amounts of text that students can understand and introducing new words in those chunks. New vocabulary should represent Beck's tier II (Beck, McKeown, & Kucan, 2013) vocabulary words—not words in conversational vocabulary or words that make up technical subject-specific vocabulary, but useful words encountered frequently. They recommend that students use their own languages to clarify ideas from the text, a process often referred to as "translanguaging" (Garcia & Wei, 2014). This will be more effective if the teacher participates only in English. During the first reading by the teacher, there is a focus on building on the background knowledge addressed in the first stage of the lesson, and reading with expression and prosody that emphasizes new vocabulary. During the second reading the teacher makes more connections to new vocabulary, and the students listen for the new words, signaling when they hear them with a sign prearranged with the teacher, perhaps an ear tug. The students then discuss new vocabulary in small groups, constructing sentences that contain the words. After the reading, the teacher asks open-ended questions that are designed to elicit students' opinions about the text, and the students respond. In keeping with the natural approach, minor errors are not corrected as students express their ideas, guided by the teacher.

Sheltered English Instruction for Intermediate-Level English Speakers

When English language learners have reached an **intermediate level** of English proficiency, they are ready to move from academic instruction in their mother tongue to academic instruction in English by using sheltered English instruction, a model that provides extensive support for comprehension. Sheltering strategies in the content areas of the curriculum add substantially to the knowledge and contextualized vocabulary that students need as a base for reading comprehension as they read and think in any language (Krashen, 1985). These strategies are consistent with the philosophy of communicative approaches to second-language acquisition, and they additionally provide access to academic areas of the curriculum in such a way that communication is maintained. Sheltered English strategies are also very appropriate in providing support for teaching Standard American English to speakers of African American Vernacular dialect; in this case, sheltered instruction should not be described as an ESL strategy.

CONTEXT: THE UNDERLYING BASIS FOR SHELTERED INSTRUCTION   Cummins (1981) provides a set of intersecting continua that are very useful for conceptualizing the issue of balancing the complexity of curriculum content with demands on language proficiency (see Figure 14.5).

The vertical continuum extends from cognitively undemanding to cognitively demanding—ranging, for example, from an art lesson to conducting a science experiment. Cummins's intersecting horizontal continuum extends from context embedded to context reduced, ranging, for example, from a mathematics lesson taught with concrete objects on the context-embedded side to participating in a debate on capital punishment on the context-reduced side. Sheltered instruction in English is most effective in subject areas of the curriculum that can be presented concretely, such as mathematics, science, art, music, and physical education. Although certain aspects of social studies can be taught concretely, such as geography and map skills, so many abstract concepts are taught that English language instruction in this area might well be delayed until students acquire additional English proficiency, especially if expository text in English is an important source of knowledge for the children.

SHELTERED INSTRUCTION: PROVIDING SCAFFOLDING TO ENABLE STUDENT COMPREHENSION   The purpose of a sheltered instruction approach to the core curriculum in English is to provide a focus on context-embedded activities, ensuring that comprehensible input is provided while treating increasingly cognitively demanding aspects of the core curriculum. Examples of sheltered instruction strategies that provide the necessary scaffolding in content areas for intermediate English language learners include the following (Crawford, 2015):

- Simplify input by speaking slowly and enunciating clearly.
- Use a controlled vocabulary within simple language structures.

Figure 14.5 Classification of Language and Content Activities by Cognitive Level and Contextual Support According to Cummins's Framework

SOURCE: Based on Cummins (1981)

	Cognitively Undemanding	Cognitively Demanding

Context Enhanced	Art lesson
	Playing football
	Telephone conversation
	  on Skype with video
	Watching the news on television
		Mathematics lesson using
		  concrete objects
		Conducting a science experiment
		  about evaporation
		Playing a board game
		Making a map of the schoolyard

Context Reduced	Beginning reading skills
	Talking on the telephone
	Listening to the news on the radio
	Reading a set of instructions
		Responding to higher-order reading
		  comprehension questions
		Participating in a debate on capital
		  punishment
		Taking the TOEFL or the IELTS

- Where possible, use cognates and avoid the extensive use of idiomatic expressions.

- Use nonverbal language, including gestures, facial expressions, and dramatization.

- Use graphic organizers, manipulatives, and concrete materials, such as props, graphs, visuals, overhead transparencies, bulletin boards, maps, and realia.

- Check understanding by asking for confirmation of comprehension; by asking students to clarify, repeat, and expand; and by using a variety of questioning formats.

- Use fist of five—students hold up the number of fingers that indicate their understanding—from one (low) to five (high).

- Repeat, rephrase, and expand when students do not understand.

- Encourage interaction between the teacher and students, and among students (see translanguaging below).

- Include content and language objectives in lessons; for example, in a mathematics lesson with a content objective about the addition of decimals and a language objective of understanding and using new vocabulary terms: more than, less than, and equal to.

- Use reading with stops by asking students to read a paragraph or two at a time, guided by a higher-order question instead of reading a large piece of text without guidance as to purpose.

- Rewrite an important and difficult text in a shorter version with easier vocabulary and less complex sentences.

- When teaching from the blackboard, face the students when speaking; the expression on the face and movement of the lips provides important information. Remember the old joke: "What does a mathematics teacher look like?" "No one knows."

- For the same reason, male teachers with moustaches should ensure that they are trimmed so children can see the upper lip.

- In addition, provide wait time after asking a question so that English language learners who know the correct answer can think about how to express it in their new second language (Stahl, 1994).

Many of these sheltered strategies are also very useful for teaching ESL lessons, even before English language learners reach the intermediate level needed for sheltered instruction in the content areas.

OTHER SHELTERED INSTRUCTION SCAFFOLDING STRATEGIES   Richard-Amato and Snow (1992) also provide valuable strategies for content-area teachers of middle school English language learners. They recommend providing a warm learning environment, recording lectures and talks for later review, rewriting some key parts of text material at lower levels, asking native-English-speaking students to share notes with English language learners, and avoiding competitive grading until students have achieved sufficient English proficiency to compete successfully with native speakers.

It is clear that many of these strategies are nothing more than effective teaching practices, but their absence is very damaging to English language learners who are struggling to learn mathematics, science, and social studies in English when they have reached an intermediate level of English proficiency.

Several other strategies provide scaffolding for English language learners in specially designed academic instruction activities in English. The highly contextualized interactions that take place in cooperative learning can make the difference between what Krashen (1985, 1991) describes as submersion, or sink or swim, and sheltered instruction, the type of scaffolded subject-matter instruction just described. Cooperative learning is most effective when, in the words of Vygotsky, more capable peers—that is, stronger speakers of English—are included in groups with English language learners at various levels.

Bauer and Manyak (2008) provide several strategies for enriching language instruction for English language learners at this intermediate stage, each stressing a focus on making input comprehensible. These strategies include the following: having instructional conversations about observations that children log about topics such as weather or the activities of a goldfish or a frog in an aquarium—what they mean; discussing cognates in two languages on the classroom word wall; and talking about a story they have read or heard from a read-aloud. The focus is the theme of the conversation, not the correctness of the grammar.

Translanguaging is an often naturally occurring communication pattern among students that can serve as sheltered instruction (Garcia & Wei, 2014). If an English language learner doesn't understand a teacher's question in English, another student may lean over and whisper the question in the other student's mother tongue. Rather than being a practice that is viewed negatively, it should be encouraged, as it helps students maintain comprehension. We discourage translanguaging by teachers in the mother tongue, however, as students will begin to wait for it, not paying attention to what the teacher is saying in English.

SHELTERED INSTRUCTION OBSERVATION PROTOCOL   The Sheltered Instruction Observation Protocol (SIOP®) (Echevarria et al., 2013) is a carefully organized professional development model that incorporates strategies you have seen in this chapter and previous chapters:

- *Preparation:* lesson planning, content objectives, instructional materials
- *Building background:* integrating student background knowledge and developing academic vocabulary
- *Comprehensible input:* teacher speech presentation strategies and multimodal techniques
- *Strategies:* scaffolding instruction and promoting higher-order thinking skills
- *Interaction:* encouraging elaborated student speech and grouping students appropriately
- *Practice/application:* activities to extend student learning of language and content
- *Lesson delivery:* delivering lessons that meet teaching objectives
- *Review/assessment:* teacher review of key language and content concepts, assessment of student learning, and feedback to students

A SIOP® lesson plan incorporates all of these elements. This model is designed for English language learners, but you can see how it would be very effective with speakers of African American Vernacular English and with any student struggling with language and literacy. As a framework for planning and teaching effective lessons, it highlights best teaching practice for all children.

All of these sheltered strategies build background knowledge that supports the reading comprehension of English language learners as they begin to read expository text in their new second language. When instruction in the mother tongue precedes the sheltered instruction in English, their background knowledge is much richer. A similar approach used in the United Kingdom and Europe is titled Content and Language Integrated Instruction (CLIL) (Coyle, Hood, & Marsh, 2010).

Watch this video that demonstrates how the SIOP model helps students who are learning English and then answer the question that follows.

 Video Exploration 14.3: **Watch the video and answer questions that reflect the content you have read.**

Linking ESL Instruction and Literacy

There is a close link between literacy and the acquisition of a second language that becomes apparent when, as a part of the natural approach, key words are written on the board in the second language, especially for older children who are literate in their mother tongue (Terrell, 1981). This corresponds to the key words to reading approach (Veatch, 1996; Veatch et al., 1979). In the early production stage of his natural approach, Terrell indicates that children may express themselves quite appropriately in one- or two-word utterances as they begin to acquire a second language. According to Crawford (1994), it is altogether appropriate that children also begin to read key vocabulary that they have expressed for their teacher to write for them. They may later produce lists of related ideas, such as foods to eat at the school cafeteria, words that describe a favorite friend, or things to do after school. These topics and this output reflect the oral language common in the early production phase of Terrell's natural approach to language acquisition, output that is well suited for children to dictate for their teachers to record and for the children to read later.

Most bilingual teachers who teach reading in the mother tongue recognize that students' motivation to begin reading and writing in English early is strong. Although it is most beneficial for students to learn to read and write in their native language (Cummins, 1986, 1989; Krashen & Biber, 1988; Snow et al., 1998), where possible, teachers can begin an early introduction to literacy in English to take advantage of that motivation. The key vocabulary and language-experience approaches should be used with caution to ensure that the second-language acquisition program does not evolve into an English literacy program presented before the student is ready. Being able to read and write in the mother tongue is always the most desirable base from which to establish literacy in English later because of the positive transfer of literacy skills to English.

As English proficiency increases, the key word approach to reading may give way to the language-experience approach described in Chapter 5. It is important that the teacher accept the language that the children use in their initial dictations. There will be incomplete sentences, missing words, and inappropriate vocabulary, but this represents the stage at which they are working in their new second language, and correction will only serve to dampen enthusiasm and diminish active participation.

Teach It! 65

Language Experience With English Language Learners

Learn how the language experience approach allows English language learners to be successful as they develop English fluency, print concepts, sight word recognition, and phonemic awareness.

Teach It! 11

Shared Reading

Extending the benefits of reading aloud in their students' new second language, in a shared reading with English language learners, the teacher demonstrates select comprehension strategies and provides guided practice in the use of those strategies *during* the read-aloud.

As mentioned earlier, big books are an excellent source of large-format illustrations for ESL lessons. Later in the process, teachers will find that many children benefit from read-alouds in their new second language, especially when these are based on the background knowledge that children have already acquired as a result of lessons using the illustrations in these big books. The big books that are of most value will be very predictable and have repetitive elements.

Other early second-language reading and writing activities that are useful in the emergence of speech stage of the natural approach include the creation of vocabulary cards, with a word in English and an accompanying illustration from a magazine or drawn by the student. These can be used for word games, including some that begin to focus on beginning sounds; this is especially productive for students who are already learning to read in their mother tongue. Children can also use their vocabulary cards for building word banks, student dictionaries, and word walls. Many children will be anxious to begin writing in their new second language. Simple poetry forms, such as the cinquain (see Chapter 11) and diamante, are useful structures for their initial attempts.

In their efforts to use the mother tongue of children in their classes, teachers sometimes provide cards with a vocabulary word in the mother tongue on one side and in English on the other. They also often provide bulletin boards in the two languages, and search out children's books with text in English on one side of the page and in the mother tongue on the other side. Although these efforts are laudable, such practices lead children to approach their new language of English through their mother tongue instead of directly. Vocabulary cards in English are a good practice, but a picture on the other side is a better choice than the word in the mother tongue. Teachers can and should provide bulletin boards in both languages, but not with both languages represented on the same bulletin board. For example, a science bulletin board can be provided in English on one side of the classroom, and the same bulletin board in the mother tongue can be placed on the other side of the room. Providing the same literature in English and the mother tongue has many advantages, but it is better provided in two separate books. Children will learn their new second language of English better if they do not approach it through the mother tongue.

Check Your Understanding 14.3: Gauge your understanding of the skills and concepts in this section.

Teach It! 64

Form Poems

For English language learners, writing form poems is a simple way to support vocabulary growth, familiarity with structured poems, and awareness of how form and meaning shape each other in poetry.

Options for Teaching the English Language Learner to Read

There are two major options for teaching English language learners to read. These correspond to the two major categories of programs: English only and bilingual education.

In English

In an English-only instructional program, the children necessarily have to learn to read in English. This is not a positive approach, but it is often the only option when a mother tongue reading instruction program cannot be offered because of a very small number of children with a common non-English language, a lack of appropriate personnel and materials, or political considerations.

Assuming that an ESL program is offered beginning in kindergarten and extending into the primary grades, the English language learners should not be placed in a formal and systematic English reading program before they have any proficiency whatsoever in English. The reading program is not an appropriate place for beginning ESL instruction, which should instead focus on understanding and speaking. When reading in English is included at the beginning stages of instruction in listening comprehension and speaking English, the ESL program all too often evolves into a formal phonics- and text-based reading program instead of an ESL program, with very negative results in terms of both language acquisition and reading. According to Lenters (2005), students cannot read with comprehension a language they cannot understand or speak.

As children gain vocabulary in English in their ESL program, they will be interested in writing the words they learn, and they will begin to learn to read them, too, especially if they are learning to read in their mother tongue at the same time. A complete treatment of teaching the English language learner to read in English is provided in Chapters 12 and 13 in two dimensions: (1) the very positive process of teaching the English language learner who has first learned to read in the mother tongue and who has also reached the intermediate level of proficiency in understanding and speaking English and (2) the less desirable, but sometimes necessary, process of teaching reading in English to an English language learner who has not learned to read in the mother tongue and/or who has not reached the intermediate level of English-language proficiency.

Finally, some families will insist that their children learn to read and write only in English, even though the children do not speak or understand that language. Often, the parents themselves can express that desire only in their mother tongue. A few parents might even believe that the purpose of using the minority language for literacy is to maintain speakers of that language in an inferior social position. In this case, teachers need to demonstrate respect for the mother tongue, and they need to assure the children and their families that they will also have the opportunity to learn to speak, read, and write English. In addition, they need to reinforce the idea that children learn to read and write only once and that learning to read and write in another language, such as English, later is a relatively simple transfer process that is well supported in research. Finally, teachers need to reinforce the idea that reading is *comprehension*, not just pronouncing or "reading" sounds. Nonetheless, some parents still insist on English only, and most schools accept that parental decision.

In the Mother Tongue

A fundamental precept of literacy for children who are English language learners is that they learn to read and write more rapidly and more effectively in their mother tongue than they will in a second language that they learn later. The first important and authoritative position taken on this issue was at a UNESCO conference (UNESCO, 1953), in which it was concluded that children learn to read better in a new second language if they first learn to read in their mother tongue. This conclusion has been corroborated by many investigators in subsequent years. Saville and Troike (1971) reported that once a child has learned to read, transferring that ability to another language is not a difficult matter. Modiano (1968) found that Maya children in Mexico learned to read more rapidly in their mother tongue of Quiché than did Maya children who learned to read in their second language of Spanish. Subsequently, the children who had initially learned to read in their mother tongue read better in Spanish than those who first learned to read in Spanish. Through succeeding years, the evidence consistently indicates that children learn to read most effectively in their second language by first learning to read in their primary language (Cummins, 1986, 1989; Krashen & Biber, 1988; Snow et al., 1998; UNESCO, 1953).

Cummins's (1986, 1989) linguistic interdependence hypothesis indicates that what students learn in two languages is interdependent. This common underlying proficiency (CUP) (Cummins, 1981) forms the basis for positive transfer of skills. Children have knowledge and skills that they have learned in their mother tongue, and they can use them in the second language. They do not have to learn this knowledge and these skills again. In fact, it is axiomatic that children learn to read only once. They can transfer reading and writing skills to their new second language, just as adults do when

The World of Reading

My 24 First Graders Speak 14 Different Mother Tongues: What Can I Do?

An increasingly common scenario in American classrooms is the presence of children who speak many different home languages. A bilingual education program usually cannot be provided for most of them for the following reasons:

- The teacher is not proficient in more than one of the languages, if that.
- Reading materials are not available in the languages.
- It would not be feasible to provide reading instruction in several languages, even with a proficient teacher and adequate materials.
- There might not be enough children with a common language at a grade level to support a full bilingual education program.

When many children at a grade level have a common language and are scattered among several classrooms, it might be possible to gather all of them into a single classroom. This is especially desirable if there is a teacher who can teach them in their mother tongue or if a paraprofessional or parent volunteer can provide mother tongue support to lessons taught in English. Usually, these children will be taught only in English in an immersion program. Because English is the only language common to most students, they acquire basic interpersonal communication skills rather quickly. Formal reading instruction is usually delayed, although children can work with key words and the language experience approach early in the process of acquiring English. Shared big books also provide excellent comprehensible input in English, as well as an early introduction to the concept of print and much valuable background knowledge.

they study a foreign language. Cummins indicates that CUP explains why children who have attended school in their country (and language) of origin tend to demonstrate higher achievement in English later than do children who lack that experience. These principles lead to the counterintuitive, but inescapable, conclusion that success in English-language proficiency is closely related to students' learning of reading, writing, and academic concepts in their mother tongue (Collier, 1989; J. Crawford, 1989; Cummins, 1989; Hudelson, 1987; Krashen, 1985; Krashen & Biber, 1988; Ramírez, 1991).

Language policy is a factor of great importance in literacy for children. Clearly, children learn to read and write most quickly and most effectively in the mother tongue. Many factors must be taken into consideration, however, before that decision is made (Crawford, 1995). For example, if skilled bilingual teachers are available, if children speak a minority language for which there is a well-developed written form, and if there are instructional materials in that language, the children can be given instruction in their mother tongue. If this is not the case, then the teacher can consider using the language experience approach in English.

If children speak a language for which there is not a well-developed written form, such as Hmong, then they must be taught to speak and understand English and later to read and write in English, probably using the language experience approach and simple predictable literature in English. If bilingual teachers are not available, then even the presence of instructional materials will not be sufficient to permit mother tongue instruction. The school can also prepare a literate speaker of the minority language as a paraprofessional who works under the supervision of a fully trained teacher who is not proficient in the mother tongue of the children.

In the case of a program of bilingual education, the children will have the opportunity to learn to read in their mother tongue. If a bilingual program is provided for that population, children who speak another non-English language will likely be placed in an English-only approach instead.

In the case of Spanish and other languages that use the Latin or Roman alphabet, there is a close correspondence between literacy skills in English and these languages and therefore much transfer of skills from reading in the mother tongue to English (Briceño (2016):

- The letters of the alphabet in Spanish are almost without exception identical to those of English, except for a few diacritical markings, such as the tilde (~) in Spanish.
- The left-to-right and top-to-bottom directionalities of the languages are the same.
- The concept of print and the alphabetic principle operate in the same way.
- Most consonant sounds and some vowel sounds are the same.

- In addition, there are significant similarities in vocabulary because of the many cognates that exist between English and Spanish (Manyak & Bauer, 2009; Montelongo, Hernández, & Herter, 2011a, 2011b). Some, however, are false cognates, such as *actual*, which means "real" in English and "present" or "current" in Spanish.

- Reading comprehension and organization skills are the same. When a child has learned to read in Spanish, these skills do not need to be learned a second time.

You can think of your own experiences in studying a foreign language. There were many new vocabulary words and grammatical elements to learn, but you did not have to learn to read and write again.

Teaching Children to Read in Spanish

Most English language learners in American schools speak Spanish at home, and almost all formal programs of bilingual education are conducted in Spanish (Fradd & Tikunoff, 1987). According to the National Center for Education Statistics (2009), 21% of students enrolled in American schools were non-English speaking, and 72% of those spoke Spanish at home. In most areas, it is only in Spanish that a wide range of instructional materials are accessible and that sufficient certified bilingual teachers are available to conduct such a program. Therefore, this section of the chapter is devoted to the teaching of reading in Spanish to these children.

As you have seen, the reading and writing processes in English and Spanish have a common alphabet and similar writing conventions. A major difference between English and Spanish is in the regularity of phoneme/grapheme relationships. In English, they are very irregular and inconsistent, especially with respect to the vowels, but in Spanish, they are very regular and consistent, especially with respect to the vowels.

Given this difference, one might expect that reading methodologies in Spanish would focus on phonics to take advantage of that regularity, and many do. But Latin American educators have found that children who learn to read using decoding as their only word recognition skill fall short in comprehension, just as occurs in English reading. Their reading is characterized as *silabeando*, that is, reading syllable by syllable. Their focus is on oral reading accuracy and speed, with little or no attention to comprehension or enjoyment. This is often observed in children who have learned to read in Spanish in Latin America.

There are many approaches for teaching reading in Spanish, just as there are in English. Major approaches are summarized in Table 14.1.

Table 14.1 Major Approaches for Teaching Reading in Spanish

Category of Approach	Methodology	Characteristics	Citation
Part-whole	Alphabetic (alfabético)	Letter names taught first; sequence of vowels, consonants, syllables, words, phrases, and sentences	Barbosa Heldt (1971) de Braslavsky (2006)
	Phonetic (fonético)	Focus on sounds; sequence of vowels, consonants, syllables, words, phrases, and sentences	Barbosa Heldt (1971) de Braslavsky (2006)
	Syllabic (silábico)	Focus on syllables; sequence of vowels, consonants, syllables, words, phrases, and sentences	Barbosa Heldt (1971) de Braslavsky (2006)
	Onomatopoeic (onomatopéyico)	Focus on auditory associations between sounds of letters and natural sounds of the environment, such as the /s/ as the whistle of a fireworks rocket; sequence of vowels, consonants, syllables, words, phrases, and sentences	Barbosa Heldt (1971) Torres Quintero (1976)
Whole-part-whole	Everyday vocabulary (palabras normales)	An analytic approach in which words are broken into syllables, then into sounds, and then reassembled	Barbosa Heldt (1971) Rodríguez Fuenzalida (1982) Rébsamen (1949)
Global	Whole word (global)	Sequence of words and sentences, with little or no phonics	Barbosa Heldt (1971) de Braslavsky (2006)
	Generated words (palabras generadoras)	Sequence of sight words, syllables, and sounds; use of these elements to create new words, phrases, and sentences	Hendrix (1952) Barbosa Heldt (1971)
Eclectic	Eclectic (ecléctico)	Combination of sight word development and phonics; typical of basal reader programs in English and Spanish	Barbosa Heldt (1971)
Constructivist	Whole language (lenguaje integral)	Focus on literature and authentic text; similar to whole-language focus in English; phonics taught implicitly and when need demonstrated (not explicit and systematic)	Freinet (1974) Solé (1994) Goodman (1989) Arellano Osuna (1992) Salmon (1995)
Eclectic	Yo sí puedo (Yes, I can)	A Cuban approach widely used in Latin America and Africa for illiterates of all ages never in school, drop-outs, and those with physical problems, such as hearing and vision	LaBash (2007) Ringo (2012)

These approaches range from those that are highly synthetic to those that are whole-part-whole, even including what is characterized as constructivist or whole language in English. A balanced approach in the whole-part-whole tradition provides for a strong, well-rounded program that is characterized by the following:

- Extensive read-aloud activities to build background knowledge and vocabulary in the mother tongue
- Use of the key words to reading approach, the language experience approach, and shared reading of authentic literature at the beginning stages to introduce the concept of print for children who do not have a rich print environment in the home
- Phonemic awareness activities emerging from vocabulary in children's background knowledge and from LEA charts and shared literature experiences
- An inductive whole-part-whole strategy for teaching phonics, with elements emerging from words the children have acquired in the activities just described
- Use of authentic children's literature in Spanish to serve as a basis for teaching reading comprehension
- Extensive and early opportunities for writing

Application of these strategies in Spanish is similar to that in English, with the exception of phonics, which is addressed later. These key instructional activities also represent the four blocks framework presented above. Beyond the beginning stages of reading instruction, they should be augmented with the many highly effective strategies described throughout the book.

METHODOLOGIES FOR TEACHING READING IN SPANISH   In *The Old Man Who Read Love Stories*, a prize-winning novel written by a Chilean author about an elderly man who lives in the rain forest of Ecuador, Luis Sepúlveda (1989) has described very accurately the way too many Latin American children read as the result of the syllabic approach to reading instruction used in almost every country in the region. They often read very slowly, pronouncing each syllable, and then repeating the entire word. It is not uncommon to find the use of similar methodologies in the United States, often in the hands of bilingual teachers who themselves were educated in Latin America, perhaps even trained as teachers there. These approaches have many limitations when used in isolation; their best use would be as an ancillary word attack skill program to use with high-quality children's literature. But as in reading English, children who read in Spanish need to employ all cueing systems in support of their word recognition efforts: the semantic, syntactic, and pragmatic systems, as well as the graphophonic system.

ISSUES RELATED TO THE SOUND SYSTEMS OF SPANISH AND ENGLISH   The sequence in which Spanish phonics is introduced is different from that of English. It begins with vowel sounds because they are few in number and regular (see Table 14.2). Consonants follow in an order that reflects their frequency and regularity.

Few word recognition problems appear in reading in Spanish, but there are several difficult points in Spanish, as in English, in which one letter represents several sounds. These are often observed in the **invented spelling** of children, as seen in Figure 14.6.

The invented spelling in the student's work presented in Figure 14.6 is very typical of children who write in Spanish, and it is also consistent with Gentry's phonetic stages (Gentry, 1981), where there is substitution of incorrect letters with similar or the same pronunciation. The word *castillo* is spelled *castio*, which yields the correct pronunciation of the word, but not the correct spelling. In the words *paresio* and *isieron*, the student substituted the letter *s* for *c*, again yielding the correct pronunciation of the word, but the wrong spelling. In addition, the silent *h* of *hicieron* was omitted. There is much confusion between the sounds of *b* and *v* in Spanish, both being pronounced similarly to the /b/ in English in the initial position and like /v/ in English when between vowels, resulting in the very typical substitution of *v* for *b* in *estava*.

Finally, there is a grammatical error that reflects a troublesome issue even for some adults. The conventions of Spanish require that the sequential repetition of a sound be avoided. Therefore, *y hicieron* should be written as *e hicieron* to avoid the repetition of the *y* (and) and the *hi* in *hicieron*, both of which carry the same sound (in Spanish, *y* followed by *hi* would sound like two English long *e* sounds in succession).

We have already discussed the issue of positive transfer of skills, that a reading skill or concept acquired in the mother tongue doesn't have to be taught again in the second language of English. Yopp and Stapleton (2008) provide evidence from a review of research and from their own work that phonemic awareness in Spanish transfers to English. They provide a variety of activities and book resources that support the kind of language play that leads to phonemic awareness in Spanish and that transfers to English.

Phonics lessons in Spanish should be drawn out of vocabulary from key words to reading lessons, language experience approach lessons, and the shared reading experiences of children. The words used in the lessons should be within the

Table 14.2 Sequence of Phonics Generalizations in Spanish

Initial Sounds	Final Sounds	Word Endings
a	a	os
e	e	as
i	o	Diminutives
o	Augmentatives	
u	d	Verbs -ar
	l	Verbs -er
m	n	Verbs -ir
t	s	
l	r	Substitution of initial consonants
p	z	
n		
d	i	Substitution of final elements
s	u	
f		
r	**CONSONANT BLENDS**	Medial diphthongs
b		
g (soft)	br	Compound words
ll	cr	
c (hard)	dr	Verb endings
j	fr	
y	pr	Homonyms
h (mute)	tr	
ch	bl	Prefixes
z	cl	
qu	fl	Suffixes
g (hard)	gl	
c (soft)	pl	Homographs
gue, gul		
güe, güi		Grades of adjectives
x (medial)		
		Syllabication

children's sight vocabulary, moving from the whole (word) to the part (element to be taught) and back to whole (word) again. Because of the nature of Spanish, elements are frequently syllables in the form of CV (consonant/vowel).

INSTRUCTIONAL MATERIALS IN SPANISH   The variety of instructional materials for reading in Spanish is almost as rich as that in English. These include formal reading programs, authentic children's literature, and electronic resources, including the Internet.

Print Resources Most major publishers that provide an English reading program also offer a parallel program in Spanish. These programs would be fairly characterized as basal, although some have anthologies of original literature instead of contrived basal reader stories or decodable text. The best programs have children's literature from the Spanish-speaking

Teach It! 70

Inductive Phonics Lesson in Spanish

This brief, highly structured phonics lesson promotes auditory discrimination, visual discrimination, and word recognition skills that can later be generalized to reading in English.

Figure 14.6 Invented Spelling in Children's Writing in Spanish

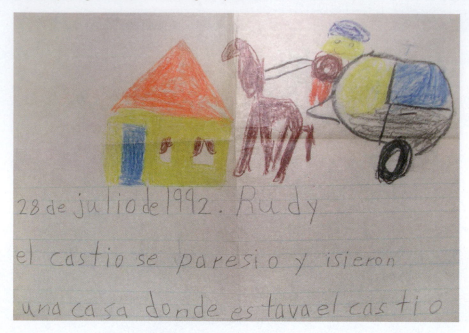

world or children's stories written in Spanish by native Spanish-speaking authors. In both of these cases, the quality of Spanish language and the cultural appropriateness should be evaluated carefully.

Most Spanish programs also contain authentic children's literature translated from English. It is important to consider carefully the quality of translation and the cultural appropriateness of these selections. The best programs also offer selections of authentic Spanish-language literature translated to English for their English versions, a demonstration of their respect for the literary traditions of both languages and cultures. A major strength of programs with parallel literature selections in two languages is that students who read a selection in their mother tongue as part of their mother tongue reading program have a powerful source of background knowledge when they later read an English version of the same story.

There is also a wealth of children's books and big books available in Spanish. The teacher who wishes to use authentic literature for a Spanish reading program instead of anthologies or basal readers will find the constantly expanding series of books on recommended children's literature in Spanish prepared by Schon (2000) to be an invaluable resource. She later published a compendium of children's books in Spanish with themes from around the world (Schon, 2001, 2002). Her final review of children's literature in Spanish was published in 2009 (Schon, 2009).

Electronic Resources for English Language Learners and Their Teachers There are Web sites that provide support to English language learners and their teachers, both in the areas of English language development and in Spanish. For example, an international school Web site registry provides the home pages of schools around the world that are interested in establishing relationships such as pen pal arrangements with other schools (Greenlaw, 2001). These have the advantage of allowing English language learners to correspond in their developing second language of English with students in other countries who are also studying English, probably as a foreign language. In addition, they may have opportunities to correspond in their shared mother tongues. One site registry is found at Penpal International. Teachers should carefully supervise this activity.

A valuable Web site for the teacher who is searching for outstanding children's literature in Spanish is the Barahona Center for the Study of Books in Spanish for Children and Adolescents, established by the late Isabel Schon, who was cited earlier for her resources on this topic. The center's Web site can be found by searching for Barahona Center, California State University, San Marcos.

Children Who Struggle Learning to Read in the Mother Tongue

Reading recovery has proven to be a very effective intervention strategy for children who experience reading difficulties in English (see Chapters 1 and 12). An authorized Spanish-language version of reading recovery, called *Descubriendo la Lectura*, has also been developed (Escamilla & Andrade, 1992). It follows the pattern of diagnosis and intervention of the

Differentiated Instruction

Teaching Older Students Who Are Preliterate

It is not uncommon for teachers of older English language learners from other countries to observe that a few of these students lack literacy skills. Some have been in refugee camps without educational services, others have been working to contribute to family income, and still others have lived in very rural or isolated areas where attending school was not possible because of the great distance to the school and inadequate transportation. Many indigenous children from Latin America leave school because instruction is only provided in Spanish, which they might not speak well, if at all. There are communities of speakers of Zapotec, Mixtec, Maya, Quechua, and many other indigenous languages living in the United States. Their Spanish might be very limited.

Other English language learners have had very limited school experience and have left school, either for the reasons just cited, or occasionally because of the poor quality of education. According to Schifini (1996), many have large gaps in instruction in the primary grades, and they struggle as nonreaders in the higher grades. Schifini recommends several strategies for meeting the needs of these older **preliterate** English language learners:

- Develop a print-rich classroom environment that reflects student interests, including advertisements, brochures, bumper stickers, comics, drawings, magazines, murals, newspapers, photos, postcards, posters, recipes, and examples of their own work.
- Include native language print in the classroom environment.
- Use reading and writing workshop strategies and shared reading and literature studies.
- Use read-aloud activities for access to the core curriculum not available through reading.
- Use writing activities such as quick-writes to connect students to background knowledge.
- Provide shared book experiences with predictable and patterned books that are of standard textbook size and have mature story lines.
- Use collaborative chart stories, language-experience charts, and other forms of shared writing.

In their SIOP model, Echevarria et al. (2013) recommend additional sheltered instruction strategies effective with preliterate older English language learners:

- Use graphic organizers, such as Venn diagrams, timelines, flow charts, and semantic maps, especially for reading in content areas of the curriculum.
- Use scaffolding techniques, such as paraphrasing or restating students' responses, and think-alouds.

original program, but in Spanish. Several adaptations to language and culture were necessary, including the need to locate children's literature in Spanish. The resulting program includes more than 300 books at 20 different levels of difficulty, with about 20 books per level.

A Spanish diagnostic survey for the identification of students includes six observational tasks: (1) letter identification, (2) a word test, (3) concepts about print, (4) writing vocabulary, (5) dictation, and (6) running records of text reading. Procedures generally parallel those in the English language program, including the rereading of familiar books, a running record of the new book from the previous day, writing, rearranging a cutup story, and introducing a new book. The program is designed for first graders in the lowest 20% of the class after one year of reading instruction in the regular classroom.

In a national study of *Descubriendo la Lectura*, Escamilla et al. (1998) found that the program had a very positive outcome with Spanish-speaking second and third graders, with more than 90% of students at each grade level scoring above average on Spanish text reading. On the SABE, a standardized achievement test in Spanish, more than 75% of students at each grade level met or exceeded the average score.

Assessing the Oral Language Proficiency and Reading Proficiency of English Language Learners

Assessing the language and reading outcomes of English language learners is accomplished in a manner similar to assessment for English speakers (Kame'enui et al., 2001). A number of measures of English language proficiency are used for placement of students in bilingual education programs or programs for English language learners, depending on their levels of achievement (see Table 14.3).

Table 14.3 Assessment Measures for Spanish-Speaking English Learners

Type of Measure	Name of Measure	Subtests	Elements Measured	Source of Measure
English language Grades K–12	Basic Inventory of Natural Language (BINL)	N/A	Oral language production, language dominance, fluency, syntax, vocabulary, structural complexity	Pearson
English-language development All LEP	California English Language Development Test (CELDT)	Listening and speaking Reading Writing	Oral language (one-on-one) Reading Writing	CTB/McGraw-Hill
English language Grades K–5	Language Assessment Scales (LAS)	N/A	Auditory discrimination, vocabulary, phoneme production, sentence comprehension, oral production of English and Spanish	CTB/McGraw-Hill
English language Grades K–12	Bilingual Syntax Measure I and II (BSM)	N/A	Syntax, language dominance, second-language level, maintenance of first language	Pearson
English language (or other language) (observation rating scale) Grades 1–12	SOLOM	N/A	Comprehension, vocabulary, fluency, pronunciation, grammar	San Jose USD
English and Spanish language For NCLB Grades 1–12	Stanford English Language Proficiency Test (ELP, SEP)	Listening, speaking, reading, writing	Listening, speaking, reading, writing	Pearson
Spanish reading (normed test) Grades 1–12	Aprenda 3: Prueba de Logros en Español	Sonidos y letras	Phoneme matching, letter identification, letter/sound correspondence	Pearson
		Lectura de palabras	Word matching with picture, word identification	
		Lectura de oraciones	Sentence match with picture	
		Vocabulario	Synonym matching, defining words in context	
		Comprensión de lectura	Reading comprehension of riddles, modified cloze tests, comprehension questions	
Spanish reading (normed test) Grades K–8	Comprehensive Tests of Basic Skills	Reading	Word attack, vocabulary, reading comprehension	CTB/McGraw-Hill
WIDA Model Grades K–12	Measure of Developing English Language	Listening, Speaking, Reading, Writing	Aligned to WIDA standards, including academic language	WIDA Consortium

In general, they measure the language production of children in English, including vocabulary, syntactical complexity, and auditory discrimination/pronunciation. State and local school district authorities typically establish criteria for the reclassification or identification of children whose English proficiency has advanced sufficiently for mainstream placement in regular classroom programs of instruction, although usually with extra support from a paraprofessional or other speaker of the mother tongue at the beginning of the transition process.

There are also several widely used standardized or normed tests of Spanish reading proficiency that usually parallel similar tests in English. The results of these tests are often used to evaluate the progress of groups of children or the effectiveness of programs, but they are not very useful to teachers in identifying the levels of children for assignment to instructional groups or levels of textbooks.

In contrast, the Informal Reading Inventory (IRI) serves the same function in Spanish as it does in English. It is an authentic measure of reading accuracy and comprehension, and the outcomes that it yields in Spanish, as in English, can be used to place children in reading groups and textbooks with some confidence. Some major publishers with Spanish-language reading programs provide IRIs for them.

Teachers can also construct their own IRIs by selecting passages from basal readers or anthologies to represent each grade level, just as is done in English. Teachers should verify the levels of the passages by using a readability graph for Spanish (Crawford, 1995) (see Figure 14.7). As in constructing an IRI in English, the teacher should ensure that the content of each passage in Spanish corresponds to background and cultural knowledge that the child has in Spanish. With a passage selected for each grade level and four comprehension-level questions developed for each passage, the teacher can employ the same process and accuracy and comprehension criteria for Spanish as for English, as described in Chapters 11 and 13. The IRI in Spanish yields frustration, instructional, independent, and capacity levels, just as it does in English and with the same criteria.

Figure 14.7 Spanish Readability Graph

SOURCE: Crawford, A.N. (1985) Fórmula y gráfico para determinar la comprensibilidad de textos del nivel primario en castellano. *Lectura y Vida 6*(4), 18–24.

Number of sentences

Number of syllables	1.0	1.5	2.0	2.5	3.0	3.5	4.0	4.5	5.0	5.5	6.0	6.5
220												4.3
218												3.8
216												3.3
214											5.3	2.8
212									9.7	7.2	4.8	2.3
210									9.2	6.7	4.3	1.9
208									8.7	6.3	3.8	1.4
206							13.1	10.7	8.2	5.8	3.4	1.0
204							12.6	10.2	7.8	5.3	2.9	
202							12.2	9.8	7.3	4.8	2.4	
200					16.6	14.1	11.7	9.2	6.8	4.4	1.9	
198					16.1	13.6	11.2	8.8	6.3	3.9		
196					15.6	13.2	10.7	8.3	5.8	3.4		
194					15.1	12.7	10.2	7.8	5.4	2.9		
192					14.6	12.2	9.8	7.3	4.5	2.4		
190			19.0	16.6	14.2	11.7	9.3	6.8				
188			18.6	16.1	13.7	11.2	8.8	6.4				
186	23.0	20.5	18.1	15.6	13.2	10.8	8.3	5.9				
184	22.5	20.0	17.6	15.2	12.7	10.3	7.8	5.4				
182	22.0	19.6	17.1	14.7	12.2	9.8	7.4	4.9				
180	21.5	19.1	16.6	14.2	11.8	9.3	6.9	4.5				
178	21.0	18.6	16.2	13.7	11.3	8.9	6.4	4.0				
176	20.6	18.1	15.7	13.3	10.8	8.4	5.9	3.5				
174	20.1	17.7	15.2	12.8								
172	19.6	17.2	14.7	12.3								
170	19.1	16.7	14.3	11.8								
168	18.7	16.2										

Approximate level of readability

Instructions:
1. Count the first 100 words in the sample.
2. Count the number of sentences in the 100 words, rounding to the nearest tenth of a sentence.
3. Count the number of syllables in the 100 words.
4. Look for the number of syllables in the left column of the graph. Trace to the right to find the number of sentences. The number at the foot of that column is the approximate grade level of the passage.
5. If the text consists of more than a few pages, take samples from every three pages and compute the mean for each variable.
6. If the proportion of sentences to syllables for each 100 words does not appear on the graph, then the readability of the passage cannot be determined.

Readability measures are often misused, and the teacher should be aware of their limitations. These measures assess only surface structure features of language, and they ignore the level of content and the background knowledge required of children. Teachers should carefully judge the content of passages they select for inclusion in IRIs for the children they will assess. Finally, teachers are often tempted to rewrite text, changing sentence length or vocabulary to raise or lower readability levels. This is a dangerous practice that should be avoided. A readability graph should be used only as a rough measure and never as a tool for writing to a level.

Check Your Understanding 14.4: Gauge your understanding of the skills and concepts in this section.

Mother Tongue Support in the Bilingual Classroom

Monolingual classroom teachers who are unable to teach in their students' mother tongue might be able to use the services of a paraprofessional who can provide this support. Those paraprofessionals' services can extend from follow-up mother tongue support of lessons taught in English by the teacher to instruction provided in the mother tongue under the close and careful supervision of the teacher.

Vignette of a Non-bilingual Teacher and a Bilingual Paraprofessional in a Bilingual Classroom

There are 26 third-grade children in Room 14. Of the 26 native Spanish-speaking children, 11 have made the transition into English reading. Ten continue reading instruction in Spanish while receiving ESL instruction. They will make the transition to English reading within a few weeks or months as they become ready. Five new arrivals to the United States speak only Spanish.

Their teacher, Mr. Scott, is a certified elementary school teacher, but he does not speak Spanish. He is a very good teacher, and he provides all ESL and English reading instruction. But the Spanish reading program is conducted by Ms. Morales, a part-time paraprofessional and university student who plans to become a bilingual teacher. She is occasionally assisted by two Spanish-speaking parent volunteers who read to the children and tell stories from their childhood.

Today, Ms. Morales is teaching a reading lesson from an anthology of stories in Spanish, part of a reading program in English and Spanish that Mr. Scott is also using with the English-speaking students. Ms. Morales begins by introducing new vocabulary that students will encounter in the guided silent reading they will do in a few minutes. In addition, she helps them to construct a semantic map so that they can share background knowledge they have about the topic of the story: a young girl who lives in the Amazon forest of South America. She guides their silent reading with higher-order questions from the teacher manual and additional questions she has formulated herself. After today's lesson, during which they read the first half of the story, the children will write predictions about how the story might end when they complete it the next day. In the meantime, Mr. Scott is teaching a word analysis lesson to the English-speaking students on the other side of the room, which will be followed by a similar literature lesson from the English version of the same anthology that Ms. Morales uses in Spanish.

Mr. Scott meets daily with Ms. Morales to help her plan instruction, to answer questions about how to use the teacher's manual for the Spanish reading program, which is provided in both English and Spanish for his convenience, and to assess children's progress in Spanish reading. As they teach in parallel through the morning, he observes and monitors her activities. She also assists in parent conferences when needed.

Mr. Scott and Ms. Morales have molded themselves into a highly effective team, both making indispensable contributions to the language and reading development of the children in the classroom. She gains much from his extensive teaching experience as they plan instruction for the next day and, on a longer-term basis, for future days, weeks, and months. At the same time, he gains insights from the valuable background she has in the children's mother tongue and their culture.

Although the two are usually teaching parallel to each other, Mr. Scott is able to supervise Ms. Morales's work from his teaching station in the classroom, and he periodically walks around the classroom to encourage and reinforce the work of the children in both groups. Although he does not speak Spanish, he finds that he is able to understand much of what is occurring in her lessons.

The parallel structure of the English and Spanish anthologies from the third-grade reading program they use has many advantages. The teacher's manual for the Spanish part of the program has English and Spanish instructions on opposite sides of the teaching manual, so Mr. Scott can quickly determine the students' progress in their lessons. In addition, they will eventually read in English the stories they are now reading in Spanish. Their prior experience with the stories and the background knowledge developed will constitute an important part of scaffolding their comprehension as they move into reading in their new second language.

Supervising the Paraprofessional Who Teaches in the Mother Tongue

It is a challenging task for monolingual teachers to supervise the instructional activities of bilingual paraprofessionals. Teachers should first model for their paraprofessionals in English the teaching manner, approaches, and strategies that are to be employed in Spanish or another language. Teachers should then observe their paraprofessionals, assessing the effectiveness of their modeling. Even though teachers might not understand the paraprofessionals' words, the teachers' knowledge of what is being taught should support good communication. A major emphasis of teachers should be to impress on paraprofessionals the importance of building up the children's self-concepts and of avoiding harsh words, which can undo the effects of even excellent teaching.

At an operational level, there should be outstanding communication between the teacher and the paraprofessional. They should meet in the morning to plan before school and again before the paraprofessional leaves at the end of the day, discussing the activities of the day and planning for lessons to follow. Because the teacher and paraprofessional complement each other so well, the development of mutual respect between them is important. The teacher has skills and knowledge about teaching, and the paraprofessional contributes vital communication skills and cultural knowledge.

Many bilingual paraprofessionals are university students who are in varying stages of teacher preparation programs. They are highly motivated to become teachers, proud of their abilities to manage two languages and two cultures, and anxious to assume leadership in their own classrooms as soon as possible. As they approach and then enter their own student teaching experience, many are able to teach parallel to the regular teacher with careful supervision.

Some paraprofessionals exhibit those same language and cultural skills, but they view their paraprofessional role as their final career goal. They are often members of the local community who might have minimal academic preparation and training as instructional aides. It is perhaps among the members of this group that teachers who do not share the language and culture with the paraprofessional must exercise their most careful judgment. Because they are not trained teachers, their strategies in interacting positively and constructively with children must be carefully monitored. And since the supervising teacher often does not understand what the paraprofessional is saying to the children, it will be important to note the tone of the paraprofessional's voice and the children's reactions.

Parent Volunteers

Parent volunteers can be an important support to the non-bilingual teacher in the bilingual classroom. An important aspect of preparation for literacy in the mother tongue and English later is oral language development in the mother tongue. Family resources in the form of stories from parents, grandparents, and extended family can make a major contribution to this part of the program. Teachers can invite these adults into the classroom to tell stories to the children that can be used as a source of content for language experience stories, for example.

McQuillan and Tse (1998) describe strategies for extending these storytelling experiences into the English language. The narratives that teachers, parents, grandparents, and other sources use constitute comprehensible input in the hands of an expert storyteller. The children are exposed to rich vocabulary and their background knowledge on a variety of valuable topics is enhanced.

McQuillan and Tse indicate that students begin to write and tell their own stories as their own language production flourishes. When stories are related in English, the children's second language, students should be allowed to listen to stories in that target language without concerns about understanding everything. They should focus on the main ideas. Four steps then follow: (1) telling a short and simple version of the story; (2) revising the story by retelling it with different characters or settings, extending the story beyond its original ending, and narrating the story from the point of view of another character; (3) creating a class story, which might involve considerable negotiation among the children; and (4) creating individual or small-group stories and books.

While McQuillan and Tse are most concerned about using the process to provide comprehensible input in English, the same strategies can be used to provide a stronger base of vocabulary and background knowledge in the mother tongue. In addition, this permits parents, grandparents, and other members of the extended family to play a valued role in the classroom. Finally, it validates and reinforces the value of the mother tongue and culture.

Watch this video in which teachers discuss methods to welcome and include bilingual parents in the classroom and in the school community then answer the question that follows.

 Video Exploration 14.4: Watch the video and answer questions that reflect the content you have read.

Check Your Understanding 14.5: Gauge your understanding of the skills and concepts in this section.

For Review

At the outset of this chapter we stated that when you reached this point in your reading and studying you should be able to:

- **Describe advantages and disadvantages of teaching reading in the mother tongue with a later transition to English reading instruction vs. teaching reading in English only from the beginning.**

It is always easiest for English language learners to learn first in their mother tongue. They are ready to learn in that language, but often not in English. This requires a bilingual teacher, or in some circumstances, collaboration between a teacher and a bilingual paraprofessional who may be able to assist in the mother tongue under careful supervision. The transition to English is almost always very smooth when the students are learning confidently in the mother tongue and when they have reached an intermediate level of proficiency in English. What they have learned in the mother tongue they will also know in the second language because of the positive transfer of skills. Sometimes it isn't possible to provide a mother tongue instructional program to a student because of school district or state policies, a lack of qualified personnel, or unavailability of materials in that language. Then academic instruction in English should be delayed until the intermediate level of proficiency in English has been reached.

- **Explain how communicative approaches to teaching English as a second language are more effective and faster than more traditional approaches**

Communicative approaches to English, such as the natural approach and Total Physical Response (TPR), resemble the process through which children learn the mother tongue at home, and always with success. There is no textbook or workbook. Authentic language is introduced by the teacher in a curriculum organized around important themes, rather than around grammatical sequences. Errors are accepted as signs of immaturity in language development, not as mistakes. Incomplete structures and sentences are a natural part of the acquisition process, and, as with young children developing their mother tongue language, those so-called errors disappear over time.

- **Implement highly effective second language instructional strategies that result in the development of students' oral communication (listening comprehension and speaking) abilities.**

In the natural/TPR approaches, the teacher begins with questions and commands that the student can respond to with gestures, and sometimes yes or no. As the student's proficiency grows after a few weeks, the teacher begins asking questions and giving commands that require a word or two in response. This continues for a few months until the student begins to respond with phrases and short sentences. The teacher accepts all attempts at speaking in English. In a group setting, the teacher needs to direct questions and commands at the appropriate level to each student. As the students listen to the teacher and to each other, proficiency increases rapidly.

- **Select appropriate strategies for teaching English language learners to read.**

English language learners should learn to read in their mother tongue. This is especially appropriate when the mother tongue is Spanish. The regularity of the sound system makes word recognition much easier in Spanish than in English. In addition, Spanish is a syllabic language, permitting students to learn the sounds of syllables (consonant and vowel) together, which is very efficient. This should be done inductively, guiding students through experiences with letters and sounds that lead them to derive rules about them. But their first experiences with reading should be in shared reading strategies in which they learn that it is the print on a page that is read, not the illustration. This can be done most effectively with big books and the language experience approach. When students reach the important intermediate level in understanding and speaking English, they are ready for formal instruction in reading in English. The transition is usually very smooth and rapid.

- **Coordinate the role of a mother-tongue-speaking paraprofessional and a teacher who speaks only English in classrooms with many English language learners.**

It is very important for a monolingual English-speaking teacher and a bilingual paraprofessional to develop a close and mutually supportive relationship. Each needs to appreciate the essential role of the other. The teacher's role is to teach, and the role of the paraprofessional is to do what is necessary to maintain positive communication between the teacher and the students. The paraprofessional's role is not to translate everything that the teacher says, as we want the students listening to the teacher. Finally, the teacher needs to use sheltered (scaffolded) strategies, such as speaking slowly and clearly in English, repeating when necessary, perhaps in a different way, and providing wait time. The teacher also needs to carefully monitor students' comprehension so that the paraprofessional can intervene when sheltered strategies are not sufficient to maintain student comprehension.

For Your Journal

1. Review the Anticipation Guide and compare your earlier answers with what you think now.

2. Find a classmate who did not speak English on arrival at the school or spoke English as a second language, but who speaks English now. Interview this person about his or her experiences in learning English and learning to read. If you have ever traveled to a foreign country and did not speak or read the language, what did you do to adjust? Discuss the feelings you might have had if you had experienced this as a child.

Taking It to the World

You should now have a very clear idea of the challenges facing English language learners in their new classrooms. If you were the parent of a 6-year-old child and you were to move to Croatia, describe the language and reading program you would want for your child. What additional information would you need before making a final decision?

Appendix A
Addressing the Common Core Standards

Reading for Information	Key Ideas and Details	Chapter 7
Reading Standards for Literature	Key Ideas and Details	Chapters 7 and 9
	Craft and Structure	Chapters 3 and 7
	Integration of Knowledge and Ideas	Chapters 7, 9, 12, 13, and 14
Reading Standards for Informational Text	Key Ideas and Details	Chapters 8 and 9
	Craft and Structure	Chapters 8 and 9
	Integration of Knowledge and Ideas	Chapters 8, 9, 12, 13, and 14
Reading Standards for Foundational Skills	Print Concepts	Chapters 4 and 14
	Phonological Awareness	Chapters 3, 4, and 14
	Phonics and Word Recognition	Chapters 3, 5, 12, and 14
	Fluency	Chapters 6, 12, and 13
Writing	Research to Build and Present Knowledge	Chapter 9
Writing Standards	Text Types and Purposes	Chapter 10
	Production and Distribution of Writing	Chapter 10
	Research to Build and Present Knowledge	Chapters 8, 10, 13, and 14
Speaking and Listening	Comprehension and Collaboration	Chapters 7, 8, 9, 12, 13, and 14
	Presentation of Knowledge and Ideas	Chapters 7, 8, 12, 13, and 14
Language Standards	Conventions of Standard English	Chapter 3
	Knowledge of Language	Chapter 3
	Vocabulary Acquisition and Use	Chapters 6 and 7

Appendix B
Teach It! Instructional Activities

Codruța Temple, *State University of New York at Cortland* and

Jean Wallace Gillet, *Fluvanna County (Virginia) Public Schools, retired*

Contents

Overview

These lessons were designed for implementation by preservice teachers or by teacher education students in a practicum setting. They include a wide variety of activities featuring oral language development, emergent and beginning reading skills and concepts, reading comprehension, writing, and vocabulary development. Each of the activities is discussed in detail in the text.

Most of the featured lessons are intended for small-group instruction within a regular classroom, and most can be readily adapted for individuals or larger groups, including whole classes. They provide opportunities for preservice teachers to practice instructional planning, lesson implementation, and classroom management while helping students develop critical language and literacy skills.

Each lesson plan includes a statement of objectives, stating what the activity is intended to teach or develop; a list of necessary materials, which should be gathered beforehand; and an estimated duration, or length of the lesson. Most lesson plans also include a list of suggested variations or extensions, which can be used to provide variety in subsequent lessons and to extend and enrich the learning experience. These can themselves become subsequent lessons, guided practice activities, or independent learning activities.

Each of these lessons can easily be modified to meet the individual needs of the preservice teacher, the supervising teacher, and the students in the classroom. Group size can be adapted and procedures and instructions can be modified to fit the needs and abilities of the students. Each activity is specific to one or more fundamental literacy skills, but each is also generic in that it can be productively retaught by changing the literature selection, writing stimulus, discussion props, and so forth. Preservice teachers should be familiar with each of these activities and be able to implement them in the classroom.

Guidelines for Lesson Planning

- Plan every lesson ahead of time. Your mental preparation will enable you to present your lesson with skill and confidence. Planning ahead ensures that all necessary materials are at hand, allowing you to focus more on the students than on yourself.
- Select lessons to implement based on students' learning needs, not on your interests, strengths, or time constraints. Every lesson has an instructional purpose; knowing it will increase your confidence and enthusiasm.
- Collect and check all materials, supplies, and equipment beforehand. Missing markers, a mislaid book, or a burned-out overhead projector bulb can sabotage the best lesson.
- Be a positive language and literacy role model. Use precise, correct language; model enthusiasm for reading and literature; and show your enjoyment of learning.
- Reinforce positive behavior and effort by specifically drawing attention to what students did, rather than using empty praise. Point out when students use a strategy, attempt something difficult, or persist when having difficulty.
- Whenever possible, allow students choices, even if the range of choices is narrow. Having choices increases students' feeling of ownership and empowerment. Encourage diversity in answers to questions, ways to show comprehension, and choices of literature.
- Encourage and foster personalization and creativity. Show that you value students' attempts to relate what they are learning about to their own lives and experiences.
- Be prepared to handle interruptions, schedule changes, and the unforeseen with poise. No lesson ever unfolds exactly as planned, and an unexpected outcome can be even better than the planned outcome! Each lesson is a journey, and the "getting there" is as important as the destination.
- Evaluate each lesson you teach, even if your evaluation is only a brief self-reflection. If possible, jot down a few notes about what went well and what you'd do differently another time in a personal journal. Self-evaluation is one key to improving your teaching.

Reading Activities for Emergent and Beginning Readers

1. Reading Aloud

Objectives: To develop children's ability to comprehend written language; to raise children's awareness of the structure of different types of texts; to expand children's vocabulary; to encourage enthusiasm for literacy

Materials: An age-appropriate book

Duration: 10–15 minutes

1. Prepare to read the book.
   a. Read the book through yourself before you read it to the children to decide whether it is suitable for your class.
   b. Decide how you want to read it—with humor, with drama, with questions to whet curiosity.
   c. If there are voices to bring to life, decide how you want to make each one sound.
   d. If you decide to stop reading to ask for predictions or for discussion, decide where the stopping places should be.
   e. If there are any words or ideas that will be unfamiliar to the children, make a note to pronounce them carefully and explain them to the children.
   f. If the book has illustrations large enough for the children to see, practice reading the book through while you hold it in front of and facing away from you, where the children will be able to read it.

2. Prepare the children.

    a. Make sure the children are seated comfortably where they can see and hear you.

    b. Remind the children, if you need to, of the behavior you expect of good listeners: hands to themselves, eyes on the teacher, and ears for the story.

3. Read the title.

4. Show the children the cover of the book, ask them what they know about the topic, and ask them to make predictions about what will happen or what they expect to find out in the book.

5. Turn to the title page. Read the author's name and the illustrator's. Talk about what each contributed to the book. Remind the children of any other books they know by this author or this illustrator.

6. As you read the book through the first time, ask for comments about what is going on and for predictions about what will happen.

7. Follow up the reading with a whole-class discussion about the book.

8. Read the book a second time through, taking more time to look at the illustrations and to talk about characters, their motives, or other things you and the students find interesting about the book.

9. Leave the book available to the children in the library corner, and encourage them to read it later during scheduled time in the reading center or between other activities. The children might especially enjoy taking turns reading it to each other.

2. Dialogic Reading

Objectives: To develop children's oral language and concepts about print

Materials: An age-appropriate book

Duration: 10–15 minutes

    A. Dialogic reading for younger children (PEER)

        1. Prompt the child to name objects in the book and talk about the story.

        2. Evaluate the child's responses and offer praise for adequate responses and alternatives for inadequate ones.

        3. Expand on the child's statements with additional words.

        4. Ask the child to repeat the adult's utterances.

    B. Dialogic reading for older children (CROWD). While reading the book to the child, ask the following types of questions:

        1. Completion questions. Ask the child to supply a word or phrase that has been omitted. (For example, "I see a yellow duck looking at _____.")

        2. Recall questions. Ask the child about things that occurred earlier in the book. ("Do you remember some animals that Brown Bear saw?")

        3. Open-ended questions. Ask the child to respond to the story in his or her own words. ("Now it's your turn: You say what is happening on this page.")

        4. Wh- questions. Ask what, where, who, and why questions. ("What is that yellow creature called? Who do you think Brown Bear will see next?")

        5. Distancing questions. Ask the child to relate the content of the book to life experiences. ("Do you remember when we saw a yellow duck like that one swimming in the lake? Was it as big as this one?")

3. Morning Message

Objectives: To help emergent readers develop familiarity with written language; to focus attention on words

Materials: Chart paper

Duration: 15–20 minutes

    1. Tell students that as a class you will write two or three things about your morning, such as the date, the weather, and anything that makes the morning special.

2. Invite students to suggest a sentence. Repeat the sentence.

3. Ask students what word you should write first. Ask what letter it should begin with and whether it should be an uppercase or a lowercase letter. Have a volunteer come forward and write some of the letters of the first word for you. Continue until you have written the complete sentence.

4. Read the sentence, pointing to each word. Have students read the sentence as you point to each word.

5. Repeat steps 2–4 to write two or three additional sentences.

6. Write some of the words that are often repeated on separate pieces of thick paper and tape them to the bottom of the chart or on the chalkboard.

7. Invite a student to come forward, pick one of the pieces of paper, and read the word on it. Then have the student find the same word in a sentence. Have her read the sentence aloud, then place the word on top of the same word in the sentence. Finally, ask the student to read the sentence again with the word in place.

8. Repeat step 7 for all of the words written on pieces of paper.

9. Have all of the students read the lines of text with you as you point to each word.

10. Have students choral-read the whole text.

11. Have students echo-read the text.

12. Invite different groups of children to read the morning message.

13. Ask individual children to come forward and point to any words they can read in isolation. Bracket each word with your hands as the child reads it, so the surrounding words cannot be seen. If the child is successful, write the word on a piece of thick paper and have the student add it to her word bank for later practice.

4. Language Experience or Group Dictated Story

Objectives: To help emergent readers develop oral language fluency, print directionality, concept of word, sight word recognition, and phonemic awareness

Materials: An object, shared experience, favorite song or book, or other stimulus for the dictation; large chart tablet or 24 × 36-inch paper on easel or chalkboard; large marker

Duration: 10–30 minutes; additional time for follow-up activities listed below

1. Select a group of 4–10 children to participate.

2. Select and prepare a stimulus for dictation: for example, an interesting concrete object, classroom pet, familiar story for retelling, or recent classroom event.

3. Invite participants to gather close to the chart paper. Introduce the activity by explaining that they will talk together about the stimulus and create statements about it that you will write for them on the chart paper. They will learn to read the sentences for themselves by rereading them together and pointing to the words.

4. Invite discussion of the stimulus, encouraging students to describe, narrate, and add verbal details. If necessary, ask open-ended questions like "What else do you notice?" "What else do you remember?" or "What happened after that?"

5. Ask for volunteers to contribute sentences for the dictation.

6. Write students' sentences verbatim, allowing changes or additions. Print neatly and clearly in large letters, with clear spaces between each word. Limit the account to 5–7 sentences.

7. Read the completed story expressively and at a natural pace, pointing to each word as you read.

8. Reread the story chorally several times until students have memorized it. Continue pointing to each word. (Keep up the pace so the reading sounds natural, not word by word.) If students have trouble memorizing the whole text, divide it into sections of two or three sentences each.

9. Invite volunteers to come to the chart and recite a part or the whole story while pointing to each word. Continue until each student who volunteers has read the story individually.

10. Point to individual words and invite students to identify the words, reading from the beginning to the target word if necessary.

5. Language Experience with Authentic Children's Literature

Objectives: To help emergent readers develop oral language fluency, print directionality, concept of word, sight word recognition, and phonemic awareness; to stimulate interest in and engagement with children's literature

Materials: A culturally appropriate piece of children's literature; chart paper or chalkboard; large marker or chalk

Duration: 15–30 minutes

1. As a stimulus for a language-experience dictation, conduct a read-aloud of a piece of children's literature that is culturally appropriate for your class.

2. During the read-aloud, share the illustrations in the book and ask questions about the unfolding story.

3. Have the children dictate their brief version of the story.

4. Accept the dictations of the children as stated, regardless of any cultural affectations, as long as other children do not suggest changes. However, spell the words correctly irrespective of students' pronunciation.

5. Make sure the children have many opportunities to read the text in a shared reading mode as the dictation is recorded and after the children's rendition of the story is completed.

6. Optionally, follow up with some of the activities suggested for the Language Experience or Group Dictated Story.

Follow-Up Activities for Group Dictated Story

- Repeat choral and individual reading and pointing on subsequent days until all students can read the story fluently and point accurately.

- Create an exact copy of the story on another sheet of chart paper. Cut the sentences or lines apart. Place in a center for students to reorder the lines and compare to the original.

- Copy each sentence onto a sentence strip. Have volunteers hold up each strip in correct order. (These can also be used for independent practice with a hanging pocket chart.)

- Create exact copies of the story on copy paper. Duplicate several copies for each participant. In different lessons, students can paste copies on construction paper or in journals and illustrate them, cut lines and sentences apart and put them in correct order, cut sentences into phrases and put them in correct order, and use sentences for handwriting practice.

- Have students find individual words they recognize in isolation and begin building individual word banks with known words on cards. Students should sort and review word banks daily.

- Have students sort words in their word banks in a variety of ways: matching beginning sounds, number of syllables, alphabetical order, and so forth.

- Select one or several familiar words beginning with consonants. Using individual letter cards or magnetic letters, show students how to "make and break" the words by removing the initial letter or sound and substituting another, creating new words. (Change THAT to HAT, PAT, RAT, and CAT; MATCH to PATCH, BATCH, and SCRATCH; MAKE to TAKE, RAKE, FAKE, and LAKE.)

- Have students write known sight words using magnetic letters on cookie sheets, individual letters cut out of sandpaper, wallpaper scraps, or felt, glue and sand or glitter, pipe cleaners, heavy yarn, macaroni letters, mini-marshmallows, dried beans, and so forth. (The more ways they practice making the same words, the more automatic these words will become!)

- Begin personal dictionaries by folding eight to ten sheets of paper vertically and stapling in the fold to create individual books. Have students write a letter at the top of each page (group infrequent letters like q, u, x, y, and z with others) and begin collecting mastered sight words in their dictionaries.

6. Big Book Lesson

Objectives: To help emergent readers develop familiarity with book language patterns, print directionality, concept of word, sight word recognition, and phonemic awareness

Materials: A big book of your choice; for follow-up activities, a Word Hider (index card), sentence strips, pocket chart

Duration: 10–30 minutes; additional time for follow-up activities listed below

1. Display the big book, closed, on an easel or display stand (so your hands are free). Invite students to gather close enough to the book so everyone can clearly see the print.

2. Read the title, pointing to the words, and encourage students' observations about the cover art. Invite predictions of what the book might be about or what might happen based on the title and cover.

3. Open to the title page and read the author's and illustrator's names, pointing to the words. Be sure everyone knows what the author and the illustrator did. Make connections to other familiar books by the author or illustrator, if appropriate.

4. Read the first page fluently and expressively, pointing to the words. Comment, or invite student comments, on the illustrations. Review previous predictions and have students revise or confirm predictions based on what is now known.

5. Repeat this step with each page, or several pages at a time, depending on the length and complexity of the text and the illustrations. Continue pointing to the words as you read. Continue inviting new or revised predictions as the story unfolds.

6. As you near the story's conclusion, invite final predictions of how it will end. Read to the end of the story.

7. Invite students' comments about the story and illustrations. Encourage them to talk about characters or story parts they liked, appealing illustrations, and so forth. You may wish to go back to particular illustrations to reexamine them, looking for details, or just for enjoyment.

Five-Day Plan for Using a Big Book

Day 1: Follow the preceding plan for the first reading. Goals for this lesson include introduction to the story, forming and revising predictions based on illustrations and unfolding plot, perusal of illustrations, and general enjoyment of the book activity.

Day 2: Either reread the story in its entirety, pointing to the words, or echo-read the story with students. (You read a sentence or two, pointing to the words, then students repeat verbatim or "echo.") At relevant points, stop to discuss predictions made during previous reading, and help students verbalize how they arrived at those predictions. Reexamine illustrations, this time for features overlooked the first time, details of colors, borders, and so forth. If appropriate, compare this book to familiar others by the same author or illustrator.

Day 3: Reread the story, inviting students to "chime in" or read along with you (choral-read) as desired. Some may be more ready to do so than others. Predictable lines, repeating refrains, and rhyming elements will support choral reading. Continue pointing to the words as you read. Emphasize comprehension in this lesson; ask questions about the story events, characters, setting, and so forth, inviting students to use both the text and illustrations to find information and justify their answers.

Day 4: Reread chorally, encouraging all students to read with you as much as they can. Many will have memorized the story by now. (If many are still unable to choral-read it, break the story into sections to work on.) Emphasize "word work" in this lesson. Point to and have volunteers identify selected words. Use the Word Hider (index card) to cover selected words, have students read from the beginning of the sentence and identify the hidden word; uncover to confirm. See how many times students can find the same word on the same and subsequent pages, find other words with the same beginning sound, or match words to familiar words on the word wall.

Day 5: Reread chorally, letting your voice "fade" so students are reading more independently. Have volunteers come forward to read one or more sentences, pointing to the words as they read. Distribute sentences on sentence strips and have students put them in order in a pocket chart. Have students act out the story and/or do related art, cooking, or other extension activities to enrich the literary experience.

7. Making Individual Small Books

Objectives: To provide students with small easily read books they can read independently at school and home

Materials: Two sheets of 8½ × 11 plain paper for each student, supply of old magazines with colorful illustrations, scissors, glue, markers, stapler

Duration: 15–30 minutes, depending on number of students participating

1. Prepare a blank book for each student by placing two sheets of paper together, 11-inch side at top, folding vertically down the middle. Staple vertically in the fold, creating a book about 5½ × 8½ with front and back covers and six inner pages.

2. Select a group of six to eight students. For larger groups, another adult is needed to assist students. Give each student a magazine, or magazine pages with colorful pictures, and scissors.

3. Select a group of eight or fewer students. If the group is larger, have another adult available to assist students. Gather around a work table where supplies have been placed.

4. Show students a premade model book: A magazine picture has been cut out and glued to each of the six pages of a book, and an adult has labeled the picture underneath with a simple phrase or sentence: "The dog is jumping," "A box is round," "A red apple," and so forth.

5. Assist students in choosing a picture and gluing it to the first page. Have them continue to complete the remaining pages. Using a marker, write the student's dictated sentence or phrase neatly and clearly under each picture. Have students copy a title onto the cover, print their names, and if desired write or draw on the back cover.

6. Assist each student in reading the entire book and practicing it so each can read his or her book fluently to the group or class during sharing time.

Variations: Give each book a theme and a title: Things That Are Round, What Is Square? (shapes); Red Is Everywhere, Things That Are Blue (colors); Animals All Around, Outdoors, We Can Play (various play activities); What Starts with B? (initial letters/sounds); It's Spring! (seasons or holidays), Foods We Love.

8. Modified Reading Recovery Lesson

Objectives: To help emergent readers develop oral language fluency, print directionality, concept of word, sight word recognition, and phonemic awareness

Materials: Individual copy of a short, predictable, clearly illustrated "little book" at Guided Reading levels A–D or Reading Recovery levels 1–8 for each participant

Duration: 10–15 minutes, depending on length and difficulty of text

1. Select one to three emergent readers to participate. (If more than one, have students take turns during the following steps.)

2. Preview the book by reading the title, encouraging student/s to examine the cover illustration and predict what might happen or what the book might be about.

3. Guide student/s in looking at the illustration on each page, naming objects and/or describing the picture, and if necessary modeling expanded oral language by repeating students' remarks in expanded form (S: "A dog." T: "Yes, there's a dog. It's a brown dog.")

4. Read and point to an important word or phrase, or repeated phrases, on each page as you examine the illustrations. (T: "Here's the word dog.") In this way you smooth the way for the reader/s to read each page independently.

5. Return to the first page and invite the student/s to read each page as independently as possible. Provide assistance on unfamiliar words, and encourage the student/s to use the picture, beginning sounds, and sentence context to attempt unknown words. Point out strategies you observe the student/s using: "You were smart to go back and read that sentence again when you got stuck," "I saw you get your mouth ready to say the beginning sound," or "You did what good readers do when you looked at the picture."

6. Choral-read the book with the student/s one or more times to gain familiarity with the sound of the sentences being read smoothly.

7. Invite student/s to read the whole book one more time with less teacher support. Encourage the student/s to reread the book several times independently at school and/or at home for fluency.

9. Guided Reading

Objectives: To develop effective strategies for processing novel text at increasingly challenging levels of difficulty; to develop students' ability to read silently

Materials: Multiple copies of leveled books

Duration: 5 minutes prior to reading; time necessary to complete reading and to respond to the story

1. Select a group of 4–6 children who are reading at about the same level.

2. Introduce a new text at students' instructional level. Encourage the students to converse about the text, to ask questions, and to build expectations.

3. Have the children read the entire text, or a unified part of it, to themselves silently (or softly in the case of younger readers). Allow them to ask for help when needed.

4. While the students are reading, observe their problem-solving strategies and provide assistance by suggesting other suitable strategies.

5. After the reading, involve the children in responding to the story through such activities as writing, discussion, paired reading, or sharing personal responses.

6. For subsequent guided reading sessions, regroup the children in accordance with outcomes that you have observed and assessed.

10. Guided Reading and the Four Blocks Approach

Objectives: To develop effective strategies for processing novel text at increasingly challenging levels of difficulty; to develop children's ability to read silently; to increase children's writing fluency; to teach word study skills in a meaningful context

Materials: Multiple copies of leveled books; optionally, a big book; chart paper for whole-class word study activities

Duration: 40–60 minutes

A. Working with small groups

1. Follow steps 1–4 of the Guided Reading strategy as described earlier.

2. Have the students respond to the story in writing. Suggest writing prompts that are appropriate to students' level of writing development.

3. Follow the writing block with 10–15 minutes of self-selected reading time. Help students select texts at their independent reading level.

4. Teach word study skills tailored to the needs of the children in the group.

B. Working with the whole class

1. Make the text accessible to all students with multiple readings involving read-aloud, shared reading, and paired reading.

2. Have the students respond to the story in writing.

3. Follow the writing block with 10–15 minutes of self-selected reading time. Help students select texts at their independent reading level.

4. In the last block, do word study with the whole class, with all students working on the same skills, or, if possible, teach appropriate skills in smaller groups.

11. Shared Reading

Objectives: To develop comprehension by modeling comprehension strategies; provide guided practice in using comprehension strategies

Materials: Fiction or nonfiction book students will read together

Duration: 10–30 minutes depending on length of book and size of group

1. Select a text for students to read. A big book can be used with younger readers.

2. Select two or more comprehension strategies to demonstrate; for example, organizing prior information before reading, predicting story outcomes, creating good questions, visualizing scenes, self-monitoring comprehension, making inferences about information not directly stated, using context to understand new words, identifying and clarifying difficult parts, or summarizing.

3. Preview the book with students; examine the title and cover illustration, predict what the topic of the book might be or what might happen in the story, and look at each page, examining illustrations and pointing out important words.

4. After previewing, read the text to or with students, depending on how well they can handle the text. Students can read predictable or repeated parts, echo-read or choral-read, or alternate reading with you.

5. While reading, "think aloud" to model effective reading: Pause to wonder or predict what might happen next, tell what a part reminds you of, wonder about word meanings, demonstrate how to use word parts or context to figure out new words, identify and reread difficult parts, and comment on illustrations. Emphasize the strategies you selected beforehand. For example, if you selected visualizing, think aloud about how you are imagining the setting, characters, and action; if you selected inferring, demonstrate making an inference from several related facts or ideas. Model what good readers do as they read.

6. Invite students' comments and predictions about the text. Ask and invite thoughtful questions.

7. Reread the text in its entirety to "put the pieces together" and experience the material as a whole. With greater familiarity, students may be able to read more of the text themselves.

8. Make the text available for students to reread independently.

Word Study Activities

12. Phonemic Segmentation with Elkonin Boxes

Objectives: To develop phonemic awareness and ability to segment phonemes in words

Materials: Elkonin boxes (series of connected squares) drawn on paper or sentence strips: two boxes for words with two phonemes, and so forth; "counters" such as poker chips or dried lima beans for the student to move; letter cards or magnetic letters

Duration: 5–10 minutes

1. Select a word with 2–4 phonemes (for example, *to, cat, trip*) to segment. Use the Elkonin box with the appropriate number of spaces. Say the word, then say the word phoneme by phoneme; as you say each phoneme, push or place a counter into a box. Have the student watch as you do this. If necessary, repeat.

2. Have the student copy what you did: Say the word, and then say each sound while pushing the counters into the boxes. If an error occurs, stop the student by placing your hand over his or hers and modeling again, saying, "Watch again. Now you try." Repeat until the student can segment the phonemes and place the counters correctly.

3. Repeat the process with another word. You may choose another word with the same number of phonemes (*to, in, at*) or proceed to a word with one more phoneme (*in, pin, spin*).

4. When the student has mastered segmenting the phonemes and moving the counters, begin using letter cards or magnetic letters instead of counters, placing the letters in the boxes. (Keep letters representing digraph sounds together; for example, *that* has three phonemes, and the letters *th* are placed together in the first box.)

5. When the student has mastered moving the letters into boxes, you can remove the boxes altogether and continue practicing using just the letters.

13. Working with Names to Teach the Alphabet

Objectives: To develop knowledge of the alphabet

Materials: Pieces of cardboard, a box

Duration: 5 minutes

1. Write each child's name on a piece of cardboard and put all the names in a box.

2. Each day draw out a name, call the child forward, and interview her (about favorite pastimes, pets, games, etc.).

3. Then put the child's name on the bulletin board and explain that this word is a name.

4. Point to the letters in the name, reading left to right.

5. Have the children count the letters.

6. Call attention to the first letter of the name. Have students notice that it is a big letter. Explain that all names begin with a big letter. Show them the lowercase letter as well. Ask if anyone else has that letter in his or her name. Write other names that contain the letter on the chalkboard.

7. Repeat the activity every day with another child's name.

14. Beginning Sounds Picture Sorting

Objectives: To develop phonemic awareness, ability to distinguish among several different beginning sounds, and ability to categorize pictures of objects with the same beginning sound

Materials: Set of commercial beginning sounds sorting cards, or teacher-made cards with clear pictures of common objects, six to eight of each of two or more initial consonant sounds; pocket chart

Duration: 10–15 minutes

1. Preselect two or more beginning consonant sounds that are clearly different; begin with two contrasting sounds, and add more as students gain familiarity with the procedure. Select pictures of objects with these beginning sounds.

2. Gather a group of 4–10 students in front of the pocket chart.

3. Hold up each card and have students name each object. Be sure all students can name each object accurately.

4. Place one card for each sound at the top of the pocket chart. Tell students they will name the object on each card and place each card below the picture that begins with the same sound.

5. Mix up the remaining cards. Hold up each one and have students name the object chorally. Give each successive card to a different student. Have the student come to the chart, say a "sorting sentence" naming the two objects such as "Basket starts like baby," and place it in the correct column.

6. As each card is added to a column, have students name all the objects in that column chorally to check that they all have the same beginning sound.

7. When all pictures have been correctly sorted, have students name all the objects in each column one more time to reinforce the beginning sound. You may leave the cards near the pocket chart for students to sort independently as time allows.

Variations: Place one example of each sound at the top of the pocket chart. Distribute the remaining cards to students. Have students holding a card beginning with one sound come to the chart, say the sorting sentence, and place their cards in a column. Repeat with the other sound(s). Or dispense with the pocket chart: Have students line up next to each other, all the students with cards beginning with the same sound in one line. Have them name all the objects with the same beginning sound chorally.

15. Word Sorting

Objectives: To learn to discern patterns of similarity among words with similar sound, spelling, grammatical, or meaning patterns

Materials: Word cards with printed words that share a particular feature; pocket chart

Duration: 5–15 minutes, depending on number of words to sort and size of group

1. From a word wall, sight word banks, spelling list, or other source of words recognized at sight, select 2–4 features to contrast (for example, different beginning consonants, beginning blends, short or long vowel patterns, or parts of speech) and 4–6 words that share the same feature for each category. When introducing a new feature, or with struggling readers, contrast only two features at one time.

2. Review all the word cards with students; hold each up and have them identify the word chorally. Discard any words not recognized quickly.

3. Select one word from each group to represent the feature; read it and place it at the top of the pocket chart. Words sharing that feature will be placed below it in vertical columns. Point out the critical feature: "Let's find all the words that begin with the same sound as ball," "… have the same vowel sound as run," "… mean more than one," or "… are adjectives, words that describe things."

4. Mix up the remaining cards and hold each one up, having students read it aloud. Have volunteers come forward to place the word in the correct column and say the "sorting sentence"; for example, "Men means more than one man" or "Pretty is an adjective."

5. When all words have been correctly sorted, have students read each column chorally beginning with the example word.

6. Leave the example words displayed, remove and mix up the cards, and leave them near the pocket chart for independent sorting.

Variations: Have students sort their word banks and create their own individual sorts on the floor or table in front of them, using the example words you give them. Have students create their own individual sorts using word bank or word wall words, and let others guess the common feature. Have students sort their spelling words and write the words in categories as a practice exercise.

16. Word Hunts

Objectives: To develop children's ability to make connections between the spelling and the pronunciation of words

Materials: Chart paper

Duration: 10–15 minutes

1. Select a short rhymed poem and write it in large print on a piece of chart paper.
2. Read the poem to the children.
3. Read it a second time with the children reading along.
4. Have the children reread the poem in partner groups.
5. Ask the children what they notice about the words at the end of each line. Elicit examples of rhyming words.
6. Tell the children you want to go on a word hunt for two words that don't rhyme. Thinking aloud, select two words that don't rhyme and, on another piece of chart paper, write them as the headings of two columns.
7. Tell the students to copy the columns and the headings into their notebooks.
8. Organize the class in pairs.
9. Tell the children that each pair has to find as many rhyming words as they can that match the top word in each column. The words can be new ones that they think of, words from the word walls, and words in the poem.
10. Have the pairs share the words they have found.
11. Talk about what makes words rhyme.

17. Making and Breaking Words

Objectives: To develop phonemic awareness and ability to segment onset (beginning sound) and rime (the rest of the word without the beginning sound)

Materials: Magnetic letters or letter cards for students (metal cookie sheets for magnetic letters, and "letter holders" [sheet of paper folded 2 inches up from bottom and stapled vertically to create three or four pockets for letter cards] are helpful but optional); a large set of letter cards for demonstration

Duration: 10–15 minutes

1. Preselect two to four common phonograms that can become several different words by changing the initial consonant; these are often called "word families." Examples are *-an, -am, -to, -ock, -in, -ake, -ike,* and *-ill.* Preselect letters for these phonograms and the beginning sounds.
2. Select a group of students. Each student needs a set of letters or cards to make the phonograms and the necessary beginning letters. Gather around a table so students can manipulate letters.
3. Use large letter cards on the table or in a pocket chart to demonstrate. Put up the letters necessary to make a word such as *man.* Then remove the *m* and substitute another letter, such as *p.* Ask students to read the new word, *pan.*
4. Have students repeat the procedure themselves, using the magnetic letters or letter cards. Have them say the initial word, then say the new word as the initial letter is substituted. On the display set, again remove the initial letter and substitute another such as *r,* this time asking, "What word did I make this time? That's right, *ran.* Use your letters to make *ran.*"
5. Continue until all real words have been made. (Avoid creating nonsense words like *zan.*)
6. Using the demonstration letters, quickly "make and break" all the words in one word family and have students read each word. Then have students use their letters to quickly make the words as you call them out. Repeat with the other word families used.

18. Making and Using Word Banks

Objectives: To develop sight word recognition

Materials: Index cards cut in half or pieces of thick paper or cardboard; a box or a zip-lock plastic bag

Duration: 5 minutes

1. Once a student has demonstrated that she can read a word out of context, write that word on a piece of thick paper and have the student put it in her word bank (a box or plastic bag that contains all the sight words a student has learned).

2. Have students practice reading the words in their word banks every day in one of the following ways:

   - By reading them to a partner or a parent volunteer;
   - By grouping the words into categories (e.g., animals, things, actions);
   - By grouping all the words that begin with the same letter;
   - By doing "word hunts," that is, looking for the same words in a children's book.

3. Have each student read the words in his or her word bank to you every week or every ten days. If a child cannot read a word correctly, put it in a special envelope inside the word bank. Have students practice reading the words in the special envelope. When a word is read correctly, add it to the word bank.

19. Word Wall Activities

Objectives: To develop automatic (sight) recognition of words

Materials: Large bulletin board or wall space for display of word collections, with room to add 5–10 new words per week; blank word cards or sentence strips; heavy black and/or colored markers

Duration: 2–3 minutes to introduce each new word; 10+ minutes for a daily review of all words

1. To create a word wall of high-utility sight words, select 5–10 high-utility or frequently occurring words per week that students can recognize; begin with the simplest, like *I, a, the, is, am,* and so forth, and continue adding words weekly as students encounter them over and over in reading and writing. Divide the word wall space alphabetically; use letter cards to create spaces so words can be added with others beginning with the same letter.

2. To add a new word, print the word in large neat letters on a letter card. Hold up the card and "say-and-spell" the word aloud: "Good. G-O-O-D. Good."

3. Have students say-and-spell chorally, clapping as they say each letter. Repeat if students had difficulty.

4. Print the word on the board, or trace each letter with your finger, spelling aloud as you go. Say the word again.

5. Have students print the word or trace the letters with their fingers on desktops, the floor, or the back of their other hand, spelling the word aloud as they write/trace and repeating the whole word.

6. Have students "help you" find the letter category the new word goes in, and attach it to the word wall. Say-and-spell it again in unison. Quickly review all the words in that letter category.

7. Review at least some of the word wall words daily; point to the word and say-and-spell chorally. Have students practice "reading the wall" independently throughout the day.

Variations: Instead of, or in addition to, sight words, word walls can be made of word families (*-ike, -op,* etc.); beginning consonants, blends, and digraphs; vowel patterns; plurals; synonyms and antonyms; parts of speech (adjectives, prepositions, etc.); unusual words; subject-area words (math, science, health, history, etc.); holidays; sports; music; homophones; contractions; base words with their derivational forms; prefixes and suffixes; words with related Latin and Greek bases (*bio-, tele-, graph,* etc.); and words from a particular work of literature.

20. Analytic Phonics Lesson

Objectives: To help students learn to recognize new words by analogy to similar known words; to help develop phonemic awareness

Materials: Chalkboard, chart paper, or transparency, or letter cards and pocket chart, or magnetic letters and cookie sheet

Duration: 5–10 minutes

1. Select a word students know that can become several different words by changing the initial consonant, or have a student suggest a word they know to make new words from.

2. Write and say the word. Then say, "If I know ____, I know ____" while you remove or cover the initial consonant or cluster and replace it with another. (For example, "If I know ship, I know slip.") Repeat the process while the students say, "If I know ____, I know ____."

3. Repeat with the other initial letters to continue making new words. Invite volunteers to come forward to move the letters and make new words while saying the sentence as above.

4. Have students practice with a partner making and reading new words using letter cards or magnetic letters.

Variations: Have students write all the new words they can make from one known word. Add words to the word wall as needed. As students are able to recognize the new words at sight, have them add them to their individual word banks. Have students use the new words in oral and written sentences. Add new words to personal dictionaries.

Vocabulary Activities

21. "Word Conversation" for Primary Grades

Objectives: Introduce students to new vocabulary; help students learn the pronunciation, meaning, and use of new words

Materials: A fiction or nonfiction book to read aloud to students; chalkboard or chart paper

Duration: 5–10 minutes for each new word taught; sufficient time to read the book aloud

1. Select a book featuring rich use of language to read to the class or group. Select one to three unfamiliar words to teach. Read the book to the group or class.

2. After the reading, print the new word on the board. Point to it as you put the new word into the context of the book by using the word in a sentence about the book; for example, "In this story (*Best Friends* by Steven Kellogg), Kathy wishes Louise would get a contagious disease so Louise could come home. Say that word with me: *contagious*." Point to the word as children repeat it.

3. Give a one-sentence definition of the word in terms the students can understand: "*Contagious* means that an illness is catching; you can catch it from someone else."

4. Give an example or two that children will be able to understand: "Colds are contagious; you can get a cold from someone else if that person sneezes or coughs near you and you breathe in the germs. Chicken pox is very contagious; if one child in a family gets it, usually the other children get it soon afterward."

5. Ask children to provide their own examples of the word: "I got chicken pox from my best friend in kindergarten." "When I got pinkeye I had to stay home because I was contagious for one day."

6. Have students echo as you say the word and its meaning again: "Contagious means that an illness is catching."

Extensions: Add the new word to a poster, bulletin board, "new word" word wall, or other display of interesting vocabulary words. Have students make up and act out brief skits to demonstrate the word's meaning. Have students write the new word and illustrate it. Have them add their illustration to individual vocabulary books they create and add to systematically. Designate it the "Word of the Day," and see how many ways students can use the word in meaningful sentences. Add the new word as a bonus word to the weekly spelling list.

22. Semantic or Concept Web for Upper Grades

Objectives: To learn specific meanings of synonyms and to categorize synonymous words by connotative meanings or shades of meaning

Materials: List of synonyms or words related by meaning; chalkboard, overhead transparency, or chart paper

Duration: 10–20 minutes, depending on number of synonyms and size of group

1. From a word wall, thesaurus, student writing, reading material, or other source, select a group of words sharing a common meaning; for example, these words relate to the concept of "more than enough": *plenty, excess, ample, lavish, copious, plethora, surfeit, myriad, superfluous, profuse.*

2. Write each word, pronounce it, and brainstorm with students what each one means. Provide several good context sentences to help them determine specific meanings.

3. Help students generate several categories into which the words can be sorted; for example, these words may suggest *many*, *enough*, and *too much*. Create a web on the board, transparency, or chart paper with circles or boxes that are large enough to write all the words in that category inside it. (Students often make their circles too small.) Or have students fold a sheet of paper to create the required number of boxes: in half for two, thirds for three, or quarters for four. They label each folded section and list the words in it that fit that category.

4. Have students sort the words into their appropriate categories; for example, "many" may include *lavish, ample, myriad, profuse, copious*, and *plethora*; "enough" may include *plenty* and *surfeit*; and "too much" may include *excess* and *superfluous*.

5. Have students come up with their own context sentences that illustrate the meanings of each word.

23. Connect Two

Objectives: Help students learn new vocabulary by predicting meanings of and relationships among key terms from a selection prior to reading

Materials: List of key terms from a selection to be read by students

Duration: 5–15 minutes depending on number and familiarity of terms selected

1. Preview a selection students will read. Collect five or more key terms from the selection, including technical vocabulary and unusual or unfamiliar uses of known words. List them on the board, a transparency, or duplicated worksheets.

2. Explain that all of the terms are used in the selection, and thinking about them before reading will help students recognize and understand them when they encounter them in the text. Pronounce each word.

3. Pair students and have each pair select two terms and use them together in a meaningful sentence. Sentences should, if possible, reflect what students think the words mean or how they are related.

4. Have students write their sentence for each pair of words and, if desired, draw a sketch to accompany it. Then have each pair share the sentences and comments about them with the larger group.

Variation: Instead of creating sentences, have students categorize terms they think go together, give each category a title or heading, and explain why they grouped them together when they share.

24. Semantic Feature Analysis

Objectives: To enrich vocabulary; help students relate a new concept to familiar concepts

Materials: Nonfiction text; chalkboard, chart paper, or transparency; marker

Duration: 10–15 minutes

1. Select a concept from a nonfiction text about which students may have limited prior knowledge or experience. Think of several related concepts about which students may know a little more to compare to it.

2. Create a chart on the board, chart paper, or transparency with a vertical (y) and a horizontal (x) axis. On the x-axis, list the new concept and the related concepts; on the y-axis, list several features of the concepts they may share.

3. Prior to reading, engage students in using what they may already know and their predictions to complete the chart. Start with the concepts they may be more familiar with, and ask if each feature is true; if the concept has that feature, mark it with a plus (+), and if the concept does not have that feature, with a minus (−). End with the new concept; students may not know if it has a particular feature but are to predict based on what they already know.

4. Have students complete the reading of the selection. Have them watch for information about the concept that they predicted about.

5. After reading, reexamine the chart. Have them compare their predictions about the new concept to what they learned from the reading and change the chart as needed. Review what is now known about the new concept.

Fluency Activities

25. Repeated Reading

Objectives: To develop children's reading fluency

Materials: A reading passage of 50–500 words, depending on the child's reading rate

Duration: 10 minutes

1. Find a text (informational or fictional but not poetry or lists) written at the student's instructional level.

2. Sit next to the student in a quiet place, and listen as the student practices reading the text repeatedly.

3. Keep a copy of the text yourself on which you can mark the student's reading errors. (Errors are words that are omitted, or for which other words are substituted, or which are mispronounced. If the student does not say a word, wait 2 seconds and say the word yourself, and count that as an error.)

4. Time the student's reading for exactly 60 seconds; then stop the student, count the total number of words read, and subtract the errors from the total.

5. Have the student practice reading the text several times—preferably until the child reaches the criterion score for his or her grade level. Remember to offer adequate praise each time.

26. Fluency Oriented Oral Reading (FOOR)

Objectives: To develop reading fluency

Materials: Copies of text at students' instructional level

Duration: Three days (10 minutes each day)

1. Assemble a group of students who are at roughly the same instructional level. Provide copies of the text to all the students.

2. *Day 1:*

   - Read the text fluently while the students are following along.

   - Think aloud: call attention to the way you read words in groups and to how you emphasize important words.

   - Briefly discuss the meaning of the text with the students.

   - Echo read the text (you read one sentence fluently and the students read it at the same pace and with the same intonation).

3. *Day 2:*

   - Pair up the students and have them take turns reading the text, each one reading a sentence or a paragraph.

   - Circulate among the pairs and provide help as needed.

4. *Day 3:*

   - Have students come back together in the original group and choral read the text with you.

Extension: Step 4 may be followed by a Readers' Theater activity.

27. Paired Reading

Objectives: To develop reading fluency

Material: Text at the less fluent reader's instructional level

Duration: 5–10 minutes

1. Match up a fluent reader (a parent volunteer, a tutor, or an older student) with a less fluent reader. Instruct the more fluent reader to carry out steps 3–6.

2. Choose a text at the instructional level of the less fluent reader.

3. The more fluent reader reads the text to the less fluent reader.

4. The two readers read the passage several times in unison.

5. The less fluent reader reads the text, while the more fluent reader monitors her reading (corrects the errors by saying the words correctly, has the partner reread a sentence in which a word was misread, models the adequate intonation for a sentence and has the partner try to mimic it).

6. Repeat step 5 once or twice.

28. Readers' Theater

Objectives: To develop students' reading fluency and comprehension

Materials: A fictional text that contains dialogue, preferably among several characters

Duration: 15–25 minutes

1. Make a photocopy of the text you plan to use for readers' theater.

2. Read through the text and mark the parts that should be read by different readers. Create a code for different readers, such as a capital letter to represent the name of each different character, and a capital N followed by a number for narrator number 1, 2, 3, and so on.

3. Put brackets [ ] around the parts that will be read by each reader, and write in a letter over each section to indicate who should read it.

4. Strike through any parts that do not need to be read. Often "he said," "she replied," and the like, can be eliminated without affecting the meaning.

5. As they prepare to read a fictional text with readers' theater, have the students discuss the setting of the text, who the characters are, and what they are like.

6. Have the students read portions of the text several times in order to read the lines fluently and with the expression called for.

7. Offer coaching, asking the students questions such as,

   • "What is your character feeling right now? How do you sound when you feel that way? Should your voice be loud or soft? Fast or slow?"

   • "What might your character think about what the other character is saying? How will your character sound then?"

   • "What is going on at this point in the story? How is your character reacting to it?"

   • "How is your character changing as the story proceeds?"

8. Offer comments and suggestions after each practice reading and invite the students to do the same.

29. Choral Reading

Objectives: To develop reading fluency in a meaningful context

Materials: Poems with a strong rhythmic pattern

Duration: 10–15 minutes

1. Prepare the children to choral-read a text by discussing the circumstances or the context in which it might be said. Ask the children to imagine the situation and to describe the sounds they associate with it. Offer suggestions as necessary.

2. Decide how the poem should be read, for example, by the whole chorus, by individuals, by pairs, or by two alternating sections; in loud or soft voices; rapidly or slowly; melodiously, angrily, giggling, or seriously.

3. Have each student or group of students practice reading their part until they can keep the rhythm perfectly.

4. Have the whole class practice reading the poem in the manner previously agreed on until they sound like a good chorus. Invite and give feedback after each performance.

30. Demonstrating Fluent Reading

Objectives: To show students what fluent reading looks sounds like

Materials: A book at the appropriate reading level written in a colorful style

Duration: Ten minutes

1. Begin by reading a passage to the students in two ways. First, read it haltingly and uncertainly, in a voice that suggests you are concerned with slashing your way through the words and getting a disagreeable experience over with—in other words, read *disfluently*. Then read the passage again, but this time with your voice full of expression and interest, with pauses and emphases. Show that you are enjoying the message of the text and not simply struggling to pronounce the words—read *fluently*.

2. Ask the students which reading they preferred and why.

3. In the discussion that follows, call attention to the qualities of fluent reading:

   - The reader is thinking about the message and not just about pronouncing the words.
   - The reader varies her voice between loud and soft, and between faster and slower.
   - The reader groups words meaningfully.
   - The reader may show emotion—enjoyment, surprise, and excitement—as she reads.

4. Later, read aloud to the students again, reading as fluently as you can and "thinking aloud" as you read. Pause to explain to the students a decision you just made—such as where to pause, what words to group together, or how to read a character's voice—in order to read fluently.

31. Becoming a Model Expressive Reader

Objectives: To provide students the target behavior they should aim for, to demonstrate to students the qualities of expressive fluent reading, with accurate word recognition, appropriate rate, inflection, and phrasing.

Materials: An appropriately leveled, interesting book.

Duration: 15 to 20 minutes, including the reading and discussion afterwards.

When you model reading aloud with prosody, observe these pointers:

Read a little slower than usual.

Read with animation:

Chunk—read in meaningful praises.

Stress—emphasize certain words for meaning.

Pause—both to show boundaries of phrases and to add suspense.

Vary—create variety in the pitch and volume of your speech.

1. Read the following text in a monotone.

   Once upon a time way down in the big woods there lived a man all by himself. His house didn't have but one room in it and that room was his parlor, his sitting room, his dining room, and his kitchen, too. In one end of the room was a great big open fireplace and that's where the man cooked and ate his supper. And one night after he had cooked and eaten his supper, there crept in through the cracks of the logs the most curious creature that you ever did see and it had a great big long tail.
   (Adapted from "The Tailypo," in Botkin, 1944).

2. Next, read by "chunking" the underlined phrases. That is, read those phrases as groups, each one at a different pitch than the one before and after, with short pauses between them:

   Once upon a time way down in the big woods there lived a man all by himself. His house didn't have but one room in it and that room was his parlor, his sitting room, his dining room, and his kitchen, too. In one end of the room was a great, big open fireplace, and that's where the man cooked and ate his supper. And one night after he had cooked and eaten his supper, there crept in through the cracks of the logs the most curious creature that you ever did see, and it had a great, big, long tail.

3. Now while you keep chunking the underlined phrases, add stresses. Say the bolded important words **more loudly** than the other words:

Once upon a time way down in the **big woods** there lived a **man** all by him**self**. His house didn't have but **one room** in it and that room was his **parlor**, his **sitting room**, his **dining room**, and his **kitchen, too**. In one end of the room was a **great, big, open fireplace**, and that's where the man **cooked** and **ate** his **supper**. And one night after he had **cooked** and **eaten** his **supper**, there **crept** in through the **cracks** of the **logs** the most **curious creature** that you **ever did see**, and it had a **great**, **big**, **long tail**.

4. Now just add some pauses. Where you see the slashes (///), pause for one or two seconds. (Remember to keep chunking the underlined words, and stressing the bolded words, too.):

Once upon a **time** /// way down in the **big woods** /// there lived a **man** all by him**self**. His **house** didn't have but **one room** in it and that room was his **parlor**, his **sitting room**, his **dining room**, and his **kitchen, too**. In one end of the room was a **great, big, open fireplace** /// and that's where the man **cooked** and **ate** his **supper**. And one night after he had **cooked** and **eaten** his **supper**, ///there **crept** in through the cracks of the **logs** the most **curious creature** that you **ever did see**, /// and it had a **great, big, long tail**.

Comprehension Activities With Fictional Texts

32. Terms in Advance

Objectives: To develop comprehension by recalling and organizing prior information before reading; enable students to predict what a reading passage might be about; familiarize students with key vocabulary and concepts prior to reading

Materials: List of key terms or phrases from the text to be read, chart paper or transparency, marker

Duration: 5–15 minutes, depending on size of group, number of terms, familiarity of terms

1. From a reading passage students are going to read, collect a group of key words and/or phrases that bear importantly on the content of the passage. Try to include both familiar and unfamiliar terms; don't just collect all the hardest or least familiar vocabulary.

2. Display the words on a chart or transparency with space around each one for recording students' ideas of what each term means and/or how it might bear on the passage they will read.

3. If your main goal for the activity is to encourage predictions about what the text to be read will be about, have students hypothesize about ways in which the terms might be related in the story. Optionally, you may allow them to write down their predictions before sharing them with the class. Accept all hypotheses or predictions encouragingly.

4. If your main goal is to introduce new vocabulary, have students dictate or write sentences explaining the meaning of one or more of the terms, or make up sentences that combine two or more of the terms in one sentence.

5. As students read the text and the meaning of various terms becomes clear, modify the chart or transparency to show what each term means in the passage and to reflect new information gained during reading. Alternatively, ask students to compare the story they read to their initial predictions.

33. Directed Reading-Thinking Activity (DRTA)

Objectives: To develop comprehension by recalling and organizing prior information before reading

Materials: Fiction selection; chalkboard, chart paper, or transparency; marker

Duration: 10–30 minutes or longer, depending on length of selection

1. Select a story with a well-structured plot that revolves around a character's attempts to solve a problem or achieve a goal, with a clear resolution of the conflict at the end.

2. Plan from two to five stopping points in the story, where students will stop reading to discuss what they have read and make predictions about forthcoming parts of the story. Plan the stops just before some major event or piece of information.

3. Explain to students that they will be making predictions, or educated guesses, about what might happen in the story, and they will base their predictions on the title, illustrations, and what they read in preceding sections. They will read up to, but not beyond, the stopping points and will not read ahead. They will justify their predictions based on what

they learn as the story unfolds. All predictions will be accepted respectfully by everyone. The process of predicting, not whether their predictions are proved or disproved, is what is important.

4. Have students read the title, examine cover art and initial illustrations, and perhaps the first section of the story. Elicit predictions by asking, "What might happen in this story?" or "What might this story be about?" and "Why do you think so?" Jot down key phrases from different predictions. Have students read the next section to find out and stop at the next stopping point.

5. After each section, have students briefly review what they know so far and new information revealed in the prior section. Review and check predictions that still seem likely or possible. Elicit further predictions about the next section.

6. Repeat this cycle of "review-predict-read to prove" to the end. At the conclusion of the story, briefly discuss with students how they used clues and events to predict the outcome.

Variation: Read the story aloud to the group as a Directed Listening-Thinking Activity, following the same procedures.

34. Dual-Entry Diary

Objectives: To encourage personal responses to literature; to develop writing fluency

Materials: Response journals

Duration: 10–15 minutes

1. Model the technique on the overhead projector or on the chalkboard. Draw a vertical line in the middle of a blank sheet of paper:

   - On the left-hand side, write a passage from the text that students are reading. Explain that you chose to write it down because you found it particularly striking (because it reminded you of your own experience, or because you disagree with it, or because it is unexpected, etc.).

   - On the right-hand side, write a comment about the passage. (Why did you write it down? What did it make you think of? What question do you have about it?)

2. Instruct students to use their response journals as dual-entry diaries and, as they read the text, to pause and make entries. You may choose to assign a minimal number of entries per text.

Extension: If students are reading a longer text, you may collect the dual-entry diaries periodically and write comments in them. You may also ask students to share some of their entries in a discussion group or use them to structure a whole-class discussion.

35. Instructional Conversations

Objectives: To develop comprehension; to develop critical thinking; to develop conversational skills

Materials: Story or passages from a book

Duration: 30–60 minutes

1. Decide on what the theme or issue for the conversation should be (a real issue that real people might wonder about, one that invites different responses, one to which students can relate and that is likely to engage them).

2. Select a story or passages from a book and have the students (re)read it/them.

3. Explain that you will have a conversation about the text and that everyone is invited to think hard about it and share ideas.

4. Clarify the rules for participation: Students do not need to raise hands; however, they need to listen to each other carefully, be respectful, and wait for others to finish before contributing.

5. Begin the conversation with an open-ended question. Make sure that the students can resort to their background knowledge, interests, and experience to answer it.

6. Keep the conversation loosely focused on the main theme. Do take the time to explore collateral issues raised by students, but tactfully steer the conversation back to the main topic.

7. As the conversation proceeds, explain points that are not clear, provide background information that you notice students do not have, provide new vocabulary that students may need to express their emerging insights in a more sophisticated manner.

8. Ask students to support their ideas with evidence from the text throughout the conversation.

36. Save the Last Word for Me

Objectives: To develop comprehension; encourage thoughtful discussion of a shared text

Materials: 3 × 5 file cards or sheets of paper cut in quarters; 1–4 cards per student

Duration: 10–20 minutes depending on size of group

1. Distribute blank file cards or papers to students.

2. After they have finished reading a selection, have them find a sentence or short section (no longer than a few sentences, or as short as one sentence) in the text that they find particularly interesting, surprising, evocative, or otherwise noteworthy and write the quotation on one side of a card. On the reverse side they write a comment or response: why they found it interesting, what it made them think about, something it reminded them of, and so forth. Older students and those reading longer or more complex texts can complete several cards in the same way; younger readers or those reading shorter texts can complete one.

3. When completed, ask a volunteer to read his or her selected quotation aloud and call on several other students to comment on or respond to the quotation. Discussion of each other's comments is allowed. After several others have commented, the first student shares his or her written comment on the quotation. No discussion follows; the original writer has "the last word."

4. Another student is selected by the first student or the teacher to repeat the procedure; read the quotation, invite others to comment, then share his or her written comment. In small discussion groups or literature circles, all students may be able to participate; in larger groups or with the whole class, only some will be able to share each time.

37. Literature Circles

Objectives: To develop comprehension; promote thoughtful discussion and interpretation of shared literature

Materials: A shared work of literature (all students in the group read the same text)

Duration: 20 minutes or longer, depending on the group size, degree of experience with the procedure, and students' interest in discussion

1. Assign students participating to read the same text; they may read a short text in one sitting or read a section such as a chapter of a longer work.

2. Convene a group of all the students reading the shared work; for best interaction, group size should not exceed five or six. If more students are reading the same text, create two groups.

3. Assign each student a role for that meeting; see textbook, Table 8.1, for a list of possible roles. The roles most often used include the Questioner, sometimes called the Discussion Director, who creates three or four thoughtful questions about the main events of the selection for the group to discuss; the Quotation Finder, sometimes called the Passage Master, who selects one or more excerpts to practice and read aloud; the Artist, or Illustrator, who illustrates the selection with written captions; and the Word Finder, or Word Wizard, who locates and explains interesting or important words, figurative language, expressions or idioms, and the like, to the group.

4. Monitor the execution of the various roles in the group discussion; model reflective questioning and responding to the text without lecturing or dominating; move the discussion forward when necessary by drawing all students into the discussion, and use literary terms such as *episode*, *climax*, *resolution*, and so forth, as appropriate.

5. If students are reading a longer work in sections, assist them in deciding how far they will read before the next meeting and when they will next meet.

6. Have all students regardless of their role write a summary, response, or other piece in their literature or reading journals about the section just discussed.

7. Rotate the roles so all students participate and have different responsibilities.

38. Shared Inquiry

Objectives: To develop comprehension and critical thinking

Materials: A shared work of literature (all students have read the same text)

Duration: 20–40 minutes

1. Choose a text or part of a text that encourages discussion (that is, one that lends itself to multiple interpretations or raises interesting or even controversial issues) and which students have read carefully.

2. Prepare four or five discussion questions that meet the following three criteria: (1) they are questions that real people would ask in real life; (2) they have more than one possible answer; and (3) they lead the discussion into the text, that is, they invite revisiting the text as a source of evidence in support of possible answers.

3. Write the first question on the chalkboard and invite the students to think about it and briefly write down their answers.

4. Invite students (including reluctant speakers) to share what they wrote. Point out differences between responses and invite their authors and the rest of the class to expand on those differences. Press them to support their views with references to the text and to restate their ideas more clearly if necessary. Do not correct any answer and do not suggest that it is right or wrong. Do not offer your own answer to the question.

5. Use a seating chart to record what each student has contributed.

6. When the discussion of a question has run its course, summarize it based on your notes and ask if anyone has anything to add.

7. Repeat steps 3–6 with each of the discussion questions you have prepared.

Extension: Have students respond to one of the discussion questions in writing.

39. Discussion Web

Objectives: To develop comprehension; promote thoughtful discussion and interpretation of shared literature; help students perceive and understand both sides of a position or argument

Materials: A shared work of literature (all students in the group read the same text)

Duration: 15–30 minutes

1. Assign students participating to read the same text; they may read a short text in one sitting or read a section such as a chapter of a longer work. Text may be fiction or nonfiction.

2. Generate a discussion question that can reasonably be argued from both sides, sometimes called a binary question; for example, "Was it wrong for _____ (story character) to _____ (act in a way that some might consider wrong, but for which he or she had a reason or rationale)?" "Was _____ (story character) _____ or _____ (two opposite or opposing characteristics, like brave/reckless, caring/selfish, or wise/foolish)?" or "Is (or was) it right or wrong to _____ (non-fiction text or subject area issue: secede from the Union, hunt whales, log the rain forest, send Japanese Americans to internment camps, etc.)?" Write the question so students can refer to it as they reflect.

3. Assign students to pairs. Have each pair answer the question from both sides of the argument, listing three reasons, examples, and so forth, to support each side.

4. Combine two pairs to create groups of four. Have students combine their lists so all positions are included. Then have each foursome reach agreement on one side of the argument and prepare to defend it.

5. Have each foursome summarize and defend its work to the larger group.

Extension: When two or more groups take opposing positions, a formal debate can follow. Groups taking the same position can join forces to share arguments and prepare to present them as forcefully and logically as possible, prepare notes, select spokespersons, and if desired conduct research on their position. Establish strict ground rules (no personal attacks, no raised voices, etc.) and time limits for arguments and rebuttal. Have each side briefly summarize its arguments in closing.

40. Debate

Objectives: To develop critical thinking skills; to give students practice in making claims and defending them with reasons

Materials: Chalkboard

Duration: 20–30 minutes

1. Find a binary question (one that has a yes/no answer) that you think will divide students' opinions roughly equally and write it on the chalkboard.

2. Give students five minutes to discuss it freely in pairs or groups of four.

3. Ask the students who believe one answer to the question is right to go stand along the wall on one side of the room, and those who think the other answer is right to stand along the wall on the other side. If there are undecided students, instruct them to stand along the wall in the middle.

4. Explain the ground rules:

   a. Argue politely!

   b. If you hear an argument that makes you want to change your mind, walk to the other side or to the middle.

5. Ask the students on each side to spend 2–3 minutes in their groups to come up with a sentence that states their position and to appoint someone to say that sentence.

6. Begin the debate by asking each team, including the undecided group, to state their position.

7. Invite students on both teams to respond—either with a counterargument/rebuttal or with more reasons in support of one of the positions expressed.

8. Ask for clarifications as needed. Offer an idea or two from the devil's advocate position to liven up the debate. Change sides when you hear a compelling argument. Encourage students to change sides if they are persuaded to.

9. When the debate has proceeded for 10–15 minutes, ask each side to summarize what they have said.

Extension: Ask the students to write down what they think about the issue and why.

41. Value Line

Objectives: To develop critical thinking; to give students practice in making arguments

Materials: A shared text (one that all the students have read)

Duration: 15–20 minutes

1. After the students have read a text carefully, ask a question about it to which the answers may vary along a continuum.

2. Give the students three minutes to write down their individual answers.

3. Stand at one end of the room and announce that you represent one pole, or extreme position, of the argument. State your position.

4. Invite a student to stand at the other end of the room to represent the other pole of the argument. Help her state that position.

5. Invite the students to line up between the two of you. Instruct them to choose a point on the imaginary line between the two poles of the argument that reflects their position on the question.

6. Tell the students to compare their views with those of the students around them to make sure they are standing in the right spots. Encourage them to move one way or another on the value line after hearing others' ideas and to continue discussing their answers until they find a group that shares the same position on the question.

7. Identify three or four clusters of students who seem to represent different views. Invite them to prepare a statement of their position and to share it with the class.

Variation: After step 6, you may want to fold the value line in the middle so that students with divergent views may debate their answers, while students with similar views may be helped to think of additional reasons in support of their position.

Extension: Have students write an argumentative or persuasive essay in response to the question.

42. Story Maps

Objectives: To develop comprehension; help students identify and sequence key story elements and events

Materials: Shared fiction text; story map graphic organizer, with key story elements for students to label

Duration: 10–20 minutes

1. Have students read, or read to them, a well-structured story that has a clear plot line including a well-defined main character; a problem, goal, challenge, or defining event faced by the main character; a series of attempts by the character to solve the problem or achieve the goal, the first several of which are unsuccessful, often referred to as the *rising action*; a final attempt that is successful, although not always as the character expected, forming the climax; and a resolution of the story, in which the character is often changed in some way.

2. Create a simple graphic organizer that labels the major parts of the story and allows students to fill in spaces on a chart, timeline, or flowchart. (There are many different kinds of premade story map graphic organizers available in teacher resource books, textbooks, basal manuals, comprehension kits, and so forth, or you can make your own.) For emergent and beginning readers, divide a sheet of paper into thirds vertically and label the sections *Beginning*, *Middle*, and *End*; students retell the story, then draw a picture to represent each part and write or dictate one or two sentences telling what happened in that part.

3. Have students include important details supporting the plot, including the setting and supporting characters.

4. Allow students to share their story maps by using them to retell the story.

Extensions: Provide students free access to a variety of types of story maps they can complete as they finish a work of fiction. Carefully completed story maps can be substituted for book reports or reviews when students must demonstrate their comprehension of a completed story. They can be shared during oral book reports. When students are writing fiction, completing a story map during the planning stage of the writing cycle helps students plan a complete story before they start and helps them structure their stories. (See "Story Maps for Writing" activity.)

43. Character Clusters and Character Maps

Objectives: To develop comprehension; help students understand characteristics or traits of story characters and relationships among characters

Materials: Shared work of fiction; chalkboard, transparency, or chart paper

Duration: 10–15 minutes

A. Character Cluster

1. Have students identify the main character in a shared work of fiction. (If a work has more than one central character, create a separate cluster for each main character.)

2. Create a web graphic organizer by placing the main character's name in a circle in the center of the web. Have students brainstorm characteristics or traits of that character (e.g., brave, funny, a loyal friend, loves wildlife, shy, etc.). Have students select three to five that are most descriptive of that character and write those traits in circles around the center circle, connected to it by lines.

3. For each characteristic, have students generate examples of the character's words, actions, and attitudes from the story that illustrate that trait. Write these examples in circles that are connected by lines to the trait circles; for example, *brave*: chased away the mean dog, told the truth about breaking the lamp.

B. Character Map

1. List with students the main and supporting characters in a work of fiction they have read or are reading. Have students identify the main character/s.

2. Write the names of the main character in a central circle and the supporting characters in circles arranged around the central one. (Leave plenty of writing space between the circles.) Have students briefly describe how the main character feels about the supporting character. Draw an arrow from the main character to a supporting character; along the line, write a sentence that describes those feelings. Repeat for the other supporting characters.

3. With student help as above, draw arrows from the supporting characters to the main character and to other supporting characters. Along the arrows, write these characters' feelings about each other.

44. Dramatizing a Story

Objectives: To encourage children to take a close look at a story by getting a real feel for the action

Materials: A story with two or more characters involved in a compelling dilemma

Duration: From half an hour to two or three class periods

The procedure for dramatizing a story is adapted from the works of Spolin (1986) and Heathcote (Wagner, 1999).

1. *Immerse students in the story.* You need to make sure the students get the story on a literal level—that they know what happened. This might mean reading the story to them or asking them to reread the part you are going to dramatize.

2. *Warm them up to do drama.* There are many warm-up activities that work well to prepare students to act with more expression:

   a. *Stretches:* Have the students stand in a circle. Now tell them to stretch their arms as high as they can as they spread their feet apart and make very wide faces. Now tell them to shrink up into tiny balls. Then stretch out big again. Have them do the same with their faces: Lion face! (expansive expression). Prune face! (shrunken expression).

   b. *Mirrors:* Have students stand opposite each other. One is the person, and the other is the person reflected in the mirror. Have the person move (slowly) as the other mirrors the person's movements. Then switch roles.

   c. *Portraits:* Have students get into groups of four or five. Have them think of something to depict that uses all of them as parts. For example, to depict a skier, children can act as poles, skis, and the person.

   d. *Superactions:* This activity is more complex. Explain to the students that when we do things with other people, we often act on two levels: what we are doing and what we mean by what we are doing. For example, when we pass somebody we know in the hallway, having just seen the person a short time before, we might nod and say, "Hi." But when we see a friend in the hallway who has just come back to school after a long illness, we might say "HI!" with more exuberance. In both cases, the action is the same: to greet the friend. But the *superaction* is different. In the first case, it is just to show the person that we know he or she is there; in the second case, it is to show that we are surprised and delighted to see the person. Now practice dramatizing superactions by setting up brief situations, such as a waiter taking a customer's order. Write superactions on small pieces of paper, and give one privately to each actor. Have different pairs of students act out the same scene, with the same actions but with different superactions, leaving time for the other students to guess what they thought the superaction was and say why they thought so.

3. *Choose critical moments.* It can be particularly useful to dramatize just a few choice scenes from a story, especially the turning points when the most is at stake. In "Jack and the Beanstalk," such a scene might be when Jack first approaches the Giant's castle, knocks on the door, and is greeted by the Giant's wife.

4. *Segment the situation.* Now assign students to take each of these roles. Invite other students to join them as they think about the situation from each character's point of view. What must be on Jack's mind when he approaches the huge door? What do the door and the walls of the castle look like? How large are they in proportion to Jack? What does Jack hear around the place? What does he smell? How does the place make him feel? What makes him pound his fist on the door? What is at stake for him? What are his choices? What will he do if he *doesn't* knock on the door? Why does he decide to do it? Do the same for the Giant's wife. How does the knocking sound to her—thunderous or puny? What does she think when she sees the small but plucky boy at her door? What thoughts go through her mind, knowing what she knows about her husband? What are her feelings as she looks down at Jack? Ask the actors to focus their minds on a few of these considerations as they prepare to act out the scene.

5. *Dramatize the scene.* Use minimal props and minimal costumes to help students think their way into their roles. Ask the other students to watch carefully and see what the actors make them think of.

6. *Side coach.* As the director, don't be passive, but take opportunities to make suggestions from the sidelines that will help children act more expressively. You might ask, "Jack, do you feel scared now or brave? How can you show us how you're feeling?"

7. *Invite reflection.* Ask the other students what they saw. What did they think was on the characters' minds? It is worthwhile to invite several groups of students to dramatize the same scene and have the class discuss the aspects of the situation that each performance brings to light.

Comprehension Activities With Nonfictional Texts

45. Think-Pair-Share

Objectives: To reflect on and thoughtfully respond to a question and share responses with a peer; encourage reflective thinking and respectful listening; develop comprehension by recalling and organizing prior information before reading

Materials: Students may write their initial responses in journals or learning logs or on scrap paper; otherwise, no materials are needed

Duration: 5 minutes or less

1. Ask an open-ended question—that is, a question that can be answered many ways depending on the opinions, experiences, predictions, or preferences of the individuals answering it. For example; "What could we do as a class to show our concern for the environment?" "How could this story character have behaved differently so the story had a different outcome?" or "What traits or characteristics make a person a good leader?" Write the question so students can reread it as they think.

2. Have students think, then write in brief form their thoughts in their journals, learning logs, or on scrap paper.

3. After a short interval for writing, have each student turn to a partner and share his or her answers to the questions, taking turns. Remind students to talk to their partners, not read their papers to them, and to listen respectfully and attentively to each other.

4. Have a few volunteers share their thoughts with the larger group or restate their partner's response instead of their own.

Variation: Paired Brainstorming In a situation where students will share factual information, for example before reading expository text when students are recalling and organizing their prior information about the topic, have individuals briefly list the information they already know during the "Think" phase. After a minute or two, each student joins a partner and the two lists are quickly combined during the "Pair" stage. Finally, a few key facts from each pair are listed on the board, chart paper, or a transparency during the "Share" stage. Students can compare what they knew before reading to information they acquire during and after reading.

46. Paired Brainstorming

Objectives: To activate prior knowledge of a topic

Materials: Journals or scrap paper

Duration: 6–10 minutes

1. Announce the topic of the lesson and ask the students to brainstorm (that is, to think of everything that comes to mind) about it and list the facts or ideas on a sheet of paper in 2–3 minutes. Tell them that they may also list questions they have about the topic.

2. When time is up, instruct the students to turn to a classmate and combine their lists.

3. Have volunteers share their ideas and make a master list on the chalkboard, arranging the ideas in categories if possible.

4. Leave the master list on the board and have students compare it to the ideas they have after they have read a text or at the end of the lesson.

47. Anticipation Guide

Objectives: To develop comprehension by recalling and organizing prior information before reading

Materials: Teacher-made anticipation guides, duplicated for each student

Duration: 5–10 minutes to complete the guide prior to reading and again after reading the material

1. Read through the material your students are going to read. Select a number of important facts, terms, and so forth, you want students to remember and understand from the reading.

2. Create a set of statements to which students will respond by agreeing or disagreeing, marking them True or False, or checking the statements they think are true; for example, "There were thirteen southern colonies," "Maple syrup is made by crushing the leaves of the maple tree," or "Only native-born U.S. citizens can become president."

3. Type each statement, preceding each one with a blank on the left side of the paper and following each one with a blank on the right side of the paper. Head the left-side column of blanks "BEFORE" and the right-hand column "AFTER."

4. Distribute the anticipation guides *before* reading or discussing the text material, and have students read and mark each statement true/false, agree/disagree, and so forth, in the BEFORE (before reading) column. (Be sure they understand they are not expected to know all the right answers, just to make an attempt at each item based on what, if anything, they might already know about the topic, and their answers will not be corrected, graded, etc.) Collect the guides and keep them for later. Briefly discuss students' responses to each statement, but do not tell them the correct answer.

5. Read and discuss the text material as you would normally do. After students have thoroughly read and discussed the material, participated in comprehension activities, and so forth, redistribute the original anticipation guides and have students respond to each item, this time marking in the AFTER (after reading) column. These responses should now represent the correct information; therefore, answers in the AFTER column may be checked for correctness or graded. Be sure students understand that their initial attempts were "best guesses," and only their responses after the reading will be checked.

6. Students can fold the BEFORE column under and keep their anticipation guides as a form of class notes or study guides on the topic.

48. Graphic Organizers

Objectives: To help students organize information in text

Materials: Blank graphic organizers for students to fill in before, during, and after reading

Duration: 5–30 minutes depending on length and complexity of text and the graphic organizer used

1. Select or create a graphic organizer that fits the organization of the text: for example, a timeline or sequential flowchart for sequences of events, Venn diagram for comparison/contrast, or web for main and subordinate categories.

2. Have students preview or skim the material to find some of the main topics or categories of information and enter them on the graphic organizer. With textbook material, chapter headings and subheadings often contain this information.

3. Have students attempt to recall and organize their prior information about these topics before reading, and note what they already know in pencil on the organizer. (If they are later disproved, these entries can easily be changed.)

4. As students read, they continue to enter new information they encounter on the organizer: for example, dates and places of historical events, short- and long-term effects of events, biographical information, and other important supporting details.

5. After the reading, have students compare their organizers in pairs or small groups, adding or moving information as needed to make their organizers clear and accurate. They can then be used as outlines for writing or for study guides.

49. Metacognitive Graphic Organizer

Objectives: To develop awareness of text organization; to assist students in self-monitoring their comprehension of non-fiction texts; to help students create a personal guide for reading and study

Materials: Article or textbook chapter

Duration: Varies with the length of the text

1. Have students place the title of the article or chapter in the center of a sheet of paper and then add the major headings as they survey the material.

2. Instruct students to look at the visual information in charts, diagrams, and so on, and add key ideas from these to the graphic organizer under the appropriate headings.

3. Have students read the text and make notes on the graphic organizer or on sticky notes as they read.

4. When they finish reading, instruct students to review the graphic and the notes made and decide whether to (a) revise the graphic (if the actual organization of the text is different from what students initially drew), (b) add subheadings (if several ideas can be grouped under one subheading), or (c) write extended notes to clarify the important ideas (if there are many new ideas). Students may choose to do any or all of these depending on their own learning needs.

Extension: Have students use their graphic organizers to write a summary of the article or chapter.

50. Know-Want to Know-Learn (K-W-L)

Objectives: To develop comprehension by recalling and organizing prior information before reading; organize new information gained by reading and relate it to prior information

Materials: Nonfiction material; chalkboard, chart paper, or transparency; duplicated K-W-L charts

Duration: 10–30 minutes or longer, depending on length of selection and students' prior information

1. Create a K-W-L chart on the board, chart paper, or transparency consisting of three vertical columns; label the left-side column K: What We Know; the center column W: What We Want to Find Out; and the right-side column L: What We Learned. Write the topic at the top. Duplicate and distribute blank charts.

2. Prior to reading, have students write some things they already know about the topic in the K column on their charts. Have volunteers share some of their ideas; record them in the K column on the group chart. Ask direct questions about important information in the passage that no one mentioned.

3. When disagreements occur or when questions arise that can't be answered prior to reading, note these in the W column. Have students generate and write on their charts one question they can't answer; write some of these on the group chart and have students include them on their charts as well.

4. Briefly review with students what they already know and are uncertain about. Read the passage.

5. After reading, review the K column with students; check those ideas that were borne out by the passage; and cross off those that were disproved, writing the correct information in the L column. Review the W column; check those questions that were answered by the passage, writing the corresponding information in the L column. Mark those questions still unanswered with a question mark for further research. Add to the L column any other new information gathered from the passage.

6. Have students reorganize and add to their own charts as you do so with the group chart.

51. What? So What? Now What?

Objectives: To help students organize facts and arguments to prepare to do persuasive writing or speaking

Materials: Blank organizer on board, chart paper, or transparency; duplicated copies of blank organizer for students to complete

Duration: 10–15 minutes

1. Prepare a model organizer for the group to complete on the board, chart paper, or a transparency. Create three columns across the top: label the left-side column WHAT?, the center column SO WHAT?, and the right-side column NOW WHAT? Explain that this chart will help them organize their facts and opinions to write or speak persuasively on an issue they have read about (e.g., environmental pollution, species endangerment, cafeteria recycling, logging of national forest lands, etc.).

2. On the left side of the chart, list factual information students have learned about the topic: for example, "Since 1950, _____ species have become endangered and _____ have become extinct," or "Species are now becoming endangered at an average rate of _____." In the central column, list students' reasons why these facts are important or why others should care about them. In the right-side column, write students' suggestions of actions that could affect or improve the situation.

3. Using the completed group chart, have students compose persuasive essays or speeches presenting the relevant facts, explaining their importance, and urging their audience to pursue a course of action.

Variations: When an issue arises that students care about, complete this chart with them to help them sort out facts from opinions, create persuasive arguments, and determine how they can act on their beliefs. Then follow through as a group on one or more actions to address the situation.

Extensions: Have students organize the information in the L column in categories and construct a web or other graphic organizer of the information. Have students use their K-W-L charts as study guides or as resources for writing summaries and reports. Gather related reading materials and have students research answers to questions still listed in the W column. Follow up with a "What? So What? Now What?" activity to help students determine actions that can be taken based on what they learned.

52. Reciprocal Teaching

Objectives: To model and practice comprehension strategies of summarizing, questioning, clarifying, and predicting

Materials: Nonfiction text; chalkboard, chart paper or transparency

Duration: 15–30 minutes or longer, depending on length and difficulty of text

1. Survey and break the text into segments for students to read; depending on the length and difficulty of the entire selection, segments may be as short as one or two paragraphs or as long as a chapter section. Students can use sticky notes to mark the end of a segment. Create groups of four students each.

2. Read the first segment with students. Then model how to use the four strategies: First, summarize the section in one or two sentences, writing them on the board, chart paper, or transparency; second, ask one or two good questions to be answered by students; third, clarify by identifying the most difficult part of the section (may be a word or phrase, sentence, example, or concept) and explain it or tell how you could figure it out (look it up, check an encyclopedia, use surrounding context, etc.); fourth, predict what the next section might contain based on what you've already read.

3. Assign each student in a group a task for the next section: summarizer, questioner, clarifier, or predictor. (Job cards help students remember what they are to do.) Read the next section with students.

4. After reading, each student is to complete his or her task following your model. Allow time for task completion. Each student then shares his or her work with the group, starting with the summary statement and ending with the prediction. The group should discuss and amend the summary as needed, use the text to answer the questions, examine the difficult part and add to the explanation, and discuss the prediction.

5. Repeat the teacher modeling of the strategies after reading the next section. Depending on time available and students' success with the procedure, you can continue to alternate teacher modeling and student practice through the remaining sections or have students work through subsequent sections as above, rotating tasks within the group so each student completes a different task each time.

53. Jigsaw

Objectives: To develop comprehension; to provide practice in using comprehension strategies in cooperative learning groups

Materials: Nonfiction text; expert sheets

Duration: 40–60 minutes

1. Before the lesson select a text, divide it into four sections, and prepare four different expert sheets numbered 1–4. The expert sheets are sets of 4–6 questions that will focus students' attention on the most important points in each section. Make sure you include not only recall questions, but also questions that invite higher-order thinking.

2. Begin the activity by explaining that everybody will be reading a text and be responsible for learning all the material. Add that each person will become an expert in one part of the text and will teach others about it.

3. Assign students to home groups of four or five members.

4. Distribute copies of the text to all students. Also distribute a different expert sheet to each student in a group. If there are more than four members in a home group, make sure that no more than two students receive the same expert sheet.

5. Have the class read the entire text. Instruct students that finish early to take notes on the section of the text that pertains to their expert sheet.

6. Reassign the students to one of four expert groups based on the number of their expert sheet.

7. Instruct the expert groups to discuss the questions on their expert sheets and take notes on the answers that the group offers to the questions. Encourage the students to clarify the material as best they can. Explain that each person in the group will be responsible for helping the others in their home group understand the material in the section to which the questions on the expert sheet pertain.

8. Circulate among the expert groups to make sure they stay on task and to provide help as needed.

9. When all the expert groups have answered their questions, have students return to their home groups. Each student should take about five minutes to present in the home group what she learned in the expert group. In addition to explaining the material in her section of the text, the expert should also ask and entertain questions from the group, to make sure everyone learned her piece of the text.

54. ReQuest Procedure

Objectives: To develop comprehension; to provide practice in asking higher-order thinking questions as a way of developing principled knowledge of the topic

Materials: Nonfiction text

Duration: 10–20 minutes

1. Select a text you want your students to read using this technique. To model the kinds of questions you want them to ask, read the first paragraph aloud and ask students to read along. Ask 3–4 questions about the paragraph (e.g., "What is the main idea of the paragraph?" "Why might this piece of information be important?" "How does this new information relate to…?" "How does this compare to…?") and have students answer them.

2. Have one student read the second paragraph aloud while the class and you read along. Have the student who has read aloud ask you questions about the paragraph. Answer those questions by referring to the text as much as possible.

3. Instruct the class to continue to read the text in pairs, paragraph by paragraph, taking turns at reading aloud and reading along. Tell them to stop after each paragraph, ask each other questions about it, and try to answer them as best they can. Encourage them to refer to the text to support their answers.

Variations: (1) When the students are familiar with the ReQuest procedure, assign them to groups of three and have them take turns reading aloud and asking and answering questions. (2) Use the Paired Reading/Paired Summarizing technique, in which the student who reads a paragraph aloud also summarizes it, while the other student asks questions that probe the meaning of the passage and that both students attempt to answer.

55. Using the Table of Contents to Predict

Objectives: Develop students' awareness of the value of the Table of Contents in guiding their reading of informational texts and help them become familiar with the structure and organization of these materials

Materials: An informational text that represents the type of texts students are reading in the content being studied. Either make copies of the Table of Contents (ToC) or display it on a screen. Create a set of questions that can be answered by perusing the ToC and print them on 3 × 5 cards. For example, if the book is about the ancient Egypt questions might include: Will this book tell about sports that were played and the kinds of teams they had? Will the book tell about gods and goddesses in ancient Egypt?; Will this book explain the roles of women in the society?; Will the book explain how King Tukankhamen was found and the kinds of artifacts that we have from his life?; Will the book explain how the ancient Egyptians wrote and kept records of their business and government? Do we have people who still practice the ancient religion of the Egyptians?

Duration: 10–15 minutes

1. Explain to students that you are thinking of including this book in the unit they are studying but you aren't sure if it is "just right" to extend their knowledge of the topic. You want them to preview the book by examining the ToC.

2. Display the ToC for the students to preview together.

3. Ask students what they think the author's purpose was in writing this book, and what focus they might expect. Ask: What questions do you think will be answered by this author? Are these the questions we have? Generate a few questions from the class.

4. Explain that you have also created a list of questions based on what you have heard from the students as they have been learning about this topic. Distribute the questions you have printed on the cards to partners and ask them to answer the question: Will this book help us find information about the question on your card? (Which chapter might include this information?)

5. Bring the class together to discuss what they learned. Ask if they have additional questions they think the book may answer that are also important.

6. Finally, guide them in making a decision about the appropriateness of this book for their unit of study.

7. If students show interest, ask if 1-2 would like to preview the actual book and report back to the class about their further examination.

Writing Activities

56. Shared Writing

Objectives: To engage students in composing a written text; to raise students' awareness of letter-sound relationships

Materials: Chart paper

Duration: 10–15 minutes

1. Choose a topic that the students are excited about (e.g., a field trip) and discuss it with the class.
2. Gather the students around an easel and ask them to help you write a few sentences about the topic.
3. Have students suggest the first sentence they want to write and have them say it several times so everyone is aware of the words.
4. Ask students to help you write the first word. Ask what the first sound in the word is, what letter needs to be written, etc.
5. Before you repeat step 4 for the second word, explain that you need to leave a blank space between the two words. Demonstrate the blank space by putting a finger after the first word.
6. Continue writing the sentence in this manner, inviting the students to come forward and supply the letters they can. Pronounce the sounds the children may skip and provide letters for them. If a child makes an error in writing, put a piece of correction tape over the error and help the children write the correct letter.

57. Sample Writing Lesson

Objectives: To teach the lay-out of print on the page, letter to sound correspondences, capitalization, and punctuation

Materials: A chalk board, white board, or chart paper and easel

Duration: 20 minutes

1. After discussing an exciting event with his students, gather young students around an easel or white board and invite them to help write about the event.
2. Get them to agree on a short sentence they want to write.
3. Have them practice saying the sentence several times so that everyone remembers the words.
4. Tell the students that they will write the first word and ask the students to name the first word they want to write, and then have them suggest letters to spell the word. Proceed by having the students name the words in order, sound out each word, and supply letters to spell each sound.
5. Correct mistakes by congratulating them on their efforts, and then pointing out the standard ways to spell the sounds.

58. Interactive Writing

Objectives: To help emergent and beginning readers and writers explore the writing system in its details

Materials: Chart paper

Duration: 15–20 minutes

1. Working with a medium-size group of students, begin by agreeing on a topic to write about. The topic might be a retelling of a story or a poem or a song, the daily news, or an idea that the class is studying.
2. Ask the children to offer a sentence about the topic.
3. Have them repeat the sentence many times and even count the words to fix them firmly in their minds.
4. Ask the children for the first word; then pronounce that word slowly, writing its letters.
5. Ask for the next word and invite a child up to write the whole word, a few letters, or a single letter. Fill in letters the children miss.

6. Point to the words and have the children read back the text. Repeat this step each time a word is added.

7. To help the children orient themselves to the text and add letters, you may write blanks where the letters should go.

8. Use correction tape to paste over letters that are poorly formed, and write them correctly.

9. As the lesson progresses, teach about words and print (remind children of words they know or almost know, remind them of spelling patterns they have seen before, remind them to leave spaces between words, and to add punctuation).

59. Pillowcase, or Me in a Box

Objectives: To introduce yourself to students by displaying objects representing aspects of your life; encourage discussion; provide springboard for personal writing

Materials: Pillowcase, bag, box, or similar container; objects representing your interests, family, pets, hobbies, and so forth, in a container

Duration: 5–10 minutes to share and discuss objects; extended time for discussion and/or writing

1. Collect a number of objects that represent things about you to share with students: for example, photos, sports trophy, dog toy, college banner, map, vacation postcards, and so forth. Put them in the container.

2. Explain that the objects you collected tell about you as a person. As you show each object, explain what it represents.

3. Have students write or dictate a few sentences about you based on what they learned.

4. Invite students to collect objects in the same way and tell the group about themselves. Schedule a few talks per day so students know when to bring in their things. (Remind them to get parents' permission before bringing anything valuable or personal to school.)

5. Have students use their collections to help them write about themselves.

Variations: Invite other teachers, the principal, or other school personnel to share in the same way. Have students draw self-portraits, or use a digital camera or school pictures from cumulative files to illustrate their writing. Collect the compositions in a class book. Display them in or outside the classroom. Make a "Students of the Week" bulletin board to display several students' writings at a time until all have been displayed. Create a web graphic organizer as you model this activity; write your name in the center, the objects in circles around it, and words or phrases explaining the objects projecting from the circles. Show how the web can help you organize your writing.

60. The Writing Workshop

Objectives: To familiarize students with the writing process

Materials: Notebooks

Duration: Sessions of 30–60 minutes scheduled at regular intervals over a longer period of time, with time set aside for five distinct activities in each session

1. *Rehearsing.* Have students think of what they might like to write about. You can do this in one of the ways listed below. For a–c, demonstrate how you yourself would settle on a topic.

   a. Have the students brainstorm possible topics. Optionally, have them create a graphic organizer, such as a cluster or semantic web, with the topic listed in the center connected to "satellites" around it.

   b. Have the students interview each other to find a story.

   c. Have the students research a topic before they write about it (by reading about it, by interviewing experts, or by doing an Internet search).

   d. Ask the students to compose one work together as a class before writing their own. This will allow you to help them if they have difficulty beginning.

2. *Drafting.* Have the students set out their ideas on paper, so they can see more of what they want to say about a topic. Tell them not to worry about spelling, punctuation, and handwriting at this stage. Remember to tell the students to write on every other line, so they can make subsequent changes to the draft.

3. *Revising.* Have students consider how their ideas can be stated more clearly. Teach revising skills through the following:

   a. Focused lessons on different aspects of writing, from word-choice issues such as showing, not telling, to composition-related issues such as ways to write strong introductions and closings. In one of the early focused lessons, show students how to use arrows, carets (^), and stapled-on sections to indicate on a draft how it should be rewritten. Remember to demonstrate how you would revise your own draft each time.

   b. Teacher-led conferences with groups or individual students. Ask students questions to help them focus on areas to improve their writing, and provide checklists of things to watch out for.

   c. Peer-led conferences. Put together a checklist of good questions to ask as students conference with each other, such as the following:
  - Did my opening lines interest you? How might I improve it?
  - Do I need more information anywhere? That is, where could I be more specific?
  - Do you ever get lost while reading my draft?
  - Do I stay on topic?
  - Do I come to a good conclusion?

4. *Editing.* Have the students check their revised drafts for spelling, punctuation, run-on sentences, and so forth.

5. *Publishing/Sharing of work in progress.* Choose two or three students to share who are far along in a draft or whose work displays an interesting issue. Different students should share each time. Model giving feedback to the writers and elicit comments from the class.

61. Descriptive Writing

Objectives: To familiarize students with the genre of descriptive writing; provide practice in descriptive writing

Materials: Excerpt from text that is vividly descriptive; paper bag containing a concrete object; journals or writing folders

Duration: 15–30 minutes depending on length of text excerpt and size of group

1. Select a descriptive passage, fiction or nonfiction, to read aloud. The passage should exemplify good descriptive writing.

2. Place an object in a paper bag for students to feel without looking at it. It should be small and light enough to be held in one hand, unusual enough so students may not recognize it instantly, and safe to feel without looking (no sharp edges, points, etc.).

3. Read the excerpt to the group. Invite students' comments about how the author used vivid descriptive language. Discuss the author's use of sensory words and images to create description.

4. Have students take turns silently feeling the object in the bag without looking at it. Caution them not to say what they think it is or what it feels like. After feeling the object, each one is to brainstorm and write in journals descriptive words or phrases to describe the object without naming it. Then they are to use their list of words to write descriptive sentences or a paragraph about the object, again without saying what it is.

5. Have students share their descriptive writing before naming the object.

Variations: Use senses other than touch to explore an object; with eyes closed, have students sniff objects like a sliced orange, blooming flower, cinnamon stick or other edible spice, school paste, ground coffee, pine or eucalyptus branch; listen to environmental or recorded sounds like wind, flowing water, heavy machinery, rain, surf, traffic; or taste safe and edible substances like toothpaste, coarse sugar, dry gelatin powder, baking chocolate, or pickles. Collect, or have students collect, small objects like keys, erasers, shells, bottle caps, or toys, and place one on each desk; give students a few minutes to write a complete description of the object, and then switch objects with someone else and repeat. Have students write what an object reminds them of rather than describing its physical features alone.

62. RAFT (Role, Audience, Format, Topic)

Objectives: To develop students' awareness of genres

Materials: Blank sheets of paper; newsprint

Duration: 40–60 minutes

1. After the students have studied a topic thoroughly, have them brainstorm 4–5 roles of people or characters that have a stake in the issue. Write down the roles on the chalkboard and have each student choose one role.

2. Assign students to groups based on their roles.

3. Explain that each group will write a message expressing their position on the issue.

4. Ask each group to choose an audience for their message out of the roles listed on the chalkboard.

5. Once all the groups have selected their audience, have them decide what format their message will take (a letter, a newspaper editorial, an advertisement, etc.).

6. Allow the groups about 15 minutes to write their message.

7. Have each group share their message with the class.

8. Engage the students in critiquing the messages. (Is the format appropriate for the targeted audience? Is the register appropriate for the audience? Is the message consistent with the characteristics of the role?)

Extension: Distribute the messages to students in the class. Instruct them to adopt the role of the audience and respond to the messages.

63. Story Maps for Writing

Objectives: To assist writers in planning a cohesive story

Materials: Blank story map on board, chart paper, or transparency; duplicated copies of the blank map for students to complete as they plan their stories

Duration: 5–15 minutes

1. On the board, chart paper, or a transparency, construct a story map containing elements similar to the following: Once there was a ____ named ____ who lived ____. He/she wanted ____. So he/she ____, but ____ (so he/she ____, but ____). Then, he/she ____. Finally, ____. So, ____. Leave plenty of space after each sentence starter.

2. Invite students to help you plan to write a story by suggesting elements to go in each blank space; for example, a boy named Sam who lived in a small apartment in the city, who wanted a dog, so he asked his parents … and so forth. Remind students that the story elements they suggest need to fit together to make sense. Select suggestions to write in the blanks that will make a meaningful story. To set off the sentence starters from the rest of the text, use a different color to complete the sentences.

3. Read through the completed story map, showing students where details could be added that would help readers visualize the story. Focus attention on the character's problem or goal, attempts to solve the problem or achieve the goal, and the final resolution of the conflict. Display the group story for students to refer to as they write.

4. Distribute blank story maps and have students generate their own stories, filling in the blanks to create a skeletal story. Allow time to share ideas and completed plans with partners or small groups.

5. Have students write their stories following their story maps. Encourage them to write several sentences or a paragraph after each sentence starter, to discourage them from recopying their maps as completed stories. Allow time for sharing of completed stories.

Variations: Before attempting to write a story solo, allow pairs to create a shared story after participating in the group story. Encourage students to revise, edit, and illustrate their stories, then display or publish them. Collect illustrated stories in a binder and place in the classroom library.

64. Form Poems

Objectives: To familiarize students with structured poems; increase students' awareness of how form and meaning can shape each other in poetry

Materials: Examples of form poems

Duration: 10–20 minutes

1. Show the students an example of a well-written poem that follows the form. (You might need to write this yourself or save it from a previous class.)

2. Discuss the formal characteristics of the poem with the class.

3. Have the students help you create a poem as a group. Discuss each choice they make so they understand the process well.

4. Have individuals or pairs write their own poems.

5. Share several of the poems, and discuss their qualities. Also call attention to the ways in which the poems followed the structure.

6. Talk about why a writer might choose to write a poem structured that way.

7. Make a wall chart in which you feature several of the students' poems; also outline the procedures for writing a poem with the structure in question.

Activities for English Language Learners

65. Language Experience with English Language Learners

Objectives: To help English language learners develop English fluency, print concepts, sight word recognition, and phonemic awareness

Materials: An object, photograph, shared experience, shared literature, or other stimulus; chalkboard, chart tablet, or transparency; marker

Duration: 10–30 minutes; additional time for follow-up activities

1. Select an individual student or a group of English language learners.

2. Select a topic for dictation: an interesting concrete object, classroom pet, familiar story for retelling, recent classroom event, and so forth. Younger students benefit from a concrete or immediate stimulus, whereas older students can talk about past events, friends, families, and other more abstract topics. Encourage students to select topics.

3. Explain that you can write what students say, that they can learn to read what was written, and that learning words in these sentences will help them learn to read and write many other words.

4. Invite discussion of the stimulus, encouraging students to use as elaborated language as they can. Ask open-ended questions that encourage extended answers. If students give brief or incomplete sentences, model elaborated language using their words: S: "Green. Fuzzy." T: "It's green and fuzzy."

5. Ask for volunteers to contribute sentences for the dictation.

6. Write students' sentences, allowing changes or additions. If you want students to learn to read each other's names, include their names in the text. Print neatly with clear spaces between each word.

7. Read the completed story expressively and at a natural pace, pointing to each word as you read.

8. Reread the story chorally several times until students have memorized it. Continue pointing to each word. (Keep up the pace so the reading sounds natural, not word by word.) If students have trouble memorizing the whole text, divide it into sections of two or three sentences each.

9. Invite volunteers to come to the chart and recite a part or the whole story while pointing to each word. Continue until each student who volunteers has read the story individually.

10. Point to individual words and invite students to identify the words, reading from the beginning to the target word if necessary.

Follow-Up Activities for English Language Learners

1. Repeat choral and individual reading and pointing on subsequent days until students can read the story fluently and point accurately. (Older students can reread and point using duplicated copies of the story rather than at a chart.)

2. Copy each sentence onto a sentence strip. Have volunteers hold up each strip in correct order. (These can also be used for independent practice with a hanging pocket chart.)

3. Create exact copies of the story on copy paper. Duplicate several copies for each student. Students can paste copies on construction paper or in journals and illustrate them, cut lines and sentences apart and put them in correct order, cut sentences into phrases and put them in correct order, and use sentences for handwriting practice.

4. Have students find individual words they recognize in isolation and begin building individual word banks with known words on cards. Students should sort and review word banks daily.

5. Have students sort words in their word banks in a variety of ways: matching beginning sounds, number of syllables, alphabetical order, words that are related by meaning, and so forth.

6. Select one or several familiar words beginning with consonants. Using individual letter cards or magnetic letters, show students how to "make and break" the words by removing the initial letter or sound and substituting another, creating new words.

7. Students can write known sight words using magnetic letters on cookie sheets, individual letters cut out of sandpaper, wallpaper scraps, felt, glue and sand or glitter, pipe cleaners, gel pens, macaroni letters, letters cut from magazines, and so forth. They can also search for known words in newspaper and magazine ads and headlines, and cut them out.

8. Begin personal dictionaries by folding eight to ten sheets of paper vertically and stapling in the fold to create individual books. Have students write a letter at the top of each page (group infrequent letters like *q*, *u*, *x*, *y*, and *z* with others) and begin collecting mastered sight words in their dictionaries.

9. As students' word banks grow, have them construct sentences with word cards.

66. Cumulative Semantic Map

Objectives: To foster vocabulary growth; help students learn meanings of related words

Materials: Large paper chart that can be displayed and added to periodically

Duration: 5–15 minutes each time new words are added

1. Have students begin collecting words that are related by meaning: for example, synonyms, color words, action words, and so forth.

2. Construct a web graphic organizer on the chart, with one or more general categories in the center and related words radiating from them. For example, a cumulative semantic web on temperature words might show HOT and COLD in central circles, with various temperature words attached to them: *burning, boiling, sizzling, blistering, icy, freezing, frigid, polar,* and so forth.

3. As students encounter related words in their reading, or as you encounter such words in literature you read to them, return to the web and have students suggest where such words might be added or where new categories might be entered. For example, a new category of WARM words could be added, to include *comfortable, mild, tepid,* and *lukewarm.*

4. Encourage students to use words from the charts in their writing and to continue to watch for words that could be added to the collection.

67. Word Origins and Derivations

Objectives: To develop vocabulary; teach meanings of bases and affixes to help students figure out meanings of unfamiliar words; engage students in language learning

Materials: Space for word walls, charts, and bulletin board words; paper and markers; resource materials (dictionaries that include word histories, thesauruses, books on idioms, etc.)

Duration: 10–15 minutes several times weekly

1. Encourage students to begin collecting words they need to learn for subject areas and interesting or unfamiliar words they encounter during reading. Have them copy the sentence in which the word occurs, or share the text, so they can practice using context as a meaning clue. Make a word wall or chart of student-selected words, their context sentences, and meanings.

2. Teach vocabulary words in groups that have a shared base or affix; for example, *ex* (out): *exhale, exclaim, expand, exorcise, expectorate, exfoliate, explode, expire; in-/im-/il-*(not): *illiterate, illogical, illegal, illegible, immature, imbalance, impassable, immortal, incapable, inappropriate, inaudible, inconvenient.* Create word families and add new words as students encounter them.

3. Teach the meanings of the Latin and Greek bases or stems that have consistent meanings: for example, *photo* (light), *graph* (write), *mega* (large), *cap* (head), *corp* (body), *ped* (foot), *manu* (hand), *scrib* (write), *retro* (backward), poly (many), *phone* (sound), *mono* (single), *bi* (two), *tri* (three), *cent* (hundred). Draw attention to these word parts and their meanings whenever they occur.

4. Avoid having students copy dictionary definitions, which they rarely understand. Instead, have them predict a word's meaning from word parts they know and context sentences before looking it up. Have them write meanings in their own words rather than a dictionary definition.

5. Have students divide word cards into three sections to include (a) the word, (b) its meaning in their own words, and (c) synonyms and opposites. On the back have them draw a sketch that illustrates the meaning, and write a caption for the drawing.

6. Limit the number of new words students have to learn each week; teach a group of related words and have students really learn fewer words rather than superficially memorize a long list.

68. Visualization

Objectives: To develop comprehension; model and practice visualizing or mentally seeing images a writer creates with words

Materials: Shared text; reading journals or literature logs; duplicated copies of the text that students can draw on; sticky notes; pencils

Duration: 5 minutes or less at various points in a text

1. Copy a short (1–2 paragraphs) excerpt of vivid or descriptive text onto the board, chart paper, or a transparency. Explain that you will model what good readers do as they visualize text.

2. Read the passage expressively; as you read it, pause and think aloud by telling students what you are mentally seeing or imagining. Mark the words, phrases, or sentences that are particularly vivid to you. Make a quick sketch in the margin that represents what you are visualizing, and explain what it means to you.

3. Distribute duplicated copies of similar text or portions of a text students are reading together. Read aloud a short section while students follow along. Have volunteers say what they visualized as you read, following your model. Have all students sketch in the margin as above, or distribute sticky notes and have students sketch on them and place them over or near the appropriate sections. Ask each student to tell briefly what they drew; they do not need to display the drawings because they are a sort of personal code.

4. In later lessons, students can write ("jot") what they are visualizing, using brief phrases, in addition to or instead of sketching. Students may prefer one method over the other; neither one is "better."

Variations: As students read longer or more difficult passages, encourage them to use the "jot" or "sketch" methods independently to help them visualize by making sticky notes available during reading, by having them jot or sketch in their reading journals at the end of each day's reading, and by periodically repeating the activity with different kinds of text. Use visualization in combination with the Think-Pair-Share activity; after visualizing and drawing, each student shares with a single partner and then each pair with another pair. Encourage students to use sketches, drawings, or cutout magazine pictures to illustrate their writing about what they are reading.

69. Using Questions to Teach English Language Learners

Objectives: Vocabulary development; to help students learning English to acquire words, follow directions, and converse with others

Materials: Props to talk about: magazine pictures, picture cards, small objects like keys, toy cars, plastic fruit and other foods from children's kitchen toys, puppets, stuffed animals, and so forth

Duration: 5–15 minutes or longer, depending on students' age, English fluency, and size of group

1. Select a group of students who are similar in English fluency. Gather pictures or props to use.

2. Determine the general fluency level of students and plan the activity to meet their English abilities: preproduction, where students understand a few words but speak little; early production, where students understand simple sentences and produce very short utterances; or speech emergence, where students understand many words and sentences and produce longer, more varied sentences.

3. For preproduction students, use very simple, repetitive sentences accompanied by gesture and sound effects: "This is an apple. Is it red? Yes, it's red. Is it green? No, not green." "Can Maria hold the apple? Yes, she can. Can Nguyen hold the apple? Yes, he can. Can I hold the apple? Yes, I can." "Who has a frog? Juan has a frog. Who has a bird? Irma has a bird."

4. For early production students, use questions that require short answers, including yes/no, here/there, either/or, how many …, what color …, and common prepositions like in/out/under: "Is this a dog or a bird? What color is the bird? Do you like birds?" "Is this the mother or the father? Where is the baby? How many children are there?"

5. For speech emergence students, ask questions requiring longer answers, description, and simple sentences. Use wordless picture books, tell what is happening on each page, and ask students to retell. Read simple versions of stories several times, and have students retell or act out the stories using puppets or a flannel board. Play direction-following games like Simon Says, and have students give each other directions to follow: Stand behind your chair; open and close the door; raise your left hand. Practice naming objects: foods, clothing, tools, vehicles, classroom objects, colors, temperature words, animals, family members, areas of the school and home, and people (teacher, principal, nurse, bus driver).

70. Inductive Phonics Lesson in Spanish

In a simple three-step inductive lesson structure, the first step of auditory discrimination serves to verify students' phonological awareness of the sound stated in the objective of the lesson. Phonics in Spanish is usually taught with a focus on syllables, as it is in this lesson. If the students are not successful in this first step, substitute phonological awareness activities for the second and third steps of the lesson. If the students are successful, as they usually will be in the first grade, proceed to the second stage of the lesson, which is to verify that the students can already read the sight words used in the first stage of the lesson and also indicate that they recognize the letter and its position in the words.

The third stage, associating the new sound with the letters, is the key step in the lesson. The students who can correctly pronounce the letters or syllable indicated in the objective in unknown words in the association stage should be able to use that skill to recognize and pronounce that sound in the same position in other unknown words.

Many of the children will be able to state a rule or generalization when asked how they know how to pronounce the target sound in the unknown word. A 6-year-old's rule might be a statement that he or she remembered other known words with that letter in the same position, thought about how it sounded in those words, and pronounced it that way in the new word. The purpose of the extra stimulus question ("If that word is 'cola,' what is this word? 'Bala.'") is for the teacher to provide the part of the word that is not the subject of the lesson objective—only the initial syllable /*ba*/ is of interest.

This model lesson is inductive in that you ask questions that lead children to think about what they already know about sounds, letters, and words. You do not tell or explain. Many children will not be able to state a rule or generalization at the beginning of this type of inductive lesson, although most will be able to correctly pronounce the target element in the words. But after a number of lessons, increasing numbers of children will be able to formulate a rule. These generalizations will be remembered and applied more easily if the children derive them. If the teacher provides them in a direct instruction activity, then the child must rely on memory to recall the rule later. When children learn to derive their own rules, they can transfer this ability to new unknown words. They can also transfer this generalized ability to English.

The instructional time required for the model lesson presented below should be about five minutes, certainly less than 10 minutes. Most instructional activities in beginning reading in Spanish should focus on comprehension through shared reading and, later, in small-group lessons in which children are reading in a directed or guided reading mode.

Clearly, this type of phonics lesson must be taught by a Spanish-speaking teacher.

Inductive Phonics Lesson Plan in Spanish

Objetivo: pronunciar el sonido inicial de palabras nuevas que empiecen con la sílaba /ba/

Materiales didácticos: pizarra o caballete con papel; lista de seis a ocho palabras con la sílaba /ba/ ya conocidas por los estudiantes; otra lista de unas tres a cuatro nuevas palabras con este elemento

Horario: 5 a 10 minutos

1. *Etapa de discriminacíon auditiva (verificar conciencia fonémica)*
   "Les voy a decir tres palabras. Escuchen bien."
       bajo   baño   bate   [Oralmente, pero no escritas en la pizarra.]
   "¿Cómo se parecen? ¿Qué tienen en común?"
   "¿En qué parte de cada palabra se encuentra este sonido?"
   "Les voy a decir tres otras palabras. ¿Cuál no pertenece a este grupo?"
       ballena   mesa   barra   [Oralmente, pero no escritas en la pizarra.]
   "¿Cuál es diferente? ¿Por qué? ¿Cómo es diferente? ¿En qué parte?"
   "¿Qué otras cosas pueden ver en el salón que empiecen con el mismo sonido?"

2. *Etapa de discriminación visual*

"Vamos a leer tres palabras."

"Levanta la mano si quieres leer la primera palabra." "La segunda." "La tercera."

   bajo,   baño,   bate   [Las palabras son escritas en la pizarra.]

"Muy bien."

"¿Cómo se parecen estas tres palabras?"

"¿En qué parte de las palabras se encuentra la letra?"

3. *Etapa de asociación*

"Ahora quiero que lean algunas palabras nuevas. ¿Quién quiere tratar de leer la primera palabra nueva? ¿Cómo sabías leerla?" Si no pueden leer una palabra entera, pregunta: "¿Cómo empieza la palabra?" O, "¿cuál es el primer sonido de la palabra?"

   bala   base   barra   ballena [Las palabras son escritas en la pizarra.]

"Si esa palabra dice 'cola,' ¿qué dice esta palabra?"   "bala"

[Las dos palabras 'cola' y 'bala' son escritas en la pizarra.]

"¿Cómo sabían eso?"

[Las palabras cola y bala son escritas en la pizarra.]

References

Abedi, J. (2002). Assessment and accommodations of English language learners: Issues, concerns, and recommendations. *Journal of School Improvement 3*(1), 83–89.

Abedi, J. (2004). The No Child Left Behind Act and English language learners: Assessment and accountability issues. *Educational Researcher 33*(1), 4–14.

Abedi, J., Hofstetter, C. H., & Lord, C. (2004). Assessment accommodations for English language learners: Implications for policy-based empirical research. *Review of Educational Research 74*(1), 1–28.

Abedi, J., & Lord, C. (2001). The language factor in mathematics tests. *Applied Measurement in Education 14*(3), 219–234.

Acheson, D. J., Wells, J. B., & MacDonald, M. C. (2008). New and updated tests of print exposure and reading abilities in college students. *Behavior Research Methods, 40*(1), 278–289.

Achieve. (2010). Understanding *the K–12 Common Core State Standards in English Language Arts and Literacy in History/Social Studies, Science, and Technical Subjects*. Washington, DC: Author. Retrieved from http://www.achieve.org/files/AchievingCCSS-ELAFINAL.pdf

Achilles, C. M. (1999). *Let's put kids first, finally: Getting class size right*. Thousand Oaks, CA: Corwin Press.

Akhondi, M., Malayeri, F. A., & Samad, A. A. (2011). How to teach expository text structure to facilitate reading comprehension. *The Reading Teacher, 64*(5), 368–372.

Alexander, P. A. (1998). The nature of disciplinary and domain learning: The knowledge, interest and strategic dimensions of learning from subject matter text. In C. Hynd (Ed.), *Learning from text across conceptual domains*. Mahwah, NJ: Erlbaum.

Alexander, P. A., & Jetton, T. L. (2000). Learning from text: A multidimensional and developmental perspective. In M. L. Kamil, P. B. Mosenthal, P. D. Pearson, & R. Barr (Eds.), *Handbook of reading research: Vol. III* (pp. 285–310). Mahwah, NJ: Erlbaum.

Alexander, P. A., Jetton, T. L., Kulikowich, J. M., & Woehler, C. (1994). Contrasting instructional and structural importance: The seductive effect of teacher questions. *Journal of Reading Behavior, 26*, 19–45.

Allard, H. (1977). *Miss Nelson is missing!* Illustrated by J. Marshall. Boston, MA: Houghton Mifflin.

Allington, R. L. (1983). Fluency: The neglected reading goal. *The Reading Teacher, 36*(6), 556–561.

Allington, R. L. (1983). The reading instruction provided to readers of differing reading ability. *Elementary School Journal, 83*, 549–558.

Allington, R. L. (1997). Overselling phonics. *Reading Today, 14*, 15.

Allington, R. L., (2011). What Really Matters to Struggling Readers, 3rd edition.

Allington, R. L. (2008*). What really matters in response to intervention*. Boston, MA: Allyn & Bacon.

Allington, R. L. (2014). How reading volume affects both reading fluency and reading achievement. *International Electronic Journal of Elementary Education 7*(1), 13–26.

Allington, R. L., & Johnson, P. H. (2002). *Reading to learn: Lessons from exemplary fourth-grade classrooms*. New York, NY: Guilford Press.

Allington, R. L., & Walmsley, S. A. *No quick fix: Rethinking programs in America's elementary schools* (1995, 2007 [preface]). Newark, DE: International Reading Association.

Almasi, J. F. (1995). The nature of fourth graders' socio-cognitive conflicts in peer-led and teacher-led discussions of literature. *Reading Research Quarterly, 30*(3), 314–351.

Anderson, J. (2005). *Mechanically inclined: Building grammar, usage, and style into writer's workshop*. Portland, ME: Stenhouse.

Anderson, R. C., & Pearson, P. D. (1984). A schema-theoretic view of basic processes in reading. In P. D. Pearson (Ed.), *Handbook of reading research*. New York, NY: Longman.

Anderson, R. C., Wilson, P. T., & Fielding, L. (1988). Growth in reading and how children spend their time outside of school. *Reading Research Quarterly, 23*, 285–303.

Andrade, H. G. (2002). *Understanding rubrics*. Retrieved from http://learnweb.harvard.edu/ALPS/thinking/docs/rubricar.htm

Archambault, J., & Martin, B. Jr. (1989). *White dynamite and the curly kid*. Illustrated by Ted Rand. New York, NY: Henry Holt.

Arellano Osuna, A. (1992). *El lenguaje integral: Una alternativa para la educación*. Mérida, Venezuela: Editorial Venezolana.

Armbruster, B. B., Lehr, F., & Osborn, J. (2001). *Put reading first: The research building blocks for teaching children to read. Kindergarten through grade 3*. Washington, DC: National Institute for Literacy.

Asher, J. J. (1982). The total physical response approach. In R. W. Blair (Ed.), *Innovative approaches to language teaching* (pp. 54–66). Rowley, MA: Newbury House.

Ashton-Warner, S. (1963). *Teacher.* New York, NY: Simon & Schuster.

Atwell, N. (1988). *In the middle,* 2nd edition. Portsmouth, NH: Heinemann.

August, D., Snow, C. E., Carlo, M., Proctor, C. P., Rolla de San Francisco, A., Duursma, E., et al. (2006). Literacy development in elementary school second-language learners. *Topics in Language Disorders, 26*(4), 351–364.

Baker, C., & Sienkewicz, A. (2000). *The care and education of young bilinguals: An introduction for young professionals.* Cleveland, U.K.: Multilingual Matters.

Banks, J. A. (2008). *Teaching strategies for ethnic studies.* Boston, MA: Pearson.

Barbosa Heldt, A. (1971). *Cómo han aprendido a leer y a escribir los mexicanos.* Mexico City, Mexico: Editorial Pax México, Librería Carlos Cesarmán.

Barger, J. (2003). *Comparing the DIBELS Oral Reading Fluency indicator and the North Carolina end of grade reading assessment* (Tech. Rep.). Asheville, NC: North Carolina Teacher Academy.

Barker, C. (2006). *How many syllables does English have?* Retrieved from http://ling.ucsd.edu/%7Ebarker/Syllables/index.txt

Barone, D. (1992). That reminds me of . . .: Using dialogue journals with young readers. In C. Temple & P. Collins (Eds.), *Stories and readers: New perspectives on literature in the elementary classroom.* Norwood, MA: Christopher-Gordon.

Barone, D., Hardman, D., & Taylor, J. (2006). *Reading first in the classroom.* New York, NY: Pearson.

Bauer, E. B., & Manyak, P. C. (2008). Creating language-rich instruction for English-language learners. *The Reading Teacher, 62*(2), 176–178.

Baumann, J., Kame'enui, E., & Ash, G. (2003). Research on vocabulary instruction: Voltaire redux. In J. Flood, D. Lapp, J. Squire, & J. Jensen (Eds.), *Handbook of research on teaching the English language arts* (2nd ed.). Mahwah, NJ: Erlbaum.

Baumann, J. F. (2009). Vocabulary and reading comprehension: The nexus of meaning. In S. E. Israel & G. G. Duffy (Eds.), *Handbook of research on reading comprehension* (pp. 323–346). New York, NY: Routledge.

Bean, R., & Lillenstein, J. (2012). Response to intervention and the changing roles of schoolwide personnel. *The Reading Teacher, 65*(7), 491–501.

Beane, J. (2002). Beyond self-interest: A democratic core curriculum. *Educational Leadership, 59,* 25–28.

Bear, D. R., Invernizzi, M., Templeton, S., & Johnston, F. (2007). *Words their way: Word study for phonics, vocabulary, and spelling instruction* (4th ed.). Englewood Cliffs, NJ: Prentice Hall.

Beck, I. L., & McKeown, M. G. (2001). Text Talk: Capturing the benefits of read-aloud experiences for young children. *The Reading Teacher, 55*(1), 10–20.

Beck, I. L., & McKeown, M. (2007). Increasing young low-income children's oral vocabulary repertoires through rich and focused instruction. *The Elementary School Journal, 107,* 251–271.

Beck, I. L., McKeown, M. G., Hamilton, R. L., & Kucan, L. (1997). *Questioning the author: An approach for enhancing student engagement with text.* Newark, DE: International Reading Association.

Beck, I. L., McKeown, M. G., & Kucan, L. (2002). *Bringing words to life: Robust vocabulary instruction.* New York, NY: Guilford Press.

Beck, I. L., McKeown, M. G., & Kucan, L. (2013). *Bringing words to life: Robust vocabulary instruction* (2nd ed.). New York, NY: Guilford.

Beck, I. L., McKeown, M. G., & Kucan, L. (2013). Exit talk: Capturing the benefits of read-aloud experiences for young children. *The Reading Teacher, 55*(1), 10–20.

Beck, I. L., & Sandora, C. (2016). *Illuminating comprehension and close reading.* New York, NY: Guilford.

Berger, M., & Berger, G. (1999). *Chomp! A book about sharks.* New York, NY: Cartwheel.

Berger, M., & Berger, G. (2002). *Snap! A book about alligators and crocodiles.* New York, NY: Scholastic.

Berger, M., & Berger, G. (2009). *Scholastic true or false: Dangerous animals.* New York, NY: Scholastic Reference.

Berthoff, A. (1981). *The making of meaning: Metaphors, models, and maxims for writing teachers.* Portsmouth, NH: Heinemann.

Betts, A. E. (1946). *Foundations of reading instruction, with emphasis on differentiated guidance.* Chicago, IL: American Book Company.

Biancarosa, G. (2012). Adolescent literacy: More than remediation. *Educational Leadership, 69*(6), 22–27.

Biemiller, A. (2009). Vocabulary development (0–60 months). In L. M. Phillips (Ed.), *Handbook of language and literacy development: A Roadmap from 0–60 Months.* [online], pp. 1–42. London, ON: Canadian Language and Literacy Research Network.

Bishop, R. S. (1999). Mirrors, windows, and sliding glass doors. Retrieved from https://www.psdschools.org/webfm/8559

Blachman, B. (2000). *Road to the code.* Baltimore, MD: Paul H. Brookes Publishing Company.

Blachman, B., & Tangle, D. M. (2008). *Road to reading: A program for preventing and remediating reading difficulties.* Baltimore, MD: Paul Brookes.

Blachowicz, C. L. Z., & Fisher, P. (2000). Vocabulary instruction. In M. L. Kamil, P. Mosenthal, P. D.

Pearson, & R. Barr (Eds.), *Handbook of reading research* (Vol. 3). New York, NY: Longman.

Blachowicz, C. L. Z., & Fisher, P. (2014). Best practices in vocabulary instruction. In L. Morrow & L. Gambrell (Eds.), *Best practices in literacy instruction* (5th ed.). New York, NY: Guilford.

Blachowicz, C. L. Z., & Fisher, P. (2014). *Teaching vocabulary in all classrooms*. New York: Pearson.

Blachowicz, C. L. Z., Fisher, P., Ogle, D., & Watts-Taff, S. (2006). Vocabulary: Questions from the classroom. *Reading Research Quarterly, 41*(4), 524–539.

Blachowicz, C. L. Z., Fisher, P., Ogle, D., & Watts-Taff, S. (2013). *Teaching academic vocabulary K–8.* New York, NY: Guilford Press.

Bleich, D. (1970). *Subjective criticism.* Baltimore, MD: Johns Hopkins University Press.

Bleich, D. (1975). *Readings and feelings: An introduction to subjective criticism.* Urbana, IL: NCTE.

Booth, D., & Schwartz, L. (2004). *Literacy strategies.* Portland, ME: Stenhouse Publishers.

Bormuth, J. R. (1968, Autumn). Cloze test readability: Criterion reference scores. *Journal of Educational Measurement, 5*(3), 189–196.

Bornstein, D. (2011, May 16). A book in every home, and then some. *New York Times.* Retrieved from http://opinionator.blogs.nytimes.com/2011/05/16/a-book-in-every-home-and-then-some/.

Bos, C. S., & Anders, P. L. (1989). Developing higher level thinking skills through interactive teaching. *Journal of Reading, Writing, and Learning Disabilities International, 4*(4), 259–274.

Bos, C., & Anders, P. (1990, Winter). Effects of interactive vocabulary instruction on the vocabulary learning and reading comprehension of junior-high learning disabled students. *Learning Disability Quarterly, 13*(1), 31–42.

Botkin, B. A. (1944). "The Tailypo." In *A treasury of American folklore.* New York, NY: Crown.

Bradley, L., & Bryant, P. (1985). *Rhyme and reason in reading and spelling.* Ann Arbor: University of Michigan Press.

Brenner, B. (1992). *Group soup.* New York, NY: Viking.

Briceño, A. (2016). Emergent bilingual readers: Making meaning from print in Spanish and English. *The California Reader, 49*(2), 20–25.

Britton, J. (1970). *Language and learning.* Harmondsworth, England: Penguin Books.

Bromley, K. (1999). Key components of sound writing instruction. In L. Gambrell, L. Mandell Morrow, S. B. Neuman, & M. Pressley (Eds.), *Best practices in literacy instruction* (pp. 152–174). New York, NY: Guilford Press.

Brooks, W. M. (2005). Reading linguistic features: Middle school students' response to the African American literary tradition. In B. Hammond, M. E. Rhodes Hoover, & McPhail, I. P. (Eds.), *Teaching African American learners to read* (pp. 253–263). Newark, DE: International Reading Association.

Brooks, W. M. (2006). Reading representations of themselves: Urban youth use culture and African American textual features to develop literary understandings. *Reading Research Quarterly, 41*(3), 372–392.

Brown, M. (1947). *Stone soup.* New York, NY: Aladdin Paperback.

Brown, M. (1949). *The important book.* New York, NY: Harper.

Brown, R. (1955). *Words and things.* Garden City, NY: Basic Books.

Brozo, W. G. (2010). *To be a boy, to be a reader: Engaging teen and preteen boys in active literacy.* Newark, DE: International Reading Association.

Buck, J., & Torgesen, J. (2003). *The relationship between performance on a measure of oral reading fluency and performance on the Florida Comprehensive Assessment Test* (FCRR Tech. Rep. #1). Tallahassee, FL: Florida Center for Reading Research.

Buehl, D. (2001). *Classroom strategies for interactive learning* (2nd ed.). Newark, DE: International Reading Association.

Burnette II, D. (2016). ESSA poses capacity challenges for state education agencies. *Education Week.* Retrieved from http://www.edweek.org/ew/articles/2016/01/20/essa-poses-capacity-challenges-for-state-education.html

Butler, A., & Turbill, J. (1985). *Towards a reading-writing classroom.* Portsmouth, NH: Heinemann.

Cain, K., Oakhhill, J., & Bryant, P. E. (2004). Children's reading comprehension ability: Concurrent prediction by working memory verbal ability and component skills. *Journal of Educational Psychology, 96*(1), 31–42.

Calkins, L. (1994). *The art of teaching writing.* Portsmouth, NH: Heinemann.

Carle, E. (1987). *The very hungry caterpillar.* New York, NY: Philomel Books.

Carlisle, J. F. (2000). Awareness of the structure and meaning of morphologically complex words: Impact on reading. *Reading and Writing: An Interdisciplinary Journal, 12,* 169–190.

Carlisle, J. F., & Katz, L. A. (2006). Effects of word and morpheme familiarity on reading of derived words. *Reading and Writing, 19,* 669–693.

Carlisle, J. F., & Stone, C. A. (2005). Exploring the role of morphemes in word reading. *Reading Research Quarterly, 40,* 428–449.

Carlo, M., August, D., & Snow, C. E. (2005). Sustained vocabulary learning strategy for English-language learners. In E. H. Hiebert & M. L. Kamil (Eds.), *Teaching and learning vocabulary: Bringing research to practice* (pp. 137–154). Mahwah, NJ: Erlbaum.

Carr, E. M., & Ogle, D. (1987). K-W-L Plus: A strategy for comprehension and summarization. *Journal of Reading, 30,* 626–631. *Castañeda v. Pickard,* 648 F.2d 989, 5th Circuit (1981).

CATESOL. (1992). *Position statement on specially-designed academic instruction in English* (sheltered instruction). Orinda: California Teachers of English to Speakers of Other Languages.

Center on International Education Benchmarking. (2012). Statistic of the month: Resilient students in PISA 2012. Retrieved from http://www.ncee .org/2013/12/statistic-of-the-month-resilient -students-in-pisa-2012/

Chall, J. (1967). *Learning to read: The great debate* (Rev. ed.). New York, NY: McGraw-Hill.

Chin, J. (2009). *Redwoods.* New York, NY: Roaring Brook Press.

Christ, T., & Wang, X. C. (2011). Closing the vocabulary gap? A review of research on early childhood vocabulary practices. *Reading Psychology 32*(5), 426–458.

Clay, M. M. (1975). *What did I write?* Portsmouth, NH: Heinemann.

Clay, M. M. (1985). *The early detection of reading difficulties: A diagnostic survey with recovery procedures.* Portsmouth, NH: Heinemann.

Clay, M. M. (1993). *An observational survey of early literacy achievement.* Portsmouth, NH: Heinemann.

Clay, M. M. (1993). *Reading recovery: A guidebook for teachers in training.* Portsmouth, NH: Heinemann.

Cleary, B. (1997). *Ramona and her father.* New York, NY: Harper Trophy.

Coiro, J., & Dobler, E. (2007). Exploring the online reading comprehension strategies used by sixth-grade skilled readers to search for and locate information on the Internet. *Reading Research Quarterly, 42,* 214–257.

Coleman, J. S., Campbell, E. Q., Hobson, C. J., McPartland, J., Mood, A. M., Weinfeld, F. D., & York, R. L. (1966). *Equality of educational opportunity.* Washington, DC: U.S. Government Printing Office.

Collier, V. P. (1987). Age and rate of acquisition of second language for academic purposes. *TESOL Quarterly, 21,* 617–641.

Collier, V. P. (1989). How long? A synthesis of research on academic achievement in a second language. *TESOL Quarterly, 23,* 509–539.

Collins, A., Brown, J. S., & Newman, S. E. (1987, January). *Cognitive apprenticeship: Teaching the craft of reading, writing and mathematics* (Technical Report No. 403). BBN Laboratories, Cambridge, MA. Center for the Study of Reading, University of Illinois.

Collins, J. L. (1998). *Strategies for struggling writers.* New York, NY: Guilford Press.

Collins, M. F. (2005). ESL preschoolers' English vocabulary acquisition from storybook reading. *Reading Research Quarterly, 40*(4), 406–408.

Common Core State Standard Initiative. (2010). *Common Core State Standards for English Language Arts & Literacy in History/ Social Studies, Science, and Technical Subjects.* Washington, DC: CCSSO & National Governors Association.

Conrad, P. (1992). *Pedro's journal.* New York, NY: Scholastic.

Cowhey, M. (2006). *Black ants and Buddhists.* Portland, ME: Stenhouse.

Coxhead, A. (2000). The learning and use of academic English words. *Language Learning, 47*(4), 671–718.

Coyle, D., Hood, P., & Marsh, D. (2010). *CLIL: Content and Language Integrated Learning.* Cambridge, U.K.: Cambridge University Press.

Crawford, A. N. (1993). Literature, integrated language arts, and the language minority child: A focus on meaning. In A. Carrasquillo & C. Hedley (Eds.), *Whole language and the bilingual learner* (pp. 61–75). Norwood, NJ: Ablex.

Crawford, A. N. (1994). Communicative approaches to second language acquisition: From oral language development into the core curriculum and L$_2$ literacy. In C. F. Leyba (Ed.), *Schooling and language minority students: A theoretical framework* (2nd ed., pp. 79–121). Los Angeles, CA: California State University, Los Angeles, Evaluation, Dissemination and Assessment Center.

Crawford, A. N. (1995). Language policy, second language learning, and literacy. In A. N. Crawford (Ed.), *A practical guidebook for adult literacy programmes in developing nations* (pp. 9–16). Paris: UNESCO.

Crawford, A. N. (2003). Communicative approaches to second language acquisition: The bridge to second language literacy. In G. García (Ed.), *English learners: Reaching the highest level of English literacy* (pp. 152–181). Newark, DE: International Reading Association.

Crawford, A. N. (2015). *Guidebook on Content and Language Integrated Learning (CLIL).* Astana, Kazakhstan: Nazarbayev Intellectual Schools (NIS).

Crawford, A. N., Allen, R. V., & Hall, M. (1995). The language experience approach. In A. N. Crawford (Ed.), *A practical guidebook for adult literacy programs in developing nations* (pp. 17–46). Paris: UNESCO.

Crawford, A. N., Saul, E., & Mathews, S. (2005). *Teaching and learning lessons for the thinking classroom.* New York, NY: Central European University Press.

Crawford, A. N., Saul, W., Mathews, S., & MaKinster, J. (2005). *Lessons from the thinking classroom.* New York, NY: IDEA.

Crawford, J. (1989). *Bilingual education: History, politics, theory and practice.* Trenton, NJ: Crane.

Cummins, J. (1980). The construct of language proficiency in bilingual education. In J. E. Alatis (Ed.), *Georgetown University roundtable on languages and linguistics* (pp. 76–93). Washington, DC: Georgetown University Press.

Cummins, J. (1981). The role of primary language development in promoting educational success for language minority students. In California State Department of Education (Ed.), *Schooling and language minority students: A theoretical framework* (pp. 3–49). Los Angeles, CA: California State University, Los Angeles, Evaluation, Dissemination and Assessment Center.

Cummins, J. (1986). Empowering minority students: A framework for intervention. *Harvard Educational Review, 56,* 18–36.

Cummins, J. (1989). *Empowering minority students.* Sacramento, CA: California Association for Bilingual Education.

Cunningham, A. E., & Stanovich, K. E. (1997). Early reading acquisition and its relation to reading experience and ability 10 years later. *Developmental Psychology, 33*(6), 934–945.

Cunningham, A. E., & Stanovich, K. E. (1998, Spring-Summer). What reading does for the mind. *The American Educator*, 8–17.

Cunningham, P. M. (1995). *Phonics they use: Words for reading and writing* (2nd ed.). New York, NY: HarperCollins.

Cunningham, P. M., & Allington, R. L. (2003). *Classrooms that work: They can ALL read and write* (3rd ed.). Boston, MA: Allyn & Bacon.

Cunningham, P. M., Hall, D. P., & Sigmon, C. M. (2007). *The teacher's guide to the four blocks.* Greensboro, NC: Carson-Dellosa.

Dahl, K. L., Scharer, P. L., Lawson, L. L., & Grogan, P. R. (2001). *Rethinking phonics: Making the best teaching decisions.* Portsmouth, NH: Heinemann.

Dahl, R. (1998). *Danny, the champion of the world.* Illustrated by Quentin Blake. New York, NY: Puffin.

Damico, J. S. (1991). Descriptive assessment of communicative ability in limited English proficient students. In E. Hamayan & J. S. Damico (Eds.), *Limiting bias in the assessment of bilingual students* (pp. 157–218). Austin, TX: PRO-ED.

Daniels, H. (1994). *Literature circles: Voice and choice in one student-centered classroom.* York, ME: Stenhouse.

Daniels, H. (2002). *Literature circles: Voice and choice in book clubs and reading groups.* Augusta, ME: Stenhouse.

Davis, F. B. (1944). Fundamental factors of comprehension in reading. *Psychometrica, 9,* 195–197.

Davis, J. H. (2015, December 11). "Revamping of no child school act is signed," *New York Times.* Retrieved from http://www.nytimes.com/2015/12/11/us/politics/president-obama-signs-into-law-a-rewrite-of-no-child-left-behind.html?_r=0

Davis, L. & Gordon, C. (2007). *The Down to Earth Guide to Global Warming.* NY: Orchard Books.

de Braslavsky, B. P. (2006). *Adquisición inicial de la lectura y escritura en escuelas para la diversidad, Tomo 1.* Buenos Aires: Fundación Perez Companc.

Deacon, S. H., & Bryant, P. (2005). The strength of children's knowledge of the role of root morphemes in the spelling of derived words. *Child Language, 32,* 375–389.

Delpit, L. (1990). Language diversity and learning. In S. Hynds & D. Rubin (Eds.), *Perspectives on talk and learning* (pp. 247–266). Urbana, IL: NCTE.

Delpit, L. (1995). *Other people's children: Cultural conflict in the classroom.* New York, NY: The New Press.

Delpit, L. (1996). Skills and other dilemmas of a progressive black educator. In L. Delpit (Ed.), *Other people's children.* New York, NY: The New Press.

Delpit, L. (2008). Introduction. In L. Delpit (Ed.), *The skin that we speak: Thoughts on language and culture in the classroom* (pp. xxii-xxvi). New York, NY: The New Press.

Denton, C. A., Enos, M., York, M. J., Francis, D. J., Barn Jianes, M. A., Kulesz, P. A., Fletcher, J. M., & Carter, S. (2015, Oct.–Dec.). Text-processing differences in adolescent adequate and poor comprehenders' reading accessible and challenging narrative and informational text. *Reading Research Quarterly, 50*(4), 393–416.

Derewianka, B. (2013). *A new grammar companion for teachers* (2nd ed). Riverwood, Australia: Primary English Teaching Association.

Dewey, J. (1913). *Interest and effort in education.* Boston, MA: Riverside.

Doyle, D., & Han, J. G. (2012). *Measuring teacher effectiveness: A look "under the hood" of teacher evaluation in 10 sites.* New York: 50CAN; New Haven, CT: ConnCAN; and Chapel Hill, NC: Public Impact. Retrieved from http://www.conncan.org/learn/research/teachers/measuring-teacher-effectiveness

Duffy, G. G., & Roehler, L. R. (1989). Why strategy instruction is so difficult and what we need to do about it. In C. B. McCormick, G. Miller, & M. Pressley (Eds.), *Cognitive strategy research: From basic research to educational applications.* New York, NY: Springer-Verlag.

Duffy-Hester, A. (1999). Teaching struggling readers in elementary school classrooms: A review of classroom reading programs and principles for instruction. *The Reading Teacher, 52,* 480–495.

Duke, N. K., Caughlan, S., Juzwik, M. M., & Martin, N. M. (2012). Teaching genre with purpose. *Educational Leadership, 69*(6), 34–39.

Duke, N. K., & Pearson, P. D. (2002). Effective practices for developing reading comprehension. In A. E. Farstrup & J. E. Samuels (Eds.), *What research has to say about reading instruction* (3rd ed., pp. 205–242). Newark, DE: International Reading Association.

Durkin, D. (1978–1979). What classroom observations reveal about reading comprehension instruction. *Reading Research Quarterly, 15,* 481–433.

Echevarria, J., Vogt, M.E., & Short, D. J. (2013). *Making content comprehensible for English learners: The SIOP® model.* Boston, MA: Pearson/Allyn and Bacon.

Edwards, P. A., McMillon, G. T., & Turner, J. E. (2010). *Change is gonna come: Transforming literacy education for African American students.* New York, NY: Teachers College Press.

Edwards, S. A., Malloy, R. W., & Verock-O'Laughlin, R. (2003). *Ways of writing with young kids.* Boston, MA: Allyn & Bacon.

Eeds, M., & Wells, D. (1989). Grand conversations: An exploration of meaning construction in literature discussion groups. *Research in the Teaching of English, 23,* 4–29.

Ehrenreich, B. (2001). *Nickled and dimed: On (not) getting by in America.* New York, NY: Owl Books.

Ehri, L. C. (1991). Development of the ability to read words. In R. Barr, M. Kamil, P. B. Mosenthal, & P. D. Pearson (Eds.), *Handbook of reading research* (Vol. 2). New York, NY: Longman.

Ehri, L. C. (1997). Learning to read and learning to spell are one and the same, almost. In C. Perfetti, L. Rieben, & M. Fayol (Eds.), *Learning to spell* (pp. 237–269). Hillsdale, NJ: Erlbaum.

Elkonin, D. B. (1965). "Personality psychology and the preschool age child." In the collection *The personality development of the preschool age child.* Moscow.

Elkonin, D. B. (1973). USSR. In J. Downing (Ed.), *Comparative reading.* New York, NY: Macmillan.

Elley, W. (1992). *How in the world do students read?* The Hague: The International Association for the Evaluation of Educational Achievement.

Elley, W. (1996). *The IEA study of reading literacy.* Oxford, England: Pergamon.

Escamilla, K., & Andrade, A. (1992). Descubriendo la lectura: An application of Reading Recovery in Spanish. *Education and Urban Society, 24,* 212–226.

Escamilla, K., Loera, M., Ruiz, O., & Rodriguez, Y. (1998). An examination of sustaining effects in Descubriendo la Lectura programs. *Literacy Teaching and Learning, 3,* 59–81.

Esparza Brown, J., & Sanford, A. (2011). *RTI for English language learners: Appropriately using screening and progress monitoring tools to improve instructional outcomes.* National Center on Response to Intervention. Retrieved from http://www.rti4success.org

Farris, P. J., Werderich, D. E., Nelson, P. A., & Fuhler, C. J. (2009). Male call: Fifth-grade boys' reading preferences. *The Reading Teacher, 63*(3), 180–188.

Federal Register. (2006). *Title I—Improving the Academic Achievement of the Disadvantaged; Final Rule. 34* CFR Part 200, September 13, 2006. Washington, DC: Department of Education.

Fernandez, M. C., Pearson, B. Z., Umbel, V. M., Oller, D. K., & Molinet-Molina, M. (1992). Bilingual receptive vocabulary in Hispanic preschool children. *Hispanic Journal of Behavioral Sciences, 14*(2), 268–276.

Finkerstaedt, T., & Wolff, D. (1973). *Ordered profusion: Studies in dictionaries and the English lexicon.* Heidelburg, Germany: C. Winter

Fisher, A. (2001). *Critical thinking.* New York, NY: Cambridge University Press.

Fisher, D., Frey, N., & Rothenberg, C. 2011. *Implementing RTI with English learners.* Bloomington, IN: Solution Tree.

Fisher, P., Blachowicz, C., & Smith, J. (1991). Vocabulary learning in literature discussion groups. In J. Zutell & S. McCormick (Eds.), *Learner factors/Teacher factors: Issues in literacy research and instruction* (pp. 201–209). Fortieth yearbook of the National Reading Conference. Chicago, IL: National Reading Conference.

Fitzgerald, J. (1995). English-as-a-second-language reading instruction in the United States: A research review. *Journal of Reading Behavior, 27,* 115–152.

Fletcher, J. M. (2006). Measuring reading comprehension. *Scientific Studies of Reading, 10*(3), 323–330.

Foorman, B. R., & Mehta, P. (2002, November). *Definitions of fluency: Conceptual and methodological challenges.* PowerPoint presentation at A Focus on Fluency Forum, San Francisco, CA. Retrieved from www.prel.org/programs/rel/fluency/Foorman.ppt

Fountas, I. C., & Pinnell, G. S. (1996). *Guided reading: Good first teaching for all children.* Portsmouth, NH: Heinemann.

Fountas, I. C., & Pinnell, G. S. (1999). *Matching books to readers: Using leveled books in guided reading, K–3.* Portsmouth, NH: Heinemann.

Fountas, I. C., & Pinnell, G. S. (2001). *Guiding readers and writers: Grades 3–6.* Portsmouth, NH: Heinemann.

Fountas, I. C., & Pinnell, G. S. (2001). *Guiding readers and writers: Teaching comprehension, genre, and content literacy.* Portsmouth, NH: Heinemann.

Fountas, I. C., & Pinnell, G. S. (2001). *Leveled books, K–8: Matching texts to readers for effective teaching.* Portsmouth, NH: Heinemann.

Fradd, S. H., & Tikunoff, W. J. (Eds.). (1987). *Bilingual and bilingual special education: An administrator's guide.* Boston, MA: Little, Brown.

Frazier, D. (2007). *Miss Alaineus: A vocabulary disaster.* San Diego, CA: Harcourt.

Freebody, P., & Luke, A. (1990). Literacies programs: Debates and demands in cultural context. *Prospect: Australian Journal of TESOL, 5*(7), 7–16.

Freeman, D. (1978). *Corduroy.* New York, NY: Viking Junior.

Freinet, C. (1974). *El método natural de lectura.* Barcelona, Spain: Editorial Laia.

Freire, P. (1976). *Education: The practice of freedom.* Danbury, CT: Writers & Readers Ltd.

Frey, N. & Fisher, D. (2009). *Learning Words Inside and Out, Grades 1–6.* Portsmouth, NH: Heinemann.

Frith, U. (1985). Beneath the surface of developmental dyslexia. In K. E. Patterson, J. C. Marshall, & M. Coltheart (Eds.), *Surface dyslexia* (pp. 310–330). London: Erlbaum.

Fry, E. (1967). Fry's readability graph: Clarifications, validity, and extension to level 17. *Journal of Reading, 21,* 242–252.

Fuchs, D., & Fuchs, L. S. (2009). Responsiveness to intervention: Multilevel assessment and instruction as early intervention and disability identification. *The Reading Teacher, 63*(3), 250–252.

Fuchs, L. S., Deno, S. L., & Mirkin, P. K. (1984, Summer). The effects of frequent curriculum-based measurement and evaluation on pedagogy, student achievement, and student awareness of learning. *American Educational Research Journal, 21*(2), 449–460.

Fuchs, L. S., & Fuchs, D. (2008). The role of assessment within the RTI framework. In D. Fuchs, L. W. Fuchs, & S. Vaughn (Eds.), *Response to intervention: A framework for reading educators.* Newark, DE: International Reading Association.

Fuchs, M. L., & Mellard, D. F. (2007). *Helping educators discuss responsiveness to intervention with parents and students.* Lawrence, KS: National Research Center on Learning Disabilities.

Galloway, E. P., & Lesaux, N. K. (2014). Leader, teacher, diagnostician, colleague, and change agent. *The Reading Teacher, 67*(7), 517–526.

Ga'ndara, P. (2010). Overcoming triple segregation. *Educational Leadership, 68*(3), 60–64.

Ganske, K. (2000). *Word journeys.* New York, NY: Guilford Press.

Garan, E. M., & DeVoogd, G. (2008). The benefits of sustained silent reading: Scientific research and common sense converge. *The Reading Teacher, 62*(4), 336–344.

Garcia, E. E. (1991, Autumn). Factors influencing the English reading test performance of Spanish-speaking Hispanic children. *Reading Research Quarterly, 26*(4), 371–392.

García, E. E. (2005). *Teaching and learning in two languages: Bilingualism and schooling in the United States.* New York, NY: Teachers College Press.

Garcia, O., & Wei, L. (2014). *Translanguaging: Language, bilingualism and education.* London, U.K.: Palgrave Pivot.

Gartland, L. B., & Smolkin, L. B. (2016). The histories and mysteries of grammar instruction: Supporting elementary teachers in the time of the Common Core. *The Reading Teacher, 69*(4), 391–399.

Gee, J. P. (1992). *The social mind: Ideology and social practice.* New York, NY: Bergin & Garvey.

Gelman, R., & Greeno, J. G. (1989). On the nature of competence: Principles for understanding in a domain. In L. Resnick (Ed.), *Knowing, learning, and instruction: Essays in honor of Robert Glaser.* Hillsdale, NJ: Erlbaum.

Gelzheiser, L. M., Scanlon, D. M., & Hallgren-Flynn, L. (2010). Spotlight on RTI for adolescents: An example of intensive middle school intervention using the interactive strategies approach-extended. In M. Y. Lipson & K. K. Wixson (Eds.), *Successful approaches to RTI: Collaborative practices for improving K–12 literacy.* Newark, DE: International Reading Association.

Gentry, J. R. (1981). Learning to spell developmentally. *The Reading Teacher, 34,* 378–381.

Gentry, J. R. (1989). *Spel . . . is a four-letter word.* Portsmouth, NH: Heinemann.

Gersten, R. (1998). Recent advances in instructional research for students with learning disabilities: An overview. *Learning Disabilities Research and Practice, 13*(3), 162–170.

Gersten, R., & Baker, S. (2000). What we know about effective instructional practices for English-language learners. *Exceptional Children, 66,* 454–470.

Gillet, J. W., Temple, C., Temple, C., & Crawford, A. (2012). *Understanding reading problems: Assessment and instruction* (8th ed.). Boston, MA: Allyn & Bacon.

Giroir, S., Grimaldo, L. R., Vaughn, S., & Roberts, G. (2015). Interactive read-alouds for English learners in the elementary grades. *The Reading Teacher, 68*(8), 639–648.

Gleitman, L. R., & Rozin, P. (1973, Summer). Teaching reading by use of a syllabary. *Reading Research Quarterly, 8*(4), 447–483.

Goatley, V. J., Brock, C. H., & Raphael, T. E. (1995). Diverse learners participating in regular education "book clubs." *Reading Research Quarterly, 30*(3), 352–380.

Goldenberg, C., Rezaei, A., & Fletcher, J. (2005, May). *Home use of English and Spanish in Spanish-speaking children's oral language and literacy achievement.* Paper presented at the annual conference of the International Reading Association, San Antonio, TX.

Goldman, S. R., & Rakestraw, Jr., J. A. (2000). Structural aspects of constructing meaning from text. In M. L. Kamil, P. Mosenthal, P. D. Pearson, & R. Barr (Eds.), *Handbook of reading research* (Vol. 3, pp. 311–335). Mahwah, NJ: Erlbaum.

Gollnick, D. M., & Chinn, P. C. (2012). *Multicultural education in a pluralistic society.* Boston, MA: Pearson.

Goodman, K. S. (1967). Reading: A psycholinguistic guessing game. *Journal of the Reading Specialist, 6,* 126–135.

Goodman, K. S. (1986). *What's whole in whole language?* Portsmouth, NH: Heinemann.

Goodman, K. S. (1989). *Lenguaje integral*. Mérida, Venezuela: Editorial Venezolana.

Goodman, Y. M. (1985). Kid watching: Observing children in the classroom. In A. Jaggar & M. T. Smith-Burke (Eds.), *Observing the language learner* (pp. 9–18). New York, NY: New York University. Co-published by the International Reading Association and the National Council of Teachers of English, 1985.

Goodman, Y. M. (2006). *Kidwatching*. Retrieved from www.reading.org/downloads/publications/books/bk558-27-Goodman_Kidwatching.pdf

Goodwin, A. P., Gilbert, J. K., & Cho, S.-J. (2013). Morphological contributions to adolescent word reading: An item response approach. *Reading Research Quarterly, 48*(1), 39–60.

Gordon, D., & Gordon, C. (2007). *The down-to-earth guide to global warming*. New York, NY: Scholastic.

Gorrell, G. K. (2009). *Say what? The weird and mysterious journey of the English language*. Toronto, CA: Tundra Books.

Goswami, U. (2000). Phonological and lexical processes. In M. Kamil, P. Mosenthal, P. D. Pearson, & R. Barr (Eds.), *Handbook of reading research* (Vol. 3). New York, NY: Longman.

Graham, S., & Harris. K. R. (2005). *Writing better: Effective strategies for teaching students with learning difficulties*. Boston, MA: Paul H. Brookes.

Graves, D. H. (1982). *Writing: Students and teachers at work*. Portsmouth, NH: Heinemann.

Graves, M. F. (2006). *The vocabulary book: Learning and instruction*. Champaign, IL: NCTE.

Graves, M. F., August, D., & Mancilla-Martinez, J. (2012). *Teaching vocabulary to English learners*. New York, NY: Teachers College Press.

Graves, M. F., & Silverman, R. (2010). Interventions to enhance vocabulary development. In R. L. Allington & A. McGill-Franzen (Eds.), *Handbook of reading disabilities research*. Mahwah, NJ: Erlbaum.

Green, J., & Gordon, M. (2005a). *Why should I save water?* New York, NY: Barron's Educational Series.

Green, J., & Gordon, M. (2005b). *Why should I recycle?* New York, NY: Barron's Educational Series.

Greenlaw, W. (2001). *English language arts and reading on the Internet*. Columbus, OH: Merrill Prentice Hall.

Gronlund, N. E., Linn, R. L., & Davis, K. (2000). *Measurement and assessment in teaching*. Englewood Cliffs, NJ: Prentice Hall.

Guthrie, J., & Ozgungor, S. (2002). Instructional contexts for reading engagement. In C. C. Block & M. Pressley (Eds.), *Comprehension instruction: Research-based practices*. New York, NY: Guilford.

Guthrie, J. T., & Davis, M. H. (2003). Motivating struggling readers in middle school through an engagement model of classroom practice. *Reading & Writing Quarterly, 19*, 59–185.

Gwynne, F. (2006). *The king who rained*. New York, NY: Aladdin Paperbacks.

Haggard, M. R. (1982). The vocabulary self-collection strategy: An active approach to word learning. *Journal of Reading, 26*, 203–207.

Hall, S. L., & Moats, L. C. (1999). *Straight talk about reading*. Lincolnwood, IL: Contemporary Books.

Halle, T., Kurtz-Costes, B., & Mahoney, J. (1997). Family influences on school achievement in low-income African American children. *Journal of Educational Psychology, 89*, 527–537.

Hansen, L. E., Auproux, J., Brown, S., Giarretto, B., & Worthington, A. (2015). Using "perfect pairs" of picture books to support English learners' academic language. *The California Reader, 48*(4), 20–26.

Harris, K., & Graham, S. (1996). *Making the writing process work: Strategies for composition and self-regulation*. Cambridge, MA: Brookline Books.

Harste, J., Woodward, J., & Burke, C. (1984). *Language stories and literacy lessons*. Portsmouth, NH: Heinemann.

Hart, B., & Risley, T. R. (1995). *Meaningful differences in the everyday experiences of young American children*. Baltimore, MD: Brookes.

Hasbrouck, J., & Tindal, G. A. (2006, 7 April). Oral reading fluency norms: A valuable assessment tool for reading teachers. *The Reading Teacher, 59*(7), 636–644.

Haselhurst, M. (2005). *Hurricane*. Boston, MA: Pearson (Celebration Press).

Hauerwas, L. B., & Walker, J. (2004). What can children's spelling of *running* and *jumped* tell us about their need for spelling instruction? *The Reading Teacher, 58*(2), 168–176.

Heath, S. B. (1983). *Ways with words: Language, life, and work in communities and classrooms*. Cambridge, England: Cambridge University Press.

Heath, S. B. (1986). Sociocultural contexts of language development. In *Beyond language: Social and cultural factors in schooling language minority students* (pp. 143–182). Sacramento, CA: Bilingual Education Office, California State Department of Education.

Helman, L. A., & Bear, D. R. (2007). Does an established model of orthographic development hold for English language learners? In D. W. Rowe, R. Jimenez, D. L. Compton, D. K. Dickinson, Y. Kim, K. M. Leander, & V. J. Risko (Eds.), *56th Yearbook of the National Reading Conference* (pp. 266–280). Oak Creek, WI: National Reading Conference.

Henderson, E. H. (1990). *Teaching spelling*. Boston, MA: Houghton Mifflin.

Hendrix, C. (1952). *Cómo enseñar a leer por el método global.* Buenos Aires, Argentina: Editorial Kapelusz.

Henkes, K. (1996). *Lilly's purple plastic purse.* New York, NY: Greenwillow.

Henkes, K. (2006). *Lilly's big day.* New York, NY: HarperCollins Children's Books.

Herbert, J. (2002). *The American Revolution for kids: A history with 21 activities.* Chicago, IL: Chicago Review Press.

Hickman, J. (1979). *Response to literature in a school environment.* Unpublished doctoral dissertation, Ohio State University, Columbus.

Hickman, J. (1981). A new perspective on response to literature. *Research in the Teaching of English, 15,* 343–354.

Hiebert, E. H., & Cervetti, G. N. (2012). What differences in narrative and informational texts mean for the learning and instruction of vocabulary. In E. J. Kame'enui & J. F. Baumann (Eds.), *Vocabulary instruction: Research to practice* (2nd ed., pp. 322–344). New York, NY: Guilford.

Hill, R., Carjuzaa, J., Aramburo, D., & Baca, L. (1993). Culturally and linguistically diverse teachers in special education: Repairing or redesigning the leaky pipeline. *Teacher Education and Special Education, 16,* 258–269.

Hinchmann, K. A., & Moore, D. W. (2013). Close reading: A cautionary interpretation. *Journal of Adolescent and Adult Literacy 56*(6), 441–450.

Ho, D. B. (1999). Using wordless picture books to support struggling sixth grade readers and writers. *The California Reader, 32,* 9–11.

Hoban, R. (1995). *Bedtime for Frances.* Illustrated by Garth Williams. New York, NY: HarperTrophy.

Hoffman, J. V. (1992). Critical reading/ thinking across the curriculum: Using I-Charts to support learning. *Language Arts, 69,* 121–127.

Hohmann, M. (2002). *Fee, fie, phonemic awareness.* Ypsilanti, MI: Highscope Press.

Holdaway, D. (1979). *Foundations of literacy.* Portsmouth, NH: Heinemann.

Hudelson, S. (1987). The role of native language literacy in the education of language minority children. *Language Arts, 64,* 827–840.

Huey, E. B. (1908). *The psychology and pedagogy of reading.* Cambridge, MA: MIT Press.

Individuals with Disabilities Education Act 1997 (Reauthorization). (1997). 20 U.S.C. 1400 et seq.

Individuals with Disabilities Education Improvement Act of 2004. (2004). 108th Congress (2003-2004) H.R.1350.ENR.

Ingraham, C. (2014, October 29). Child poverty in the U.S. is among the worst in the developed world. *The Washington Post.* Retrieved from https://www .washingtonpost.com/news/wonk/wp/2014/10/29/ child-poverty-in-the-u-s-is-among-the-worst-in-the-developed-world/

International Reading Association. (2001). *Second-language literacy instruction: A position statement of the International Reading Association.* Newark, DE: Author.

International Reading Association. (2009). *Response to Intervention: Guiding principles for educators from the International Reading Association.* Newark, DE: Author.

International Reading Association and the National Council for the Accreditation of Teacher Education. (2006). *Standards for reading professionals.* Newark, DE: Author.

Iser, W. (1978). *The act of reading.* Baltimore, MD: Johns Hopkins University Press.

Iverson, S., & Tunmer, W. (1993). Phonological processing skills and the Reading Recovery program. *Journal of Educational Psychology, 85*(1), 112–126.

Ivey, G., & Broaddus, K. (2001). "Just plain reading": A survey of what makes students want to read in middle school classrooms. *Reading Research Quarterly, 36,* 350–371.

Jeffers, O. (2005). *Lost and found.* New York, NY: Philomel Books.

Jenkins, S. (2008). *What do you do with a tail like this?* Boston, MA: Sandpiper.

Jepsen, C. (2009). *Bilingual education and English proficiency: Discussion Paper Series.* University of Kentucky Center for Poverty Research, ED505041.

Jepsen, C. (2010). Bilingual education and English proficiency. *Education Finance and Policy,* v, 200–227.

Jerome, K. B. (2002). *Exploring space.* Washington, D.C. National Geographic Society.

Jian, YC. (2016). Fourth graders' cognitive processes and learning strategies for reading illustrated biology texts: Eye movement measurements. *Reading Research Quarterly, 51*(1), 93–109.

Johnston, F., Invernizzi, M., & Juel, C. (1998). *Book Buddies: Guidelines for volunteer tutors of emergent and early readers.* New York, NY: Guilford.

Johnson-Coleman, L. (2001, May). *Keep on keepin' on: Motivation for the young and young at heart.* Keynote address presented at the annual conference of the International Reading Association, New Orleans, LA.

Johnston, P. (2010). An instructional frame for RTI. *The Reading Teacher, 63*(7), 602–604.

Jones, V. G. (2008). *Marian Anderson: A voice uplifted.* New York, NY: Sterling.

Judge, G. (2009) *The timeline history of the English language.* Yokohama, Japan: Cogno Graphic Publishers.

Juel, C. (1988). Learning to read and write: A longitudinal study of 54 children from first through fourth grades. *Journal of Educational Psychology, 80,* 443–447.

Kagan, S. (1994). *Cooperative learning*. San Clemente, CA: Kagan.

Kagan, S. (1997). *Cooperative learning*. San Clemente, CA: Kagan.

Kame'enui, E. J., Simmons, D., Cornachione, C., Thompson-Hoffman, S., Ginsburg, A., Marcy, E., Mittleman, J., Irwin, J., & Baker, M. (2001). *A practical guide to reading assessments*. Washington, DC: U.S. Department of Education.

Katzir, T., & Pare-Blagoev, J. (2006). Applying cognitive neuroscience research to education: The case of literacy. *Educational Psychologist 41*(1), 53–74.

Kawakami-Arakaki, A. J., Oshiro, M. E., & Farran, D. C. (1988*). Research to practice: Integrating reading and writing in a kindergarten curriculum*. Champaign, IL: University of Illinois at Urbana-Champaign—Center for the Study of Reading.

Kelly, M. (2000). *Of dreams and new realities: Mexican immigrant women in transition*. Unpublished doctoral dissertation. National-Louis University.

Kieffer, M. J., & Lessaux, N. K. (2010). Morphing into adolescents: Active word learning for English language learners and their classmates in middle school. *Journal of Adolescent and Adult Literacy, 54*(1), 47–56.

Klein, A. (2015). ESEA reauthorization: The Every Student Succeeds Act explained. *Education Week*. Retrieved from http://blogs.edweek.org/edweek/campaign-k-12/2015/11/esea_reauthorization_the_every.html

Klenk, L., & Kibby, M. W. (2000). Remediating reading difficulties: Appraising the past, reconciling the present, constructing the future. In M. L. Kamil, P. B. Mosenthal, P. D. Pearson, & R. Barr (Eds.), *Handbook of reading research* (Vol. 3, pp. 545–562). Mahwah, NJ: Erlbaum.

Klingner, J. K., Soltero-González, L., & Lesaux, N. (2010). RTI for English-language learners. In M. Y. Lipson & K. K. Wixson (Eds.), *Successful approaches to RTI: Collaborative practices for improving K–12 literacy*. Newark, DE: International Reading Association.

Knoell, D. (2010). Selecting and using nonfiction in grades K–12 social studies and science. In K. Gansky & D. Fisher (Eds.), *Comprehension across the curriculum*. New York, NY: Guilford.

Kolln, M., & Gray, L. (2013). *Rhetorical grammar: Grammatical choices, rhetorical effects*. (7th ed.). Boston, MA: Pearson.

Koskinen, P. S., & Blum, I. H. (1986). Paired repeated reading: A classroom strategy for developing fluent reading. *The Reading Teacher, 40*, 70–75.

Krashen, S. D. (1981). Bilingual education and second language acquisition theory. In California State Department of Education (Ed.), *Schooling and language minority students: A theoretical framework* (pp. 51–79). Sacramento: California State Department of Education, Office of Bilingual Bicultural Education.

Krashen, S. D. (1985). *Inquiries and insights: Second language teaching, immersion and bilingual education, literacy*. Hayward, CA: Alemany Press.

Krashen, S. D. (1991). *Bilingual education: A focus on current research*. Washington, DC: National Clearinghouse for Bilingual Education.

Krashen, S. D. (1991). The input hypothesis: An update. In J. E. Alatis (Ed.), Georgetown University Round Table on Languages and Linguistics 1991, *Linguistics and language pedagogy: The state of the art*. Washington, DC: Georgetown University Press.

Krashen, S. D. (2004). *Principles and practices in second language acquisition*. New York, NY: Pergamon Press.

Krashen, S. D., & Biber, D. (1988). *On course: Bilingual education's success in California*. Sacramento: California Association for Bilingual Education.

Krashen, S. D., & Terrell, T. D. (1983). *The natural approach: Language acquisition in the classroom*. New York, NY: Pergamon/Alemany.

Kucan, L. (2012, March). What is most important to know about vocabulary. *Reading Teacher, 65*, 360–366.

Kuhn, M. (2004). Helping students become accurate, expressive readers: Fluency instruction for small groups. *The Reading Teacher, 58*(4), 338–344.

Kuhn, M. R., & Stahl, S. A. (2003). Fluency: A review of developmental and remedial practices. *Journal of Educational Psychology, 95*, 3–21.

LaBash, C. (2007). *Cuba teaches the world to read*. New York, NY: Workers World. Retrieved from http://www.workers.org/2007/world/cuba-0111/

Labbo, L. D., & Teale, W. H. (1990). Cross age reading: A strategy for helping poor readers. *The Reading Teacher, 43*, 363–369.

Labov, W. (1970). *The study of non-standard English*. Champaign, IL: NCTE.

Labov, W. (1972). *Language in the inner city: Studies in Black English vernacular*. Philadelphia, PA: University of Pennsylvania Press.

Ladson-Billings, G. (2009). *The dream-keepers: Successful teachers of African American children*. San Francisco, CA: Jossey-Bass.

Lambert, W. E. (1975). Culture and language as factors in learning and education. In A. Wolfgang (Ed.), *Education of immigrant students*. Toronto: O.I.S.E.

Landrum, J. (2001). Selecting intermediate novels that feature characters with disabilities. *The Reading Teacher, 55*, 252–258.

Langer, J. A. (2011). *Envisioning knowledge: Building literacy in the academic disciplines*. New York, NY: Teachers College Press.

Langstaff, J., & Parker, N.W. (1991). *Oh, a-hunting we will go*. New York, NY: Aladdin. *Lau v. Nichols*, 414 US 563 (1974).

Layton, L. (2014, January 16). Majority of U.S. public school students are in poverty. *The Washington Post*. https://www.washingtonpost.com/local/education/majority-of-us-public-school-students-are-in-poverty/2015/01/15/df7171d0-9ce9-11e4-a7ee-526210d665b4_story.html

Lehr, F., Osborn, J., & Hiebert, E. (2006). *A focus on vocabulary*. Honolulu, HI: Pacific Resources for Education and Learning.

Lehr, S. S. (1991). *The child's developing sense of theme: Responses to literature*. New York, NY: Teachers College Press.

Lems, K., Miller, L. D., & Soro, T. M. (2010). *Teaching reading to English language learners: Insights from linguistics*. New York, NY: Guilford.

Lennon, C., & Burdick, H. (2004). *The Lexile Framework as an approach for reading measurement and success*. Durham, NC: MetaMetrics.

Lenters, K. (2005). No half measures: Reading instruction for young second-language learners. *The Reading Teacher, 58*, 328–336.

Leslie, L., & Caldwell, J. (2005). *Qualitative reading inventory* (4th ed.). Boston, MA: Allyn & Bacon.

Leu, D. J., Coiro, J., Castek, J., Hartman, D. K., Henry, L. A., & Reinking, D. (2010). Research on instruction and assessment in the new literacies of online reading comprehension. In C. C. Block & S. Parris (Eds.), *Comprehension instruction: Research-based best practices*. New York, NY: Guilford Press.

Leu, D. J., Zawilinski, L., Castek, J., Banerjee, M., Housand, B., Liu, Y., & O'Neil, M. (2007). What is new about the new literacies of online reading comprehension? In L. Rush, A. Berger, & J. Eakle (Eds.), *Secondary school reading and writing: What research reveals for classroom practices* (pp. 37–68). Chicago, IL: NCTE/NCRL.

Levi-Strauss. C. (1970). *Structural anthropology*. Garden City, NY: Basic Books.

Liebfreund, M. D. (2015, Oct.–Dec.). IRA outstanding dissertation Award for 2015: Success with informational text comprehension: An examination of underlying factors. *Reading Research Quarterly, 50*(4), 387–392.

Linan-Thompson, S., & Vaughn, S. (2007). *Research-based methods of reading instruction for English language learners, grades K–4*. Alexandria, VA: ASCD.

Lipson, M. Y., Chomsky-Higgins, P., & Kanfer, J. (2011). Diagnosis: The missing ingredient in RTI assessment. *The Reading Teacher, 65*(3), 204–208.

Loban, W. (1976). *Language development: Kindergarten through twelfth grade*. Urbana, IL: National Council of Teachers of English.

Louie, B., & Sierschynski, J. (2015). Enhancing English learners' language development using wordless picture books. *The Reading Teacher, 69*(1), 103–111.

Lourie, P. (2011). *The manatee scientists: Saving vulnerable species*. Boston, MA: Houghton Mifflin Harcourt.

Luke, A., & Freebody, P. (1999). A map of possible practices: Further notes on the four resources model. *Practically Primary, 4*, 2.

Luria, A. R. (1976). *Cognitive development: Its cultural and social foundations*. Cambridge, MA: Harvard University Press.

Lysaker, J. T., Tonge, C., Gauson, D., & Miller, A. (2011). Reading and social imagination: What relationally oriented reading instruction can do for children. *Reading Psychology 32*, 520–566.

Macrorie, K. (1988). *The I-Search paper revised*. Portsmouth, NH: Boynton/Cook.

Mandler, M. J., & Johnson, N. S. (1977). The remembrance of things parsed: Story structure and recall. *Cognitive Psychology, 9*, 51–91.

Manyak, P. C., & Bauer, E. B. (2009). English vocabulary instruction for English learners. *The Reading Teacher, 63*(2), 174–176.

Manyak, P. C., Von Gunten, H., Autenrieth, D., Gillis, C., Mastre-O'Farrell, Irvine-McDermott, E., Bauman, J. F., & Blachowicz, C. L. A. (2014). Four practical principles for enhancing vocabulary instruction. *The Reading Teacher, 68*(1), 13–23.

Manzo, A. V. (1969). The ReQuest procedure. *Journal of Reading, 13*, 123–126.

Marsh, G., Friedman, M., Welch, V., & Desberg, P. (1981). A cognitive-developmental theory of reading acquisition. In G. MacKinnon & T. Waller (Eds.), *Reading research advances in theory and practice*, volume 3. New York, NY: Academic Press.

Marshall, E. (1994). *Fox and his friends*. Illustrated by James Marshall. New York, NY: Puffin.

Martinez, M., Roser, N., & Strecker, S. (1999). "I never thought I could be a star": A readers' theatre ticket to reading fluency. *The Reading Teacher, 52*, 326–334.

Marzano, R. J. (2004). *Building background knowledge for academic achievement: Research on what works in schools*. Alexandria, VA: ASCD.

Marzano, R. J., & Pickering, D. J. (2005). *Building academic vocabulary: Teacher's manual*. Alexandria, VA: Association for Supervision and Curriculum Development.

Mayer, M. (2002). *Beauty and the beast*. Illustrated by Mercer Mayer. New York, NY: Macmillan.

McGee, L. M., & Richgels, D. J. (2003). *Literacy's beginnings: Supporting young readers and writers* (3rd ed.). Boston, MA: Allyn & Bacon.

McGee, L. M., & Schickedanz, J. A. (2007). Repeated interactive read-alouds in preschool and kindergarten. *The Reading Teacher, 60*(8), 742–751.

McKenna, M. C., & Kear, D. J. (1990, May). Measuring attitudes toward reading: A new tool for teachers. *The Reading Teacher, 43*(9), 626–639.

McKeown, M. G, Beck, I. L., & Sandora, C. (2012). Direct and rich vocabulary instruction needs to start early in vocabulary instruction (2nd ed.). In E. J. Kame'enui & J. F. Baumann (Eds.), *Research to Practice*. New York, NY: Guilford Press.

McKissack, P. C. (1997). *Ma Dear's aprons*. New York, NY: Alladin.

McQuillan, J., & Au, J. (2001). The effect of print access on reading frequency. *Reading Psychology, 22*, 225–248.

McQuillan, J., & Tse, L. (1998). What's the story? Using the narrative approach in beginning language classrooms. *TESOL Journal, 7*, 18–23.

Mehan, J. (1979). *Learning lessons*. Cambridge, MA: Harvard University Press.

Meier, T. (2015). The brown face of hope. *The Reading Teacher, 68*(5), 335–343.

Mesmer, E. M., & Mesmer, H. A. E. (2008/2009). Response to intervention (RTI): What teachers of reading need to know. *The Reading Teacher, 62*(4), 280–290.

Meyer, J. B. F. (2003). Text coherence and readability. *Topics in Language Disorders, 23*(3), 204–224.

Moats, L. C. (2009). *Language essentials for teachers of reading and spelling: Module 3 – Spellography for teachers: How English spelling works*, 2nd edition. Boston, MA: Sopris West Educational Services.

Moats, L. C. (2010). *Speech to print: Language essentials for teachers* (2nd ed.). Baltimore, MD: Paul H. Brookes.

Modiano, N. (1968). Bilingual education for children of linguistic minorities. *American Indígena, 28*, 405–414.

Moffett, J. (1976). *Teaching the universe of discourse*. New York, NY: Holt, Rinehart & Winston.

Moline, S. (2011.) *I see what you mean*. Portland, ME: Stenhouse.

Montanari, D. (2004). *Children around the world*. Toronto, ON: Kids Can Press.

Montelongo, J. A., & Hernández, A. C. (2013). The teachers' choices cognate database for K–3 teachers of Latino English learners. *The Reading Teacher, 67*(3), 187–192.

Montelongo, J. A., Hernández, A., & Herter, R. J. (2011a). Identifying Spanish-English cognates to scaffold instruction for Latino ELs. *The Reading Teacher, 65*(2), 161–164.

Montelongo, J. A., Hernández, A. C., & Herter, R. J. (2011b). Using cognates to scaffold context clue strategies for Latino ELs. *The Reading Teacher, 64*(6), 429–434.

Moore, J., & Whitfield, V. (2009). Building schoolwide capacity for preventing reading failure. *The Reading Teacher, 62*(7), 622–624.

Moore, P. J., & Scevak, J. J. (1997). Learning from texts and visual aids: A developmental perspective. *Journal of Research in Reading, 20*(3), 205–223.

Morris, A. & Hevman, K. (1989). *Bread, bread, bread*. New York, NY: HarperCollins.

Morris, R. D. (2005). *Case studies in beginning reading*. New York, NY: Guilford.

Morris, R. D. (2006). *The Howard Street tutoring manual* (2nd ed.). New York, NY: Guilford.

Morris, R. D., Blanton, L., Blanton, W. E., Nowacek, J., & Perney, J. (1995, November). Teaching low-achieving spellers at their "instructional level." *Elementary School Journal, 96*(2), 163–177.

Morris, R. D., Nelson, L., & Perney, J. (1986). Exploring the concept of "spelling instructional level" through the analysis of error types. *Elementary School Journal, 87*, 181–200.

Morris, D., Tyner, B., & Perney, J. (2000). Early Steps: Replicating the effects of a first-grade reading intervention program. *Journal of Educational Psychology, 92*(4), 681.

Morrow, L. M., & Gambrell, L. (2004). *Using children's literature in preschool: Comprehending and enjoying books*. Newark, DE: International Reading Association.

Munoz Ryan, P. (2002) *When Marian sang*. New York, NY: Scholastic.

Murray, D. (1985). *A writer teaches writing*. Boston, MA: Houghton Mifflin.

Muth, J. (2003). *Stone soup*. New York, NY: Scholastic.

Myhill, D., & Watson, A. (2014). The role of grammar in the writing curriculum: A review of the literature. *Child Language Teaching and Therapy, 30*(1), 41–62.

Nagy, W. E., & Anderson, R. C. (1984). How many words are there in printed school English? *Reading Research Quarterly, 19*, 304–330.

Nagy, W. E., Anderson, R. C., & Herman, P. A. (1987). Learning word meanings from context during normal reading. *American Educational Research Journal, 24*, 237–270.

Nagy, W. E., Anderson, R., Schommer, M., Scott, J., & Stallman, A. (1989). Morphological families and word recognition. *Reading Research Quarterly, 24*, 262–282.

Nagy, W. E., Berninger, V. W., & Abbott, R. D. (2006). Contributions of morphology beyond phonology to literacy outcomes of upper-elementary and middle-school students. *Journal of Educational Psychology, 98*(1), 134–147.

Nagy, W. E., & Townsend, D. (2012). Words as tools: Learning academic vocabulary as language. *Reading Research Quarterly, 47*(1), 91–108.

Nathan, R., Temple, F., Juntunen, K., & Temple, C. (1988). *Classroom strategies that work: An elementary teacher's guide to process writing*. Portsmouth, NH: Heinemann.

National Assessment of Educational Progress. (2011). *Reading Report Card, 2011*. Retrieved from http://nationsreportcard.gov/reading_2011/nat_g4.asp.

National Center for Education Statistics. (1999). *Digest of education statistics, 1998*. Washington, DC: U.S. Department of Education.

National Center for Education Statistics. (1999). *The condition of education*. Washington, DC: U.S. Government Printing Office. Retrieved from http://nces.ed.gov/programs/coe/

National Center for Education Statistics. (2009). *The condition of education: Participation in education*. Alexandria, VA: U.S. Department of Education.

National Center for Education Statistics. (2009). *Parent and family involvement in education*. Retrieved from <http://nces.ed.gov/programs/coe/2009/section4/indicator30.asp>

National Center for Education Statistics, National Assessment of Educational Progress [NAEP]. (2009). *The nation's report card*. Washington, DC: U.S. Department of Education.

National Center for Education Statistics. (2015). The condition of education 2015. Washington, DC: Author. Retrieved from http://nces.ed.gov/programs/coe/

National Center for Learning Disabilities. (2014). *The state of learning disabilities* (3rd ed.). New York, NY: National Center for Learning Disabilities. Retrieved from http://www.ncld.org/wp-content/uploads/2014/11/2014-State-of-LD.pdf

National Clearinghouse for English Language Acquisition. (2011). Retrieved from http://www.ncela.gwu.edu/files/uploads/9/growingLEP_0809.pdf.

National Literacy Panel on Language–Minority Children and Youth. (2006). *Developing literacy in second–language learners: Report of the National Literacy Panel on Language–Minority Children and Youth* (D. August and T. Shanahan, Eds.). Mahwah, NJ: Erlbaum.

National Reading Panel. (2003). *Reports*. Retrieved from http://www.nationalreadingpanel.org

National Reading Panel. (2000, December). *Teaching children to read: An evidence-based assessment of the scientific research literature on reading and its implications for reading instruction*. (Reports of the Subgroups). Washington, DC: National Institute of Child Health and Human Development, National Institutes of Health.

NEA [National Education Association]. (2004). *NCLB: The intersection of access and outcomes*. Washington, DC: Author.

Neuman, S., & Wright, T. (2014, Summer), The magic of words. *The American Educator*, 4–13.

Neuman, S. B., & Celano, D. (2001). Access to print in low-income and middle-income communities: An ecological study of four neighborhoods. *Reading Research Quarterly, 56*, 8–28.

Neuman, S. B., & Celano, D. (2010, November). Roadblocks on the information highway. *Educational Leadership, 68*(3), 50–53.

Neuman, S. B., & Celano, D. (2012, Fall). "Worlds apart" One city, two libraries, and ten years of watching inequality grow. *American Educator, 36*(3).

Newkirk, T. (2012). How we really comprehend nonfiction. *Educational Leadership, 69*(6), 29–32.

Nichols, W. D., Rupley, W. H., & Rasinski, T. (2009). Fluency in learning to read for meaning: Going beyond repeated readings. *Literacy Research and Instruction, 48*(1), 1–13.

Nunes, T., Bryant, P., & Bindman, M. (2006). The effects of learning to spell on children's awareness of morphology. *Reading and Writing, 19*, 767–787.

O'Connor, R. E., & Davidson, S. J. (2014). Teaching students with learning disabilities to read words. In C. A. Stone, E. R. Silliman, B. J. Ehren, & G. P. Wallach (Eds.), *Handbook of language & literacy: Development and disorders* (pp. 428–450). New York, NY: Guilford.

O'Leary, D. (2002). *2002 widening achievement gap*. Tucson, AZ: League of Latin American Citizens (LULAC).

Obama, B. (2004) *Dreams from my father: A story of race and inheritance*. New York: Broadway Books.

Ockey, G. (2010). *Assessing English language learners' silent reading*. Chicago, IL: Annual Convention of the International Reading Association.

OECD. (2010). *PISA 2009 results: What students know and can do—student progress in reading, mathematics and science* (Vol. 1). Retrieved from http://dx.doi.org10.1787/9789264091450-en

OECD and Statistics Canada. (2005). Learning a living: First results of the Adult Literacy and Life Skills Survey. http://www.oecd.org/education/innovation-education/34867438.pdf

Ogle, D. (1986). K-W-L: A teaching model that develops active reading of expository text. *Reading Teacher, 40*, 564–570.

Ogle, D. (1991). The know, want to know, learn strategy. In N. Muth (Ed.), *Children's comprehension of text: Research and practice* (pp. 22–23). Newark, DE: International Reading Association.

Ogle, D. (2000). Make it visual: A picture is worth a thousand words. In M. McLaughlin & M. Vogt (Eds.), *Creativity and innovation in content area teaching*. Norwood, MA: Christopher-Gordon.

Ogle, D. (2016). Literacy practices of a cultural history In T. DeV Wolsey & D. Lapp (Eds.), *Literacy in the disciplines: A teacher's guide for grades 3–12*. New York: Guilford, 2016.

Ogle, D., & Blachowicz, C. (2001). Beyond literature circles: Helping students comprehend informational texts. In C. C. Block & M. Pressley (Eds.), *Comprehension instruction: Research-based best practices*. New York, NY: Guilford Press.

Ogle, D., & Correa, A. (2010). Supporting English-language learners and struggling readers in content literacy with the "partner reading and content, too" routine. *The Reading Teacher, 63*(7), 532–542.

Olson, M. W., & Gee, T. C. (1988). A review of story grammar research. *Childhood Education, 64*(4), 302–306.

Ogle, D., & Lang, L. (2011). Best practices in adolescent literacy instruction. In L. Gambrell, L. Morrow, & M. Pressley (Eds.), *Best practices in literacy instruction.* New York, NY: Guilford.

Organization for Economic Cooperation and Development. (2009). *Programme for International Student Achievement: PISA 2009 key findings.* Retrieved from http://www.oecd.org/pisa/pisaproducts/pisa2009/pisa2009keyfindings.htm

Overturf, B. (2015). *Inside the Common Core classroom: Practical ELA strategies for Grades 3–5.* Boston, MA: Pearson.

Owocki, G., & Goodman, Y. (2002). *Kidwatching: Documenting children's literacy development.* Portsmouth, NH: Heinemann.

Palincsar, A. S., & Brown, A. L. (1986). Interactive teaching to promote independent learning from text. *The Reading Teacher, 39,* 771–777.

Palmer, F. R. (2001). *Mood and modality.* New York, NY: Cambridge University Press.

Parish, P. (1992). *Amelia Bedelia.* Illustrated by Fritz Siebel. New York, NY: HarperCollins.

Patterson, E. (1984). *Language, letters, and learning.* Lecture at Hobart and William Smith Colleges, Geneva, NY.

Pearson, P. D., & Anderson, R. C. (1985). A schema theoretic view of the learning to read process. In P. D. Pearson, R. Barr, & P. Mosenthal (Eds.), *Handbook of reading research: Volume 1.* New York, NY: MacMillan.

Pearson, P. D., Cervetti, G. N., & Tilson, J. L. (2008). Reading for understanding. In L. Darling-Hammond et al., *Powerful learning: What we know about teaching for understanding* (pp. 71–111). San Francisco, CA: Jossey-Bass.

Pearson, P. D., & Gallagher, M. (1983). The instruction of reading comprehension. *Contemporary Educational Psychology, 8,* 317–344.

Pearson, P. D., Hiebert, E., & Kamil, M. (2012). Vocabulary assessment: Making do with what we have while we create the tools we need. In E. J. Kame'enui & J. F. Baumann (Eds.), *Vocabulary instruction: Research to practice* (2nd ed.). New York, NY: Guilford.

Peer-Assisted Literacy Strategies (PALS) Series. (2010). Retrieved from http://smu.edu/education/readingresearch/interventions/pals.asp

Perfetti, C. A. (1985). *Reading ability.* New York, NY: Oxford University Press.

Perfetti, C. A. (1992). *Reading ability.* New York, NY: Oxford University Press.

Pilkey, D. (2000). *Captain Underpants boxed set.* New York, NY: Scholastic.

Plecha, J. (1992). Shared inquiry: The Great Books method of interpretive reading and discussion. In D. Temple

& P. Collins (Eds.), *Stories and readers: New perspectives on literature, the elementary classroom* (pp. 103–114). Norwood, MA: Christopher-Gordon.

Policy Almanac.org. (2002). *Almanac of policy issues.* Retrieved from http://www.policyalmanac.org/education/archive/literacy.shtml

Pomplun, M., & Omar, M. H. (2001). The factorial invariance of a test of reading comprehension across groups of limited English proficient students. *Applied Measurement in Education 14*(3), 261–283.

Preece, A. (2009). *Reading Liberia: Guidebook for trainers.* Monrovia, Liberia, and Ottawa, Ontario, Canada: We Care Library/CODE.

Pressley, M. (1999). Self-regulated comprehension processing and its development through instruction. In L. B. Gambrell, L. M. Morrow, S. B. Neuman, & M. Pressley (Eds.), *Best practices in literacy instruction.* New York, NY: Guilford Press.

Pressley, M. (2000). What should comprehension instruction be the instruction of? In M. L. Kamil, P. B. Mosenthal, P. D. Pearson, & R. Barr (Eds.), *Handbook of reading research* (Vol. 3, pp. 545–562). Mahwah, NJ: Erlbaum.

Pressley, M. (2002). Metacognition and self-regulated comprehension. In A. E. Farstrup & S. J. Samuels (Eds.), *What research has to say about reading instruction* (pp. 291–309). Newark, DE: International Reading Association.

Pressley, M., & Afflerbach, P. (1995). *Verbal protocols of reading: The nature of constructively responsive reading.* Hillsdale, NJ: Erlbaum.

Pressley, M., Rankin, J., & Yokoi, L. (1996). A survey of instructional practices of primary teachers nominated as effective in promoting literacy. *Elementary School Journal, 96,* 363–384.

Pressley, M., Wharton-McDonald, R., Mistretta, J., & Echevarria, M. (1998). The nature of literacy instruction in ten grade 4/5 classrooms in upstate New York. *Scientific Studies of Reading, 2,* 159–191.

Purcell-Gates, V. (1996). Stories, coupons, and the *TV Guide*: Relationships between home literacy experiences and emergent literacy knowledge. *Reading Research quarterly 31*(4), 406–428.

Purugganan, M., & Hewitt, J (2004). How to read a scientific article. Retrieved from owlnet.rice.edu/~cainproj/courses/HowToReadSciArticle.pdf.

Rabinovitz, J. (2013, January 13). Poor ranking on international test misleading about U.S. student performance, Stanford researcher finds. *Stanford News*. Retrieved from http://news.stanford.edu/news/2013/january/test-scores-ranking-011513.html

Radcliffe, R., Caverly, D., Hand, J., & Franke, D. (2008, February). Improving reading in a middle school science classroom. *Journal of Adolescent and Adult Literacy, 51*(5), 398–408.

Raphael, T. E., Goatley, V., McMahon, S., & Woodman, D. (1995). Teaching literacy through student book clubs. In N. Roser & M. Martinez (Eds.), *Book talk and beyond: Children and teachers respond to literature* (pp. 66–79). Newark, DE: International Reading Association.

Raphael, T. E., & McMahon, S. I. (1994). Book club: An alternative framework for reading instruction. *The Reading Teacher, 48,* 102–117.

Rappaport, R. A. (1999). *Ritual and religion in the making of humanity.* New York, NY: Cambridge University Press.

Rasinski, T. V. (2003). *The fluent reader: Oral strategies for building word recognition, fluency, and comprehension.* New York, NY: Scholastic.

Rasinski, T. V., & Padak, N. (2005). *Three-minute reading assessments: Word recognition, fluency, and comprehension.* New York, NY: Scholastic.

Rasinski, T. V., Reutzel, D. R., Chard, D., & Linan-Thompson, S. (2011). Reading fluency. In P. D. Pearson, M. Kamil, E. B. Moje, & P. Afflerbach. *Handbook of reading research, Volume IV.* New York, NY: Routledge.

Read, C. (1975). *Children's categorization of speech sounds in English* (Research Report No. 17). Urbana, IL: National Council of Teachers of English.

Rébsamen, E. C. (1949). *La enseñanza de la escritura y lectura en el primer año escolar: Guía metodológica.* Paris: Librería de la Vda de Ch. Bouret.

Reichle, E. D., & Perfetti, C. A. (2003). Morphology in word identification: A word experience model that accounts for morpheme frequency effects. *Scientific Studies of Reading, 7,* 219–237.

Reutzel, D. R., Jones, C. D., Fawson, P. C., & Smith, J. A. (2008, November). Scaffolded silent reading: A complement to Guided Repeated Oral Reading that Works! *The Reading Teacher, 62*(3), 194–207.

Richard-Amato, P., & Snow, M. A. (1992*). The multicultural classroom: Readings for content area teachers.* New York, NY: Longman.

Rickford, J. R. (1999). *African American Vernacular English.* Malden, MA: Blackwell Publishers.

Rickford, R. R., & Rickford, A. E. (1995). Dialect readers revisited. *Linguistics and Education, 7,* 107–128.

Ringo, J. (2012). "Yo sí puedo"—Cuban Literacy Method Benefits Six Million People around the World. Retrieved from https://youthandeldersja.wordpress.com/2012/05/31/yo-si-puedo-cuban-literacy-method-benefits-six-million-people-around-the-world/

Roberts, K. L, Norman, R. R., Duke, N., Morsink, P., Martin, N. M., & Knight, J. A. (2013). Diagrams, timelines, and tables—Oh my! Fostering graphical literacy. *The Reading Teacher, 67*(1), 12–24.

Roberts, T. A. (2008). Home storybook reading in primary or second language with preschool children: Evidence of equal effectiveness for second-language vocabulary acquisition. *Reading Research Quarterly, 43*(2), 103–130.

Rodríguez Fuenzalida, E. (1982). *Metodologías de alfabetización en América Latina.* Pátzcuaro, Michoacán, México: UNESCO/ CREFAL.

Rosen, M. (2003). *We're going on a bear hunt.* Illustrated by H. Oxenbury. New York, NY: Alladin.

Rosenblatt, L. (1978). *The reader, the text, and the poem.* Carbondale, IL: Southern Illinois University Press.

Roser, N. L., & Hoffman, J. V. (1992, January). Language charts: A record of story talk. *Language Arts, 69*(1), 44–52.

Ross, T. (1992). *Stone soup.* New York, NY: Dial Books.

Routman, R. (2002). *Reading essentials: The specifics you need to teach reading well.* Portsmouth, N.H.: Heinemann.

Rowe, M. B. (1974). Wait-time and rewards as instructional variables: Their influence on language, logic and fate control: Part one—Wait time. *Journal of Research in Science Teaching, 11*(2), 81–94.

Rueda, R. S., August, D., & Goldenberg, C. (2006), The sociocultural context in which children acquire literacy. In D. August & T. Shanahan (Eds.), *Developing literacy in second-language learners: Report of the National Literacy Panel on Language-Minority Children and Youth* (pp. 319–339). Mahwah, NJ: Erlbaum.

Saddler, B. (2012). *Teacher's guide to effective sentence writing.* New York, NY: Guilford.

Salmon, K. (1995). *Lenguaje integral: Una alternativa para la enseñanza-aprendizaje de la lecto-escritura.* Quito, Ecuador: Abrapalabra Editores.

Samuels, S. J. (2007). Afterword for B. W. Riedel. The relation between DIBELS, reading comprehension, and vocabulary in urban first-grade students. *Reading Research Quarterly, 42*(4), 546–567.

Samuels, S. J., & Farstrup, A. E. (Eds.). (2006). *What research has to say about fluency instruction.* Newark, DE: International Reading Association.

Sanacore, J. (2004). Genuine caring and literacy learning for African American children. *The Reading Teacher, 57*(8), 744–753.

Santa, C. M. (1988). *Content reading including study systems: Reading, writing and studying across the curriculum.* Dubuque, IA: Kendall Hunt.

Saville, M. R., & Troike, R. C. (1971). *A handbook of bilingual education.* Washington, DC: Teachers of English to Speakers of Other Languages.

Scarcella, R. (1990). *Teaching language minority students in multicultural classrooms.* New York, NY: Longman.

Schifini, A. (1996). Reading instruction for the pre-literate and struggling older student. *NABE News, 20,* 5–6, 20, 30.

Schlagal, R. C. (1989). Constancy and change in spelling development. *Reading Psychology, 10*(3), 207–232.

Schön, D. (1983). *The reflective practitioner: How professionals think in action.* New York, NY: Basic Books.

Schon, I. (2000). *Recommended books in Spanish for children and young adults, 1996–1999.* Lanham, MD: Scarecrow Press.

Schon, I. (2001). *Los niños y el mundo:* Children's books in Spanish from around the world. *The Reading Teacher, 54,* 692–698.

Schon, I. (2002). From Pulgarcito to Shakespeare. *Language, 2,* 28–30.

Schon, I. (2004). *Recommended books in Spanish for children and young adults, 2000 through 2004.* Lanham, MD: Scarecrow Press.

Schon, I. (2009). *Recommended books in Spanish for children and young adults, 2004–2008.* Lanham, MD: Scarecrow Press, 2009.

Schon, I., & Corona Berkin, S. (1996). *Introducción a la literatura infantil y juvenil.* Newark, DE: International Reading Association.

Schwanenflugel, P. J., & Knapp, N. F. (Eds.). (2016). *The psychology of reading: Theory and applications.* New York, NY: Guilford.

Schwartz, R., & Raphael, T. (1985) Concept of definition: A key to improving students' vocabulary. *The Reading Teacher, 39,* 198–205.

Scieszka, J. (2005) *Baloney!* New York, NY: Puffin.

Scott, J., Miller, T. F., & Finspach, S. L. (2012). Developing word consciousness: Lessons from highly diverse fourth-grade classrooms. In E. J. Kame'enui & J. F. Baumann, (Eds.), *Vocabulary instruction: Research to practice* (2nd ed., pp. 169–188). New York, NY: Guilford.

Scott, J. A., Flinspach, S. L. & Vevea, J. L. (2011, December). *Identifying and teaching vocabulary in fourth and fifth grade math and science.* Paper presented at the Literacy Research Association Conference, Jacksonville, FL.

Scragg, D. G. (1974). *A history of English spelling.* New York, NY: Barnes & Noble.

Selinker, L., Swain, M., & Dumas, G. (1975). The interlanguage hypothesis extended to children. *Language Learning, 25,* 129–152.

Sepúlveda, L. (1989). *The old man who read love stories.* New York, NY: Harcourt Brace.

Serafini, F. (2014). Exploring wordless picture books. *The Reading Teacher, 68*(1), 24–26.

Shanahan, T. (2002). *A sin of the second kind: The neglect of fluency instruction and what we can do about it.* PowerPoint presentation at A Focus on Fluency Forum, San Francisco, CA. Retrieved from www.prel.org/programs/rel/fluency/Shanahan.ppt

Shanahan, T. (2016). *Meeting the challenge of Common Core: Planning close reading in close reading shift kit.* Normal, IL: Illinois State University: Center for the Advancement and Support of Educational Initiatives.

Shanahan, T. & Shanahan, C. (2008) Teaching disciplinary literacy to adolescents: Rethinking content-area literacy. Harvard Education Review. 78, 40–59.

Shaw, R., & Shaw, D. (2002). *DIBELS Oral Reading Fluency-based indicators of third grade reading skills for Colorado State Assessment Program (CSAP).* (Tech. Rep.) Eugene, OR: University of Oregon.

Shaywitz, S. E., Escobar, M. D., Shaywitz, B. A., Fletcher, J. M., & Makuch, J. R. (1992). Evidence that dyslexia may represent the lower tail of a normal distribution of reading ability. *New England Journal of Medicine, 326,* 145–150.

Shinn, M. R. (Ed.). (1989). *Curriculum-based measurement: Assessing special children.* New York, NY: Guilford.

Short, K., Harste, J., & Burke, C. (1996). *Creating classrooms for authors and inquirers.* Portsmouth, NH: Heinemann.

Short, K., & Kauffman, G. (1995). So what do I do? The role of the teacher in literature circles. In N. Roser & M. Martinez (Eds.), *Book talk and beyond: Children and teachers respond to literature* (pp. 140–149). Newark, DE: International Reading Association.

Simon, S. (2007, June 1). Teaching kids right from left. *The Los Angeles Times.* Retrieved from http://articles.latimes.com/2007/jun/01/nation/na-kidbooks1.

Simpkins, G., Holt, G., & Simpkins, C. (1974). *Bridge: A cross-culture reading program.* Boston, MA: Houghton Mifflin.

Skerry, B. (2010). *Face to face with manatees.* Washington, DC: National Geographic Society.

Slavin, R. E., Madden, N., Calderón, M., Chamberlain, A., & Hennessy, M. (2010). *Reading and language outcomes of a five-year randomized evaluation of transitional bilingual education.* Retrieved from http://www.edweek.org/media/bilingual_pdf.pdf

Smith, C. B. (1997). Vocabulary instruction and reading comprehension. *ERIC Digest.* ERIC Clearinghouse on Reading English and Communication #126.

Smith, F. (1973). *Psycholinguistics and reading.* New York, NY: Holt, Rinehart & Winston.

Smith, F. (1986). *Keynote address: How education backed the wrong horse.* Presented at the meeting of the California Reading Association, Fresno.

Snow, C. E., Burns, M. S., & Griffin, P. (Eds.). (1998). *Preventing reading difficulties in young children.* Committee on the Prevention of Reading Difficulties in Young Children. Commission on Behavioral and Social Sciences and Education, National Research Council. Washington, DC: National Academy Press.

Snowling, M. J. (2000). *Dyslexia.* London, England: Blackwell.

Snyder, L. (2010). Reading expository material: Are we asking the right questions? *Topics in Language Disorders, 30*(1), 39–47.

Solé, I. (1994). *Estrategias de lectura.* Barcelona, Spain: Graó Editorial.

Souriau, E. (1955). *Les deux cent milles situations dramatiques.* Paris, France: Flamarion.

Spache, G. (1981). *Diagnosing and correcting reading disabilities* (2nd ed.). Boston, MA: Allyn & Bacon.

Spandel, V. (1996). *Seeing with new eyes.* Portland, OR: Northwest Regional Educational Laboratory.

Spandel, V. (2000). *Creating writers through 6-trait writing assessment and instruction* (3rd ed.). Boston, MA: Allyn & Bacon.

Spandel, V. (2012). *Creating writers: 6 traits, process, workshop, and literature (6th edition).* New York: Pearson.

Spinelli, J. (1990a). *Maniac Magee.* Boston, MA: Little, Brown.

Spinelli, J. (1990b). *Maniac Magee.* New York, NY: Scholastic. Large-print version from Library Reproduction Service, ISBN 0-590-45203-7.

Spolin, V. (1986). *Theater games for the classroom.* Evanston, IL: Northwestern University Press.

Stahl, R. J. (1994). Using "think time" and "wait-time" skillfully in the classroom. ERIC Digest, ED370885.

Stahl, S.A. & Nagy, W.E. (2006). *Teaching word meanings.* Mahwah, N.J.: Erlbaum.

Stahl, K. A. D., & Stahl, S. A. (2012). Young word wizards!: Fostering vocabulary development in preschool and primary education. In E. J. Kame'enui & J. F. Baumann (Eds.), *Vocabulary instruction, research to practice* (2nd ed.). New York, NY: Guilford Press.

Stanovich, K. E. (1986). Matthew effects in reading: Some consequences of individual differences in the acquisition of literacy. *Reading Research Quarterly, 21,* 360–407.

Stanovich, K. E. (1992). Are we overselling literacy? In C. Temple & P. Collins (Eds.), *Stories and readers.* Norwood, MA: Christopher Gordon.

Stanovich, K. E., & Siegel, L. S. (1994). Phenotypic performance profiles of children with reading disabilities: A regression-based test of the phonological core variable-difference model. *Journal of Educational Psychology, 86,* 24–53.

Stauffer, R. (1975). *The language experience approach to the teaching of reading.* New York, NY: Harper.

Steele, J. L., & Meredith, K. E. (1997). *Critical thinking.* New York, NY: Open Society Institute.

Stein, N. L., & Glenn, C. F. (1979). An analysis of story comprehension in elementary school children. In R. O. Freedle (Ed.), *New directions in discourse processing: Vol. 2. Advances in discourse processes* (pp. 53–120). Norwood, NJ: Ablex.

Sternberg, R., & Powell, J. (1983). Comprehending verbal comprehension. *American Psychologist, 38,* 878–893.

Stevens, R. A., Butler, F. A., & Castellon-Wellington, M. (2000). *Academic language and content assessment: Measuring the progress of English language learners* (CSE Technical Report No. 552). Los Angeles: University of California, National Center for Research on Evaluation, Standards, and Student Testing.

Strickland, D. S. (1991). Cooperative, collaborative learning for children and teachers (emerging readers and writers). *Reading Teacher, 44,* 600–602.

Stritikus, T. (2006). Making meaning matter: A look at instructional practice in additive and subtractive contexts. *Bilingual Research Journal, 30*(1), 219–227.

Strunk, W., & White, E. B. (1999). *The elements of style* (4th ed). Boston, MA: Pearson.

Suárez-Orozco, C., Suárez-Orozco, M. M., & Todovora, I. (2008). *Learning in a new land: Immigrant students in American society.* Cambridge, MA: The Belknap Press of Harvard University Press.

Sulzby, E. (1985). Kindergarteners as writers and readers. In M. Farr (Ed.), *Advances in writing research: Vol. 1. Children's early writing development* (pp. 127–199). Norwood, NJ: Ablex.

Sutherland-Smith, W. (2002). Weaving the literacy web: Changes in reading from page to screen. *The Reading Teacher, 55,* 662–669.

Taylor, B., Pearson, P. D., Clark, K., & Walpole, S. (1999). *Beating the odds in teaching all children to read.* Ann Arbor, MI: CIERA. Retrieved from http://www.ciera.org/library/reports/inquiry-1/1-010/1-010.pdf

Taylor, B. M. (2008). Effective classroom reading instruction in the elementary grades. In D. Fuchs, L. W. Fuchs, & S. Vaughn (Eds.), *Response to intervention: A framework for reading educators.* Newark, DE: International Reading Association.

Taylor, B. M., & Pearson, P. D. (2005). Using study groups and reading assessment data to improve reading instruction within a school. In S. Paris & S. A. Stahl (Eds.), *Children's reading comprehension and assessment* (pp. 237–255). Mahwah, NJ: Erlbaum.

Taylor, W. L. (1953). Cloze procedure: A new device for measuring readability. *Journalism Quarterly, 45,* 415–433.

Teale, W. H., & Sulzby, E. (1987). Literacy acquisition in early childhood: The roles of access and mediation in storybook reading. In D. Wagner (Ed.), *The future of literacy in a changing world* (pp. 111–130). New York, NY: Pergamon Press.

Temple, C., Crawford, A., & Gillet, J. W. (2009). *Developmental literacy inventory.* Boston, MA: Pearson.

Temple C., & MaKinster, J. (2005). *Intervening for literacy.* Boston, MA: Allyn & Bacon.

Temple, C., Martinez, M., & Yokota, J. (2014). *Children's books in children's hands* (4th ed.). Boston, MA: Allyn & Bacon.

Temple, C., Nathan, R., Burris, N., & Temple, F. (1993). *The beginnings of writing* (3rd ed.). Boston, MA: Allyn & Bacon.

Temple, C. A., Nathan, R., and Temple, C.F. (2012). *The beginnings of writing*, 4th edition. New York: Pearson.

Temple, C., Nathan, R., & Temple, C. (2013). *The beginnings of writing* (4th ed.). Boston, MA: Pearson.

Temple, F. (1992). *Tiger soup*. New York, NY: Orchard.

Temple, F. (1995). *Tonight, by sea*. New York, NY: Harper Trophy.

Temple, F. (1996). *The Beduin's gazelle*. New York, NY: Orchard.

Terman, L. (1916). *The measurement of intelligence*. Stanford, CA: Stanford University Press.

Terrell, T. D. (1977). A natural approach to second language acquisition and learning. *Modern Language Journal, 6*, 325–337.

Terrell, T. D. (1981). The natural approach in bilingual education. In California State Department of Education (Ed.), *School and language minority students: A theoretical framework* (pp. 117–146). California State University, Los Angeles: Evaluation, Dissemination and Assessment Center.

Terrell, T. D. (1982). The natural approach to language teaching: An update. *Modern Language Journal, 66*, 121–122.

TESOL. (1997). *Policy statement of the TESOL board on African American vernacular English*. Arlington, VA: Center for Applied Linguistics.

Texas Education Agency. (2009). Retrieved from http://ritter.tea.state.tx.us/teks/

Thomas, W. P., & Collier, V. (1997). *School effectiveness for language minority students*. Washington, DC: National Clearinghouse for Bilingual Education.

Thomas, W. P., & Collier, V. P. (2002). *A national study of school effectiveness for language minority students' long-term academic achievement final report: Project 1.1*. Santa Cruz, CA: Center for Research on Education, Diversity and Excellence.

Tileston, D. W. (2011). *Closing the RTI gap: Why poverty and culture count*. Bloomington, IN: Solution Tree.edu/eecearchive/digests/2000/tomlin00.pdf

Tompkins, G. (2000). *Teaching writing: Balancing process and product*. Columbus, OH: Merrill.

Topping, K. J. (1987). Paired reading: A powerful technique for parent use. *The Reading Teacher, 40*, 608–614.

Torres Quintero, G. (1976). *Método onomatopéyico*. Mexico City: Editorial Patria.

Trelease, J. (2006). *The read-aloud handbook* (6th ed.). New York, NY: Penguin Books.

Trieman, R. (1985). Onsets and rimes as units of spoken syllables: Evidence from children. *Journal of Experimental Child Psychology, 39*, 161–181.

Tripplet, C. (2014). *TESOL releases statement on Every Student Succeeds Act*, TESOL. Retrieved from https://www.tesol.org/news-landing-page/2015/12/04/tesol-releases-statement-on-every-student-succeeds-act

Trout, B. (1993, November). Little dogies, lay down. *Highlights for Children*.

U.S. Census Bureau. (2011). *Overview of race and Hispanic origin*. Retrieved from http://www.census.gov/prod/cen2010/briefs/c2010br-02.pdf

U.S. Department of Education. (2000). *Report of the National Reading Panel: Teaching children to read, an evidence-based assessment of the scientific research literature on reading and its implications for reading instruction*. Washington, DC: U.S. Government Printing Office.

U.S. Department of Education. (2001). *No child left behind*. Retrieved from http://www.ed.gov/offices/OESE/esea/

U.S. Department of Education. (2004). *No Child Left Behind: Toolkit for teachers*. Retrieved from http://www2.ed.gov/teachers/nclbguide/nclb-teachers-toolkit.pdf

U.S. Department of Health and Human Services. (2006). *Quick guide to health literacy*. Retrieved from http://www.health.gov/communication/literacy/quickguide/about.htm

UNESCO. (1953). *The use of vernacular languages in education*. Paris: Author.

Urrea, L. A. (1996). *By the lake of sleeping children: The secret life of the Mexican border*. New York, NY: Anchor Books.

Vacca, R., & Vacca, J. (1986). *Content area reading*. Boston, MA: Allyn & Bacon.

Vacca, R., & Vacca, J. (1996). *Content area reading* (5th ed.). New York, NY: HarperCollins.

Valencia, S., Hiebert, E. & Afflerbach, P. (1993). *Authentic reading assessment: Practices and possibilities*. Newark, DE: International Reading Association.

VanDoren, C., & Adler, M. (1972) *How to read a book*. New York, NY: Touchstone Books.

Vaughn, J., & Estes, T. (1986). *Reading and reasoning beyond the primary grades*. Boston, MA: Allyn & Bacon.

Vaughn, S., & Fuchs, L. S. (2003). Redefining learning disabilities as inadequate response to instruction: The promise and potential problems. *Learning Disabilities Research & Practice, 18*(3), 137–146. doi:10.1111/1540-5826.00070.

Veatch, J. (1996). From the vantage of retirement. *The Reading Teacher, 49*, 510–516.

Veatch, J., Sawicki, F., Elliott, G., Flake, E., & Blakey, J. (1979*). Key words to reading: The language experience approach begins*. Columbus, OH: Merrill.

Veenendaal, N. J., Groen, M.A., & Verhoeven, L. (2015). The contribution of segmental and suprasegmental phonology to reading comprehension. *Reading Research Quarterly, 51*(1), 55–66.

Vellutino, F. R., & Scanlon, D. M. (2001). Emergent literacy skills, early instruction, and individual differences as determinants of difficulties in learning to read: The case for early intervention. In S. B. Newman & D. K. Dickinson (Eds.), *Handbook of early literacy research.* New York, NY: Guilford Press.

Vellutino, F. R., Scanlon, D. M., Sipay, E. R., Small, S. G., Pratt, A., Chen, R., & Denckla, M. B. (1996). Cognitive profiles of difficult-to-remediate and readily remediated poor readers: Early intervention as a vehicle for distinguishing between cognitive and experiential deficits as a basic cause of specific reading disability. *Journal of Educational Psychology, 88*, 601–638.

Verhoeven, L. (1990, Spring). Acquisition of reading in a second language. *Reading Research Quarterly, 25*(2), 90–114.

Vernon-Feagans, L., Hammer, C. S., Miccio, A., & Manlove, E. (2001). Early language and literacy skills in low-income African American and Hispanic children. In D. K. Dickenson & S. B. Newman (Eds.), *Handbook of early literacy research.* New York, NY: Guilford.

Vogt, M.E., & Echevarria, J. (2015). Reaching English learners: Aligning the ELA/ELD Framework with SIOP. *The California Reader, 49*(1), 23–27.

Vygotsky, L. S. (1976). *Thought and language.* Cambridge, MA: MIT Press.

Vygotsky, L. S. (1978). *Mind in society: The development of higher psychological processes.* Cambridge, MA: Harvard University Press.

Vygotsky, L. S. (1982). *Thought and language.* Cambridge, MA: MIT Press.

Wagner, B. J. (1999). *Dorothy Heathcote: Drama as a learning medium.* Portsmouth, NH: Heinemann.

Wagner, R. K., Torgesen, J. K., & Rashotte, C. A. (1994). The development of reading-related phonological processing abilities: New evidence of bidirectional causality from a latent variable longitudinal study. *Developmental Psychology, 30*, 73–87.

Walsh, D.J., Price, G. G., & Gillingham, M. G. (1988). The critical but transitory importance of letter naming. *Reading Research Quarterly, 23*, 108–122.

Walton, R. (2011). *Bullfrog Pops! Adventures in verbs and direct objects.* Layton, UT: Gibbs Smith.

Watson, A. (2013). Conceptualisations of grammar teaching: L1 English teachers' beliefs about teaching grammar for writing. *Language Awareness, 24*(1), 1–15.

Weaver, C. (2008). *Grammar to enrich & enhance writing.* Portsmouth, NH: Heinemann.

Weinberg, S., Martin, D., & Monte-Sano, C. (2012). *Reading like a historian.* New York, NY: Teachers College Press.

Wheeler, R., Cartwright, K. B., & Swords, R. (2012). Factoring AAVE into reading assessment and instruction. *The Reading Teacher, 65*(5), 416–425.

Whipple, G. (Ed.). (1925). *The twenty-fourth yearbook of the National Society for the Study of Education: Report of the National Committee on Reading.* Bloomington, IN: Public School Publishing.

White, E. B. (1980). *Charlotte's web.* New York, NY: Harper Trophy. (Original work published in 1952.)

Whitehurst, G. J. (1994). *Dialogic reading for parents: Headstart, K, and pre-K* (available from G. J. Whitehurst, State University of New York at Stony Brook, Stony Brook, NY 11794–2500).

Whitehurst, G., & Lonigan, C. (2001). Child development and emergent literacy. *Child Development, 69*, 848–872.

Whitehurst, G. J., & Lonigan, C. J. (2001). Emergent literacy: From pre-readers to readers. In S. B. Neuman & D. K. Dickinson (Eds.), *Handbook of early literacy research.* New York, NY: Guilford Press.

Wiggins, G., & McTighe, J. (2005). *Thinking by design, expanded edition.* Washington, DC: Association for Supervision and Curriculum Development.

Wilder, P. (2016). *Promoting student self-assessment: A strategy guide.* Newark, Delaware. International Literacy Association and National Council of Teachers of English: *Read/Write/Think.*

Wilhelm, J. D., & Smith, M. W. (2014). Reading don't fix no Chevys (yet)! *Journal of Adolescent & Adult Literacy, 58*(4), 273–276.

Willems, M. (2003). *Don't let the pigeon drive the bus!* New York, NY: Hyperion.

Williams, S. (1991). Classroom use of African American Language: Educational tool or social weapon? In C. Sleeter (Ed.), *Empowering through multicultural education* (pp. 199–215). New York, NY: State University of New York.

Wilson, J. (2005). *The relationship of Dynamic Indicators of Basic Early Literacy Skills (DIBELS) Oral Reading Fluency to performance on Arizona Instrument to Measure Standards (AIMS).* Tempe, AZ: Tempe School District No. 3.

Wilson, P. (1992). Among non-readers. In C. Temple & P. Collins (Eds.), *Stories and readers.* Norwood, MA: Christopher—Gordon.

Wixson, K. K., & Lipson, M. Y. (2012). Relations between the CCSS and RTI in literacy and language. *The Reading Teacher, 65*(5), 387–391.

Wixson, K. K., & Valencia, S. W. (2011). Assessment in RTI: What teachers and specialists need to know. *The Reading Teacher, 64*(6), 466–469.

Wolf, M. K., Herman, J. L., Bachman, L.F., Bailey, A.L., & Griffin, N. (2008). *Recommendations for assessing English language learners: English language proficiency measures and accommodation uses: CRESST Report 737.* Los Angeles, CA: UCLA.

Wong-Fillmore, L., & Snow, C. (2000). *What teachers need to know about language.* Washington, DC: U.S. Department of Education, OERI.

Wood, S., & Jocius, R. (2013). Combating "I hate this stupid book." *The Reading Teacher, 66*(8), 661–669.

Woodson, J. (2014). *Brown girl dreaming.* New York, NY: Nancy Paulsen Books.

Wylie, R. E., & Durrell, D. D. (1970). Teaching vowels through phonograms. *Elementary English, 47,* 787–791.

Yap, M. J., Balota, D. A., Sibley, D. E., & Ratcliff, R. (2012). Individual differences in visual word recognition: Insights from the English Lexicon Project. *Journal of Experimental Psychology: Human Perception and Performance, 38*(1), 53–79.

Yopp, H. K. (1988). The validity and reliability of phonemic awareness tests. *Reading Research Quarterly, 23,* 159–177.

Yopp, H. K., & Stapleton, L. (2008). Conciencia fonémica en español (Phonemic awareness in Spanish). *The Reading Teacher, 61*(5), 374–382.

Young, J. P., & Brozo, W. G. (2001). Boys will be boys, or will they? Literacy and masculinities. *Reading Research Quarterly, 36*(3), 316–325.

Zambo, D. (2007). Using picture books to provide archetypes for young boys: Extending the ideas of William Brozo. *The Reading Teacher, 61*(2), 124–131.

Zambo, D., & Brozo, W. G. (2009). *Bright beginnings for boys: Engaging young boys in active literacy.* Newark, DE: International Reading Association.

Zarrillo, J. (2010). *Are you prepared to teach reading?* (2nd ed.). Englewood Cliffs, NJ: Prentice Hall.

Zehr, M. A. (2008). *Ten-year anniversary of bilingual education.* Retrieved from http://blogs.edweek.org/edweek/learning-the-language/2008/06/tenyear_anniversary_of_proposi.html

Zemach, H. (1964). *Nail soup.* Chicago, IL: Follett.

Zutell, J. (1999). Sorting it out through word sorts. In I. C. Fountas & G. S. Pinnell (Eds.), *Voices on word matters* (pp. 103–113). Portsmouth, NH: Heinemann.

Zutell, J., & Rasinski, T. (1991). Training teachers to attend to their students' oral reading fluency. *Theory Into Practice, 30,* 212–217.

Glossary

ABC framework—a structure for comprehension instruction that includes **A**nticipation, **B**uilding knowledge, and **C**onsolidation of ideas

Academic vocabulary—words that occur in school contexts during content learning

Acrostic—poem created by listing the letters of a name vertically and then elaborating on the poem's theme with words and phrases for each key letter in the order in which they occur

Additive program—a program in which a second language is added to the mother tongue that the student already knows; the goal is a bilingual/bicultural individual; it is the outcome of a maintenance transitional model for bilingual education in which the student adds to mother tongue proficiency, which is maintained after the transition to English

Affix—a prefix or a suffix

African American Vernacular English (AAVE)—a dialect of English spoken mainly by African American students; it has a unique and regular vocabulary and grammatical structures different from those found in Standard American English, but consistent in application

Alphabetic phase of word recognition—a phase in which children read words by decoding

Alphabetic principle—the system of representing phonemes with graphemes

Alphabetic writing system—a writing system in which the characters represent phonemes

Amazing Fact Sheet—a graphic template on which young children record information they want to share from a text they have read

Analytic reading—careful reading to determine how the author has structured the ideas and what evidence is presented to support his or her argument or point of view

Anthology—a collection of readings

Anticipation—in comprehension instruction, *anticipation* refers to the period immediately prior to reading a text, when students are reminded of their prior knowledge, are pre-taught vocabulary, and are prepared to make sense of the text

Antonym—word with meaning opposite of the target word

Appositive—a phase that follows a word to explain the meaning of that word

Assessment—in reading, assessment entails gathering, analyzing, and interpreting information to determine how well a student reads

Assimilated prefix—a prefix whose final consonant has changed to match the pronunciation of the first consonant of the base word

Authentic assessment—an approach to assessment that involves both informal and structured observations and work sampling, including portfolios

Authentic literature—literature written for the reader to enjoy, not text written for use in the teaching of reading

Automaticity—a level of performance where little conscious effort is required

Background knowledge—readers' existing knowledge and experiences about a topic

Base word—a word to which affixes have been added

Basic interpersonal communication skills (BICS)—basic interpersonal communication skills, the ability to converse in a second language at a conversational level, which is thought to be different from academic language

Behaviorist, reductionist—an approach to psychology that considers human behavior through scientific observation; in learning, it is often viewed as part-whole

Benchmark—a standard that achievement is measured against

Bidialectical—a student who is proficient in two dialects of a language, such as an African American student who can switch easily and confidently between African American Vernacular English and Standard American English, and who knows when to use each dialect

Book clubs—an approach to discussing books in which students are encouraged to take the lead in sharing their impressions of a work

Bound morpheme—a morpheme that must combine with other morphemes to form a word

Buddy reading—a method to develop reading fluency in which students pair up, take turns, and practice reading a text aloud

Building knowledge—refers to the phase of reading the text for comprehension, and the inquiry and thinking that occurs while the text is being read

Chapter graphic organizer—a visual diagram showing the title of a chapter and the main headings that can be used while reading to add notes and indicate questions and key ideas

Character cluster—a semantic map for exploring character traits with evidence of those traits

Character map—a graphic organizer displaying relations among characters

Chunking—reading groups of related words—clauses and phrases—together

Close reading—attending carefully to and analyzing a text; this process involves several readings of the same text and is usually guided by a teacher to build greater understanding of how an author has structured ideas and developed arguments or a point of view

Cognitive academic language proficiency (CALP)—cognitive academic language proficiency; sufficient second language proficiency to learn to read, write, and learn academic subjects

Cognitive apprenticeship—teaching by modeling proficient behavior for the students to imitate

Collocation—the phenomenon of words that often occur together

Communicative approaches to second language acquisition—thematic approaches to second language acquisition that attempt to replicate the successful language learning environment of the child at home; they include the natural approach and the total physical response approach (TPR)

Complex sentence—a sentence with a main clause and one or more subordinate clauses

Compound sentence—a sentence made up of two or more main clues

Comprehensible input—oral input to a student that is made understandable by the teacher and that is accompanied by a small amount of new information, such as a new word that is understood in a familiar context; it is often expressed as CI + 1

Comprehension-level question—a question that is at a higher level than simple recall; for example, "How did the author tell you that the main character was frightened?"; the reader must make an inference, as the word *frightened* does not appear in the text

Concept cluster—a visual array of words associated with the key concepts

Concept ladder—a visual tool students use to arrange similar words in meaningful hierarchies (such as types of, results of)

Concept of Definition Map—a graphic organizer that positions a key word in a larger frame: the category of the term, words that describe it, and examples are included; often students also draw a picture or illustration of the term's meaning

Concept of word—awareness that language comes in units of words, and that in print, words are represented by clusters of letters with spaces on either end

Concepts about print—knowledge of the features of print that orient children to the tasks of learning to read

Connect Two—an activity to focus attention on new vocabulary terms; students are asked to connect two new words into a single sentence that highlights the meanings of both words

Connected word web—a visual diagram of words that are associated by their morphemes

Connotation—the associations or feelings that a word communicates in addition to its literal meaning, and that can be positive or negative

Consolidation—refers to the phase immediately after reading the text for comprehension, when the reader reflects on, interprets, applies, or debates the meaning of the text

Consonant assimilation—the changing of one consonant to match the consonant that follows

Constructivism—refers to a theory of learning that holds that readers create meaning partly from their own prior knowledge and concepts with clues from the text

Constructivist view—creation of meaning through individual constructs; in learning, it is often viewed as whole-part-whole

Content validity—the degree to which a test measures what is claimed for it to—that is, the similarity between an item on a test and the skill or behavior under real-world circumstances that the item purports to evaluate

Context clues—information provided in the text that helps define new terms: the sentence and surrounding paragraph, examples, appositives and synonyms, and visual displays

Conversation poster—a newspaper-sized color poster based on a topic from a thematic curriculum, such as the classroom, transportation, or major holidays

Critical literacy—the activity and accompanying disposition of examining the social, political, and cultural purposes and values that are reflected in the texts being read

Critical thinking—a process of reasoning and reflecting that is done in order to decide what to believe or what course of action to take

Curriculum-based measurement—a system of testing based on standards that is administered periodically and sometimes frequently to make sure students are making desired progress in learning

Decoding—using knowledge of phonics to read a word by sounding it out

Decontextualized language—language that refers to things that are not present in one's immediate surroundings

Denotation—the literal meaning of a word

Derivational phase of spelling—the most advanced level of spelling development in which children are learning that spelling is influenced by words or parts of words that are derived from other words, sometimes ancient words or affixes from Latin or Greek

Derivational phase of word recognition—phase or stage in which readers recognize words that are derived from each other, including some awareness of word histories

Derivational affix—a prefix or suffix that changes the part of speech of the base word

Dialogic reading—a structured procedure for discussing a book with young children

Digraph consonants—spellings of single consonant phonemes with two letters

Diphthong—a double vowel sound

Domain-specific vocabulary—words that occur almost exclusively in a specific academic context (mathematical processes, scientific terms, geographic labels, etc.)

DRA—Directed Reading Activity, where the teacher calls out questions before important parts of a text and asks students to read and find answers to them

DRTA—Directed Reading-Thinking Activity, where the teacher asks students to make predictions before each section of a text, and read to find if the predictions were correct

Dual-entry diary—a response journal kept in two columns, with quotations on the left, and comments on the right

Early phonemic phase of spelling—an immature level of spelling in which letters are used to spell some sounds in words, but incompletely

Early production stage—the stage in the natural approach to language acquisition during which students begin to respond with yes/no, single words, and pairs of words

Emergence of speech stage—the stage in the natural approach to language acquisition during which students begin to respond with phrases or short sentences, instead of just a word or two

Emergent literacy—an early stage in reading instruction where students develop the concept of print and the concept of word

Engagement—taking charge of one's own learning with a clear purpose and motivation

English language learner (ELL)—a student whose mother tongue is not English and who is learning English as a second language

Envisionment—a term from literary criticism that means "calling up in the mind's eye"

Etymology—word origin

Expressive vocabulary—words one can use in speaking and writing

External features—the visible elements that highlight text organization and content; they include the table of contents, headings, sub-headings, highlighted terms, and visual and graphic displays

Fluency oriented oral reading (FOOR)—a method that combines a demonstration of fluent oral reading by the teacher, practice by pairs of students, and choral reading in a group

Formative assessments—assessments done while instruction is going on, in order to see how well the instruction is working

Frayer Model—four-part graphic organizer for new words with boxes for essential and nonessential characteristics/examples and nonexamples

Free morpheme—a morpheme that can stand alone as a word

Frustration reading level—the level of challenge of reading material that is excessively challenging for a particular child

General academic vocabulary—words that are encountered in a variety of academic contexts

Genres—types or varieties of text; examples include folktales, realistic fiction, legends, poetry, persuasive essays, etc.

Grade equivalent score—when a student's performance on a test is reported as similar to that of students performing adequately at a particular grade level

Gradual release of responsibility—a model of teaching that ranges from having the teacher writing or reading and the children observing to just the opposite

Grammatical suffix—(See inflectional suffix)

Grand conversations—a discussion strategy in which deep and open-ended questions are posed to a group of students

Grapheme—a small unit of written language that represents a speech sound (e.g., a letter or a cluster of letters)

Graphics—visual features within texts designed to explain information; these include diagrams, tables, and charts

Guided reading—an instructional process in which the teacher guides the reading and poses questions before a paragraph or a page; text is often chunked or broken into smaller pieces than an entire story or informational text to make it less burdensome to developing readers

Guided Repeated Oral Reading (GROR)—a method that combines a demonstration of fluent oral reading by the teacher with oral reading practice by the students

Homographs—words that are spelled the same but have different meanings, and sometimes different pronunciations

Homophones—words that sound the same but have different meanings

I-Chart—the inquiry chart is a graphic organizer grid on which key questions students ask are listed on one axis and several texts that are pertinent are listed on the other. Students find how each of the texts addresses the questions and record those answers on the grid before creating their own summary of what they consider the answer to each question

I-R-E—Initiation, response, and evaluation are the three moves teachers traditionally make when engaging students in responding to texts; they ask questions, seek one response, and provide an evaluation without extending opportunities for probing the question

Ideographic writing system—a writing system in which the characters directly represent ideas

Idiom—a phrase whose meaning cannot be predicted from the meaning of the individual words

Immersion instruction—teaching English language learners in the areas of reading and academic subjects in English only; sometimes called submersion instruction

Inclusion—in schools, the practice of placing special education students in regular classrooms for as much of the school day as is appropriate; the purpose is to avoid segregating special education students all of the time

Incremental growth—word learning that occurs over time; words vary in their meanings and appropriate usage and this requires multiple encounters

Independent reading level—the level of challenge of reading material that a particular child can read on his or her own, without the support of a teacher or other more skilled readers

Inflectional suffix—an affix that adds grammatical information to the base word

Informal reading inventories—individually administered commercial or teacher-made tests consisting of text samples and word lists on graduated levels of difficulty, with comprehension questions and measures of fluency and word recognition

Informational text—also called nonfiction; a text presenting accurate information that was written to instruct readers

Instructional reading level—the level of challenge of reading material that is moderately challenging for a particular child

Inter-rater reliability—measured when an instrument such as a rubric is used by different raters to assess the same student, and the results are compared

Interlanguage—also called telegraphic speech, where students speak in truncated phrases as they develop proficiency, such as " doggy big"

Intermediate level—the level that follows emergence of speech; the level at which students are ready for formal reading instruction in English and sheltered instruction in academic subjects

Internal organization—the way an author organizes ideas and information; common patterns include chronology, description and details, compare/contrast, problem/solution, and sequence

Invented spelling—spellings generated by children who have not been taught to spell those words

Jigsaw text—readers divide the task into sections based on chapter headings and share what they learn; together they "solve the puzzle" of the ideas an author presents

Kidwatching—a structured form of informal observation of learning

KWL—Know, Want to Know, and Learn; a strategy used for guided comprehension of informational text in which teachers guide students to first activate what they **K**now, raise questions about what they **W**ant to Know, and then record what they **L**earn

KWL+—KWL with the added components of organizing what has been learned graphically and then writing a summary; this helps students internalize new knowledge and ideas

Language experience approach (LEA)—an approach to beginning reading instruction often used in second language instruction; students dictate text to be read later to the teacher, who faithfully writes it down on a chart; students develop the concept that what they say can be represented by print

Language form—any formal aspect of language, such as pronunciation, spelling, morphological structure, sentence structure, or text organization

Letter name phase of spelling—an early level of spelling development in which letter names are matched with the phonemes children wish to spell

Lexile Framework—a widely used-computer-based system of measuring readability, accompanied by lists of books rated according to their levels of challenge or Lexiles

Literacy—a set of concepts and skills that enable a person to make sense of and communicate messages through the medium of written language

Literature circles—a cooperative discussion strategy in which students are pre-assigned different roles (to pose questions, to make inferences, to explore vocabulary, etc.)

Logographic phase of word recognition—a phase in which children read words as wholes, without any decoding

Matthew Effects—a reference to the Biblical passage in the Gospel According to Saint Matthew about the rich getting richer and the poor get poorer; the analogy to reading is that those who develop early reading skills will avidly practice reading and gain more skills, while those who lack early skills will avoid practice and fall behind

Mentor text—a short text that clearly illustrates one aspect of the writer's craft

Metacognition—thinking about one's own thinking and learning processes

Metalanguage—language about language; linguistic terminology

Metalinguistic awareness—the ability to analyze and reflect on language structure and language use

Monitoring—the process of metacognitively checking to insure that one understands what one is reading and that one's purposes are fulfilled

Monophthong—a single vowel sound

Morpheme—the smallest meaningful part of language

Morphological phase of spelling—a spelling stage in which children are taking note of word parts whose spellings influence their meanings

Morphological phase of word recognition—phase or stage in which readers correctly pronounce morphemes in words, and understand the effects of morphemes on word meanings

Morphology—the study and identification of meaning-bearing units of language

NAEP—The National Assessment of Educational Progress, a federally administered test of reading and other subjects given in the United States to students in fourth, eighth, and twelfth grades

Natural approach—a communicative approach to language acquisition in which students proceed through three stages: pre-production, early production, and emergence of speech; correction is minimized

Nested command—one natural approach command inside another one; for example, "If Mario is wearing a red sweater today, stand up, Juan. If Margarita has brown shoes, put your finger on your nose, Marisela"

New Literacies—making meaning from non-print forms of communication, forms that are emerging so rapidly they are called "literacies" instead of "literacy" because new media may require new reading and writing strategies

Nonverbal behavior—communication behavior conveyed without speaking, such as gestures and facial expressions

Norm-referenced tests—also called standardized tests, are tests with performance levels that have been established by collecting and averaging scores of large numbers of subjects

Noun—the name of a person, place, or thing

Onset—the consonant/s preceding the vowel in a syllable; in a spoken syllable, the beginning consonant sound

Orthographic phase of spelling—a spelling stage in which children begin to spell clusters of letters such as rimes or phonogram patterns correctly

Orthographic phase of word recognition—a phase or stage in which readers analyze words into onsets and rimes

Orthography—a set of rules for spelling. A *shallow orthography* is a spelling system where each grapheme regularly represents the same phoneme, and vice versa. A *deep orthography* is a spelling system that may have a discernible structure, but not a simple relationship between letters and sounds

Paired reading—a method of having students practice reading for fluency in which a stronger and a weaker reader work together and support each other

Paired reading/paired summarizing—a reading technique in which one student reads a paragraph aloud and summarizes it, the other student asks questions about the passage that both answer, and then they change roles with the next paragraph

Percentile scores—scores based on a 99-point scale that tell what percentage of the students in a comparison group received a lower score than a particular child

Phoneme—the smallest sound unit of speech, which makes a distinction between different words

Phonemic awareness—awareness of the phonemes or sounds in spoken words

Phonics—an umbrella term for explicit, implicit, and systematic ways to teach children how the print-to-speech and speech-to-print system works

Phonogram pattern—another term for a rime, or a vowel plus consonant in a syllable

Phonological awareness—awareness of the smaller units of spoken language, including syllables, onsets, rimes, and phonemes

PIRLS—Progress in International Reading Literacy Survey, a literacy test administered to fourth graders in 54 OECD countries or administrative areas (for instance, Shanghai and Hong Kong are treated separately)

PISA—Programme for International Student Assessment—a test of reading, mathematics, and science administered to 15-year-olds in 70 countries

Polysemous—describes a word that can have more than one meaning

Portfolios—collections of children's works gathered according to the objectives of the teacher's instruction

PRC2—a partner reading and learning activity based on children reading two-page spreads together, with each taking charge of their page, reading it orally, asking a question, and discussing the answer

Predictive validity—the power of a test to predict the student's future performance on related tasks

Preference ranking—a communicative approach activity in which students indicate preferences, such as colors or ice cream flavors; these are placed in a chart on the x-axis with students' names on the y-axis; this provides a base for extended conversations in the second language

Prefix—a morpheme added at the beginning of a base word, and which changes the meaning of the base word

Preliterate—students in upper elementary grades, junior and senior high school grades, and adults who are not literate; common among refugee families and immigrant students of extreme poverty from developing countries

Prephonemic phase of spelling—the least mature level of spelling in which the letters bear no apparent relation to sounds

Preproduction stage—the stage in the natural approach to language acquisition that corresponds to the silent period of young children, when they express themselves with actions and gestures rather than language; it is also the stage at which total physical response (TPR) instruction is conducted

Principled content knowledge—familiarity with a topic and understanding in depth about its components and how the topic is related to a larger field of knowledge

Print environment—the extent of the presence of print materials in the home of a student, such as books, magazines, newspapers, religious books

Prosody—the sound contours of larger segments of spoken language.

QAR—Question–Answer–Relationships is a framework for evaluating questions based on reading a selection and determining what is needed to answer them fully. Some questions can be answered *right there*; others are characterized as *think and search, author and me*, or *on my own*

Radio reading—an approach in which students practice reading the same text multiple times as a preparation to performing it in front of the class

Rate Your Knowledge chart—a tool to help students identify their levels of knowledge of targeted vocabulary

Raw scores—the number or the percentage of items that students answered correctly on a test

Read-alouds—a lesson in which a teacher reads a big book or story aloud to children, making reference only to illustrations during the reading

Readability—a term applied to the level of difficulty of text, often expressed in grade levels or lexiles

Reader response criticism—the literary version of schema theory, that holds that readers create their own understanding of literary texts through the interaction of textual clues and prior knowledge and associations

Readers' theater—a method of dividing up a text with roles for many students, who practice reading the text and then perform it as if it were a play, but with reading aloud instead of memorizing lines

Reading fluency—the ability to read a text accurately and quickly and with proper phrasing and expression

Receptive vocabulary—words one can identify when heard or read

Reciprocal teaching—teachers model and then turn over to students discussion of short text segments focused on four strategies: summarizing, questioning, clarifying, and predicting

Relative clause—a clause that is related to another word and serves to explain it or elaborate on it

Reliability—a measure of the likelihood that the results of the test are stable and dependable

Repeated reading—having students read the same short text multiple times, while measuring rate and accuracy, and seeking to improve their fluency

ReQuest—partners read a text paragraph by paragraph, taking turns asking questions about each paragraph and co-constructing responses

Resilient students—those who overcome difficult circumstances and succeed in school

Response to Intervention (RTI)—an approach to special education in which educators work as a team to meet the needs of special education students, including special education teachers, regular classroom teachers, reading specialists, school psychologists/counselors, administrators, and parents; assessment begins as soon as student achievement indicates a potential problem

Restrictive clause—a clause that explains a word in such a way that is essential to the meaning

Rime—in a spoken syllable, the vowel and any consonant that comes after the vowel

Roaming around the Known—a phrase coined by Marie Clay to warn teachers to take testing results tentatively until further instruction bears out their accuracy

Root—a bound morpheme of Latin or Greek origin that carries the meaning of a word

Rubric—a chart used in evaluation, that lists qualities with examples of inferior, average, and superior works or actions that exemplify those qualities

Running records—an informal assessment done by scoring words read correctly in a moderately challenging text

Scaffolded Silent Reading (ScSR)—a method for supporting students' fluency as they read silently

Schema theory—a theory that holds that understanding is created as cues, and that clues from a text lead a reader to summon up her own prior knowledge, organized as schemas, or mental frameworks

Schemas—concepts and other associations stored in memory (also known as **schemata**)

Self-selected reading—students select books they want to read from a classroom or school library

Semantic feature analysis—a matrix on which attributes of similar words are compared and contrasted

Semantic web—a graphic way to organize words by their meaningful relationships

Shared inquiry—a relatively structured approach to guiding inquiry into texts

Shared reading—a lesson in which a teacher reads a big book or story aloud to children, making references to the illustrations and also sweeping her hand under each line as it is read out loud

Shared writing—an activity in which teacher and children collaborate in writing the words in a text letter by letter

Sheltered English instruction—a scaffolding approach to teaching the second language at the intermediate level of second language proficiency; support is provided to students in lessons in the second language and also in academic subjects through sheltered strategies, such as speaking slowly, enunciating clearly, checking frequently for comprehension, providing wait time

Sheltered Instruction Observation Protocol—a system of teaching language and content subjects to students with limited proficiency in English

Sight words—words that are not decoded, but recognized instantly

SIOP—Sheltered Instruction Observation Protocol®; a program of sheltered (scaffolded) instruction for English language learners

Skills—automatic processes used habitually without conscious attention

Split-half reliability—measured when samples of a student's performance on different items of the same test are compared with each other

Standard American English (SAE)—the English spoken by most native speakers of English; the mainstream dialect of American English

Standards-based tests—measures that are designed to test performance on learning standards that are part of a statewide or local curriculum

Stanine scores—scores based on a 9-point scale that tell roughly how a student's scores match those of a comparison group; the spread of scores represented by each number is based on a normal curve of distribution

Story grammar—a plot pattern that is both the organizing framework of a story and a set of expectations or rules for story organization that resides in a reader's memory

Strategies—processes or routines used with conscious selection and monitoring

Structural analysis—morphological analysis; analysis of morphemes, or meaningful parts of a word, to determine the word's meaning

Subtractive bilingual education—a program in which a second language is substituted for the mother tongue that the student already knows; the goal is a monolingual individual; it is the outcome of a transitional model for bilingual education in which the student transitions from the mother tongue to English only

Suffix—a morpheme added at the end of a word or root

Summative assessments—assessments done after instruction is completed to see what the instruction accomplished

Suprasegmental phonology—like prosody, refers to sound contours of language at units larger than phonemes and syllables

Syllabic sonorant—an unstressed syllable with *M, N, R,* or *L,* which is often spelled without a vowel by inventive spellers

Syllabic writing system—a writing system in which the characters represent spoken syllables

Synonym—a word with a meaning that is similar to that of another word

Syntax—the set of rules that order words of different types and their inflections meaningfully in sentences

Taxonomy—an organized framework for the total corpus of activities or ideas showing relationships and hierarchies

Test-retest reliability—measured when the same students are given the same test within a short interval, to see if the results are similar

Text coding—assigning students certain kinds of items to look for in a text and lightly marking in the margin where those items are found

Text complexity—a measure of the challenge of a particular piece of text that includes measures of the text's features, its conceptual density, and the task to which a reader will be asked to put it

Text structure—the way an article or book is organized both visibly and internally

Think-aloud—an activity in which a skilled reader reads aloud a passage of text and talks through her cognitive processes as she makes sense of the text

Topical content knowledge—surface level knowledge about a topic

Total physical response (TPR)—a communicative approach to second language acquisition that focuses on students responding to commands and questions with gestures, rather than by speaking; it relates to the silent period, before students begin to speak, but after they begin to understand; it also corresponds to the pre-production phase of the natural approach

Two-page spread—printed materials are organized and presented so the two facing pages can be considered a unit

Unrestrictive clause—a clause that provides more information about a word, but not essential information

Validity—the extent to which a test measures what claims that it measures

Visuals—features in texts that complement verbal presentations, including pictures, illustrations, cartoons, charts, graphs, and maps

Vocab-O-Gram—a visual organizer that students use to identify words in a story by story elements (character, setting, plot, etc.)

Vocabulary Detective Bookmark—a tool that guides students in using important sources of information in determining meanings of new words

Voice choir—a group of students who practice and perform a text, usually a poem, with varied parts

Wait-time—a brief interval of a few seconds that a wise teacher provides after a question so that students can think for a moment before responding

WCPM—the number of words read correctly per minute; a way of measuring oral reading fluency

Webbed questions—three basic questions to ask of new vocabulary: what is it?, what is it like?, and what are some examples?

Whole-part-whole teaching—beginning by practicing reading or writing in a real context, focuses on teaching a limited concept or skill, and then returns to practicing reading or writing in a real context again

Word consciousness—attentiveness to words and interest in how they function and are formed

Word knowledge—a broad term that includes phonics knowledge but also involves knowledge of other aspects of how written words work, such as the morphemes or meaningful word parts out of which they are constructed, their relations to other words, and their histories

Zone of proximal development (ZPD)—from the late Russian psychologist Lev Vygotsky, the area of learning for a student that is not so difficult that it cannot be learned, not so easy that the student needs no help at all, but is the level at which the student can learn with support from an adult or student peer

Name Index

Subject Index